Story of a Hanged Man

By

Parker Anderson

© 2016 Parker Anderson. All rights reserved.

Cover and interior design: Kubera Book Design, Prescott, AZ

ISBN: 978-0-692-75353-8

No part of this book may be reproduced or transmitted in any form or by any means, electronic or mechanical, including photocopying or recording, or by an information storage and retrieval system, without permission in writing from the publisher.

Cover photographs are courtesy of the Sharlot Hall Museum and David Schmittinger.

Acknowledgments

A story such as this is never possible without the assistance and input of many individuals, and I wish to extend my deepest thanks and gratitude to the following people, without whom this book would not exist:

Michael Wurtz, Juti Winchester, Lorri Carlson, Terry Munderloh, Ryan Flahive, Scott Anderson, and the rest of the staff at the Sharlot Hall Museum Archives in Prescott, Arizona, who granted me unlimited access to their holdings during the researching of this book;

Linda Terrin, Anna Daniel and the staff of Mohave Museum of History and Arts in Kingman, Arizona, for providing me with material from their archives;

Professor John D. Tanner, Jr. of Palomar College, Fallbrook, California, for sharing his own research on Parker with me; including much on Parker's early life in Chapter 1;

Linda Offeney, ranger at Yuma Territorial Prison State Historical Park;

Allene Alder of Jerome Historical Society, Jerome, Arizona;

John Burton and the staff of Prescott Public Library, Prescott, Arizona;

Nancy Sawyer and Patricia Roeser of Arizona Department of Library, Archives, and Public Records, Phoenix;

Dora Silberman, the great-granddaughter of Louis C. Miller, who shared a great deal of information on her notorious ancestor's later life, despite being blindsided by the revelations of who he really was;

Carol Powell, who shared much of her detailed research on the family of her husband Glenn, whose ancestors included Louis C. Miller;

Gene Norris, who provided much input on his ancestor, Erasmus Lee Norris;

Gretchen Eastman, a volunteer at Sharlot Hall Museum who assisted me with research on Abe Thompson;

Staff of the Clerks of Superior Court in Mohave and Cochise Counties, Arizona;

Kathryn Vohs, Deputy Recorder, Yavapai County Recorder's Office;

Joseph P. Samora and the staff of California State Archives in Sacramento;

Justin Russell, Deputy Clerk of Tulare County Superior Court;

Terry Ommen of Tulare County Historical Society;

Lisa Gezelter of the National Archives—Pacific Southwest Region, Laguna Niguel, California;

Lori Cox-Paul, Education Specialist for the National Archives—Rocky Mountain Region, Denver, Colorado;

R. Chandler of Wells Fargo Historical Services, San Francisco;

Marilyn Chambers of the Lafayette County (Wisconsin) Historical Society;

Michael Work, distant relative of the Work/Parker families, for his research and insight on his ancestors;

Also many thanks to the following for various assistance and support: my mother, Darla R. Anderson; my dear friend Jody Drake of Blue Rose Historical Theater; Donna Baldwin; Sue Schnell; Pat Atchison.

The contributions of the above-named people made my work a lot easier. I am grateful to all of them.

Contents

Foreword by Melissa Ruffner and Elisabeth Ruffner — vii
Introduction — ix

Chapter 1: *Early Life* — 1
Chapter 2: *George C. Ruffner* — 31
Chapter 3: *The Abe Thompson Gang* — 35
Chapter 4: *The Rock Cut Train Robbery* — 50
Chapter 5: *The First Posse* — 88
Chapter 6: *L. C. Miller and Cornelia Sarata* — 130
Chapter 7: *Jailbreak and the Second Posse* — 169
Chapter 8: *The Trial* — 264
Chapter 9: *The Long Road to the Gallows* — 304
Chapter 10: *Life After Parker* — 386
Chapter 11: *Myths, Legends, and Unverifiable Stories* — 468
Chapter 12: *Other Writings* — 477
Epilogue — 518

Foreword

by Melissa Ruffner and Elisabeth Ruffner

The Fleming Parker saga has become a legend of the real West for decades. The capture, conviction and hanging accounts in fact, in film and song, have captured the imagination of the public as no fictional account could. The original photographs, diaries and family stories have given vivid reality to a romantic version of an account of a real life cowboy, train robber, murderer and convict beyond any stretch of the imagination.

The Ruffner Family Archives, now formalized in Sharlot Hall Museum in Prescott, Arizona and at Longwood University in Farmville, Virginia, are original sources for Parker Anderson, a young man who in his research and writing has once again proved his stature as an author, bringing real stories of the West of this country to life on the printed page.

The Ruffner family has played a significant role in the recording and collection of the family archives and the founding of this nation. Melissa Ruffner, great-grandniece of Sheriff George C. Ruffner, and Elisabeth, her mother, widow of Sheriff Ruffner's beloved nephew, Lester Ward Ruffner, are privileged to collaborate with this author as historians and writers who commend this remarkable story to live on in the words of Parker Anderson, friend and colleague.

Introduction

Whenever he is written about in periodicals of Old West lore, Fleming Parker (alias James Parker or Jim Parker) is usually described as an obscure outlaw. It is true that Parker has yet to have a movie made about him, and he does not have active scholars devoting their lives to studying him, and it is also true that he does not command the frightened awe that such legendary badmen as Jesse James receives. To my knowledge, only one other book has been written about Parker's life, although it has been the subject of chapters in anthology works.

But Fleming Parker is or was hardly an obscure outlaw. In his lifetime, his crimes were written about in newspapers across America. Since his 1898 hanging, his story has been retold countless times in Western magazines and nostalgic newspaper columns. Numerous untrue legends have sprung up about him. Most serious students of Western lore know the basics of his story. Fleming "James" Parker was many things, but obscure is not one of them.

So what gives the Parker story its lasting appeal? Arizona yielded up many hardened criminals in the 19th century—many committed crimes even grislier than Parker's. After careful study and consideration, I think the answer is this: Parker behaved differently than many badmen of the era. His crimes had an in-your-face audacity that frightened his contemporaries and fascinated subsequent historians. He did not show any remorse for his deeds, based his court appeals on legal technicalities instead of begging for mercy, and was probably the most calm, composed person at his own hanging. He did not even seem human, and this terrified many people. This undoubtedly contributed to his hanging during a period when numerous Arizona murderers were getting off fairly lightly.

And yet, in retrospect, there is something human about Parker that cries out from the recesses of his story to this day. He had a family who loved him; sisters who could not believe their brother was truly guilty of the crimes for which he was accused. Ranchers and other country residents, including the venerable Henry F. Ashurst, would be quoted by newspapers as saying that Parker was a friendly, civilized, reliable ranch hand, and that they were stunned when they came to realize he was a member of the gang that had been persecuting them. Until the truth about him became known, Parker seemed like the last person in the world to have ice water in his veins.

Fleming "James" Parker was a true jigsaw puzzle of a man, someone that a present day psychologist would have had a ball analyzing. It is my intention in this book to present as complete an account of his life as I possibly can, based on what material has survived. I have tried to refrain from using undocumented legends as much as possible, although some of them will be discussed separately in Chapter 11. I believe this to be the fullest, most detailed account of Parker's life and crimes to be published to this day.

Some readers may be surprised at my use of original newspapers as source material in many instances. For many years, Western historians have dismissed old newspapers as inaccurate, unreliable, and in some cases, deliberately untruthful. Because of this, many researchers have ignored them, preferring instead to keep repeating the many hand-me-down legends that exist about the era.

I strongly disagree. While inaccuracy existed to a certain extent due to poor communications, I do not find these first-hand accounts to be as worthless as all that. In fact, I find just the opposite. Nineteenth-century newspapers are surprisingly detailed, as reporters took great pains to seek out eyewitnesses. Within the last few years only, some other historians have also discovered that original newspapers are treasure troves of information, offering quotes from notable people, publishing official documents, etc.

So, why have original newspapers been regarded with disdain for so long? At the risk of making some people angry, I strongly believe it is because the original, first-hand accounts do not always corroborate the romantic legends that have been so popular and profitable for so many.

To cite the most famous example, primary news coverage of the Gunfight at the OK Corral describes an event that sounds much different than the one folklorists and Hollywood have depicted for so many generations. So which is more reliable, the original news coverage, or the oral and written folklore tales of the era? I believe it is the newspapers.

Many different newspapers are quoted in this book, as different journalists managed to acquire different details of the Parker story. Putting them all together, they form a fairly complete picture. Needless to say, Prescott's two newspapers, the *Arizona Journal Miner* and *Prescott Courier,* had the heaviest Parker coverage (both papers were intense rivals, and wasted a lot of ink calling each other dirty names during their existence. The *Courier* still publishes). Other Arizona papers with strong interest in the case included the *Arizona Republican* (today the *Arizona Republic*), the *Arizona Gazette* (precursor to the *Phoenix Gazette*), and the *Phoenix Herald*. The *Flagstaff Sun-Democrat* and the *Mohave County Miner* (from Kingman) also weighed in heavily. Tragically, newspapers from Williams and Jerome, which would have also had heavy Parker coverage, have not survived.

There was surprising interest in Parker in California as well. Naturally, papers from Visalia were interested in what was happening with their home town boy, but the various periodicals from Los Angeles and San Francisco weighed in as well, seeking out interviews with case participants, including the robbed trainsmen, as well as Parker himself. Wire service reports of the case reportedly went as far East as Chicago.

A few things need to be said about the style of newspapers from the 19th century so there is no confusion. Many newspapers, including Prescott's *Arizona Journal Miner* and *Courier*, utilized a publishing process that has been long since abandoned. They would print daily editions, and then once a week, they would publish a "weekly" edition which was comprised of the contents of the past week's dailies verbatim! Therefore, in the weekly editions, you often had different and sometimes conflicting dispatches on the same story in different parts of the same paper. This made sense to readers then, most of whom subscribed to both formats.

Today, however, this style has caused problems for researchers. In cases of papers like the *Phoenix Herald*, both the daily and weekly editions have survived. In other cases, such as the *Journal Miner* and the *Courier*, only the weekly editions have survived and are available for perusal. But the above stated format of these weeklies has confounded researchers for years, who sometimes have missed certain dispatches because they expected that issue's coverage of a certain story to be all in one place.

It has also led to confusion concerning dates of events. It is important to remember this, because certain newspaper dates do not seem to add up or correspond with each other at first glance in the text of this book. This is the reason why.

I always smile when I hear politicians of today complain bitterly about perceived "media bias." Any bias that exists today has got nothing on the press bias of the 19th and early 20th centuries. This is not to say this made the stories inaccurate, but journalists of the era very much upheld society's notions of right and wrong, and they did it in the actual news articles and not on the editorial page.

For example, men whom society automatically regarded as "the good guys" were always described in the papers as "courageous," "fearless," and "honorable." By contrast, accused criminals and other "bad guys" were forever being denounced as "desperate," "cowardly," and even "worthless." It is jarring to read this today, and even more jarring to realize that such descriptions were genuinely considered to be impartial back then.

Printer's ink was an expensive commodity in those days as well, and led to certain abbreviations in writing that are also no longer practiced. In many cases, newspapers recorded news items about certain local individuals without describing who they were, the presumption being that readers already knew who they were. Also, in dispatches regarding ongoing events, previous developments were not recapped each time as most newspapers do today, the presumption being that readers remembered what had come before.

Because everyone tried to make expensive ink last as long as possible, newspapers many times referred to individuals by their initials instead of their full names! This was done nearly 85% of the time. For example, Sheriff George Ruffner was almost always publicly referred to as G.C. Ruffner. For the same reason, this practice was also utilized on court documents and legal certificates in the majority (though admittedly not all) of the cases.

This practice of using people's initials started to die out in the larger cities in the early 20th century, but it was still actively utilized in the more rural areas as late as the 1940s.

It is against this backdrop that we begin our examination of the life of one of Northern Arizona's best known outlaws . . .

CHAPTER 1

Early Life

Unlike many Old West badmen who seemed to come out of nowhere when they did their crimes, the early life of Fleming Parker is surprisingly well-documented, no doubt due in large part to a decided interest in his background beginning already in his lifetime. As much of the documentation in this book is reprinted in general chronological order of when it was originally written, we shall return to details of Parker's earliest days later on. But here are the basics:

According to his own words as well as other sources, Fleming Parker was born in 1865 (exact date unknown) in Tulare County, California, the son of a small-time farmer and his wife, whose spread was just outside of Visalia. Fleming was the second of four children. He had an older sister, Sarah Jane (usually referred to as Sadie), born December 18, 1862, and two younger sisters, Martha (born in 1872), and Margaret (usually referred to as Maggie), born February 13, 1868.

This is an unidentified parade in downtown Visalia, California, circa 1880s. Fleming Parker knew these streets well. (Courtesy of Tulare County Historical Society)

Fleming Parker's maternal grandfather, Fleming Work, arrived in California in 1852, after having been born in Tennessee, according to his later obituary. A land deed which has survived, dated September 28, 1859 in Tulare County, shows him selling some land to a J. W. Reynolds and Ann Reynolds, his wife, for the sum of $40. The land is described as *"All that certain tract of land on the Kaweah River, swamp land survey $454 in the southwest ¼ of the southeast ¼ of section 15 in township 18 south range 26 east, containing 40 acres."* The deed is recorded in Book A of property titles, p. 530, in the Tulare County records.

Fleming Work had two daughters, Mary and Litha, and a son, William. His daughter Mary Elizabeth Work married Daniel D. Parker, a native of Laurel County, Kentucky, on Christmas Eve, December 24, 1860 in Tulare County. Some later accounts of the family's life erroneously list Mary's name as Harriet. According to information provided to me by Michael Work, family historian, Daniel and Mary were actually first cousins.

After Work's daughter married Dan Parker, Work sold him some land. A deed dated November 28, 1863 shows a land sale between the two for the sum of $15,000, a considerable sum in its day. The land that Daniel Parker bought from his father-in-law is described as "*West ½ and NE ¼ of SW ¼ of section 18, township 16 south of range 26, east of Mt. Diablo baseline and meridian*" in Visalia. Recorded in Book M of property Titles, p. 595, in the Tulare County records.

The Tulare County census of 1870, which is far less detailed about households than later censuses would be, lists Daniel Parker at age 36, with occupation as farmer. Mary Parker is listed as being 21, which is clearly an error. They undoubtedly meant 31.

While Parker was still very young, his mother died April 23, 1875 shortly after giving birth to her fifth child, a boy named Hopkins Parker, who also died a few weeks later on June 30, 1875, and was buried at the foot of his mother's grave (the name Hopkins ran in the family—there are two men, both named Hopkins Work, buried in the Visalia Cemetery). After that, Parker's father, Dan Parker, sold his farm and moved himself and his children to live with his wife's father, Fleming Work. According to Sarah Jane (Sadie)'s later letters, she tried to alleviate the bad situation a bit by marrying a local young man named Curtis Jackson Boyd (referred to as Jim Boyd, possibly erroneously, in some accounts), even though she was only about 15. Tulare County records show this marriage occurred on Christmas Eve, December 24, 1877.

Dan Parker was inconsolable with grief over the death of his wife. Although his daughters encouraged him to remarry, which he later did (I have been unable to locate the record; it must have occurred in another county), he never recovered, and it eventually drove him insane. This finally came to a head, and the following item appeared in the *Tulare Weekly Times* newspaper of February 8, 1879:

Suicide

Daniel Parker, a citizen of this county who lived in Stokes' Valley up in the foothills, committed suicide last Tuesday near Tulare city, under circumstances that lead to the belief that he was suffering from temporary insanity. He came from his home down to Elbow Creek near Visalia on Monday and stopped that night at the residence of a brother-in-law. Here he wrote a note directed to his wife and left it on the mantle-piece weighted down with a silver coin. The note said that he felt as though he must die or else go to Stockton. The next day Parker was seen wandering about in the neighborhood of Tulare acting in a strange manner, and later a stranger found him near the road leading toward Lemore in a dying condition. Parker told the man that he had taken strychnine and was going to die and requested him to stay with him until he did die. The end came in a few moments and the stranger went to Tulare and reported, when citizens of that place went out and brought the body in. A coroner's jury was impaneled and rendered a verdict in accordance with the foregoing facts. Parker was about 40 years old and a good citizen, much liked by his neighbors. He left several children, some of whom are as old as his second wife whom he married only a few weeks ago. He was buried in the Visalia cemetery last Wednesday.

I visited the Visalia Cemetery in August of 2008 and found the graves of Daniel and Mary Parker. I noted with interest that at the base of Daniel's tombstone, near the ground in tiny, obscure letters, was an inscription that reads:

He who plants within our hearts
All This deep affection,
Giving when the form departs
Fadeless Recollection.

These are the graves of Daniel and Mary Elizabeth Parker, the parents of Fleming Parker, in the Visalia Cemetery. Daniel's name is misspelled "Danuel" on his tombstone. Mary's tombstone has fallen over at some point over the years. (author's photo)

By the age of 14, Fleming Parker had lost both of his parents. Fleming Work was apparently unable to handle raising his four grandchildren, particularly his namesake Fleming Parker, who was rapidly becoming incorrigible. In an apparent attempt to give him some semblance of family life again, the Boyds took in young Fleming and youngest sister Martha, while Maggie went to live with an aunt and uncle. For the moment, Fleming Work was free of his burden.

The 1880 Tulare County census lists the Boyd household, with C. Jackson Boyd listed as 21 years of age, and a native of Arkansas. His occupation is listed as "farmer." His wife, Sarah Jane, is listed as being 17 at this time, with "orphans" Martha Parker, ten years old, and Fleming Parker (with name misspelled Flemming), listed as 15 years old, both living in the household. The census records a servant, Gelia (or perhaps Delia?) Gregg living with them also.

A rare surviving newspaper notice from the *Tulare Weekly Times* of May 17, 1883 records the marriage of Parker's sister Maggie to a William A. Welch on May 14. Justice of the Peace William B. Wallace performed the ceremony. The marriage is also recorded in Tulare County records.

Fleming Parker apparently did not get along with Sadie's husband, Curtis Jackson Boyd, so he eventually ran away, and seems to have spent his remaining teenage years alternating between his grandfather's home, and just drifting around the state, learning the vices and sociopathic attitudes that would shape his adult life. It is probable that he started to learn some of his skills with cattle and horses during this period, working as a hired hand on Tulare County ranches. Despite an existing legend to the contrary, it is highly unlikely (though not impossible) that he made his first foray into Arizona at this time.

Although it is widely believed that Parker got in and out of various scrapes with the law as a teenager, his first documented hard crime came in the Spring of 1885, when the young man was only 20 years old. He and a partner, Philo Johns, were arrested for (prophetically enough) stealing livestock. Virtually nothing is known about Johns, except that he was from Missouri and was three years older than young Fleming. It is reasonable to assume that Johns was just another ne'er-do-well, looking for excitement and fast money, just like Parker. It is not known whose idea it was to stage the theft.

Fleming Parker's court papers from this theft have survived, but they are scattered. Most of them are on microfilm at the Tulare County Courthouse in Visalia today, but a few are in the California State Archives in Sacramento, while one very pertinent document somehow wound up in the Sharlot Hall Museum Archives in Prescott, Arizona. This scattering undoubtedly was caused by roving souvenir hunters many years ago, who likely grabbed a few documents after Parker's later infamy. Considering their age, we are lucky they have survived at all, and despite some illegibilities due to advanced age, we can reconstruct Parker's trial quite well.

The original criminal complaint against Parker and Johns was filed over a month after the theft, and reads as follows:

> Personally appeared before me this 24th day of May 1885, L. W. Holder of Visalia in the County of Tulare, who being first duly sworn, complains and says: That Philo Johns & Flem Parker of Tulare County, on or about the 9th day of April A.D. 1885, and before the filing of this complaint in the County of Tulare, did willfully and feloniously steal, take, and carry away a certain steer, said steer being then and there the personal property of H.D. Woodard.

The complaint was signed by Holder before Justice of the Peace A. C. Neil. It is unclear who Holder was.

Fleming Parker was picked up and lodged in the Tulare County Jail by Deputy F. M. Bell. Parker's bail was set at one thousand dollars, a considerable amount of money in

Chapter 1: Early Life

The Visalia jail, c. 1890s, where Parker was undoubtedly held while awaiting trial in both 1885 and 1890. He probably spent time here for various unrecorded altercations as well. The jail was very small, for a small town where crime was rare. (Courtesy of Tulare County Historical Society)

1885. In retrospect, it is difficult to read Parker's bail bond without feeling an overwhelming sense of sadness:

> "An Order having been made on the 24th day of May 1885 by A. C. Neil, a Justice of the Peace of Visalia Township, Tulare County, that Fleming Parker be held to answer and to appear for examination before the said Justice at his office in City of Visalia in said County and State on the 2nd day June 1885 upon a charge of Grand Larceny upon which he has been admitted to bail in the sum of one thousand dollars, and which charge is pending in that Court against him, in behalf of the people of the State of California.
>
> "Now we Fleming Work, a resident of Tulare County and by occupation a farmer; and C. P. Brown, a resident of Tulare County and by occupation a farmer, hereby undertake that the above named Fleming Parker will appear and answer the charge above mentioned, in whatever Court it may be presented, and will at all times hold himself amenable to the orders and process of the Court, and if convicted will appear for judgement and render himself in execution thereof; or, if he fail to perform either of these conditions, that we will pay to the people of the State of California the sum of one thousand dollars."

Parker's aging grandfather had come to his rescue, and had apparently persuaded a friend to go in with him on the bail money, a sum that neither one probably could afford.

A summons for a venire of jurors was issued, and reads in part:

> "I hereby certify that I received the Within writ of Venire on the 24th day of June 1885, and personally served the same by summoning the following named persons to be and appear before the Superior Court in the City of Visalia, Tulare County forthwith to serve as trial jurors as I am commanded by said writ, to wit:
>
> | | | |
> |---|---|---|
> | H.T. Young | D. Douglass | E. A. Carothers |
> | G. C. Dean | W. L. Pratt | L. W. Gregg |
> | Joseph Cecil | R. S. Nearman | T. J. Spencer |
> | Thomas Preisker | | |
>
> A. Balaam, Sheriff
> By M. A. Keenan, Deputy

The old Visalia jail still stands but has been moved to the grounds of the Tulare County Historical Society. Author Parker Anderson is seen standing in the doorway. (author's photos)

These jurors did not last, because the start of the trial was delayed.

In Parker's surviving court papers, there is an affidavit sworn by the Deputy who arrested him. It reads as follows:

> F. M. Bell, being duly sworn, deposes and says that on the (illegible) day of May 1885, he was duly appointed a deputy sheriff of the County of Tulare, that after being duly qualified and while legally acting as deputy sheriff, a warrant signed by A. C. Neil, Justice of the Peace of Visalia township county of state aforesaid, ordering the arrest of Fleming Parker and Philo Johns on a charge of felony, was placed in his hands by Sheriff A. Balaam of Tulare County with directions to affiant to search for said Fleming Parker and said Philo Johns, and if possible to serve said warrant upon each of them, that in pursuance of such instructions he proceeded in search of said Parker and Johns, that he found and arrested said Fleming Parker, that he inquired of said Parker the whereabouts of said Philo Johns, that said Parker then told affiant that he, Parker, said Johns, and a girl named Mattie Slater were together for a week a short time before said Parker was arrested, on Pine Ridge at (illegible; possibly "sheep camp") which is in the County of Fresno, that Parker said further that said Johns had been a true friend to him and he would not tell where he then was and remarked to affiant "You wouldn't give a friend away, would you," Parker further said to affiant and W. L. Elam, "Boys, I won't tell where Philo is. You've got the warrant and if you want him, go and hunt him as you did me."

F. M. Bell

Subscribed and sworn
Before me this 24th day of June 1885
(name illegible)
Clerk

At some point while awaiting trial, Parker apparently realized he was up the creek, and he proceeded to do just what you might expect—he turned on his friend Philo Johns. Parker's affidavit in response to that of Bell reads as follows:

> Fleming Parker, said defendant, being duly sworn says: That he has heard read the affidavit of F. M. Bell herein. That affiant did not state to said Bell at any time "that he, Parker, said Johns, and a girl named Mattie Slater were together for a week a short time before said Parker was arrested on Pine Ridge at a (illegible; possibly "sheep camp") which is in the County of Fresno, or anything to that effect, and the same is not true in fact. That affiant did not state to said Bell at any time that he, affiant, would not tell where said Philo Johns was. That affiant did not then, at the time of affiant's arrest know the whereabouts of said Philo Johns and has not at any time since that date known where said Philo Johns was and does not now know (illegible). That said Philo Johns is and from three years last (illegible) has been a resident of this Tulare County.
>
> That said Sheriff has returned said subpoena in this (illegible) with his return (illegible) to the effect that, after diligent search, he cannot find said Philo Johns in this County.
>
> That defendant expects to (illegible) by said Philo Johns the following facts to wit: That on the 30th day of March 1885 at said County of Tulare, this defendant, for a valuable consideration, bought from said Philo Johns the steer mentioned and described in the information in this action, and said Philo Johns sold and delivered said steer to this defendant, and that said Philo Johns claimed to be the owner of said steer at that time.
>
> That affiant does not know of any other person or persons by whom he can (illegible) the foregoing facts.
>
> That said Philo Johns resides in the mountainous (illegible) of this County and as short a time has (illegible) this cause was set down for trail, the Sheriff has not had sufficient time to effect a service of said subforma.
>
> That this application is not made for delay merely, but in good faith, that justice may be done in the (illegible) and affiant (illegible) believes that if this cause is continued until the September session of this court, he can (illegible; possibly "provide") the attendance of said Philo Johns at the trial in this court.
>
> Fleming Parker
> Subscribed and sworn
> To before me this 24th day of June 1885
> (name illegible)
> Notary Public

This bit of legal maneuvering by Parker and his lawyers was strange and risky. It can only mean one of two things—either Parker was telling the truth and he really was

Exterior of the Tulare County Courthouse in Visalia, California. Young Fleming Parker was put on trial twice here for various thefts. This building is no longer standing. (Courtesy of Tulare County Historical Society)

framed by Philo Johns (which seems highly unlikely, considering his subsequent track record), or he was trusting that Johns successfully made it out of the County and would never be caught.

Legal technicalities contributed to the confusion, especially in historical retrospect. From the *Tulare Weekly Times* of June 25, 1885,

> Flem Parker, charged with grand larceny, was acquitted this morning in the Superior Court on the ground of variance between the information and the proof. He was detained by Judge Cross and the District Attorney was directed to draw up another information.

While Parker was undoubtedly guilty, the zealousness to prosecute a first offender cattle thief can only be attributed to its era. One can almost understand Parker's later assertions that he was being persecuted during his early life.

Since Johns could not be found, Fleming Parker was reindicted separately. A new criminal complaint was sworn out against him, this time by Homer D. Woodard, the owner of the steer. It reads:

> Personally appeared before me, this 24th day of June 1885, H. D. Woodard of Tulare County, in the County of Tulare, who, first being duly sworn, complains and says: That one Fleming Parker of Tulare County, on the 7th day of June*; in the County of Tulare, did feloniously steal, take, and carry away a certain steer branded (illegible; possibly "T.G.") on left hip, said steer being then and there the personal

---

* This date is obviously an error, the cause of which is no longer known.

property of M. Woodard and H. D. Woodard who were doing business at the time alleged under the firm name of Woodard and son."

The surviving court papers show a second bail bond for one thousand dollars, dated June 25, 1885, and being met by Parker's grandfather Fleming Work and his friend C. P. Brown. It is unclear whether this paper was a formal continuation of Parker's original bond, or whether Work had to come up with <u>another</u> grand.

With Parker's trial approaching, another summons went out for a venire of jurors. Sheriff Balaam acknowledge it as follows:

> I hereby certify that I received the within and hereunto annexed writ of Venire on the 24th day of June 1885 and personally served the same by summoning the following named persons to be and appear in the Superior Court in the City of Visalia forthwith to serve as trial jurors as commanded by said within annexed writ, to wit:
>
> | | | |
> |---|---|---|
> | Ed Hinds | D. F. Carter | A. Prother |
> | Felix Miller | C. M. Tubbo | W. C. McAdams |
>
> A. Balaam, Sheriff
> By (illegible), Deputy

Due to more delays, these jurors did not last either.

After months of delays, probably due to the disappearance of Philo Johns, young Fleming Parker was finally arraigned on the charges in the Tulare County Superior Court. The surviving notes of the arraignment are as follows:

> Monday, August 3, 1885
> Presiding: Hon. W. W. Cross, Judge
> The People
>   Vs.
> Fleming Parker
> Grand Larceny
>
>   The District Attorney with the Defendant and his counsel Messrs. Atwell & Bradley came into Court and Defendant by his counsel waived the reading of the Information filed in this Cause: Whereupon the Clerk delivered to said counsel a certified copy of said Information. Defendant upon being asked if Fleming Parker was his true name replied in the affirmative.
>   Whereupon the Defendant waiving time in which to plead and wishing to plead at this time; he thereupon entered his plea of Not Guilty as charged in said Information:
>   and with the consent of counsel the Court Ordered that this case be set for trial on Tuesday the 8th day of September 1885 at 10 o'clock a.m.

Now the story gets complicated. In the interim, Philo Johns was evidently apprehended, apparently having been not intelligent enough to flee the county. But instead of validating

This is the courtroom of Judge William W. Cross in the Tulare County Courthouse. Parker was tried and convicted for two felony thefts here. Judge Cross is 4th from left, with Tulare County District Attorney William B. Wallace just below him. (Courtesy of Tulare County Historical Society)

Parker's story (which would have required him to take the blame himself), he apparently agreed to turn State's evidence against Parker in exchange for the dropping of charges against him! This can be surmised through the record, which shows Philo Johns testifying as a witness for the prosecution at Parker's trial, as well as the fact that Johns was never tried for stealing Woodard's steer. The two one-time friends had truly turned on each other.

On September 8th, 1885, the People vs. Fleming Parker went to trial in the Superior Court of Tulare County, with Judge William W. Cross presiding. In those days, trial testimony was often not recorded, and when it was, it usually ended up not being saved unless there was clear indication that a convicted defendant planned to appeal his sentence to a higher court, in which case the original court would provide the transcript to show that the defendant had indeed received a fair trial. Consequently, trial testimony has not survived for this case.

The official court record of the trial has survived, however, and it reads as follows:

> This cause coming on regularly for trial, the District Attorney and T. M. McNamara, Esq. Appearing as counsel for the prosecution and the Defendant appearing with his attorneys Messrs. Atwell & Bradley. Thereupon the parties being ready for trial, the following persons drawn from the regular Venire, being accepted, were sworn as jurors to try the Matter pending, to wit: Jesse Hoskins, John Mangan, J.

W. Bozeman, Jacob Spear, Wm. Ragle, John McKiernan, Andrew Monroe, R. H. Renick, J. A. Bacon, Spencer Fay, John Hilton, and D. L. Clotfelter.

The Information filed against the Defendant in this action was thereupon read and the Defendant's plea thereto stated by the Clerk to the Jury, and after the Statement of the case by the prosecution, the following witnesses were sworn and examined on part of the People Viz: Thomas Gaines, Myron Woodard, H. D. Woodard, Susan Woody, John W. Slater, Stonewall Slater, Henry McGee, Wm. Cortner, D. E. Cason, A. Frazer, J. N. Bowhay, Wm. Elam, F. M. Bell, and Philo Johns.*

Whereupon the defense having no evidence to offer, the cause was with the consent of counsel for both parties submitted upon the instruction given by the Court to the Jury—without argument.

The Jury thereupon retired in charge of the Sheriff to deliberate upon a verdict:

And after a short deliberation, the jury came into court and through their foreman declared the following verdict, to wit:

We, the Jury find the Defendant Guilty of Grand Larceny.

John McKiernan, Foreman

Which said verdict upon being rendered was read by the Clerk to the Jury, and they were asked if it was the verdict of them all: To which they all assented. The Court thereupon ordered that Saturday, September 12th, 1885 at 10 o'clock a.m. be the time fixed for pronouncing judgement against said Defendant, Fleming Parker. The Defendant was then remanded to the custody of the Sheriff of Tulare County.

When September 12 came, Parker was sentenced to one year in the State Prison at San Quentin. It was a comparatively light sentence, considering the nature of the crime and the time period in which it occurred. The California State Archives has informed me that the full prison records for San Quentin have not survived for that period, but the prison register has. It states that Parker was received on September 18, 1885. He was prisoner #11839.

The register also gives us the earliest recorded description of Parker. It lists his age at 20 (which was correct), and gives his occupation as a Teamster. This prison register states he was 5 feet 8 inches tall, light complexion, gray eyes, brown hair.

On September 9, 1885, the day after he was convicted of Grand Larceny for stealing Woodard's steer, Fleming Parker took his revenge on his ex-friend Philo Johns for testifying against him. Parker swore out a complaint of his own, accusing Johns of other cattle thefts! This original complaint reads as follows:

Personally appeared before me this 9th day of September 1885, Fleming Parker of the County of Tulare,, who, being first duly sworn, complains and says: That one Philo Johns of Tulare County on or about the 3rd day of March A. D. 1885,

---

* Except for Philo Johns, Deputy F. M. Bell, and the Woodards, it is not known how these other witnesses figured into the case. The two Slaters were probably related to the previously invoked friend of Johns, Mattie Slater. Today, one just aches for more information, which sadly has not survived.

and before the filing of this complaint, at the County of Tulare did willfully and feloniously steal, take, and drive away one white steer, with black ears and black mark on neck, marked with (illegible) and two splits in one ear and crop and split in the other ear, being the property of Taylor Archer; one red heifer about 2 years old, small, with white spot in forehead, branded K2 and marked in both ears, being the property of Wm. Kinkade; one (illegible) steer, 3 years old, white spot in forehead, branded (illegible), 2 (illegible) in one ear and (illegible) in other ear, being the property of unknown owner.

All of which is contrary to the form of the Statue in such cases made and provided and against the peace and dignity of the people of the State of California.

"Said complainant therefore prays that a warrant may be issued for the arrest of the said Philo Johns, and that he may be dealt with according to law.

Subscribed and sworn to before me this 9th day of September A.D. 1885.
Fleming Parker

Fleming Parker,[*]

A. C. Neil
Justice of the Peace

It is not known how Parker excused away his detailed knowledge of these thefts without admitting to his own probable involvement, but despite the fact that he had just been convicted of a felony, Parker somehow convinced District Attorney William B. Wallace that his charges were valid. He did claim to have been a witness to the sale of the stolen cattle to a George Bunch of Kingsburg, but how he did that without admitting complicity in the thefts is unknown. Wallace proceeded to order the arrest of Philo Johns, who was indicted on September 13th, 1885 (by the time the official indictment was written out, Wallace had determined that the last stolen steer had been the property of a James Halstead).

If Parker was involved in all of these thefts, and it is likely that he was, it would seem to indicate that he and Johns had attempted to start a little cattle rustling business. Parker's involvement with this kind of thievery certainly began early; it is significant to remember this, as a number of Western history revisionists of recent years have attempted to depict Parker as an upstanding citizen until his involvement in the Rock Cut Train Robbery. Such is clearly not the case.

From the *Tulare Weekly Times* of September 24, 1885:

Flem Parker, who was sentenced by Judge Cross to one year's imprisonment in the State boarding-house, was conveyed thither last Thursday night, in charge of Special Officer J. J. Hanafin, Jr.

From the *Tulare Weekly Times* of October 1, 1885:

---

[*] This is the signature of Fleming Parker, from his court papers in 1885 after he was arrested for stealing a steer. (Tulare County Superior Court—public record)

District Attorney Wallace has filed three informations in the Superior Court against George Washington Fry for burglary, and one against Philo Johns for grand larceny.

On October 1st, Judge William W. Cross set Johns' bail at $1,000, which he did not (and probably could not) pay. On October 5th, his attorney filed a demurer to the charges, arguing why they should be dismissed by the court:

> Now comes the defendant in the above entitled cause, by his Attorney Oregon Sanders, and demurs to the Information filed herein on the following grounds to wit: That it appears upon the face of said Information that more than one offense is charged therein to wit: the offense of grand larceny committed in stealing and driving away one white steer with black ears, the property of Taylor Archer, the offense of grand larceny committed in stealing and driving away one small red heifer, the property of William Kincade; and the offense of grand larceny committed in stealing and driving away one large, red, (illegible) steer, the property of James Halstead.
>
> That it appears upon the face of said Information that the same does not conform to the requirements of Section 950 of the Penal Code of the State of California in this, that it does not contain a statement of the acts constituting any offense known to the law of California in ordinary or (illegible) language or in such a manner as to enable a person of common understanding to know what is intended;
>
> That it appears upon the face of said complaint that it does not conform to the requirements of Section 952 of the Penal Code of this State in this; that it is neither certain nor direct as it regards the offense charged or the particular circumstances of it.
>
> Oregon Sanders
Atty for Defendant

What all of this legal jargon really meant was, attorney Sanders was protesting the legal propriety of charging Philo Johns with a single count of Grand Larceny, while incorporating three different thefts into the one-count indictment. Today, such behavior by a District Attorney would indeed be grounds for a dismissal of the charges, but Sanders' plea fell on the Court's deaf ears in 1885.

But the star witness against Philo Johns had already been shipped to San Quentin to begin his one-year prison term, so District Attorney Wallace had to petition the Tulare County Superior Court to order the temporary transport of Fleming Parker back to Visalia to testify against his ex-friend. The paperwork for this act makes for interesting reading:

> In the Superior Court of the County of Tulare, State of California
> The People, Plaintiff
>   Vs
> Philo Johns, Defendant
> State of California
> County of Tulare

W. B. Wallace, District Attorney of Tulare County being duly sworn says, that Fleming Parker, a prisoner imprisoned in the State Prison at San Quentin in Said State, is a necessary and material witness for the People in Said cause; that the facts he expects to prove by Said witness are that he Fleming Parker saw the property alleged in the Information in Said cause at the time said property is alleged to have been stolen, and at all times thereafter until said property was sold and delivered to George A. Bunch at Kingsburg in Fresno County; that the testimony of said witness in not cumulative, and the facts sought to be proved by him cannot be proved by any other witness within reach of the process of said Court.

"Wherefore he prays for an order for the temporary removal of said Fleming Parker from said State Prison, and for his production before said Court at the trial of said cause on the 15th day of October 1885 at 10 o'clock a.m.

W. B. Wallace

Subscribed and Sworn to
Before Me this 7th day
Of October 1885
L. Gilroy, Co. Clerk
By John L. Knox, Deputy
State of California
County of Tulare

Upon reading the foregoing affidavit, it is Ordered by the Hon. W. W. Cross, Superior Judge of Tulare County, that the witness therein named to wit: Fleming Parker, be temporarily removed from said State Prison and produced before the Superior Court of Tulare County, said State, at 10 o'clock a.m. on the 15th day of October 1885, and the Sheriff of said Tulare County is hereby authorized and directed to bring the said Fleming Parker before said Court at said time, to safely keep him, and when he is no longer required as a witness to return him to said State Prison; and the Warden of said State Prison is hereby authorized and directed to deliver into the custody of said Sheriff the said Fleming Parker, upon his application in pursuance of this order.

Dated Visalia   W. W. Cross
Oct. 9th, 1885   Superior Judge

The *Tulare Weekly Times* found all of this amusing as well. From the October 18, 1885 edition:

Sheriff Balaam, who went to San Quentin last Friday for the purpose of bringing Flem Parker from the State Prison to Visalia, where he is wanted as a witness in the Philo Johns case returned with his charge last Tuesday. It will be remembered that Parker was sent up for one year for grand larceny. During his short stay within the prison walls he has been following the legitimate occupation of driving a team, and as soon as his testimony is taken in the Johns case, he will be returned to the penitentiary and allowed to resume his honorable calling.

Surviving records for the trial of Philo Johns are not as complete as they are for Parker, so it is not known what other witnesses besides Parker were allowed to testify (although George Bunch was surely among them.)

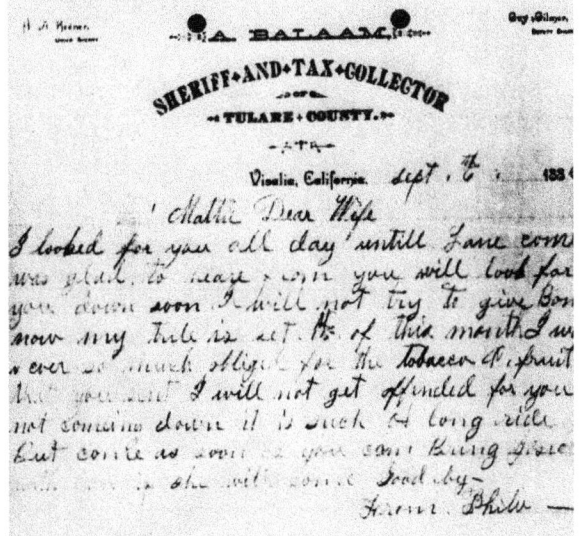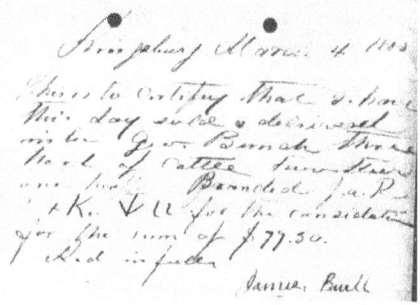

These two scraps of paper, a bill of sale and a letter from Philo Johns to his wife, were admitted into evidence in Johns' trial. It is difficult to know why, unless the District Attorney was trying to show similarities between the handwriting, and there isn't much. (Tulare County Superior Court—public record)

What has survived are two pieces of material evidence used against Johns, and in the retrospect we have today, they raise some interesting questions.

The first, titled Exhibit A, is a bill of sale for the stolen cattle, acknowledging that George Bunch paid $77.50 for the animals in question to James Burll (presumably the alias used by Johns when transacting the sale). The document is signed by Burll. It is dated March 4, 1885.

The second document, Exhibit B, is a letter written from jail by Philo Johns to his wife, identified as Mattie. Is this the Mattie Slater alluded to in F. M. Bell's sworn affidavit in Fleming Parker's trial? If so, Johns and Mattie must have hurriedly gotten married in the interim. The letter was obviously never mailed, and must have been seized by Sheriff Balaam for use as evidence. Written on the Sheriff's own stationary, it reads as follows:

> Mattie Dear Wife
> I looked for you all day until Lane come was glad to heare from you will look for you down soon. I will not try to give Bonds now my trile is set 15 of this month. I was ever so much obliged for the tobacco & fruit that you sent. I will not get offended for you not coming down it is such a long ride. But come as soon as you can. Bring Josie with you if she will come. Good by
>
> From Philo

It is not at all clear why this letter was considered prime evidence against Johns. There isn't a single thing incriminatory in the contents that I can see. The only possibility is that the letter was used to show that Philo Johns' handwriting matched that of James Burll on the bill of sale. If this is the case, District Attorney Wallace must have been counting on the illiteracy of the trial jurors to put it over, because even the naked eye can tell you that the two handwriting samples bear very little resemblance to each other. While I am not a handwriting expert, I do have to add (with historical hindsight guiding me) that the writing of "James Burll" on the bill of sale actually resembles the later surviving handwriting samples of Parker himself! This is very interesting.

Again, court papers for the People vs. Philo Johns are spotty, but they indicate that the jurors summoned for the case were G. M. Caldwell, J. A. Miller, R. J. Rogers, F. G. Miller, John Miner, J. D. Langley, Ed Hinds, P. Byrd, W. W. Kelley, Samuel Berkley, B. Shaver, C. P. Murry. One of these jurors must have been replaced, as the verdict is signed by a foreman named A. F. Thompson.

Philo Johns was found guilty of Grand Larceny. His attorney quickly filed a motion for a new trial:

> Now comes the defendant in the above entitled cause by his attorney Oregon Sanders and before the entry of judgement herein moves the court to grant him a New Trial of (illegible) on the following grounds to wit:
> That the court misdirected the jury in matters of law and erred in the decision of questions of law arising during the course of the trial.
> That the verdict was and is contrary to law.
> That the verdict was and is contrary to the evidence.
> Oregon Sanders
Atty for Defendant

This motion was about as routine as you can get, and was quickly denied. Philo Johns was sentenced to two years in the State Prison at San Quentin. Again, the detailed records of San Quentin have not survived, but the surviving prison register shows that Johns was admitted October 30, 1885 as Prisoner Number 11897. He was listed as having originally come from Missouri, and like Parker, listed his occupation as a Teamster. The register describes Johns as having been 23 years old, 6 feet, 2 inches tall, light complexion, brown eyes, and black hair.

Following Johns' trial, the *Tulare Weekly Times* carried this item on October 22, 1885:

> Sheriff Balaam went to San Quentin Tuesday morning, having in his custody George Washington Fry, recently convicted in the Superior Court on a charge of burglary and sentenced by Judge Cross to serve three years in the State Prison. Flem Parker was also in charge of the Sheriff to be returned to the penitentiary.

One wonders if Fleming Parker and Philo Johns ever encountered each other in prison!

Philo Johns, who had received a much stiffer sentence than Parker had, was released from San Quentin on June 30, 1887, about 4 months shy of his full sentence. His whereabouts after that are unknown. Most ex-cons in those days usually left their old haunts in an attempt to start over someplace where no one knew their past. Perhaps Philo Johns (and his wife Mattie) did just that.

Chapter 1: Early Life

Fleming Parker was released from San Quentin on July 17, 1886, roughly two months before his full sentence would have been up. After that, he wasn't heard from for a few years. Unlike many of the ex-cons I alluded to above, it is known that Parker did return to Visalia and his family, but whether he did so right away or not is unclear.

Many Western historians are adamant that Parker made his first foray into Arizona at this time, beginning his cowboying stints, and befriending George C. Ruffner (see Chapter 2). He may well have done so, but there is no evidence to prove it. One legend—a beautiful but nevertheless unproven legend—contends that Parker and Ruffner both entered the first July 4th rodeo in Prescott, Arizona (Prescott lays claim to hosting the world's oldest annual rodeo) in 1888.

Tulare County records show that Parker's sister Martha married a local man named Wallace Rockwell on January 9, 1888.

A deed in the Tulare County Courthouse does show that Parker sold some land to his grandfather, Fleming Work, in Visalia, on October 3, 1888. How Parker came to own the land is unknown, although he probably inherited it from his father (Dan Parker's probate records have apparently not survived). Fleming Work paid his wayward grandson $500.00 for the land, which is described as *"the southeast ¼ of section 8, township 17 south, range 27 east of Mt. Diablo baseline meridian—160 acres."*

That is quite a bit of land for only $500.00, even at 1888 prices. For reasons unknown, Parker apparently needed money badly.

Whether Parker was in Arizona during this period, or whether he returned to Visalia and stayed there, he did manage to stay out of trouble for a few years. At least, he didn't do anything he was caught at. But Fleming Parker was definitely in Visalia in late 1890.

On November 22, 1890, a farmer named George Ditman swore out a routine complaint in Tulare County against an unknown thief or thieves that had broken into his barn. It was a seemingly ordinary crime, and the complaint simply reads:

> Personally appeared before me this 22nd day of November 1890, G. E. Ditman of the County of Tulare, State of California, who being first duly sworn, complains and says:
>
> That one John Doe on or about the 20th day of November A.D. 1890, and before the filing of this Complaint, at the County of Tulare, State of California, did willfully and feloniously, with intent to steal, break into the barn of this affiant, on the Simmons ranch in said township, and did steal and carry away about fifty sacks of wheat of the value of $85.00.
>
> All of which is contrary to the form of the statue in such cases made and provided and against the peace and dignity of the people of the State of California.
>
> Said complainant therefore prays that a warrant be issued for the arrest of said John Doe, and that he may be dealt with according to law.

The complaint was signed by Ditman and Justice of the Peace C. Bingham. The unknown John Doe was soon apprehended and identified as W. B. Brown (also referred to as Walter Brown), and he was formally indicted for Grand Larceny on November 28, 1890, by District Attorney W. R. Jacobs.

As with Philo Johns, virtually nothing is known of the background of Walter Brown. In all likelihood, he was either another drifting cowboy, local low-life, petty thief, or even all of the above, the sort of unsavory character Parker was always hanging around with.

One small bit of evidence as to Walter Brown's character has recently come to light—something that Fleming Parker himself probably didn't know about his friend. Brown had, in 1887, served a term in San Quentin prison for a burglary committed in Shasta County.

The Shasta County Courthouse has informed me that they no longer have court papers from the era, and I was unable to glean anything from the area's old newspapers, so the exact details of Brown's crime are unknown. What is known is that, based on records at the California State Archives, Brown committed his burglary on December 28, 1886, pleaded guilty to the crime and was sentenced to one year in prison.

The surviving San Quentin registry shows that he entered the facility on January 21, 1887 as Convict No. 12372. It described him as having come from Illinois, that he was 28 years old at that time, and that he worked as a "laborer." He was 5 feet, 9 ¾ inches tall, complexion "florid," with gray eyes and red hair. He was further described as having a "large scar under right ear close to cheek, mole on left collar bone, (several words illegible), broad shoulders, stout built."

Brown was released from San Quentin on November 21, 1887, and probably just roamed around after that, eventually ending up in Tulare County, and participating in the robbery of George Ditman's wheat in 1890.

Although the details are lost to history, Brown struck a deal with W. R. Jacobs. In exchange for leniency, Brown agreed to turn State's evidence against his accomplice in the burglary—Fleming Parker.

Fleming Parker was quickly picked up. Ditman was asked to refile his complaint, which he did on November 26th, 1890. Parker was formally indicted on November 28 by District Attorney Jacobs.

As with the previous case, the surviving court papers from the People vs. Flem Parker are scattered, caused, no doubt, by early 20th century souvenir hunters. Most of the papers are still available at the Tulare County Courthouse in Visalia, but one key document eventually wound up in the archives of the Sharlot Hall Museum in Prescott, Arizona. Put together, we once again get a fairly full picture of this episode in Parker's early life.

Parker acquired an attorney, possibly paid for by his grandfather again. There is no surviving bail information. The attorney, James S. Clack, immediately filed the usual motion to dismiss charges:

Motion to set aside the information filed herein on the 28th day of Nov. 1890.
    Comes now the defendant in said action and moves the Hon. Superior Court aforesaid to set aside information in this case filed on the 28th day of Nov. 1890, and to discharge this defendant from custody upon the following grounds:
    1stst That before the filing thereof, that is before the filing of said (illegible) had not been legally committed by a magistrate.
    2nd That before the filing of the said information, said defendant had not been legally committed for the offense charged in said information or any public offense by a magistrate.
    Wherefore Defendant prays that said information may be set aside and dismissed and that this defendant may be released from custody.
                                     J. S. Clack
                                     Attorney for Defs.

From the *Tulare County Times* of November 27, 1890:

Flem Parker and W. B. Brown were brought to this city from Traver last evening and incarcerated in the county jail to await trial in the Superior Court on the charge of stealing 69 sacks of wheat from the ranch of George Dittman, near Smith's mountain. The wheat was brought to this city on Friday last and disposed of at the flouring mill. Mr. Dittman does not live on the ranch from where the wheat was stolen, but at Traver, but on going to the ranch missed the wheat and informed Constable W. F. Russell of the fact. The officer got on the track of the men named, and arrested them. They had a preliminary examination before a Justice of the "Peace" at Traver, and were bound over to appear before the Superior Court. The evidence against the men is said to be sufficient to convict them.

Here, the details of the case get murky, with precious little clarifying evidence. At some point, a man named James Hamilton was also arrested in connection with the Ditman burglary, and Brown apparently agreed to turn state's evidence against him as well. From the *Tulare County Times* of December 4, 1890:

James Hamilton, arrested on the charge of implication with Flem Parker and W. B. Brown in stealing wheat from the ranch of George Ditman, in the 76 country, was before Justice Neill for trial yesterday. As the Sheriff's office refused to let Brown appear in the Justice's Court, without an order from the Superior Court, and as Brown was the principal witness in the case, District Attorney Jacobs moved the dismissal of the charge against Hamilton, and he was allowed his freedom.

As will be seen, Parker would later try to use Hamilton as an alibi, but exactly who he was and what role he played in the robbery are apparently lost to history.

Having agreed to a plea bargain to turn state's evidence against Parker, Walter Brown proceeded to plead guilty to the Ditman robbery. December 16, 1890 was originally set for his sentencing, but this was later postponed for unknown reasons until December 31. At that time, Judge William W. Cross sentenced him to 2 ½ years in San Quentin, or 30 months. He entered the prison as convict 14375 on January 4, 1891. The description of him on the prison register is virtually identical to his earlier one, except that he was now 32 years old. He was released from prison on January 4, 1893, two years to the day of his entry. Nothing further is known of him after that. He probably continued his drifting ways, and for all we know, may have gotten in trouble elsewhere. But with no evidence of where he went, his whereabouts and his fate are virtually impossible to trace.

As explained before, there are no surviving verbatim transcripts of the courtroom proceedings and testimony in many cases from this era, and Parker's case is no exception. A summary of the proceedings in the People vs. Flem Parker has survived. Judge William W. Cross presided over the case once again. From Parker's arraignment on November 29, 1890:

> The Defendant appeared in Court with his Attorney J. S. Clack Esq. and waived the reading of the Information, and the clerk delivered to him a certified copy thereof. Thereupon the Defendant was asked by the Court if Flem Parker was his true name, and he replied in the affirmative. Whereupon the Court ordered that the Defendant have until Monday December 1st, 1890 at 10 o'clock A. M. to plead to said information.

From the record of the December 1st session:

> This being the tome fixed by the Court for the Defendant to plead to the Information filed against him; the District Attorney with the Defendant and his counsel J. S. Clack Esq. Appeared in Court. Thereupon the Defendant by his counsel moved the Court to set aside the Information on the grounds that said Defendant had never been legally committed by the Committing Magistrate, which motion, after argument by counsel for the respective parties, was by the Court denied, to which ruling and Order of the Court, the Defendant by his counsel then and there duly excepted. Thereupon the Defendant by his counsel pleads that he is not guilty as charged in said information.

At the December 3rd session, Judge Cross ordered that Parker's trial be set for December 30th, 1890.

Parker's attorney filed an affidavit with the court requesting a postponement of the trial, to no avail. They argued that James Hamilton could completely clear Parker, but that they were having trouble finding him:

> Flem Parker, being first duly sworn, deposes and says that his name is Flem Parker; that he is the defendant in the above entitled action; that the said defendant has fully and fairly stated the case in this action and the facts thereof to J. S. Clack his Counsel and Attorney in this case above entitled, and after such statement, he is advised by his said counsel, and verily believes that he has a

good and substantiated defense to said action on the merits, that he cannot safely go to trial at this term of the Court, or at this setting of the Court, because and on account of the absence of James Hamilton, who is a material and necessary witness for Defendant. That subpoena was duly issued by the Clerk of said Court on the day that said case was set down for trial, to wit: On the 3rd day of Dec. 1890, or thereabouts and by this defendant immediately placed in the hands of the Sheriff of the County of Tulare aforesaid for service upon said witness James Hamilton and said sheriff did on 29th day of Dec. 1890 return said subpoena to said Court unserved upon said witness James Hamilton, stating in his return that he, said sheriff, made due and diligent search and inquiry for said witness James Hamilton at said Tulare County and that he, said sheriff, has been and was unable to find him, said witness James Hamilton, at or in said Tulare County, a copy of which subpoena is hereunto annexed and marked Exhibit "A" and made a part of this affidavit and the same is hereby referred to as a part of this affidavit together with all the endorsements and returns thereon of said sheriff.

That witness is a young man of about the age of twenty years; that he, said witness, is now and has been for several months last a permanent resident of the said County of Tulare; that he, said witness, is a property owner of and in said County of Tulare, he having an (illegible; possibly "undenied") interest in the Estate of Martha J. Hamilton deceased and therein he, said witness, owns and possesses personal property in said County; that said witness James Hamilton, as the defendant is informed and believes and therefore states the fact to be, is absent in the Eastern part of Tulare County aforesaid hunting. That said witness James Hamilton is a respectable & well appearing young man & will make a good appearance on the witness stand. That the evidence and testimony of said witness James Hamilton is material and necessary for the defense of this defendant (illegible). That he, said witness James Hamilton, will testify and (illegible; possibly "state") upon the witness stand under oath the following state of facts to wit:

That his name (name of witness) is James Hamilton, and that his age is about 20 years; that he is a laborer by occupation and resides in the County of Tulare, State of California, and owns an undivided interest in the Estate of his mother Martha J. Hamilton now deceased, besides he, said witness, owns personal property in said County of Tulare and is a permanent resident of said County& has been for more than six months last (illegible); that he knows Flem Parker, the defendant in this case & has known him for seven years last (illegible); that he knows one W. B. Brown who has been informed against by the District Attorney of Tulare County is said (illegible; possibly County) of the commission of the crime of Burglary to which said Brown has pleaded guilty, the same being the same offense with which said defendant is accused of having committed on or about the 20th day of Nov. 1890 in company & in conspiracy with said Brown.

That said offense of which said Brown pleads guilty of having committed and of which defendant is also accused of was not perpetrated or committed prior to the night of Nov. 20th 1890; that he, said witness James Hamilton, and said Brown and Defendant Flem Parker were together in an eating house in the City of Visalia, said County & State, on the evening of the 20th of Nov. 1890 and before said alleged offense was committed by said Brown as aforesaid, and said three parties being the only persons present, said James Hamilton heard a conversation between said Brown and Defendant Parker and there and then agreed to pay him, said Parker, the sum of $3.00 per day to assist him, said Brown, to haul some grain from one George Ditman's Ranch is said County; that there and then Brown did pay said Parker the said sum to assist him, said Brown, for helping haul grain as aforesaid; he, said Brown, stating there and then that he had agreed to deliver the said grain on the following day in the City of Visalia. Brown, in said conversation said: I'll give you $3.00 to go & help me load up the grain & he paid him. No other persons were present as said conversation (illegible) Parker Defendant, then and there said he would go if he would pay him. He paid him as aforesaid, Brown then and there said he had bought the grain.

That the evidence of said witness James Hamilton is material and necessary for the defendant' defense in said action; That the said facts which defendant expects to prove, can prove, and will prove by said absent witness James Hamilton cannot to this affiant's knowledge be proved by any other person or persons or witness or witnesses. That this application is made in good faith and the same is not made merely for the purpose of delay but that Justice may be done in the (illegible), and affiant verily believes that if this cause be Continued for this term, this time set apart for the trial of criminal actions by said Court, or for a reasonable time, he will be able to have the said witness present in court at such reasonable time that said court may fix for and to which this case may be postponed by said Court.

[signature]

The affidavit was signed by Parker and sworn before the Deputy Clerk of the Court. It is a perfect example of how lengthy and didactic legal terminology already was in 1890. If it were in the present day, the continuance would have most likely been granted by the court, but in 1890, it was denied and the trial of Flem Parker went on as scheduled.

So who exactly was James Hamilton? Would he have truly provided an alibi for Parker? These questions are lost for all time, I fear, but there is a bizarre footnote: Many years later, in 1964 to be precise, an author named Tom Coleman would write a heavily romanticized after-the-fact account of Parker's life for *True West* magazine, in which the author would drop the name of "Jim Hamilton" as a partial alibi for the 1897 Rock Cut Train Robbery (see Chapter 10)! Could Hamilton have followed Parker to Arizona later on? Not likely; it is more reasonable to conclude that this footnote in Parker's life inadvertently spilled over into another event in the mind of Coleman.

As for the contention that Parker was framed by one of his friends for the crime, it was now the second time and second crime for which Parker made the allegation. Although certainly not impossible, it is still very difficult to believe that he could have had such a run of astoundingly bad luck, especially in retrospect, knowing what we know now of his hideous track record in Arizona. For her part, Parker's sister Sadie never stopped believing in her brother, and in her surviving letters (reprinted later), she would continue to contend that her brother was set up for these Tulare County crimes.

---

* Fleming Parker's signature.

On December 30th, 1890, the case of The People vs. Flem Parker commenced, with Judge William W. Cross presiding. Again, no transcript of the testimony survives, but the official record of the proceeding has. It reads:

> The District Attorney with the Defendant and his Counsel J. S. Clack Esq. Came into Court. Counsel for the Defendant moved for a continuance of the trial of this case on the ground of absence of a material witness on part of the defense and filed the affidavit of the Defendant in support of his Motion. Whereupon the District Attorney resisted said motion, and filed counter affidavits thereto. After argument of Counsel, said motion was by the Court denied, to which ruling of the Court the Defendant by his Counsel duly excepted. Thereupon, the following named persons were drawn from the regular Venire and being accepted were sworn as Jurors to try the case at bar, to wit: Charles Wilbur, S. Townsend, T. E. Winsett, C.R. Hawley, A. J. Wood, G. Q. Gill, E. Harrison, J. W. Kellum, C. G. Hough, J. A. Howell, John Cowing, and W. McFadden.
>
> The Information filed herein was read and Defendant's plea thereto stated by the Clerk to the Jury. Thereupon the following witnesses were sworn and examined for the prosecution, G. W. Ditman, W. B. Brown, W. E. Russell, C. Eder, G. H. Tyson, and R. C. Hardin* and the Prosecution rests;
>
> Counsel for the Defendant moved the Court to instruct the jury to acquit the Defendant on the ground of the variance between the proofs and charge contained in the Information, which motion after argument of Counsel was by the Court taken under advisement until Wednesday, December 31st, 1890 at 10 o'clock a.m.; to which time the Court took a recess.

The trial resumed the following day, on schedule. Again, from the official record:

> The Defendant and the Jury and Counsel being present and the Court being now sufficiently advised in the matter or Defendant's Motion to instruct the jury to acquit the Defendant, ordered that said motion be denied, to which ruling of the Court the Defendant by his Counsel duly excepted. Thereupon Flem Parker, J. W. Slater, & S. J. Slater** were sworn and examined for the defense, and Defendant rests, and W. B. Brown was called in rebuttal by the Prosecution. The Evidence closed, and case argued by Counsel for the prosecution and defense and submitted after the instructions given by the Court to the Jury for consideration and decision.
>
> The Jury thereupon retired in charge of the Sheriff to deliberate upon a verdict, and after deliberating the Jury returned into Court and asked for further instructions and again retired to deliberate.
>
> And after due deliberation, the Jury came into Court and declared the following verdict:
>> We the Jury find the Defendant guilty of Burglary in the first degree.
>> J. Woods, Foreman
>
> Defendant remanded and January 12th, 1891 at 10 o'clock a.m. set as the time for pronouncing Judgement.

---

*   Again, it is unclear who those last three witnesses were.

** The recurring presence of the Slater family in Parker's early crimes is a mystery.

Parker's surviving court papers show that on January 12, 1891, attorney Clack petitioned the Court for a one week delay in sentencing, which was granted. For reasons that are unclear, it was postponed for yet another week, but on January 26, 1891, Flem Parker was sentenced to five years in San Quentin prison. The stiffness of the sentence was undoubtedly due to the fact that this was Parker's second offence. Prior to sentencing, attorney Clack petitioned the court for a new trial, which was denied (naturally).

For the second time in his young life, Fleming Parker was admitted to the California State Prison at San Quentin. He was received on January 27, 1891, and became prisoner #14402. This time, his full prison record has survived, although it is at the Sharlot Hall Museum instead of in California. Whatever early-day souvenir hunter grabbed it did us all a huge favor, as virtually no detailed San Quentin records have survived from this period.

On Parker's 1891 San Quentin record, his age was listed as 26 (correct), and his occupation was still listed as a Teamster. His physical description was largely the same as in 1885—height 5 feet, 7 ½ inches (a half-inch difference from his previous record), with light complexion, brown hair, and gray eyes. His weight was listed at 165 pounds, his foot size measured at 6 ½, and his forehead described as "full high." His religion was listed as Protestant, and, most interestingly, his mental culture was described as "poor."

This surviving prison record gives us the most detailed description of Parker in existence. It goes on to list him as having medium features, straight nose, small round chin, and square shoulders. His teeth are described as "fair." Under a listing for scars and deformities, a surprising number were recorded as follows:

> 1 small back right hand, 1 left side head, 1 small inside right forearm, 1 right thumb, numerous forfinger right hand, 1 small middle finger right hand, 1 underpart right hand, 1 back head.

Either Parker had an unusual run of work injuries, or, far more likely, he had been in a lot of fights!

This prison description of Parker concludes by noting that he had a mole on the back of his neck and a vaccine mark on his right upper arm.

If young Parker were inclined toward sociopathy to begin with, and it appears that he was, two stays in San Quentin before he reached 30 certainly would have finished the job.

An interesting sidelight to the case: In Parker's surviving court papers is a sworn deposition by a W. W. Moore that was apparently not used during the trial. Exactly why is unclear, but it is rather ambiguous. At first glance, it seems very damning to Parker, but the evidence seems to not be strong enough to have really accomplished anything. For interest's sake, it reads as follows:

> W. W. Moore being first duly sworn, deposes and says: That his name is W. W. Moore, that (illegible) is 44 years of age & is now & has been a resident of said County since 1859 & owns personal property in said county, and by occupation a lumberman.

Affiant further says under oath, I am well acquainted with defendant Flem Parker, have known him about fifteen years last (illegible): have known the witness W. B. Brown who testified in the said case against defendant at his trial on the 30th and 31st days of last (illegible)—Dec. 1890—about eight months last (illegible) & have known said Brown to have been engaged in the occupation of making & selling posts from the mountains in said county.

Affiant states further that he had 3 or 4 conversations with said Brown, some before & some after the offense in said case is & was alleged to have been committed. One conversation that I had & heard from Brown aforesaid make was after he had delivered the wheat in said question to the mill in the City of Visalia, said county & state. Was in front of said mill in the presence of one Al Downing and on the 22nd day of November 1890, or thereabouts the time after the said Brown had delivered the wheat in question to said mill, Brown then and there said to said Downing, "You have a bad opinion of me. Downing said Why? Brown said, I understand you said I am guilty of stealing wheat, said Brown further, I never stole anything in my life; I traded posts for this wheat, the wheat that I sold to the mill (illegible).

After this conversation, Brown aforesaid & I went (illegible) straight to (illegible; possibly name of a town) in said County, and in the immediate vicinity thereof & then, I heard him Brown said to Defendant, I want you to be in town, meaning Visalia, by one o'clock. Speaking to Defendant, you can clear me, he Brown said.

Parker did not serve even one year of his five year sentence. His attorney, James S. Clack, appealed the case to the California State Supreme Court on legal technicalities. The case was 20806. The details have not survived; the California State Archives has informed me that the case file is now missing, even though they have most of the Supreme Court records from that period. Again, it was undoubtedly pilfered by a souvenir hunter after Parker's later infamy, but it has never turned up elsewhere.

The Supreme Court found merit in the case, and overturned Parker's conviction. A text of the opinion still exists in the Visalia copy of Parker's court file, and it reads as follows:

> The People, Respondent,}
>   vs   No. 20,806
> Flem Parker, Appellant }

An information was filed charging the defendant with the crime of burglary.

Before pleading he moved to set aside the information upon the ground "that he had not been legally committed by a magistrate." Upon the hearing of the motion it was shown that G. W. Ditman filed a sworn complaint before a magistrate alleging "That one Flem Parker, on or about the 20th of November, 1890, and before the filing of this complaint, at the county of Tulare, State of California, did willfully and unlawfully enter a barn with intent to commit larceny, said barn being located on the Simmons ranch in said Kaweab township," etc.

There were no other depositions in the case, and upon the complaint was endorsed the following commitment:

"It appearing to me that the offense in the within deposition mentioned has been committed, and that there is sufficient cause to believe the within-named Flem Parker guilty thereof," etc.

The information charges that: "The said Flem Parker, on or about the 20th day of November, 1890, and before the filing of this information, at the county and State foresaid, did willfully, unlawfully and feloniously enter a certain barn, the property of one G. W. Ditman, with intent then and there and therein to commit the crime of larceny."

The motion to set aside the information should have been grated, for the foregoing record discloses that the defendant was never committed by a magistrate for this offense charged in the information.

Under the law as declared in People vs. Ah Chuck, 66 Cal., 063, and People vs. Vierra, 67 Cal., 231, the district attorney is allowed to file an information based either upon the offense set out in the commitment or upon the facts disclosed by the depositions, and that is the limit of his authority.

This information is based neither upon the commitment nor the facts set out in the complaint or deposition.

It alleges that the defendant entered a certain barn, the property of one G. W. Ditman, with the intent, etc.

The record is entirely silent as to any such state of facts, and the district attorney in framing his information is bound by the record.

It be insisted that the allegation of ownership of the barn is G. W. Ditman is immaterial, and therefore harmless.

While is charging the offense of burglary, it may not be necessary in all cases to allege ownership of the property entered, yet in this case, it was a secondary allegation, for it constituted the entire and only description of the barn which the defendant is charged with feloniously entering.

Let the judgement be reversed, and the cause remanded, with directions that the information be set aside.

Garoutte, J.

We concur:
DeHaven, J.
Sharpstein, J.
McFarland, J.
Harrison, J.
Beatty, C. J.

(Concurring Opinion)

If the question were an open one, I should say that information could not be sustained unless it charged the offense charged in the complaint, and for which he was examined and committed by the magistrate. Such appears to me in the view of the Supreme Court of the United States in Hurtardo vs. California, 110 U.S., 516. Our own cases, however, hold that the district attorney may prosecute for any offense shown by the depositions taken on the preliminary examination. I therefore concur.

Paterson, J.

The *Tulare Weekly Times* noted the event with an eerily prophetic news item on September 17, 1891:

The case of the People vs. Flem Parker, tried in the superior court of this county last December, when Parker was convicted of burglary, was appealed to the supreme court by his attorneys, J. S. Clack and Olias G. Lamberson, and last week the supreme court in Bank reversed the case with directions that the information be set aside. It is not probable that the case will be tried again, as the principal witness for the prosecution is confined in San Quentin and the district attorney cannot bring him here to attend a preliminary examination. Parker has a bad reputation, and the cattle growers of the county will regret that the information was incorrectly drawn by the former district attorney of this county.

Parker was released from San Quentin on October 6, 1891. It is unclear what caused the delay after his conviction was overturned, but according to letters later written by his sister Sadie (in Chapter 8), Parker did not return to Visalia and his old haunts this time. Instead, he rode off for Arizona and infamy. Whether he had ever been to the Arizona Territory before is a matter of some debate, but this time he went for certain.

On February 4, 1892, the *Tulare Weekly Times* carried the following on the declining health of Parker's grandfather, Fleming Work:

> Flem Works is at the home of Joseph Patnot, very ill with pneumonia. This morning there was a slight change for the better.

Fleming Work knew he was dying, and on February 4, 1892, disposed of his estate while he was still alive. Papers filed in the Tulare County Courthouse showed that he divided his land among his children and grandchildren, William Work, Litha A. Boyd, Sarah Jane Boyd, Margaret Welch, Martha Susan Rockwell, and Fleming Parker, who received a 1/12th undivided interest in the land. Work's land was described as *"South ½ of section 8 and south ½ of north ½ of section 8, Twp. 17 south, range 27 east of Mt. Diablo. 480 acres more or less."*

Fleming Work died three days later, on February 7, 1892, at the age of 77. The *Tulare Weekly Times* carried the following:

> One by one, the pioneers go. Flem Work came to California in 1852, and located in Yolo county, after which he came to Tulare. He was born in Tennessee seventy-seven years ago. He was an old school Democrat, having voted that ticket at every election since his majority. His family consists of a son, W. M. Work, and a daughter, the wife of J. M. Boyd. Mr. Work was a lover of good horses and owned several noted racers at different times. He leaves many friends.

According to a later letter by Sadie, Parker did not return to Visalia to attend to his grandfather's estate. She would also say that, in the ensuing years, he returned occasionally to assist her after her divorce from Curtis Jackson Boyd.

The grave of Fleming Work, loving grandfather of Fleming Parker, who tried unsuccessfully to straighten his incorrigible grandson out. (author's photo)

Parker did not finish paying his attorney's fees after getting out of prison, and as a result, James S. Clack filed a lawsuit against him to collect on November 28, 1892. The suit reads as follows:

> In the Superior Court of the County of Tulare,
> State of California
> J. S. Clack,
> Plaintiff,
>
> Vs.
>
> Flemming Parker,
> Defendant
>
> The plaintiff above named complains of the above named defendant, and for cause of action alleges:
>
> That said defendant is justly indebted to said plaintiff in the sum of Three hundred and seventy-five ($375) Dollars for balance due plaintiff for legal services rendered by said plaintiff as an attorney at law for said defendant at said defendant's special instance and request, within the two years last past immediately prior to the commencement of this action, at the agreed price of Four hundred ($400) Dollars, Twenty-five ($25) Dollars of which has been paid.
>
> That no part of said sum of Three hundred and seventy-five ($375) Dollars has ever been paid, and the whole thereof still remains due, owing and unpaid from said defendant to said plaintiff.
>
> Wherefore said plaintiff demands judgment against said defendant for the sum of Three hundred and seventy-five ($375) Dollars and costs of suit.
>
> Bradley Fainswotth
Attorney for Plaintiff
>
> State of California)
>   ) as
> County of Tulare)
>
> J. S. Clack being duly sworn, deposes and says: That he is the plaintiff in the above entitled action; that he has heard read the foregoing complaint and knows the contents thereof, and that the same is true of his own knowledge.
>
> J. S. Clack
>
> Subscribed and sworn to before me
> This 28th day of November, 1892
> (illegible)
> Notary Public

At the same time, Clack filed a writ of attachment on the land that Parker inherited from his grandfather, which directed Tulare County Sheriff Eugene W. Kay to seize the land until the court would presumably award it to Clack in the suit. The Sheriff's official response reads as follows:

> Sheriff's Return on Attachment
> J. S. Clack, Plaintiff
> Vs.
> Flemming Parker, Defendant
> State of California
> County of Tulare
>
> I, E. W. Kay, Sheriff of the County of Tulare, hereby certify and return that I received the hereunto annexed Writ of Attachment on the 28th day of November 1892, and by virtue of the same did on the 29th day of November 1892, attach all the right, title, claim and interest of Flemming Parker, Defendant, of, in and to the following described real estate, situated in the County of Tulare, State of California to wit: The undivided one-twelfth (1/12th) interest in and to the South half and South half of the North half of Section Eight (8) in Township Seventeen South range twenty-seven East MDBYM situated in the County of Tulare.
>
> Said real estate standing on the records of said County of Tulare in the name of Flemming Parker was attached as follows: By filing with the Recorder of said county on the 28th day of November 1892, a copy of the writ together with a description of the property attached, and a notice that it is attached and by leaving a similar copy of the writ, description and notice with Mrs. Wm. Works, an occupant of the property:
>
> Dated, Visalia, this 29th day of November A.D. 1892,
>
> E. W. Kay, Sheriff
> By G.W. Mitty, Deputy

However, both Clack and Sheriff Kay were too late. Parker obviously anticipated this, and three days earlier, on November 25, had sold the land in its entirety to his brother-in-law, Curtis Jackson Boyd, for $450.00, according to surviving land records in the Tulare County courthouse. Clack could no longer acquire the land in lieu of his bill. It is not known if Mrs. Work, who was obviously a relative (possibly Parker's aunt) whom Parker was renting to, was allowed to stay.

Parker undoubtedly returned to Arizona after this, where he was out of Clack's reach. The lawsuit was never settled, and Clack was never paid for getting Parker out of prison. According to Sadie, Parker did return to visit her occasionally.

While in Arizona, Parker hired out as a ranch hand to many of the spreads in the northern part of the territory, where he reportedly developed quite a reputation as a top cowboy. He also joined up eventually with the Abe Thompson Gang and their group of petty thieves. Parker, not having learned anything from his prison terms, still had his eyes out for easy money.

For awhile, the son of Sadie's second husband (Sadie's stepson) reportedly went to Arizona for awhile to learn about cowboying from his "uncle," but returned to California soon after, repulsed by Parker's nefarious crimes with the Thompson Gang.

After moving to Arizona, Parker changed his name, as most ex-cons did when they relocated. From this point on, he called himself James Parker, or Jim Parker, and he stuck with that name until his death. With the sole exception of a Wells Fargo wanted poster, Parker would never again be publicly referred to as Fleming, or Flem, in his lifetime.

The first documented appearance of Jim Parker in Arizona appears in the *Mohave County Miner* newspaper of March 18, 1893. In those days, many newspapers regularly reprinted hotel registers for some reason, and this edition lists Jim Parker of Peach Springs checking in at the Commercial House hotel in Kingman. It had to be him. Also checking in was a man named Lovel Maron of Peach Springs—it is reasonable to surmise that this was a typographical error for Parker's outlaw buddy, Love Marvin, who we will meet in Chapter 3.

Over a century of Parker folklore has contended that, in addition to being a top ranch hand, he entered numerous rodeos in Northern Arizona, often winning top prizes. Few old rodeo records have survived, so this story is largely unverifiable, although it is probably true, since the story was first spread by old-timers who had known Parker. However, there is one interesting news item in the *Coconino Sun* (of Flagstaff, Arizona) from the edition of July 5, 1894. It is a lengthy account of Flagstaff's July 4th celebrations, including bands, games, and a rodeo, all of which went on despite inclement weather. In commenting on the rodeo part of the celebration, the article reports:

> In the broncho riding, Charley Hollingshead, Jim Parker and Ed Gaddis showed up in the above order. This caused excitement, especially among the tenderfeet, who saw the show for the first time. The judges gave the first prize, $30., to Parker, and the second, $10., to Gaddis. Gaddis had two falls, doing no harm.

True, Jim Parker was and is a common name, and readers might wonder if it was Parker himself. But Parker was in the area as we know, and he was a great horseman, to say nothing of the fact that old-timers said he entered rodeos. It had to be him.

CHAPTER 2

George C. Ruffner

Perhaps the single most legendary law enforcement figure in Northern Arizona history is George C. Ruffner, who served as Sheriff of Yavapai County from 1894-1898, and then again in his advancing years, from 1922-24 and 1926 until his death in 1932. He has been written about numerous times in latter-day magazines of western lore, and also in anthology books of Arizona history. Many of these pieces are heavily romanticized, as numerous legends about Ruffner have grown up over the years. Despite his fame, it is this author's considered opinion that the definitive biography of George C. Ruffner has yet to be written.

George C. Ruffner was born in Mason, Illinois in 1862. He had four brothers and three sisters. Of his brothers, three of them, Lester, Edward, and Walter, would later follow him to Arizona when he made good.

It is unclear just when and why Ruffner decided to come to the Arizona Territory. Some accounts state, and it may well be true, that he came West to visit his uncle Marion Andrew (Andy) Ruffner, who had a mining claim in the Cleopatra Hill-Jerome area. Or perhaps young George simply heard the call of "Go West, Young Man" and went. Whatever his reasons, he stayed on.

The year of Ruffner's arrival in Northern Arizona is also unclear. Some popular histories have him arriving as early as 1873, while others put his first appearance as late as 1890. The most reliable accounts (including Ruffner's obituary, reprinted in Chapter 10) put his first appearance in Arizona in 1880, and this supposition seems reasonable. At any rate, once he was there, the rugged young man began to hire himself out as a ranch-hand and cowboy, working on many of the spreads in the area. Needless to say, no employment records for the area's ranches from this era have survived, but hand-me-down stories have placed Ruffner at the Hat Ranch in Williams, the King Ranch in Chino Valley, and the Double O Ranch near Seligman, among others. He also made forays into mining and freight-hauling.

It has often been said over the years that, while he was out cowboying on the various ranches of Northern Arizona, George C. Ruffner struck up a close friendship with the cowboy who now called himself Jim Parker. Popular legend has contended that the two ranch-hands rode together, bunked together, drank together, patronized saloons together, played cards together, and womanized together. It has also been contended that Parker taught the young George some tricks about horsebreaking, and that they entered rodeo tournaments together.

These stories lasted for many years, but some contemporary researchers of the Parker story have been dumbfounded to discover that there is surprisingly little corroborative evidence to show that the two men had even known each other at all prior to the events of 1897, let alone been close friends. Because of this, the legend has shown signs of fading in recent years. This is a shame, because this author believes there is at least some validity to it, and I will proceed to explain why shortly.

Several 20th century authors, in writing about Parker, depicted a romantic scene of the young Ruffner and Parker, fast friends, riding into the city of Prescott together in 1881, the first time either man laid eyes on the place. I love the imagery—who wouldn't?—but in 1881, Parker was only 16 years old. It is highly unlikely that he made his first foray into Arizona already then. If Ruffner and Parker did ride into Prescott, it had to have either been during Parker's undocumented (and therefore not necessarily true) first foray into the Territory in the late 1880s, or during Parker's first known appearance in Arizona in the early 1890s. Either way, George Ruffner had been in the area for some time, and doubtlessly would have visited Prescott long before he met Parker. The "first ride into town" is a beautiful legend, but I fear that's all it is.

But the question remains: Were George Ruffner and Parker friends during their cowboy days? There is a certain amount of evidence that strongly suggests they were, although whether the friendship ran as deep as the legends say is not known. As shall be seen in subsequent chapters, Sheriff George Ruffner seemed to take a heavier than usual interest in the Parker case. Although apparently nothing was made of it, Ruffner seemed to flout his jurisdictional authority by taking Parker to the Yavapai County jail after capturing him following the train robbery, instead of turning him over to Mohave County Sheriff John C. Potts.

During the period of his incarceration, Parker developed an almost irrational hatred of Ruffner, openly making threats against his life. Why Parker would feel this strongly against George and not the other lawmen and Sheriffs who dogged him is unclear—unless Parker felt betrayed by a man he once considered a friend.

The night before Parker was hanged, the newspapers reported that Ruffner spent most of the night with him, talking. It seems hard to believe that the Sheriff would have done that for just any murderer about to be hanged. There seemed to be some genuine feeling.

All of this is circumstantial, of course (the specific events will be dealt with in detail in the ensuing chapters). But what of the other side of the coin? If George Ruffner and Parker were friends, would there not be stronger surviving evidence? If Parker hated Ruffner so strongly after his arrest, why didn't he try to discredit his former friend by publicly boasting of their past? Parker, who did make statements to reporters on occasion, had ample opportunity to do so.

There are no answers to these questions. However, it must be noted that there is nothing to say that Parker didn't try it. Even though Prescott's two newspapers, the *Courier* and the *Journal Miner*, detested each other, both were strong supporters of Sheriff

Ruffner. It is unlikely either paper would have printed any allegations about his past, especially coming from a source as unsavory as Jim Parker. Or, failing that, perhaps for psychological reasons even he couldn't understand, maybe Parker had no desire to discredit his ex-friend in the public eye, even though he wished to kill him.

This is all conjecture, of course. But the strongest piece of evidence that Ruffner and Parker were friends in their cowboy days came 32 years after Parker's hanging. The February 11, 1930 edition of the *Arizona Journal Miner* noted the anniversary of the Rock Cut Train Robbery with an article headlined: "ANNIVERSARY OF FAMOUS MAN HUNT IN WHICH SHERIFF TRAILS FORMER PARTNER RECALLED BY G. C. RUFFNER." What followed was an article recounting the Parker story—although it offered no direct quotes from Ruffner (who was Sheriff again when this appeared), the headline strongly implies that a *Journal Miner* reporter had interviewed him for this article.

This article (which is reprinted in its entirety in Chapter 10) contains the following statements:

> It was the anniversary of Sheriff George C. Ruffner's start on the night of Feb. 10, 1897 to capture Jim Parker, train robber and only five years previous to that date a saddlemate and partner in many a cattle roundup in the country north of here.
>
> In 1892 Sheriff Ruffner was pushing cows for old man King, founder of the present King outfit in Chino Valley. Parker was a cowpoke for the old Thornton outfit in the same district at the same time. During roundups, both frequently found themselves working the same country together, eating from the same chuck wagon, and sleeping side by side.
>
> **WERE CLOSE FRIENDS**
> A close friendship grew between them and there was considerable mutual respect and liking.

Considering the apparent source for this write-up was George C. Ruffner himself, this is quite compelling, and there is no evidence that he disputed the contents of the article after it saw print either. It also seems to give a firm time period when Ruffner and Parker rode together—during Parker's first documented appearance in Arizona in the early 1890s.

It is unknown exactly what drove Ruffner and Parker apart as friends, but it probably had a lot to do with the direction each was taking his own life. By 1893, George C. Ruffner had worked himself up to a solid position of respectability. He owned a small spread of his own, a lucrative freight business in Prescott, and a large livery stable across the street from the Yavapai County Courthouse. Parker, on the other hand, continued his spiral into lawlessness, legitimately working ranches by day, but joining Abe Thompson in rustling horses and cattle by night.

Ruffner was also a married man by this time, having wed Mary (Molly) Birchett in 1891. And the year 1893 proved to be a pivotal one in the young cowboy's life—he was

This photo from 1897 is probably the best known image of Yavapai County Sheriff George C. Ruffner, clearly posing for the camera in his office. He remains one of Arizona's best-known and respected lawmen. (Courtesy of Sharlot Hall Museum)

appointed a Deputy under Yavapai County Sheriff James Lowry. The following year, he was elected Sheriff in his own right. Although his first stint in the office would be marred by the Jim Parker case, he was regarded as the most effective lawman the area had seen in a while, diligently hitting the trail to bring in the pettiest of lawbreakers no matter how far they had gotten away. It may be an overstatement to say (as some have said) that he always got his man, but any failures were not for lack of trying on his part.

While I have tried to give some detailed biographical data on other men who played important roles in the life of Jim Parker, I have not attempted to do so with George Ruffner. This decision is not intended to downplay his role in the story (indeed, Parker's life may have ended much differently without Ruffner), or his role in Yavapai County history. Rather, the Sheriff's life was so full, so rich, and so detailed that it would be impossible to do justice to it in a single chapter, and I will not insult his memory by trying. The life of George C. Ruffner is a book waiting to be written, and this author hopes it will happen someday.

CHAPTER 3

The Abe Thompson Gang

In its February 18, 1897 edition, the *Flagstaff Sun-Democrat* reported on the capture of Jim Parker following the Rock Cut train robbery (to be recounted in the next chapter). In that article, the newspaper also described some of the problems facing the ranchers of Northern Arizona:

> Bally Creighton, "Kid" Marvin, and Abe Thompson, together with Jim Parker, had for several years terrorized the law-abiding ranchmen in the vicinity of Peach Springs and kept up a continual round of pilfering and petty stealing, frequently breaking into the cabins of the ranchmen thereabouts.

Because of the onslaught of Parker folklore in later years, the tentacles of the ruffians collectively known as "the Abe Thompson Gang" have been exaggerated, although there is no doubt that the gang existed. In retrospect, the gang is barely a footnote in the Southwest, certainly not as large or as organized as the Jesse James gang, or Butch Cassidy's the Wild Bunch.

The Abe Thompson Gang seemed to content themselves with petty burglaries and cattle and horse rustling on a small scale. There is surprisingly little documentation surviving as to their specific activities, or specific crimes they were known to have committed prior to the train robbery. There were no rewards out for them, and they weren't "Wanted" by name by the law. There are multiple reasons for this.

First, in real history, cattle rustling was much different than it has been depicted in western movies. It was usually done on a much smaller scale than widely believed. Sometimes only a few cows or horses were taken at a time, in the belief (often true) that ranchers would take longer to notice them missing. The idea of huge herds of cattle being "long-rode" across the whole southwest by rustlers is largely an invention of Hollywood.

Nevertheless, rustling was a very real problem for ranchers, whose cattle were being pilfered on a regular basis and being sold to unscrupulous buyers in other counties and occasionally other states. The problem was so common that most of the time ranchers did not even bother to report the thefts to the authorities unless they could positively identify the thieves. Suspicions undoubtedly abounded as to the thieves' identities, but Sheriffs generally did not make arrests unless there was solid evidence linking the thieves to the crimes. The same held true for the petty burglaries, the booty of which

Portrait of Abe Thompson, taken at a studio in Prescott, probably in the early 1890s. (Courtesy of Sharlot Hall Museum)

ended up being used by the thieves for their own needs, or again, sold to shady buyers in neighboring counties.

As long as they were careful and did not bite off more than they could chew with their crimes, the members of the Abe Thompson Gang were able to stay out of jail. They were undoubtedly able to go into Peach Springs, Kingman, Williams, or even Prescott whenever they wanted supplies, liquor, or women, without incident. Some townspeople undoubtedly would have suspected, or even knew outright, who they were, but were unable to do anything in the absence of proof. Incidents of mob rule and lynch law were still very common in many parts of America, but were almost unheard of in Arizona. For whatever reason, Arizonans were a high-toned people, not prone to taking the law into their own hands.

Second, many ranchers and country settlers did not report their troubles to the local authorities because they distrusted "city folk." They didn't believe that anyone from the city would really care about them, and more often than not, told themselves they would eventually handle things their own way, which, of course, they seldom did. Why this distrust came to be is unclear, but in some areas, it still exists down to this day. As shall be seen, Parker took full advantage of this distrust during his second flight from Arizona law, during which he was aided by a number of settlers and cowboys.

Only five people are known with certainty to have ever belonged to the Abe Thompson Gang, although some historians have suggested that a number of Mexicans and "half-breeds" were involved as well (if so, they dispersed very quickly following the disastrous train robbery). This may be true, as it is hard to believe so few men could have pulled off all of their thefts and rustlings by themselves, but there is no solid evidence anymore as to their membership.

Nothing is known about Charles "Bally" Creighton, except that he made a fast exit from the gang once they started talking about expanding to train robbery. Creighton was undoubtedly just another saddle-bum who joined up with Abe Thompson for fast money and excitement. If he later read about the failed train robbery in the newspapers, it is reasonable to assume that he rode as far away from Arizona as he could possibly get. After leaving the gang, he was replaced by a friend of Parker's, the man who would ultimately be killed at the Rock Cut, and whose identity remains unknown to this day.

Nothing is known about Love Marvin as well. He, too, was probably just the usual drifting tramp looking for money and kicks. In various accounts, Marvin has also been referred to as Lovell Marvin, Lowell Marvin, Lane Marvin, Kid Marvin, and Pug Marvin. Kid Marvin is the only alias he is definitely known to have used; the other names may be misnomers due to faulty memories. But he was called Love Marvin in his later court papers, and he did not dispute it, so that is what we shall call him here. A photo of him survives, reprinted in this chapter.

The only known photo of Love Marvin, clearly taken at the same studio as the opposite photo of Abe Thompson. Although it is not known if they were taken at the same time, it is fun to envision the two outlaws going into Prescott together to have their pictures taken. (Courtesy of Sharlot Hall Museum)

Williams historian Thomas E. Way believed that a man known as Windy Wilson also belonged to the Abe Thompson Gang. As Way based much of his writings on the recollections of old-timers who had known Parker, this may well be true, but there is no surviving solid documentation that Wilson even existed or belonged to the gang. It is one of those details that cannot be either confirmed or denied, and I certainly do not dispute it. If Wilson was a member of the gang, he obviously was not sought by the law in connection with the train robbery after it happened. Perhaps he had joined Creighton in leaving the gang once train-robbing came under discussion. Nor can it be ruled out that Wilson was the dead train robber—Thomas Way speculated that he was. The answer will probably never be known for sure.

By contrast, there is a surprising amount of surviving information about Abe Thompson, the self-styled leader of the gang. Just enough information exists, in fact, to make it frustrating that there isn't even more. Virtually nothing is known of his early life. In his later prison record, Thompson claimed to have originally come from Wisconsin. A later newspaper clipping would also indicate that he had relatives in Kentucky.

According to research supplied to me by Gretchen Eastman, a volunteer at Sharlot Hall Museum, Abe Thompson appears as a 19-year old in the 1880 Federal Census, living in Gratiot, Wisconsin, in the house of John and Betsey Thompson, along with a lot of other Thompsons—Samuel, Thomas, Mont, and Eugene, who seem to have been children or foster children to John and Betsy. At first glance, it would seem that Abe was the son of John and Betsey, but on the Census, he is listed as a farm hand in the household.

Marilyn Chambers of the Lafayette County (Wisconsin) Historical Society provided me with some data on John Thompson, including a brief local article on him written in 1881, stating that he had come to Wisconsin from Pennsylvania in 1837 with his first wife Lydia, who bore him 6 children—John, Robert, Wesley, Philander, Lydia, and Rachel, who at that time were all grown and living in Kansas. After John married Betsey, she bore him one son, Eugene, and that they adopted a son, Samuel. This account does not mention Abe or Mont.

The Lafayette County Historical Society also provided me with information from John Thompson's will and probate, filed when he died on March 28, 1889 (he and Betsey are buried in Gratiot). In it, he provides for his widow, Betsey; his son Eugene Randall Thompson; Samuel Black, a legatee; his daughter Lydia Bowlsby and her 7 children living in Concord, Nebraska; his daughter Rachel Bracken; his sons Philander and George in Antelope County, Nebraska; another daughter named Rachel Taggert also living in Antelope County, Nebraska; his sons Wesley and Robert Thompson in Nebraska; his son John Thompson in Madison, Dakota Territory; and a list of grandchildren and great-grandchildren. While the legalese of the probate is difficult to decipher today, Abe Thompson appears to be listed as one of John's grandchildren! He and Samuel Thompson, listed as a legatee, are noted as living in Peach Springs, Arizona.

It is hard to probe the complicated genealogy of this very large family, so I am not ready to state with certainty that Abe Thompson was John's grandson instead of his son or foster son, even though this may well be the case. If any genealogists wish to tackle this further, please feel free to do so, and I would be very grateful for the information.

The year of Abe Thompson's arrival in Arizona is not known, but when he arrived, he settled down in Peach Springs in Mohave County. There, he slowly eked out a life as a respectable citizen. As we shall see, he became a sheep rancher, and worked at various times as a fireman and as Constable of Peach Springs! On his Yuma prison record, he listed "engineer" as his occupation, indicating that at some point in his early life, he had worked for the railroad. How such a man would end up leading a gang of bandits and thieves is nothing short of bizarre.

The first documented appearance of Abe Thompson in Arizona occurred in 1885. The April 26, 1885 edition of the *Mohave County Miner*, in its court news, listed the following case:

> On Thursday and Friday, the Court was occupied with the examination of the case of the Territory against J. H. Farlee, who was charged with grand larceny in having killed one or more steers belonging to F. Garner. The examination resulted in the defendant being held to answer, with bail fixed at $1,000 which was promptly furnished. The District Attorney and J. W. Stephenson appeared for the prosecution, and Messrs. Williams & Hyde conducted the defense.

Following that, in which Thompson was not mentioned, the *Mohave County Miner* described Farlee's trial on June 7, 1885:

> Court met June 4th. Minutes read and approved.
> Territory of Arizona
>   Vs.
> J. H. Farlee
> On trial. The following witnesses were sworn and examined for the prosecution: R. L. Frazier, D. L. Hollister, Abe Thompson, J. N. Nelson, and Wm. Harper.
>   The prosecution rest.
>   Samuel Crozier and H. J. Farlee sworn for the defendant.
>   The defense rest.
>   T. F. Garner, H. H. Partirdge, and Abe Thompson recalled for the prosecution.
>   The jury instructed by the Court and the case argued by the respective counsel.
>   The jury retired for deliberation and soon afterward returned into Court with the following verdict:
>   We, the jury, find the defendant, J. H. Farlee, not guilty.
>   G. W. Beecher, Foreman"
> Ordered that the defendant be discharged and his bail exonerated.
> Ordered that the witnesses in attendance receive $2 per diem and 30 cents mileage one way.
> Ordered that the Sheriff and Clerk receive extra compensation at the rate of $5 per session for two evening sessions and that the Sheriff be paid $10 for a special deputy for services in taking care of and preparing a certain beef hide for evidence.
>   Court adjourned.

It is not known what testimony Abe Thompson provided or what he was a witness to. Farlee's court papers have not survived, although it is unlikely they would have shed any light on it.

The December 31, 1887 edition of the *Mohave County Miner* prints the guest roster from the Kingman Hotel that week, including an "A.L. Thompson" from Peach Springs, and an Abe Thompson from New York! The typesetters likely got the two similar names reversed.

On February 22, 1888, an incident occurred in Kingman wherein a prostitute named Kate "Kitty" Blonger shot and killed a blacksmith named Charles Hill, who burst in on her while she was conducting "business" with a Prescott resident named Dayton M. "Kid" Fay. Hill had apparently become a bit possessive of his favorite lady of the evening, and got angry over her other customers. News accounts have survived; today, an entire Internet web page is devoted to this case. You can find it at *www.blongerbros.com*.

The court papers can be found on this website, and they show that when Kitty Blonger's trial began in April 1888, Abe Thompson was among the venire of jurors who were summoned. There are no details, but he did not make it on to the final jury. However, ironically, future Mohave County Sheriff John C. Potts did, and he became the jury foreman.

The most likely reason Abe Thompson was excused from the jury is that he was later summoned as a witness for the defense by Kitty Blonger's attorney, Earl M. Sanford (who would later represent Jim Parker for a short time in Prescott). Neither the court papers nor surviving news accounts detail what Abe Thompson testified to. Perhaps he was in the brothel, or in a neighboring one, at the time of the shooting, and heard something. If so, remember that he was not married yet, and in those days, while prostitutes were considered the scum of society, no man ever lost respectability by visiting one. It is a double standard that still exists today to a certain extent. Interestingly, J.N. Cohenour, who would later be on the Mohave County posse following the Rock Cut train robbery, was summoned as a witness for the prosecution.

The jury found Kitty Blonger not guilty of murder. The reason for the verdict is unknown, but it was fairly common in those days for prostitutes to be acquitted of various charges whenever they were arrested. In all such cases, it probably was because jurors thought they might be rewarded with some free "favors" in exchange for their verdict. At any rate, Abe Thompson's presence in the case is just a footnote to it.

On June 2, 1888, the *Mohave County Miner* reported:

Abe Thompson, fireman, is laid up with rheumatism, and has taken a lay-off for ten days.

On October 6, 1888, the *Miner* recorded the results of the local Republican primaries, and printed the list of all of the Party's delegates from Mohave County. Listed for representing Peach Springs were J. L. Nelson, J. N. Cohenour, Alex McDonald, and Abe Thompson.

From the *Mohave County Miner* of June 1, 1889:

Abe Thompson and Ida Baldwin were married at Peach Springs one day this week.

Chapter 3: The Abe Thompson Gang

These two portraits of Abe Thompson and wife Addie (or Ida, there is confusion on her name) were likely taken in Peach Springs in the early 1890s. They have been posted on *Ancestry.com* by someone known as "Shadowen" who is a distant relative of the Thompson family.

Other sources have listed her name as Ada and Addie. It is listed as Addie on the official record. A Thompson family tree posted on the popular genealogy website Ancestry.com lists her as Ida.

Thompson was most assuredly on the way up. He was married, active in local politics, and held respectable jobs. And it didn't end there. The *Miner* reported on June 21, 1890:

> Abe Thompson is in Yavapai County after a drove of 2,000 sheep, which he will keep at Pine Springs, northeast of here. He has a fine range in that section, and there is no doubt but what he will be successful with his sheep ranch.

Sheep were the basis for a strange court battle Abe Thompson became involved in. In the fall of 1890, he filed suit against Flagstaff-area rancher William Nellis, charging him with having apparently stolen 150 of Thompson's sheep! Why this became a civil case instead of a criminal case is unclear—apparently Thompson was unable to prove the sheep in Nellis' possession were actually his. Coconino County had not yet been formed, so Flagstaff was still part of Yavapai County at that time. Therefore, the suit was originally filed in the District Court of the Third Judicial District in and for the County of Yavapai. The court documents were mostly handwritten, and the writing by Court Clerk J.M. Watts is hard to decipher, but the original complaint, in the case of Abe Thompson vs. William Nellis, reads:

> The plaintiff, Abe Thompson, complains of the Defendant William Nellis, and alleges that, on the first day of March 1890, he was, has ever since been, and is now the owner of one hundred and fifty head of sheep of the Spanish breed and of the Marino breed, and that he is entitled to the immediate possession of the same.
> That said sheep are of the value of (illegible; looks like $2,701 but that is not possible) each and of the aggregate value of $412.50.

That said sheep (illegible) branded with three bars, thus--///--on the left side of the nose, and (illegible) of the same branded thus—X on opposite side of nose, and ear marked as follows: The ewes with under half crop in right ear and the (illegible) with under half crop in left.

That on the ___ day of March 1890, the said Defendant, with force and arms, and against the will of Plaintiff and without right, unlawfully seized and took into his possession all of said sheep and since said date has unlawfully withheld said sheep and each and every of the same from the possession of Plaintiff and still does the same.

"(inserted) That Defendant has changed the said /// brand on said sheep from said /// brand to this brand VIX, and has also changed the ear mark of (illegible), as Plaintiff is informed and believes, and (several words illegible).

That Plaintiff has demanded from Defendant possession of said sheep, and he refused to deliver the same, since said unlawful seizure aforesaid.

That Plaintiff has been damaged for being kept out of the use of said sheep by loss of clipping of wool (illegible) the sum of $200, and for lambs yielded by said ewes since said seizure, $100.00, which Defendant has (illegible) to his own use, and for the expense and loss of time in looking after the farm, $100.00.

Wherefore, Plaintiff prays Judgment for the possession of said sheep, and for the sum of $300, his damages (illegible) sustained, and in the failure of Plaintiff to have and obtain Judgment for restitution of said sheep, as (several words illegible) have and obtain Judgment for the sum of $412.50, the value of the same. For the sum of $500. for his (several words illegible) general relief.

              Wilson and Norris
              Attorneys for Plaintiff

The case is bizarre, inasmuch as there is no surviving evidence of a criminal investigation of the incident. Thompson's attorneys were "Wilson and Norris," the latter undoubtedly being Thomas G. Norris, while William Nellis retained the services of "Baldwin and Johnston," the latter likely being T.W. Johnston.

After the suit was filed, the Court directed Yavapai County Sheriff William O. "Buckey" O'Neill to go to Nellis' ranch and take possession of the sheep and return them to Abe Thompson until the matter could be settled. Although it surely was not an enviable job, Sheriff O'Neill dutifully did as he was directed, and pursuant to the law, filed an affidavit with the court (describing the sheep in greater detail) attesting that he had done so:

I, William O. O'Neill, Sheriff of the County of Yavapai, in the Territory of Arizona certify, that I received the annexed writ of Replevin on the 29th day of August 1890, and personally served the same on the 2nd-3rd and 4th days of September 1890, between Challender and Williams, at the Residence of the within named Defendant, William Nellis, and as follows, to-wit, I carefully examined, do hereby the Sheep of the within named Defendant Wm Nellis, and selected therefrom all of said Sheep claimed by the Plaintiff, Abe Thompson, and as follows, One (1) Ewe, Branded III on left side of the Nose, and marked Upper bit and Swallow Fork in the right and Under Slope in the left Ear-and One (1) Ewe marked Over half crop in left, and square crop off the right Ear-and One (1) Ewe branded VIX on left side of the Nose, and X on right side of the Nose, and marked Overslope off left, and straight crop off right Ear, and One (1) Ewe Branded III on left side of the Nose, and marked Underslope off left, and under bit off right Ear, and One (1) Wether Branded III on left side of the Nose, and marked Upper half crop off left, and square crop off right Ear, and One One Ewe Branded VIX on left sifde of the Nose, and X on the right side of the Nose, and marked Overslope off left and square crop off right Ear, and One (1) Ewe Branded III on left side of the Nose, and marked straight crop off left, and split and over bit off right Ear, and One (1) Ewe, Branded VIX on left side of the Nose, and X on the right side of the Nose, and marked Overslope off left, and straight crop off right Ear, and One (1) Ewe Branded III on the left side of the Nose and marked square crop off each Ear, and One (1) Ewe branded VIX on the left side of the Nose, and X on the right side of the Nose, and marked Overslope off left and square crop off right Ear, and One (1) Ewe branded III on the left side of the Nose, and marked Under half crop off right Ear, and One (1) Ewe, branded III on the left side of the Nose, and X on the right side of the Nose, and marked Under slope and over bit off left, and split in right Ear, and One (1) Ewe Branded VIX on left side of the Nose, and X on the right side of the Nose, and marked overslope off left, and square crop off right Ear, and One (1) Ewe branded III on the left side of the Nose, and marked over Half crop off the left, and square crop and under bit off right Ear, and One (1) Ewe branded VIX on the left side of the Nose, and X on the right side of the Nose, and marked smooth crop off Right, and overslope off left Ear, and One (1) Ewe branded VIX on the left side of the Nose, and X on the right side of the Nose, and marked overslope off left and and smooth crop off right Ear, and One (1) Ewe branded VIX on the left side of the Nose, and X on the right side of the Nose, and marked Overslope off the left, and smooth crop off the right Ear, and One (1) Ewe, marked Under Half crop off right Ear, and one (1) Ewe, branded III on the left side of the Nose, and marked Upper Half crop off left and crop and under half crop of right Ear. Making a total of Nineteen Sheep, taken from the Possession of the within named Defendant William Nellis, and delivered into the Possession of the within named Plaintiff Abe Thompson, And that I put upon the front of the Nose of each of said Sheep, this T Brand, to be able to identify said Sheep in the future.

Dated Prescott A.T. September 7th 1890

       Wm. O. O'Neill
       Sheriff of Yavapai County Arizona Territory
       By M. W. Guernsey (?) chief Deputy

These were 19 out of 150 alleged stolen sheep. What happened to the rest of them? For this service, Abe Thompson had to sign a legal document promising that he would pay Nellis $850.00 and return the sheep if he should lose the case. This worked both ways; Arizona Territorial law had some quirks, one of which allowed Nellis, as the holder of the sheep at the time they were seized, to file a bond with the County allowing him to retain the sheep until the matter was settled. The court papers show that prominent ranchers George F. Thornton and D. Levy helped Nellis to pay this $825.00 bond, and presumably Sheriff O'Neill had to go and seize the sheep again and take them back to Nellis!

While all of this was going on, the layout of the Territory was changing, and Flagstaff-area businessmen (including Ralph H. Cameron) had succeeded in their long quest to form a new county, Coconino County, broken off from the Northern part of Yavapai County. When this occurred, many civil and criminal cases in the Yavapai County courts were transferred to the new Coconino County, closer to where the original incidents had taken place. The case of Abe Thompson vs. William Nellis was just such a case, and on December 1, 1890, it was transferred to the newly formed District Court of the Fourth Judicial District of the Territory of Arizona, in and for the County of Coconino.

Over a year had passed since Abe Thompson had filed his lawsuit, but in the fall of 1891, the case was about to go to trial, with Judge Edmund Wells presiding. Thompson subpoenaed a man only identified as "Domingo" (a Mexican), William McInyre, James A. May, William Hull, Joe Monty, Gus Rimer, and Gregorio Chavez. It is not known who these men were or what they testified to, although it is reasonable to assume that the Mexicans were ranch-hands for Abe Thompson. William Nellis subpoenaed Ferdinand Nellis, George F. Thornton, J.B. Tappan, L.P. Nellis, John Donovan, and Joseph Moritz. Again, aside from Thornton, it is not known who these men were, although two were obviously family members of William Nellis. All subpoenas were served by new Coconino County Sheriff J. W. Francis, who took the office under cloudy circumstances after Ralph Cameron had served only about four weeks (Cameron would later return to the position).

The *Coconino Sun* newspaper reported on September 5, 1891:

> Abe Thompson, of Peach Springs, is in town this week, attending court.

The same edition reported in its court column that the case was continued for the term. Time dragged on. The *Coconino Sun* reported March 17, 1892:

> Abe Thompson, of Peach Springs, is in town this week.

The same edition reported the case was set for trial March 21.

After that, nothing. The surviving court papers are incomplete and do not show the outcome of the case. Likewise, the case ceased to be mentioned in the *Sun*'s court column. So what happened? Perhaps Thompson and Nellis settled out of court, but this seems unlikely given the circumstances. We simply do not know how this event ended.

The case of Abe Thompson vs. William Nellis leaves many questions. There was clearly more to the story than the surviving data indicates. Was Abe Thompson really the victim of rustling? If so, is it possible that this incident put the idea in his head that rustling was profitable? Was William Nellis, a respected rancher, really a rustler on the side? That seems far-fetched, but who knows—look at what became of Abe Thompson himself!

Regardless of the outcome, Abe Thompson was still a highly respectable citizen in Mohave County at this time.

Chapter 3: The Abe Thompson Gang

The January 3, 1891 edition of the *Mohave County Miner* lists Abe Thompson as a guest at the Hubbs House, a hotel in Kingman (these were the days when small newspapers printed such information on town visitors). A Dr. J.R. Baldwin from San Francisco is also listed on the register, making one wonder if perhaps this was Abe's father-in-law.

In those days, newspapers often printed the local property tax rolls, so everyone would know who owned what, I suppose. On the tax roll printed in the *Mohave County Miner* on January 31, 1891, was the following:

> Thompson, Abe. Frame cottage in Peach Springs, 100 00; personal property 70 00 .... 29 (taxes)

Yes, life was mighty fine for Abe Thompson. During this period, his wife Addie, or Ida, bore him two children; a son, Charles Samuel Thompson, and another whose name has not survived. He was also appointed or elected (it is unclear which) Constable of Peach Springs!

No records have survived to indicate exactly when Thompson became Constable, although it was probably circa 1891. Oftentimes even the newspapers failed to report the changing of a Constable. The job was one of the most minor in law enforcement in nearly all cities that had one, consisting mostly of nightwatchman-style duties, serving insignificant arrest warrants, and only occasionally doing more important chores, if the Constable happened to be in the right place at the right time

The first reference to Abe Thompson as Constable appears in the *Mohave County Miner* of July 25, 1891. A recounting of the minutes of a meeting of the Mohave County Board of Supervisors includes the following notation:

> Bill of Abe Thompson, constable fees for $5, returned to be itemized.

Thompson's respect in Mohave County led to all manner of positions. From the *Miner* of April 18, 1891:

> The suit of T. F. Garner, of Peach Spring, against the Atlantic & Pacific railroad company, has been settled by arbitration. The claim was for sixty head of cattle which were killed by the cars. In the settlement Garner receives between fifteen and sixteen hundred dollars, he to pay his own costs in the matter. Abe Thompson was chosen by Garner and Jerry Sullivan by the railroad company and W. E. Frost was agreed upon as the third arbitrator. The terms of the settlement seem to be agreeable to both parties.

A note of irony here, in that some after the fact accounts of the Parker story claim that Jim Parker at some point worked for a rancher named Jerry Sullivan. The same edition of the *Miner* noted elsewhere that *"Frank Garner and Abe Thompson were down from Peach Springs Tuesday."*

The *Coconino Sun* of July 18, 1891 printed a list of 21 Northern Arizona citizens who were called to Prescott to serve on the Grand Jury for the United States District Court (the Federal court). They included prominent men like Ralph H. Cameron, Coles Bashford, J.M.W. Moore, George Schuerman, Charles Genung, Benjamin Belcher, and Abe Thompson. The July 29, 1891 edition of the *Arizona Journal Miner* in Prescott records a formal protest signed by some (not all) members of this Grand Jury (including Abe Thompson), and filed in court with Judge Edmund W. Wells, alleging they had been mistreated because of court delays in discharging them when there was nothing further to do.

There was a day when Constable Thompson's duties were a little more exciting than usual. From the *Mohave County Miner* of December 26, 1891:

A Christmas Tragedy
The Christmas festivities at Peach Springs were marred by what seems to have been a cold-blooded murder, caused principally by an overload of whiskey.

The particulars, so far as we have been able to learn, are as follows:

Some time during last Thursday a Mexican whose name has not been learned, arrived in Peach Springs from Williams, to go to work in the cinder pit at the round house. During the day he made the acquaintance of a party of his countrymen, among whom was the murdered, Nicolas Carbgall. In the course of the day they all got full of whiskey and Carbgall found out that the stranger had come to Peach Springs to take his job in the cinder pit and was very much incensed. He drew a knife and made threats that he would be revenged; he said as he had just lost his job he had as well loose his life.

Constable Abe Thompson captured the knife and supposed that the trouble was over, but in this he was mistaken. About 4 a.m. he was called from his room by a Mexican who told him that Carbgall had shot the stranger, and on repairing to the scene of the shooting he found the deceased lying on the floor of the house with two bullet holes through the head, one shot having entered at the top of the nose and the other entered just back of his right ear, and both passed through his head. He lived until 1 o'clock to-day.

The constable started in search of the murderer, and located him in an old adobe house. On approaching the house, he was met by a Mexican who informed him that Carbgall had a pistol and would shoot whoever tried to come in. The constable approached near enough to talk to the fugitive, who finally agreed to come out and surrender.

He was brought to Kingman this evening and is now in the county jail. He will have a preliminary examination Monday.

From the same edition:

Abe Thompson came down from Peach Springs this afternoon having in charge the Mexican who killed another Mexican at that place last night.

The killer's name was actually Nicholas Carbajal, and he was eventually sentenced to 25 years in Yuma Territorial Prison. He was pardoned by the Governor in 1894 already, after serving only two years. Contrary to popular belief, many murderers did get breaks during this period, although Carbajal's prison term was unusually short even under those circumstances. It is unlikely that Abe Thompson played any further role in the case.

The March 24, 1892 edition of the *Coconino Sun* ran an article about a gala ball hosted by the Brotherhood of Railroad Trainmen at La Prade's Opera House in Winslow, Arizona. The paper printed the names of everyone who attended from all over northern Arizona, with guests coming from as far away as Gallup, New Mexico and Albuquerque. Among them were Henry F. Ashurst, Mr. And Mrs. W. Nellis (almost certainly William Nellis), and Mr. And Mrs. A. Thompson of Peach Springs. Considering the location, it had to be them.

The minutes of a Mohave County Board of Supervisors meeting appeared in the *Miner* of May 21, 1892, and contained a reprint of the county's budget, which contained the following item:

This is the Yuma Territorial Prison mugshot of Nicholas Carbajal, who was arrested by Constable Abe Thompson for murder in Peach Springs. (Courtesy of Pinal County Historical Society)

 Abe Thompson, Constable fees, expense fund......................14 30

That was the last reference to him as Constable, and there is no surviving record of when or why he ceased to hold the position. Except for incidents like the Carbajal case, no one really cared who their Constable was.

The Property Tax Assessment rolls were printed in the *Miner* again on February 4, 1893, and included the following listing:

 Thompson, Abe. 10 head cattle 70, furniture 50, dwelling houses in Peach Springs 75, improvements on possessory rights 5 .... 7 30

The list also includes an entry for a Samuel Thompson as a property owner, undoubtedly his brother or foster-brother, whatever the case was. The entry:

 Thompson, Samuel. Farmture 25, residence in Peach Springs 50 ....2 73

Then came the event that may have been the turning point in Abe Thompson's life—the sudden death of his wife Addie, or Ida. The *Mohave County Miner* relayed the tragic details for its readers on April 8, 1893:

> A Sad Death
> Tuesday morning the quiet town of Peach Springs was startled by the report that Mrs. Abe Thompson was found dead in her home at that place. Mr. Thompson had gone up to Ash Fork Monday to secure the services of several sheep shearers. He returned early the next morning and repaired to his home. He was horrified on entering to find the lifeless form of his wife stretched full length on the floor. The baby (one year old) was sitting in a high chair almost stiff with cold, while the older child was peacefully sleeping beside the form of its mother. Mr. Thompson gave the alarm and sympathetic neighbors were soon on hand ministering to the little ones and caring for the dead.
>
> Dr. Lappetis, of this place, was sent for and made a post mortem examination. He found that the deceased lady had been suffering for several days with an acute attack of neuralgia in the face and the supposition is that it suddenly went to the heart stopping the life pulsation forever. She had fallen face downward on the floor, her hand clutched over her heart. Her face was bruised by the fall and death must have been instantaneous as little blood flowed from the wounds.
>
> She was a most estimable woman and was loved and respected by all who knew her. Her two little children will be cared for by the ladies of Peach Springs until their father can obtain a permanent abode for them.
>
> Rev. W. G. Blakely went up to the Springs Wednesday afternoon and conducted the funeral service.
>
> Nearly every man, woman and child followed the remains to the grave.
>
> The sympathy of the whole community is extended to the bereaved father and husband in this sad affliction.

It was about the last time Abe Thompson appeared in the press as a respected citizen. Although there is no documentation as to exactly when, it is generally believed that he formed his gang and engaged in acts of burglary and rustling not long after this. This sudden change in his personality is unexplained; perhaps the trauma of finding his wife dead in such horrible circumstances knocked a few shingles off his roof.

How Abe Thompson recruited Charles "Bally" Creighton, Love Marvin, and Jim Parker is also unknown. As Thompson had been a sheep rancher, perhaps they had worked for him at one time. Some historians believe that once he was in the gang, Parker deposed Abe Thompson as leader, although Thompson stayed with the bunch. This is partially confirmed in interviews with men such as Henry Ashurst (to be printed later in this book), who said it was their understanding that Parker was the leader of the gang.

Thompson appeared one more time on the Mohave County property tax rolls, published March 3, 1894, in the *Miner*. Some of this was repeated in the March 24, 1894 edition as well. By this time, his holdings seem to have depleted somewhat:

Thompson, Abe .... work horses 157 50, 1 saddle hores 29 25, wagon 25 00, harness 10 00, set of furniture 50 00, 20 head of stock cattle 119 00, frame building at Peach Springs 150 00.

He must have sold all of this off soon after as well, for at the time the gang was arrested for the Rock Cut train robbery, all Abe Thompson seemed to own was a cabin outside of Peach Springs in the country. The newspapers made references to "Thompson's Cabin" as a hideout for outlaws, and the same papers seemed to assume that everyone knew what and where it was, and that they should avoid the location at all costs.

On February 8, 1897, the Abe Thompson Gang, most likely under the leadership of Parker, made the move that would ultimately finish them off as a unit.

CHAPTER 4

The Rock Cut Train Robbery

It is not known why the Abe Thompson Gang decided to move on to bigger things than burglary and rustling. Perhaps they got ambitious. Perhaps they had heard of something extremely valuable on the train—a popular legend contends that old No. 1 was carrying a shipment of gold the night it was robbed.

Whatever the reason, it is reasonable to assume that robbing a train was Parker's idea, as he seemed to be the most ambitious member of the gang (and, as previously noted, he may have taken over leadership from Abe Thompson). It is pretty much established that Charles "Bally" Creighton left the gang around this time, apparently spooked when talk turned to train robbery. Ready for any occasion, Parker brought one of his friends into the gang to replace Creighton, a man whose identity has never been concretely established. Love Marvin would later claim that Parker's friend was introduced to the gang as "John Clayton," but different accounts have given many other names to the man, not one of them ever confirmed or denied with any certainty.

In his confession (to be printed in its entirety in Chapter 5), Love Marvin would claim that part of the plan was for he and Abe Thompson to go into Peach Springs, and make themselves conspicuous, thus giving the impression that the whole gang was in town at the time the robbery was occurring. Popular legend has contended that Parker very publicly left Peach Springs on a train a couple of days before (thus giving him an alibi), and then sneaked back on horseback by night. This cannot be confirmed or denied, but at any rate, the gang seemed to be taking strong precautions for what would be their biggest heist yet.

The train robbery was a failure so spectacular it made news throughout the Southwest. In the next few pages, we will recount the event from several different regional viewpoints—it is important to see how it was perceived in different areas, and this gives one a complete picture of the important event.

Peach Springs was far from Prescott. Contrary to legend, Parker was not a well-known citizen in Prescott. The people of Prescott had no idea just how much of a Prescott story this would turn into, nor did the newspapers. Nevertheless, it seems appropriate to begin documenting the Rock Cut Train Robbery from Prescott's point of view. The *Arizona Journal Miner*, one of Prescott's two competing newspapers, carried this account on February 10, 1897, two days after the robbery (remember, these are weekly editions):

Chapter 4: The Rock Cut Train Robbery

Contemporary photo from 2012 shows a train going through a rock cut between Peach Springs and Nelson. It is not known if this was the rock cut where the infamous 1897 train robbery occurred, as there are several along the line. (Courtesy of David Schmittinger)

A Dead Train Robber
Four Men Hold Up an Atlantic & Pacific Train Near Peach Springs

Express Messenger Summers Shoots and Kills One Robber While The Others Finish the Job and Escape

Ash Fork, Feb. 9—[Special to the Journal-Miner]—The Atlantic & Pacific overland train number one, west bound, was held up last night by four men seven miles east of Peach Springs.

After forcing the watchman in a rock cut to flag the train, they compelled Fireman Bar* to uncouple the mail and express car from the train. While this was being done, Express Messenger Summers and his helper Randall, each jumped from opposite side doors of the express car and ran back toward the train. Summers came suddenly upon one of the robbers standing on the rear platform of the express car, and without hesitation, fired twice. The first ball passed through the robber's body just above the heart. The second ball from Summers' 45-caliber Colts' revolver struck the robber before he fell, entering his left eye and coming out of the back of the head. By this time the engine and two cars had started. Summers and Randall were unable to get on them. The cars, which were the mail and express cars, were stopped at Nelson siding, and while one robber guarded the engineer and mail clerk, another went through the registered mail, taking eight packages of registered mail. The express car was not molested. The dead robber weighed about 147 pounds and was about 40 years old. Special Officer Selvy and Deputy Sheriff Fairchilds are on the trail of the escaped bandits.

---

* His name was actually Nelson Bartoo.

All that is left today of the town of Nelson is a small cemetery. Possibly the dead train robber is buried here in an unmarked grave, but this is not known for sure. (Courtesy of David Schmittinger)

The dead robber is thought to be a cow boy, formerly in the employ of the Arizona Cattle Company, near Flagstaff. Indian trailers were started out this morning in pursuit of the three robbers who escaped.

The *Prescott Courier* also printed the following account, on February 12, 1897:

News was received at the Sheriff's office yesterday morning that four men had held up westbound train No. 1, seven miles east of Peach Springs, Monday night. The hold-up was near a cut where a watchman is kept on guard. Robbers made watchman flag train, and boarded train when it was stopped. They then forced the fireman to uncouple the mail and express car and started for Nelson siding. Express Messenger Summers and his assistant sprang from the express car side doors. Summers fired twice, both times with fatal effect upon a robber on the rear platform of the express car. At Nelson siding the robbers rifled the registered mail. The express car was not molested. The identity of the dead robber is, as yet, only a matter of conjecture. Mohave and Coconino county officers, with Indian trailers, took the field immediately upon receipt of news of the robbery. Sheriff Ruffner and Deputy Munds, with their horses, took the northbound train yesterday afternoon to join in the pursuit.

The interesting thing about almost all of the initial accounts is the contention that three or four robbers were involved. Love Marvin would later say that only Parker and his deceased friend actually pulled off the robbery, and historians generally believe that. In fact, as shall be seen, the three posses would soon conclude that they were only chasing one man.

It is interesting to compare these news articles with the account published in the *Flagstaff Sun-Democrat* on February 11, 1987, told from the viewpoint of Coconino County law enforcement, and Coconino County Sheriff Ralph Henry Cameron:

> The overland passenger train, No. 1, with Engineer William Daze at the throttle, which left here at 3:35 Monday, had an encounter with train robbers when a few miles this side of Peach Springs. After forcing the watchman in the rock cut to flag the train, they compelled Fireman Bart to dismount and uncouple the mail and express car from the train. Express Messenger Summers and his helper Randall each jumped from opposite side doors of the express car and ran back toward the train. Summers came suddenly upon one of the robbers standing on the steps of the rear platform of the express car and immediately opened fire with his 45-caliber Colt's revolver on the bandit. The first shot passed through the robber's body, just above the heart, and another entered his left eye, coming out at the back of the head. The robber rolled off onto the ground. While this was going on the other bandits had succeeded in getting the mail and express cars uncoupled and conveyed with all speed to Nelson siding, where the mail car was gone through and eight registered packages consigned to Uncle Sam's care appropriated. The two robbers then made their escape. Deputy Sheriff Fletcher Fairchild was on No. 2 coming up from Kingman with Tom Sims, the Mexican cook, wanted here as a witness in a larceny case, and ordering his prisoner to proceed for Flagstaff, got off at Peach Springs and started on the trail of the robbers. Sheriff Cameron left here Tuesday morning for the scene. The dead bandit has been identified as a cowboy formerly in the employ of the Arizona Cattle Company here. It is impossible for the bandits to escape, owing to the topography of the country adjacent to Peach Springs, and their speedy arrest is expected.

In the same issue, in a section devoted to news from the Coconino County city of Williams, the *Sun-Democrat* noted the following:

> Deputy Sheriff Bugglin left Tuesday night for the scene of Monday night's train robbery near Nelson.

Martin Buggeln was one of the pioneer lawmen of Williams, who was constantly having his name misspelled by the press, so keep that in mind.

Needless to say, the *Mohave County Miner*, the newspaper closest to the scene of the crime, had the most detailed coverage, including the first news of the posses. Naturally, Mohave County Sheriff John C. Potts joined Yavapai Sheriff George C. Ruffner and Coconino County Sheriff Ralph H. Cameron on the trail of the fleeing bandit. The *Miner* ran the following account on February 13, 1897:

Two Robbers Stop A Train
_____
Bold Holdup of Uncle Sam's Mail
_____
One Robber Killed
The Other Outlawed and Fleeing for Life

Last Monday evening at 8:30 No. 1, west bound passenger, was held up two miles west of Nelson siding by two masked men. The watchman at a big rock cut had been pressed into service by the holdups and under the frowning mouth of a sixshooter used his red light to bring the flying train to a sudden stop. Almost before the wheels had ceased to turn two men sprung lightly onto the engine and while one covered the engineer with a gun the other ordered the fireman to cut off the express and mail cars from the train. The fireman, under escort of the robber, walked back to cut off the cars and while the work was being done the robber kept an eye on the movements of the train hands. The sudden stoppage of the train, of course, caused the brakeman and conductor to go out to investigate the cause, but they were ordered back to the car with a volley of oaths and a flourish of gun by the robber. The express messenger, A. C. Summers, took in the situation and ordered his assistant to drop out of the door on one side of the car and he went out of the other. He found himself on the ground on the side opposite to the robber, and as it was dark he managed to slip to the end of the car where he saw the robber standing on the car steps on the other side. As the robber was giving the order for the train to pull ahead, he quietly raised himself on the lower step and fired at the man across the platform. The robber loosened his hold on the handrail, reeled backward and fell face downward on the ground. In falling his gun was fired into the air. The messenger thinking the fellow might be playing "possum" fired two more shots at him. The other robber, unconscious of his partner's fate, was speeding down the road with the baggage and express cars. A hasty examination of the robber by Summers disclosed the fact that he was dead. At first it was thought that he was shot through the head, but the fact is he was shot through the left breast, the bullet passing entirely through the body. He was examined by trainmen and passengers and a Winchester rifle, revolver and a dozen sticks of giant powder found on him. In his coat pocket was a book containing many brands and a small notebook containing snatches of poetry and selections from letters presumably from a woman. The names Katie Howell and _____ Dilly also are in the book.

    The other robber, after taking the cars to Nelson siding ordered the engineer to go with him to the baggage car and break it in. Passing around the car he said, "I am two men shy, but guess I will do this job up myself." Not being able to break open Wells Fargo's safe he passed on to the mail car and ordered the clerk to open the door. The registered mail was called for and several letters were handed over. His partner not showing up, he told the engineer to run back up the road for about a mile and not discovering him the run was made back to the siding, where he jumped from the train and disappeared.

    The engineer ran back to his train, coupled on and taking the body of the dead man on board arrived in Peach Springs about two hours late. Sheriff Potts was notified and at once sent Deputies Smith and Lovin with three Indian trailers to Peach Springs to take up the trail of the remaining robber at daybreak. Horses were to be in waiting for them but owing to the fact that no horses could be obtained in Peach Springs the posse did not get away until two o'clock in the afternoon of Tuesday, horses having to be sent by special train from Kingman. The posse consisted of Smith and Lovin of Kingman, Cade Selvy, A. & P. special officer, and Les Fairchild of Coconino county, with the Indian trailers. Smith and the Indians had trailed the bandit to the Pine Springs road in the morning on foot and the trail was taken up at the point left off. About twenty miles north of the starting point they observed a horseman coming toward them from the north. (Illegible) who he was as the horseman commenced to shoot at long range. The chase for ten miles was an exciting one. The outlaw was mounted on a fleet animal and he would ride well ahead and then wheel his horse around and deliberately aim at his pursuers. The bullets sang a melancholy tune as they sped by the little posse, but bullets were showered with lavish hand by the pursuers and as night came on they passed Thompson's cabin, on up a rocky gulch and into the timber. Here the robber found himself in a trap and abandoning his horse disappeared in the tangled forest. The posse captured the horse and returned to Thompson's cabin, where they remained for the night. Here they found a miscellaneous assortment of plunder, stolen from neighboring ranches. Among the other things they found a pair of pants belonging to the suit worn by the dead robber and on the box in which they lay was the name of a Mr. Ayres. The posse, having no feed for their horses, returned to Peach Springs. The dead robber could not be identified, but Mr. Ayres claimed the coat and vest worn by the robber had been stolen from his cabin at Pine Springs a month ago and that Charles Creighton had been seen in Peach Springs wearing them. Thursday another posse left Peach Springs well mounted, armed and provisioned to spend considerable time on the trail of the robbers. Sheriff Potts, with deputies Cohenour and Harris, left the Springs in the evening to take up the trail anew. They will stay to a finish.

The country where the holdup occurred is a wild and picturesque region and to the north a man could lose himself in the labyrinthine windings of the Grand and Diamond canyons. Snow covers the ground along the ridges of the mountain and close to the valley the ground is soft and slushy. A ten mile run through the snow and slush is worse on man and horse than a fifty mile ride over an ordinary country road. The snow is fast disappearing but the nights are cold and frosty. The officers are not finding the job a picnic.

A drummer relates a story of the panic into which the passengers were thrown by the holdup. They were nearly all eastern people and they had read of the wild and wooly outlaws of Arizona and they feared the worst. Momentarily they expected to be lined up alongside of the train with pistols the size of young canons leveled at their heads, while a fierce looking outlaw searched their persons for loose change and jewelry. One lady moaned, "Where! Oh where, will I hide my diamonds." A gentleman across the isle from her suggested that if she hid them in her bosom the usual Arizona highwayman was too gentlemanly to make a search for them in that particular place. She made several ineffectual attempts to unbutton her dress and then implored the gentleman to come to her assistance, which he gallantly did.

Kingman's other newspaper, the much smaller *Our Mineral Wealth*, carried news of the train robbery and the first movements of the posse on February 12, 1897, but their account was not much different from that of the *Miner*, so there is no need to reprint it here.

We will return to the chase in Chapter 5.

Also on February 13, 1897, the *Winslow Mail* (from the town of Winslow, far east of Flagstaff) carried an account of the robbery that contained some variations. With the exception of the presence of a third robber at the train, the variations do not contradict the other accounts—whether they are true or just products of faulty communications, we will never know for certain, but the article is worth repeating:

The Hold-up on the A. & P.

On Monday night last No. 1 passenger train going west was held up about 8:30 p.m. nine miles east of Peach Springs by three men. There are a series of deep cuts where the hold-up took place which necessitates the employment of a track-walker. The train robbers captured him as he came from one of those cuts and held him until the train came along, when they forced him to flag it. As soon as the train stopped two of the robbers, with Winchesters in hand, jumped on the engine and covered engineer Daze and fireman Bartoo, while the third man was shooting along side the train to prevent the arrival of assistance. Then Messrs. Daze and Bartoo were commanded to climb down and were lined up alongside the trackwalker.

The next move was to cut the train, which they proceeded to do, but made a mistake of cutting it between the mail and express cars, and commanded Mr. Daze to get on his engine and pull up. Mr. Daze says he hadn't moved more than a car length when the mistake was discovered and he was ordered to stop and back her.

Mr. Somers, the express messenger, took advantage of these little mishaps and prepared himself to give them a warm reception. When the mail car was backed down, the first man who showed himself was shot down. This frightened another one of the robbers, who saw the shot fired and his partner fall, and he, undoubtedly thinking discretion the better part of valor, took to the rocks. The one who appeared to be the leader, was in the mail car while this was going on, but it took him only a few seconds to discover that he was unsupported, when he snatched a few registered letters and decamped also.

On occasions of this kind there are always more or less amusing, as well as ludicrous, incidents happen. The engineer and fireman in this case, however, took the matter very coolly. One of the robbers commanded Mr. Daze to block the engine, which he proceeded to do very leisurely, when a sharper order came to hurry up. Mr. Daze replied that he was getting along in years and besides was a cripple—that he couldn't hop around like a kid. Directly afterward he was ordered to climb up and look into the window of the mail car, to see who was in there. "Oh, I can't climb up there," was the answer. Then they wanted him to go into the express car, but the step was too high for him to mount.

One of the robbers had fireman Bartoo covered with a pistol and was firing down the train with another in the other hand, when the Kid cautioned him to be a little careful which gun he pulled off. After the robbers had left, thinking they might return, Bartoo went into a passenger coach and inquired if any of the passengers

Chapter 4: The Rock Cut Train Robbery

Today, this lime manufacturing plant sits on the site of the former town of Nelson, Arizona. There is nothing else left of Nelson itself. (Courtesy of David Schmittinger)

had guns. He was shown all sizes from a .22 to a .41. He informed the owners that none of them were any good in such an emergency, when a man crawled out from under a seat and pulled a double-barreled shotgun after him loaded with buckshot.

The train then pulled into Peach Springs, gave the alarm, and we are informed there was a posse on the ground the next morning at five o'clock with bloodhounds ready to take the trail.

Train robbers will learn, after they receive a few more lessons such as the last attempts have proven, to give the Atlantic & Pacific a wide-birth. This is the second attempt made on this road at holding up a train, both of which proved failures and in both of which the robbers lost a man.

Later—Thursday 11th—Posse with Deputy Bayless in charge, accompanied by One-eyed Riley, a well known and fearless plainsman, left Flagstaff on the night of the 10th to assist Sheriff Cameron in his hazardous undertaking of capturing the men who are supposed to have held up the train Monday night near Peach Springs. Cameron, with his two fearless deputies, Fairchilds and Buggeln are on the right track and as usual to the front. It is reported they had arrested two men early Thursday morning, near Peach Springs, who, it is pretty certain, were connected with the robbery. It is almost a certainty now that four men were engaged in the robbery. One is dead, two are under arrest, and the officer were so close on the trail of the fourth man that they felt confident of capturing him before night.

Again, we will return to the arrests and the posse in the next chapter.

News of the botched robbery and the death of one of the bandits was on the front page of the *Arizona Republican* (today the *Arizona Republic*) of Phoenix on February 10, 1897:

> One Bandit Less on Earth
> A Hold-Up on the A. &. P.
> Mohave County
>
> ———
>
> One of the Robbers Killed by an Express Messenger and the Other
> Trailed by Indians Toward the Grand Canyon

Kingman, Ariz., Feb. 9—The westbound passenger due here at 11 last night was held up seven miles east of Peach Springs at 8:30. The robbers had forced a watchman at what is known as the Big Rock cut to signal the train down, and when it came to a stop one of the men ordered the fireman to get off and cut the mail and express car out. The brakeman came out on the platform of the day coach and was ordered "to get back there, d---n you, or I will shoot." The robbers stood over the fireman while he cut the coupling.

The express messenger realizing that the train was help up jumped from the car on the side opposite the robbers and scrambling up the side of the cut fired down on the robbers. He fired three shots and a robber fell dead, his gun exploding as he fell. The fireman had cut the train and the robber on the engine ordered the engineer to pull out. After going two miles the robber ordered the engineer to break in the express car, but failed. The mail car was then entered and several registered letters were taken, but were supposed to contain no money.

When the engine pulled away Messenger A. C. Somers of Los Angeles entered the train and said, "I got one of them and got him good." There was a general rush to see the dead robber. The shot struck him in the left breast just below the heart. Death was instantaneous. A Winchester rifle, sixshooter and twelve sticks of dynamite were found on the body. A brand book showing many cattle brands was found in the pocket of the dead robber and it is supposed that he was a cowboy.

Great excitement prevailed among the passengers while the shooting was being done and valuables were hid in every conceivable place in the cars. One lady with many valuable diamonds was so badly frightened she could not unbutton the bosom of her dress to hide them, and asked a gentleman to do it for her. The conductor and brakeman ran down the track in the direction the engine had gone and soon encountered it coming back. The train was coupled together and the dead robber taken to Peach Springs.

Deputy Sheriff Smith and three Indian trailers left at 5 o'clock this morning to take the trail at daybreak. Another posse left on a special at 11 this morning. The robbers cannot escape, as there is snow on the ground and the Indians are better than bloodhounds on the trail. The country where the holdup occurred is a wild, rocky region contiguous to the Grand canyon and the robbers will probably try to get into the rocky defiles of the canyon before night. It will be almost impossible to get them if they get in there.

Mr. Juda of San Francisco, a drummer, who was on the train, says there were only two men in the holdup and the dead one having the dynamite in his possession caused the failure to get at Wells-Fargo treasure. Many wealthy eastern people were on the train, but were not molested.

TRAILING THE BANDIT
Kingman, Ariz., Feb. 9—The Indians who are on the trail of the men who robbed the westbound passenger train near Peach Springs last night are headed north toward the Grand canyon of the Colorado, the robber riding a horse and leading another. It was snowing all day, making the trail dim.

It is supposed that Donovan, who held up the Southern Pacific and killed a messenger over a year ago, is concerned in the robbery. He is known to have been hiding near the Grand canyon for a year. The dead robber is not identified. He wore clothes and carried a rifle stolen from a rancher in the vicinity a month ago. He answers the description of one Baldy Creighton.

That last paragraph represents one of the reasons many historians misguidedly scoff at primary sources. They were prone to hear rumors and repeat them. We know of course, that "Donovan" was not involved at all, and I have not researched his case yet for that reason. The data on the dead train robber is more excusable, since his identity remains murky to this day, but we do know he was not Charles "Bally" Creighton ("Baldy Creighton," no less!).

The *Phoenix Herald* of February 9, 1987 gave virtually the same account, almost word for word with a few exceptions. The February 10, 1897 *Arizona Gazette* (later the *Phoenix Gazette*) also covered the robbery but with no variation in details, ditto for other newspapers around the state. Accounts were published in St. Johns, Safford, Holbrook, and other Arizona locations far from the site of the robbery. This hold-up made news undoubtedly because it was unusual for one of the robbers to be killed while in the commission of his crime.

It is interesting to note that the *Albuquerque Citizen*, in its February 9, 1897 edition, had some better detail than most Arizona papers did, including the presence of only two robbers at the train, which we now know to be true. Here is the *Citizen's* account:

> Early this morning reports of hold-ups on the Atlantic & Pacific reached the city, and C. H. Young, the efficient division superintendent and local agent for Wells Fargo Express company, received the information that the No. 1 Los Angeles express, which left here yesterday morning, was held up by two masked men near Peach Springs, Arizona, at 11:30 last night; that the messenger, A. C. Summers, had shot and killed one of the robbers, and the body of the dead man had been taken to Peach Springs. The other robber pilfered the mail car after the killing, and the news received by Mr. Young further stated that Cade Selvy, special officer on the Atlantic & Pacific, who was on the train, was in pursuit of the escaped robber, with several Indian trailers.
>
> According to a recent order issued by the Wells-Fargo Express company, Messenger Summers will receive $1,000 for shooting and killing the robber.

FACTS FROM CLERK WALKER
These facts, so stated above, were obtained from Mr. Young, but, in order to obtain

more definite information, THE CITIZEN representative called upon Chief Clerk Walker, and the following was secured:

Paassenger train No. 1, on the Atlantic & Pacific, which left here Monday morning, was held up at Peach Springs, Ariz. Last night by two train robbers. One of them boarded the express car and when Expressman Alex Summers learned the purpose of his visit, he gave him a warm welcome in the shape of gunshot, well aimed. The robber dropped dead in his boots.

The pal of the dead robber forced the engineer to cut off the mail car and then went through it. There were some registered letters in the car, but the amount which the robber realized is not known.

The dead train robber has not yet been identified, but his dress indicates that he was a cowboy.

The following special dispatch, from near the scene of the hold-up was received this morning.

FURTHER FACTS

Special to the Citizen

Flagstaff, Ariz.—Feb. 9—As train No. 1 rounded the curve about five miles west of Yampai last night, Engineer Wm. Daze was signaled down by a red light. Thinking something wrong with the track, he came to a standstill, when his engine was boarded by two or three robbers with guns in hand, ordering Daze to do their bidding, and taking the fireman with them they ordered him to cut the express and mail car loose.

Express Messenger Alex Summers, thinking something was wrong, after taking in the situation, blew out the lights and got outside where he could have an even break with the robbers. As the detached cars began to move forward, Summers jumped on the rear end of his car, one of the robbers getting on the opposite side of the platform. Summers got the drop and killed him instantly, hitting him just over the heart. The others went with the cars to Nelson where they robbed the mail car, getting some registered packages, and rapidly disappearing in the darkness. Had it not been for the rapid and quick work of Summers, their plunder would certainly have been of larger amount. The sheriff from Kingman, with posse, is already on their trail and will soon have them in custody. Sheriff Cameron left here this morning to assist. The robbers are believed to be known in this vicinity.

ON THE TRAIL

Special to the Citizen

Kingman, Ariz. Feb. 9—Indian trailers and deputy sheriffs started before daylight on the trail of the train robber who escaped after holding up the train at Nelson last night. It is supposed that the trailers will have no trouble in running down the robber.

The identity of the robber killed by Messenger A. C. Summers is still unknown. He was a cowboy. The mail clerk insists that there were several robbers, but the engineer and fireman saw only one after the shooting by the messenger. The robber secured nothing but a few registered packages and letters from the mail car, through pouches being unmolested.

Chapter 4: The Rock Cut Train Robbery

News of the robbery and the shooting of one of the bandits by Messenger Summers spread like wildfire, and preceded the train in its arrival in Los Angeles. Up and down the line, Summers was hailed as a hero, and as noted in the *Albuquerque Citizen's* account, Wells Fargo immediately announced that it would give Summers a $1,000 reward for the slaying. As difficult as it is to believe today, the issue of vigilantism was never considered. If someone killed a "bad guy," it was a cause for celebration. As sophisticated as Territorial law was at that time, it was surprisingly low level in this area. Morals and standards were much different in those days, and it is as simple as that.

When the train arrived in Los Angeles, it was mobbed by reporters and curiosity seekers. Passengers and crew were sought after for newspaper interviews. Summers and Mail Clerk Albert S. Grant gave several, and artist sketches of the men appeared in several papers.

A number of the interviews will be reprinted here. Much of it is repetitive, but as these are the only surviving first-hand accounts of the robbery, it is important to preserve them. The *Los Angeles Times* of February 10, 1897 ran statements from both Summers and Grant:

> The overland Santa Fe train, which was held up Monday night at Rock Cut, about six miles east of Peach Springs, in Arizona, on the line of the Atlantic and Pacific Railroad, arrived in this city yesterday afternoon at 2 o'clock, only half an hour behind schedule time. The train was met at the depot by a crowd of curious persons, who were anxious to hear the story of the train-robbery direct from the lips of those who were present.
>
> Wells-Fargo messenger Alexander C. Summers, who shot and killed one of the robbers, was the center of attention, but he modestly sought to avoid unnecessary publicity and escaped to his home at No. 137 West Thirty-second street, at the first opportunity.
>
> The passengers, who had been saved from danger almost before they knew of the hold-up, had a variety of thrilling stories to relate, most of which dealt chiefly with their personal sensations.
>
> Of those who were actually connected with the fight and train-robbery, Messenger Summers and Mail Clerk Albert S. Grant were the only persons who came on with the train as far as Los Angeles. The crew in charge of the train was changed at Barstow, which is at the end of the division. Engineer William Hase, who pulled the engine and express and mail cars ahead after the train was stopped, and the fireman and Brakeman Moore, do not run in here.
>
> Messenger Summers is a well-built man, rather above medium height, and is 34 years of age. He has a quiet manner, and it not inclined to boast of his latest achievement, but he has the appearance of being a man who moves deliberately and keeps a cool head. His conduct during the time of the hold-up certainly bears out that belief.
>
> When he was seen at his house that night, he deprecated the idea that he was not alarmed when he first realized what was happening.
>
> "When the train stopped I supposed we had been flagged, and I had no thought of a hold-up until I heard a shot fired outside. The first thing I did was to turn out the two lights over my desk, at the same time I jumped for my .45 Colt's

and Randall, my assistant in the express car, grabbed the sawed off shotgun which we always carry.

By this time and before the train had come to a stop, one of the robbers started to uncouple the mail and express cars. Randall caught sight of one of the robbers, and was about to fire through the side door of the car, but I checked him, thinking it might be one of the train crew.

I told Randall to get out of the car on the left side towards the front, and I climbed out quietly on the other side by the rear door. There was no one in sight on my side and I made up my mind to try and get on the break-beam as we started to move slowly forward.

I caught the side edge of the platform and just as I rose up, I spied one of the robbers on the lower step of the opposite side of the platform. He did not see me at all, as he was watching Randall and was about to throw down on him. He had a short double-barreled shotgun in his hand.

I took deliberate aim at him and fired. He pitched forward without a word and fell to the ground. At the same moment I dropped off the car and the engine and two cars pulled ahead.

The train-robber was lying motionless on the ground, but not feeling satisfied that he was dead, I fired two more shots at him. Then I called to him to throw up his hands and moved up towards him.

He was dead. The bullet had gone in at the back of the head above the left ear. He wore a short mask that came down below his nose. Otherwise, his dress and appearances was that of a cowboy.

His coat was lined with sticks of giant powder, which he evidently intended to use in blowing down the express car.

The people in the cars left behind were badly rattled. The only person I could find who was willing to come out and help me look for the rest of the robbers was a fireman whose name I do not know. Together with Randall, who had hidden in some brush near the track, we started ahead, but soon discovered that whatever number of robbers remained had ridden ahead with the engine.

We had to tramp about two miles before we came up with the cars, which we found standing in charge of Engineer Hase and Mail Clerk Grant. The robbers, of whom there were two, had skipped out. Grant opened the door when we called to him and told us about his experience after they pulled ahead.

After their partner, who carried the giant powder, was killed, the robbers were unable to blow open my safe, so they got nothing there."

Summers was made a hero of on his arrival here, but he got away from the crowd as soon as possible and went to his home.

Albert S. Grant, the mail clerk, was the only man who came on to this city with the train who saw everything that happened after Engineer Hase was ordered to pull ahead. He told the following story:

"When the train slowed up, the first thing I saw was a man climbing over the tender. Just then another man showed on the front platform of my car. I thought they were tramps until I heard some shots fired. Then I knew what was up.

"The first thing I did was to put out the lights. Then I looked around for a place to hide out.

"When we stopped, after running ahead for some distance, a man came to the door and asked to be let in. He would not give his name, but made the engineer act as spokesman. In obedience to his command I came out and stood beside the engineer, while the robber entered the car. He carried a lantern, and after a few minutes ordered me into the car and demanded the registered packages. I replied that this was a United States mail car, and refused to get the packages for him. He leveled his gun at me, however, and compelled me to open the drawer, from which he took nine registered packages. I do not know their value. A dozen registered pouches which I had concealed beneath some mail sacks just before he entered the car escaped his attention. After he left the car I heard several shots fired, and soon afterward Mr. Summers came to the door and told me the robbers were gone. They had a team about twenty feet away from the point where we stopped. We were held there an hour and a quarter. The robber who came into my car spoke like a man of good education and did not use any profanity."

It seems rather hard to believe that the dead robber was actually going to shoot one of the trainmen (especially since Summers did not relay that important bit of information in every interview). As a rule, train robbers were not murderers, and no member of the Abe Thompson Gang had ever been known to have killed anyone up to that time.

The *Los Angeles Herald* took a much more sensationalistic approach to the robbery, including its own interview with Summers and Grant. Following are excerpts from that coverage of February 10, 1897. I have edited out a few paragraphs that repeat verbatim information that obviously came from Arizona papers:

The Overland Train Hold-Up in Arizona
Full Details of the Bandits' Daring Deed
ROBBER WHO CARRIED THE DYNAMITE
―――――――――
Was Shot to Death by Brave Summers
A FUSILLADE OF BULLETS
―――――――――
Terrorized the Train Crew and All the Passengers
―――――――――
Mail Agent Grant Also Had His Head With Him
―――――――――
He Hid Away the Registered Mail Pouches
The Would-be Robbers Were Green Hands—Excitement Among the Passenger
―――――――――

Train robbing in the west is becoming such a hazardous occupation that people who engage in it are no longer good risks for life insurance companies. In The Herald yesterday was printed the news of a daring but unsuccessful attempt to rob a Santa Fe overland train near Peach Springs, Ariz. And the fatality that attended the boldness of one of the robbers, owing to the cool courage of Express Messenger A. C. Summers, who made a good shot. That the robber did not succeed in getting away with much of value is owing first to the express messenger's killing the bandit who carried the dynamite which had been provided for blowing up the cars and secondly to the mail agent, who, though naturally scared, retained enough presence of mind to hide the valuable mail pouches.

The train that was held up Monday night arrived in Los Angeles yesterday, only seventy-five minutes late, though it had been detained at Peach Springs something like two hours. Of the train hands, the only ones who came through west of Barstow were the express messenger, the mail clerk and the Pullman car people. To meet the train at the La Grande station were a number of railroad men, express messengers and newspaper reporters who all hailed the muscular little Summers as a hero.

The story of the stirring episode is being told in the words of the two men who were most directly concerned and are here given.

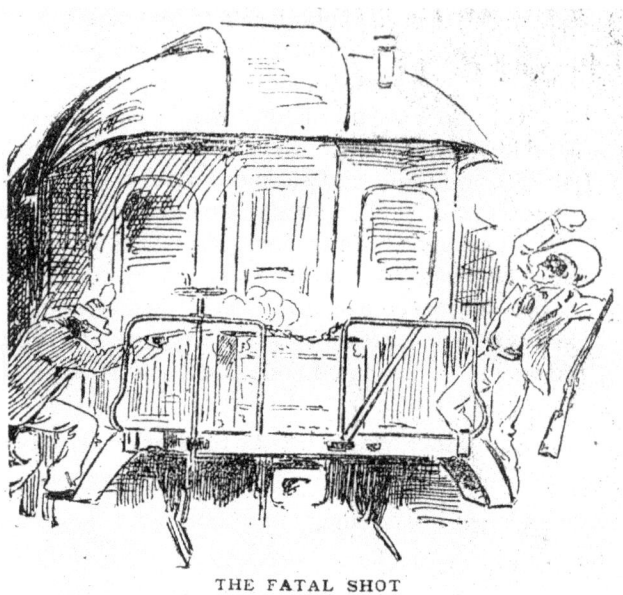

Newspaper artist's rendering of the train robber being shot, which appeared in the *Los Angeles Herald,* February 10, 1897. (Author's collection)

ON THE SPOT

A Terrible Wreck Averted by the Lateness of the Freight Train
Special to the Herald
WILLIAMS, Ariz., Feb. 9—Train No. 1, leaving here at 5:50 p.m. was held up at Rock cut between Yavapai and Nelson about 9 o'clock. The train was flagged by the watchman who patrols the track in that vicinity.

When Engineer Daze stopped, he was covered by one of the robbers and told to do whatever was requested. Fireman Bartoo was told to get down and cut off the engine. He was somewhat slow, and one of the robbers abruptly kicked him and said: "Why the _____ don't you hurry up?"

Just as the train was cut off Messenger Summers, who had not lost any time in hiding what he could and closing the door of his car, was sitting on the brake beam watching every move they made. Just as they cut off the car and bade Bartoo goodbye, he took aim and shot at the big man. Summers' aim was good and his man fell bleeding over the eye; and as he fell his gun was discharged. The other man, unconscious of his partner's fate, went through the mail car, taking several packages of registered mail.

The man on the engine kept Daze going back and forth up the track. He joined the man on the engine and said: "We are a couple of men short."

A panic reigned among the passengers and top berths were at a premium. Luckily they were not molested. The place where the hold-up took place starts in a canyon and the track circles many times. Generally a freight follows the passenger. Last night it was late. Otherwise there might have been an awful wreck.

THE DEAD ROBBER

The dead robber is a man six feet tall, with sandy complexion, had light mustache and weighed 147 pounds; also had a very small head and piercing eyes. He had on three suits of clothes, three suits of underwear, a heavy black overcoat; wore a black mask lightly drawn over his face. He was not recognized by anyone, but was seen here several weeks ago and tried to sell Tyner, the saloonman, a rifle.

Near the car was found enough dynamite to blow up a mountain. It is presumed that if their comrade had not met his deserved fate they would have opened the through safe. The three men walked up and down in company with the watchman for several hours before the arrival of the train and chatted quite pleasantly. They went to the engine and when nearly to Nelson told Daze to go back and get his train. This morning the trainmen coming this way noticed fresh horse tracks, so they must have doubled back.

ON THE TRAIL

The company's detective, Selvey, was on the ground on the arrival of No. 5. Soon after he went to Peach Springs and gathered a posse. The night was bright and only a slight fall of snow. The officers should have no trouble in tracking them. Sheriff Cameron and Deputy Buggeln and Chas. McGary left on the first train, all acquainted with the country and will give them a hot chase.

WHAT SUMMERS SAYS
He Modestly Relates the Part He Took in the Drama

He won't talk to you about it—he is very reticent." That is what an express messenger told a Herald reporter who was waiting to hear from A. C. Summers the story of his thrilling experience at Peach Springs on Monday night. Summers is a man of strictly business principles, not only in disposing of would-be robbers, but in handling the goods and valuables entrusted to him by the Wells-Fargo Company. That is why when he was accosted at the Santa Fe station upon the arrival of the Santa Fe overland at 1:55 p.m. yesterday, he begged to be allowed to first deliver his valuable freight and report to the office before he could say anything about the Arizona incident in which he unconsciously figured as a hero. He went directly to the Arcade depot, where he was met by a large number of his fellow-messengers, who greeted him with cheers. Some of them had themselves been held up and they could not only understand the ticklish position of Summers, but could also appreciate the bravery and coolness he had displayed.

Mr. Summers is a stockily built man, muscular, good-natured, deliberate in speech and just the type of a man who would keep cool in the most trying emergency. His home is at No. 137 West Thirty-Second Street in this city. He is about 34 years old and has been in the employ of the Wells-Fargo Company for ten years past. Though he had taken his life in his hand in facing and killing the train robber, and in so doing displayed commendable bravery, Summers showed no elation over the act or pleasure in the contemplation of a reward that is sure to come to him.

With few words the express messenger told to the Herald reporter the facts of the experience to this effect:

HOW IT HAPPENED

It was about 9 o'clock last night, said he, when the Santa Fe Overland was proceeding westward near Peach Springs, Ariz. At about ten miles east of Peach Springs the train slowed up. I did not then know the cause of the stopping, but I soon learned it was done by the signal of the track walker who is kept on duty there, and who had been captured by robbers and compelled to flag the train, after he had been their prisoner for two hours.

IN FOR IT NOW

The train stopped and we heard a shot. I said to my helper, Randall, "We are in for it now" and put out the lights. We could hear someone uncoupling our car from the coach that was next to it. The car we were in was the express car, and followed the mail car, which was the first on the train. We didn't know it then, but we learned later that the robbers had made the fireman climb out of his cab and go back under guard of one of the fellows to cut off the mail and express car from the rest of the train. We could hear the work of uncoupling, and Randall jumped out of one side-door and I from the opposite side of the car. Randall had a sawed-off shotgun, loaded with buckshot, and he displayed great nerve in going for the one robber who was there. When the uncoupling had been done, the robbers sent the fireman back into a coach and told him to stay there, so he was out of the way.

WITH THE FIRST SHOT

The robber saw Randall get out of the car and was watching him. I kept my eyes on the robber and crept up as close as I could to him. He was about to get up on the lower step of the real platform of the express car when I got up on the corresponding step on the other side and fired my revolver at him. My first shot must have hit him in the head and killed him instantly. As he fell, the gun he was carrying was discharged. I thought at first he was firing at me. I was not then certain I had hit him and as I dropped down beside the track, I saw his form lying down on the opposite side. Thinking he might be playing the same tactics that I was, I fired two more shots at him.

The first shot I fired across the platform between the end of the car and train box. The robber and I both dropped to the ground and the two cars and engine went on ahead for two miles. When I had fired my third shot, I ran toward the dark figure on the ground and cried, 'Hands up'. Then I saw he was dead, with brains spattered over his face. Randall was on the other side of the robber and would have shot at him but for fear of hitting me. When we had realized our situation the trainmen came up and four of us, Randall, Conductor Rice, the fireman and myself, walked to the engine and two cars that had been hauled two miles westward to a siding. Grant, the mail clerk, can tell you what happened there. He knows all about it.

THREE ROBBERS

When we reached the engine, we found that the engineer and the track-walker had been kept in the cab at the point of a robber's revolver, the engineer being compelled to run the train to the siding and that Grant had had an experience. His car had been entered by the other robber. Grant's robber had run away when he found that his partner could not join him. There were three robbers altogether—the one who was shot, the one who had the engineer covered, and another who was at the siding with some horses. The two surviving robbers took to flight and disappeared in one of the canyons nearby.

THE DEAD MAN'S AMMUNITION

The dead robber was found where he had dropped. He had been armed with a rifle and a large revolver. Inside his coat was a quantity of dynamite sufficient to blow up a whole train.

If one of my shots had hit the dynamite, I don't know what would have happened. The robber was masked when he found him. When the mask was taken off, he was seen to be a rather good looking fellow, 25 or 20 years old and apparently a cowboy. We picked him up and took him to Peach Springs where we left him.

Now I am dirty and awfully hungry," said Summers, "and I must go home to clean up and get something to eat.

When he had succeeded in breaking away from his fellow messengers whose congratulations and joshing nearly overcame him, he made a break for home.

THE MAIL CLERK
How A. S. Grant Saved Several Sacks of Registered Mail

The through mail clerk in the car just ahead of the express car was A. S. Grant, and when the car was hauled away from the scene of the shooting he went along with it, locked safely from the inside. He did not kill a robber, but he displayed presence of mind that resulted in saving much valuable mail. He was at work in his car when he heard the shooting and surmised the cause. He double locked his door and put out the light.

When we arrived at the siding about two miles from where the train was stopped," said he, "somebody pounded on the door of my car. I asked who was there, when a voice I recognized as that of the engineer told me to open up. I expostulated when the engineer told me he was being guarded by a robber and was commanded to order me to open up. When I realized the situation, not knowing but that the engineer would be shot for my refusal and the car probably blown up by dynamite, I finally opened the door. The masked robber in a low tone told the engineer to order me to get out, which I did, and then in the same way I was asked if there was anyone else in the car. When I said, 'No,' I was told to get back in and the robber followed me.

A SUCCESSFUL RUSE

He asked me for the registered mail and I told him there was none. He found nine registered packages and took them with him. Their value I know nothing about. He would have found more but for the fact that while we were parlaying through the closed door I had hid four sacks of registered mail beneath a lot of other sacks. When the fellow had gathered up all that he could find that he considered valuable he went out again and fired a number of shots in the air as signals to the companions he had left behind. He did not know that the other man was killed and he wanted him to come with the dynamite so they could rob the express car. When he found that the man with the dynamite would not show up, he ran away, joining the other fellow, who had kept in the dark.

While the fellow was firing signals in the air to call the others, I went back in the car, closed the door and kept it locked until Summers came and said the robbers were gone.

Was I scared?" Of course I was and I am not ashamed to admit it. If it had not been that Summers shot the man who had the dynamite, something more serious would have happened and the loss would have been greater.

A SLEEPING CAR CONDUCTOR
Was Not in the Fight but He Knew of It

A. B. Holmes is a conductor of one of the Pullman sleeping cars that were on the train. Neither the trainman nor any of the passengers were disturbed by the robbers, but the curiosity of the former almost led him into a scrape. As a rule, sleeping car conductors have no business to meddle with robbers of express and mail cars, but when Train Conductor Rice and Pullman Conductor Bellman heard the shooting, they went forward to reconnoiter, but they lost interest in the affair when someone with a gun told them to go back where it was more comfortable.

The brakeman had the good sense to run back to flag a train that was due to follow the waylaid passenger and thus prevent a collision. Conductor Holmes says that after the mail and express cars had been cut off the train the two express messengers jumped out and Summers first hid on the brakebeam of the car; afterwards he came out and shooting across the rear platform, hit the robber.

The train conductor took a Winchester rifle, a big revolver, and belt with eighty cartridges and eight sticks of dynamite from the body of the dead robber.

Conductor Holmes and other trainmen unite in saying that too much praise cannot be given to Summers for his bravery. The passengers on the train had little knowledge of what was going on, though they heard the shots.

EXPERIENCE OF PASSENGERS
To Most of Them it Was a Startling Incident

A hold-up is not usually as dangerous to passengers as a wreck might be, and consequently as a diverting incident on a transcontinental journey it has its advantages. To the tourists who have promised to write letters from every station to their friends, a hold-up wherein passengers had not been made to pungle up their purses, is something worth going across the continent to experience.

Richard Prendergrast and wife of Chicago, were passengers in a Pullman. Mrs. Prendergrast fainted dead away when she heard the shooting. She was all alone at the time, her husband being in the smoking car and she feared for his safety. Mr. Prendergrast, being in the smoker, was near the scene of the shooting and had exceptional opportunity to give a passenger's version. When the train stopped he walked to the front of the car to see what was the matter, when someone remarked that there was probably a hold-up.

"When the shooting began," said Mr. Prendergrast, "no one seemed anxious to investigate into the cause. After the shooting was over, the fireman came rushing in and asked for a gun. Somebody gave him one and he hurried out, but by that time the engine was steaming off down the track with the cars and he could do nothing and came back. We all went up to look at the body of the dead robber."

The passengers in the sleepers, being further away, did not have as good an opportunity to know what was going on, but they know all about it now.

"I heard the first shot and that was what startled me, and when the porter came running into the car and said we were being held up, I thought we would be shot, and was glad when the porter pulled down the curtains and put out the lights," said Miss L. Frazier of Dorchester, Mass. "Yes, indeed, I was frightened and don't want to take another trip like it. None of us saw the robbers. It was too dark, but it sounded as though there were half a dozen and all shouting. Oh, I guess, there must have been seven or eight shots fired."

Mrs. F. C. Shield of Providence, R. I. said: "As soon as the train came to a standstill and I heard that first shot my whole dream came back to me and I said to Miss Frazier, 'It is a hold-up.' A moment after the porter rushed in and confirmed what I said. No, I wasn't a bit frightened and I was the only woman to go up and see the dead robber."

Others whose experience was more or less exciting were Joseph Smith of Cincinnati who first learned from the porter that the train was held up. Dr. J. J. Siegel of Portsmouth, O., was present and he made an examination of the dead robber which convinced him that the bandit was thoroughly converted. He says that Summers' bullet went through the robber's head. "The fellow was a half-breed," said the doctor, "about 30 years old, smooth face and a muscular man weighing about 150 pounds. His features were not bad. I am perfectly willing to let other passengers have the robberies," said the doctor laughingly. "It isn't funny to feel that you may be a target for a couple of bullets any minute."

WHERE THE CAR WAS HIT
One Little Scar Furrowed in the Woodwork

The express car in which Messenger Summers and his helper were is No. 650. The only mark of the fray that can be found is on the rear end of the car about eight inches above the handrail on the left hand side, where there is a furrow in the wood, plowed out by a bullet of generous size. The groove is only about two inches long, but it marks the spot where someone's bullet struck and glanced off. As Summers feels certain it was his first shot that proved fatal, and the robber did not fire at him, it may have been one of the express messenger's subsequent shots that hit the end of the car as it was being hauled away toward the siding.

The small mark in the woodwork of the car is insignificant in size but it tells a story.

The discrepancy as to what exactly the unidentified robber was doing when Summers shot him is most revealing—it was almost as if Summers did indeed have some worries about what people might think of him. Nevertheless, it remains a clear statement about 1897 life that no one thought anything of Summers firing two more shots into the robber's corpse to make certain he was dead! There was never any talk of arresting him for murder or manslaughter. He was a hero simply because he had killed a "bad guy." Life was viewed in black and white absolutes in those days.

When the *San Francisco Chronicle* came calling for an interview, Summers returned to his self-defense story. That paper ran detailed coverage of the robbery also on February 10, 1897, much of it clearly culled from the Arizona dispatches we have already seen. Alexander Summers' interview with the *Chronicle* reads as follows—as a lot of the wording (but not all of it) is similar to that of the *Los Angeles Times* interview, we cannot rule out the possibility that Summers made interviews with the two reporters at the same time:

> When the train stopped I supposed we had been flagged, and I had no thought of a hold up until I heard a shot outside. The first thing I did was to turn out the two lights over my desk. At the same time, I jumped for my revolver and Randall, my assistant in the express car, grabbed the sawed-off shotgun which we always carry.
>
> By this time and before the train had come to a stop one of the robbers started to uncouple the mail and express car. Randall caught sight of one of the robbers and was about to fire through the side door of the car, but I checked him, thinking it might be one of the train crew. I told Randall to get out of the car on the left side toward the front, and I climbed out quietly on the other side by the rear door. There was no one in sight on my side, and I made up my mind to try and get on the brake-beam as we started to move slowly forward.
>
> I caught the side rods of the platform, and just as I rose up I saw one of the robbers on the lower step of the opposite side of the platform. He did not see me at all as he was watching Randall and was about to throw down his gun on him. He had a short double-barreled shotgun in his hand. I took deliberate aim at him and fired. He pitched forward without a word and fell to the ground. At the same moment I dropped off the car and the engine and two cars pulled ahead. The train-robber was lying motionless on the ground, but not feeling satisfied that he was dead I fired two more shots at him. Then I called to him to throw up his hands and moved toward him, but he was dead. The bullet had gone in at the back of the head above the left ear.
>
> He wore a short mask that came down below his nose. Otherwise his dress and appearance was that of a cowboy. His coat was lined with sticks of giant powder, which he had evidently intended to use in blowing open the express car.
>
> After seeing that the bandit was dead I went into the smoker, where I found the passengers in a state of the wildest excitement. The only person I could find who was willing to come out and help me look for the rest of the robbers was a fireman whose name I do not know. Together with Randall, who had hidden in some brush near the track, we started ahead, but soon discovered that if any of the robbers remained they had ridden ahead with the engine. We had to tramp about two miles before we came up with the cars, which we found standing in charge of Engineer Hare and Mail Clerk Grant. The robbers, of whom there were two, had skipped out. Grant opened the door when we called to him and told us about his experience after they pulled ahead. After their partner who carried the giant powder was killed the robbers were unable to blow open my safe, so they got nothing there."

STORY OF THE MAIL CLERK

How the Registered Pouches Were Saved

LOS ANGELES, February 9—Albert S. Grant, the mail clerk, was the only man who came on to this city with the train who saw everything that happened after Engineer Hare was made to pull out with the engine and mail car. He told the following story:

"About ten miles east of Peach Springs the train began to slow up. Almost at the same instant I noticed a man climbing over the tender. At the same time a second man appeared on the front platform of my car. I first took them to be tramps, but when the first shot was fired I realized what was coming. To say that I was scared was to put it mildly.

"I proceeded at once to extinguish the lights in my car and went to the rear end and concealed myself behind some mail pouches. When we came to the siding, some one approached my door and demanded admittance. I went to the door and asked who was there. The robber did all his talking through the engineer who told me to open the door and come out. I obeyed the command and was ordered to stand up beside the engineer when one of the robbers, of whom there were two, sprang into the car.

"He had been there but a few moments when he ordered me to climb in. He had a lantern in his hand. He asked for the registered packages. I told him that he could get them as well as I could. At the same time I said to him this is a United States mail car. He replied that he knew what he was about, leveling his gun on me. I told him I only had a few little packages, which were in the drawer. He stepped to the drawer and took out nine packages of registered matter, the value of which I know nothing about. Just before he entered the car, as I was ordered to the door, I threw several small sacks over a dozen registered pouches, which he fortunately did not discover.

"The robber appeared to be a well-educated man, used good language and never uttered an oath while in the car. After he left several shots were fired, and the next intimation I had was when Messenger Summers knocked on my door and told me they were gone. We were held there one hour and fifteen minutes. The fireman and brakeman were back in the smoker, the engineer and myself being alone with the robbers at this point. Upon investigation we found that the robbers had a team within about twenty feet of where we stopped.

The same edition of the *Chronicle* contained a few more passenger statements:

Stories of the Passengers

Frantic Efforts to Put Valuables Out of Sight

LOS ANGELES, February 9—The holdup caused a panic among many of the passengers in the sleepers. Several women fainted, others made frantic efforts to conceal their valuables and to place themselves beyond danger from flying bullets. One woman fell to her knees to pray. Another was so badly frightened that she had to appeal to a gentleman to assist her in unbuttoning the bosom of her dress that she might hide her diamonds. The porters added to the panic among the women by turning out the lights so that the robbers would not fire into the cars.

Richard Prendergast of Chicago, ex-Judge of the County Court of Cook County, Ill., was one of the passengers. He said:

> "When the train stopped some one said, laughingly, that it must be a hold-up, as no station was in sight. A moment later we heard the shots and realized that it was indeed an attempt to rob the train. We felt the train jar as the cars were uncoupled and then the fireman came rushing in and asked for a gun. He got one from one of the passengers, but it was too late for him to do anything, as the engine was already steaming down the track. We all went out then and saw the dead body of the train robber."
>
> Dr. J. J. Singel of Portsmouth, O., examined the dead man within five minutes after he was shot. He said that death had been instantaneous, as the bullet passed directly through the man's head.

The *Chronicle* on the same day ran an editorial on the opinion page, praising Summers' heroics:

> The express messenger on the Santa Fe train that was held up in Arizona proved to be of the right mettle. He didn't stay in his car and wait for the robbers to force him out with dynamite, but got out with his assistant. As soon as he saw one of the bandits he blazed away and brought down his man, thus ruining the plans of the criminals and probably saving the passengers from loss. The express company should give him not only a handsome money present but some testimonial that he may keep as a sign of his bravery."

As if that weren't enough, the *Chronicle* on Feb. 12, 1987 ran artist renderings of Summers and Grant (as had some other papers), and included this caption beneath the portraits:

> A. C. Summers, the Wells-Fargo messenger who killed one of the robbers in the Arizona hold-up, is a young man, and has been in the express service ten years. He is very quiet and, as one of his friends expressed it, "the last man in the world who would be expected to make a gun fight."
>
> A. S. Grant has been in the United States railway mail service for a number of years and has been on nearly every big run in America. He has had two most remarkable escapes from death in collisions. In the winter of 1892, at Blue Water, N.M., an east-bound mail train collided with a Raymond & Whitcomb west-bound train. Six persons were killed outright and fourteen were severely injured. Grant, who was in the mail car, was thrown into a sand bank and rendered unconscious. But his car was crushed to fragments and the ruins caught fire. A year later, near Kingman, a train on which Grant was mail clerk ran into the rear end of a freight train, killing two men. Grant's car was completely telescoped, but he was unhurt. In addition to having had many narrow escapes, Grant is well known as a whistler. He is a duet whistler and has only one rival in the world in that line.

On the same day, William Randolph Hearst's *San Francisco Examiner* also covered the robbery in some different and interesting (though not necessarily contradictory) detail. Note that this statement from Summers contains no allegation of self-defense at all:

Chapter 4: The Rock Cut Train Robbery

Took Good Aim Before He shot
Express Messenger Summers Tells How He Killed a Train Robber
Potted the Bandit as He Stood on the Car Platform

Coolly Planned With His Assistant Just What was to Be Done

SAYS HE WAS BADLY FRIGHTENED
Indian Trailers and Sheriffs of Three Counties Now in Pursuit Of the Other Bandit

LOS ANGELES, February 8—When the Santa Fe train from Chicago arrived this afternoon Express Messenger Alexander C. Summers was given an ovation by the Wells-Fargo people and railway men, for he has introduced a new feature into train robbery, that of killing the robber.

This was the train that was held up last night near Peach Springs, Arizona. Mr. Summers tells his story in the simple, modest way characteristic of brave men, and did not seem to realize that he had done anything out of the ordinary duty of express messengers. The story told by the man who killed the robber as told by himself is as follows:

Artist's rendering of Alexander Summers, the Express Messenger who killed the unidentified train robber., which appeared in the Examiner, *San Francisco, February 12, 1897. He was considered a hero for this, even though the dead man never had a chance. (Author's collection)*

"A short time after the train left Peach Springs I felt the brakes take hold. In a few minutes I heard a shot, and I said to my helper, J. Randall, 'We are in for it.'

"Randall took the shotgun and I grabbed my Colt's six shooter and we agreed to make a fight. Randall went to the forward side door, and I to the opposite rear one, both intending to get out and give battle.

"As Randall opened his door he saw a man and was about to drop him, but I stopped him, as we could not be sure that it was not one of the train crew. I got out and dropped to the ground, intending to get on the brake beam, as the car was still moving, and when it stopped get the drop on the bandits. I had grasped the side rods when I saw one of the robbers on the lower step of the same platform on the opposite side.

"I aimed long and carefully at his head and fired. He made no sound but instantly fell off, and I dropped off to make sure of him, and the car moved away, leaving us together.

"I ordered him to put up his hands, but he did not move, and on approaching him I found that he was dead. My bullet had struck him in the back of the head just above the left ear. I took his mask off, and the face was that of the typical cowboy,

Artist's rendering of Albert S. Grant, the Postal Inspector held up by Parker during the Rock Cut Train Robbery, which appeared in the *Examiner*, San Francisco, February 12, 1897. (Author's collection)

with possibly a strain of Indian blood in him. Under his coat he had a bag containing a number of sticks of dynamite.

"I went back to the smoking car and the fireman offered to help fight the other bandits if we gave him a weapon, so I dug him up a gun and we joined Randall, who was scouting about, and we went down the track to the cars, and I notified Mail Clerk Grant that the robbers had gone. The robbers had entered my car, but as their pal with the dynamite was not in a condition to assist, they could not get into the safe, so they got nothing.

"I don't mind saying that I was badly scared and all the time wished I was back in Los Angeles. It is an ugly situation to be in, and I only did the best I could under the circumstances."

Story of the Mail Clerk
For ten years Albert S. Grant has been in the railway mail service, and this was his first experience with robbers. He said:

"As soon as the train commenced to slow down I saw a man on the tender and another on the front platform of my car. I supposed at first they were hoboes, but there was a shot and then I realized what was up. I put out the lights and did all I could to hide the registered mail, but the engineer soon knocked at the door and repeated to me the robbers' order to open the car.

"I stepped down and was soon up alongside the engineer, and one of the men entered the car. He came back to the door and ordered me to come in and show him where the registered mail was. I said, 'You can get them yourself. Do you know this is a United States mail car?' He answered, 'Yes, I know what I am about,' and he put his pistol against my head and marched me to the desk where there were a few little packages. The others I had covered up with mail pouches.

"The bandit seemed to be a cultivated man. He used excellent English and did not swear or use any foul language. As he left a number of shots were fired. The next intimation I had about our situation was when Messenger Summers came to the car and told us the robbers had gone. The bandits had a team within twenty feet of where we were."

How the Train Was Stopped
Details of the hold-up, which were so difficult to obtain last night, show that the plan of the robbers had been carefully prepared. The train, which is known as West-bound No. 1 was due at Peach Springs, Arizona at 9:15 last night.

Two hours before the arrival of the train at Nelson siding two masked men appeared in the deep cut (two miles east of there) and held up the watchman at the cut, keeping him under cover of their Winchester rifles for two hours. On the arrival of the train they compelled the watchman to signal it to stop. The engineer, seeing the signal of the watchman and at a dangerous part of the road, brought his train to a standstill.

Immediately both men covered the engineer and fireman with rifles and compelled the watchman to get on the engine. The fireman, in company with the taller robber, then uncoupled the mail and express cars from the balance of the train and upon a signal from his pal that all was ready the other man on the engine ordered the engineer to pull out. The engineer replied that the air was stuck and he could not move the train.

"Jim, cut off that air," came from the engine and the little fireman promptly cut it off as "Jim" motioned with the muzzle of his Winchester what was expected of him, as soon as the brakes were released. Bill, the short robber on the engine, said to the engineer, "I guess you can go now all right." As the engine pulled out the tall robber, "Jim," climbed onto the rear platform of the express car, leaving the fireman standing on the ground.

The Shot of the Messenger

Slowly at first the cars moved, and when half a car length was passed there was a sharp crack of a pistol, a little red flash and "Jim" sank down on the platform and then rolled to the ground.

All oblivious of his comrade's fate, "Bill" went on to Nelson siding, stopped the train and proceeded to go through the mail car.

When the train first stopped the express messenger, learning the real cause, quietly opened the door of his car and dropped to the ground on the opposite side of the car. He waited, six-shooter in hand, until the train started up, and then fired across the platform at the unconscious bandit, as he stood on the steps holding the rail.

On the arrival of the cars at Nelson Siding the robber named Jim ordered the watchman into the express car.

"I am liable to get killed in there," was his response.

"You might just as well get killed in there, as out here, partner," was the way in which the bandit put it, and then the watchman climbed into the car and reported no one there. At the orders of the robber the watchman said that he could not find anything of value, and the bandit then paid his attention to the mail car.

In the Mail Car

"Open that door," he called to the mail clerk.

"All right, gentlemen, I will open it for you," came the polite reply, and the door was opened.

The robber went inside the door, guarding the mail clerk and the people outside.

"Give me the registered mail," he demanded.

Eight packages of local registered mail were handed over, and putting them in his pockets, the man climbed down and looked for his companion. Not finding him he compelled the engineer to back up again about one mile and stop. He then fired several shots as a signal, and receiving no reply ordered the engineer to run back to Nelson where a final search was made and then he left in the darkness after firing more shots.

The train reached Peach Springs two hours' late, the body of the dead robber being on board. An inquest was held today. The dead man is six feet tall, about thirty-five years of age, weighed 160 pounds, had blue eyes, light hair, red and very small mustache. Forehead high and narrow. He had a peaked face, narrow between the eyes, and a very long, pointed nose.

On the Trail

At daylight a Deputy Sheriff left Kingman with J. A. Smith, Henry Lovin and three Hualapai Indian trailers, who took up the trail. The trail took a direction north, toward Pine Springs, forty-five miles distant on the Hualapai reservation.

It was snowing at Peach Springs to-night, and unless the trailers and deputies catch the bandit to-night, it is feared that the trail will be obliterated. Eight miles from the scene of the robbery the bandit took the wagon road to Pine Springs. The deputies and trailers had to go on foot, and this morning two of them returned, secured horses at Kingman and started at 2 p.m. This gives the robber fifteen hours' start, and unless he stops at Pine Springs it may be a long chase.

The Sheriff of Yavapai county, George C. Ruffner, and the Sheriff of Coconino county, Ralph Cameron, with deputies, three horses and an outfit will be at Peach Springs to-night. Sheriff Potts from Kingman is there now. Twenty men will be on the trail before to-morrow morning. There is $2,300 reward for the capture of the escaped bandit, dead or alive.

The laws of Arizona make train robbery or attempt at train robbery a capital offense, and this makes the attempt at arrest a desperate undertaking. A month ago a sheep-rancher's house near Pine Springs was broken open and clothing, a rifle and provision stolen. To-day the owner of the house was at Peach Springs and identified the coat and vest on the dead robber and the Winchester rifle as those stolen from him.

The latest reports from the vicinity of last night's hold-up near Peach Springs lead the officers to believe that the hold-up was planned by one Johnnie Donovan, who about one year ago was implicated in a train robbery on the Southern Pacific. Donovan is thought to be hiding in the northern part of the Territory, between the Atlantic and Pacific Railroad and the Grand Canyon, and it is believed that he, with some cowboys, are the ones implicated in this robbery. The dead robber has not yet been identified.

The weather has turned colder and it is snowing, making it very hard trailing, but two of the best Indian trailers in this part of the country are on the track of the robber. Parties who know the country well in that vicinity say that the robber has a very good chance to escape.

The "Donovan" theory, which appeared in a number of newspapers, disappeared within a couple of days. One interesting thing about the *Examiner's* account was that it was the only one to report that one of the robbers was named Jim—before Parker had been identified. Only problem is, Jim Parker was NOT the dead robber! Yes, inter-newspaper communications were not so good in those days, although as you can see from these accounts, the discrepancies are not that serious and seldom were with any story. The derision that many Western historians regard old newspapers with is unjustified.

Also on February 10, 1897, the *San Francisco Call* ran their own account as well. They identified the dead robber as the "leader," procured their own interview with Summers, ignored Albert Grant, and also took a statement from Pullman Car Conductor Holmes:

> GRIT OF THE MESSENGER
> Saved the Express Car Treasure by Killing the Leader
> LOS ANGELES, Cal., Feb. 9—The Santa Fe overland train which was boarded by outlaws near Nelson, Ariz., last night, when one of the robbers was killed by Express Messenger Alexander Summers, arrived in this city only thirty minutes late this afternoon. It was well crowded with passengers, each of whom had his own tale of experience to relate. Some ludicrous scenes were described, but the spectators were not in a frame of mind to enjoy them. Many of these stories exaggerated the attempted "hold-up" to a wonderful degree, one woman claiming that fifty shots were fired.
>
> The passengers one and all praise the courage and coolness of Express Messenger Summers. There is nothing too good for that modest and unassuming gentleman here to-night.
>
> He has been overwhelmed with congratulations. Crowds gathered at nearly all the stations on the route to Los Angeles to yell for "Good boy Alex." Messenger Summers, who has been in the employ of the company for ten years, described his exciting experience to a Call correspondent this afternoon.
>
> "As we slowed up," he said, "one of the robbers proceeded to uncouple the mail and baggage car from the balance of the train. Just then Randal, my assistant, said that one of them could be seen from my car side door and remarked, 'I can bring him down.' I said, 'Hold on, don't shoot; it may be a railroad man.' There are two doors on each side of the car. Randal went to the forward side-door to the left to get out, while I took the one on the right, nearest the rear end of the car. I opened it cautiously, and not seeing anyone, dropped down carefully to the ground and was going to crawl under the car and get on the brakebeam.
>
> "The two cars had been uncoupled and were moving along at this time. I am quite up to jumping brakebeams, and as the end of the car moved up to me I grasped hold of the side rods, at the same time observing one of the robbers standing on the lower step of the same platform on the opposite side. When I had drawn myself up I took good aim with my revolver and fired. He tumbled headlong off the step. He had in his hand a small cut-off double-barreled gun and was looking forward at the time, endeavoring to get a bead on my helper, who was trying to get down on the opposite side.
>
> "As soon as I fired I dropped to the ground, and the engine and mail and express cars moved away. I could see my man lying on the ground, but not knowing whether he was dead or alive, I fired two more shots at his body. I then went up to him and found that he was dead. The first bullet had entered the back of the head, just above the left ear. I lifted his mask and came to the conclusion that he was a cowboy. I also found under his coat a bag which was fastened around his waist. It contained several sticks of dynamite."

Pullman Car Conductor Holmes made the following statement, which he declares is absolutely correct:

"The robbers corralled the watchman at Nelson, a station six miles east of the springs for four hours, waiting for No. 1 to come along. When the train showed up they made the watchman flag the engineer with a white light. Stopping the train the robbers compelled the fireman to get out and cut the mail and express cars off. The train conductor, Rice, was in the sleeping-car with Conductor H. Bellman of the sleeper. Both went forward to see what the trouble was. They were ordered back. Conductor Rice had reached the ground and was compelled to return, the brakeman running to the rear to flag No. 3 following.

"After the express and baggage cars had been cut off, the two messenger agents jumped from the express-car. Agent Summers crawling under the car, hid on the tracks. As the car passed the air brakes held so the cars stopped.

"Summers, getting out and stepping on the rear steps of the express-car, saw the robbers, who had commanded the fireman to cut the train loose, step up on the opposite step. Taking his revolver and steadying it on the chest on the rear platform, he fired, killing the leader of the gang. The cars commenced to move and Summers jumped off.

"The robbers (there were two left) took the engine and two cars, with the engineer and mail clerk still on, and ran ten miles west, one guarding the engineer and the other the mail agent. The engine was backed up twice to see if the leader would not show up, during the time the robbers ransacked the mail. They were at the work for two hours, taking all the registered letters.

"The conductor got the shotgun, a revolver, eight sticks of dynamite and a belt with eighty cartridges off the dead robber. Then, with Express Messenger Summers, the fireman and one other man, armed with what weapons they could borrow from the passengers, they went forward to find the engine and cars coming upon them two miles away. The robbers, seeing them coming, left the train and fled to the mountains.

"Too much praise cannot be given Messenger Summers, who is a brave man. By the killing of the leader the train was saved, as the remaining two robbers had no dynamite to blow open the safe or cars. The passengers of the coach and sleepers were terribly frightened. The engine and cars were backed to the train. The dead robber was placed upon the rear platform of the express-car and brought to Peach Springs, where the body was left. The train proceeded on to Los Angeles, arriving her about on time."

On February 11, 1897, the *Call* ran the following editorial:

CHECKING THE BANDITS

The courage of Express Messenger Alexander Summers not only prevented the robbery of the Santa Fe overland train in Arizona on Monday night, but put an end to the life of the leader of the gang. Rarely has a shot been more effectually fired than that which killed the bandit who carried the dynamite with which it was intended to blow open the safe of the express-car and postoffice-car. If a few more such feats are performed the trade of holding up trains will be rendered so hazardous that it will cease to attract the minds of adventurous villains.

The feat of the express messenger was one of more than ordinary daring. He had to get out of a car in a train which had been held up and make his way to a position where he could get a sure shot at the robber. To effect this he was compelled to crawl under the car and get on the brakebeam, and from that place draw himself up to a place where he could take good aim with his revolver, and after making sure that he had the right man kill him with one shot.

Too much praise cannot be given to Messenger Summers for the service which by his valor he has rendered not only to the express company but to the public generally. He has done much to put an end to train-robbing, and if his example is followed by others the time will not be far distant when travel on the railway trains of the United States will be safe from any danger of molestation by any gang of bandits however reckless and bold they may be.

The *San Francisco Bulletin* seemed to be the least interested in the robbery as far as that city's four main newspapers went. They printed only spotty details, no interviews, and no variations worthy of reprinting here.

Our Mineral Wealth from Kingman ran the following February 19, 1897:

Train men say that A.C. Sommers, who killed the train bandit, was so badly frightened after he (illegible) through the cars with a cocked pistol in his hand and his eyes standing out on his cheeks. That may be so but he knocked over the hold up first.

Interestingly, the *Holbrook Argus*, of Holbrook, Arizona (west of Winslow) printed a statement from Alexander Summers as well. As it seems unlikely that a reporter from Holbrook would have been in Los Angeles to interview the messenger, the *Argus* must have pulled it from wire service reports, whom Summers apparently spoke with as well. It is very ironic to note that the tiny *Argus*, far away from Peach Springs or Los Angeles, would become the only Arizona newspaper, to my knowledge, to print a statement on the robbery from Summers or any of the trainsmen for that matter:

TRAIN WRECKERS
They Attempt to Hold Up an A & P Train—One of the Robbers Killed
Train No. 1, west bound was held up by three mask men Monday night between Yampai and Nelson. One of the robbers was killed by Alex Summers, a Well-Fargo messenger, who gives the following account of the affair:

"The first intimation that I had of the hold-up was the train stopping about ten miles east of Peach Springs. At first I thought the train had been flagged for orders. Then a shot was fired. I turned out the lights over my desk, grabbed my revolver and Randall, my helper, grabbed the shotgun. As the train slowed up one of the robbers uncoupled the mail and baggage car from the train. Randall took one door and I took the other, which I opened cautiously. Not seeing any one I dropped to the ground and swung on the brake beams as the car moved off, at the same time observing one of the robbers standing on the lower step of the platform. I took good aim and fired and the robber tumbled headlong from the step. He had in his hand a small cut-off doubled barreled gun and at the time was trying to get a bead on my helper who was trying to get down on the opposite side. As I fired I also dropped to the ground and the engine, mail and express cars moved away.

"The bullet entered the back of the outlaw's head just above the left ear. I found under his coat a bag which contained several sticks of dynamite. I then went into the smoking car, where the utmost confusion prevailed.

"The fireman was the only one who would accompany me, and learning there were no more robbers in the vicinity, we walked down the track and found that the robbers who accompanied the cars had entered the express car but were unable to get into the safe owing to the fact that the man who had the dynamite failed to respond to their calls."

Naturally, with communications being what they were in those days, the further you were away from the train robbery, the more sketchy and inaccurate the details became.

The *Denver Post* of February 9, 1897 contained several headlines on the robbery, including the words, "The Boldest Attack Ever Made." The *Post's* article then recounted the known details of the heist, and then it got very interesting:

The post office inspector's department was surprised this morning by the receipt of a message from Los Angeles, California, recounting a most sensational hold-up of the Santa Fe West-bound train late last night. According to the message, one bandit is dead and a valuable mail package has disappeared.

The details are meager, but sensational enough to have caused Chief Postoffice Inspector McMechen to immediately telegraph to the postmaster at Peach Springs, Arizona, for confirmation and more details. Up to a late hour no answer had been received. The information in possession of Mr. McMechen leads him to believe that one of the two dead bandits, possibly the one who met death, was the famous Musgrove, the New Mexican "blood-drinker," as he is referred to by the Mexicans whose settlements he has ravaged. The story received by the inspector is as follows:

As the Santa Fe West-bound train No. 1 was proceeding toward California over the Arizona deserts last night, two masked men sprang on the track at some distance ahead and by wildly waving red lanterns caused the engineer to come to a standstill. The point was on the Atlantic and Pacific tracks a few miles from Peach Springs, a small settlement boasting of a post-office, general store and a few scattered dwellings.

As soon as the train came to a standstill the engineer was covered with a revolver in the hands of one of the robbers, who ordered him to keep quiet. The other robber then uncoupled the mail and express car and with his companion sprang on board the engine and ordered the engineer to run up the road for two or three miles. Here the train was stopped and the robbers proceeded to open the door of the mail car.

Messenger Summers was in the car at work at the sacks, when the man with the mask sprang beside him and ordered him to throw up his hands. This was done. A revolver lay on the shelf near the messenger, escaping the robber's observation by being covered with several small sacks. As the man turned his back to rip a leather mail bag containing registered letters, Summers quickly reached for the weapon and as the robber attempted to leave the car shot him in the head, the man dying instantly. The other robber, who had grabbed a bundle of registered letters in the meanwhile made his escape.

The train was ran back to Peach Springs with the dead robber, where his body now awaits identification. The corpse is described briefly in the telegram as being of athletic build, the face covered with a short beard and wearing "schapps" of Mexican manufacture. The train which was held up was due at Los Angeles, California, at 1:30 o'clock this afternoon.

"I am strongly of the belief," said Postoffice Inspector McMechan, "that one of the two men is Musgrove, who robbed numerous postoffices in New Mexico and Arizona. Waterbury and the deputy United States marshals placed them in the Oscura mountains in New Mexico and killed all but two, Musgrove and a companion. These two escaped to Old Mexico where they have since been living in hiding. I should not be surprised if they had made their way up from Mexico, entered Arizona and endeavored to hold up the Santa Fe train. In fact, it is very probable, for the daring and recklessness of the thing is similar to his former escapades."

Peach Springs, the scene of the robbery, is in Mohave county, Arizona, a lonely place on the Santa Fe route to California. The desert reaches off in long sandy swells, broken occasionally by dwarfed cacti or sage-brush to Red Lake, a body of clear water, lying to the northwest. The station is fifty-one miles from Kingman, Arizona, the first large town. The country is exceedingly wild.

Inspector McMechen continued to shoot off his mouth for other reporters as well. The February 10, 1897 *Rocky Mountain News*, also of Denver, carried the following paragraphs in its coverage of the train robbery:

It is the opinion of Postoffice Inspector McMechen that the robbers were the remainder of the gang of five which started out in New Mexico several months ago, terrorizing the country.

There were five in the gang at the outset," said the chief, "but two of the gang were killed, one was captured, and Musgrove and his partner escaped. Judging by the way the work was done, I am of the opinion that Musgrove was in charge at the time of the train robbery. Black Jack was made a prisoner at El Paso, and Cole Estes and Bob Hayes were shot previously. I have no doubt at all that the whole band will be brought to justice.

Likewise, the *El Paso Daily Times* of February 9, 1897, ran the following sentences in its coverage of the robbery:

The robbery is to be investigated by the postal authorities here. Chief Postoffice Inspector McMechen started a detective out to the scene of the robbery this afternoon. Chief McMechen says that from the information he has he believes the dead robber to be Jack Musgrove, who was concerned in the White Oaks, New Mexico, robbery some time ago.

It does not speak well of Postal Inspector William M. McMechen that he would proclaim almost immediately that he knew the identity of the robbers without the slightest

This photo of the corpse of the unidentified dead train robber was taken the morning after the hold-up occurred. It was widely circulated in the hope that someone might be able to identify him. (Courtesy of the Ruffner family)

bit of evidence. Perhaps it was wishful thinking on his part—perhaps the failure to have captured Musgrove (whose name was George, not Jack) was a thorn in his side, and his desperation to remove it caused him to speak out prematurely.

McMechen's erroneous views traveled quickly, and soon other offices who were nowhere near Peach Springs jumped on the bandwagon. From the *Santa Fe Daily New Mexican* of February 9, 1897:

> Marshal E. L. Hall received a telegram from Peach Spring, A. T. this morning stating that train No. 1 was held up eleven miles west of that station last night by robbers who secured eight packages of registered mail. There were three men in the gang, one of whom was killed by the express messenger. A posse started on the trail of the other two at daylight this morning. Mr. Hall judging by the description of the men sent him thinks they are Black Jack, George Musgrave and Tom Anderson and if these are the men Anderson was the one killed.

The dead train robber, Parker's pal whom he brought into the Abe Thompson Gang, was never identified to anyone's satisfaction. In the days following the failed robbery, a volley of different names were attributed to him. Most of the time, the names probably came from people who thought they had seen someone like him somewhere, sometime.

After bringing his body into Peach Springs, the authorities propped the robber up and took his picture. An inquest was held later, but I have been unsuccessful in locating the records, and I presume they have not survived. On February 26, 1897, the *Prescott Courier* reported:

> Pictures of the dead Rock Cut train robber have been received at the sheriff's office. The pictures show eyes of deep blue, a large round head, high forehead, sinister smile, exposing a row of handsome teeth. Officers say the man was about

thirty-five years of age and had a yellow white mustache. His pockets were filled with cigarettes. Before the arrival of the train, he talked with the Rock Cut watchman for several hours and smoked cigarettes all the while. He was evidently a habitual cigarette smoker.

As to his identity, the *Courier* reported February 12, 1897:

> A telegram was received at the Sheriff's office yesterday from Sheriff Ruffner, stating that the robber killed near Peach Springs is supposed to be a man who formerly worked at Smith's slaughter house, near Prescott.

On February 17, 1897, the *Arizona Journal Miner* chimed in with this bit of news:

An artist's rendering of the photo of the dead train robber, which appeared in the *San Francisco Examiner* February 13, 1897. (Author's collection)

> The train robber killed near Peach Springs a few days ago, has been identified as Williams Daylon. He was employed a few month ago as a sheep herder for W. H. Smith of this city.

Daylon was apparently very much alive and very angry, for the *Journal Miner* retracted almost immediately. From the same edition:

> Daylon, the former Prescottite was not the robber killed the other day at Peach Springs. The rumor was unfounded, and was circulated on account of his resemblance.

As shall be seen in the next chapter, California papers would variously identify the dead man as Charles Douglass and Dan Collins. Love Marvin would later claim that he knew the man as John Clayton.

Still later, the *Mohave County Miner* printed the following on March 27, 1897:

> From a photograph the dead Rock Cut train robber has been positively identified as Jack Williams, of Cedar, Iron county, Utah. Williams was well known to the cowboys around the county, having brought a band of horses from Utah almost two years ago.

The name Williams stuck, somehow. After Parker's later jailbreak, Wells Fargo would issue a Wanted poster for him, describing his criminal history and identifying his dead partner as Jim, alias Harry, Williams. If the famed bank had any solid data to back up that claim it has been lost. Some after-the-fact accounts of the Parker story, many years later, would attribute still other names to the dead man.

So who was the dead train robber? It is unlikely we will ever know for certain. He may not have even been a bad man per se, just misguided. But in the 19th century, people universally saw everything in black and white absolutes. To them, the man tried to rob a train, so he richly deserved the death that befell him. Parker, for reasons known only to him, steadfastly refused to divulge his friend's name, right down onto his own death. He would later tell a reporter it was because the man had come from a good family, and he didn't want them to know their loved one had gone bad. Whether this is true or not will never be known.

It is not known for certain how the body was disposed of. In all likelihood, the dead man was unceremoniously dumped into a pauper's grave near Nelson or Peach Springs. That is how such matters were usually handled, especially in the absence of a confirmed identity.

For many years, the amount of money Parker got from the train robbery remained cloudy. In Parker's later court papers, the railroad estimated the loss at around $100. Some historians have put the figure as low as $5.00. Since the dead robber was weighed down with dynamite and blasting caps, it is clear that the bandits were anticipating finding something extremely valuable.

But in the year 2001, Professor John D. Tanner, Jr. of Palomar College, California, embarked on his own research of the Parker story, and looked where no historian had thought to look before—at the National Archives in Washington. There, in the Records of the Post Office Department from 1877 to 1903, he found the most important discovery regarding Parker that had been uncovered in many years—a letter from Denver post office inspector A.C. Frederick to his superior officer, William M. McMechen. Written after Parker's arrest (which will be recounted in the next chapter), it gives exact detail on the amount of money in the registered letters that Parker grabbed. Professor Tanner informed me that the file was thick with dust, indicating it had not been looked at possibly since being filed in the Archives, and I am grateful to him for sharing this and other research with me. The text, fascinating in its detail, reads as follows:

Denver, Colorado, April 18th, 1897

Hon. Wm. M. McMechen,
Inspector in Charge,
Denver, Colorado
Sir:—
I have the honor to report the arrest of James Parker, on Feb. 15th, 1897, for train

robbery near "Nelson siding," Arizona, also Abe Thompson, and Lovell Marvin, on Feb. 10th, 1897, who were accessories to said crime: all of the above mentioned parties were arrested about 30 miles north of Peach Springs, Ariz. By Geo. C. Ruffner, Sheriff of Yavapai County, Ariz.

On Feb. 8th, 1897, Train #1, Atlantic & Pacific Railway, was "held up" near "Nelson Siding, Ariz. By two masked men, one of whom was instantly killed by the Wells Fargo Express Messenger, (the identity of the dead robber has never been ascertained) the other robber detached the mail car from the train, and proceeded with same about one mile west, where he ordered the engineer to stop, he then entered the mail car and held up the Railway Postal Clerk, and ordered him to deliver over all registered matter: the clerk had presence of mind enough to secrete the through registered pouches under some empty tie sacks, where they remained undisturbed, but he was compelled by "force of arms" which consisted of a #45, "BullDog" revolver, to deliver over to the robber (Mr. Parker) what local registers he had on hand, which were as follows.

Registered letter #84, R.P.E.#80, mailed Feb. 6th, 1897, at Winslow, Ariz., writer, Kim Sing, addressed to San Francisco, Cala. Contents $5.00 in currency. Registered letter #86, R.P.E.#86, mailed Feb. 6th, 1897, at Ft. Apache, Ariz. Writer Wm. Wooster, addressed to "Crocker Woolworth" National Bank, San Francisco, Cala. Contents $364.76 in checks. Registered letter #75, R.P.E.#72, mailed Feb. 8th, 1897, at Williams, Ariz. Writer Mrs. Wm. Hayward, addressed to Wm. Hayward, San Francisco, Cala. Contents $40.00 in currency. Registered letter #84 R.P.E. #77, mailed Feb. 7th, 1897, at Congress, Ariz. Writer Richard Urin, addressed to Mrs. Bessie Kendall, San Francisco, Cala. Contents not yet ascertained. Registered letter ?, R.P.E.#60, mailed Feb. 7th, 1897, at Big Bug, Ariz. Writer unknown, addressed to San Francisco, Cala. Contents not yet ascertained. Registered letter #3 R.P.E.#3, mailed Feb. 8th, 1897, at Bluewater, New Mexico, writer J. S. VanDoren, addressed to Montgomery Ward & Co. Chicago, Ills. Contents $5.45 in cash. Registered letter #334 R.P.E.#334, mailed Feb. 8th, 1897, at Prescott, Ariz. Writer G. H. Schueman, addressed to H. Thurman, Ransburg, Cala. Contents $3.00 in currency. Registered letter #327 R.P.E.#327, mailed Feb. 8th, 1897, at Prescott, Ariz. Writer J. D. Shipp, addressed to G. Levy, Signal, Ariz. Contents $15.00 in currency. Registered letter #335 R.P.E. #335, mailed Feb. 8th, 1897, at Prescott, Ariz. Writer Jack Sims, addressed to "Man Wo Sang & Co." Hong Kong, China, contents $20.00 currency, and $50.00 check.

All of the above described registered letters, are covered by registered cases numbered from 104219-to-104227-"A" inclusive. The sum of $41.00 in currency was found upon James Parker, when arrested, which amount is now in the hands of Sheriff Ruffner, and he declines to turn over the same to your office, until so ordered by the court, which will necessarily delay the return of the above mentioned "A" cases.

The Indian trailers found a one dollar bill near where Parker was captured, said bill has a diamond shaped piece cut or torn out of the upper side of same, and which will no doubt constitute very material evidence against said Parker, as the same was found near where he had camped the evening before his arrest.

In conclusion would say, that the evidence thus far secured against Parker, Thompson, & Marvin, will be presented to the Territorial Grand Jury, at Prescott,

Arizona, June 1897 term, and there is no questions but that they will be indicted, and convicted for the above mentioned crime.

Very respectfully,
A. C. Frederick
P. O. Inspector

It was a small haul, to be sure, and what happened to most of it is unknown. The $41.00 Parker had on him when captured was still lower than the amount stolen, but no record exists as to if it was ever determined what Parker did with the rest while on the run.

The "evidence" of Parker leaving behind dollar bills with diamond shapes cut out of them is truly bizarre—would Parker really have taken the time to stop and do that while on the run? Maybe it had some kind of symbolic meaning to him, or perhaps it was even an attempt at evidence-planting by some overzealous deputy or posse member who feared the captured man might beat the rap. As Parker would never stand trial for train robbery, this was never brought up again.

Months later, when on the run from posses following the jailbreak, Parker would tell country settlers he had gotten thousands of dollars from the robbery. This claim was probably just used by Parker to induce the settlers to help him, implying that he might share his treasure with them.

The February 12, 1897 edition of Kingman's small mining newspaper, *Our Mineral Wealth*, ran a small item which, if true, was surprisingly underreported:

> No. 1 Again in Trouble
>
> As No. 1, Monday night, was bowling at its usual rate of speed, it found an open switch at Luna, a small station 28 miles west of Albuquerque and before it could be stopped, jumped the track throwing the engine over on its side and nearly demolishing the mail and baggage cars. The engineer was the only person hurt and it is not thought he is badly wrecked. Passengers state that stones were also piled on the track ahead of the train. This was probably the work of hobos as no masked man appeared to ask for donations.

It is not known if No. 1 was ever repaired and recommissioned.

Express Messenger Alexander C. Summers enjoyed his 15 minutes of fame to the hilt. The following article appears to have originated in the *Kansas City Star*, but it went out over the wire services, and this reprint is taken from the *Aspen Tribune* in Colorado, from the November 21, 1897 edition:

TRAVELS OF AN OLD HAT

From the Kansas City Star: There drifted into the office of Wells Fargo & Co's express in Kansas City was other day an old hat that had seen much of the country. Completely covering its sides, crown, and brim, were express tags from Mexico to the Yukon and to Kansas City. Last night it left for New York, and will undoubtedly reach its destination if there remains room to attach the necessary tags.

Inside of the hat, securely wired and sealed, are some photographs---one of Jim Parker, an outlaw, who attempted to "hold up" the Atlantic and Pacific express at Peach Springs, Ariz., last February. He was captured, but escaped, after killing his jailer. He was recaptured and is now in jail at Prescott. There is also the photograph of a dead train robber, made an "angel" by A.C. Summers, an express messenger on the Albuquerque and Los Angeles division of the Atlantic and Pacific railway. The hat was worn by Summers, who started it out for Mexico with the injunction pasted inside for all messengers to attach their stickers and forward, and with the information that the hat would eventually be presented to Mr. McKinley. The hat started for Mexico and came back loaded down with messages, humorous and otherwise, from the agents of the company. To some of the tags are attached with sealing wax Mexican corn husk cigarettes, to others small bottles of pulque and mescal; a Mexican 43-cent silver dollar is wired to the bottom, also a copper centavo. Nearly all the messages are in Spanish and there are small photographs of Mexican bull fighters, pulque gatherers, and comic pictures from the Mexican papers. There is also a rabbit's foot, a key, wax matches, aluminum tags, tin tops from beer bottles, car seals and tin types. The route the hat took can be traced all through Mexico, Arizona, Colorado and the northwest, back through Nebraska, Iowa, Topeka, Kan., and now to Kansas City. On several of the tags are earnest injunctions to keep the hat well iced en route. It is an expressman's joke and carries well. Where the old hat will come to a stop it is hard to say, because it is quite likely that when there is no more room left for tags an addition will be sewed on and it will travel some more.

Fun and games in the 19th century! There is no record of whether Summers' hat was actually given to President William McKinley or not.

The eventual fate of Alexander C. Summers, as well as most of the rest of the train crew, is unknown at this time.

CHAPTER 5

The First Posse

The Rock Cut Train Robbery was a failure. Of the two men known to have been direct participants, one was dead and the other was on the run. Posses were quickly formed in three counties to join in pursuit of the fleeing bandit. Sheriff John C. Potts of Mohave County headed up the first one, while Sheriff George C. Ruffner of Yavapai County, and Sheriff Ralph H. Cameron of Coconino County soon joined with posses of their own.

The *Arizona Journal Miner* of February 17, 1897 carried the following dispatch:

> "KINGMAN, Ariz., Feb. 11,—The sheriff's posse returned this morning without the Peach Springs robber. They ran across him Tuesday, but he rode on a well known race horse, and after a running battle for miles, he escaped in the dense brush on foot. He was recognized as Jim Parker, a well known desperado.

Undated portrait of John C. Potts, who was Sheriff of Mohave County at the time of the Rock Cut Train Robbery. He led one of the three posses in pursuit of Parker after the failed heist. (Courtesy of Mohave Museum of History and Art)

Portrait, c. 1890s, of Ralph Henry Cameron, who was Sheriff of Coconino County at the time of the Rock Cut Train Robbery. He led one of the three posses, and later falsely claimed to have captured Parker himself. (Library of Congress)

And so, the identification was made. If there was anyone left in Mohave County who had doubted that cowboy Jim Parker was involved in nefarious activities, those doubts were now gone. The same edition of the *Journal Miner* carried the following update:

> Ash Fork, Feb. 11.—[Special]—Telegraphic reports today from Peach Springs say that a running fight took place last night between officers in pursuit and the train robbers, at a point about twenty miles north of the railroad. About fifty shots were exchanged without any casualty, except the slight wounding of a deputy sheriff's horse. The robbers dismounted when rough ground was reached. The fight occurred on the edge of Prospect valley, and it would seem that the robbers are endeavoring to reach the Grand Canyon cliffs and cross over. There is said to be a great volume of water running down the Colorado river at present and it is impossible to ford it. There is but little hope now of the robbers escaping, and their capture is foregone, as they have nothing to subsist on, and are afoot in a very rough country. The fight was conducted at a range of from 200 to 400 yards.

The details of the posse chase remained big news in the newspapers around Arizona, and in California. It would be soon that the posse would realize they were only chasing one man. The *Arizona Republican* ran this dispatch on February 12, 1897:

A RENEWED PURSUIT

> Kingman, Ariz. Feb. 11.—J. C. Potts, sheriff of Mohave county, and posse are now starting on another attempt to capture the Rock Cut train robber. He is thought to be still in the vicinity of Pine Springs, half way between the A. & P. road at Peach Springs, and the Grand canyon of the Colorado. Indian trailers will accompany them.

SUSPECTS ARRESTED

> Kingman, Ariz., Feb. 11—This morning Sheriff Cameron of Coconino County, arrested Abe Thompson and Love Marvin at Peach Springs as accessories in the holdup of the passenger train. They were taken to Flagstaff this evening."

And so, Abe Thompson and Love Marvin, who had gone into Peach Springs to draw attention to themselves and thereby provide an alibi for the gang, had been connected to the robbery as conspirators after all. The evidence used to arrest them will be revealed shortly. At any rate, the robbery had been such a disaster that it spelled the end of the Abe Thompson Gang. If there had been any other unidentified members of the gang, they undoubtedly and understandably fled the area once Abe Thompson himself had been arrested.

The *Los Angeles Times* carried these details February 11, 1987:

{BY ASSOCIATED PRESS WIRE}

> KINGMAN (Ariz.,) Feb. 10.—Under Sheriff James Smith of Mojave county, Under Sheriff Fairchild of Coconino county, Deputy Henry Lovin, Kade Selvery, special officer of the Atlantic and Pacific road, and three Walapai Indian trailers are now hot on the trail of the train-robber. The snow on the ground makes the trail easy

to follow, and, as the direction is north, the snow will increase. It is now sure that there were only two robbers in the hold-up. The booty of the escaping man is seven packages of registered matter.

EXCHANGED SHOTS

KINGMAN (Ariz.,) Feb. 10. — The posse returned from the pursuit of the train-robber this afternoon, completely worn out. They had followed the trail through the snow two feet deep, and early in the morning closed in on the fugitive about forty miles north of the railroad. The robber was pressed so close that he abandoned his horse and took to the woods. Several shots were exchanged, but no one was injured. Sheriff Cameron of Coconino county will have a carload of fresh horses in the morning to take up the trail, and before night will have the man surrounded. He is known, and is, a desperate character. Warrants are out for the arrest of several men suspected of being accessories. An inquest was held on the dead robber at Peach Springs this morning, but the remains are not yet identified.

The *Times* followed up with the following article on February 12, 1897:

ARIZONA TRAIL-ROBBERS

THE IDENTITY OF THE BANDITS AT LAST ESTABLISHED

The Dead Man Was a Cowboy Named Charles Douglass—His Fleeing Pal is Jim Parker a Notorious Desperado—Posses in Pursuit

[BY ASSOCIATED PRESS WIRE]

KINGMAN (Ariz.,) Feb. 11.—The Sheriff's posse returned this morning from chasing the Rock Cut train-robber. They ran across the man twenty miles north of Peach Springs. The robber rode a racehorse, well known in this section, and after running awhile, would stop and shoot at the posse. A running fight was kept up through the deep snow until after dark Tuesday night when the robber abandoned his horse and took it afoot. All of Wednesday the trail was followed, but at last the drifting snow covered the trail, and the Indians could follow it no longer. Under Sheriff Fairchild and Kade Selvey will again take up the hunt this morning. The fleeing robber was recognized as Jim Parker, a notorious desperado. The name of the robber killed by Messenger Somers is Charles Douglass, a cowboy.

A FRESH START

KINGMAN (Ariz.,) Feb. 11.—J. C. Potts, Sheriff of Mohave county, and a posse are now starting on another attempt to capture the Rock Cut train-robber. He is thought to be still in the vicinity of Pine Springs, half way between the Atlantic and Pacific road at Peach Springs and the Grand Cañon of the Colorado. Indian trailers will accompany them.

TWO SUSPECTS ARRESTED

KINGMAN (Ariz.,) Feb. 11.—This morning Sheriff Cameron of Coconino county, arrested Abe Thompson and Love Marvin, at Peach Springs, as accessories in the hold-up of the passenger train. In Thompson's cabin, thirty-five miles north, were found many things stolen from neighboring ranchers, among them trousers belonging to a suit worn by the dead robber and stolen from the Ayers ranch a month ago. Thompson and Marvin were taken to Flagstaff this evening.

At noon a posse composed of the best officers in Arizona, with Indian trailers left Peach Springs to take up the train where the robber abandoned his horse. Later in the afternoon rapid firing was heard to the north by section men at Nelson, and it is thought that the robber has been surrounded. Sheriff Potts and posse left at 9 o'clock this evening to assist in tracking the man down. The dead man has not been positively identified.

Following the *Journal Miner*'s earlier coverage, this was the second appearance in news reports of a "well known race horse" that Parker was allegedly riding to make his getaway. Exactly where he got it is unclear—if the reports are accurate, he most likely stole it. Some later dispatches would claim it belonged to Abe Thompson, which seems unlikely. It would also later be reported to belong to a man named Frank Garner. As for the dead train robber, we have already discussed that many different names were ascribed to him during this time, and Charles Douglass was simply one of them.

Over in San Francisco, the *Examiner* covered the "running fight" in this fashion on February 11, 1897:

KINGMAN (A.T.), February 10—Two Deputy Sheriffs from the pursuing party returned to Peach Springs late to-night after fresh horses and provisions. They will return in the morning. They report having caught up with the robber at 6:20 p.m. of the 9th in a pine forest near Pine Springs. A running fire was kept up for six miles, but no one was hit. Over fifty shots were fired.

Darkness prevented the capture of the robber. His trail was followed all night by moonlight. At noon to-day the trail was lost out of the snow and had not been found when Deputy Smith left the party for Peach Springs.

The posse got close to the robber to identify him. His name is Jim Parker, a well-known Northern Arizona cowboy, a rustler and a hard case.

Now that he is known, his escape is considered impossible.

The horse captured is owned by Abe Thompson of Pine Springs, and the saddle belongs to Jim Parker.

Sheriff Cameron of Flagstaff wired to-night for warrants for robbery for Abe Thompson and Love Marvin. Both are in Peach Springs. A remark made by the robber while searching for his dead comrade indicates that two more men were to have taken part in the robbery and failed at the last moment.

Parker is a desperate man and knows the country thoroughly, and it is not believed that he will be taken alive. Thompson and Marvin will be arrested to-night and taken to Flagstaff.

It is believed the plan was laid for Thompson and Marvin to join the other two men at the scene of the robbery and that their courage failed them. Marvin is not over twenty years of age. Thompson has two children at Peach Springs and is a widower.

The *Examiner* followed up on February 12, 1897:

KINGMAN (Ariz..), February 11.—Deputy Sheriff James A. Smith and Henry Lovin returned to Kingman early this morning from the pursuit of the train robber. Two Indian trailers returned with them. They left Sheriffs Cameron and Ruffner, Deputies Fairchilds and Munn, Detective Selvy and Deputy United States Marshal Frank Morrell on the trail of the robber. Sheriff Potts, with two deputies, fresh horses and trailers, left to-day to take the places of the returned deputies.

The place where the pursuing party overtook the bandit is only twenty miles north of Peach Springs, a few miles from Abe Thompson's ranch. Upon discovering his pursuers the bandit spurred his horse into a run. He was riding the best horse in that part of the country and his pursuers could not catch up with him. Fairchilds' horse, the fastest among those of the pursuers, came within one hundred and fifty yards of the bandit, who stopped, wheeled his horse, took deliberate aim and fired, the bullet passing close to Fairchilds' head. Then the bandit wheeled and galloped off. Fairchilds' horse was unruly and the officer could not get a shot at the man.

An Indian trailer and Jim Hardy were riding parallel with the bandit on the ridge and the bandit was in a little ravine. The Indian fired his Winchester, emptying nine shells. Whenever the bandit saw a good opportunity he stopped, wheeled, fired and then spurred his horse and galloped away from his pursuers.

He was first discovered at 3 p.m. and was kept in sight every little while through the timber until dark.

The robber's abandoned horse was caught by his pursuers and is now in Kingman. It is Abe Thompson's race horse and Jim Parker's saddle.

The pursuers positively identified the bandit as Jim Parker. Yesterday they trailed the bandit on foot until he got out of the snow and then they lost his trail near Thompson's ranch. They found where the robber had camped, half a mile from Thompson's. All the provisions, bedding, etc. stolen from Ayers' sheep ranch one month ago were found there.

Thompson and Marvin were arrested to-day.

Every hour it is expected that the posse will return with the dead bandit, as they do not expect to take him alive. The dead robber has been identified as Charles Douglass, a cowboy and hard case, who had worked in Apache, Yavapai and Coconino counties, and who had trouble in Colorado or Montana.

"Jim Hardy" was a Hualapai Indian trailer who was often employed by Mohave County authorities, and it is difficult to know if he was the same Indian trailer known as Captain Jack Hardy (a silly name undoubtedly given him by his white "employers") who reportedly lived in this section. Further confusion can be had because one of Mohave County's best known historical pioneers was a white man named Captain William H. Hardy—perhaps Captain William was "Captain Jack's" employer, or "Jim's" employer.

The *Los Angeles Herald* was keeping abreast of the developments as well. From the February 13, 1897 edition:

CAPTURE IS CERTAIN

The Arizona Railroad Robber Cannot Long Avoid the Officers
KINGMAN, Ariz., Feb. 12.—The sheriff's posse is close on the trail of the robber. Today they picked up a Winchester rifle, coat, boots, blankets, saddle, hat and provisions. The bandit is heading south. When the carrier left the posse was six miles from Peach Springs. The boots and saddle are identified as the property of Jim Parker.

Officers along the line of the railroad were wired to look out for Parker, as it is thought he will try to get away on a train from some siding. He is on foot, and is probably worn out and footsore. Being a cowboy he can hardly go much further. The snow has gone from the ground and he is easily tracked in the soft soil. If it does not snow this evening the posse will surely make the capture tomorrow. Scouts have been sent out in all directions to head off the fugitive.

The *Herald* followed up on February 15, 1897:

HOT ON THE TRAIL

Bloodhounds Will Follow Him into the Grand Canyon
KINGMAN, A. T., Feb. 14.—Bandit Parker was trailed by the officers to Milk Weed springs eighteen miles north of Hackberry this afternoon. Parker held up two Indians at the springs and took their rifles from them. Bloodhounds will be put on the trail to-morrow and the robber followed into the Grand canyon.

Marvin, who was arrested, has offered to confess and will implicate several people now at large. Marvin purchased the powder and cartridges found on the body of the dead robber in Kingman Sunday last. Many things purchased by Marvin have been found, implicating him in the hold-up. A posse will go out this evening to guard the ferry over the Colorado river. Parker's people live in Utah and he may try to reach his home. A brother of his was hanged a few years ago for horse stealing.

Here we have a perfect example of why some historians look upon old newspapers with derision. They did occasionally print rumor as they tried to get the details of a story. We know of course that Parker did not come from Utah, and that he did not have a brother who was hanged for horsestealing. It is interesting to speculate, however, that this dispatch (which appeared in a few other newspapers as well) may have eventually evolved into the untrue legend that Jim Parker was Butch Cassidy's brother (see Chapter 11)—Cassidy had come from Utah, and his real name was Robert Leroy Parker.

The *Los Angeles Times* ran the following on February 14, 1897:

THE FLEEING TRAIN ROBBER

He Gets a Mount and Will Probably Escape
[BY ASSOCIATED PRESS WIRE.]
KINGMAN (Ariz.,) Feb. 13.—The Nelson or Rock Cut train-robber was trailed by

the posse to twenty miles west of Peach Springs today. At dark, a squaw reported in Hackberry that she was out in the hills five miles southeast of town riding a horse and that a man with a rifle took the horse away from her, mounted it and rode off in a southerly direction. Her description tallies with that of the outlaw Parker. Indian scouts are on his trail and will follow it as long as the moon is above the horizon. Sheriff Smith's posse will go south in the morning. Cameron's posse will remain on the trail until assured that the two trails were made by the same party. The robber is now wearing shoes, but is without saddle or bridle. Cowboys will be inclined to shield the bandit, as they look upon his grit with admiration. He knows the country like an open book, and may possibly elude his pursuers. The outlaw can now supply himself with good horses at every ranch and the chase will be a long one if he gets to the first ranch on Big Sandy Creek.

While a few of these dispatches are contradictory, it should again be noted that rumor was rife about the ongoing pursuit. The differing stories about Parker bushwhacking Indians could all be true, or they could be mutations of a single incident. They could even be mutations of the following incident, which is definitely accurate.

For several days, in the freezing cold, snow, and ice, and without adequate clothing, supplies, or provisions, Parker had defied all odds and managed to elude the giant posse that was relentlessly pursuing him. It wasn't long, though, and his luck would start to run out. Parker was captured—but they didn't keep him very long. From the *Phoenix Herald* of February 15, 1897:

A RASCALLY DEPUTY

He Captures the A. & P. Robbers and lets him Get Away
KINGMAN, Ariz. Feb. 15.—Sheriffs Cameron and Ruffner with a posse followed the trail of the Rock Cut train robber to the grand Canon of the Colorado. When the trail got hot the intrepid sheriffs sent one man ahead with the Indian trailers while they rested. The trailers found the robbers asleep by a fire and covered him with their guns capturing him. The white man's name with the trailers is Rogers. Rogers told the Indians to gather wood to make coffee and stack their guns. While the Indians were gathering wood the robbers jumped for their guns breaking one over a log, and threw one into the river and kept two others will all the ammunition, ordering the Indians to "git" which they lost no time in doing. It is supposed the man Rogers stood in with the robbers as he is a cowboy of unsavory fame. The whole posse abandoned the chase and returned to the railroad. Sheriff Potts of Mohave county has left the false trail of the fugitive with Smith of the railroad and is now camped at Milk Springs in the Music Mountains about twenty miles from where the bandit was last seen. Under Sheriff Smith at Kingman sent a courier to him this morning and before noon they will be on trail of the hold-up. Sheriff Potts and posse are determined and brave men who will take the man or kill him if he is found.

With the exception of the *Herald's* plural use of "robbers," this incident matches all other accounts of it, and is undoubtedly true.

John Rogers was actually a jailed convict awaiting trial in Coconino County on a charge of illegal branding—that is, he stole a cow and attempted to alter the brand on it. I have copies of his court papers, but since they are not pertinent to the Parker case, I won't reprint them. Exactly why Sheriff Cameron would take one of his prisoners on a posse with him is unknown, and is certainly bizarre behavior. Perhaps Cameron thought that Rogers had a sincere desire to be helpful, or perhaps Rogers had expressed interest in working for the County in exchange for leniency.

In reading the accounts of the incident, it seems to me that John Rogers got a bum rap with Parker. After capturing the bandit, it appears that Rogers made the mistake of turning his back on him, giving Parker the opportunity to grab a gun. But in 1897, no one believed that Rogers, an accused criminal, could be that stupid, and the automatic presumption was that Rogers had deliberately allowed Parker to escape. But if that were so, why did he try to capture Parker in the first place?

I have been unable to learn anything of the background of John Rogers. Presumably he was still another drifting petty criminal, like so many of the characters in the Parker story. I have encountered references to a man named John Rogers throughout Arizona during this period, including two who did time in Yuma Territorial Prison. But since John Rogers was an exceedingly common name, it is impossible to know if any of these men were the same John Rogers who botched his capture of Parker.

On February 17, 1897, the *Phoenix Herald* ran the following letter to the editor, written by an anonymous citizen (newspapers printed anonymous letters in those days):

KINGMAN, Ariz., Feb. 15, 1897.
Editor Herald:—After a day at this place I can state that the reports I can get from the mines and business man that times in Mohave county were never better, and a regular mining boom is now on. There is a great difference between a boom in land and farm products, or even in general business, and in gold mining. Gold when taken out from the ground or from rock that has to be crushed, when it is in bar, or in a crude state, it is money. It passes and has a fixed value. There is now at least thirty teams, mostly large, six to twelve horse or mule teams, hauling freight to the mining camps north of Kingman and the prospects are now that these teams will be kept busy for months to come.

There has been a real hold-up on the railroad east of this place, one highwayman killed and a chase after another; last accounts has it that the sheriff and posse came up to the hold-up; the hold-up played possum and when an opportunity came he jumped and grabbed the officer's gun and held him and the posse up, took their Winchesters, threw them in the river or broke them and ordered them to "git." There are some funny stories out about this affair. I have heard of the hound getting ahead of the fox, but there are real facts and cold truths that reflect greatly against the officials of two or three counties in this end of the Territory. The Legislature should vote a chromo to some of the officials. The worst part of the story as it is told on the street is that the officials are in with the hold-ups. It is no greater disgrace to Arizona to have a train help up than in older states, but to have officials in with the help-ups and shield and feed them is rather rough on Arizona's name. H.

Apparently there were rumors on the streets of Kingman that Mohave County law enforcement officials were in cahoots with the train robbers. Such rumor-mongering was undoubtedly started by the Rogers incident, plus the failure of the posse to apprehend Parker immediately, and possibly even the revelation (as we shall soon see) that Mohave Deputy Asa Harris had sold Love Marvin some of the ammunition that was used in the robbery!

From the *Phoenix Herald* of February 18, 1897:

Yesterday afternoon the city police force took their bloodhounds out for a test of their powers. They started a man out three hours ahead of the dogs. The man covered some five miles and was treed near the river by the bloodhounds who took the trail readily and followed it to the finish. The dogs had hardly been returned to their kennels when a telegram was received from Sheriff Ruffner, of Yavapai county, asking that the dogs be sent to him for the purpose of trailing the lone train robber who is afoot in the wilds of the northern portion of the Territory. The dogs were placed on the train and will be used by Sheriff Ruffner to track the robber.

Apparently impressed by bloodhounds, the *Arizona Gazette* had this to say on the same subject, February 16, 1897:

On Sunday, in response to a telegram from Sheriff Ruffner, J. B. Moore sent his two bloodhounds to Peach Springs to assist in trailing the train robber. These dogs are well trained, and on Sunday they, with the four pups belonging to the Phoenix police force, were given a nine mile chase, going down by the river and returning to a place near the M. & P. depot where the man was treed. The use of bloodhounds will soon be a great factor in catching criminals.

And so, the pursuit continued. But not for much longer.

For all of his resourcefulness, stamina, and determination, Parker's flight from the law was beginning to take its toll on him in the freezing cold, snow, and without food or sleep. Sheriff Ruffner went on ahead of his posse at one point, and through happenstance, came across his old friend, and it was over. The *Arizona Journal Miner* recorded the details February 17, 1897:

CAPTURED BY RUFFNER

The A. & P. Train Robber Falls into the Clutches of Yavapai's Courageous Sheriff

A Pretty Piece of Criminal Work Performed in the Face of Danger and Hardships

The closing chapter in the railroad tragedy at Peach Springs just one week ago was enacted in Prescott this morning. By it Sheriff Ruffner again ascends the pedal of fame in the daring criminal successes of the coast, and Jim Parker, the unfortunate cowboy, who fails by his own folly, is landed behind the bars of everlasting shame and disgrace.

Chapter 5: The First Posse

The first tidings of Sheriff Ruffner's capture reached Prescott last night in a private dispatch and with that morbid feeling people have in anticipation of seeing a highhanded criminal, half of the eagerly inclined of the town jammed the depot platform to suffocation to see after all only a poor and dejected wretch hobbling shackled face to face with the scorn and stain of his fellow men. Such is human nature, and in this instance the nerve of the victim in holding up an overland train was intensified only the more so in daring and cunning by the big crowd that was (illegible) to see and behold something their imagination weighed as out of the ordinary.

In conversation with Sheriff Ruffner nothing but meager details are given of the capture by him, as he said "I have been in the field for four nights and days without sleep and without rest, and I must go to bed." He says, however, that he and Deputies Buglin and Riley effected the capture yesterday at 1 o'clock in diamond canyon, laying north of Peach Springs, no assistance being given him by Indians or any others besides the above named, although there were many others in the field. In regard to the capture the sheriff said Parker had no opportunity to use his weapons and when I told him to throw up his hands he did so hastily.

Leading up to the capture of Parker, the following will prove of interest: It seems that on Sunday afternoon Ruffner fell back on the trail to kill a beef, while Deputy Rogers and the Indian trailers continued the pursuit. Later Rogers and the Indians ran onto Parker and took him as a prisoner. With the robber camp was made, Ruffner and his deputies not joining them up to that time. It was while the prisoner and his captors were sitting in camp that Parker seeing an opening jumped forward and getting hold a Winchester aimed it at Rogers, who at once retreated, and as he fled a bullet whizzed past him. The Indians stampeded at once and west in the direction of where they had left Ruffner and deputies. Hearing of what had happened, and coming upon the fleeing ones the next morning, Ruffner, Buglin and Riley started up Diamond Creek. They had not gone far when they saw Parker coming down that stream evidently making his way into the Grand Canyon. Ruffner secreted himself on one side and Buglin and Riley were together on the opposite side. When Parker reached Ruffner, the latter said, "Hands up!" when Parker raised his gun for action and looked in the direction of the sound. Immediately Buglin and Riley gave a similar command, when Parker, in a confused manner, turned his head around also toward them. He was simply at the mercy of Ruffner and gave up. When in custody the first time he took a rifle and broke it over a boulder, and the weapon was brought here as a trophy by the sheriff.

Sheriff Ruffner says that he and his deputies conducted the chase most of the time on foot, owing to the rugged nature of the country, which together with the weight of their weapons, lack of food and loss of sleep, not to mention the perils and anxiety of being intercepted at any moment, totally exhausted each officer and taxed them to the utmost.

Parker, the robber, is a cowboy and since his arrest maintains an indifference when asked of the hold-up of the association of any accomplices. He is below the average in stature, somewhat heavy set, of a determined expression and with a light moustache. His physical bearing in short is of a typical wild and wooly cowboy.

This good of work on the part of Sheriff Ruffner is certainly a pretty piece of criminal doings, and carries with it official sagacity and courage that is deservedly commendable. He is a hard one on lawbreakers and never sleeps when in the field. And in this particular instance conquering as he did in a county outside of his own, and unfamiliar as he was with the topography of the same, is to be lauded only the more so.

The crime of train robbery in this territory is punishable with death, but in previous cases executive clemency has interfered with carrying out the letter of the law.

Rewards in this case aggregate it is said nearly $4,000.

The *Prescott Courier* recounted the capture in this manner on February 19, 1897:

Sheriff Ruffner arrived in Prescott yesterday with Parker, the accused train robber and lodged him in jail. Parker is an every day looking cowboy and looked as if he had been on a long round-up or drive when he entered the jail. The particulars of the capture are in brief, as follows:

The running fight before spoken of, took place last Wednesday between Parker and Mohave county officers. There were three Indian trailers. Country approaching canyon was very rough and officers were unable to keep up with the Indians. Saturday night before sundown, the three Indians and Deputy Rogers, of Mohave county, surprised, got the drop on and captured Parker, who was well fagged, and broke down while walking back to camp with captors. Having camped, just before the moon went down and as the Indians were cooking coffee, Parker sprang forward, grabbed a gun, fired at Deputy Rogers, who fell, the bullet passing close to his head. The Indians fairly tumbled over one another in their flight, during which Parker laughed neatly. When Parker was captured, he was commanded to drop his pistol on the ground. Instead, he threw it into the Colorado river and it exploded when touching the water. He now proceeded to rearm himself. He broke Rogers' rifle and took his six-shooter. After the escape of Parker, Ruffner, Munds and others appeared upon the scene and offered the Indians $100 apiece to trail Parker, but the Indians were frightened and refused. One Indian said he must return and see his sick son, another had sore feet. The Indians took the back track. Saturday morning the Ruffner party were 23 miles from Peach Springs and their horses had given out. The partly split; Munds went back and telegraphed for bloodhounds. Sunday night the party camped at Soda Springs. From there they went to Diamond canyon. Chas. McGrary went down the canyon and Ruffner up the canyon; the two calculating to meet halfway. McGrary came in sight at a rapid gait, said he had seen Parker, but the latter had not seen him. At this time, Buglin and Riley came up. The horses were hurriedly hidden. Buglin hid on the rim of a cliff 150 feet below. In a little while Ruffner saw Parker walking slowly up the canyon, pistol in belt and rifle across shoulders. Parker walked by Ruffner, who called "Throw up your hands," Parker made no reply. He was 125 yards from Ruffner. Twice more Ruffner called on Parker to throw up his hands, with no response. When Ruffner called out: "Look here, this is the last time, put up hands," Parker's hands went slowly up. Then Ruffner ordered Parker to walk 40 or 50 feet from his guns, which he did, with hands still up. This move brought Parker within sight of the deputies hidden above and Riley fired at Parker, but did not hit him. Then the men came down and surrounded Parker, while Ruffner kept him covered with his rifle. The capture was made at 1 p.m., Monday. Parker had $11 on his person. About this time, Ralph Cameron, who had gone back for provisions and new Indians, came up and the famished party had a feed. Parker had not eaten since Saturday morning. Munds got his dogs, and he, Morrell and Fairchilds struck out for Milk Weed Springs. The dogs made a run of 40 miles in one day. Parker left his horse in a rock cabin near Pine Springs. The officers and trailers followed him 40 miles the first day. Parker said he laid on a rock point overlooking a ravine one day and night, and from that vantage ground could have picked off all the officers had they appeared. The officers found about ten pounds of flour at each of the camps left by Parker. While on foot Parker carried 40 pounds of flour, two overcoats, two dress coats, two pairs of boots, two (illegible) of double blankets, a (illegible) and his arms. He did not know of the killing of the other robber until he was captured and had led the dead robber's horse ten miles from the scene of the robbery. The robbery occurred in Yavapai county. Sheriff Ruffner feels very thankful for the assistance rendered by the officers of other counties and says that equal credit is due to all. Ruffner needs no praise from the Courier as his work speaks for itself.

It is interesting to continually read how Indian trailers were regarded simply as property in those days. It is the sort of oppressive era that is difficult for many people to imagine today. "New Indians," no less.

Interestingly, the *Flagstaff Sun-Democrat* ran the most informative account of Parker's capture in its February 18, 1897 edition:

BANDIT JIM PARKER CAPTURED

An Exciting Chase After the Yampai Train Robber

Captured at the Mouth of Diamond Creek Canyon—
Barefoot and Wading in the Water

Arizona's nine days' wonder has culminated in the arrest of the only surviving bandit in the daring hold-up near Peach Springs.

The robbery occurred on Monday evening, February 8, a few miles this side of Peach Springs. Immediately after the hold-up the facts were telegraphed to Sheriff R. H. Cameron and to the Sheriffs of Yavapai and Mohave counties. Posses were organized at once and Sheriff Cameron left Monday morning for the scene.

Under Sheriff Fletcher Fairchild was on his way from Kingman with one Tom Sims, a Mexican cook, wanted here on a charge of embezzlement, and when at Peach Springs placed Sims in the care of the railway employes and got off.

Procuring a horse Mr. Fairchild joined the posse then organizing and early Tuesday morning started on the trail of the bandit.

The trail was taken up a few miles out of town, several Wallapai Indians being pressed into service to do the tracking, and Tuesday evening, when about nine miles from Peach Springs, Under Sheriff Fairchild, who was riding far in advance of the rest of the posse, suddenly came upon the mounted bandit, near the edges of a "park" and among the cedar skirting the edge.

The Indians, who were keeping up with Fletcher, opened fire on the outlaw. The robber returned the fire, and a running fight was kept up between Fletcher and his Indians and the bandit. Mr. Fairchild pressed steadily on in pursuit of the fleeing criminal, who was dodging in and out among the timber, sending back a shot here and a shot there, keeping protected by the trees as much as possible.

These random shots done no damage and it was Mr. Fairchild's aim to get close enough to the bandit to exchange shots with him with some degree of accuracy. It was twilight and getting darker every minute, but when capture by the bullet seemed almost certain, the robber, who had been fully identified by this time as Jim Parker, a cowboy and all around tough man, disappeared behind the ridge into the canyon, through which the road from Peach Springs to the Grand Canyon passes.

The posse had stayed behind during the skirmish and the Indians had fled. As it was growing darker and the trail could be followed no longer, Mr. Fairchild was compelled to turn back. The posse refused point blank to proceed any further, and Mr. Fairchild returned with them to Peach Springs.

Sheriff Cameron had left here Monday night for the scene and Tuesday a telegram was received from him at Peach Springs asking for more horses. A shipment was made up at once and sent to the Springs. Deputy Sheriff W. C. Bayless and Will Riley* accompanied them.

Arriving at Peach Springs, another posse was organized, consisting of Sheriff Cameron, Under Sheriff Fairchild and Will Riley of Flagstaff, Deputy Sheriff Bugglin, United States Marshal Morrell and Charley McGerry of Williams; Sheriff Ruffner and Deputy Sheriff Munds of Prescott; John Rogers, who was recently incarcerated in the county jail here, and three Wallapai Indians.

Will Riley, who was to the front throughout the chase and who assisted in the capture, gives us, in substance, the following account:

"Wednesday, the man-hunters left Peach Springs, following the same trail that the other posse had taken to Thompson's cabin. Here they came upon the horse and saddle of the bandit, and a little farther on, about a mile northward, a large quantity of supplies, consisting of five fifty-pound sacks of flour, a sack and a half of sugar, bedding, etc. was discovered cached. It was evident that the intention of the train robbers was to escape to this vicinity, load these provisions on their pack horses and cut across the country into Utah.

"The sharp-eyed Indians took up the trail again from this point, noting that the hunted man had cunningly wrapped his feet with blankets to give the tracks the appearance of Indian footprints. Parker's cowboy boots were found nearby.

"All day long the Indians followed the zigzag trail, into canyons and along the roadside. The posse went into camp Wednesday night, and Thursday morning continued the exciting chase.

"The bandit, after leaving Thompson's cabin, and tying his boots up with blankets, went in a northwesterly course for about fifteen miles. Here he had discarded his boots, which were afterward found by the posse, and then turned southwest, toward Peach Springs, continuing in this direction for about twenty-five miles, striking Diamond creek canyon at a point almost due north and within nine miles of the Springs. This canyon goes south from this point for about a mile, bending north again, virtually doubling on its course. Parker followed the canyon around the bend and when directly opposite from the point where he entered, made a circuitous march from the canyon to a high ridge about a

---

*   Will Riley may be the deputy referred to as "One-eye Riley" in later accounts.

quarter of a mile away, overlooking the point where he entered and also where he emerged from the creek. Right here the bend in the creek is so sharp that the distance from the section of the canyon running south to the one running north is only a quarter of a mile.

"Parker's reasons for returning so near to Peach Springs seems to have been that he was expecting aid from an accomplice, possibly the dead robber, and this supposition is borne out by the fact that up to the time of his capture Monday night, Parker was unaware of the fate that befell his unfortunate partner.

"This ridge upon which he was camped overlooked the Diamond creek canyon road to the Grand Canyon of the Colorado, affording him a full view up and down the canyon and also across to the trail which he had so recently made. The Indians coming over the hills on his trail would have been clearly visible long before they could see him and he could easily shoot them down, as well as the posse, before they could get their guns to bear on him. However, the posse came not, and escaped the ambush thus skillfully laid for their destruction.

"Thursday morning the bandit left his stronghold on the ridge, after discarding another pair of boots, an overcoat and a blanket, and started up Diamond creek canyon, following alongside the wagon road toward the Grand Canyon. He trudged along his wearisome way, walking among the rocks that lined the roadside, which made tracking him a difficult task for even the Indians.

"Thursday night, after doubling back on his trail for about two miles, he established his camp behind a 'chimney' on the mesa overlooking the canyon road. He was enabled from this position to command a view up and down the road, and had thus arranged a most effective ambuscade. The posse had not yet caught up with him and Friday morning he resumed his tramp, after discarding another overcoat and one or two other garments.

"Parker was nearing the Grand Canyon now and reached it sometime that evening. The posse was then but six hours behind him and the trail was plainly marked in the roadway. The posse put spurs to their horses and galloped on with all speed, the three Mohave Indians keeping ahead and pointing out the trail. Very sensibly whenever one of those 'chimneys' or abrupt corners of a mesa hove in sight the on-rushing Indians discreetly reined in and allowed the white men to proceed and reconnoiter. These 'chimneys' are excellent places to afford protection and concealment to an outlaw with murder in his heart and the Indians did not propose to take any changes of being ambushed.

"All Friday afternoon the posse kept up the chase and camped that night at a cabin about a mile from the juncture of Diamond creek canyon and the Grand Canyon of the Colorado.

"Saturday morning the Indians set out, accompanied by John Rogers, following the Diamond canyon down to the Colorado river. Here they caught sight of Parker, who was some distance ahead, proceeding down the river. They followed him for fully fifteen miles, when they caught up with him, and before Parker was aware of being followed at all four Winchesters were leveled at him at close range and he was compelled to surrender.

"Rogers and the Indians with their prisoner camped Saturday night under a sheltering wall of the Canyon. Sometime during the night, while the watchers were asleep or off their guard, Parker jumped up, grabbed a Winchester and firing a few shots at Rogers and the Indians, who fled in the darkness, started up stream, making for the Diamond creek canyon, intending no doubt to proceed south to secure a horse and also learn what had become of his partner.

"The Indians returned direct to the posse's camp near the mouth of Diamond canyon, reported the escape and quit the camp.

"Sheriff Cameron left at once (Sunday morning) for Peach Springs, and reaching there telegraphed for the bloodhounds belonging to the Territorial Prison at Yuma. It was supposed that Parker had started down the river and it was Sheriff Cameron's plan to cut across the country with the hounds in a northwesterly direction from Peach Springs and head off the desperado should he attempt to leave the Canyon and go south. The posse was instructed to watch the river at the intersection of Diamond creek and thus prevent him escaping by that route.

"Monday noon, as Sheriff Ruffner was patrolling Diamond creek toward the Grand Canyon he noticed the figure of a man wading up stream from the Colorado river. Concealing himself, he waited until the man, who proved to be Parker, had passed by on his way up the stream, and when abreast of Deputy Sheriff Martin Bugglin and Will Riley, who were concealed near the bank of the creek and who had previously received a signal from Ruffner, the command rang out from the Yavapai Sheriff to 'Halt!' Parker did not halt and was about to fire, when a shot from Riley and Bugglin caused him to throw up his hands. The latter two disarmed the robber and handcuffed him. He was then conveyed to Peach Springs, and from there to Prescott, where he now languishes.

"John Rogers was placed under arrest for abetting Parker's escape from the Indians, it being alleged also that he was implicated with Parker in a number of other shady transactions.

"No small amount of credit is due the intrepid posse, who followed the robber through a rough and perilous country for six days, going without sleep and suffering from the cold, to an extent that would have resulted fatally to less hardy men."

Thursday's Arrests

Bally Creighton, "Kid" Marvin and Abe Thompson, together with Jim Parker, had for several years terrorized the law-abiding ranchmen in the vicinity of Peach Springs and kept up a continual round of pilfering and petty stealing, frequently breaking into the cabins of the ranchmen thereabouts.

Shortly before the train robbery a number of cabins were burglarized and a large part of the stolen stuff cached near Abe Thompson's cabin, where the headquarters of the gang appeared to be.

The supposition is that just before the plans for the robbery were consummated Bally Creighton withdrew from the gang and skipped the country. A stranger took the place of Creighton and the plans for the robbery were proceeded with. Young Marvin was sent into Peach Springs after a supply of dynamite and cartridges.

The dynamite was afterward found on the body of the bandit killed by Express Messenger Summers. The box containing the cartridges purchased by Marvin was found in Thompson's cabin and identified by the clerk who sold it to Marvin, the identification being made complete by the recognition of the cost-mark on the box. Some of the dynamite was also found in the cabin.

On the body of the dead robber were the coat and vest stolen from the cabin of John Ayers and a shirt stolen from George L. Selsor, whose cabins had been broken into in their absence, a few nights before. The clothing was identified by these gentlemen, as was also some camp utensils and provisions found cached about a mile from Thompson's cabin.

These circumstances led to the arrest at Peach Springs on last Thursday—three days after the robbery—of Abe Thompson and Love (alias Kid) Marvin on the temporary charge of burglary. They were brought here Friday morning in charge of Deputy Sheriff W. C. Bayless and Detective Cade Selvy, and lodged in the county jail.

Messrs. John Ayers and George L. Selsor, the Peach Springs ranchmen, were brought here as witnesses against the suspects on the burglary charge, but it is now evident that the intention of the prosecuting officers is to have them give incriminating evidence against the prisoners, connecting Thompson and Marvin directly with the robbery or at least as accessories, which it seems is not hard to do.

Death for Train Robbers

The bill which is before congress providing that the penalty for train robbery shall be death has merit, in view of the fact that during the past six years there have been 186 stoppings of trains for criminal purposes, as the result of which seventy-five persons were killed and fifty-eight wounded by shots—Indianapolis Journal.

The same edition contained the following items, including a reprint from the *Albuquerque Democrat*:

Ralph Cameron, the energetic Sheriff of Coconino county, Arizona, who has been after the men who held up the Atlantic & Pacific train near Peach Springs, lived in Albuquerque a few years ago.—Albuquerque Democrat.

Sheriff R. H. Cameron, Under Sheriff Fairchild and Will Riley returned Tuesday morning from their seven days' hunt after the Yampai train robber. Their personal appearance showed that they had experienced a very rough time.

The same edition ran this item of irony from Williams:

Friday evening, about 9 o'clock, while the proprietor of the Williams House, Mr. Aultman, and other gentlemen were seated in the office discussing the late train robbery near Nelson, a man stepped in the door, covering all three with a gun, ordering hands up and faces to the wall. This being complied with he handed them a sack apiece to pull over their head, then proceeded to search them, obtaining about $400 in cash. After securing what cash he could find, the robber fired one shot, which passed between Mr. Aultman and one of his companions through the partition, striking Mrs. Aultman who was in the adjoining room, inflicting a flesh wound near the ankle. The robber escaped, leaving no clue. This is the second robbery in Williams the pas six weeks. Some action should be taken to thin out this class of individuals and for the protection of citizens and property.

The *Mohave County Miner* of February 20, 1897, included a few more details of the capture, but considering the events were so nearby, their account is surprisingly brief:

The Train Robber Caught

Jim Parker, the bandit, was caught last Monday at 1:30 in Diamond Canyon by the Yavapai and Coconino sheriff posses. The chase had been kept up with unabating vigor from the day of the robbery until the capture. Sheriff Potts and deputies Cohenour and Harris had been lead away on a false trail or they would have been in at the capture. As it was, but for an accident, they would have got the bandit anyway. Sunday morning the chase after the bandit lead the officers into the neighborhood of Diamond Canyon where the trail had to be followed slowly and carefully. The Indians were sent on ahead and the two posses of officers laid down to get an hour's rest. While the officers were sleeping a man by the name of Rogers, who was with the Cameron posse as a guide, slipped away after the Indians. He had no trouble in overtaking them and along in the afternoon came upon the bandit lying by a fire sound asleep. The Indians wanted to kill the outlaw but Rodgers told them that they had the man and would take him back alive. He awakened Parker and told him that the officers were on his trail and that his comrade was dead. When told of the death of his partner in the holdup Parker pulled his hat down over his face and the tears rolled down his cheeks like rain. Rogers told the Indians to set their guns against a rock and gather wood to build up the fire and make a cup of coffee. When this was done Parker watched the opportunity given him and sprang to where the rifles were stacked and ordered the Indians to throw up their hands. Rodgers fell to the ground, crying out not to shoot him. The Indians were divested of their ammunition, one of the guns was broken and another thrown into Diamond Creek and then the red men were told to take the back track, which they did. Rodgers talked with the outlaw for an hour and then went back to camp with the pitiful story of being held up by Parker. Rodgers knew that the Potts posse was in ahead of Parker and the outlaw doubled on his track. The Indians reported that he was worn out and would not travel much farther, that he could not get his shoes on and was traveling barefooted. The next day at 1:30 the posse sighted him a few miles from where the Indians had overtaken him. He was wading up Diamond Creek and when ordered to throw up his hands came ashore and threw away his gun. He was handcuffed and taken to Peach Springs. Sheriff Ruffner took him to Prescott, where he will be tried. He refused to talk although he admitted his guilt. When asked the identity of the dead robber he refused to disclose it and it seemed to grieve him greatly. It is thought that the man was a brother or relative.

It is a fact worthy of note that so far no train robber in northern Arizona has ever escaped although one was followed over six hundred miles before he was captured. This holdup will put a quietus on train robbery in this part of Arizona for many years to come.

Marvin and Thompson, who have been arrested in connection with the train robbery, have so far refused to make a confession, although it has been so reported. Asa Harris identified the cartridge box as one he had sold Marvin the day before the holdup. The cartridges were found in the belt of the dead robber. The belt was sold by the W. H. Taggart Mercantile Company but they have no recollection to whom.

There is considerable discussion as to whether the robbers will be tried before the territorial of U.S. courts, but Uncle Sam will probably do the business. A preliminary examination will be held in Prescott next Monday.

It is significant to note that this account, so close to the location, identifies Mohave Deputy Asa Harris as the man who sold Love Marvin some of the ammunition. He must have been burned by this, for sixty years later, as we shall see, Harris would attempt to rewrite the Parker story with himself as the star, and Marvin and Thompson not even appearing as characters.

In account after account, poor John Rogers was branded an accomplice of Parker who "allowed" him to escape, when such was almost certainly not the case. Rogers was also taken to Prescott and jailed for aiding and abetting a criminal.

Kingman's other newspaper, *Our Mineral Wealth*, covered the capture this way on February 19, 1897:

> The much hunted train hold up, Jim Parker, has been captured and he made no fight either. He was walking up Diamond creek, which is a tributary of the Grand Canyon of the Colorado, when Sheriff Ruffner, of Yavapai county, and his deputies ambushed him and told him to hold up his arms, which he did after the third command without making an attempt at resistance. Instead of being the bad man as expected, he was tame as an oyster and if his actions after the hold up are correctly reported, he has about as much brains as that bivalve.
>
> Under-Sheriff Jas. Smith and posse first after the robbery sighted the robber and chased him into the night, capturing his horse and putting him afoot which enabled other officers to capture him. Sheriff Potts and his deputies, J.N. Cohenour and Asa Harris, were still out looking for the man at the time of his capture having been thrown out of their course for a time by getting on the trail of a man supposed to be the fugitive but who turned out to be someone else. All the officers were working together and working hard, and the sequel shows that it is unhealthy for train robbers to ply their trade in Northern Arizona.
>
> Several men are arrested as accomplices of the real hold ups and before they get through they will be convinced that it pays to be honest and to run their shebang on the square.
>
> To further show the stupidity of the outfit and the mistake they made in the selection of their calling, one of their number, Love Merwin, just prior to the hold up came to Kingman and at Gaddis & Perry's purchased from Asa Harris the rifle and pistol cartridges which were used in the job of train robbing. This could have led to the detection of the man even had there been no other "comedy of blunders".
>
> Holding up trains and endangering the lives of passengers is poor murderous business and our officers should be praised for their part in the running down of the gang.
>
> The reward for Parker's capture is up into the thousands, and as the plan of capture was arranged among the officers from each county engaged in the hunt it will be an even whack.
>
> It is said the robber's feet were badly swollen, yet he only walked about 6 miles per day.

The *Phoenix Herald* ran two letters to the editor on February 22, 1897, both concerning the capture of Parker, as well as John Rogers:

Kingman, Feb. 16, 1897

The excitement about the hold-up begins to die away and officers are returning home.

It seems that the train was help-up in Coconino county near the line of Mohave county, a part of the train, after being cut, moved into Mohave county, where the mail was tampered with. The Sheriff of Mohave county was the first to reach Peach Springs, armed and provided with Indian trailers. Soon a Sheriff's party came from Coconino county; also from Yavapai county. That evening word was received at this place that the last robber had been run down and captured.

It was a rough job to trail through snow and slush, as the country around Pine Springs is a high, bleak plateau. The last robber was actually "worn out," his feet frost-bitten, blistered and in fact bare when caught. Arizona is not exempt from bandits—we have our share, but here is a point we will make, that our officials staid with the tracks, received the shots of the bandits and still pursued. We have no record of man who followed bandits where more bravery and staying qualities were shown, it is a warning to hold-ups to shun Arizona and try a country where the officials are less vigilant.

At Kingman there is now a gang of hobos, sports and all sorts, seven saloons seem to be doing a flourishing business, with thirty to forty teams hauling freight, with prospectors coming and going, gives an appearance of a new mining camp. Mining business never looked better than today in Mohave county.   H.

Kingman, Feb. 18, 1897

EDITOR HERALD,—It now appears that the cowboy Rogers that ran into the highwayman Parker was not a regular deputy sheriff but had been employed as a guide or helper. After he had allowed Parker to take the rifles, ammunitions, provisions, etc., he was placed under arrest as being accessory and soon turned states evidence.

This is a point for Arizona to make. In every case where a train have been held up all of the hold-ups has been captured, while in the states none have been captured. Much of this success in capturing must be credited to Indian trailers. They have never failed to get their man when allowed to have their way. Train robbery in Mohave county will never be profitable as long as there is one hundred Indian trailers at hand. There is now three Indian schools in Mohave county. The Indians are learning ideas not to steal but to work for a living. They are always ready to join a sheriff's posse. It was a fearful cold job to follow the hold-up Parker over the rough, (illegible) mountains, but the officials had staying qualities that are rarely found in men. Four days and nights with light bedding will try men of nerve.

Wm. H. Hardy

The author of the second letter is, of course, Mohave County's near legendary pioneer and Indian fighter, "Captain" Hardy. History has not been kind to the Captain, owing to his typical-of-the-era hatred of Indians, and even this letter does not flatter him by today's standards. As for Rogers turning state's evidence, this must have been yet another rumor on the streets of Kingman, as there is no evidence to back it up. Such a rumor implies that Rogers confessed to deliberately helping Parker, which was not the case.

In the ensuing years, the question of legal jurisdiction has risen as well. The train robbery occurred in Mohave County. How then did Yavapai County officials get jurisdiction? Why did Ruffner take Parker to Prescott instead of turning him over to Mohave Sheriff John C. Potts? Why didn't Potts protest and demand the turnover of a prisoner who was rightfully his? Why did Coconino County Sheriff Ralph Cameron arrest Abe Thompson and Love Marvin for a crime committed in Mohave County?

There are no ready answers to these questions. Perhaps Ruffner held on to Parker because he thought he could better look out for his old friend (who certainly didn't appreciate the gesture). Since County courts were already clogged, perhaps Potts simply decided that if Yavapai wanted Parker, they could bloody well have him. At any rate, since George Ruffner insisted on bringing the case to Prescott, Coconino Sheriff Ralph Cameron decided to give Abe Thompson and Love Marvin, now in jail in Flagstaff, to him as well. Reported the *Arizona Journal Miner*, February 24, 1897:

> Sheriff Ruffner and Deputy Munds left for Flagstaff this afternoon to bring down Thompson and Marvin who are charged with complicity in the Peach Springs train robbery.

The question of jurisdiction was not limited to the counties. Robbing the United States Mail was a Federal offense—would the three men be charged under local or Federal law? The *Arizona Gazette* issued a comment February 18, 1897:

> The question of jurisdiction in the Peach Springs train robbery cases is still in doubt. The government has issued warrants of arrest but the county of Yavapai refuses to give exclusive jurisdiction. The arrest was made by officials of that county.

Eventually, as shall be seen, Parker, Thompson, and Marvin would be indicted under BOTH Territorial and Federal law, although none of them were ever brought to trial on the Federal charges.

In California, where initial interest in the Rock Cut Train Robbery had been so high, the newspapers carried largely wire service accounts of Parker's capture. Typical of these were the ones that appeared in the *Los Angeles Herald* on February 16, 1897:

PARKER IS NOW A PRISONER

And the Penalty of His Crime Is Death

The Stone Cut Train Robber Utterly Worn Out, Suffers Himself to Be Taken Without Resistance

KINGMAN, Ariz., Feb. 15.—Sheriffs Cameron and Ruffner, with a posse, followed the trail of the Rock Cut train robber to the Grand Canyon of the Colorado. When the trail got hot the intrepid sheriffs sent one man ahead with the Indian trailers while they rested. The trailers found the robber asleep by a fire and covered him with their guns, capturing him.

The white man's name who was with the trailers was Rogers. Rogers told the trailers to gather wood to make coffee, and to stack their guns. While the Indians were gathering wood the robber jumped for their guns, breaking one over a log, throwing one into the river and keeping the other two, with all the ammunition, and ordering the Indians to "git," which they lost no time in doing.

It is supposed that the man Rogers sided in with the robber, as he is a cowboy of unsavory fame. The whole posse then abandoned the chase and returned to the railroad. Sheriff Potts of Mohave county has left the false trail of the fugitive. Smith of the railroad is now camped at Milk Springs in the Music mountains, about twenty miles from where the bandit was last seen. Under Sheriff Smith at Kingman sent a courier to him this morning, and before ???? they will be on the trail of the hold-up. Sheriff Potts and posse are determined and brave men, who will take the man or kill him if he is found.

CAPTURED

Deputy Sheriff Munds of Williams at 1:30 this afternoon captured James Parker, the Nelson train robber, twenty miles north of Peach Springs. When overtaken he was wading in the middle of diamond creek and offered no resistance. The bandit was completely worn out. His feet had been frozen and were badly blistered. He said he had been without food for fifty hours. The posse arrived in Peach Springs with the prisoner at 7:30 this evening. He will be taken to Prescott for trial. Rogers, who assisted Parker to hold up the Indians, was arrested and will also be taken to Prescott.

The penalty for train robbery in Arizona is death. The officers who assisted at the capture are Sheriff Ruffner and Deputy Munds of Yavapai and Deputy Fairchilds of Coconino.

Newspaper sensationalism was nothing new, even in 1897. It is true that train robbery was legally punishable by death in Arizona, but the sentence was never imposed. There is no record that I have seen of anyone being hanged exclusively for a train robbery in all of the Arizona Territory. Parker didn't really have much to worry about in that area at this point.

The *Los Angeles Herald* followed up with another dispatch February 17, 1897 with a headline that single-handedly won it a place in this book:

A SICK SHERIFF

Ruffner Has Earned the Right to Lie in Bed Awhile
PRESCOTT, Ariz., Feb. 16,—Sheriff Ruffner of this county arrived today from Mohave county, having in custody Jim Parker, the highwayman who held up the Atlantic and Pacific train at Peach Springs one week ago. Ruffner was tendered an ovation as he stepped from the platform with his prisoner, the greater portion of the population being on hand at the depot. Parker refused to say anything to the Associated Press reporter, being worn out and ugly in disposition. He is personally

Yavapai County Deputy John L. (Johnny) Munds in the 1890s. He would later become Sheriff of Yavapai County. (Courtesy of Sharlot Hall Museum)

known to many in this city, and is a fearless and daring cowboy and a hard character generally. Ruffner's daring is commended highly and he is confined to his home, suffering from the privations and hardships of his long chase.

The *San Francisco Examiner* carried the following account of Parker's capture on February 16, 1897, with a few inaccuracies, particularly concerning poor John Rogers:

PEACH SPRINGS (A.T.), February 16—Sheriff George C. Ruffner, with three deputies, arrested the train robber Jim Parker at 1:30 to-day and arrived in Peach Springs with the prisoner at 7:20 to-night and soon after left for Prescott, where Parker will be placed in jail.

After escaping from Rogers and the Indians yesterday Parker doubled on his trail and went back up the Colorado river fourteen miles to the mouth of Diamond creek and took a course up the creek towards his rendezvous at Thompson's ranch.

Ruffner, who has camped on the trail of the robber for seven nights, never having abandoned it once, was near the mouth of the creek and discovered the trail and followed. Parker had entered the creek and was wading in water kneedeep with his boots on when he was overtaken about five miles above the mouth of the creek. Parker was unconscious of the approach of the posse. He carried a 38-caliber Winchester belonging to Sheriff Cameron, taken from one of the Indians who had arrested him yesterday, also a sixshooter and a belt full of cartridges.

"Throw up your hands," Ruffner called.

Parker wheeled, took in the situation, and hesitated whether to shoot or surrender. There were six of the pursuing party, and they were so close that refusal to surrender meant certain death.

It was simply a case of give up after so long a tramp and surrender, or be killed. Four times the order to "Throw up your hands" was repeated, while the bandit calmly contemplated the situation before him. At last his decision came. Throwing his rifle on the bank up went his hands and the chase was over.

Parker was soon relieved of his pistols and searched, but nothing of value was found on him. The Sheriff started at once with his man for the railroad, twenty-two miles away.

Parker looks grim and maintains a determined silence. He was seen to-night but said he had nothing to say. He had eaten nothing for fifty hours when caught, but was trudging bravely on towards his cave in the diamond creek canyon, where he has provisions, bedding and a complete outfit.

John Rogers, who allowed Parker to escape after the Indian caught him yesterday, is in Peach Springs, where he will be detained. He knows all about the robbery and the operations of the dangerous gang are now effectually broken. He has told Sheriff Ruffner all he knows, and in consideration of this service he will not be prosecuted. The rendezvous of the robber gang was in Coconino county, the train was stopped in Yavapi-county and the robbery was committed in Mohave county.

Parker will be tried at Prescott, Yavapai county. Couriers are out in all directions to-night calling in posses and guards are stationed at different places. Parker's home is in California. Friends of the gang are trying to get Thompson and Marvin out on bail at Flagstaff.

The *Arizona Journal Miner* reported the following on February 24, 1897:

Two photos of Jim Parker, the alleged train robber, were taken yesterday and forwarded to the San Francisco Chronicle by request of that paper.

Indeed, the *Chronicle* ran an artist's sketch of Parker based on the photos on February 21, 1897. Accompanying the sketch was a caption that described Parker as "below the average in stature, weighs about 175 pounds, and has a light mustache." The *Chronicle* also noted that Parker "talks in a manner typical of the frontiersman."

Below the sketch, the *Chronicle* ran an interview with Parker, the only one of its kind from this period prior to the jailbreak. Somehow the *Chronicle* succeeded in getting a reporter to Parker in jail where other reporters had failed. The interview reads as follows:

DENIES THAT HE IS A TRAIN ROBBER

STORY OF SUSPECT PARKER

HE SAYS HE IS A COW PUNCHER OF PEACH SPRINGS

Thought He Was Pursued by Cowboys Who Had a Grudge Against Him

Special Dispatch to the "Chronicle"
PRESCOTT (A. T.), February 20—In an interview with James Parker, the man arrested for holding up the Atlantic and Pacific express and passenger train on February 9th, near Peach Springs, Yavapai county, he gave the following statement:

"My occupation is what you would call a cowpuncher. I was born in California and my age is 33 years. I have been working on the ranges around Peach Springs for several years and have had some trouble with one or two fellows. One is named Coner.

"The first that I knew that anybody was after me was on February 10th, while on my way to Peach Springs. I was riding along the road and when within a few miles of the town I saw several men riding along behind me several hundred yards away. Not knowing but what they were some of the fellows with whom I had trouble, I slacked up my horse and turned out of the road. I saw the party divide as though they were laneing cattle, and I stopped and dismounted near a cedar tree. I waited there a few minutes and again mounted my horse and took the trail to what they call Thompson's cabin. While crossing the open country I heard a shot, and looking around I saw this crowd following me and shooting. I wheeled my horse to the left and threw my six-shooter in the air and fired three shots, thinking that the party were Coner and his crowd, but have since learned that the party consisted of Fairchilds and posse.

This artist rendering of Parker appeared in the San Francisco Chronicle on February 21, 1897 and was taken from his mugshot after he was arrested. The actual photo no longer survives except on his later "wanted" poster. (Author's collection)

"I then rode on to the Thompson's cabin, dismounted, unsaddled my horse, turned it loose and hid my saddle. I camped there for awhile and then made for the canyon. I left a few provisions with my saddle, as I intended to keep out of town for a few days until I could find out what was the matter. After walking for several hours Sunday I lay down to rest and while sleeping I was covered by three Indians and a white man named Rogers. They called on me to throw up my hands, and of course I could do nothing but surrender. We took the back trail for about one mile and then struck camp.

"In the meantime one of the Indians went for the posse to tell them that they had found Parker. We made some coffee, I having about five pounds of flour with me and coffee and bacon. Then, after cooking some coffee, the Indians and myself laid down to rest while Rogers stood guard. I woke up just as soon as the moon was setting and stood at the fire, while Rogers sat on the ground. Seeing that I had the best of him, I jumped for the guns and got a rifle and covered Rogers, who threw up his hands. The Indians broke for the rocks. I made Rogers keep his hands up until I had captured all the guns. Then I threw a six-shooter into the Colorado river and broke Rogers' Winchester over a rock. Then I told Rogers to find another job, as trailing was not in his line. In jumping for the arms a Winchester was discharged and the bullet whistled close to Rogers, which, of course, scared him a bit, no doubt.

"Then I broke camp and made for Diamond canyon, a branch of the Grand, and was making up the canyon on Monday with a Winchester over my shoulder, when I heard a command to throw up my hands, and thinking that it was Frank Morrell I threw up my hands, as I knew that he was an officer and that I would be in safe hands. But I afterward found out that it was Sheriff Ruffner of Yavapai county who called to me. I threw up both hands and the Sheriff, who was above me, told me to drop my guns, which I did. He then told me to walk away from them. I walked about fifty feet and then stopped. He told me to raise my hands higher, but I told him that I could not, as I was sore from exposure. In the meantime one of the posse above us fired, and Ruffner called, "Do not shoot; he has his hands up," and then he came down and searched me.

"I am no train robber and do not follows train robbery as an occupation. I will be able to prove my innocence, and the only reason that I made a fight was that I do not believe any one can arrest another when he has not done a thing to warrant arrest. I have no use for an Indian, and I would have shot the Indians if they had not run when they did. I was on my way to give myself up when taken."

Students of the Parker story may be disappointed to learn that Parker's first known statement on the affair was a defiant denial of any involvement in the robbery. But considering when the interview took place, it makes perfect sense. Parker would ultimately plead not guilty to the train robbery charge, so of course he would publicly deny involvement. As for "Coner," there probably was no such man, and if there was, Parker simply used him as an alibi.

So, how did all of this play in Visalia, California—Parker's home town? He had changed his name from Fleming to Jim—did the old folks of Tulare County realize the Arizona train robber was one of their own?

They did, but it took them a few days to make the connection. Finally, the following write-up appeared in the *Tulare County Times* on February 25, 1897:

FLEM PARKER UNDER ARREST

A Former Tulare County Man Charged With Train Robbery

In the Sunday Chronicle appeared a picture of Jim Parker, the cowboy who has been arrested in Arizona on a charge of train robbery. It is said Parker's real name is Flem Parker, and that he was once a resident of Tulare county. Flem Parker is a son of Dan Parker, who lived during his lifetime in Stokes valley. Flem was named for his grandfather, Flem Works, of Antelope valley. All the old residents of this part of the country know of these families.

After his father's death Flem Parker was a great deal of trouble to his grandfather, and the old man spent many hundreds of dollars upon him trying to make something of him and to keep him out of the trouble he was always getting into. From Tulare county Flem went to Arizona, developed into a cowboy, and if reports are true, into a full-fledged train robber. He is accused of being in the train robbery on the 8th of this month near Peach Springs, Arizona.

Parker was sent up to San Quentin to serve a small sentence for stealing cattle in the foothills near where he used to live, northeast of Visalia. That was perhaps fifteen years ago.

Tulare County's other newspaper, the *Visalia Daily Delta*, had been the one to initially make the connection, and they carried a more detailed account of the revelation and recounted Parker's early life. In addition to some wire service reports describing the train robbery and chase, the *Delta* ran the following February 21, 1897:

ANOTHER BAD MAN

A FORMER RESIDENT OF THIS COUNTY A TRAIN ROBBER

FLEM PARKER AND PAL ROB A TRAIN IN ARIZONA

The Pal Killed by the Messenger—Parker Escaped, but was Captured After a Seven Days' Chase—Stole Cattle and Wheat in Tulare County and Served Time in San Quentin

It was Sheriff Cunningham of Stockton who once said that if a train was held up or a stage robbed, he would at once telegraph to the Sheriff of this county to ascertain if any of our "good" citizens were missing from their accustomed haunts.

Tulare county has been the home of a number of desperadoes, who have done their utmost to give the county a hard name. The Daltons, Evans and Sontag, John Keener, and others of the ilk have transgressed the laws of our State and injured the county in reputation abroad by the fact that these criminals resided here.

On Thursday night, February 8th, a Santa Fe train was held up and robbed. One of the highwaymen was killed by the express messenger; the other was more fortunate, for a time at least. Just one week afterwards, Monday, February 15th, the fugitive outlaw was captured.

The bandit was identified as James Parker. His real name is Flem Parker. He was raised in Tulare county and is well known to people in Visalia and the northern part of the county.

Parker was a grandson of Flem Works, an old resident of this county, who lived in the foothills northeast of Visalia.

A CRIMINAL CAREER

Parker Started in to be a Bad Man at an Early Age

Flem Parker early started on a criminal career, and has served two terms in San Quentin. After his escapades here he went to Arizona, where he engaged in the cattle business. It is reported that when he ran short of cattle, he had no conscientious scruples in making raids to replenish his own bands.

During Sheriff Balaam's term of office Parker and Philo Johns were arrested for stealing a steer from Homer Woodard's ranch northeast of Visalia. Parker was sentenced to a year's imprisonment in San Quentin. He served out his time and came back to this county to live. He worked at anything he could get to do, but was given to lawlessness of a petty nature.

On November 26, 1890, he and Walter Brown were arrested by Deputy Sheriff W. E. Russell on a charge of stealing forty-nine sacks of wheat from George Dittman's ranch near Smith mountain. The two thieves brought the wheat to Visalia and sold it to J. M. Fox, proprietor of the flour mill. Parker, however, was not known in the transaction, as he got off the wagon in the outskirts of town. Brown sold the wheat, but was arrested and he confessed the crime, implicating Parker. Brown pleaded guilty to the crime and turned State's evidence against Parker, who was tried and convicted. He was sentenced to San Quentin for five years by Judge Cross. J. S. Clack of this city was his attorney during the trial. Brown was given a light sentence.

Parker's case was appealed to the Supreme Court, and after serving six or seven months he was released on a technicality that developed in the trial. Another warrant was issued for Parker's arrest. The youthful criminal fled from the country and it was afterward learned that he was a cowboy on a ranch in Arizona. No effort was made to recapture him, as the officers were satisfied he would never remain in this county.

A few years ago, Parker's grandfather, Flem Works, died. Parker came here to settle up the estate. J. S. Clack made an effort to collect his fees from Parker for defending him on the wheat charge. Mr. Clack, however, was unsuccessful.

Parker returned to his home in Arizona, where he became an all-around bad character. C. J. Boyd of Los Angeles, who formerly resided in Traver, married Flem Parker's sister. Mr. And Mrs. Boyd moved to Los Angeles, but owing to the family differences they separated. Boyd's oldest son went to Arizona to live with his uncle, Flem Parker. The boy, however, did not remain in Arizona long, and returned to his father in Los Angeles. He told his father that he did not like the cattle business. It is presumed that Flem Parker was engaged in the hazardous occupation of stealing cattle, and young Boyd was not inclined to follow in the footsteps of his uncle in rounding up steers that did not belong to him. He said that his uncle went by the name of "Jim" Parker, having dropped the surname "Flem."

Mrs. Boyd obtained a divorce from her husband and moved to San Jose, where she married a man by the name of Barker. They lately sold out there for the purpose of going to Arizona to engage in the butcher business. Mrs. Barker (Flem's sister) was heard to say recently that "it would only be a short while before they had all the money they wanted." Whether the statement had any connection with Parker's attempt to hold up a passenger train in Arizona is not known, but the remark and the daring crime are in conso with each other.

J. A. Boyd of Traver married a sister of Flem Parker's mother, who is well spoken of by those who know her. Her daughter, who married Johnny Johnson, the leader of the gang of "Forty Thieves" who have terrorized the Traver country for years, resided in Visalia for a while, and fell desperately in love with Obie Britt, the young man who turned State's evidence in the case of train robbery in which Dan McCall and Si Lovren were the principal parties. Britt and the Johnson woman are now employed in the International Hotel in San Francisco. It is reported they are married.

Of course, it is difficult to believe that Parker's sister, Sadie Baker (not Barker, as the newspaper said), had any knowledge at all of her brother's plans to rob the train, let alone approved of it. Nothing further ever came of the allegation.

The most interesting revelation in this article is that Parker had some distant relatives through marriage who were outlaws and petty criminals. Whether these folks had any influence on Parker in his youth is not known. It certainly could not have helped his upbringing.

The February 22 issue of the *Delta* has not survived, so it is not known if they ran any more details the next day. However, the following appeared on February 23, 1897:

FLEM PARKER, OUTLAW

He Went to School to W. B. Wallace, Who Later Sent Him to Prison

The news that James Parker, the desperado who held up the Santa Fe train in Arizona, and Flem Parker, formerly a resident of Tulare county, were one and the same person, as detailed in Sunday's Delta, has been a fruitful source of conversation.

As a boy Parker was a stupid fellow. He attended a school taught by W. B. Wallace of this city. It was his duty as District Attorney for Judge Wallace to prosecute his pupil several years afterward on a charge of cattle stealing. Parker was tried and convicted and sentenced to a year's imprisonment.

In 1890, Parker was arrested, tried and convicted of stealing wheat. He was defended by J. S. Clack of this city. Mr. Clack's fee was $400, and Parker and his relatives promised to pay it, but they never did. Mr. Clack appealed the case to the Supreme Court and secured a reversal of the judgment.

It is reported that another resident of Tulare county was or is implicated with Parker in holding up the train. One of the robbers was killed, and the identity of the highwayman has not yet been established. It may be that the dead robber is the Tulare county man referred to.

Ah, yes, speculation continued over the identity of the dead train robber.

In those days, individuals arrested for crimes would have a "preliminary examination" before a Justice of the Peace, who would then determine if there was sufficient evidence to forward the case to the Grand Jury. This is no longer done in the present time, as the redundancy of two separate hearings to decide if prosecution was justified became more and more apparent as the years went on.

The following dispatches preceding Parker's preliminary examination appeared in the *Journal Miner* on February 24, 1897:

> A. S. Grant, of the railway mail service, whose car was robbed at Peach Springs in the recent train robbery, arrived yesterday to be in attendance at the preliminary examination of Parker, who is accused as one of the robbers. Mr. Grant is one of the veteran employees of the government, and in addition to thoroughness as an official, possesses the traits of good fellowship, which make him popular "all along the line."

From the same edition:

> Deputy U.S. Attorney Albert M. Franklin, came up from Phenix on last night's train for the purpose of prosecuting the case against Jim Parker for robbing the United States mail. If Parker is prosecuted under the United States law for robbing the mails, the government will pay all expenses of the trial. The penalty, if convicted, is from ten years to life in the penitentiary. If he is prosecuted and convicted for train robbing, the penalty is death, hence the chances for conviction are much less, while the county will have to bear all the expense of the trial.

From the same edition:

> Marvin and Thompson, charged with being accessories to the Peach Springs train robbery, were brought down from Flagstaff on Saturday night, and lodged in jail, pending their preliminary examination.

From the same edition:

> The preliminary examination of Parker, the alleged train robber is set for Monday at 10 o'clock. Marvin and Thompson will have their examinations on Tuesday.

From the same edition:

> Ralph Cameron came in on today's train to attend the preliminary examination of the alleged train robbers.

Chapter 5: The First Posse

From the same edition:

Wm. Daze, a veteran railroader of the A. & P. railroad is in Prescott, to attend the preliminary examination of the Peach Springs train robbers. Mr. Daze was manipulating the throttle of the engine of the train which was robbed.

The preliminary examination of Jim Parker, the alleged train robber was postponed today till tomorrow at ten o'clock. It will take place before Justice J. M. W. Moore. The examination will be held in the court house. District Attorney H. D. Ross will conduct the prosecution.

The *Prescott Courier* of February 26, 1897 reported:

Detective Silvey of the A. & P. is in Prescott looking into matters bearing on the recent train robbery.

Parker's hearing went pretty much as expected. Despite Parker's denial of involvement, the case seemed pretty open and shut. The February 24, 1897 edition of the *Journal Miner* gave the details:

MUST STAND TRIAL

Jim Parker's Examination Results in His Being Held to Answer to the Grand Jury.

The Story of the Rock Cut Train Robbery Graphically Told by The Train Men

Soon after the town clock struck the hour of ten this morning, the court room was filled with people seemingly anxious to get a look at the man charged with the train robbery at Rock Cut, on the night of February 8, and to hear the testimony in his preliminary examination.

Justice J. M. W. Moore presided at the examination. District Attorney H. D. Ross was assisted in the prosecution by T. G. Norris, while E. M. Sanford represented the prisoner. Jim Parker, the accused, was dressed in a heavy sack coat of a bluish color, with a sort of checkered trousers, both looking the worse for wear, while in his hand he held a regulation cowboy white hat. His feet seemed to be pretty badly swollen, as great slits were cut in his boots to relieve the pressure on his feet.

Parker is a determined looking man, but does not have the appearance of a desperado at all. He is a man apparently about 30 or 35 years old of medium height, stout in build, dark hair, but has a light colored mustache and blue eyes. During the examination of the witnesses he did not seem to take any special interest in the proceedings.

The first witness called was Edw. Allen, the watchman, who was help up and compelled to flag the train. He stated that two men wearing black masks came up to him about 7:15 o'clock on the evening of the robbery, and after telling him their mission, proceeded to stand guard over him until the arrival of the west bound passenger train at 8:50. During the time they were with him, two freight trains passed. The man who was killed by Express Messenger Summers, he stated, was very talkative during the time they were waiting, but the other man said little, or nothing, and remained some distance away from him, and walked up and down the track to keep warm.

When the passenger train appeared in sight, he signaled it to stop, his signal being answered by the engineer. The place where the train was stopped is about eight miles from Peach Springs, and the express and mail cars were cut loose from the rest of the train and taken to Nelson Siding, about two miles further west, where the robbery was committed. His account of what happened after the cars were cut loose, was substantially the same as has been published. He stated that he did not know that the other man had been killed until the engine and express and mail cars had backed up to the other part of the train. Nothing new was elicited in the cross-examination.

Wm. Daze, the veteran engineer of the Atlantic & Pacific railroad, who has run on the road ever since 1883, and who is known to every one along the line, and to a large number of the people who have traveled over the road was the next witness. After a few preliminary questions which in answer to, he stated that he was in charge of engine No. 85, pulling train No. one west bound when near mile post 457 he was signaled by the watchman to stop. He then proceeded to tell the story of the robbery by saying that he answered the signal by two blasts from the whistle, and brought the train to a stand still, the drivers being just alongside of the watchman. Instead of the letter being on the side of the track where the engineer was, as is customary, he was on the fireman's side of the engine. He asked the watchman what the trouble was, but received no reply. He inquired then of him if there was any obstruction on the track, but still no reply. Just about this time a man appeared on the tender with a gun and made the fireman get off the engine. After some delay the train was cut in two, and the man with the gun, who wore a mask, ordered him to pull out for Nelson siding at the rate of 15 miles per hour. During the delay in cutting the cars off, four or five shots were fired off towards the rear end of the train, while the man on the engine fired one in the air, apparently as a signal.

Arriving at Nelson siding the man compelled them to block the engine, and compelled the watchman to get in the express car. The robber also went into this car, but came out soon. He then made Daze back up the track for a mile or so, and fired off four shots in rapid succession, all the time apparently expecting an answer to his signals and looking north of the track as if expecting some one. After he had fired three shots and receiving no reply, he ordered the engineer to return again to Nelson siding and said "get out of here as soon as God will let you."

The engine and cars were again run down to the siding, when the robber entered the mail car and came out with a big package shoved partially under the waistband of his pants.

During the time he was marching and counter marching the train men around the train, he heard the man say in an undertone, "I am short two men." Mr. Daze gave a lucid and thrilling account of the occurrence. From the time the watchman's lantern was swung across the track in front of him, til it was all over, and he pulled out again on his run, but aside from some minor incidents, there was little in the testimony that has not already appeared in print in connection with the robbery.

Fireman Bartoo was the next witness, but he told substantially the same story, except that he said when the robber ordered him off the engine, he was told to hurry up, and the robber emphasized his remark by shooting twice towards his feet, and said: "If you don't hurry up, I will shoot off your heels." This witness cut the train in two, and was in the act of doing so when Express Messenger Summers shot the other robber. When Summers shot, the robber was standing on the steps of the rear platform of the express car; as the shot rang out, the robber threw up both hands and fell to the ground. Several sticks of dynamite, a revolver and a Winchester were found on him. The witness was not present at the robbery of the mail car, as he failed to get on the car when it pulled out.

A. S. Grant, the mail clerk, told of the robber demanding the registered mail, and of his getting nine packages. He stated that he remembered the voice of the robber and recognized the voice of the prisoner as that of the robber.

At this stage in the proceedings, an adjournment was taken till 2 o'clock this afternoon, when the officers were placed on the stand to tell of the trail of the robber being taken up, and of his pursuit and capture.

Sheriff Ruffner, of Yavapai, and Deputy Sheriff Fairchild, of Coconino, testified this afternoon, and at the conclusion of their testimony, Justice Moore held the prisoner without bail to answer to the grand jury.

The examination of Marvin and Thompson was commenced immediately on the conclusion of Parker's examination.

Sheriff Cameron, of Coconino county, who came down today to attend the preliminary examination, states that Parker has resided in the vicinity of Flagstaff for several years, and that he is a professional horse breaker and cowboy. He says he thinks Parker took part in the "bronco busting" tournament in Prescott during the Fourth of July celebration in 1895. A number of our citizens who have seen him seem to think that they recognize familiar features in him, and this probably accounts for it.

The identity of the dead robber is still shrouded in mystery, and the only man, probably, who can clear it up, professes ignorance, and persistently refuses to divulge any information in regard to him.

Interestingly, the *Courier* seemed less interested. Their entry on the examination results, on February 26, 1897, read as follows:

Train robber Parker had his preliminary examination before Justice J. M. W. Moore yesterday, and was held to appear before the grand jury, without bail. District Attorney H. D. Ross, assisted by Hon. T. G. Norris, appeared for the prosecution, while E. M. Sanford represented defendant. Parker looked cool and collected and was frequently noticed whispering suggestions to his attorney. Few, if any, facts were elicited which have not already been published. The preliminary examination of Marvin and Thompson follows that of Parker.

From the *Journal Miner*, March 3, 1897:

The examination of Abe Thompson and Kid Marvin, on a charge of being accessories to the Rock Cut train robbery, has been in progress today before Justice J. M. W. Moore. The interest in this examination is much less than was manifested yesterday in the examination of Parker, as not to exceed a dozen and a half spectators were present. Up to the hour of the noon recess, practically the same testimony as that introduced at Parker's examination had been introduced, and nothing to connect the accused with the crime had been introduced. The examination was concluded this afternoon, and both prisoners were held without bail to answer to the grand jury."

The *Flagstaff Sun-Democrat* was also losing interest in the case. They summed up their coverage this way, on February 25, 1897:

The preliminary examination of Jim Parker, the alleged train robber, occurred at Prescott Tuesday and resulted in his being bound over to the Grand Jury. The examination of Marvin and Thompson followed, and they were also held to await an indictment by the Grand Jury. Sheriff Cameron and Under Sheriff Fairchild were present and testified. This winds up the train robbery case for a few weeks. The identity of the robber killed by Messenger Summers is still shrouded in mystery.

From the same edition:

Sheriff Ralph Cameron and Under Sheriff Fletcher Fairchild returned this morning from Prescott.

From *Our Mineral Wealth* of February 26, 1897:

"Under Sheriff Smith is back from Prescott where he has been giving testimony in the preliminary hearing of the train robbers."

The train robbery and its failure were both spectacular, but the culprits were safely imprisoned, their convictions were a foregone conclusion, and everyone, including the reading public, became complacent. The Grand Jury would not be impaneled before June, so there was not much to say about the case. From the *Journal Miner*, March 3, 1897:

A. S. Grant, the mail clerk whose car was robbed in the recent train robbery, is a whistler of quite an extended reputation. He gave an exhibition of his whistling ability last night to a select audience at Cook & Bell's jewelry store.

From the *Courier*, February 26, 1897:

It is stated that Parker felt much depressed upon receipt of the news of the death of the Rock Cut train robber, but up to date he has not divulged the dead man's name.

Back in Visalia, California, interest was still high in what had become of their home town boy, and intensified when Detective Selvey, informed that Parker had prior criminal records, arrived in town to search for more information. The *Visalia Daily Delta* reported the following on March 13, 1897:

DIGGING UP RECORDS

FLEM PARKER'S CRIMINAL CAREER IN TULARE COUNTY

THE IDENTITY OF HIS DEAD COMPANIION NOT ESTABLISHED

Arrival Here of Special Officer Selvey of the Atlantic and Pacific—The Dead Robber Had a Book Containing Jasper Harrell's and Sands Baker's Cattle Brands Therein

C. Selvey of Albuquerque, New Mexico, a special officer in the employ of the Atlantic and Pacific Railroad, arrived here Thursday morning and was accompanied by O. J. Meade of Bakersfield, a special officer of the Southern Pacific.

Mr. Selvey is engaged in securing evidence in the case against Flem Parker, who was arrested in Arizona on February 15th on a charge of being one of the robbers who held up and robbed the west-bound Santa Fe train near Peach Springs on the night of February 8th. As Parker formerly lived in this county, Mr. Selvey came here for the purpose of looking up his criminal career in this county.

It will be remembered that during Sheriff Balaam's term of office, Parker and Philo Johns were arrested on a charge of stealing a steer from Homer Woodard's ranch northeast of Visalia. Parker was tried and convicted, and he served one year's imprisonment in San Quentin.

On November 26, 1890, Parker and Walter Brown were arrested on a charge of stealing wheat from George Ditman's ranch near Smith's mountain. Brown turned State's evidence and escaped with light punishment, while Parker was sentenced to serve five years' imprisonment. Parker's case was appealed to the Supreme Court and he was released from the penitentiary, after serving six months, on a technicality.

He did not tarry long in this part of the country, but went to Arizona, where he entered the business of stealing cattle from the neighboring ranges. Little was heard of him until he held up the train in Arizona, and then his identity was somewhat clouded, as he gave the name of "Jim" Parker. The Delta established his identity as a former resident of this county. The Visalia correspondent of the Examiner wired the details of his identity. This telegram in the Examiner was read with considerable interest by the Arizona officers, and it was this clue to the train robber's identity that brought Mr. Selvey, the railroad special officer, to this city to investigate further.

Parker's preliminary examination has been held in Prescott, Arizona, and he has been held to answer the charge of train robbery in the higher court. He was bound over without bond, as train robbery in Arizona is now a capital crime. His trial has not yet been set.

It will be remembered that one of Parker's accomplices was shot and killed by the express messenger of the train held up and robbed. The identity of the dead man has not yet been established, as Parker refuses to divulge his name. It is believed that he formerly resided in this part of the country, and it reasonable to suppose so for several very good reasons. When the body of the dead robber was searched a book, containing a number of cattle brands, was found on his person.

Officer Selvey brought the book containing the brands to Visalia, and two of them are identified as being the brands of Jasper Harrell and Sands Baker. The latter resides near Dunlap, Fresno county.

Mr. Selvey also brought a picture of the dead man, taken several days after he was shot. The picture was shown to John Bennett, a cattle-raiser, who lives near the foothills, and he says he has seen the man, but where or when he does not know. The face of the dead man is also familiar to City Marshall Collins, but he cannot place him.

At the time of the train robbery, it was reported that the dead man's name was Rogers.

It is believed that Parker and his train-robbing gang made their headquarters in a cave up the Diamond Creek canyon, which opens into Grand canyon, about twenty-one miles north of Peach Springs. Parker was captured while wading up this creek in order to hide his trail. It is believed he was on his way to his hiding place. Deputy Sheriff Buggeler of Coconino county made the arrest. As soon as he saw Parker wading the creek, he covered him with his rifle and commanded him to throw up his hands a surrender. The bandit hesitated a moment and then slowly brought up his hands above his head. Parker was completely worn out, his feet had been frozen and were badly blistered. He had been without food for fifty hours.

Certified copies of the records in the criminal cases against Parker have been made by Deputy County Clerk Gilmer, and they will be taken back to Prescott by Mr. Selvey. There is no doubt that the bandit will be convicted, as he has been positively identified by the train men.

It is reported by those who know that the picture of the unidentified dead robber looks like a man by the name of Dan Collins, who formerly resided here. It is known that he went from here to Arizona.

Friday evening's issue of our contemporary contained the following:

"Bud Sherman also identified the picture and pronounced it the exact reproduction of the features of Collins. He had met Collins at Mineral King in the summer of 1895, and had become acquainted with him there."

Mr. Sherman, in an interview with a representative of the Delta, says that he did not see the picture of the dead man and did not identify the dead train robber as being Collins, whom he knew in this county. He says the article did him an injustice in that a statement is made concerning him that is not borne out by the facts.

And so another name was added to the list of names that was growing about the dead robber. The *Tulare County Times*, on March 18, 1897, reported it this way:

THAT DEAD ROBBER
Dan Collins Supposed to Have Been Shot in Arizona

Two or three days ago Detective Silvey arrived here from the south and set about the work of identifying the train robber who was shot dead in the attempt that was made near Peach Springs, Arizona, two or three months ago. He had with him the photographs of the dead man who had been the partner in crime of Flem Parker, who was arrested after a long chase, and is now in jail awaiting trial.

Several men in this city have identified the photo as being that of a man by the name of Dan Collins, who formerly lived in this county. Victor Stolz is positive the picture is that of Collins. He described Collins' appearance to the detective, and it tallied exactly with the description of the dead robber, with the single exception of weight.

Bud Sherman also identified the picture and pronounced it the exact reproduction of the features of Collins. He had met Collins at Mineral King in the summer of 1895, and had become acquainted with him there.

Collins came to California from Illinois, where he left a daughter, who is now grown. He was about 50 years old. There is a reward of $50 for the positive identification of the dead robber, and if Mr. Stolz proves to be correct he will be given the reward.

But like William Daylon before him, Dan Collins was alive, well, and very angry when he heard he had been identified as both a train robber and a corpse. From the *Tulare County Times* of April 8, 1897:

Collins is Alive but Mad

It will be remembered that a detective from Arizona was in Visalia some time ago with a photograph of the dead robber who was killed near Peach Springs station while attempting to rob a train. The photograph was claimed by some here in town to be that of a man by the name of Dan Collins. That was a bad mistake, for Collins is alive and well and located at Santa Monica. A copy of the "Times" containing the opinion of a Visalian as to the photograph brought here from Arizona was sent to Collins and a gentleman of this city has received a letter from him in which he says that he is ready to prove to the man who recognized him as a dead robber that he is very much alive and about the best fighting corps that he has ever seen.

Collins is well known here. His real name is Napoleon B. Collins, but he always went by the name of Dan. His friends here are sorry that his name was ever mixed up in that train robbing case. He was always a straight-forward, honest man, and bore a good reputation.

The identity of the robber continued to remain as mysterious as ever.

And this is where we shall leave the Visalia newspapers. Strangely, they seemed to lose interest in Parker after this. Yes, they covered the jailbreak right up to his hanging, but they relied on wire service reports exclusively. Visalia reporters did not seek out statements from people who had known Parker, or statements from his family, as they might have done today. In retrospect, this is too bad, as such analysis from Parker's hometown would be fascinating today.

Briefly going back to earlier press dispatches that stated Parker escaped the posse because "he rode on a well-known race horse," it is still unclear where he obtained such an animal, unless it had been stolen by the Abe Thompson Gang. At any rate, the *Mohave County Miner* added this footnote on March 27, 1897:

Frank Garner was in Kingman Monday and Tuesday this week. He took back with him to Peach Springs the race horse captured by the sheriff's posse while pursuing Jim Parker, the train robber.

Was the horse really Garner's? Probably, but who really knows for sure?

After the entire gang (as far as anyone knew) was in jail, Love Marvin started to get nervous. As already seen, some news accounts stated that he offered to confess early on, but he finally struck a deal with District Attorney Henry D. Ross in March of 1897. In exchange for leniency, Marvin agreed to turn state's evidence against his friends Parker and Abe Thompson.

Love "Kid" Marvin was very young, and probably panicked at the thought of going to prison. The fun of stealing horses and cattle, as well as burglary, harassment and being a tough guy, were over for good; now it was time to pay the piper. If he had confessed because of an attack of conscience, it might seem honorable, but in actuality, he almost certainly did it to save his own neck.

The text of Marvin's confession has survived, and it is the only genuine glimpse into how the Abe Thompson Gang operated, as well as how they planned the train robbery. It reads:

> Statement of Love Marvin's Confession.
> Dated in City Jail, Prescott, Arizona
> March 22, 1897:
>
> Love Marvin told H. D. Ross and T. W. Johnston, the following story concerning the holding up of A. & P. Train on February 8th, near the Rock Cut, Yavapai County, Arizona, to-wit:—
>
> Parker, Chas. Creighton, Abe Thompson and myself, near the first of December, 1896 burglarized and stole the property that was cached near the "Thompson cabin," from the houses of Manker and Ayers: Got two Winchesters, suit of clothes of Ayers', part of a suit from Mankers', sugar, coffee, flour, bacon, and some shirts. We got the Selsor shirts from Mankers cabin. The masks worn by John Clayton (dead man) and Parker were made from the same shirt, and the shirt was taken from one of the cabins above, that is from Mankers or Ayers.
>
> I paid Parker for his interest in a partnership with Thompson and me $380, and the same or the next day he left for California. Creighton left in two days after Parker left, and came to Jerome.
>
> On January 27, 1897 Parker and another man, whom Parker introduced to me and Thompson came to the "Thompson Cabin," where we were camped. This man with Parker was introduced under the name of John Clayton. He came from Nevada, as did also Parker, as they stated, and across the country, swimming the Colorado River. They came across with a pack. Clayton was a cowboy. Said he had been one of Buffalo Bill's actors, and had gone all over the country with him.
>
> January 28, 1897, they sent me to Peach Springs to get some money that they claimed was to be sent me for them, either by postoffice or Express. I went

and enquired but found nothing. Went back to camp, and they, Parker, Clayton and Thompson said to me we are going to hold up a train. Do you want in on it? I told them I did not. This was on the 28th. January, 1897, and the following morning, 29th. They brought up the same matter again, and Clayton told me that they didn't want me to help at the train; that he and Parker would attend to that, but that they wanted me and Thompson to help them out in getting away. I agreed to it.

Then it was agreed that Thompson and I should get the cartridges and Dymamite. So we went to P.S. I sold some cattle and horses to Garner; got some money, and went the same evening to Kingman and got some cartridges; bought the 40-60 at Watkins Drugstore, and the 44's and 49's at Taggart's. Thompson got the dinamyte in Mickey Nelson's barn, at P.S.

The day before the train was held up, Thompson and I went out away from P.S.; got two horses, switched around P.S. and went over to "Thompson's Cabin", and took the cartridges and dynamite, and the two horses, and turned all over to Parker and Clayton. The morning of the night that the train was held up we started for P.S. and Parker and Clayton came with us out seven miles or thereabouts, and Thompson and I came into P.S.

Thompson and I were to remain in Peach Springs and the other two were to hold the train up. We did stay in town and made ourselves as conspicuous as possible, going all around during the evening and night. It was agreed that either Thompson or I would be on the top of the hill just above Peach Springs after the holdup, to which place the other parties were to ride the horses. Then we were to divide the gains and we were to bring the horses down into town and turn them loose. I muffled my feet with the saddle-blanket that was afterwards found under Nelson's barn and went on to the hill as agreed, and was there (illegible), and Thompson went to bed, I think. I waited on the hill but no one came, then I went back to town and was preparing to go to bed when Thompson came in and said let's go down to the train. After we got out of the house, Thompson said they made a failure of it, and John was killed. It was agreed that if the hold-up was successful that Parker and Clayton should hold us up on our way to the ranch, and take our horses from us, and then go towards Nevada, swim the Colorado River and go to some Spring that I knew well north of the river and wait there until Thompson and I should come after them in ten or twelve days.

Clayton and Parker had kept out of the way since coming into the country the last time. The Indian Hiawatha or (Hellwater) was the only person that saw them both, to their knowledge. Clayton went into Peach Springs once and bought some lunch at Nelson's, Parker staying out of town.

Parker and Clayton each had one Winchester and one sixshooter, - the Winchesters were stolen from Makers and Ayers cabins and the sixshooters belonged - one to me and the other to Thompson. The first day I went to town P. and C. asked me to pick up a played out horse of theirs, left by them between there and P.S., and throw him back out of the way so that no one would see him. It was a well known horse to me. I had known him in Nevada when up there the year before.

Thompson and I were to get part of the proceeds of the undertaking; there was to be a division; were furnish the necessary poder and cartridges and secure the needed horses and in fact any and all things we could to forward the project.

We four were all that were in it. There just two men at train.

So yet another name was hung on the dead train robber. Whether the name of John Clayton is any more accurate than the others will never be known.

It was unknown at the time, but Ross would not need Marvin's confession. Parker would never be tried specifically for the train robbery, and Abe Thompson would ultimately decide not to fight it and plead guilty. But, a deal was a deal. A few months later, on May 7, when the district court, with Judge John J. Hawkins presiding, was in session, Marvin's case came up. The *Prescott Courier* reported it as follows:

> Territory vs. Love Marvin; robbery; defendant arraigned; waived time and plead 'guilty as charged'. Sentence suspended.

It is not known what became of Love Marvin after that. Again, like so many lawbreakers of the era, he probably left the Territory once he was out of trouble, never to be heard from again. Marvin had also been indicted on Federal charges for the train robbery, but was never brought to trial on those charges either. Instead, his case was carried over from term to term of the U.S. Court until July 7, 1909, when the U. S. Attorney asked that the case of United States vs. Love Marvin be dismissed.

Although everyone believed that John Rogers helped Parker to escape, there was apparently not enough evidence to indict him on that charge. So, he was returned to Flagstaff to face his original charge of illegal branding. Reported the *Flagstaff Sun-Democrat* on March 25, 1897:

> Indictments have been found by the Grand Jury against John Rogers for illegal branding, Frank McCarthy for grand larceny.

The next news item pertaining to Rogers stupidly got his name wrong, but it is unquestionably the same man. The *Sun-Democrat* of April 1, 1897 simply reported:

> The case of the Territory vs. Frank Rogers, charged with horsestealing, tried yesterday, resulted in a verdict of guilty.

That wasn't the end of it. Appeals occurred, and the *Sun-Democrat*, making the same name error again, reported:

> Frank Rogers, who was found guilty Wednesday of illegal branding, was turned loose Thursday on a writ of habeas corpus, it being shown that the District court had no jurisdiction in the premises but that it was a case for the Federal courts.

As the United States Court held its sessions in Prescott, this meant transferring Rogers. According to the *Prescott Courier*, April 9, 1897:

> Sheriff Ruffner yesterday brought in from Coconino county a prisoner named Rogers, an United States prisoner, charged with stealing horses on the reservation. Rogers is the man who figured as a deputy sheriff in the pursuit of Train Robber Parker, and who, at the head of Indian trailers captured Parker, only to allow him to escape later on. It was suspected at that time that Rogers and Parker were in sympathy. They are said to be friends.

From the *Arizona Journal Miner*, April 14, 1897:

> John Rogers, who was arrested last Monday, charged with horse stealing, will have his preliminary examination next Monday. Rogers is the man who first arrested Parker, the alleged train robber, and who was charged with allowing him to escape. His examination will be held before United States Court Commissioner H. T. Andrews, as the alleged crime was committed on a reservation and comes under the jurisdiction of the United States Court.

From the *Courier*, April 8, 1897:

> Deputy Sheriff Munds left for Mohave county yesterday after witnesses in the case of a man named Rogers, charged with horse stealing.

The *Flagstaff Sun-Democrat* ran their own account April 22, 1897, which included a quote from the *Mohave County Miner*:

> The Federal court has become interested in the fate of John Rogers and is now trying him in Prescott for the same charge upon which he was convicted here at the last term of court. He may yet suffer for his crime. The Kingman Miner says: "Rogers, the fellow who was arrested for mixing up in the train robbery business near Peach Springs, and who was tried a few days ago in Flagstaff for horse stealing, but was discharged (after being found guilty by the jury) because the crime was committed on the Wallapai Indian reservation, is again in limbo, and will be tried by the United States court at Prescott.

In the end, nothing much came of Rogers' Federal trial. In recording the events in the United States Court, the *Arizona Journal Miner* of July 14, 1897 simply reported:

> U. S. vs. John Rogers, grand larceny. Case dismissed on motion of United States attorney.

No explanation for the dismissal has survived.

One year later, on June 4, 1898, ironically the day after Parker was hanged, the *Mohave County Miner* carried this item:

> John Rogers was given ten days in jail a few days ago by Judge Redman for using bad language on the street. Rogers is the man who assisted in the chase of Parker and allowed the outlaw to take his arms and those of the Indians away from them.

Nothing further is known of John Rogers. Again, like most petty criminals and saddle-bums, he undoubtedly left the area for parts unknown in due time.

Readers up to this point are probably asking themselves about Abe Thompson. He had two young children—what became of them? They probably stayed at Thompson's Cabin with their father and the rest of the bandits after the death of their mother, but what about after Abe Thompson's arrest for the train robbery?

Regrettably, no information has survived as to the fate of Thompson's youngest, who was probably placed in foster care by the Mohave County authorities. But as for Thompson's eldest son, we do have some sketchy information. Since George Ruffner had chosen to take jurisdiction over the entire Rock Cut Train Robbery case, including all of the known participants, the Mohave authorities decided to palm the boy off on Ruffner.

From the *Arizona Journal Miner*, April 28, 1897:

> Charles Samuel Thompson, a six-year-old boy, came in on this morning's train, with a tag attached to him, directed to Sheriff Ruffner. He was sent from Mohave county. The little fellow's mother is dead, and his father, Abe Thompson, is in jail here, charged with complicity in the train robbery at Rock Cut in February last. He has no friends or relatives to care for him, but Sheriff Ruffner and wife will probably give him a home.

From the same edition:

> Mrs. G. C. Ruffner has fitted her little ward, Charles Samuel Thompson, out with a new suit of clothes and a supply of books and started him to school today. The little fellow is quite bright.

Less than two months later, the following appeared in the *Mohave County Miner* on June 19, 1897:

> Sheriff Ruffner, of Yavapai county, last Sunday, sent the little boy of Abe Thompson (who is in the Yavapai county jail on a charge of train robbery), to Kingman. He was consigned to no one, and as he has no relatives here, the sheriff must have thought that God would care for him. This might be all right if the little fellow was consigned to heaven, but in Kingman small boys have to eat and drink. W. A. Laswell took charge of the little one until another home can be found for him. He is properly a charge of Coconino or Yavapai county and the proper one should be compelled to care for him.

This dispatch, shocking by today's standards, was reprinted in the *Journal Miner* and numerous other Arizona papers. Apparently the Sheriff at some point simply put him on the first train back to Kingman. While Ruffner's conduct can be called into question here, the incident must be scrutinized by the standards of 1897.

In the first place, there may have been more to the story than the newspapers knew. And even if there wasn't, it must be remembered that times were different. Laws defining child abandonment were many years in the future, and since Ruffner had not harmed the boy, most people did not think anything of the incident. The Sheriff simply presumed that someone would take care of a stranded child, and while I do not excuse his behavior here, it was not an unlikely supposition.

Another thing to take into consideration was that little Charles had spent nearly three years living with a gang of bandits and thieves. This could not possibly have been good for a child so young, and may have had a strong negative effect on him. Child psychology was many years in the future, and in the era of 1897, any parents or other people who had children that were troubled, unmanageable, or mentally ill, were on their own. There was no help for parents or guardians in this position, and they either toughed it out or abandoned the child, which tragically happened all too often.

It is not my intention to excuse Ruffner's abandonment of little Charles Thompson, and I'm only speculating, but if Charles had mental or emotional issues from his horrible upbringing, perhaps George and Molly felt they just couldn't deal with it, and took the only option they felt was open to them.

Finally, George C. Ruffner helped make Yavapai County what it is today, contributing much toward the progress of Prescott in particular during his lifetime. His influence on Prescott can still be seen, and one incident of poor judgement does not erase that.

On August 21, 1897, the *Mohave County Miner* reported the following:

> The little boy of Abe Thompson, who has been living with the family of W. A. Laswell for several months past, was sent by the board of supervisors, last Tuesday night, to a relative in Louisville, Kentucky.

Nothing further is known of Charles Samuel Thompson, who in theory, could have possibly been alive as late as 1990. There is a draft registration card for him from 1942 on *Ancestry.com*, listing his birthplace as Peach Springs, so it is undoubtedly him. He was drafted out of Libertyville, Illinois, where he was employed at Hawthorn Farm as a worker. No other data exists on him from the area, so he may have been just a traveling ranch hand.

As for James Parker, as he was now universally known as, he continued to wait for his trial for train robbery. Sheriff Ruffner had him in custody, but he didn't keep him very long. On May 9, 1897, Parker broke out of jail.

CHAPTER 6

L. C. Miller and Cornelia Sarata

At this point, we will take a detour from the Parker story, and go back a few years to do what most after-the-fact accounts of Parker's life have never done—examine the backgrounds of Louis C. Miller and Cornelia Sarata, Parker's accomplices in the jailbreak.

In recalling the escape of Parker, Miller, and Sarata, most western writers have simply dismissed Miller as "a forger," and have never bothered to research further. In actuality, he was a pretty notorious character in Prescott history, already known for causing trouble long before he crossed paths with Jim Parker. Historian Carol Powell, whose husband Glenn is a great-grandson of Louis Miller's brother William, has told me that Louis Clair Miller was born in 1870 in Texas, named after his father Louis Miller, a Dutch immigrant.

Miller's mother, Clara Olmstead, had previously been married to a man named Franklin Howard, and had six children by him who were half-siblings to Louis Miller. Their names were Fred, Herbert, Franklin Jr., Estella, Curtis, and Pearl, who would marry future Coconino County Deputy Fletcher Fairchild.

I am unclear as to what happened to Clara's first husband, but she later married Louis Miller (Sr.) and bore him more children, including Louis. The other children were Otto, Baldwin (nicknamed Tobe), William, Charles, Florence, and Minnie.

According to the Powells, Louis and Clara Miller decided to move to Arizona after the birth of their last child, where Louis was killed by Indians near Fort Huachuca, leaving Clara to finish raising her large brood of children alone. Although some drifted away as they grew up, most of the Miller siblings stayed in various parts of Arizona as they grew to adulthood. Some would become minor figures in the Parker story, thanks to their wayward brother Louis, the black sheep of the family.

It is not known exactly when Louis C. Miller arrived in Prescott, but he first came to the public eye when he became Constable of Prescott precinct around 1892 or 1893.* As noted before with Abe Thompson, the position of Constable was a comparatively minor

---

* I have been unable to ascertain the exact time that Miller became Constable. Records for such a minor position have not survived, and the newspapers did not seem interested in carrying such trivia.

law enforcement position in virtually any city that had one; the job consisted of little more than night-watchman duties, unless ordered to do more by superior officers.

Constable Miller made a few minor arrests during his term. From the *Arizona Journal Miner*, November 8, 1893:

> Constable Miller arrested Ben Lindenbaum last evening for pulling a gun on a man named Clark, and took him before Judge Fleury for an examination. The judge let him off with ten dollars and a reprimand on account of hard times and cheap silver.

From the *Prescott Courier*, Jan. 5, 1894:

> Constable Miller had a warrant yesterday and was on the trail of a man accused of beating a Granite Street French woman.

Such was the life of a Constable. All of that would change for Miller soon after, when he became involved in a violent confrontation with Prescott Chief of Police Miles Archibald.

Now, Chief Archibald was a much-liked, highly respected member of the community. According to his obituary many years later (see Chapter 10), he had come to Prescott from Nova Scotia, presumably with his family. In my files I have a photocopy of a newspaper clipping I have not been able to identify, purportedly dated February 24, 1892, which records some District Court proceedings, and notes:

> Miles Archibald was admitted to citizenship.

That same obituary noted that at the time of his death, he had an ex-wife, Virginia, living. Since two other marriages of Archibald are well-documented, Virginia must have been his first wife, and that marriage and divorce must have occurred prior to his appointment as Chief of Police of Prescott, as (judging by the news coverage) he was clearly not married at the time of the incident with Miller. In fact, for several years, the newspapers strongly implied that Miles Archibald was living with his (apparently divorced or separated) mother, the one-time wife of Prescott Postmaster J. W. Archibald.

The January 11, 1893 *Journal Miner* ran a lengthy article on the wedding of H. D. Aitken and Mattie B. Tuttle, and listed all of the wedding gifts the newlyweds received, including a China ice cream set, given by "Mrs. Archibald and Miles Archibald,"— mother and son.

Miles Archibald continued to rise in Prescott. From the *Journal Miner*, January 25, 1893:

> Miles Archibald has passed a very satisfactory examination and has been admitted as a member of the Order of Railroad Conductors.

From the *Journal Miner*, August 16, 1893:

> Miles Archibald returned today from a trip along the A. & P., and says that less freight is being hauled by that road than ever before, owing to the prevailing panic everywhere in the east.

Then came the moment that would ultimately lead to the incident with Constable Miller. From the *Journal Miner*, October 25, 1893:

> At the meeting of the City Council last evening, Miles Archibald was appointed chief of police. City ordinance No. 72, licensing women employed as musicians in saloons was passed."

It is no longer known what qualifications Archibald had to get such an appointment. Perhaps none at all, as it was much easier to get into law enforcement back then than it is today. Oftentimes, all one needed was a sense of enthusiasm and a respectable position. But like Miller, the new Chief's duties were largely menial, compared to the more prominent position of Sheriff. The November 8, 1893 *Journal Miner* noted:

> Chief of Police Miles Archibald yesterday arrested Wallace Hamilton for stealing blankets. He had his trial this morning before Justice Andrews and was sent to the county jail for ten days.

Such was the life of a Chief of Police. But Miles Archibald had no idea how soon this new career in law enforcement would end. He had no idea of what kind of man his Constable, Louis C. Miller, would prove to be.

It started out as just another Saturday night in Prescott, but before it was over, everyone in town knew exactly who Constable Louis C. Miller was. It is entirely possible that bad blood had already existed between Miller and Archibald, but if so, it all came to a head that fateful night. The *Arizona Journal Miner* of January 10, 1894 gave the following account, and the events leading up to it:

A BLOODY AFFRAY

A Shooting Scrape Between Two of the City's Peace Officers

Constable Miller Fires Two Shots into Chief of Police Miles Archibald

> An unfortunate shooting affray occurred on Saturday night in which the participants were two young men, who were sworn to preserve the peace of the city, being Miles Archibald, chief of police of Prescott, and Louis C. Miller, constable of Prescott precinct.

The origin of the trouble was the arrest on Saturday by Miller of a man in the county hospital who was virtually in the custody of the chief of police. The man, known as "Red," was arrested several days since by Archibald, charged with disturbing the peace. As he was suffering at the time from a burned hand, Archibald permitted him to be taken to the hospital for treatment. At the same time that he committed the offense against the peace and dignity of the city he is also alleged to have committed a battery on a woman, and it was for this offense that a warrant was issued and placed in Miller's hands to serve. Miller went to the hospital, arrested the man and took him before Justice Fleury, where he was convicted and sentenced to twenty-five days in the county jail.

About 10 o'clock on Saturday night Miller was engaged in playing cards in Bob Connell's saloon, when Archibald entered, and seeing Miller went up and asked him what they did with "Red." Miller replied that they gave him twenty-five days, when Archibald left. A short time afterwards the two met on the sidewalk when the shooting occurred.

MILLER'S STORY

Miller was seen in the county jail and gave his version substantially as follows: "I was standing on the sidewalk with Ralph Dillon and John Livingstone when Miles came along and said:

"What did you arrest that man for today, when you know he was my prisoner!"

"I replied, by saying: I did not know he was your prisoner. I arrested him because I had a warrant for him."

"Well you would not have arrested him if I had been there," answered Miles. To which I said, "I don't think that would have made any difference." Further words followed in which I called Archibald a liar, when he advanced towards me and struck me in the face with his left hand, and pulling his gun with his right hand he aimed it at my head and fired. Just as he fired I raised my right hand and pushed the gun to one side, and the ball grazed my thumb and powder burned my hand. By this time I had my gun out and commenced shooting."

ARCHIBALD'S VERSION

Miles Archibald was seen at his home this morning and gave his version of the affair, which is materially different in many respects. As to the conversations which occurred previous to the shooting there is but little difference in the two statements. Archibald states however that he did not strike Miller; nor did he succeed in firing his gun at all. When Miller called him a liar, he advanced towards him, and instantly there was a flash of a gun. He thinks that Miller either had his gun in his hand, or in his overcoat pocket, at full cock, as he did not have time to pull it from his scabbard. The gun was prematurely discharged, the bullet entering the sidewalk.

"I then walked a step or two," he said, and attempted to pull my gun which was in the scabbard underneath my vest. I had to take both hands to it, and while I had my back partially towards Miller, I received a shot in my left shoulder. Turning around still further in attempting to get my gun, and just as I succeeded in getting it out of the scabbard, I was struck in the right shoulder, and the gun dropped from my hand in the snow in the street. It may have been discharged, but I am not sure that it was.

HIS WOUNDS SERIOUS

As near as can be learned there were four shots fired. Three of these were apparently from Miller's gun and one from Archibald's just as he was hit the last time. The latter had a hole through one sleeve of his coat and shirt and one through the front of his overcoat and the lapels of it. One bullet entered his left shoulder from behind and passed clear through him, grazing the upper part of his left lung, the bullet being found inside of his clothes in front. Another bullet entered his right shoulder from behind and has not yet been located by the physicians. While the wounds are considered quite serious, it is thought now that they may not prove fatal, although at first the physicians expressed but little hope for the wounded man.

Both men are quite young, neither being over twenty-five years old, and both are sober in their habits.

For some reason or other, there has been more or less friction between Constable Miller and the city's officers all the year. Under the administration of M. Fagin, as chief of police, several conflicts occurred, and the precinct and city officers did not work in harmony, although nothing of a serious nature occurred.

Miller was taken before Justice J. M. W. Moore this afternoon and held until next Monday, awaiting the result of Archibald's wounds.

Excitement over the affair has by no means subsided yet and the sentiment of the community so far as it has been expressed within hearing of the Journal-Miner, is adverse to Miller.

It is alleged that he has previously shown a disposition to use his gun, or at least draw it, on the very slightest provocation.

The *Prescott Courier*, dated January 12, 1894, gave the following account:

UNFORTUNATE AFFAIR

About 10 o'clock last Saturday night, the town was startled by the rapid firing of pistols, and soon after the news spread that Constable Miller had shot Chief of Police Miles Archibald. The shooting took place on Montezuma street, just a little north of Robt. Connell's place. There are many conflicting reports regarding the matter. As far as the Courier can learn, there were only two witnesses present, who say in effect that Archibald came up to Miller and engaged him in conversation regarding a certain arrest which Miller had made, which ended in Archibald challenging Miller to fight and advancing on Miller, struck him about the neck with one hand and reached for his pistol with the other hand. Miller dodged the blow, falling against the building, when immediately two shots rang out simultaneously in the air, witnesses being unable to tell which man fired first. After exchanging shots, Archibald turned and ran, and fell on his hands and knees off the sidewalk. Miller fired two shots at Archibald after he turned. This is the substance of the statements of witnesses. Archibald claims that he did not fire a shot, that he advanced on Miller with the intention of slapping him, when Miller drew his gun and commenced to shoot. Dr. Davis, who examined Archibald, is certain that one bullet entered his back, and thinks the other one did. Miller's left hand is cut and powder burned, which, he says, was caused by the explosion of Archibald's pistol, which he seized and threw up as it was discharged. Archibald was first taken to the Mountain City Drug Store, and then to his home. One bullet passed through his body, coming out on the other side. The other bullet is still in his body. The wounded man is considered to be in a critical condition, with some chances for recovery. Miller was immediately arrested by Nightwatchman Burton and is now in jail. Archibald states that Miller drew his pistol from his overcoat pocket, while he had his in a scabbard behind him and had trouble to get it out, and that Miller shot him in the shoulder before he did get it out. Witnesses state that the men were not over four feet apart when the shooting commenced and not over ten feet apart when it ended.

Although unrelated to the Miller-Archibald shooting, there was more excitement in Prescott that night as well. It is interesting to note the following, from the *Journal Miner*, January 10, 1894:

A Saturday Night Fire

While excitement was still high, on Saturday night, over the shooting of Miles Archibald, and almost before the wounded man had been placed under the care of physicians, an alarm was sounded for a fire in C. A. Dake's store on the west side of the plaza. The department was out with its usual promptness, but on account of the extreme cold, the thermometer registering at the zero notch, together with difficulty in ascertaining the exact location of the fire, experienced considerable delay getting on an effective stream. When they did finally get the fire located, it was soon extinguished.

The fire started, apparently, from a defective chimney recently constructed in the rear portion of the store, and that part of the building as well as the contents of it are a total loss. The stock in the front of the building is also badly damaged by fire and smoke.

Mr. Dake had recently purchased the building and stock of goods from J. G. Campbell. During the past week he had the inside of the building painted, and was still engaged in making improvements to it, and the loss falls quite heavily on him. He estimates his loss between $6,000 and $10,000, between $1,000 or $5,000 being covered by insurance.

Mr. Dake has requested the Journal-Miner to express thanks for him to the fire department and citizens for their services rendered subduing the flames.

Nightwatchman George Burton lodged Miller in jail, and filed the official criminal complaint against him. The text, complete with all of the complex legal phrasing we have seen before, reads as follows:

In the Justice Court, Prescott Precinct, Yavapai County, Arizona Territory
Territory of Arizona,
Against
L. C. Miller
Territory of Arizona;}
County of Yavapai, } as:
George Burton being duly sworn, according to law, upon his oath complains

of L. C. Miller, the above named defendant, and charges him with the crime of, Assault with intent to commit murder, committed as follows, towit: On the 6th day of January, 1894, at the City of Prescott, in the County of Yavapai, and Territory of Arizona, the said defendant did, unlawfully, feloniously, willfully, deliberately, premeditatedly, and with malice aforethought, upon the body of one Miles Archibald, then and there being, commit an assault with a deadly weapon towit, with a pistol, generally called and known as a six-shooter, the said pistol then and there being loaded with gun-powder and charged with divers leaden bullets, which said pistol, he the said L. C. Miller then and there, in his hand had and held he the said L.C. Miller then and there unlawfully, feloniously, willfully, deliberately, premeditatedly and of his malice aforethought, did discharge and shoot off, to, at, against and upon the said Miles Archibald, and the said L. C. Miller, with the leaden bullets aforesaid, out of the pistol aforesaid, then and there, by force of the gun-powder aforesaid, by the said L. C. Miller discharge and shot off as aforesaid, then and there unlawfully, feloniously, willfully, deliberately, premeditatedly, and of his malice aforethought, did strike, penetrate and wound him the said Miles Archibald, in and upon the body of him the said Miles Archibald, giving to him, the said Miles Archibald, then and there, with the leaden bullets aforesaid, he as aforesaid discharged and shot out of the pistol as foresaid by the said L. C. Miller, in and upon the body of him the said Miles Archibald two wounds; the said L. C. Miller then and there having the ability to discharge and fire the said leaden bullets out of the said pistol, at, into and upon the body of him the said Miles Archibald, with the wilfull, unlawful, felonious, deliberate, premeditated and malicious intent him the said Miles Archibald then and there to kill and murder;

Contrary to the form and effect of the statutes of the Territory of Arizona, in such cases made and provided and against the peace and dignity of the territory of Arizona.

Subscribed and sworn to before me this 8th day of January, 1894

Geo. Burton
J. M. W. Moore
Justice of the Peace.

From the *Courier*, January 12, 1894:

"Justice Moore yesterday fixed Constable Miller's bail at $2,000, pending his preliminary examination."

Four of Miller's friends came to rescue, apparently each contributing a share of his bail. His bail discharge document states:

The Territory of Arizona,}	Territory of Arizona
The County of Yavapai, } as.	Against
	L. C. Miller

A complaint having been made on the 8th day of January 1894, before J. M. W. Moore a Justice of the Peace for said County, that said L. C. Miller be held to answer before him on the 15th day of   1894 on a charge of assault with intent to commit murder upon which he has been admitted to bail in the sum of Two Thousand dollars, we, L. C. Miller, as principal, and E. A. Rogers* by occupation a Printer, residing in said County and Territory, and Joseph Dougherty, by occupation a Merchant residing in said County and Territory, and Sarah E. Taylor by occupation a lodging House Keeper, residing in said County and Territory, and M. J. Hickey*, by occupation a Hotel Keeper residing in said County and Territory, as sureties, undertake as follows, to wit: the said L. C. Miller, in the penal sum of Two Thousand dollars, and E. A. Rogers, in the sum of Two Thousand Dollars, and Joseph Dougherty in the sum of Two Thousand dollars, and Sarah E. Taylor in the sum of Two Thousand dollars, and M. J. Hickey in the sum of Two Thousand Dollars, and   in the sum of   dollars, that the above named L. C. Miller will appear and answer the charge above mentioned in whatever court it may be prosecuted, and will at all times hold himself amenable to the order and process of the Court; and if committed to answer said charge before the grand jury of the District Court of said County will appear for judgment, and render himself in execution thereof; or, if he fails to perform either of these conditions, that he will pay to the Territory of Arizona the sum of Two Thousand dollars.

Witness our hands and seals, this, the 8th day of January 1894.

> L. C. Miller (SEAL)
> E. A. Rogers (SEAL)
> Joseph Dougherty (SEAL)
> Sarah E. Taylor (SEAL)
> M. J. Hickey (SEAL)

Territory of Arizona, }
The County of Yavapai}

Before the undersigned authority personally appeared   and E. A. Rogers and Joseph Dougherty and Sarah E. Taylor and M. J. Hickey, who each being duly sworn, for himself deposes and says: That he is a resident householder in said Territory; that he is a surety in said undertaking, and worth, exclusive of property exempt from execution, the amount for which he has become surety in said undertaking.

> Subscribed and sworn to before me, this   [E. A. Rogers
> The ninth day of January 1894   [Joseph Dougherty
> J. M. W. Moore Justice of the Peace.   [Sarah R. Taylor
>   [M. J. Hickey

I approve the above undertaking, and hereby order the discharge of the defendant, the 9th day of January 1894.

J. M. W. Moore, Justice of the Peace
Endorsed: "Filed January 9th. 1894. J.M.W. Moore J.P."
Endorsed: "Filed Feb'y 10th. 1894, at 4 o'clock P.M. A. J. Herndon, Clerk."

---

* Edward A. Rogers was publisher of the Prescott Courier, and judging by that paper's coverage of Miller's problems, a very good friend of the Constable. Michael Hickey had also once been a Deputy Sheriff. Joseph Dougherty was a local businessman who owned Prescott's old Governor's Mansion for a while after it ceased to be a Government facility. Sarah Taylor was a boarding house owner—perhaps Miller's landlady?

The *Courier* of January 12, 1894, affirmed:

"Constable Miller, having given satisfactory bail, was released from custody yesterday."

It is interesting to note that Miller was not suspended from duty, pending his examination, as he would have surely been today. As shall be seen, he simply returned to his patrols after being released from jail. The presumption of innocence was taken more seriously in those days than it is today.

That same issue of the *Courier* also contained quotes from a speech given by Prescott Mayor J. L. Fisher before the City Council. Among those remarks:

> The shooting of our chief of police is to be greatly deplored, and I reflect your feelings, gentlemen, in the matter of extending heartfelt sympathy to him and to those most dear to him.

The *Courier* also felt the need to editorialize on the issue. From the same issue:

> With a nightwatchman, a constable, and the sheriff's office here, Prescott has about as much use for a chief of police as a wagon has for five wheels. That $100, a month expended in lighting the streets with electricity or paying city indebtedness would be much more in order.

It is shocking to this day to see the *Courier* kicking Archibald when he was down like that, but it would later be seen that Miller had some strong friends and supporters at that paper.

As he was regarded as a pillar of the community, the newspapers kept very close tabs on Miles Archibald's recovery. There was an update almost every day in the *Journal Miner*, and all were reprinted in the weekly editions (the only copies to have survived). From January 17, 1894:

> Miles Archibald's condition still seems favorable, although he is experiencing a soreness in his left hung now. His left arm still continues paralyzed, and he is unable to move it, and has no feeling whatever in it. Whether this will prove only temporary or not the doctors are unable to determine.

From the same issue:

> Miles Archibald continues to improve.

From the same issue:

Archibald's Condition

Miles Archibald's condition still continues favorable, and unless some unforeseen and entirely unexpected complications now arises, his recovery seems almost certain. Dr. Dawson, one of the attending physicians, had charge of the Alameda County hospital, in California, for two years, and has studied this case closely. On account of the weak condition of his patient on the night of the shooting, the physicians were unable to make as careful and extensive an examination for the second bullet as they would have wished to do. After studying the case closely noting the symptoms of his patient, Dr. Dawson came to the conclusion that the second bullet did not enter Archibald's body, and an examination confirmed this theory. The bullet struck the shoulder blade and glanced upwards under his clothing, passing around over his shoulder and lodging in front under his clothes. It was this bullet that was found on the night of the shooting, the other one passing clear through his body, and his clothes as well.

Archibald also obviously tendered his resignation as Chief of Police, as the *Courier* reported on January 19, 1894:

The appointment of chief of police is set for January 30, 1894.

Meanwhile, the same issue reported:

The appointment of Livingstone as deputy constable by Constable Miller was made on the first of this month. He was appointed special to go to the Verde to serve some papers, which Miller did not have time to attend to.

The usual legal delays kept Miller's case from proceeding expeditiously. From the *Journal Miner*, January 24, 1894:

The examination of Constable Miller was again postponed today for another week.

From the same issue:

Miles Archibald is able to sit up some now.

Although it has nothing to do with Miller, it is notable how common shooting incidents seemed to be. The *Journal Miner*, also January 24, 1894, sadly reported the following:

Another Shooting Scrape

It was just two weeks ago last Saturday night since Constable Miller shot Chief of Police Miles Archibald, and on the aforesaid night another shooting scrape occurred. In this instance the "shootee" was a soldier named Riley, said to be a recent arrival at Whipple. The ball struck him in front just over the right eye and glancing around his skull plowed a furrow through his scalp, coming out behind. A small artery was cut by the ball in its passage causing very profuse bleeding but the wound is not considered a dangerous one. The shooting occurred on Granite street and it is said that Riley attempted to force an entrance to a house there, and the ball which struck him was fired from a pistol, by an occupant of the room. Frank McQuilkin, a gambler, was arrested and charged with having done the shooting. He was taken before Justice Fleury who placed his bonds at $250. Later he was re-arrested and taken before Justice J. M. W. Moore who fixed his bond at $1,000 which he readily furnished and was released from custody.

McQuilkin's examination is set for next Monday at 10 o'clock a.m. awaiting the result of Riley's wounds."

The same issue, quite understandably, editorialized:

Two shooting scrapes within as many weeks is not a very desirable record for any town.

On a happier note, the *Courier* reported February 2, 1894:

Miles Archibald appeared on the street yesterday with his arm in a sling.

The ex-Chief of Police was recovering surprisingly well.

Also from the *Courier* on February 2, 1894:

The investigation of the Archibald-Miller shooting scrape commenced before Justice Moore in the Court House yesterday. Brog. May testified to Miller's condition when he was placed in jail; said he heard five shots, three of them heavier than the other two. Further hearing will be had today.

L. C. Miller's preliminary examination had finally begun, but strangely enough, the *Courier* was disinterested in reporting any of the details, with the exception of the above dispatch. As would later be seen, Miller had friends at the *Courier*; perhaps they were already trying to protect him from inflammatory public opinion. The *Journal Miner* picked up the slack, printing testimony from the subpoenaed witnesses in great detail (although I am unclear as to who "Brog. May" was, as he was not mentioned by the *Courier*'s rival).

As official transcripts of the hearing have not survived, we are indeed fortunate that the *Journal Miner* showed the interest that they did. Their February 7, 1894 coverage follows, reprinted here for the first time (to my knowledge) since the original paper hit the streets. It is ironic to note the participation of jailor Robert Meador and attorney Thomas G. Norris, both of whom would later figure in the Parker case:

Constable Miller's Examination

The examination of Constable Miller for the shooting of Chief of Police Archibald was continued yesterday afternoon before Justice J. M. W. Moore, the hearing being held in the court house.

The first witness called was Dr. Davis. He testified substantially as follows:

My name is E. B. Davis, am a resident of Prescott. On January 6, I was called to see Mr. Archibald at the Mountain City drug store. He was lying in the back room wounded in both shoulders—in left shoulder in front and below shoulder blade; the bullet's exit was in front just beneath collar bone. The other wound was in the right shoulder a little further up and to the right. Both wounds were penetrating. There was no exit to the wound in the right shoulder. At the time I arrived he had some clothes on. He also had a contusion on left forearm between elbow and wrist. There was no powder burning about that. It might have been caused by a bullet or a fall against an object. About fifteen or twenty minutes after I heard the shooting I was called. There is a difference between the entrance and exit of a bullet. I did not probe the wound in the right shoulder. I cannot tell the course of the bullet. It could not have been a direct shot. I think the contusion was made by a bullet.

MR. ARCHIBALD—On January 6 I was chief of police in Prescott. As 10 p.m. I met L. C. Miller in front of Young's saloon on Montezuma street. I met Miller, Livingstone and Dillon on the walk. I had just come from the Cob Web intending to go up the street. As I met the three men Dillon was against the building; Miller on the edge of sidewalk, and Livingstone on the edge of the sidewalk standing north of Miller. I did not see them until I got alongside of them. When I noticed who it was I stopped and began to talk about a man I had arrested and put in the hospital and whom Miller had taken out. I questioned his right to do so and he then called me a liar. He then ran to the house and put his back against it. I started toward him. I was about five feet from him when I noticed he had his gun in his hand and just then it went off. The bullet struck the sidewalk. When I saw he was going to shoot I reached for my gun and just then heard another shot and my left arm fell to my side. I had gotten my gun by this time but as I was hit I dropped the gun and it went off. I stooped to pick it up but could not find it. I think Miller fired four or five shots. I know I felt two bullets. I had no show to shoot. I did nothing when he called me a liar.

The clothes Mr. Archibald wore were then introduced. He identified them.

It was about one or two minutes after the shooting when Mr. Vanderbilt helped me to the drug store. Miller and I always spoke prior to the shooting. I did not strike him at all. I not try to pull my gun until he shot in the sidewalk.

A. VAN NOY—I live in Yeager canyon twenty-one or twenty-two miles northeast of Prescott. On January 6 was stage driver on the Jerome stage. I slept at the Gray Eagle stables. Between 9 and 11 I started to go to the stable. I left either the Cabinet or Palace; don't know which. Just above the Cob Web I heard a murmur of voices and saw a man raise his arm to strike another who was standing on the inside of the sidewalk. I don't know whether he struck or not. Just then a shot was fired from the inside. It was fired out and down. The second shot came from the inside. Then I turned and went the other way faster than I went up. There were five shots fired. I recognized Archibald by the flash of the gun.

James Maxwell testified to hearing the shooting and to seeing Miller fire the last shot up the street.

An adjournment was then taken till 10 a.m. today.

The examination was resumed again at 10 o'clock this morning. The first witness called was J. F. Mahoney, who testified as follows:

Was in Brisley's drug store when shooting commenced, heard three shots before I left the store; I ran up the street. The first persons I saw was George Burton and Miller; I could not say that there were more than 4 shots; the flash of the last shot seemed to be from the middle of the sidewalk; there might have been three or four seconds between the first and second shots; I heard Burton say "Miller is shot"' did not see Miller until the shooting was over.

T. G. NORRIS—As I was going home I saw Archibald in Brisley's drug store; I was in the drug store when the clothes were taken off of Archibald; we looked to see the result of the shooting; there was a wound in left side in front; on the right side of back I saw a fresh wound; I picked up a bullet from under his clothes.

R. MEADOR—I was the jailor Jan. 6; I saw Burton and Miller; they came to jail; Burton gave me a revolver; revolver introduced in evidence; there are four empty shells and two loaded cartridges in it.

The case for the Territory was here closed.

The first witness for the defense was John H. Livingstone, I know Miller and Archibald; at 10 p.m. Jan. 6 I was in Miller's company. I remember of Archibald being shot; sometime before the shooting Miller, Reese and I were playing whist; Archibald came in and asked what was done with Red; after we got through we came out and found Dillon; we three were talking when Archibald came out of the Cob Web; I think he came towards us; Archibald came up and asked Miller what right he had to arrest Red. He said if Archibald wanted Red to go to Mr. Morrison and try and get him; Archibald sounded to be angry and said he could lick Miller; he then struck at Miller; I do not know whether he struck him or not; both then pulled their guns; I do not know who fired first; Miller was standing near the middle of the sidewalk when the shot was fired; I can account for but four shots; when Miller fired first shot he did not get his gun up far; Miller and I had been together since between 7 and 8 that night; I first saw Archibald come out of the Cob Web when Archibald said he could lick Miller the latter called Archibald "a damn liar"; they were about five feet apart at this time; Archibald then struck at Miller; he then grabbed at Miller's throat; Miller did not grab for his gun until Archibald grabbed for his throat; I do not think Miller moved at all during the shooting; he shot all the time from the middle of the sidewalk; they could not have been over three feet apart when the first shot was fired.

RALPH DILLON—I remember of Mr. Archibald being shot; Archibald walked up from the Cob Web saloon.

Archibald said, Why did you arrest that man of mine? Miller said I had a warrant. Archibald said, If I had been there you wouldn't have got him. Archibald said, I can lick you. And struck at Miller with his left hand and reached for his gun with his right. Miller reached for his gun and grabbed Archibald's gun with his other hand. They both fired. I don't know who shot first. During the shooting, Archibald fell off the sidewalk on his hands and knees, but got up with a bound and ran a little way. Miller did not move at all during the shooting. I next saw Archibald in front of Gus Williams' saloon. I think there were five shots. Miller fired three shots; Archibald fired one, I know. I saw Archibald come out of the Cob Web and come toward us. As Archibald struck Miller, I said, "Hold, boys!" Miller's hands were by his side. Archibald's were likewise. There was a tone of anger about Archibald.

He acted very determined. Miller did not appear to be angry. When Miller called Archibald a liar, Archibald immediately said, "What?" and Miller repeated, "You're a damned liar." Archibald then struck at Miller. I could see the right side of Miller's body all of the time until Archibald struck at Miller with his left hand and reached for his gun with his right hand. Miller commenced to reach for his gun when he saw Archibald reach for his; Archibald had his gun out first; Miller took hold of Archibald's gun and the bullet went down. The first shot from Miller's gun was horizontal and toward Archibald. I think there were five shots fired. I retreated down to Schlessinger's bay window; Archibald and I had not spoken but once or twice during my time of working in the Courier office; we had not been friends nor exactly enemies.

Recess until 2 p.m.

At the afternoon session of Justice Moore's court, on Wednesday, in the hearing of the Miller-Archibald shooting case, the defendant, L. C. Miller, was placed on the stand and testified as follows:

On January 6, I was a constable in this precinct. I know Mr. Archibald. I first saw him that evening in Connell's saloon. Bob Connell, Curley Reese, Livingstone and myself were playing cards. Mr. Archibald came in and wanted to know where that man "Red" was. I said he got 25 days. After five or six minutes after, I went out with Livingstone and we met Dillon. I saw Mr. Archibald come from the north.

The conversation was here repeated, the same as before reported by other witnesses.

I arrested the man "Red" on a warrant.

The warrant and complaint were introduced.

I executed the warrant about three days after the issue of it.

After I called him a liar he made a lunge at me and struck me on the cheek. As he struck at me with his left hand, he put his right hand behind him, with his left he grabbed me and then pulled his gun with his right hand, and as he came over with his gun I grabbed the muzzle and pushed it down and it went off. I then got my gun and shot it.

The pistol was introduced and identified, and it was shown how it was carried on the night of the shooting. It was carried in his right hand overcoat pocket.

Mr. Archibald's gun went off first. After the first shot he kind of wheeled, and shot. He fired again and wheeled and I fired again, and as he turned again I fired again. I was arrested about one minute after the last shot was fired. I did not say that I threw the gun up. When I grabbed it, the flash went up instead of down.

J. J. CURLEY—I know L. C. Miller; I heard five shots on Jan. 6 in the evening; one side of Miller's face was a little swollen when he was brought into the jail. I think the swelling was on the right side; he had a handkerchief wrapped around his thumb; there appeared to be blood on the handkerchief; I am in jail awaiting the action of the grand jury on a charge of burglary; there appeared to be evidence of a powder burn on his thumb when I saw it.

J. W. JACKSON—I know the defendant by sight; I saw him at the O.K. Corral. Evidence thrown out.

ROBERT CONNELL—At 10 p.m. Jan. 6 I was about twenty-five feet from the shooting; I guess I staid pretty near all the time; Miller, Livingstone, Reese and myself were playing whist; Archibald came in and asked what they did with Red; Miller said he got twenty-five or thirty days, I do not know which; I think that there were five shots fired during the shooting; I don't think one man could have fired all of the shots.

W. H. TEAGUE—On Jan. 6 I was in the Cabinet saloon; "The Kid," Burton and myself hunted for Archibald's gun and I found it twelve or fifteen feet from the edge of the sidewalk in front of the restaurant next to Gus Williams.

CHAS. MITCHELL—I remember the shooting of Archibald; Teague, Burton and myself hunted for Archibald's gun and found it in front of the restaurant near Gus Williams and about fifteen or twenty feet from the sidewalk.

L. C. MILLER, recalled—I said in the presence of Osenburg and Anderson, "that will be all right: I ain't through with this thing yet." This was said with regard to the canvass of myself and Archibald for chief of police; the reason I made the remark was that I intended to contest the election; I did not say that I would like to bump into Archibald on the Friday or Saturday night previous to the election.

Adjourned till 10 a.m. Thursday.

The examination was resumed at 10 o'clock this morning when Harry Brisley took the stand and testified as follows: Am a druggist in Prescott; I recall the shooting of Mr. Archibald; I heard Mr. Archibald say substantially that he ought not to have made a pass at Miller when Miller called him a liar; I could not say that he made that remark in the first five minutes he was in the store or in the first half hour; my relations with Mr. Archibald were not friendly.

GEO. N. GLADDEN—I do not know either Miller or Archibald; there were five shots fired; Mr. Archibald fired the first shot; there were a few words passed before the shooting. I recognized Mr. Archibald by the flash of the gun; the second and third shots were so close together I do not know who fired them; that first shot was down into the sidewalk.

Defendants case here rested.

J. C. MARTIN*—Called in rebuttal; interviewed Miller in the jail Sunday or Monday after the shooting at the door of the county jail; Miller said that Archibald drew his gun and aimed it at Miller's face and he struck the gun up and the shot went into the air; he also said that the first shot he (Miller) fired went into the sidewalk; I do not remember whether he said who fired first.

The following is the closing testimony in the Miller examination taken Thursday;

CHARLES BIDDINGER: I know L. C. Miller and Ralph Dillon. On the Friday or Saturday night before the election, at Charley Wallace' saloon, in referring to Archibald, Miller said he wanted to get a chance to bump into Archibald. Dillon said, "All you want is to bump into him once." Miller said, "Yes." Wallace was standing near at this time. I am friendly to both parties concerned. I do not remember whether it was Friday or Saturday night.

H. H. CARTTER: I am a deputy sheriff. I examined the bullet hole in the side walk in front of Jim Young's saloon. The bullet was fired from near the double doors of Young's saloon. The man who fired the pistol must have fired toward the road. The bullet hole was about two inches in length, but was not over half an inch in depth.

CHARLES WALLACE, called for defendant: I know Miller, Biddinger, and Dillon. I remember on the Friday or Saturday night before the late city election, of

---

* Editor of the *Arizona Journal Miner*.

Chapter 6: L. C. Miller and Cornelia Sarata

these three gentlemen being in the saloon; I did not hear Miller say "I want to get a chance to bump into him," meaning Archibald. I did not hear Dillon say to Miller, "All you want is one chance." I do not know what these gentlemen said, as I did not hear anything that was said. I know that they were conversing, but what was said I don't know.

Miller recalled by the defense; I did not use the words "I should like to bump into Archibald once." I did not hear Dillon say "All you want is one chance." I was not in town on the Saturday night previous to the shooting.

H. H. Cartter recalled by the defense: The bullet hole could have been made by a man having his hand twisted around and pointed at the side walls.

J. R. Dillon recalled by the defense: On the Friday or Saturday night before the election, in the presence of Miller, Biddinger and Charley Wallace at the (illegible) I did not hear Miller say in reference to Archibald, "I want a chance to bump into him." I did not say, "All you want is one chance." I don't remember that we were there that particular night.

Court adjourned until 1:30 p.m.

The afternoon session of Justice Moore's court, Thursday, was devoted to argument of counsel in the examination of Constable Miller, no testimony being introduced. Andrews & Ling have been employed to assist District Attorney Morrison; while T. W. Johnston represented the defense at the examination. The argument was opened by R. M. Ling, for the prosecution, followed by Mr. Johnston for the defendant, and was closed by District Attorney Morrison. At the close of the argument, Justice Moore announced his decision, binding the defendant over to appear before the grand jury, as announced in Thursday's issue, bonds being fixed at $2,000. The bond formerly given was continued.

Miller's surviving court papers show that George Burton, Robert Avey (?), a Professor Schlesinger, Michael Boland, Frank Emmal, Tom McCormick, W. W. Vanderbilt, Archie Varray (?), Joe Valentine, Juan (?) Vigeal, W. G. Barker, Busch Anderson, R. B. May (possibly the Brog. May referred to by the *Courier*), and a couple of other men whose names are illegible today on the handwritten subpoenas, were called to testify. Who these men were, what they testified to, or even if they testified at all after being subpoenaed, is unclear. The Court papers also show that witness Michael Boland petitioned the court for reimbursement of his traveling, board, and lodging expenses—$7.50.

The testimony was confusing and, at times, contradictory, and this almost certainly was the main factor in the Grand Jury's later decision not to indict Miller.

Also from the February 7, 1894 edition of the *Journal Miner*, a report of Prescott City Council proceedings, which included the following:

On motion of Marks, the bill of Miles Archibald, for $100. salary as chief of police for January, was allowed, all voting aye, except Goldwater.

Why prominent ex-Mayor and City Councilman Morris Goldwater opposed paying Archibald is not known.

After being released on bail, Miller returned to his Constable duties. But he didn't stay out of trouble very long. Within two weeks he was arrested again, this time for shooting a drunk. The details were even more confusing, helped in no small way by the behavior of Prescott's two rival newspapers, who each printed diametrically opposite accounts of the affair. Miller clearly had friends at the *Prescott Courier*, which printed this account, favorable to Miller, on February 23, 1894:

> About nine o'clock last Saturday evening, two shots in quick succession were heard and the news soon spread that Constable Miller had shot a man in that questionable quarter of town where bad spirits do seem to most congregate. There were many conflicting reports regarding the shooting, but all agree that the man was shot while resisting arrest for very boisterous and dangerous conduct. From the most reliable information the Courier can gather, the tragedy came about in this way: One Wallace, a powerful man about six feet in height, and of splendid physique, a recent arrival from the railroad grade, was full of whiskey and in a maniacal frame of mind when he entered one of those rooms in the Sorg block, north of the Union Saloon, inhabited by the unfortunate women of the town. He approached the occupant of the room in a threatening manner, drew a knife, and compelled her to jump over the stove. Constable Miller passed at this time and the woman called for protection. Miller went in, when Wallace put his knife up. Miller did not see the knife. Miller got the man out and pacified him, as he thought. Miller then went into the Royal saloon, when someone on the outside called him, saying he was needed. He went out, found Wallace boisterous, told him that he was an officer, and to consider himself under arrest. Wallace, with most emphatic profanity, said all the officers in Prescott could not arrest him, and he suddenly seized Miller by the throat.
>
> Miller struck Wallace alongside the head with his revolver, but failed to loosen Wallace's giant grip on his throat. Miller called for help, saying he would have to shoot Wallace. No help was afforded. Wallace continued to choke Miller. Miller's wind was completely shut off, and he sank to his knees with his back against a post. Wallace drew his knife. With a spasmodic effort, Miller rose to his feet; two shots rang out on the night air and Wallace fell to the ground with two bullet holes through his body, both entering above the heart about two inches apart, the bullets passing entirely through his body and lodging in the building near by. Miller was immediately taken into custody and Wallace afforded medical treatment. Wallace's wounds are serious. At the hour of going to press, his condition was reported somewhat better than it was in the morning. Wallace is said to be a good citizen and hard working man when sober, but is made crazy by liquor. His railroad comrades think a good deal of him and have raised a purse, we are informed, to see that he is well cared for. The affair is certainly a much to be regretted one. The knife taken from Wallace is in the sheriff's office. It is a case knife with the point broken off.

Even in newspapers of the era, it is highly unusual to see such vivid, flowering, and descriptive verbiage. The unknown reporter seems to have had a good time writing the piece.

Any city resident who happened to read both newspapers (something most newspapers believe no one ever does) were probably startled to find an entirely different account of the incident in the *Arizona Journal Miner* of February 21, 1894:

SHOT DOWN!

A Drunken and Almost Helpless Man Shot Twice by Officer Miller

Statements of Eye Witnesses Damaging to the Shooter

Prescott, on Saturday night, had the disgrace of another shooting scrape added to the already unusually long list of such affairs within the past few weeks. Commencing with the shooting of Chief of Police Miles Archibald, January 6, by Constable L. C. Miller, and since that time four shooting scrapes have occurred. Three of them including the one on Saturday night occurred within fifty feet of each other on Granite street, at or near the Royal saloon. In two of them Constable Miller, a peace officer of Prescott precinct, has figured as the shooter.

The shooting on Saturday night occurred about fifteen minutes past nine o'clock. The particulars of it as learned from two eye witnesses by representatives of the Journal-Miner will be found below. One of the parties interviewed was within ten or fifteen feet of both parties when the shooting occurred and the other was within three or four feet. As both of them have been subpoenaed to testify at the preliminary examination, their names are not given. Their stories are corroborative of each other and neither knew of the Journal-Miner's interview with the other as it has been the object of this paper to get at all the facts as nearly as possible.

THE TWO STATEMENTS

Are substantially as follows: John Wallace, the man who was shot, was almost hopelessly drunk. He had visited one of the places in the vicinity and had had trouble with a woman and was ejected from her rooms, barefooted, bareheaded and without a coat. His clothes were thrown out to him on the street. Wallace was inclined to be boisterous and noisy just as many men, in the degree of intoxication in which he was in, are. He imagined that his clothes were still in the room from which he had been ejected and he was kicking the door with his bare feet asking for his clothes. Constable Miller came along and told him to dress and keep quiet or he would arrest him. Wallace then picked up his clothes and had his shoes in one hand and his coat over his arm when he told Miller that he could not arrest him and that all the officers in Prescott could not do so. He made a pass at Miller and caught hold of him when the latter drew his gun and placing the muzzle in Wallace's face told him to go slow. Wallace then released his hold on Miller and the latter put the gun in his pocket. Wallace then said "you are a shooting s—of—a—b---are you" or a remark of a similar import when he again grabbed him, and Miller drew his gun again and hit once or twice with it when he fired twice.

BOTH BALLS TOOK EFFECT

In Wallace's left breast entering the body within two inches of each other passing clear through the lung.

One ball came out of the back just to the left of the spine and the other also on the left side of the spine but its exit was several inches from the exit of the other. The pistol was held at such close range that Wallace's clothes were set on fire by the powder and his skin was also powder burned. Wallace was taken to Brisley's drug store and cared for immediately after the shooting in the same shoeless, hatless and coatless condition in which he was shot down, but was afterwards taken to the county hospital in West Prescott, where he has been under the care of Dr. Sewall ever since. Drs. McCandless and Davis were also called in last evening to see him. All agree that his condition is very critical, but not entirely hopeless.

District Attorney Morrison being informed yesterday that he was likely to die, went to the hospital and took

WALLACE'S ANTE-MORTEM STATEMENT

The substance of it was that he was shot without provocation, and also went to show the almost helpless state of intoxication that he was in at the time, as he imagined that the trouble occurred in the woman's room from which he had previously been ejected.

The statement has been made that Wallace drew a knife on the constable, but neither the circumstances or the statement of eye witnesses seem to justify this. The parties interviewed state positively that they did not see any knife drawn, while the only knife found about him was taken from his pocket after he had been removed from the scene of the shooting, up on Montezuma street. This was a harmless broken case knife. Had he drawn it on the officer, he would never have been able to return it to his pocket after receiving two such wounds as were inflicted on him.

Wallace had been at work with the track laying force of the S. F. P. & P. railroad, and is a large, powerful man. Several of his fellow workmen were seen yesterday, all of whom state that he is as harmless and innocent as a child. They also state he served for three years on the police force of St. Louis. He is about 30 or 33 years of age.

The Journal-Miner man did not attempt to get any statement from Miller, in regard to the shooting, as he was dragged into court as a witness in the Archibald shooting case, to contradict Miller's statement on the stand, which was at variance with the one given to the Journal-Miner just after the shooting occurred. Not desiring a repetition of this, it refrained from asking any statement from him.

It was an hour or more after the shooting occurred before Miller was arrested. It was not until M. J. Hickey, who is on Miller's bond, for his appearance to answer for the shooting of Miles Archibald, went to the sheriff and gave notice of his withdrawal from the above bond, and demanded that he be taken into custody that he was arrested. It is also stated that while his victim was lying on the sidewalk and supposed by all to be dying, Miller stood near rolling a cigarette to smoke, as nonchalantly as though it was an every day occurrence for him to shoot a man.

After learning the particulars of Saturday night's shooting Joseph Dougherty who was also on Miller's bond for the shooting of Miles Archibald withdrew from his bond, his remaining two sureties being E. A. Rogers and Mrs. S. E. Taylor.

Miller's friends were active yesterday in trying to secure a new bond for him.

The wounded man was reported, by Dr. Sewall this morning, as having passed a reasonably comfortable night, and his condition favorable for recovery.

> The shooting of this man is generally condemned as being wholly unjustifiable and considerable indignation has been expressed over it even by those who have been Miller's friends heretofore, while on the other hand of course there are those who defend the act as being one of self defense.

The official complaint was sworn out by Wallace (whose first name was John) himself, but the legal terminology, charging Miller with assault with intent to murder, is virtually the same as in the Archibald shooting, negating the need to reprint it here.

Miller's friends were unable to raise a new bond, and he did remain in jail until his eventual trial. The *Journal Miner* continued to express outrage over the incident. From the same issue:

> The shooting on Saturday night, by Constable Miller of a poor drunken, harmless man seems to call for his immediate removal as a peace officer. An officer who is unable to make an arrest of a man in such a helpless state of intoxication as Miller's latest victim seems to have been, is certainly not fit for the position. The usual plea of self defense has already been raised, and it is stated that a rusty, broken old case knife will be introduced in the case as the deadly weapon which threatened the officer's life. When a man reaches a certain degree of intoxication he often imagines that it would require a whole army to "take him in" and he often makes a great show of resistance. An officer who can not manage such a subject without shooting him should surrender his insignia of office. Even the clubbing of such characters, with a gun, except the very worst of them is seldom necessary, and the shooting of them is nothing short of murder. The peaceable law abiding citizens are becoming quite disgusted and indignant over the repeated shooting scrapes which have occurred within the past few weeks and their indignation found expression on Saturday night in threats of lynching. Had this latest victim of this "shooting officer" not been an entire stranger, those threats might have resulted in an attempt, at least, to carry them out.

Again, from the same issue:

> Prescott has no need for officers who shoot unarmed men, even though they may resist arrest.

Also, from the same issue:

> John Wallace, the last victim of Constable Miller, is reported to be resting easy today. He now thinks that he will recover.

It was the first time that Wallace's first name was used.

L. C. Miller's examination before Justice J. M. W. Moore took place within a few days of the Wallace shooting, much faster than it had occurred in the Archibald incident.

Again, because no official transcripts have survived, we are very fortunate that the *Journal Miner* was interested enough in the hearing to print details of the witnesses' statements. And again, I believe this to be the first time the coverage has been reprinted in its entirety since it first hit the streets. The following coverage appeared in the *Arizona Journal Miner* of February 21, 1894. Note the presence in the story of then-Deputy George C. Ruffner:

CONSTABLE MILLER'S EXAMINATION

The examination of Constable L. C. Miller, for shooting his latest victim, was commenced at 10 a.m. this morning before Justice J. M. W. Moore. Only two or three weeks have elapsed since his examination for shooting Chief of Police Miles Archibald, took place, which goes to show how readily a determined officer can make business for the courts. Few men succeed, within so short a time, in getting two appearances before a justice of the peace for a preliminary examination on charges of attempt to murder.

The first witness placed on the stand to-day was Ike Morrison, who happened to be within a few feet of Miller and his victim when the shooting occurred, who testified to seeing the injured man lying on Marie Castro's floor, apparently drunk.

MARIE CASTRO testified that the injured man was in her house previous to the shooting. That he was drunk and abusive. That she made him go out, and Miller tried to make him dress and go away. And when the man refused and resisted, Miller shot him.

GEORGE RUFFNER—There were men standing on the outside of the walk, and when they would get back I could not see anything. The man who had his coat off was standing on walk. I heard some one say, "put on your shoes." The first blow was overhand; I did not start for the walk until Miller reached for his gun, and then I recognized Miller; I then went towards him; this man was a large man, he would weight 185 or 190 pounds. Two of us then helped the man who was shot; we did not have to carry until we got to Fisher's alley; I would not say there was a coat on his arm, there was something; the man who was shot was talking; I don't know what he said; I saw Miller raise his pistol and hit the man; I could not see where the man hit Miller; I cannot say whether the man had his hand on Miller's throat or not; I heard the man who was shot say: "You are a gun man, are you?" Miller said: "That's what I am," and then Miller put his hand back and two shots were fired just as quick as a man could pull the gun; they were under the porch and there was an electric light which throws quite a light for forty or fifty feet; when I first saw Miller make a motion for his gun I was forty or fifty feet away; when the shots were fired they were about two feet and a-half from the wall; they must have been five feet from the post; I was about twelve or fifteen feet away; just before Miller struck the man I could see all of Miller; the men were right together when Miller hit him.

KITTY MARKS—I know this woman; she lives four doors south of the Royal saloon; I passed the man before the shooting; he had no shoes or socks on and was vomiting; the trouble could not have been over two minutes; I went right into the Royal saloon by the ladies entrance.

ALBERT WEBER—On last Saturday night I was present when Miller shot the man; the shooting was on Granite street just south of the Royal saloon; when I came there Miller was telling the man who was afterwards shot to put his shoes on and the fellow would not; Miller said if he did not, he would arrest him; the man said he could not and all the officers in the town could not arrest him; Miller then drew his gun out and then put it back; the man said: "You're a gun man, are you?" Miller said: "That's what I am," and the man grabbed Miller with his left hand and Miller drew his gun again and struck him three times, once hard and twice easy; Miller then shot him; when the shooting took place the man must have been about three feet from the house; when I went there the man had no shoes or socks on, and no coat or vest on; he had his coat on his arm and his shoes in his hand; when Miller drew his gun the man said: "_____ _____ you are a gun man, are you?" When the man grabbed Miller he took hold of him with his left hand; the first blow Miller struck him he hit him hard; the man was in toward the wall and Miller was on the outside.

WILLARD MARTIN—I know Miller; Adolphus Blair and I went out of the Union saloon and started for the Royal saloon; we saw this man and he said he would kick down the whole d___d house; the woman then locked the door and went in the house; we went on to the Royal saloon and seeing Miller said: "There is a job for you outside." Miller told the man to put on his clothes or he would run him in; the man said: "You can't arrest me or any other officer." Miller then pulled out his gun and the man said, "You are a gun man, are you?" Miller said "Yes; no." The man then grabbed Miller and forced him to the post; Miller then drew his gun again and hit him twice; the blows did not stagger him; Miller then shot him; the man then let go of Miller. Miller's conduct was gentlemanly, and the man's conduct was very rough. When the man had his hand on Miller's throat I could not see his other hand.

CHANCEY E. WEST—I am stationed at Whipple; I was present when Miller shot this man; I was in the Royal saloon and I heard a man say, "I guess there is a scrap outside." We went out and heard Miller talking to a drunk, telling him to put on his clothes; the man said he could not make him; the man had hold of Miller's coat; Miller pulled his gun; the man who was shot said, "You are a gun man, are you?" Miller said "That's what I am," and then put his gun back; the man grabbed Miller by the throat, and Miller then pulled his gun and hit the man with it; the blows had but little effect on the man; he continued to push Miller back; Miller then fired; the shots were quick; after the shots were fired, the man let go.

"The examination was concluded this afternoon, resulting in Miller's being held under $2,000 bonds."

Miller was unable to find anyone to raise another $2000 bond for him, and he remained in jail.

Because of the intense public interest in the case, the Journal Miner printed further testimony from that same examination. From the February 28, 1894 edition:

"CONSTABLE MILLER'S EXAMINATION

The balance of the testimony given at the examination of Constable Miller will be found below:

ALBERT W. BEHAN*—I am stationed at Whipple Barracks; I was talking with Miller, and a man came in and said, "There is a job for you outside." I then walked back into the saloon with two friends; some one said "There is a scrap outside, let us go outside and see it." We went outside and saw a man with no

---

* Albert Behan was the son of lawman and fabled enemy of Wyatt Earp, John Behan.

coat or vest on or shoes. Miller told him to put his clothes on, or he would have to go with him; the man said, "No ____ ____ ____ can make me go with him." He had hold of Miller's coat, and Miller told him to let go; the man did not do so; Miller then pulled his gun, and then put it back; the fellow grabbed Miller and pushed him backwards; Miller then drew his gun and hit him twice, and as he continued to push him back there were two shots fired; I think the man had hold with the left hand.

C. N. BEATTY—I am stationed at Whipple Barracks; was in the Royal saloon with two friends; Miller came up and said, "Who of you is named Beecham?" Beecham responded, and they went to the bar; a few minutes after, a man came in and said to Miller, "You are wanted outside," then went out; some one said "There is a scrap outside," we then went out to see it; when we got out, Miller was trying to persuade a man to put on his clothes. The balance of his testimony was simply corroborative of other witnesses in regard to the shooting.

ADOLPH BLAIR—Will Martin and I went out of the Union saloon; went down the street and saw this man talking to a woman; she told him to go away, but he refused; this man was drunk; just in a fierce mood; we went to the Royal saloon, and seeing Miller told him there was some work for him outside; he said "All right," and went right out. [The conversation was again repeated by the witness.] The fellow then grabbed Miller by the coat, and Miller broke his hold and put his hand back for his gun; the fellow said, "You are a gun man, are you?" Miller said, "I am not." Miller said, "Give me some help," but I did not do anything; the man then grabbed Miller by the throat, and Miller pulled his gun and hit him; the man had something in his left hand. I think it was a knife; Miller then hit again, and as the man continued to push him back Miller shot; I did not help Miller at all; when he called for help I did not help him; I was about three feet away; he grabbed Miller with his right hand and hit at him with his left hand; he had a knife in his hand.

R. M. Ling testified to having taken an old knife out of Wallace's right hip pocket when he was lying on the sidewalk.

Lester Jackson testified to receiving the knife from Ling, and that it was taken from his right hip pocket.

The knife was introduced in evidence. It was a caseknife, about three and one-half inches long.

George Ruffner, recalled—After the shots were fired, I was the first man to reach the wounded man; the man was kind of doubled over; his hands were by his left side; Charley Sanders and I helped him up to the Mountain City drug store; it might have been a quarter of a minute before I reached the man; I heard Miller say something about fire, and I started to put out the fire.

L. C. MILLER, called for the defense—Last Saturday night I was constable of Prescott precinct; I shot a man on that night; I was going to Charles Wallace's saloon to find a man who stole an overcoat; there was a man lying in a door, three doors south of Wallace's saloon; the woman Castro asked me to get him out; I told him to get up, dress and behave himself; he said, "Who the h_ll are you?" I said, "I am an officer," some conversation took place; I went on down to Wallace's saloon and went through a soldier to see if he had a gun on; I tried to find Frank McQuilliken, to see if he could identify this drunk, in the door, spoken of before; while in the saloon, Adolph Blair came in and said "You are wanted outside," I went out and this man was on the walk, cursing and making a noise; I told him he must stop or I would run him in if he did not. He said I could not do so; the man grabbed me by the coat; I could not make him let go; I drew my gun, then put it back; he said, "You are a ___ ___ __ __ of gun man, are you?" I said, "No, I am not, but I have a right to carry a gun." He then grabbed me by the throat, and he struck at me; I thought he had a knife in his hand; I put my hand up to push him off, and with the other drew my gun. I said to Blair, "Dolph, I want your assistance." No one came to my assistance; I struck at this man twice with my gun, and I know I hit him once; I dropped my hand that held the gun; I was bent clear back and I fired twice about as fast as a man could fire a single action gun; I staggered off the walk, and as soon as I could get my wind I told Blair to put out the fire; whether he did or not I don't know. I walked up around the block and there was a big crowd around the drug store; I kept the crowd back; I helped take the man to the hospital, and then came back with Deputy Sheriff Ruffner. The man seemed to be in a very dangerous state of mind before I shot him; the gun used has a 44-caliber Smith and Wesson double-action. [Marks on throat and cut in vest were shown by defendant.] I saw a knife in the wounded man's pocket while he was at the drug store; R. M. Ling took it out of his pocket; I did not stay around more than a minute; I turned to the crowd and said, "You fellows saw this, didn't you?" They said, "Yes." The cut was not in my vest prior to the shooting.

So which account was true? Even today, the various conflicting statements are confusing, and it is unlikely the truth will ever be known for certain. The *Prescott Courier*, however, was buoyed by certain witnesses corroborating their account of the shooting, and they proceeded to lash out at their journalistic nemesis, the *Journal Miner*. From the February 23, 1894 edition of the *Courier*:

In its issue of the 19th, under the title of 'Shot Down', the Journal-Miner, upon the unsworn statements of two unnamed witnesses, tried, convicted, and condemned Constable Miller for shooting Wallace last Saturday night, reaching the conclusion that without justification Miller had shot a hopelessly drunken man. The motive is immaterial; the result of the publication, uncontradicted, will be of incalculable damage to Miller in causing the community to prejudge his conduct, harmfully and unjustly to him, hence follows a careful, conservative statement of the facts as sworn to by three soldiers, five civilians, two deputy sheriffs, and two women at the preliminary examination yesterday before Justice Moore, all introduced by the prosecution, and ignoring entirely the statement made by Miller:

About nine o'clock Saturday night, a man named Wallace, tolerably drunk, was lying on the floor of Maria Castro's room, near the (illegible) door, exposed to passers by, without shoes, hat, coat, or vest, because, as he said, he was tired and sleepy. Maria tried to induce him to leave; he refused, whereupon she said that if he did not leave she would call an officer and have him put out. He said that neither she nor the officers could put him out, whereupon the woman stood in the open door, complained of the man's presence, and upon inquiry of Officer Miller informed him that she wanted the man put out. Miller spoke to the man; he jumped up and wanted to know what Miller had to do with it; was told by Miller that he was an officer and that if he did not come out of there, put on his clothes and behave himself, he would be arrested. He then defied and denounced Miller, but came out, went to the edge of the sidewalk and puked.

His clothes were handed out of the door and it was closed, and Miller left.

Immediately thereafter, Wallace, in a loud, boisterous, disorderly and obscene manner, without shoes, hat, coat, or vest, stood on the public street, near the woman's door, and said that he would kick in the door, kill the woman, burn up the house, and damned the officer villainously.

Two men passed by, and, fearing that he would harm the woman, and seeing his disorderly condition and conduct, hunted for an officer and found Miller about fifty feet away, in Wallace's* saloon, and told him of Wallace's actions and sayings, and asked his arrest. Miller, followed by about five men, including three soldiers, went out to arrest Wallace. Miller weighs about 150 pounds, Wallace is a powerful man of 190 pounds.

As Miller approached Wallace, he was still talking and acting and clad as before, and Miller told him that unless he put on his shoes, got off the streets and behaved himself, he would arrest him. Wallace asked Miller, "Who are you?", Miller replied, "I'm an officer, as I have already told you." Wallace refused to put on his clothes and leave the street, but started back towards the woman's door, abused Miller, calling him a son of a b_____, and saying that neither he nor all of the d_____d officers in Prescott could arrest him. Miller prevented his going towards the woman's door, and said, "I'll run you in." Wallace then caught Miller by the coat. Miller tried to loosen his hold, but could not. Miller pulled his pistol, and then Wallace's hold gave way and he said to Miller, "You son of a b_____, you are one of those gun men, are you?", Miller replied, "Yes, I am", "Yes—no," the witnesses differing as to this, and Miller's statement being counted.

Miller then placed his pistol in his scabbard, whereupon—some said with his right, others said with his left—hand, Wallace viciously and violently grabbed Miller by the throat, cursing and denouncing him, and telling that he could not arrest him, pushing toward the edge of the sidewalk, near a post. Miller tried to loosen his hold, pulled his pistol and struck him certainly once, probably twice, possibly three times over the head, but it did not cause him to release his grip from Miller's throat. He was getting the better of Miller all of the time. While holding Miller by the throat, Wallace struck at Miller, had something in his hand which looked like a knife. Miller called on the bystanders to help him arrest the men, after he had struck him and while the man was still choking him, and getting no assistance, and being about to fall backward from the choking, and having his wind nearly shut off by Wallace, fired two shots rapidly through Wallace's body, whereupon Wallace released his hold, groaned, had the fire on his burning garments put out, walked about 50 yards between two men and then was carried to the drug store, and there a strong case knife, about two inches of blade gone, well whetted and sharpened, was taken from his right hand hip pocket.

On Miller's throat are the physical marks of violence, the same on his left hand, on the left side of his vest below his left nipple a cut in his vest about one inch long.

At both interviews between Miller and Wallace, the former's conduct was civil and courteous, and he tried to persuade the man to put on his clothes, behave himself and avoid arrest; the latter's conduct was violent, disorderly, and refusing to be arrested, and his language was very abusive, obscene, and insulting.

---

* The saloon owner was Charles Wallace, presumably unrelated to John Wallace, the drunk.

> Miller was in the sheriff's custody within twenty minutes after the shooting, of his own volition.
> The above statement is simple justice to Miller and is due the community. Let justice be done though the heavens fall.

The journalistic war of words continued. The *Journal Miner* wasted no time in firing back. The February 28, 1894 edition ran a column which opened with a quote from the *Courier* piece, and then continued:

> Following the above is a column or more purporting to be testimony taken at the examination. Some of the assertions made never appeared during the examination.
> The Journal-Miner has no desire to enter into a discussion over this affair, but since forced to do so by the Courier it will defend the position assumed after a full, thorough and impartial investigation of the affair.
> It even goes further than its contemporary, as it not only gives a synopsis of all the testimony against Miller, but gives that of himself and witnesses also. The testimony of the several witnesses differs but little, except as to the presence of a knife, and the witness who testified to Wallace having a knife previously said that he did not see any. Four or five other witnesses as close to Miller's victim, and whose eyesight was equally as good as his, swear that he had no knife. Miller himself did not swear positively that he had.
> Circumstances prove conclusively that he had no knife in his hand. The witness who testifies to it says it was in his left hand. It must have been there when this man was shot according to this man's testimony. Every sane man knows it was a physical impossibility for him to have gotten that knife from his left hand around to his right hand hip pocket after being shot before he was reached by Deputy Sheriff Ruffner.
> The entire testimony resolves itself down to a plain proposition.
> The man was almost helplessly drunk. Miller tried to arrest him. The man resisted. Five or six men according to Miller's testimony were standing near. A deputy sheriff was within forty or fifty feet and would have come to Miller's rescue if he had called for help. All those present except one testify that he did not ask for help. Is an officer justified under these circumstances in shooting a man down?
> The Journal-Miner holds human life too sacred a thing to be taken or to be even attempted under such circumstances. An officer must not expect a drunken man to implicitly obey his command, and an officer who will shoot, under the circumstances, as detailed by the testimony taken at this examination, is not competent to fill the position. Constable Miller should be removed from office and disarmed.

Throughout the confusing details, and despite the fact that the *Courier*'s version of the story sounds convincing, the *Journal Miner* did raise a very excellent point that rings truer today than it did in 1894—in historical retrospect, it is impossible to believe that Deputy Sheriff George C. Ruffner, within earshot, would not have come to Miller's aid if Miller had indeed started screaming for help.

In the same edition, the *Journal Miner* also thundered:

A person who reads the evidence introduced at the examination of Miller can see strong symptoms of perjury in a portion of it. It will probably be the subject of a legal investigation, as it certainly should be. When one goes on the witness stand and swears "to tell the truth, the whole truth and nothing but the truth", he should suffer the penalty of any deviation from it.

From the same edition:

Constable Miller had not given bonds at a late hour this afternoon.

From the same edition:

The condition of the man shot on Saturday night by Constable Miller continues favorable for recovery.

From the same edition:

Dr. Davis says his patient, Wallace, is improving daily, and may recover. The doctor is an experienced person on gun-shot wounds, and has an excellent reputation in this line of his calling.

Also in the same edition, the *Journal Miner* reprinted a comment on the case from the *Mohave County Miner*, and proceeded to comment on it:

The Courier and the Journal Miner do not view the shooting of John Wallace by Constable Miller, at Prescott last Saturday night, in the same light. The Courier says the shooting was justifiable, and the Journal Miner says that it was unjustifiable. The evidence given before the preliminary examination was in favor of Miller."—Mohave Miner. The man who penned the above is always consistent in one thing, and that is in his inconsistency. The testimony introduced at the above examination was very similar in its character to that introduced at the examination of George Blaine, in Mohave county, for shooting a drunken man. In the latter case, the Miner was very pronouncedly in favor of hanging Blaine.

John Wallace did recover. From the March 7, 1894 *Journal Miner*:

John Wallace, who was shot by Constable Miller, is recovering.

From the *Journal Miner*, March 28, 1894:

Jack Wallace, who was shot by Constable Miller, is able to be around again.

Up to this point, Miller was luckier than he was smart.

Chapter 6: L. C. Miller and Cornelia Sarata

Things were much different in 19th century Arizona than they are today, even in legal proceedings. Grand juries were only empaneled at certain times of the year, at which times they examined the cases of everyone who had been arrested in the preceding months to determine if a "true bill," or indictment, was in order. Consequently, it was not until June that a grand jury got around to the two charges of attempted murder lodged against Louis C. Miller. In the District Court column of the *Journal Miner* (which reported all of the court's doings) on June 13, 1894, the paper referred to the June 6 presentation of the Grand Jury's presentation to the court, excerpted as follows:

> Territory vs. L. C. Miller; charge ignored in the Archibald shooting, and case dismissed, but defendant held to answer on another charge of assault to commit murder on Wallace.
> Territory vs. L. C. Miller; arraigned at 2 p.m.

In retrospect, it is astounding that the Grand Jury refused to indict Miller for shooting Miles Archibald, but did so in the Wallace assault. The evidence against Miller in the Archibald case was, if anything, stronger than the evidence in the Wallace incident. In reporting this development, the *Prescott Courier* kept up its drumbeat of support for Miller, writing on June 8, 1894:

> The first charge against Constable Miller was ignored by the grand jury. He was indicted on the second charge of assault to commit murder. Miller was one of the most ambitious young peace officers this section has ever had; he was ever on the alert to do what he considered his duty, and his last trouble was brought on by rushing in when called upon for assistance, where an old hand at the business would have turned his back with the mental reservation that "they are a tough crowd and I will let them fight it out." Miller is a young man without means, and has been in jail for months under a heavy bond.

And what about Miles Archibald? The *Courier*, predictably ignored him from this point, no doubt due to publisher Edward A. Rogers' obvious friendship to Miller. But in the ensuing months, the *Journal Miner* gave periodic updates on his recovery. He left for San Francisco where he clearly felt there were better physicians. His mother accompanied him, while his sisters remained in Prescott. From the *Journal Miner*, June 20, 1894:

> Miles Archibald, who is now in San Francisco, consulting eminent medical men in the hope of having his arm restored to usefulness again, writes that he will enter a well known hospital there and submit to an operation. He has secured the services of two surgeons, and states further that they insure his permanent relief, although the operation will be a very painful and trying one on him, but without danger, necessarily.

From the *Journal Miner*, June 27, 1894:

A letter was received by Miss Sadie Archibald last evening from her mother in which the latter speaks very hopefully of the condition of her son, Miles. The doctors, on an examination of his old wound, discovered that the motor nerve had not been cut, but had been pinned down to the flesh and muscles, by the ball, and they state that he will regain the use of his arm again, within a month or two. His many friends here will rejoice to learn this encouraging news.

From the *Journal Miner*, July 4, 1894:

Another letter was received today from Mrs. Archibald in which she states that the condition of Miles is quite serious. Since having the operation performed he has been troubled with congestion of the lungs accompanied by spitting of blood. The attending physician however still gives her assurance that he will get along all right.

From the *Journal Miner*, July 18, 1894:

A letter was received to-day by F. E. Andrews from Miles Archibald in San Francisco, which stated that the latter had sufficiently recovered from the recent operation performed on him to permit his removal from the hospital to private rooms. He also stated that while very weak still, he was rapidly gaining strength and that the use of his left arm, he believed, would again be given him soon.

From the *Journal Miner* of August 1, 1894:

Miles Archibald was recovered the slight use of his arm again. He can now raise it to his head and can bend his elbow.

From the *Journal Miner*, September 12, 1894:

Miles Archibald is slowly recovering the use of his arm under treatment in San Francisco, but as yet he cannot move his fingers.

In the archives of the Sharlot Hall Museum in Prescott, there is a file on Miles Archibald, consisting mostly of some (not all) of the news clippings reprinted here. In this folder, some anonymous filer from years back has scribbled that Archibald was a "morphine fiend" who never returned to Prescott. I have seen no evidence to support or deny the first charge (personally, I doubt its veracity), but it is patently untrue that he never returned to Prescott.

From the *Journal Miner*, September 26, 1894:

Mrs. J. W. Archibald and her son Miles returned to-day from San Francisco. The latter's condition is improving, and he expects soon to have the use of his arm again.

Miles Archibald participated in the Yavapai County Republican Convention that October. From a long, detailed summary of convention activities that appeared in the October 16, 1894 *Journal Miner* was this notation:

> For recorder, Samuel Hubbard named Joseph I. Roberts, and Miles C. Archibald nominated F. A. Tritle. The ballot resulted as follows: Roberts 34, Tritle 27.

Still, Archibald's arm did not seem to recover as quickly as doctors had hoped. Some time later, from the *Journal Miner* of May 20, 1896:

> Deputy Recorder Archibald left yesterday for San Francisco, where he goes to have an operation performed on his wounded arm, it being the intention of his physicians to break several fingers of his left hand and by which they agree to restore the full use of that member.

From the *Journal Miner* of June 3, 1896:

> Miles Archibald has written a letter to his mother, saying that the doctor would perform the first operation on his hand on last Monday. Another operation will be performed in two weeks, and the physician attending him is very hopeful of greater beneficial results, giving him greater use of his arm and hand.

As we shall see also, accounts of the Parker jailbreak noted that Archibald was on the street near the Courthouse when it happened. Later, he would also be hired to participate in the deathwatch on Parker.

I have been unable to ascertain with any certainty whether Archibald ever fully recovered the use of his left arm. Whether he did or whether he did not, he lived a long active life. With that, we shall leave him for now and return to the main subjects of this book. We will pick up Archibald's denouement in Chapter 10.

The trial of Louis C. Miller for "Assault with intent to Murder" commenced shortly after his formal indictment. Attorney T. W. Johnston represented Miller. The case papers have survived, including the indictments, subpoenas, and requested jury instructions from both the prosecution and defense, which will not be reprinted here due to space considerations. The *Journal Miner* reported on June 20, 1894:

> There was a large attendance of spectators in the district court room this afternoon, the occasion being the trial of L. C. Miller for shooting Wallace.

From the same edition:

> Territory vs. L. C. Miller; assault to commit murder: the following jury was impaneled to try the case, and the trial was commenced at 2 p.m.:

Frank Genung*, P. W. Strahan, Z. T. Stone, Fred Plumb, F. H. Lamb, John A. Bryant, C. L. Parker, P. V. Springer, Henry Johnson, J. C. Forest, W. C. Atkinson, W.A. Heisler.

The transcript of the trial has sadly not survived in the case papers. In those days, while transcripts of testimony were written down, they were not saved unless it seemed likely that a defendant would appeal his conviction to a higher court (which, believe it or not, was not as common then as it is today). If such an appeal did materialize, the transcripts were given to the appellate court to show that the defendant had indeed received a fair trial. If there was no appeal, the transcripts were apparently tossed.

It is virtually certain, however, that Miller's attorneys pleaded self-defense, as Miller had done at his preliminary examination. The jury obviously bought the story, as they acquitted him with very little deliberation.

The *Arizona Journal Miner*, undoubtedly burned by this turn of events, gave it as little attention as possible, noting only briefly, in their June 20, 1894 edition:

> The jury in the Miller case retired this afternoon to deliberate. They brought in a verdict of acquittal soon after.

The *Prescott Courier*, naturally, gloated over the verdict:

> Constable Miller is again a free man. A jury of 12 intelligent and just Americans decided that he was not guilty as charged.

As for John Wallace, who obviously recovered from the gunshot wound, nothing further is known of him. Railroad workers and drunks were a dime a dozen in most towns of the era, and most of them drifted from town to town, moving on eventually. Wallace most likely did the same. He may well be buried somewhere in America under his own name, but without any further data on who he was and where he originally came from, it is virtually impossible to trace his movements following his shooting.

One final, irreverent note regarding Marie Castro, the prostitute at the center of the Miller-Wallace shooting. The June 20, 1894 *Journal Miner* reported the following incident:

> Marie Castro amused herself by smashing in some windows on Granite street. Later in the day she amused Justice Moore by paying $20 for her fun, that being the value of it according to his estimate.

Well, if you were trying to quietly sell your "wares" and were suddenly thrust into the county wide glare because of a shooting incident, it might make you a little crazy, too.

---

* Juror Frank Genung was the son of legendary Yavapai County pioneer, miner, and Indian scout Charles Genung.

One side note to all of this—while Constable Miller was fighting these attempted murder indictments, he was also being sued! There was no mention of it in the newspapers, but court papers have survived which show that around January 5, 1894, around the same time he had shot Miles Archibald, Miller seized a shipment of furniture belonging to one W.E. Hall, and refused to release it! Why he did so is not known—maybe the impetuous young lawman thought he had uncovered a furniture-smuggling ring? The complaint in the suit of W.E. Hall vs. L.C. Miller reads:

> The Plaintiff in the above entitled action, complaining of the defendant in said action, alleges:
> That on the fifth day of January 1894, Said plaintiff was the (illegible) and entitled to the immediate possession of the following goods and Chattel, of the value of—to wit, one wardrobe of the value of $10.00, one chair 50c, one bed (illegible) $3.00, two blankets $5.00, one pillow and sheet $3.00, one clock $2.57, one lamp $2.50, one (illegible) $10.00, one trunk $2.50, one glass $1.00, one mattress $2.00—All of the value of forty-two dollars.
> That the defendant, without the consent of said plaintiff, now detains such goods and chattel from the possession of said Plaintiff.
> That before the commencement of this action, to wit: On the 19th day of January A.D. 1894, the Plaintiff duly demanded of this defendant possession of said goods and chattel. But to deliver the possession thereof the defendant refused, and still refuses.
> That said defendant still unlawfully withholds and detains said goods and chattel from the possession of the Plaintiff, to his damage in the sum of forty-two $42. dollars the value of said property, and the further sum of twenty dollars for detention thereof.
> Wherefore, the Plaintiff demands judgment against the defendant for the (illegible) of the possession of said goods and chattel, or for the sum of forty-two dollars, the value thereof, in case a delivery cannot be had, together with twenty dollars damages for detention thereof, and costs of suit.
> John Howard
Atty. For Plaintiff

Robert E. Morrison assisted John Howard in representing W.E. Hall. Miller had the same attorneys, Harris Baldwin and T.W. Johnston, for this suit as he did for the shooting incidents. They filed for dismissal of the suit, but incredibly, this bizarre case went to trial on February 3, 1894 in Justice Court of Prescott Precinct, in front of Justice of the Peace Henry W. Fleury, and a jury which included Ed Hoagland.

It did not take the jury long to find in favor of Hall, and Miller was ordered to either release the furniture or pay Hall the amount it was worth. Miller refused to do either and defiantly told the Court he planned an appeal. However, two of the young Constable's friends, A.J. Head and Robert Burmister (both very prominent citizens in

Prescott) decided they had better save Miller from himself. They paid Hall the amount the jury had awarded him, and the case was dismissed.

So.....what was that all about????

Having beaten the rap for both shootings, Constable Louis C. Miller returned to his duties, which once again included the usual rinky-dink arrests, and menial assignments.

From the *Journal Miner* of July 11, 1894:

> Constable Miller arrested a colored woman last night on a charge of malicious mischief. She is accused of breaking the windows in a house belonging to G. Hathaway.

From the *Prescott Courier* of August 3, 1894:

> Constable Miller, accompanied by Wm. Linn and Clarence Howell, returned yesterday from the line of the live railroad, where they have been guarding bridges.

From the *Journal Miner* of August 8, 1894 (remember, this was a weekly issue):

> William Linn, L.C. Miller and Clarence Howell returned today from doing duty on the Prescott railroad, guarding bridges. J.M. Dodson and Joseph Engle remained there. They have been out since July 13.

From the *Courier* of August 16, 1894:

> Constable Miller arrested two bloods who were beating an old Frenchman yesterday. They are out under $100. bonds each.

From the *Arizona Journal Miner* of August 29, 1894:

> Constable Miller arrested a railroader this morning for battering up a French woman last night. Justice Fleury arbitrated the matter and enriched the county twenty dollars.

From the *Courier* of September 7, 1894:

> Constable Miller returned from the Middle Verde country yesterday, which section he reports flooded with water, but very slight damage done.

From the *Journal Miner* of September 12, 1894:

> Constable Miller returned last evening from Weaver, having in custody Francisco Contreras, who was charged with assault with a deadly weapon. The latter had his examination to-day and was discharged, there being no evidence to hold him.

And, in a dispatch that evokes its era better than almost anything, the *Courier* reported on September 21, 1894:

> Constable Miller arrested two female Gila Monsters for using obscene language. Judge Fleury fined them $10 each, which was paid.

But Miller was ambitious, and his victories in court had boosted his ego considerably. Shortly before the Yavapai County Republican Convention in October, L. C. Miller announced his candidacy for Sheriff. His announcement "card" appeared in the September 26, 1894 *Journal Miner*, while the *Courier* continued its love affair with Miller by writing on September 21, 1894:

> Constable Miller announces himself as a candidate for the nomination for Sheriff, subject to the action of the republican convention. Miller has the record of a good and fearless officer to his credit. He is in all probability the strongest man yet announced on the republican side of the house.

But memories of the Archibald-Wallace shootings had not faded from public memory in so short a time, and there is no evidence that Miller for Sheriff aroused any serious interest. At the Republican Convention, he withdrew from the race in favor of a more popular nominee, and ran instead for re-election as Constable. From the *Courier* of October 5, 1894:

> Constable Miller, W. H. Hall, and Wm. De Witt were candidates for sheriff. The latter two were placed in nomination, Miller having previously withdrawn in favor of Hall. Hall received 48 votes and De Witt 37. Hall was declared the nominee.

From the same edition:

> Louis Miller, Jake Webber, and John Fitch were placed in nomination for constables. Miller and Webber were declared the nominees.

Strangely enough, although both papers would carry detailed County election results in November, the race for Constable was not mentioned, and I have not located records elsewhere either. Apparently the results were not considered that important, since Constable was such a minor law enforcement position. However, Miller disappeared from view after that, so, in the face of no surviving documentation to the contrary, I am concluding at this point that Miller was defeated by whoever the Democrats put up for the position (whose candidacy was also strangely unrecorded by the press).

Democrat George C. Ruffner defeated Republican W. H. Hall for Sheriff (owing to newspapers typos, this could possibly be the same Hall who sued Louis C. Miller over furniture a couple of years earlier). In context, it must be noted that while Yavapai County is a solid Republican block today, the Democrats ran the show in the late 19th century, and it stayed that way until the early 1960s.

While on trial for the shootings of Miles Archibald and John Wallace, Louis C. Miller had hired Harris Baldwin and T.W. Johnston as his attorneys and agreed to pay them $375.00. He paid them $75.00 at some point, but never paid off the rest of his legal bill, so Baldwin and Johnston sued him! Only the court papers survive—upon being served with the suit on June 1, 1896, Miller must have come up with the money somehow, for the suit was withdrawn shortly after it was filed.

The Rock-Cut train robbery and Jim Parker's arrest had already occurred when Louis C. Miller resurfaced in April of 1897, out of work and out of money. He apparently got drunk one night and decided to obtain money the easy way—by stealing it. He forged and cashed a check in the name of his old friend J. R. "Ralph" Dillon, and then fled Prescott. The *Arizona Journal Miner* picked up the story on April 28, 1897:

> L. C. Miller, a former constable of Prescott, was arrested in Tucson yesterday by Sheriff Ruffner, charged with forgery. The particular act alleged against him is the passing of a check calling for $50 at one of the saloons in Prescott, the check having what purported to be the signature of J. R. Dillon, of Jerome. On presentation of it at the bank, it was pronounced a forgery, and a warrant was immediately issued for Miller's arrest.
>
> A peculiar feature of the case is that Miller went into a certain business house in town, and called for paper and ink, saying he wanted to do some writing. The writing material was furnished, and he was asked if he wanted paper, when he replied "No, I have paper." He went to a table and sat down, pulled a slip of paper out of his pocket and commenced writing, and shortly afterwards took the slip of paper in his hand and held it up in front of him in the presence of the party giving him the pen and ink, and read it, and then passed out. The party in the store who noticed the operation remarked after he went out, that he believed Miller had forged a check, but the person he made the remark to laughed at him, and nothing more was said.
>
> It is thought that he was intending to go to Mexico, but was overtaken before he reached the line.

From the same edition:

> Sheriff Ruffner returned from the south last night, having in custody L. C. Miller, charged with forgery. When arrested at Tucson, the officers report that he offered to pay the amount of the check that he forged—$50., if they would let him go. Of course, this offer was refused. He had about $60 on his person when arrested. His destination was Minas Prietas, in Mexico. He was accompanied by another man from Prescott. The money was garnished in the hands of the sheriff by the party who cashed the check.

The criminal complaint against Miller, presumably filed by the banker who took the check, reads as follows:

> In the Justice's Court of Prescott Precinct, Yavapai County, Arizona.
> Territory of Arizona,
> Vs.
> L. C. Miller
> W. A. Cline being first duly sworn, deposes and says; that the defendant L. C. Miller is guilty of the crime of forgery, committed as follows, to-wit:
> That at the County of Yavapai, Territory of Arizona on the 10th. Day of April, 1897, the said defendant, L. C. Miller did falsely and feloniously, make, forge and counterfeit a certain writing on paper, the tenor, purport and effect whereof is as follows:
> Prescott, Arizona, Apr. 19th. 1897, No._____
> THE PRESCOTT NATIONAL BANK,
> Pay to the order of L. C. Miller $50.00
> Fifty Dollars _____ 50,00 Dollars.
> Ralph Dillon,"
> And endorsed on the back thereof his name as follows; "L. C. Miller," with the intent to defraud the said Ralph Dillon, The Prescott National Bank, a corporation organized under the laws of the United States, and the affiant.
> Contrary to the form and effect of the statute in such case made and provided, and against the peace and dignity of the Territory of Arizona.
> W. A. Cline
> Subscribed and sworn to before me this 20th. day of April, 1897.
> Donald Campbell
> Justice of the Peace.

The April 28, 1897 edition of the *Journal Miner* reported on Miller's preliminary examination:

> The examination of L. C. Miller on a charge of forgery took place today before Justice Campbell and resulted in his being held to answer to the grand jury under bonds in the sum of $500. At a late hour this afternoon, the bond had not been given.

The *Prescott Courier* was not so quick to rush to Miller's support this time. They reported on the examination in this manner:

> Justice Campbell held L. C. Miller in $500 to appear before the grand jury. Miller is said to have remarked that some others were liable to suffer along with him. His remark kept all present guessing as to who he referred to, and what those referred to had been guilty of.

The surviving court papers from the examination read as follows:

> In Justice Court Prescott Precinct
> Yavapai County Arizona

> Territory of Arizona
>   Vs
> L. C. Miller
>
> Criminal complaint sworn to by W. A. Cline charging L. C. Miller with crime of forgery. The (illegible) of the forged check is as follows.
>
> Prescott Arizona April 19th, 1897   No.
> The Prescott National Bank
> Pay to the order of L. C. Miller $50.00
> Fifty dollars $50.00   Dollars
>   Ralph Dillon
>
> Defendant brought into court and the charges read to him, and he was advised of his right to employ counsel and the hearing in the was set for the 26th of April 1897 at 11 o'clock.
>
> Case came on for hearing, both Parties answering ready; the following witnesses were sworn and testified for the Territory: J. R. Dillon, W. A. Cline, Ed Shummate, whereupon the Territory rested its case. Defendant being asked if he wished to make any statement answered no, and being further asked if he had any evidence to offer in his own behalf again answered no, whereupon the case closed.
>
> The Court being fully advised as to the law and the evidence being fully convinced of the guilt of the defendant as charged in the complaint held him to await the action of the Grand Jury on a bond of $500.00 and committed him to the care of the sheriff of Yavapai County.
>
>   Donald Campbell
>   Justice Peace
>
> This is a true transcript of the proceedings in this case as recorded in my docket.
>   Donald Campbell
>   Justice Peace

It must be presumed that Shummate was the store clerk who witnessed Miller forge the check. Miller's previously mentioned companion in Tucson was never identified, and clearly not indicted.

And so, it was this simple forgery charge that placed Louis C. Miller in the Yavapai County jail with Parker when the latter made his break for freedom. As he probably would have drawn a fairly light sentence, it is not known why Miller participated in the jailbreak. In fact, as shall be seen, he would later be accused of planning the act. It must therefore be attributed to his already documented impulsiveness, fiery temper, and a clear determination to avoid going to prison at any cost.

The November 4, 1896 *Arizona Journal Miner* contained a very small, insignificant news item that read as follows:

> A Mexican, whose name was not learned, it is alleged, fired two shots at a saloon keeper named Stephens, at Crowned King, recently, and a warrant has been issued for his arrest.

The young man's name was Cornelia Sarata (there have been many variations of the spelling of his name both at the time and in subsequent years), and he was a member of the American West's beleaguered Mexican population. It is not widely remembered, and rarely addressed by historians, but Hispanics lived under almost the same conditions of separation, revulsion, and social servitude that Blacks were enduring in the Deep South at the time.

The attitudes of the times are reflected by the newspapers of the era. Week after week, month after month, year after year, the press regaled the reading public with countless crimes allegedly committed by Mexicans, far too many to be believable today. Undoubtedly, some of the accused men were guilty, while others no doubt had the misfortune to be in the wrong place at the wrong time when a crime was committed, and got the blame because of it.

Nothing is known of the background of Cornelia Sarata. In those days, births and marriages of Mexicans were not recorded. Deaths were only recorded by the counties in cases of accidents, murders, or other questionable events. Mexicans were not allowed to hold elective office in most areas, and were not allowed to pursue "respectable" careers in cities. Newspaper coverage of Mexican activities was almost always limited to negative reports of crime, drunkenness, and other ill behavior. Prescott and Yavapai County were not exceptions.

The criminal complaint against Sarata, sworn out by saloon owner P. Stephens, reads:

In the Justice's Court
    Prescott Precinct, County of Yavapai, Territory of Arizona.
    The Territory of Arizona,
    Plaintiff,   }
        Vs.   }
    Cornelia Sarata,   }
    Mexican Defendant }
Personally appeared before me, this 29th day of October, 1896 P. Stephens who being first duly sworn, complains and says: That one Cornelia Sarata, a Mexican, on or about the 27th day of October 1896, in Yavapai Precinct, County and Territory aforesaid, committed a felony as follows, to-wit:

The said defendant did unlawfully and feloniously make an assault upon the said P. Stephens with a deadly weapon, commonly called six shooter. Said six shooter being there and then loaded and charged with gunpowder and divers leaden bullets. The same being there and then a weapon likely to (illegible) great bodily injury. All of which is contrary to the form of the Statute in such case made and provided and against the peace and dignity of the Territory of Arizona.
                                                            P. Stephens
Subscribed and sworn to before me, this 29th day of October 1896
                                                            J. M. W. Moore
                                                            Justice of the Peace of said
                                                              Precinct

As the shooting incident was considered no big deal, Prescott's newspapers did not even report on Sarata's eventual arrest, but his surviving court papers show that Yavapai County Sheriff George C. Ruffner caught up with him in Globe on December 22nd, 1896. Ruffner continued his reputation of tracking down any lawbreaker no matter how far away they went. Under arrest, Sarata was brought back to Prescott and lodged in jail.

For reasons no longer clear, Cornelia Sarata's preliminary examination did not take place immediately. Eventually, the *Journal Miner* reported on February 3, 1897:

> A Mexican named Cornelia had his preliminary examination today before Justice Moore, on a charge of assault with intent to commit murder, and was held to appear before the grand jury, with bail fixed at $300. The alleged crime was committed at the Crowned King mine last fall.

Nothing further is known of Stephens. Cornelia Sarata had not yet been brought to trial at the time of the jailbreak.

Why did Sarata participate in the jailbreak? Attempted murder was a serious offence, and guilty or not, he undoubtedly knew he didn't stand much of a chance in the white man's court. He probably felt he had nothing to lose—he had no way of foreseeing that the break would result in one of the most notorious murders in Yavapai County history. Ironically, as shall be seen, he would be the only one to truly succeed in escaping, one way or the other.

CHAPTER 7

Jailbreak and the Second Posse

Even though train robbery was legally punishable by death in the Arizona Territory, the sentence was never imposed on anyone for such a crime. Parker would have almost certainly drawn a fairly light sentence—maybe five years with the probability of parole. So why did he risk his future by breaking out of jail?

Parker would later claim that he did so because his attorney, E. M. Sanford, was taking his money and preparing an inadequate defense on the train robbery charge (a ridiculous excuse—even if it were true, Parker was still not looking at the gallows). More likely, Parker had been in prison twice before in his life, and he was determined not to go back again.

The May 9, 1897 jailbreak in Prescott is what Parker remains best known for today. Like everything else he touched, it turned into a disaster. The *Arizona Journal Miner* recorded the horrifying details. From the May 12, 1897 weekly edition:

DESPERATE JAIL BREAK THIS AFTERNOON!

Train Robber Parker, L. C. Miller and a Mexican Escape From the County Jail at One O'Clock—Jailor R. W. Meador Overpowered by Them When They Request a Bucket of Water

---

Lee Norris, Who Comes to Meador's Assistance, Shot Down by Parker, with a Charge from a Shot Gun—Horses Secured from Sheriff Ruffner's Stable to Make Their Escape.
(From Our Extra of Sunday Afternoon.)

One of the most daring jail breaks ever attempted by desperate men was successfully made at 1 o'clock this afternoon from the county jail.

It was accomplished by the probable fatal wounding of Lee Norris, assistant district attorney of the county, and brother of T. G. Norris.

At the hour above named the prisoners in the jail called Jailor R. W. Meador, stating that they wanted a bucket of water. Meador opened the jail door, permitting a Mexican, who was confined on a charge of attempted murder, at Crowned King, to pass out with the bucket, to secure the water. No sooner had he passed outside

The South side of the Courthouse in Prescott, Arizona. It is this side that the three escaped prisoners were believed to have exited from. This building no longer stands, although a different large courthouse remains on the same site. (Courtesy of Sharlot Hall Museum)

of the door, and before Meador had a chance to close it than he grappled the jailor and prevented him from closing the door. Meador screamed for help and fought desperately with the Mexican to free himself from his iron grasp, and to prevent the other prisoners from escaping. In the tussle the Mexican wrested the big key from Meador's hand and dealt him a murderous blow on the head causing a severe scalp wound from which the blood poured in torrents.

While the struggle between the Mexican and Meador was in progress, Parker, charged with train robbery, and L. C. Miller, charged with forgery, made their escape from the inside. Parker went into the jailor's room adjoining the entrance and secured a double barreled shot gun, a Winchester rifle and a six shooter. Just as he came into the corridor of the jail with the weapons, Lee Norris, attracted by the cries for help from Meador, came down the stairway. On seeing the armed and desperate prisoners he must have turned to flee up stairs again and as he did so Parker discharged one barrel of the shot gun, the charge taking effect in Norris' back and in his left side.

By this time the Mexican released his hold on Meador and with Parker and Miller started to run. As they left Meador fired three shots at them, but without effect.

They went up stairs in the court house through the hall, passing out of the south door and went directly to Sheriff Ruffner's livery stable, where they held up the stable keeper and took two fine horses, one of them belonging to a man named Yeomans, of Big Bug, and the other the favorite white horse belonging to the sheriff. They did not take time to secure saddles. As they left they said to the stable keeper, "Just tell them that you saw us."

Chief of Police Prince and ex-Chief of Police Archibald, who were in front of the Corner drug store when the affair happened, rushed up to the livery stable, arriving there just as the men were mounting the horses in the yard back of the stables, but as neither of them was armed they were compelled to let them pass unmolested.

After mounting they rode down the alley, south, between Marina and Cortez streets to Carleton near Judge E. W. Wells' residence, where they rode west to Cortez street going south on that street.

Near R. Mosher's residence Miller and the Mexican, who were riding Yeoman's horse, fell off, but quickly remounted and they started over the hill in full view of hundreds of people who by this time had been attracted by the shooting and the excitement.

Fully fifty people were in the vicinity of Ruffner's stable before they left there, but as none of them were armed they were powerless to do anything to prevent their escape.

A posse was immediately organized and from fifteen to twenty men started in pursuit. W. J. Mulvenon who has had the arms of the old Prescott Grays stored at his place turned these guns over to the posse and Sam Hill furnished ammunition for them. J. D. Moore joined the posse armed with a rifle and took his blood hounds along to trail the escapes.

The key with which the Mexican struck Meador belonged to the outside door.

The plan was evidently for the Mexican to secure this key, overpower Meador and then lock him in between the outer and inner doors, secure arms from the jailor's room and escape unnoticed.

At the livery stable one of the guns taken from the jailor's room was left and another one taken from the stable.

All three of them were armed, having two rifles, a shot gun and six shooter.

Jailor Meador was alone in the sheriff's office at the time they made the request for a bucket of water, Sheriff Ruffner being in Congress and Under Sheriff Dillon and Deputy Munds being at home.

At this writing, an hour after the occurrence, Lee Norris' wounds are not considered as dangerous as was at first thought as the gun was loaded with bird shot instead of buck shot. He is resting easy and the physicians have hopes of his rallying. The other cartridges belonging to the gun were opened and all found to contain buck shot, by some unaccountable accident this one alone having been charged with small shot.

Sunday's Journal-Miner Extra was eagerly sought and read by all.

Yavapai County had been the scene of a number of grisly crimes over the years, but the populace of Prescott had never seen anything like this before. It was the subject of almost all conversation that afternoon.

Deputy District Attorney Erasmus Lee Norris, brother of Thomas G. Norris who had represented the Territory at Parker's preliminary examination, had the bad fortune to be in the wrong place at the wrong time. In the heat of the action, Parker had simply gunned him down without batting an eye. We shall return to this.

From the same edition:

PURSUIT OF THE OUTLAWS!

Deputy Munds and Horace Yeomans Overtake Them on Lynx Creek and in a Fight Wound Lew Miller

---

The Mexican Deserts the Other Two.
The Posse Hot on Their Trail Today Going Towards Agua Fria.

From Monday's Daily

An extra issued from this office yesterday afternoon and published in this issue, gives details of the jail break which occurred yesterday as they were hurriedly obtained immediately after the occurrence. J. D. Moore's blood hounds were given the trail in the south part of town and followed it with unerring accuracy to the vicinity of Vincent Frost's mining camp near the head of Groom creek when they became exhausted, on account of not being used to the work, and were brought back to town.

Deputy Munds was the first to start in pursuit but lost some time in getting on the trail but when he struck it he had little difficulty in following it. He was accompanied by Horace Yeomans, the well known packer, and after a four hours ride the two men came up with the outlaws on Lynx Creek about 5 o'clock when a fight ensued resulting in the wounding of Miller. The Mexican was not with them when the posse overtook them and it is supposed that he abandoned them on the summit. Miller was riding the horse previously ridden by the Mexican when the brush with the officers took place and a shot from Yeomans' rifle brought the horse to earth, when another from Deputy Munds' rifle brought Miller down. The latter crawled behind a bush where Parker was concealed and threw up his hands as a signal that he would surrender. This action, it is said, brought forth a volley of oaths and curses from Parker's lips who denounced Miller for his lack of nerve. Parker, who was mounted on Sheriff Ruffner's white horse then drew Miller on behind him and they rode off.

The officers, previous to this engagement, had dismounted, leaving their horses some distance behind and being unable to pursue them on foot retraced their steps to their animals, which were exhausted from the long hard ride and they returned to Prescott for fresh horses. After mounting fresh horses they returned and expected to be able to take the trail again this morning.

Deputy Sheriff F. E. Burt, of Ash Fork, and Deputy George Merritt, of Jerome came in on this morning's train and were provided with horses, arms and ammunition, and left about 11 o'clock this morning to join the others of the posse.

About twenty-five or thirty armed men, from Chaparral, also took the field last night.

A telephone message was received just before noon today from Chaparral, from ex-Sheriff Lowry, who is out with the posse, stating that the trail had been struck this morning leading towards Hildebrand's Ranch on the Agua Fria. Lowry's horse gave out near Green's ranch, and he went to Chaparral to secure a fresh animal, and he sent this message. He stated that when he left the posse they were on a slow trail, but he got a view of them some time afterwards, when they were all on the run. He stated that the white horse ridden by the robbers had lost a shoe, and as he gets lame easily when bare footed, it was thought they would run him down before night, unless he secured a fresh animal at one of the Agua

The only known photograph of Yavapai County Deputy District Attorney Erasmus Lee Norris, taken from an old yearbook at the University of Michigan, before he came to Arizona. (Courtesy of Gene Norris)

Fria ranches. It was the opinion of the posse that Parker had gotten rid of Miller and was alone, though the reasons they had for entertaining this opinion was not given, as no trace of Miller had been seen.

A telegram was received at the sheriff's office just before noon, stating that Deputies Fairchild and Buggelin, of Coconino county, who participated in the original pursuit and capture of Parker in February, were just leaving Winslow for the Tonto Basin country, in order to intercept Parker, should he succeed eluding the posse from here, as it now seems as if he was heading in that direction.

Otto Miller, Dolph Blair, John Fitch and Ward Pritchett were arrested yesterday afternoon, presumably in connection with the case. Later in the day, Fitch and Pritchett were released, as there was not the least shadow of evidence so far as known, to connect them with the case. Miller and Blair were still in jail this forenoon. Whether the officials have any testimony to connect them with the case can not be ascertained.

Ben Rybon, who went out with the posse yesterday afternoon, returned last night and after a few hours sleep today left this afternoon in a buggy with J. D. Moore, the latter taking his blood hounds along. They intend going to the scene of last evening's fight, for the purpose of getting the dogs on the trail, in the hope of locating Miller if the theory of his having been deserted by Parker is correct.

Lee Norris, the unfortunate victim of Parker's murderous aim, developed alarming symptoms Sunday afternoon, just after the issue of the Journal-Miner extra, when he commenced having hemorrhages. At times he seemed to rally sufficiently to inspire hope among his physicians and friends that he might rally and recover when he would be attacked with sinking spells, and hope would give way to fear. His condition was such for hours, that hope alternated with fear with those who were tenderly caring for him, until about dark, when the physicians pronounced his case hopeless, and he died just about midnight. All that medical skill on the part of his physicians and loving care on the part of his friends could suggest was done for him without avail. From the very first, he seemed to realize that his wound was a fatal one, and so stated to his friends. His brother, T. G. Norris, was called to his bed side within a few minutes after he was shot and remained with him till the end came, and is completely prostrated over his death. Before he died he requested that his body might be sent back to Green Forest, Arkansas, and buried beside his parents, and in accordance with this request, his remains are being embalmed and will be shipped on tomorrow afternoon's train.

Deceased was only 28 years old, and although he had resided here less than a year, he was universally respected and liked by all who knew him. His brother and other relatives, both here and abroad, have the most profound sympathies of the community in their sad bereavement.

Owing to the indisposition of T. G. Norris, as well as on account of his family, J. C. Herndon, his law partner, will accompany the remains east.

Funeral services will be held in Prescott tomorrow, prior to their shipment. These services will be held at the South Methodist church, West Prescott at 3 o'clock p.m.

Sheriff Ruffner, who was en route to Congress, was intercepted at Congress Junction by a telegram informing him of the affair and he secured the locomotive of the Congress Gold Company which was run to Kirkland station, on the S. F. P. & P. railway, where he caught a special stock train, arriving at Prescott about 7 o'clock. He immediately started in pursuit alone, joining other members of the posse at Lynx creek.

It is stated that the outlaws left without ammunition hence did not return the fire of the officers last evening.

The *Prescott Courier* of May 14, 1897 carried the jailbreak in this fashion:

One of the exciting incidents in the history of Prescott had its origin within the walls of the county court house yesterday. A little before 1 p.m. Jailor Meador heard the prisoners rattling the iron doors of the jail, and went down the stairs. They said they wanted water. As this was a daily occurrence about this time, Meador thought nothing of it, and as was his custom, unlocked the door and allowed Cornelius, a large Mexican, to come out with the two empty buckets, relocked the door, went on to the iron door opening into the inner hall, unlocked that and accompanied the Mexican to the well under the court house steps, where the latter drew the water, and, accompanied by Meador, who walked alongside him, re-entered the inner hall, Meador relocked the door and walked in a few feet further to the door of the jail. As Meador turned the key in the lock, the Mexican dropped both buckets of water and grappled with Jailor Meador. There was not a prisoner in sight when Meador turned the key, but the instant that Cornelius, the Mexican, grabbed him, Parker, the train robber and Louis Miller, a forger, rushed through the door, Parker leaping into the jailor's room and rushing out with shot gun in hand. Meador and the Mexican still fought. The Mexican had gotten hold of a large jail key and beat Meador over the head with it until the blood ran down Meador's face into his eyes, blinding him. Meador called loudly for help all the while, and Lee Norris started the stairs just as Parker rushed out of the jailor's room, shot gun in hand. Parker was at the foot of the stairs and Norris about half way down the stairs, when Parker, without a word, fired a load of shot into Norris, who fell heavily on the stairs. Norris had turned when Parker fired. Parker and Miller then ran up the steps passing over the prostrate body of Norris; when they were on the steps, the Mexican let loose of Meador and sprang up the stairs, followed by three shots from Meador's pistol, none of which took effect, as Meador's face and eyes were filled with blood. Meador's first care was to lock up the other prisoners and attend to the wounded man, as the alarm, had by this time, become general. Having reached the top of the stairs the prisoners dashed through the court house, with Parker in the lead, he carrying the shot gun. They made straight for Ruffner's Livery stable, and they entered the office, where Cornelius and Miller grabbed a couple of Winchester rifles and were examining them while Parker told Mr. Osborn to hurry and saddle him a horse. Osborn replied that he was not there to hurry; Parker had the muzzle of the gun in line with Osborn's body and punched Osborn twice in the ribs with the muzzle of the gun as he made Osborn and Chas. Thurbur get out of the office into the stable. While Parker urged the saddling of a horse, he noticed Sheriff Ruffner's horse standing in a stall, already saddled and immediately mounted the horse, while Cornelius and Miller got a horse out in the corral back of the stable. Parker left his hat in the livery stable office. While they were in the corral, citizens, all unarmed, gathered around the outer fence, John Lawler among them. Lawler told Miller he would kill him if he had a gun. Miller made no reply, but drew a gun on a young man named Taylor, who thereupon fell off the fence. The Mexican threatened to shoot Will Ruffner, but Parker told him to desist as Ruffner would get the horse for him. Miller and the Mexican mounted one horse and dashed out of the gate of the corral and up the ally, Parker being in the lead on Ruffner's horse. When going down the hill by Judge Wells' place, the horse bucked Miller and the Mexican off, but they immediately remounted. Parker did not stop, but kept his horse at full gallop. Hon. J. C. Herndon, from the front porch of his residence, saw the horse buck the two men off, but did not know who they were. By this time crowds of excited citizens could be seen gathered here and there. Deputy Munds and Ed. Ruffner quickly took the trail of the robbers. They were about 25 minutes behind them.

Not less than 50 armed horsemen and many men on foot were soon scouring the hills. A man who came in from the Senator says the escapes passed him. That Ed. Ruffner was close enough behind them to hear the beat of their horses' hoofs and that Ruffner was putting his horse to its best speed.

Lee Norris was shot in the rear of the left side below the ribs, the shot ranging upward. The shot, to the surprise of everybody, proved to be bird shot, the supposition being that the gun was loaded with buckshot. Several cartridges to the gun were opened and found to contain buckshot. At this writing 16 shot had been taken from Norris' body and he was resting as easily as could be expected.

Later—Deputy Munds returned about 11 o'clock last night. Having left their horses on the divide, Munds and Horace Yeoman, on foot, overhauled Parker and Miller below the Lynx creek divide. The Mexican was not with them. Shooting commenced. Yeoman shot Miller's horse and Munds shot Miller off the horse. Miller dragged himself to where Parker was behind some bushes. Miller threw up his hands, when Parker cursed him for having no nerve and pulled Miller upon to his horse and rode off with him. Several shots were fired at Parker, to each of which he replied with a defiant Indian yell. Munds and Yeoman trailed Parker and Miller in the direction of the Agua Fria. The direction taken by the outlaws is that indicated by J. D. Moore's bloodhounds, which followed the trail some miles early in the day.

Lee Norris died at 11:55 last night.

The killing of Lee Norris changed the attitude of the Prescott populace from fascination with the audacious train robber to outrage over the murder of a highly respected citizen. Parker was now a murderer, and despite some fanciful legends to the contrary, this was the first and only time Parker was known to have killed anybody. Lee Norris was much loved, and from a prominent family—Parker could not have picked a victim that would have made his situation much worse.

As we already know, Parker would later be tried, convicted, and hanged for first degree murder. Interestingly, few historians have ever questioned the justice of this. Parker was breaking out of jail, in a hurry. Lee Norris walked through the door, turned, and ran. In the heat of that terrible moment, Parker impulsively gunned down the young attorney. It is not my intention to justify Parker's terrible crime in any way, but given the circumstances, the killing should be viewed more as a case of voluntary manslaughter, or second-degree murder. There was no premeditation; Parker had no idea anyone would come walking through that door. Considering that hangings were much less common in Arizona than pulp writers would have you believe, it must be surmised that Parker went to the gallows for WHO he killed as much as the circumstances surrounding the shooting.

Historians have puzzled for years over the gunfight on the Lynx Creek divide. How could Parker and Miller, in plain view of Deputies Johnny Munds and Horace Yeoman, have simply ridden off without being shot by the lawmen? There are no easy answers to that one; most likely the two Deputies were afraid that if they continued shooting under those circumstances, a stray bullet might have hit Sure-Shot. Sheriff Ruffner would not have taken kindly to that.

The theft of the Sheriff's prize horse caused almost as many tongues to wag as the shooting of Norris, and today it remains one of the details most often repeated when the Parker story is retold. Most storytellers believe that the escaping Parker deliberately picked Ruffner's prize gelding to make his getaway on, but this is unlikely. Since Parker and Ruffner were now enemies, it is unlikely they would have conversed in jail about what kind of horse Ruffner owned; Parker likely had no idea Sure-Shot belonged to his ex-friend. Judging by the speed of the jailbreak and escape, as well as the eyewitness accounts, the three convicts seemed to have simply grabbed the first horse they saw.

If it were humanly possible to overstate the terrible events of May 9, the *Flagstaff Sun-Democrat* managed to do so. In the May 13, 1897 edition, a journalist who remains mercifully anonymous wrote about the tragedy this way:

THREE PRISONERS ESCAPE

Prescott The Scene Of The Shameful Tragedy

Train Robber Parker, Forger Miller And a Mexican Charged With Attempted Murder Break Jail at 1 o'clock Sunday—Lee Norris Fatally Shot by Parker—Jailor Meador Brutally Beaten

> The citizens of Prescott were horror stricken Sunday afternoon at what was one of the most cold blooded murders and the boldest jail delivery now on record. Jim Parker, the bold and noted train robber, who held up the Atlantic & Pacific train at Rock cut in February last, has made another chapter in his history of crime by taking the life of an innocent young man. It was the most daring deed ever performed by man. No doubt the scheme had been previously entered into by these desperate criminals, and Jim Parker was the principal actor in the bloody tragedy. Deep dyed in iniquity, hardened in crime, heartless in feeling, desperate in mind, three men had made a determination to be released from Prescott's prison—even though it cost the blood of one of Yavapai's best and most honorable young men.

The remainder of the article was a verbatim reprint of the *Journal Miner*'s coverage. The *Mohave County Miner* likewise culled its coverage May 15, 1897 from the Prescott newspapers.

Kingman's *Our Mineral Wealth* also carried the news in routine fashion May 14, 1897, but added:

> A telegram received by Sheriff Potts this morning from Under Sheriff Smith states that Parker, the escaped train robber, has been tracked to within a few miles of Williams.

From the same edition:

> Asa Harris and Henry Loven with two Wallapais left immediately on receipt of the news that the Parker gang had broken out to join in the pursuit.

From the same edition:

> It looks like the officers who are after Jim Parker are on the wrong trail. T.L. Garner of Peach Springs claims to have picked up near there the horse rode by Parker, and that the outlaw passed near Peach Springs Monday under full gallop bound for the direction of Utah. If this is the case, Jim Parker ere this is among the Mormons.

Of course, we now know that Garner, whoever he was, did not have Sure-Shot, but he would return later to crow that he was right about Parker's trail, as unlikely as the claim seems.

The *Arizona Republican* also carried news of the escape on May 11, 1897, and while the article errs in its description of Sure-Shot, it is interesting to read the story from the viewpoint of Phoenix and Maricopa County Sheriff Lin Orme, who is not usually mentioned in retellings of the Parker story:

WEARY OF PRESCOTT

Jail Delivery and Murder on Sunday Afternoon

―――――――――――

THE TRAIN ROBBER GONE
And Two Other <u>Desperate Characters</u> With Him

―――――――――――

Assistant District Attorney Norris Shot Down—The Trustfulness of Jailor Meador Grossly Abused and His Head Hammered

―――――――――――

Three unworthy persons in the Prescott jail abused the confidence of the jailor last Sunday by leaving the jail, murdering a county official, holding up a livery stable and riding out into the country. They further repaid the beautiful and childlike trustfulness of the jailor by hammering him on the head with a heavy iron key with so great energy, not to say actual violence, that it is feared that his skull has been fractured. Two murderers, one a desperate train robber, and a forger, are out and gone and at midnight nobody knew where, but nearly all the officers of two counties were riding in the night, over the mountains and bloodhounds were yelping on a trail.

AN ALARM FROM THE NORTH

A little after 1 o'clock a telegram was received at the sheriff's office here from the under sheriff at Prescott, saying that a jail delivery had occurred there. That the jailor had been badly beaten, Assistant District Attorney Lee Norris had been shot, and three prisoners, Jim Parker, the Peach Springs train robber, L. C. Miller, the forger, and a Mexican murderer, Cornellia, were at large and going south. An hour later another telegram describing the prisoners in detail was received. Late at night, Sheriff Ruffner himself telegraphed requesting Sheriff Orme to spare no expense and send out men on all (illegible). Parker was said to be riding a gray pacing horse, and one thousand dollars would be paid for his living or dead body.

The sheriff organized a posse and left town with William Doheney and Al Galpin a little before midnight. They intended to go to Castle Creek, thinking the outlaws might reach that place by breakfast time the next morning. No word has since been received from the posse.

Early yesterday morning another party consisting of W. H. Buck, Dick George, Lin Orme, Jr. and N. J. Hale started out to cut across all northern roads. None of the members of this party had returned at 1 o'clock this morning. The particulars of the delivery, which is the most important since Price and Young left the Phoenix jail, and the most disastrous that ever occurred in Arizona, were first learned yesterday morning.

STORY OF THE ESCAPE

Parker, Cornellia and Miller, the first with hardly a hope between him and the gallows, the last two with no hope at all between them and long terms at Yuma, were occupying a single cell in the Prescott jail. About 1 o'clock in the afternoon Jailor Meadows heard them rattling the cell door of the jail and went down stairs (the jail proper is reached by a short flight of stairs from the ground).

They wanted some water. But they had wanted water every day so long about this time of day that the jailor was disarmed of suspicion. He unlocked the outer iron door, then unlocked the cell door, permitting the Mexican to come out with two empty buckets. He accompanied him to the place where the water was obtained and back through the outer door, which was relocked. They went on to the cell door. While the jailor was unlocking that to readmit him the Mexican sprang upon him. The rest was easy. Parker and Miller ran out, the former to the jailor's room where he armed himself and came back. The fight between the jailor and the Mexican was nearly over, for the latter had gotten hold of the heavy iron key and was reducing the jailor to subjection. The jailor's cries for help alarmed Assistant District Attorney Norris, who ran down the stars and met the armed desperados, for by this time they had secured a revolver, two Winchesters and a shotgun. Norris turned, but half way up the stairs Parker poured a charge from the shotgun into his back and he fell. It was a charge of bird shot, but it was delivered at such short range that it was as deadly as buckshot. Norris died shortly before midnight.

AN ORDERLY TOWN

The noise of this shot and the cries of the jailor, who, blinded by blood, ineffectually fired three shots, must have created an alarm. However, the desperados passed on without loitering (illegible) Sheriff Ruffner's livery stable, (illegible) engaged in a colloquy with the keeper and finally induced him at the point of a gun to give up two horses. Parker mounted one and the Mexican and Miller the other. They rode away, Parker shouting back gaily the refrain of a topical song, "Just tell them that you saw us."

The chief of police of the city of Prescott right here in Arizona came upon the outlaws as they were concluding their negotiations for the horses, but he didn't have his gun. A great many other people were standing around, but there wasn't a gun in the crowd. One night not a great while ago eighteen men were crowded about a peaceful faro game in Phoenix. A careful statistician made an investigation and said he discovered that fifteen of them were armed.

The desperadoes rode out into the country pursued half an hour later by a respectable posse of fifty men. Sheriff Ruffner was at Congress when he heard of the delivery. He went back on a special engine and directed a further pursuit.

At nightfall a part of the posse overtook the outlaws at the Lynx creek divide, a man named Yeoman shot Miller's horse and Deputy Sheriff Munds shot Miller. The train robber lifted Miller behind him and rode away yelling defiantly to reply to shots from the posse. They were going toward the Agua Fria with the possible intention of crossing into the Verde country where Parker is supposed to have friends. Deputy Sheriff Ben Rybon and "Sure Shot" Moore left Prescott yesterday afternoon with Moore's bloodhounds. The dogs took the trail, which the officers the night before believed the outlaws had taken. The officers did not think Parker would carry Miller far. The course he will likely take is a matter of the merest conjecture, but the conjecture is that if he does not immediately seek refuge among friends in the Mogollons he will spend some time in hiding amid the impenetrable recesses of Bloody Basin.

ARRESTS FOR COMPLICITY

Amid the excitement which immediately followed the shooting and the escape several young men were arrested at Prescott for expressing sympathy and hope for the welfare of the robbers. This led to a supposition that they had in some way facilitated the break. The newspapers there are engaged now in pointing out the advantages of lynch law under certain circumstances. Reports have been arriving there that the outlaws have taken this direction on that one. It was said that they were near the Senator mine on Sunday night. In that case they were probably striking for the Verde country. The Mexican had separated from his companions before the encounter in the Lynx creek divide. He was believed to be on the road to the Crowned King.

PERSONNEL OF ACTORS

Lee Norris, the murdered man, is a younger brother of Hon. T. G. Norris. He was graduated from the University of Michigan last year and came directly to Arizona. He was less than thirty years old, a young man of promise and well liked. He had been connected with the office of the district attorney since the first of the year.

The history of Parker is so well known and his exploits as a train robber are so recent as to hardly warrant a further description. From what is known of him there is little doubt that his capture will involve at least the death of himself, if not that of one or more of his pursuers.

Miller, the forger, was arrested at Tucson two weeks ago and was kept over night in the jail here. He was a constable at Prescott three years ago and at that time shot Miles Archibald, then chief of police. The Mexican, Cornellia, was in jail for a shooting at the Crowned King.

On May 12, 1897, the Republican reported:

Tom Cannon and young Mr. Turnbull left Prescott yesterday heavily armed and mounted on two cayuses to earn that $1,000 reward offered for the capture of the outlaws.

It would be interesting to know if "Mr. Turnbull" was the same Milton Turnbull who witnessed the notorious Goddard Station murders six years later.

The *Arizona Gazette* May 11, 1897 repeated most of the same information, but reprinted a couple of telegrams it had received:

About 10 o'clock yesterday morning the following telegram from Under-Sheriff Dillon, at Prescott, was received at the sheriff's office:

"Prescott, May 10.—Posse had fight with the outfit last night. One horse was killed and Miller wounded. Parker took Miller on his horse with him and are headed towards Black Canyon. The Mexican is on foot and going in the direction of Crown King."

In relation to the encounter the Gazette last night received the following special telegram from its Prescott correspondent:

"Prescott, May 10.—Deputy Sheriff Munds returned last night from the chase, reported that he and Horace Yeoman, having left their horses on the divide, they started on foot and over-hauled Parker and Miller below the Lynx Creek divide. The Mexican was not with them. Both sides immediately commenced shooting and Yeoman shot Miller's horse, while Munds winged Miller. The latter fell from his animal and dragged himself to some bushes behind which Parker was hidden. Upon the officers calling to the two to surrender, Miller threw up his hands. Parker cursed him for lacking in nerve and placing Miller on his horse they rode off. Several shots were fired at them but Parker showed disapproval by defiant yells.

"Munds and Yeoman trailed them in the direction of Agua Fria, but owing to the darkness the fugitives escaped."

A second dispatch stated that Lee Norris who was shot by Parker, expired at 11:55 the preceding night. The excitement in Prescott is intense over the killing of Norris, and lynching is probable in case of the capture of the fugitives.

There is already a reward of $4,500 for Parker, on account of the A. & P. hold-up, and as Sheriff Ruffner is not anxious to lose such a valuable prisoner he will stay on the trail until he is either re-captured or killed. He has offered a reward of $1,000 for the capture of the escapes, dead or alive.

Miller, Parker's companion, is a hard character, who distinguished himself some years ago by the shooting of Chief of Police Archibald, of Prescott. The latest offense for which he was confined was the forging of the name of Ralph Dillon to a check for $50. He is a brother of Otto Miller, who several years ago was a printer on one of the Phoenix papers.

The May 12, *Gazette* added the following:

The S. F. P. P. company has aided largely in the attempt to effect the capture of the escaped outlaws. Superintendent Wells gave Sheriff Ruffner the use of a special train to take him from Congress to Prescott, and placed another special at his disposal last night to carry him from Jerome Junction to Ash Fork.

From the same edition, the following snide editorial comment:

Parker, the escaped train robber and murderer, will soon become as ubiquitous as the famous Apache Kid, unless his career is brought to a sudden termination.

The jailbreak made the newspapers in California as well, with most of them carrying wire service reports that were culled from Prescott newspapers. Some of them had minor erroneous data not worth reprinting here, with the exception of the *San Francisco Call*, which mangled its data so badly that it bears note. From their May 10, 1897 edition:

BULLETS FLY IN PRESCOTT'S JAIL

Three Convicts Escape From the County Prison

Shoot the Jailer With His Own Revolver and Dash for Liberty

Assistant District Attorney Norris Wounded in an Attempt to Check Them

---

Prescott, Ariz., May 9.—Three prisoners made a successful break for liberty from the County Jail at noon to-day and when last seen were riding southward, mounted on stolen horses procured at the point of the pistol. At the jail were found Assistant District Attorney Lee Norris, thought to be fatally wounded by a pistol bullet in the break, and Jailor Robert Meador, beaten on the head and also suffering from a bullet wound.

The escapes are "Jim" Parker, who, with his partner, who was killed on the spot, held up the Atlantic and Pacific train at Rock Cut, near Peach Springs, several months ago, a Mexican named Cornelli, accused of murder, and L. C. Miller, a forger arrested a week ago at Tucson. The Sheriff and a strong posse are in pursuit. The trail is a plain one.

It is not believed that either Parker or Miller will be taken alive. The former was captured near the Grand Canyon of the Colorado, only after he had been deprived of strength by starvation, while Miller is a notorious desperado, who shot City Marshal Miles Archibald of Prescott several years ago, and narrowly escaped the gallows.

The escape is believed to have been due to the carelessness of Meador, who has been jailer for many years. He entered the jail corridor armed, and was seized by the prisoners, shot with a bullet from his own pistol and pounded into insensibility. Norris, who is a young man lately admitted to practice, was at the jail door to see a prisoner. He attempted to stop the escaping criminals, and was shot down with the jailer's pistol. The escapes are believed to have had help from the outside and to have been supplied with weapons other than those they took from the jailer. One thousand dollars reward is offered for the men dead or alive.

This silly nonsense prompted the *Prescott Courier* to comment on it May 14, 1897:

The individual who sent the Prescott special to the San Francisco Call, of May 10, regarding the jail break at this point, must have been excited or in a highly imaginative state of mind, judging from the inaccurate details given regarding the escape.

The *Courier*'s blood enemy, the *Arizona Journal Miner*, reprinted the above and added their own comments May 19, 1897:

The above special was never sent from Prescott but was sent from Phenix. A few ambitious press correspondents endeavor to cover the whole territory in sending news. Gathering very meager news, but no particulars of the jail break Sunday, they immediately drew on their imagination for details and fired their imaginary news over the wire. Some of the Denver papers contain specials sent in the same way which are as wide of the mark as the special referred to above.

Even in a time such as this, the two papers had to snipe at each other.

The jailbreak and murder of Lee Norris caused a number of editorials to be written, most of them decrying the state of the justice system in Arizona. On May 14, 1897, the *Prescott Courier* thundered:

> There is a crying need for a little hanging of outlaws and murderers in this section. Our taxpayers are over-burdened with expenses incurred in the prosecution and keeping of these outlaws, who, even when convicted, seldom stay convicted, owing to executive clemency or some other cause; and who, when in jail, are even then a menace to life, law and order, as was shown by yesterday's tragedy in the court house, when three outlaws, broke from jail and shot one of our most highly respected citizens—perpetrating one of the most unprovoked attempts at murder imaginable. Popular indignation was such that these three men would have been hung on short notice had they fallen into the hands of a justly indignant populace. Our people are patient and long suffering in the way in which outlaws have gone unwhipt of justice and have commenced "to think," both as a matter of financial and personal safety, that many of these fellows would be more serviceable as fertilizers of grass roots, than by any other use to which they could be put.

Not to be outdone, the *Journal Miner* reprinted the above and decided to take the thought even further. From the May 12, 1897 edition:

> The above voices the sentiment which has been time and again reposted in these columns without apparent avail. Since the last execution for murder committed in this county no less than forty or fifty cold blooded murders have been committed and with few exceptions every last one of the murderers is enjoying his liberty today. Technicalities of courts, false sentiment among jurors, and abuse of the pardoning power, have been the agencies employed to defeat justice.
>
> Not satisfied with all of these agencies to aid red handed murderers to escape the penalty of their crimes, a democratic legislature enacted a law last winter whereby such criminals, it is said, will escape by the wholesale from answering to offended justice for the heinousness of their deeds. This law, enacted by a democratic legislature, none of whom were lawyers, hence could not realize the sweeping effects of the law passed, was signed by a democratic governor, who is a lawyer and who should have had the legal acumen to have forseen the results.
>
> No special blame can attach to the legislature, as the real intent of (illegible) was hidden beneath its (illegible), and none but a legal (illegible) have detected it. (Illegible) who drew it up, whoever he was, no doubt fully understood the effect it would have and the governor who signed it should have been able to bring his legal training into bearing in its consideration, with the result of vetoing it.
>
> In this connection it may be asked whether the community, as an aggregation of citizens, has any duty to perform? If so is that duty to sit idly by and see human being after human being wantonly murdered, while justice is handcuffed by legal meshes? Let each individual answer these questions according to his own conscience.

The law referred to was known as the Norton Act, designed to redefine in legal terms what constituted a homicide. The problem was a technicality; once the law was passed, murderers who had committed their crimes PRIOR to the passage of the Act, but had not yet been tried, could not be indicted for murder—the best Arizona counties could do was to bring them to trial on manslaughter charges. A number of murderers escaped lengthy prison time and even the gallows because of this gaffe.

On May 14, 1897, *Our Mineral Wealth* editorialized:

> If the Arizona legislature did repeal the law to punish murderers, which we don't believe, Judge Lynch has still a law on the statute books that never has been repealed, and while we are not in favor of Judge Lynch, he may be of service on some occasions.

Perhaps the most surprising editorial came from the *Phoenix Herald*, was came perilously close to accusing jailor Robert Meador of helping the inmates to escape! From the May 12, 1897 edition:

> The escape of the train robber, Parker, from Prescott last Sunday at midday, is a lesson of which county officials, especially jail officials, should make a note. Several years ago a murderer confined in the county jail in this city escaped under exactly similar circumstances, except that he killed no one in doing so; but that was purely because no one happened to appear in his way in the building. That a jailor will do as was done by that official in each of these cases, shows either criminal carelessness or collusion with the criminals themselves and either one should be sufficient under our laws to send the men to Yuma who make it possible for the escape of desperate criminals, the murder of innocent men, and the vast expense the people of the county are put too to re-capture such criminals. A jailor permitting such a thing, should at once be placed under arrest and subject to the most scrutinizing examination and the fact of the escape of a criminal, under such circumstances, sufficient evidence of criminal negligence, if nothing more. The law we believe could be made to cover such a case, as it stands.

The *Arizona Journal Miner*, shocked by this "very severe stricture," reprinted it and commented:

> So far as Jailor Meador is concerned, nothing could be farther from the truth than even an intimation of any collusion with the prisoners. It was extremely lucky for him that he escaped as he did, as there is no doubt he would have met the same fate that Mr. Norris did if he had been in the way of Parker, or if the Mexican had had anything to have killed him with.
>
> Mr. Meador has always treated the prisoners kindly and with consideration and in this way has gained their friendship and good will, on account of which he has no doubt placed too much confidence in them. Desperate men with death or a long term of imprisonment staring them in the face do not stop to consider friendship or kindness that stands between them and liberty.

The *Prescott Courier* also responded to the *Herald*'s accusations on May 14, 1897:

Chapter 7: Jailbreak and the Second Posse

These two reward notices, from Sheriff George C. Ruffner and Arizona Governor Benjamin J. Franklin, appeared in the *Prescott Weekly Courier*, May 14, 1897 and May 21, 1897

The comments of the Phoenix Herald on Jailor Meador, of Prescott, would not have appeared had the Herald man been personally acquainted with Jailor Meador and the daily routine of his duties. No more faithful, conscientious or braver man can be found than Meador. He made a gallant fight when beset by overwhelming odds. While the escape is to be deplored, the fact remains that even more daring and successful escapes have been made from the most impregnable prisons in the world. It is not an overly wise man who talks from views taken from his hindsight. We can all point out the defects and mistakes after the calamity, but how many of us are there who would have stood up and made the fight which Meador did against such great odds, and most of us would have been caught in the same way, for the plot to escape was planned with far more than ordinary shrewdness. There is no man in this community who is more cast down in mind over this sad affair than Jailor Meador, and the Courier knows that he would willingly lay down his life if he could obliterate this tragic chapter in the history of Yavapai county. Yes, Mr.

Herald, where would you be, or where would any other man be, if, according to your suggestion, we were all arrested and placed on trial for our mistakes. No man on earth could escape arrest. There would be no unarrested man to act as judge, and God alone could act in that capacity, and, for this very reason, He does and will act in that capacity. Meador did the best he could under the circumstances; no power on earth or above it can do more.

And speaking from a historical point of view, the *Herald*'s allegations are as ridiculous now as they were then. There was never any evidence to back up the notion that Robert Meador, a respected and much-loved citizen of old Prescott, aided the escape of Parker, Miller, and Cornelia Sarata.

Sheriff George C. Ruffner's offer of $1,000 reward, as it appeared on the front page of the *Prescott Courier*, appears in the illustration opposite. The reward offered by Territorial Governor Benjamin J. Franklin, which appeared in newspapers throughout Arizona, reads as follows:

Proclamation of Reward
_____

Territory of Arizona.   }
Executive Department   }

To all whom these presents shall come:

Whereas information from authentic source has been received by me that James Parker, L. C. Miller and one Cornellia (Mexican) who each stand charged with the commission of a crime and were each arrested and imprisoned therefore in the county jail of Yavapai county, this Territory,

And whereas it has come to my knowledge that said James Parker, L. C. Miller and Cornellia (Mexican) did on the 9th day of May, 1897, escape from the said jail, and, in making their escape, did murder Lee Norris, the deputy district attorney of Yavapai county.

Now, therefore, I, Benjamin J. Franklin, Governor of the Territory of Arizona, by virtue of the power and authority in me vested, do hereby offer the following rewards for the apprehension of said fugitives from justice, to-wit:

Five hundred dollars, for the apprehension of said James Parker, and his detention in any jail of the United States.

Five hundred dollars, for the apprehension of said L. C. Miller, and his detention in any jail of the United States.

Two hundred and fifty dollars for the apprehension of said Cornellia (Mexican), and his detention in any jail of the United States.

(Seal)   In testimony whereof I have hereunto set my hand and caused the Great Seal of the Territory to be hereunto affixed.

Done at Phoenix, the Capital, this 12th day of May, A. D. 1897.

>By the Governor,
>B. J. Franklin

Charles M. Bruce,
Secretary of Arizona"

The newspaper *Our Mineral Wealth*, from Kingman, responded with an editorial:

> "Gov. Franklin has offered a large reward for Parker, the train robber, and the others who broke jail with him, but we have not heard that he offered any reward for Mouse, the Piute Indian who in cold blood murdered Davis and Stearns in this county several months ago.

Whenever the Parker story is repeated, Parker's victim, Erasmus Lee Norris, is usually given short shrift. This is unfortunate, and is probably due to several factors. First, victims are rarely remembered as widely as their killers. Second, having only served as Deputy District Attorney for only a very short time, there is little surviving record of Norris in Prescott. Third, authors of after-the-fact accounts knew that their readers wanted to hear about Parker himself—Lee Norris was only a name to them, the name of the man Parker murdered and nothing more. Constrained by space, they left it at that.

But Lee Norris was very well-liked and respected in Prescott, almost as much as his brother, Thomas G. Norris, whose position as an attorney is remembered in Prescott down to this day. Finally, at along last, we have some hard data on the unfortunate Lee Norris, provided to me by his great-great-grandnephew, Gene Norris of Oklahoma. I am deeply grateful to him for providing me with much of his family history, which will be utilized in this section. The following background data on Lee Norris was written by Gene Norris of Oklahoma, and is reprinted here with his permission:

> Erasmus Lee Norris was born 14 Aug 1868 in a small log cabin home about one half mile east of what is now Green Forest in Carroll County, Arkansas. He was the youngest of 14 children born to Jonathan and Mary Jane (Cannon) Norris. His parents came to Carroll Co., AR in Nov 1850 from Overton Co., TN. Jonathan was born 21 Oct 1818 in Wilkes Co., NC, a son of Gilbert and Rachel (Chambers) Norris. His mother was purported to be one quarter Cherokee but the family could not prove it factually, just as a handed-down story.
>
> Jonathan moved to Overton Co., Tn with his parents and family from Wilkes Co., NC, late in 1835.
>
> Jonathan was married to Mary Jane Cannon 7 Apr 1843 near the Oak Hill Community in Overton Co., TN. She was born 5 Jan 1822 in Overton Co., Tn, a daughter of Thomas and "Patsy" (Lee) Cannon. Her father was a hatter by trade.
>
> Jonathan Norris was a farmer, stockman, and self-taught stonemason. They moved to Carroll Co., AR, in 1850 where the last eight of their 14 children were born.
>
> He built a log cabin home east of what is now Green Forest. He raised horses, cattle, apples and corn. All of their children received a basic education. The only

two children to further their education were their sons, Thomas Gilbert Norris, 1856-1932, and Erasmus Lee Norris, 1868-1897.

Lee attended his first years of school in a one-room schoolhouse called Douglas School just east of the family farm. When he was 16, in 1884, he received a certificate to teach and taught one term of school at Douglas. His brother, Tom, had recently graduated from the University of Iowa Law School and had set up his first practice west of Green Forest in the Carroll Co. seat of Berryville.

Lee liked to run foot races. It was said the only way he could out run anyone was in his bare feet. He always won the short distance races but if he ran any long distance against his brother, Tom, Tom would always hide from Lee and Lee would never win. He entered himself in the Harrison High School where he graduated in 1890.

By this time, his older brother, Tom, was now practicing law in Flagstaff, AZ, then Prescott, AZ. Lee would spend his summers in Flagstaff and Prescott.

According to Gene Norris, Lee Norris' mother Mary died in 1891. Following this, young Lee left for Flagstaff, Arizona to live with his brother Thomas. Various articles about him would appear in the newspaper of Green Forest, Arkansas, the Tribune.

From the Green Forest Tribune of August 10, 1893:

Lee Norris came in from Flagstaff, Arizona, Sunday and will visit friends and relatives for a week or ten days.

From the Green Forest Tribune of August 17, 1893:

Lee Norris, who came in recently from Flagstaff, Ariz., to visit friends and relatives, leaves in a few days for Ann Arbor, Mich., to enter the law department of the University of Michigan. He expects to remain in school there three years. He goes by way of Chicago, and will spend a week seeing the sights at the World's Fair. Lee is a promising young man and he has our best wishes for his future success.

Young Lee did indeed stay in the prestigious law school for three years, and while there, he became engaged to another University student named Burnice Smith. From the Green Forest Tribune of July 9, 1896:

E. L. Norris arrived Monday from Ann Arbor., Mich., where he has been attending a law school the past three years, graduating last week. Lee is now fully equipped for the profession and we predict for him a grand future. His many friends here are pleased to meet him. He will remain some weeks visiting and then go to Arizona to enter his profession.

From the Tribune of July 16, 1896:

E. L. Norris left Tuesday for Prescott, Ariz., where he will join his brother, T. G. Norris, in the practice of law. Lee has hosts of friends here who will rejoice to hear of his future success. His brother, Ben, accompanied him to Eureka Springs.

It is a hard fact of life that one never knows how the most innocuous decisions can affect one's life or even end it. In this case, needless to say, young Lee Norris, anticipating a long and bright future, had no way of knowing that his decision to join his brother in Prescott would ultimately mean his death.

The May 18, 1897 edition of the Green Forest Tribune covered the murder of their home town boy this way:

LEE NORRIS MURDERED

The Sad News Reached Here Monday

Monday noon J. E. Norris received a telegram from his brother, T. G. Norris, Prescott Ariz., bearing the startling intelligence that their brother, Lee, had been shot and killed by a jail breaking prisoner. The telegram also stated that it was Lee's request to be buried beside his father and mother.

His remains will reach Eureka Springs Saturday and will be accompanied by J. C. Herndon, T. G. Norris' law partner.

A special dispatch was sent to the Globe Democrat giving the particulars of the murder. As will be seen from it the shooting took place Sunday just after 12 o'clock and Lee must have lived several hours as no telegram was sent here until Monday.

Prescott, Ariz., May 9.—Jim Parker, one of the robbers who held up an Atlantic and Pacific train in February, escaped from the county jail at 1 o'clock this afternoon, in company with a Mexican charged with attempted murder and L. C. Miller, in for forgery, all three being desperate, determined, men.

They selected the hour when no attaché of the sheriff's office, except the jailer, was on duty. They asked him for some water and the Mexican was let out with a bucket to get it. As soon as he reached the outside of inner door he grabbed the jailer, and taking the key from the outer door dealt him a murderous blow on the head with it. The jailer screamed for help. His cries attracted the attention of Assistant District Attorney Norris, who happened to be in an office in the upper part of the court house. Norris came to the jailer's assistance just as Parker procured a shotgun from an adjoining room, and the latter fired at Norris, the charge taking effect in his back, near the left kidney, producing a wound which it is feared may prove fatal.

The three men then went to the Sheriff's livery stable less than half a block distant, stole two horses and rode out of town in the presence of 100 persons, who had been attracted by the shooting. A posse of 50 men, heavily armed, are in pursuit with blood hounds.

This sad and deplorable news has cast a gloom over the entire community. Lee Norris was born and reared here, however he had spent some of his time in the West but for the past eight years had been continually in school until last June when he graduated with high honors from the Ann Arbor, Michigan, school of law, after which he visited relatives a short while here and then went to Prescott, Ariz., where he secured the position of assistant district attorney under Henry D. Ross, also a former Carroll county boy.

To be thus cut down by a vile criminal with the bright prospects that his merits deserve makes it all the more deplorable.

> Lee Norris was our old schoolmate and trusted friend, and we shall speak more fully of him in the future.
> Ben, Jim and Granville Norris go to Eureka Springs Friday and it is expected that they will return with the corpse Saturday night and that the funeral will take place Sunday.

Lee Norris was well-loved in Prescott as well. During his short time there, he had made many friends and earned the respect of his brother's prominent colleagues. When the news of his murder broke out, virtually the whole town of Prescott seemed to take the time to weep. From the *Arizona Journal Miner* of May 12, 1987:

> On account of the condition of Lee Norris last evening, the Prescott Brass Band did not give their usual Sunday evening concert.

From the same edition:

> The tragedy enacted in the court house yesterday has caused a gloom to overshadow the town. Lee Norris, the victim, was an exceptionally peaceable and well liked young man, and the manner of his death, in the very bright morning of his manhood, causes additional sadness to the occurrence.

From the May 19, 1897 edition of the *Journal Miner*:

> A short session of the district court was held yesterday, at which the following committee was appointed to draft suitable resolutions in regard to the death of the late Lee Norris: H. D. Ross, R. E. Sloan, E. M. Sanford, H. T. Andrews and R. E. Morrison. The committee will report in open court tomorrow, May 13.

The resolution, after being adopted, was printed in the May 19, 1897 *Journal Miner*, and the May 14, 1897 *Courier*:

> There was a session of the District Court yesterday morning, during which the following resolutions were adopted to voice the feeling of the bar upon the untimely death of the late Lee Norris; Judge Sloan delivered an eloquent, and touching, tribute to the worth of deceased. He was followed in like vein by R. E. Morrison. Judge Hawkins also made a few very appropriate remarks.
> WHEREAS, E. L. Norris, late a member of this bar, while in life gained the admiration and respect of all, and by his exemplary conduct, scholarly attainments, amiable disposition and thoughtful traits of character, gave promise of future usefulness and distinction in his chosen profession and in social spheres; and
> WHEREAS, in early manhood and in the full vigor of mental and social power, our brother was suddenly stricken down while chivalrously, in trepidly and nobly responding to an urgent appeal to defend the assailed; now, therefore, be it
> Resolved, That the bench and bar of the Fourth Judicial District of the Territory of Arizona, in the departure of our brother from among us, have suffered the substantial loss of an esteemed and worthy member of our profession, and be it further

Resolved, that we condole with the sorrowing family and tender them our sympathy in their affliction; be it further

Resolved, That these resolutions be spread upon the minutes of this Court and that a copy be sent to the bereaved family.

> H. D. Ross
> R. E. Sloan
> H. T. Andrews
> E. M. Sanford
> Robt. E. Morrison
> Committee

As we have already seen, E. M. Sanford was Parker's attorney for the train robbery; by today's standards, his presence on this committee would represent a major conflict of interest, but in 1897, no one thought a thing of it.

From the *Courier* of May 14, 1897:

> The death of Lee Norris has cast a pall of sadness over this community, for none knew him but to respect and like him, and his unprovoked murder, cutting him down in the strength of his manhood and flower of his youth has caused an outpouring of sympathy from every heart for his bereaved friends and relatives, and feelings of indescribable horror at the atrocity of his murder. His brother and many friends remained at his bedside from first to last and everything that medical science and loving hands could do was done to save him. Deceased was 28 years old, and had resided here about one year and was acting as assistant district

The Methodist Church on Marina Street in Prescott in the late 19th century. The funeral of Erasmus Lee Norris was held here. (Sharlot Hall Museum)

attorney at the time of the tragedy. He requested that his body be sent to Green Forest, Arkansas, and buried beside those of his parents. The remains will be shipped this afternoon and will be accompanied by Hon. J. C. Herndon, partner of Hon. Thos. Norris, brother of deceased, who is prostrated with grief. The funeral services will be held at 1:30 p.m. today, at the M. E. Church South, West Prescott.

From the same edition:

Funeral services over the remains of the late Lee Norris were held at the M. E. Church South yesterday at 1:30 p.m. The church was crowded; in fact, many who went were unable to get in owing to the large turnout of citizens. About 20 vehicles were noticed standing around the edifice. Rev. G. L. Pierson delivered the funeral discourse, and paid a deserved tribute to the manly worth of the departed. Rev. Wykoff assisted Rev. Pierson. The pallbearers were Harry Kaiss, Fred Tritle, Jr., Paul Hastings, John Robinson and Frank Frantz. The body was shipped east for interment with parents of deceased in the family graveyard at Green Forest, Ark. Hon. J. C. Herndon accompanied the remains East.

From the same edition:

A photograph was taken of the interior of the M. E. Church South yesterday during the funeral obseque of the late Lee Norris. The casket was beautifully decorated with flowers, the church crowded, and all surroundings such as to make it an impressive picture.

Sadly, the photograph is not known to have survived.
The grief of the Norris family over the loss of their loved one is illustrated by the following note, which also appeared in the May 14, 1897 *Courier*:

Card of Thanks
As I am unable to individually thank all the noble people who were so kind to me during those saddest of hours when my brother was painfully passing to the other shore, and to thank all those whose outpouring of sympathy, when all was lost, was a never-to-be-forgotten, grateful support to the mind bowed with grief. I take this method to try to express my thanks, which are greater than can be conveyed by word or pen. I thank you all from the bottom of my heart.
Respectfully, T. G. Norris

And from the May 26, 1897 *Arizona Journal Miner*:

Card of Thanks
Green Forest, Ark., May 16, 1897—Editor, Journal-Miner, Prescott, Ariz: I desire upon the part of myself and in behalf of the other brothers and the sisters of Lee Norris, to express our sincere thanks to his loving friends in Prescott for the kindness shown to him during his last hours and for the beautiful floral decorations that adorned his casket, and especially do we feel grateful to your honored citizen,

Mr. J. C. Herndon, who accompanied our brother's remains to Arkansas. May heaven's richest blessings attend you all.

Respectfully, B. F. Norris

Finally, it should be noted that even the *Flagstaff Sun-Democrat* made a note about Lee Norris without even mentioning Parker by name. This entry, touching in its simplicity, is from the May 13, 1897 edition:

> J. C. Herndon passed through on No. 2 yesterday for Eureka Springs, Arkansas. He was in care of the remains of A. L. Norris, whose body was shipped back to Green Forest for interment.

In Arkansas, the Green Forest Tribune covered the arrival of Lee Norris's remains, and covered the funeral there in chilling detail, the like of which is rarely seen any more. From the May 20, 1897 edition of the Tribune:

FUNERAL OF LEE NORRIS

Followed To The Grave By Hundreds of Sorrowing Friends

A Brief Sketch of the Awful Murder, and Resolutions of Respect

Friday noon B. F., O. N. and J. E. Norris, accompanied by Dr. D. F. Ray, M. S. Coxsey, A. J. Russell, G. M. Wallace and E. C. Lanier left for Eureka Springs to meet and take charge of the remains of Lee Norris, who was murdered by a jail breaking train robber at Prescott, Ariz., an account of which appeared in last week's issue of The Tribune.

Saturday morning at 9:11 o'clock Hon. J. C. Herndon, T. G. Norris's law partner, arrived with the corpse.

He was met at the depot by the above named gentlemen, also the Eureka Springs bar and a part of the Berryville bar were there in a body and escorted the remains up town where Mr. Herndon took a final leave of his silent charge.

Owing to force of circumstances Mr. Herndon could come no further, which he very much regretted. He left on the afternoon train on his return.

At 10:30 o'clock the party left Eureka Springs, arriving at Green Forest at 4:30 p.m. The corpse was taken to J. E. Norris' residence where the many relatives and friends viewed it.

The body was in a perfect state of preservation, having been embalmed in a beautiful metallic casket, hermetically sealed.

Loving hands in the far West had placed many wreaths of beautiful flowers about the casket, among which was a large bouquet sent by a lady friend from Los Angeles, California. Over the breast was a plain silver plate bearing the simple inscription, "Lee Norris."

Sunday afternoon his remains were consigned to their last resting place in the family burying grounds near the Norris homestead. Rev. R. A. Martin conducted beautiful funeral services at the cemetery in the course of which he remarked, "By searching the pages of history we find more than one instance where men who have attained to high positions have been slain by the ruthless hand of criminals. Such is the case with this noble young man, who lies cold in death before us. He was born and reared among us, but had taken up his abode in the distant West. He had equipped himself for the prosecution of violators of the laws of our land and country, but in the prime of his youth he was shot down by one of the worst criminals in all the land.

After the funeral services the vast throng of fully one thousand people and perhaps more than one hundred relatives took a last parting look at the face of Lee Norris.

The grave of Erasmus Lee Norris, in the Norris Cemetery in Green Forest, Arkansas. (Courtesy of Gene Norris)

The particulars of the murder do not differ materially from our last week's report, but as best we can will again relate it as Mr. Herndon told it to us on his arrival at Eureka Springs.

Sunday afternoon about 1 o'clock, May 9, Lee went to his office in Prescott, Ariz. He was engaged in writing a letter to his sweetheart in Ann Arbor, Mich., when he heard some one screaming down stairs. Rushing down the stairs he discovered that the prisoners had broken jail, at the same time Jim Parker, in for train robbery, immerged from the Sheriff's rooms with a shot gun presented. Lee exclaimed, "For God's sake don't shoot me," and immediately started to retrace his steps up the stairway, but the murderous aim of the desperado was unerring, the ball taking effect over the left kidney and side. When Lee was picked up he was lying on the stairway near the foot.

For the first few hours, the doctors were hopeful that the shot was not fatal, but Lee insisted from the first that he could not live and repeatedly requested that his body be shipped to Arkansas for burial beside his father and mother.

There being no hemorrhage of the lungs the doctors still expressed faint hope, but that all vanished when Lee gave a slight cough and spitting on a handkerchief remarked, "There it is, boys, I knew it was there."

Lee was perfectly conscious to the very last, did not appear the least excited and fully realized that he must go.

The article then launched into a verbatim reprint from the *Journal Miner*, and then concluded thusly:

Resolution of Respect

The members of the bar of Carroll County were at Eureka Springs on the 13th day of May, 1897, when A. Davis was elected chairman and O. W. Watkins was elected Secretary. The following proceedings were had:

> Whereas we have heard that Lee Norris, a young man born and raised in this county and who had recently graduated at the University of Michigan and had become one of the leading members of the Prescott, Ariz. Bar, was killed by an outlaw on the 9th day of May, 1897, therefore be it
> Resolved: That we tender our heartfelt sympathy to the family of our professional brother, and especially to his brother, T. G. Norris, of the Prescott, Ariz. Bar, who was admitted to practice in this county and who is highly esteemed by us all.
> Resolved. That a copy of these resolutions be sent to the family of the deceased and that the papers of the county be requested to publish the same.
>
> A. Davis,   O. W. Watkins,
> Chairman   Secretary

In my files, I also have an undated clipping from an unidentified newspaper that seems to be of Michigan vintage:

> E. L. Norris, a former high school student and graduate of the Law department class of '95, was shot and killed at Prescott, Ariz., last Sunday morning by escaping convicts. Mr. Norris was a native of Arkansas and while in school was highly esteemed by his fellow students and teachers, both as a gentleman and scholar. He was one of the best young lawyers of his state and was pushing rapidly to the front, being, at the time of his death, district attorney.—Times.

The pain shows through over a century after Lee Norris' death. Nothing further need be said.

But Parker, Miller and Sarata were still at large, with posses from all over the Territory trailing them. California newspapers kept up the story as well, although most of them continued to rely on Associated Press wire dispatches. The *Los Angeles Times* ran this update May 11, 1897:

> Prescott (Ariz.) May 10—Lee Norris, the victim of yesterday's jailbreak, died early this morning, and gloom has settled over the town, as he was a young man popular with every one. Ward Pritchett and John Fitch, arrested yesterday, have been discharged, as there is no evidence whatever to connect them with the escape. It is generally believed that Parker intended to kill Sheriff Ruffner at the latter's livery stable, as the latter arrested him in February and Parker realized that he is a dangerous man in pursuit of a criminal.
> The Sheriff's livery stable is located between his residence and the courthouse, and it is his habit to stop at the stable about 1 o'clock every day when in town, as he comes from his lunch to the office. When the criminals entered the stable for horses, Parker asked twice where Ruffner was, and was very abusive when told by the man in charge that he did not know. As it happened, the Sheriff was out of town at the time. Sheriff Ruffner has posted a reward of $1000 for the arrest and detention of the fugitives in any jail in the United States, of upon satisfactory proof of their death.

The general feeling is that the posse in pursuit will make no effort to take them alive, but will shoot them down on sight if overtaken. When Miller was wounded in last evening's fight, he crawled behind a bush where Parker was and threw up his hands as a signal that he surrendered, when Parker let out a perfect volley of oaths for his lack of nerve and cowardice. Parker then remounted his horse and pulled Miller up behind him, and as the posse fired, Parker replied with a defiant yell at the officers. In their haste to get away they failed to secure ammunition, and unless they hold up some ranch or mining camp for ammunition, they will be unable to make much of a fight. Important news is momentarily expected from the posse.

A telephone message received from Chaparral from ex-sheriff J. R. Lowry, one of the posse in pursuit of the outlaws, states that the posse struck the trail early this morning, and the fugitives are headed toward Agua Fria Valley, where are several ranches, and from which they may secure fresh horses. The posse thought Parker had deserted Miller and was alone, the Mexican apparently having left the other two yesterday morning afoot. The horse ridden by Parker had lost one shoe, and as he goes lame easily when barefooted, they had hope of soon overtaking him unless a fresh horse is secured.

Deputy sheriffs from different parts of the county were called to Prescott today and another posse organized and started in pursuit on fresh horses just before noon. Feeling here is very much worked up since the death of Norris was announced, and cool-headed, conservative men talk of lynching the outlaws if captured alive. This feeling is intensified on account of the passage by the last Legislature of a law which virtually acquits all murderers where the crime was committed prior to the passage of the law.

Two prisoners, now in jail here, who have been convicted, sentenced to death, afterward granted a new trial by the Supreme Court, and another whose trial has not yet taken place, will be cleared through the operation of this law. The new law enacted defines murder and provides punishment, and all former laws are repealed without a saving clause excepting cases then pending. From forty to fifty murders have been committed in this county in the last six or seven years without adequate punishment.

A telegram has been received at the Sheriff's office, stating that Deputies Fairchild and Buggelin of Coconino county, who assisted in the pursuit and capture of Parker in February after the train-robbery left Winslow this forenoon for the Tonto Basin country toward which Parker was heading, in order to intercept him, should the posse from here fail to overtake him.

Nothing has been heard from the posse in pursuit of the outlaws since noon. Deputy Ben Rybon and J. D. Moore left this afternoon with the latter's bloodhounds for the scene of yesterday afternoon's battle, where the dogs will be placed on the trail in the hope of running down Miller, if the officers' theory is correct, that Parker has deserted him. As he is known to be wounded, it is thought that no trouble will be experienced in running him to earth. The posse is now away beyond telephone and telegraph communication.

Parker had shown an uncharacteristic sense of honor by saving Miller from the Lynx Creek firefight instead of just abandoning him to the law. Whether Parker later

Chapter 7: Jailbreak and the Second Posse

actually deserted Miller, or whether they just agreed to split up, will never be known for certainty, especially since Miller would later audaciously deny that he was at the firefight at all.

From the *Phoenix Herald* of May 11, 1897:

> Very little was heard today from the officers or fugitives who left Prescott Sunday afternoon in the desperate chase which is now going on in the northern portion of the Territory. Since the word was received that the officers and outlaws had had a battle, during which Miller was wounded but escaped with Parker, both being on the same horse, nothing has been heard of an interesting nature, both the pursued and pursuers being evidently far from a telegraph office or place from which word could be received. This morning word was received that the fugitives were headed towards the Tonto Basin and that the Sheriff of Gila county had left Globe with a posse for the purpose of heading them off in the basin.
>
> Not a word has been received from Sheriff Orme who left this city Sunday night or the posse which left here Monday morning, and it is supposed that they are still making an effort to come up with the outlaws.
>
> The Mexican has evidently dropped entirely out of sight as nothing has been heard from him since he left the other two men on foot going in the direction of the Crowned King mine.
>
> Tomorrow will most likely end the chase as by that time the officers will have surrounded their men and secured them.
>
> A rumor this afternoon to the effect that Miller had been captured could not be traced to an authentic source and is believed to be a canard.

Needless to say, Miller had not yet been captured. The following strange paragraph appeared in the *Arizona Journal Miner* on May 12, 1897:

> It is reported that the three desperadoes who escaped from jail yesterday held up Mike Hermann on Groom Creek for a bottle of whiskey each.

Hermann was kind of a local old codger, judging by other news coverage of him over the years. He was a veteran of the Civil War, and probably liked to tell tall stories. As his alleged bushwhacking was never brought up again, it may be surmised that the story was later deemed to lack credibility: Hermann may have simply been trying to draw attention to himself. It is hard to believe that the fleeing outlaws, with a posse right on their heels, would take the time to steal liquor (to say nothing of the fact that Groom Creek is in a different direction than the outlaws were known to be going. Cornelia Sarata, who seems to have parted with his comrades early on, may well have headed in Hermann's direction, but not all three of them.)

From the same edition:

OUTLAWS STILL AT LARGE

No Information Received From the Sheriff's Posse For Over Twenty-four Hours
From Today's Daily

All manners of wild rumors have been afloat during yesterday and today in regard to the pursuit of the outlaws who escaped from jail on Sunday, but up to a late hour this after noon nothing definite had been received at the sheriff's office.

Fred Stevens, the Camp Verde Stage driver, who arrived last night, stated that two men had camped on Sunday night in a gulch south of Martin Rust's place on Ash creek leaving at daylight on Monday morning. Sheriff Ruffner and others of the officers party arrived there about seven hours behind them and kept on their trail.

It is now pretty well known that Parker is heading for the Mogollon mountains where it is said he has lots of friends who will assist him.

Dolph Blair, another of the four who were arrested on Sunday, has been released as there was absolutely no evidence to connect him with the affair. The fact is now demonstrated to almost a certainty the plot to escape was planned in the jail, and no outsider knew anything of it, or had anything to do with it. It is thought that probably Thompson and Rogers may have been in the plot to escape but even this is only surmise. They appeared at the jail door with the other prisoners, being naturally attracted there by the scuffle between Meador and the Mexican, and the cries of the former.

Ex-Sheriff Lowry, who was out with the posse, returned yesterday. He states that a man named McFaddon, who was about one hundred yards from Miller and Parker when they were fired upon by Munds and Yeoman, says Miller was shot in the knee. It is also stated that on Sunday evening, two or three hours after Miller was wounded, two miners saw Parker at a point about four miles east from where Miller was shot and that Parker was alone and was leading his horse. He did not speak to the men.

George Merritt telephoned last evening from Chaparral that he has struck the trail of the Mexican leading towards Turkey Creek and that he was afoot. It is stated that the Mexican has a brother living in Turkey Creek and is well known to the Mexicans generally. Under-Sheriff Dillon telephoned to Merritt to take the trail and follow it, if necessary into Mexico.

Turnbull and Cannon, who went out yesterday, returned last night. They also reported having struck the Mexican's trail on Lynx Creek and to have followed it past the old smelter and down the Chaparral road to a Mexican cabin, where they found three empty Winchester cartridges boxes.

A gentleman who was out on the Lynx Creek road yesterday on private business reports that at a point this side of the smelter the road was strewn with empty cartridges.

Funeral services were held this afternoon at 1:30 o'clock at the South Methodist church, over the remains of the late Lee Norris, which were attended by a large concourse of sympathizing friends, the church being crowded. Rev. G. L. Pearson conducted the services and paid a glowing tribute to the worth and character of the young man. Rev. E. D. Wyckoff delivered a very fervid and eloquent prayer. In addition to the singing by the choir, Rev. E. D. Wyckoff sang a solo and Messers. Wydkoff, Johnston, Aitken and Burmister rendered a quartette.

The body was taken to the depot and shipped on the afternoon southbound train to the former home of deceased at Green Forest, Arkansas, for interment besides his parents. J. O. Herndon, the law partner of T. G. Norris, accompanied the body east.

The May 14, 1897 *Prescott Courier* also carried the following tidbits:

John Coker called at the Courier last evening and stated that the outlaws were in the Lynx creek hills, about five miles from senator. That they would probably try to get over the Lynx creek divide during the night, but chances were against them doing so.

From the same edition:

Several young men were locked up yesterday in connection with the Court House tragedy. There was probably, no specific charge against them. It is said they had indulged in some rather indiscreet and foolish sympathetic talk about the outlaws. This at least one of them, with whom the reporter talked, denies. The reporter does not believe that any one of them knew anything about the criminal affair before its concurrence. They may have talked favorably for the outlaws, and thus brought suspicion on themselves, but the fact of their reported talk and the fact that they had been in the habit of associating with one of the principals in the tragedy, caused their arrest. The Courier believes this is the status of matter. We certainly hope so.

As already seen, these men were later released, but the *Courier*'s take on the incident was interesting. From the same edition:

Not much of tangible interest occurred yesterday in the matter of the pursuit of the outlaws. Armed men from almost every portion of the county, were scouring the country in search of the fugitives. Deputy Sheriff Burt of Ash Fork and Deputy Sheriff Merritt of Jerome, came in and joined in the chase. A little before noon, ex-Sheriff Lowry telephoned in from McCabe that the trail had been struck, heading toward Hildebrandt's ranch, on the Agua Fria. Lowry had to leave the posse on account of his horse giving out. When he last saw the posse, they were riding fast. The horse ridden by Parker had lost a shoe. The posse thought Miller was not with Parker. Munds, Yeoman, Prince, Ruffner and others were of this posse. A telegram was received at the sheriff's office, stating that Deputy Sheriff Fairchilds and Buggelin, of Coconino, were leaving for the Tonto Basin country to intercept Parker. These officers were among the trailers of Parker after his train robbery. Ben Rybon and J. D. Moore left yesterday afternoon with Moore's bloodhounds for the scene of Sunday afternoon's fight. Messrs. Cannon and Turnbull also went out yesterday morning, returned about six o'clock in the evening. They claim to have trailed the Mexican in the neighborhood of the old smelter and down the Chaparral road; traced his course to a Mexican cabin where they saw three empty Winchester cartridge boxes. There were all sorts of wild stories all out on the streets which could be traced to no credible source.

From the same edition:

Geo. P. Harrington telephoned from Crowned King to the sheriff's office, that he believed Cornellia, the Mexican escaped prisoner, was in that neighborhood. Under Sheriff Dillon requested him to put a mounted posse on the trail.

From the same edition:

Hon. T. G. Norris is said to have received a telegram from W. A. Clark, of Fools Gulch, stating that he thought Cornellia, the Mexican escape, had been in that neighborhood. As this man is on foot, he most probably passed through the various camps where he is supposed to have been seen.

From the same edition:

City Marshal Prince, who went out with the Ruffner posse, returned last evening. He is quoted as saying that when he left the posse they were in the Black Hills and on Parker's trail. They were very close to him last Monday, as could be seen by the fresh horse signs in the road. They would have overtaken him had they not lost the trail for about three hours. The trail indicates that Parker was lost, as it frequently led to the top of the most elevated points, where Parker seemed to have ridden to get his bearings. The impression with the posse was that Parker would make for Black Canyon or Cherry Creek pass.

Deputy Assessor Rybon and J. D. Moore returned last night from the scene of the battle on Upper Lynx creek. They ascertained that Parker dropped Miller from his horse after carrying him about 400 yards. It will be remembered that Parker drew Miller upon his horse and rode off with him when Miller was shot. Rybon says that Parker rode over the hill and dropped Miller in the next gulch, as the horse was unable to carry double up the next hill over which Parker rode. Miller is supposed to be on the head of Big Bug, where he has friends who may doctor his wounded leg. Rybon went out again last evening.

From the same edition:

Jack Nelson and Deputy Sheriff Merritt are in the Crowned King section hunting Cornellia, the Mexican.

From the same edition:

There were no new developments of note in the outlaw chase yesterday, as is generally known. Sheriff Ruffner telegraphed in from Jerome Junction Tuesday evening for fresh horses. These were immediately forwarded him and he left Jerome Junction yesterday morning on Parker's trail, who is said to have passed through that section. After the Ruffner posse left Jerome Junction, two deputy sheriffs and three Indian trailers arrived from Peach Springs and followed the Ruffner party. Ruffner had telegraphed for these trailers. It is stated that Parker had passed east of Jerome Junction and headed in the direction of Campbell and Baker's ranch. As usual, there were all sorts of reports as to what Parker did, where he slept, etc., but the above is the straight at information that could be gained up to the date of this writing, 7 p.m.

The first few days after the escape seemed endless. Everyone presumed the three armed and dangerous men would be captured in short order. When this did not happen, people became edgy. From the *Arizona Journal Miner* of May 19, 1897:

A DAY OF SUSPENSE

No Tidings Whatever From the Pursuers of Parker—The Whereabouts of Miller and Cornelia Still Unknown

From Wednesday's Daily

Up to the hour of going to press nothing had been heard at the sheriff's office from the posse in pursuit of Parker. The only fresh rumor on the street today was brought in by a passenger from Ash Fork on last night's train, stating that Parker had passed near there yesterday, riding a bay horse and headed towards Peach Springs. The rumor may or may not be true, but the sheriff's office has received no notice of it. If true, Parker had evidently secured a fresh animal. The fact that no word has been received from Sheriff Ruffner is construed by many to mean that Parker has traded his tired horse off for a fresh one, as otherwise the sheriff's posse could scarcely have failed to overtake him yesterday. At 2:30 this afternoon Sheriff Cameron, of Coconino county, telegraphed from Ash Fork, asking that the blood hounds be sent up there. A. W. Galpin arrived from Phenix on the early train this morning with three young dogs, and those, with J. D. Moore's two, were sent up on this afternoon's train in charge of Mr. Galpin.

A telephone message was received later in the afternoon from deputies Merritt and Burt, from Crowned King, saying that they had failed so far to locate the Mexican.

No news whatever has been received from parties in pursuit of Miller.

Governor Franklin yesterday issued rewards of $500 each for the capture of Miller and Parker, and $250 for the Mexican.

The *Phoenix Herald* of May 12, 1897 reprinted some of the *Journal Miner*'s coverage, but added some extra details from their area:

Sheriff Orme and posse returned last evening from the Castle Creek Hot Springs, at which place they had received word of the whereabouts of the fugitives, and knowing that they could not catch up with them and could do no good where they were.

This morning the following telegram was received by Sheriff Orme:

"Ruffner advises me that he is sure of getting Parker today. He has his trail in the Black Hills and is close behind him. The three have separated, Miller and the Mexican trying to get south. Keep all roads to the north guarded.

Dillon

Sheriff Orme at once sent Deputy McPheal west to guard the roads leading south, and as Mr. McPheal is thoroughly posted on that section of country, it will be impossible for the outlaws to pass him.

> The other posse which left here Monday has not been heard from and it is believed they are with the pursuing posse from the north.
> A special left Ash Fork last night with the three Indian trailers who assisted in the capture of Parker some time ago. They are Captain Jack Hardy, Indian Kate and Indian Lester, and it is said they are the best trailers on the American continent today, being better to keep the trail of a man afoot over any mountain in the country better than blood hounds. They left the train at Jerome junction and went up into the Black Hills where they will join Ruffner and run their man to earth.

The Indian trailers, of course, bore ridiculous names hung on them by their white "masters." The practice of "using" Indians to trail fugitives was actually in its last days in America at this time. In fact, at this time in Arizona, it was primarily Mohave County authorities who actively engaged in the practice yet, with its heavy Hualapai population. In fact, even though Mohave Indian trailers were used to track Parker during the First Posse, there is evidence that Yavapai's Sheriff Ruffner scoffed at the idea that there was any benefit to this. From *Our Mineral Wealth* of May 21, 1897:

> Jim Parker is still spending his summer vacation in the cool shades of waving pines. Indian Hardy was not allowed by the Sheriff of Yavapai county to trail the robber's horse when he pulled the shoes from it else Mr. Parker might now be in hock once more."

The *Arizona Gazette* covered much of the same territory regarding the pursuit May 12, 1897, but added the following:

> At a late hour last night the following dispatch from Sheriff Ruffner to Prescott officials was duplicated to the Gazette:
> "Jerome Junction, May 11.-After leaving Prescott Sunday night I caught traces of Parker where the fight with the posse occurred the previous evening. Got track of him in the Lynx creek mountains about 10 o'clock yesterday morning.; Trailed him from there to Black Hills, and stayed in Black Hills last night. I think Parker saw us yesterday evening just before dark. Have trailed him forty-five miles today. He could not have been more than three hours ahead of us. His horse is very tired. Neither Parker nor the animal have had anything to eat for about fifty hours. We found two shoes that were cast by the horse. His feet are getting sore.
> "Ruffner."
> Another special dispatch as follows was received:
> "Prescott, May 11.-Late tonight R. E. Wells, general manager of the S.F., P & P., received a telegram from Sheriff Ruffner at Jerome Junction, requesting a special train from the Junction to Ash Fork and return. This has been arranged for. The plan outlined by the sheriff is to have three Indian scouts taken to Jerome Junction and chase Parker further. Ruffner wants the same scouts he had when he trailed Parker the last time."
> Just what the special train was wanted for the telegram does not state, but it is presumed that it was for the purpose of conveying the Indian scouts to Jerome Junction to take up the trail without delay. Sheriff Ruffner does not state anything

about Miller in his dispatch, and it is probable that Parker left him and is traveling alone."

From the same edition:

A report reached here yesterday that Dick George, who was a member of the posse that left here to go on the trail of the escaped jail birds from Prescott, was dismounted and continuing the chase on foot. It is a safe bet that if Dick comes up with Parker he will have the latter's horse.

The *Arizona Republican* had this to say May 12, 1897:

CLOSING IN ON THE OUTLAW

Sheriff Ruffner Says He Will Have Parker Before Night

The Desperado Bewildered and Starving-Return of Sheriff Orme Last Night-A Hint from Prescott of a Prospective Lynching

No authentic report was received here yesterday announcing the capture of Jim Parker, the train robber and murderer. The authorities, both here and at Prescott, think, though, that he has been either killed or taken, since it seems impossible that he should escape. No fugitive in Arizona was ever before so furiously hunted or tried to escape against greater odds.

Sheriff Orme, Al Galpin and William Doheney, who went to Castle Creek hot springs on Sunday night expecting to intercept the fugitive there, returned late yesterday evening. The driver of the Castle Creek stage who meets the driver on the other end of the line at Briggs, returned to Castle Creek at midnight of Monday. The other driver told him that the outlaws had gone east on Groom creek, closely pursued. They were expected to emerge near Chapparal. A telephone message had been sent on Sunday night to Joe Meyers' ranch several miles from Chapparal alarming the country and directing that the neighborhood be closely guarded. The posses, both before and behind the outlaws, were constantly increasing.

Word was sent to Sheriff Orme that he need not follow. He would have gone on, but in order to reach the part of the country in which he could be of any service it would have been necessary to make a detour requiring two days. The hunt he believed would be over within less time.

Parker was badly mounted, beside being encumbered by the wounded Miller. His horse was a pacing horse, unable to stand a long chase. He was without a saddle, and riding a bareback horse is killing. The advantage he and Miller had gained in the darkness of Sunday night had been lost and they were being closely pressed. Parker was known to be without Winchester cartridges and there was no likelihood of his being able to obtain any along the route. He and Miller have had no time for rest or sleep, not even enough time to look for food or water, if indeed any were to be found. There are said to be no horses in the country through which they were going, so that it has been impossible for them to secure a remount on their way.

A telegram was received at the sheriff's officer yesterday saying that the Mexican, Cornelia, was not with Parker and Miller and had probably gone southwest. If Sheriff Orme had received that information at Castle Creek he would have crossed into the San Domingo country, the region in which Cornelia would most likely have sought refuge and the one in which he would most likely have found it. The settlement is made up largely of outlaws, among whom are a lot of Gila river Mexicans who fled into that country years ago and have never left it since. They live by placer mining on a small scale. The adjacent ranges supply them with beef. A report reached here yesterday morning that having been abandoned by Parker, Miller had been captured. The report could not be traced to its source and nothing was known at Prescott of the incident.

The only apparent hope of the fugitives seems to be in being able to hide from their pursuers. But that is a forlorn hope, for the posse from Prescott is attended by Moore's bloodhounds.

Since the news of Norris' murder has been spread abroad the country, interest in the chase has been deepened and it is said that if Parker is taken alive Sheriff Ruffner will have a hard time landing him in jail alive. The sheriff has a double reason for avoiding a lynching. The first is that it would blot his official record and the other is that the $4,500 offered for Parker's conviction of train robbery would go glimmering if he should die before his trial.

A later telegram at the sheriff's office yesterday afternoon said that the desperadoes were going northeast, headed evidently for Utah or New Mexico.

LATEST FROM THE PURSUIT

The following dispatch from Prescott was received at The Republican's office late last night.

"Prescott, Ariz., May 11.-At 9 o'clock tonight a message just received from Sheriff Ruffner locates his posse twenty-three miles north of town, on a fresh trail of Parker, the train robber and murderer. They are camped for the night, awaiting the arrival of three Indian trailers.

The other two jail breakers cut loose from Parker and have gone in an opposite direction. A big posse leaves tonight on the train with fresh animals. Parker since Sunday has been without food and is evidently so closely pursued that he has become bewildered. A fight to the death will certainly follow before he is captured. There are over fifty officers out from this city and the country is thoroughly aroused. Ruffner telegraphs that he will have his man before sundown on Wednesday. The city is quiet, but nevertheless is determined if a capture is affected."

From the Republican of May 13, 1897:

The only definite information received here yesterday from the pursuit of Parker, the train robber and murderer, was afterward found to be untrue. Early in the morning a telegram from Under Sheriff Dillon of Yavapai county containing in substance the dispatch to The Republican the night before was received at the sheriff's office. The under sheriff had had assurance from Sheriff Ruffner that Parker would be captured before night. It was added that Miller and the Mexican were going south and the authorities here were directed to watch all roads.

Harry McPhaul started west to intercept the fugitives if they should attempt to pass in that direction. Dr. Helm received a telegram from Prescott asking him if he could start for there on the next train. It was indefinite and it was inferred that word had reached there of a fight in which a member of the posse had been wounded. W. H. Buck, N.J. Hale, Dick George and Lin Orme,Jr., who left town on Monday morning, returned late yesterday afternoon from an extensive circuit, embracing Castle Creek, Goddard and Humbug without having heard anything of the outlaws.

As a matter of fact nobody knows what direction Miller has taken. In the eagerness of the pursuit after Parker, he has been lost sight of and it is only supposed that he is traveling south. There seems little doubt, though, that the Mexican went in the direction of the San Domingo country, where it will be hard to locate him. It appeared late in the afternoon that Parker's capture was not as close at hand as it seemed twenty-four hours before. Sheriff Ruffner telegraphed for the city bloodhounds and Al Galpin left with them yesterday evening. He will go to Jerome Junction, where he will be met by a buckboard and taken northeast where the posse is now supposed to be on the trail.

The posse already had Moore's bloodhounds, besides three Indian trailers, who joined the party yesterday morning. It is supposed here that the other dogs had either given out or had been killed by Parker."

The same edition editorialized on the prevalence of rumors concerning the chase:

The Prescott jail delivery and the pursuit of the fugitives has contributed to the development of the liar in Phoenix. Startling rumors originate and newspaper reporters and other dupes who try to follow them back find they pinch out before they reach a telegraph office or other reliable medium of communications with the scene of the disturbance.

Again, the *Arizona Gazette* covered much of this same territory, but added their own observations May 13, 1897:

Parker, the train robber and murderer, at last accounts was still at liberty and heading towards the Mogollon mountains. How he has managed to elude the officers so long is a mystery, and he must be endowed with wonderful powers of endurance, for so far as is known he has been without food since he made his escape. He has been so closely pressed that he has had no time to seek food or rest.

From the same edition:

Conductor Kipper of the S. F., P. &P. said yesterday that he met Sheriff Ruffner at Jerome Junction Tuesday night, and the officer told him that during the day he could not have been more than ten miles behind Parker, and that the latter was making slow progress on account of the condition of himself and the horse he was riding. The sheriff's clothes were in tatters, the result of trailing the outlaw through the brush. The officer was hopeful, and said it would be a miracle if Parker escapes. The entire northern country is aroused, and the outlaw can look for assistance from no one in the Black Hills. The only fear is that he may elude his pursuers long enough to reach the Mogollons, where he has friends who will hide him from his pursuers.

From the same edition:

The posse composed of Will Buck, Dick George and Lin Orme, jr., that left here Monday morning, returned yesterday afternoon. The posse struck out for Goddard's station and then went to Tiptop, where it was learned that the outlaws were surrounded and capture certain, so the posse returned to Phoenix by way of Castle creek. Sheriff Orme is now waiting to hear from Prescott before sending a posse north to Wickenburg to cut off the Mexican and Miller should they be traveling toward the San Domingo country.

There is heavy irony to note that six years later, the well-known stage stop of Goddard Station would cease to exist, owing to the brutal murder of its owner, Charles Goddard, and his assistant Frank Cox. The two murderers would be hanged on the Courthouse Square in Prescott, just as Parker ultimately was.

From the same edition:

That jaunt Al Galpin took with the posse that was on the trail of the Prescott jail breakers served to reduce him in weight and impart to his complexion a decidedly burnt appearance.

Galpin apparently *rejoined* the posse, for the May 14, 1897 *Gazette* reported:

Al Galpin has gone north with the city bloodhounds to take the trail of Parker. The bloodhounds, although pups, have on several occasions shown remarkable sagacity on the trail, and they will no doubt assist largely in running the outlaw to earth.

From the same edition:

Parker, the outlaw, has thus far managed to successfully elude his pursuers, and how he has done so is a mystery, as he has three of the best Indian trailers in the country following him up, and the entire northern country is out to head him off. The last authentic news received of him was that Sheriff Ruffner and posse had trailed him to within twelve miles of Ash Fork, and he was headed towards Pine Springs. Sheriff Cameron of Flagstaff has left with a posse to head off the outlaw. Parker has now reached a country where he has friends, and there is now no certainty that he will be captured.

The same edition ran the following editorial:

We need different jails or more watchful officers. The sad ending of one of Prescott's most promising young men, Lee Norris is proof of this. While not criticizing the officials in Prescott, these escapes occur annually all over the territory and a different system ought to be inaugurated.

In its May 15, 1897 edition, the *Santa Fe Daily New Mexican* reported:

> A.P. Frederick, postal inspector, passed through to southern Arizona on Thursday morning with the intention of intercepting Jim Parker, whom he, Frederick, thought was heading for Mexico. Mr. Frederick detailed some good news, which I will try to put in shape for the next letter.

Newspapers in California covered much of this same territory via wire services dispatches, but the *San Francisco Call* reprinted another telegram from Sheriff Ruffner in their May 13, 1897 edition:

> At midnight last night the following information was received from Sheriff Ruffner:
> "I ran Parker out of Lynx Creek Mountains about 10 o'clock yesterday morning; trailed him to the Black Hills and stayed in the hills last night. Think Parker saw us yesterday evening just before dusk. Tracked him about forty-five miles to-day. He could not have been more than three hours ahead of us at any time. His horse is evidently very tired and neither he nor his horse has had anything to eat for over fifty hours. Think we have a sure thing in the morning."

The *Call* added these cryptic thoughts the following day:

CAMPING ON PARKER'S TRAIL

> Officers and Bloodhounds Pursuing the Arizona Train-Robber
> Prescott, Ariz., May 13.-Parker, the escaped train-robber is now not far from Ash Fork and seems to be heading for his old haunts in the region of the Grand Canyon of the Colorado. Sheriff Ruffner, with a strong posse, including three expert Indian trailers, is closely following the fugitive, and it is marveled that he has not caught him yet. Two young bloodhounds from Phoenix have been added to the party, though with what success is not known. If Parker is captured alive it is not believed he will be taken back to Prescott. The temper of the people here is at a dangerous heat. Several murderers now in jail are apt to escape the extreme penalty through a defect in the murder law passed by the last Legislature and Parker's lynching would be accompanied by at least two others.

But, of course, it was the Prescott newspapers that carried the most detail. The posse on the trail of Parker and his comrades was one of the most extensive in Arizona up to its time. From the *Arizona Journal Miner* of May 19, 1897:

ON PARKER'S TRAIL

The Sheriff's Posse Re-inforced With Fresh officers, Horses and Indian Trailers
From Thursday's Daily.

The first news received from the sheriff's posse in pursuit of the outlaws since Sunday night was received at the sheriff's office last night. It came in the shape of a telegram from Sheriff Ruffner from Jerome Junction and was to the effect that the posse had followed the trail for about forty-five miles and had Parker located in the Black Hills. It was apparent that neither he or his horse had had anything to eat since leaving Prescott, except such as the could pick up on the way.

In response to a telegram from the sheriff John Denair, division superintendent of the A. & P. railroad run a special train from Peach Springs to Ash Fork last night and from there a special was run to Jerome Junction. It contained two officers, two expert Indian trailers and four fresh horses.

The train arrived at Jerome Junction at 4 o'clock this morning and the officers and trailers immediately started out to join Ruffner and party and it was confidently expected that they would be able to run Parker to earth before night today.

Parker lost his bearings on Monday night and leaving the mountains road across the upper end of Lonesome valley within a mile and a half or two miles of Point of Rocks or within nine or ten miles of Prescott, arriving there probably about daylight when realizing his location doubled and headed back to the Black Hills.

The officers found where he had tied his horse and where he had lain down to sleep. From the point where he had camped he took a north-easterly course, his trail going about four miles east of Jerome Junction, and at dark last night where they left it he was heading directly towards Campbell & Baker's lower ranch on the Verde. As his horse showed signs of being tired out it is more than probable that he would secure a fresh horse there last night. It is rumored that he formerly worked there but this could not be traced to any reliable source.

During a portion of the time yesterday the officers figured that they were not more than three hours behind him judging by certain signs. Another evidence that Parker was lost is the fact that he frequently rode to high points in the mountains in order to get his bearings, as well as to take a view of the country to watch for his pursuers. Sheriff Ruffner telegraphed that Parker had evidently seen them on Monday night.

J. D. Moore and Ben Rybon returned yesterday from their hunt for Miller. They found the trail and followed it for some distance but it was too old for the dogs and they were compelled to return. They state, however, that Miller separated from Parker within one hundred yards or less from where they were when the fight with Munds occurred. It is still thought that Miller is in the neighborhood of Big Bug or Chaparral.

A telephone message was received from Crowned King yesterday stating that it was thought that the Mexican was in that vicinity and Deputy Sheriff Jack Nelson and two or three others started from there in search of him.

Prisoners in the county jail charged with murder have grown extremely nervous over the events of the past few days and seem to realize that the proper thing for the citizens of Prescott to do would be to have a general hanging bee. At any rate whatever their thoughts may be, they requested the jailor last night to send to Whipple for a detachment of troops stationed to guard the jail and protect them. In addition to Thompson and Rogers confined for complicity for train robbery, there are two men there who have been convicted and sentenced to be hanged, but granted a new trial by the supreme court, and Richard Cross, the red handed murderer of Jones, at Jerome. The latter, it is said, manifests the greatest degree of nervousness, as he relies on the law passed by the last legislature to save his worthless neck, and he specially dreads meeting justice at the hands of an outraged community.

Parker left the jail without either coat or hat, but it is stated he had a supply of biscuits and meat stored away in his shirt.

It is shocking to this day to see a major newspaper like the *Journal Miner* openly call for a lynch mob to storm the jail and dispatch its inhabitants into eternity. Some people were shocked even in 1897, for the *Arizona Republican* on May 14, 1897 reprinted the "hanging bee" comment and then proceeded to scold the Prescott paper:

That is not the right kind of talk, neighbor. Arizona's reputation in the money centers is already bad enough. We don't need the kind of advertisement that a first class lynching would be.

People were amazed at Parker's resourcefulness, and they puzzled over how he could have eluded capture for so long. Undoubtedly he was aided, either forcibly or voluntarily, by some of the country settlers in northern Arizona, and this would later be corroborated. Country settlers often had a deep mistrust of "city folks," and sometimes considered any enemy of the "city folks" to be their friend. Also, Parker undoubtedly had friends strewn all over the area from his days as a ranching cowboy.

But several days had passed without any positive eyeball sightings of him. That was bound to change, however. From the *Arizona Journal Miner* of May 19, 1897:

PARKER NEAR WILLIAMS

He Held Up a Sheep Camp, Got a Fresh Horse and Replenished His Ammunition
From Friday's Daily

Sheriff Cameron of Coconino county, telegraphed to Under Sheriff Dillon after midnight last night asking the latter to notify Sheriff Ruffner to go to Williams. What reason he had for sending this word was not given. As Mr. Dillon had not heard from his chief for forty-eight hours, it would have been about as impracticable to send the word to him as to have sent to Parker.

A telephone message was received from Chaparral last evening saying that Miller had been seen in Eugenia Gulch yesterday and they hoped to capture him today. The report of his being wounded in the leg was confirmed by this message.

Cornellia was reported to have been seen in the vicinity of Crowned King on Wednesday night, but it was not the officers who saw him.

Joe Tappan, who is visiting Prescott, says he is acquainted with Parker and that he is a desperate man. In the cattle and sheep men's troubles some years ago in northern Yavapai, Parker was on the side of the cattlemen and was considered a bad man. He is also said to have stolen several horses, but no attention was paid to the crime for fear of Parker and his ever ready gun.

The first definite news received from the sheriff's posse, came about 10:30 this morning in the shape of a telegram from Williams from Sheriff Cameron of Coconino county. It stated that Sheriff Ruffner and posse had left Williams this morning. The telegram stated further that they knew positively where Parker was located, and that he and posse would leave in a few minutes with the pack of blood hounds, and were certain would capture him within two days.

As explanatory of the two telegrams received from Cameron what seems like authentic information was received this morning stating that Parker had stopped last night at a sheep camp near Williams. That he had secured a fresh horse and a Winchester rifle and fifty rounds of ammunition. This information was received at Ash Fork last night and it was acting on it apparently that Sheriff Cameron left there this morning for Williams.

The story of Parker robbing the sheep camp would later fall into dispute, especially the part about Parker securing a new horse and abandoning Sure-Shot. The *Arizona Republican* covered the story this way on May 15, 1897:

Very little was heard here yesterday of the chase after Parker. A note was received at the sheriff's office from Al Galpin, who said he was about to leave with his bloodhounds with Sheriff Cameron's posse. The note was delivered by the conductor of the north and south train, but he did not say from what point it had been sent. It was afterward learned that the party was at Williams. The conductor of the evening train reported that Parker had visited a sheep camp near Bill Williams' mountain and had obtained a fresh horse, a Winchester rifle and fifty rounds of cartridges. This was afterward confirmed by an Associated Press dispatch to The Republican from Prescott. It was also reported that Sheriff Ruffner's horse, which Parker rode away last Sunday, returned to Prescott yesterday. It is beginning to be doubted now whether Parker will be captured at all. His flight had been admirably conducted. With a start of only twenty minutes and pursued by fifty men from the outset, so far as is known, until he visited the sheep camp he had not been seen since the fight on the Lynx creek divide on Sunday afternoon. His journey has described half a circle around Prescott and three days after his escape he was within twenty-three miles of the town. The whole country had long before been alarmed by telephone or telegraph and one telephone line crossed the arc of the circle he was making. He was so closely followed that he had not even time to eat if he had food. His horse was fatigued and every chance seemed to be against him. Now he is in a country with which he is more familiar than any of his pursuers. He is also well mounted and among persons who are more or less friendly to him.

The *Arizona Gazette* reported it this way, complete with a telegram reprint, on May 15, 1897:

PARKER HEARD FROM

Stopped at a Sheep Camp and Secured Ammunition

Another day has passed and still outlaw Parker is a free man, although the minions of the law are pressing him on every hand. Each day his chances of capture are growing slimmer for he is now in a country where he has friends who will throw every obstacle in the way of his pursuers.

Sheriff Ruffner, with the untiring energy for which he is noted is still on the trail and those who know him say that he will not retire from the chase until Parker is either captured or killed. It is a mystery how the outlaw has managed to evade capture for so long a time for since the day he made his escape he has been handicapped in every way. His knowledge of the country has stood him in good hand for an unacquainted person would long since have famished from thirst. His powers of endurance must be wonderful, for the first three days of his liberty it is not known that he had anything to eat, as he was too closely pressed to do anything but travel continuously. The only authentic news that has been heard concerning Parker was a telegram received by Sheriff Orme yesterday from Al Galpin at Ash Fork. The telegram reads as follows:

"Parker stayed on Bill Williams mountain last night (Wednesday) at a sheep camp. He got a Winchester and fifty rounds of ammunition from the herders. I leave in thirty minutes with five dogs on the trail. Am at present with Sheriff Cameron's posse."

This would indicate that Parker is now better equipped than at any time since he broke jail and he has a much better show of making a fight should he be surrounded.

The gray horse belonging to Ruffner's livery stable that he stole when he broke jail has returned to Prescott. Parker has evidently secured a fresh mount and turned the other horse loose.

But the reports that Sure-Shot (who, of course was NOT gray) had returned to Prescott on his own were not true, and this is the chief reason why the sheep camp story is not regarded as accurate—or, quite possibly, a friend of Parker's who was a sheepman told this story to the posse to throw them off Parker's trail. This was later speculated as well.

From the *Arizona Journal Miner* of May 26, 1897:

The white horse stolen by Parker from Sheriff Ruffner's livery stable has not been returned, as reported by one or two Phenix papers. So far as known, Parker and the white horse are still keeping company.

The fact that Ruffner was not able to make good on his boast to have Parker captured "by nightfall" did not pass unnoticed. The *Los Angeles Times* put it this way May 15, 1897:

RUFFER TALKED TOO SOON
The Sheriff Has not Got Fugitive Parker Circumferenced
(By Associated Press Wire)

Prescott (Ariz.) May 14.—Telegrams received at the Sheriff's office today, stated that Sheriff Ruffner of this county and Sheriff Cameron of Coconino county, left Williams early this morning, with a large posse, accompanied by bloodhounds, on a hot trail after Parker.

From other sources, it is learned that Parker held up a sheep camp near Williams last night, got a fresh horse and Winchester rifle with fifty rounds of ammunition.

The chances for his capture were greatly lessened by this act, as he is now in a country well-known to him, and is well-mounted and armed. Miller and Cornelia still manage to elude the pursuers.

And what of Louis C. Miller and Cornelia Sarata? Sarata seemed to have dropped off the face of the earth, but there was one sighting of Miller prior to his capture. From the *Arizona Gazette* of May 15, 1897:

MILLER NEAR JEROME

He Was Met by Two Prospectors in the Verde Valley

James Conlon arrived yesterday evening from Jerome and gives the information that Lou Miller, one of the Prescott jail breakers was seen Wednesday afternoon in the Verde valley about 15 miles southwest of Jerome. He was met by a couple of prospectors who had been in the hills and knew nothing of the jail delivery. The prospectors assert that they came upon Miller suddenly. He was sitting down in the shade of a tree and appeared very much alarmed when he saw the prospectors. He appeared to be in a famished condition and was so weak that he could hardly stand up. The men furnished him with something to eat and when he stood up they noticed that he was very lame, in fact could hardly move his left leg. His clothes were badly torn and in places the skin was exposed. To the quire of the prospectors as to how he came to be in such a dilapidated condition, Miller evasively replied that he had been prospecting and was thrown from his horse, injuring his leg. His story was so rambling that the suspicion of the prospectors were aroused, but not knowing anything of the jail breaking they formed no conclusion until they arrived at Jerome and gave a description of the man who proved to be Miller. After leaving Miller the prospectors saw him limp off in the direction of the hills. It is supposed that Miller is trying to communicate with friends in Jerome and is hiding in the neighborhood for that purpose.

A very quiet report is being circulated that Miller has already been captured and is being kept quietly in jail at Prescott for fear that an attempt will be made to lynch him. From a dispatch received here last night it was learned that Cornelia was last seen near the Crowned King mine.

This particular dispatch is remarkable historically in that it appeared in the *Gazette* and no other papers that I know of, despite the fact that it is almost certainly true. The article places Miller in the vicinity of Jerome very shortly before his capture there, and yes, as it turned out, he was indeed trying to reach either friends, or his sister and her husband who lived there.

On the night of May 15, 1897, Louis C. Miller was captured in Jerome. Not much more than that is known with certainty; his capture was affected in circumstances that remain controversial and confusing to this day, and continue to have historians (including myself) tearing their hair out. Several newspapers gave radically different accounts of the capture, and it is not known how such widely varying stories could get into print so fast with so much detail. Some journalists in Prescott recognized the problem even then, for that city's papers reprinted some of the differing accounts so the public could decide for itself. It is the sort of situation that has caused many latter-day historians to denigrate the

The mountain town of Jerome, Arizona, c. 1914, clinging precariously to the hillside. It would have looked about like this in 1897 when Louis C. Miller was captured there. (Author's collection)

For comparison, this is Jerome, Arizona today. (Courtesy of David Schmittinger)

usefulness of old newspapers as source material. See if you can wade through this mess. From the *Arizona Journal Miner* of May 19, 1897:

MILLER CAPTURED AT JEROME LAST NIGHT

He is Wounded but Says that Jailor Meador Fired the Shots and That he was not with Parker at Lynx Creek

He Confesses to a Most Murderous Plot on the Part of the Prisoners Involving the Robbery of the County Treasurer

From Saturday's Daily

L. C. Miller, who escaped from jail on Sunday was arrested last night at Jerome by Deputies Fletcher Fairchild and Cade Silvey. By his request he was taken to Flagstaff where he will be kept for a time in jail until excitement in Prescott over the tragic event subsides.

Miller gives a version of the escape and fight which throws an entirely different light on the entire affair. While he is wounded in the left leg and in the left side he received them from bullets from R. W. Meador's pistol as he was coming up the stairway from the jail to the court house instead of from Deputy Munds' rifle. He also states that Meador hit the Mexican too, the bullet passing through his body, but did not strike a vital part. Miller further stated to the officers that he left his two companions within fifteen minutes after their escape and went up by the city reservoir and hid in the brush remaining there till night when he worked his way to Point of Rocks where he remained hidden all day on Monday. There he got on the railroad and followed it till nearly Jerome Junction when he cut across the country to the Jerome road and followed it till near Jerome, when he again took to the brush and remained concealed.

He further states that six prisoners were involved in the plot to escape, their plans having been laid for the previous day, but he refused to divulge the names of the other three. He says the plot as originally planned was to hold up the county treasurer's office and take everything in sight and to spare no one who came between them and liberty, but through some cause or other the opportunity did not present itself. He says that Parker's ambition particularly was to get Sheriff Ruffner. Miller thinks that the Mexican was seriously wounded and that they may find his dead body.

Otto Miller was released from custody this morning there being not a scintilla of evidence to connect him even in the remotest degree with the escape, and he has been made to suffer on account of his brother. It has been apparent from the first that the escapes had no aid whatever from the outside, and Miller corroborates this. The plot was planned entirely on the inside of the jail and executed from there without any outside aid or assistance and without the knowledge of any one on the outside. He says that when the Mexican came out for the water, Parker was concealed from the view of Jailor Meador. That he (Miller) stood at the end of the table in the jail corridor, with a paper in his hands, and that the signal agreed upon by them was that when the Mexican grappled with Meador, he was to drop the paper when all were to rush to the door. This he did but only himself and Parker succeeded in getting through the door.

From an extra issued by the Jerome Reporter last night the following additional particulars are gleaned:

At about 10 o'clock tonight, Friday, forger and jail breaker, L. C. Miller, gave himself up to justice and law at the home of his sister, Mrs. Fred Haas, of this city.

Under Sheriff Fletcher Fairchild, of Coconino county, a brother-in-law of Miller's, had been sent for from Flagstaff and to him Miller surrendered.

It was through the efforts of his sister that Miller, who had been hiding in an old tunnel at the Winningham camp, just above town, in Deception Gulch, for the past two days, was induced to give himself up. He is in a pitiable condition—weak from his wounds which are not, however, of a serious nature, Miller having walked the greater portion of the distance to this city. When he reached the friendly shelter of the Black Hills, and felt that the mine where he worked before he left here—about a month ago—was within reach, he could scarcely muster courage to reach the place where he has been cared for since Wednesday morning.

One of the men who gave Miller shelter in the Winningham camp, is said to be a brother-in-law to Parker.

Miller was at once taken by Fairchilds, in a private conveyance, from town, as he was very much afraid of being lynched. Although his crime itself is but a small one, his association with one of the most foul murders that has ever blotted the pages of the history of our territory, is enough to hang him in the old way in which justice had often been administered in early days, and he implored to be taken some place further from the scene of crime, and is now well on his way to Flagstaff, accompanied by Fairchilds and another officer.

Above all things, Miller had no wish to see Prescott, and for many reasons it was deemed advisable to take him to Flagstaff.

Little can be learned from the people instrumental in his surrender here, as they refused to talk to or see a reporter, and it was only in the first excitement of the news, which was kept very quiet, that any facts of the case could be learned, but Miller is known to have been in town last night (Thursday) at the Haas residence, which is in the business portion of town, but in a very quiet place. Most of the inhabitants were either at the lodge, or at the show, and the coast in that part of town was comparatively clear.

Miller also remarked that the jail breaking was a piece of "d—d foolhardiness on their part"—his especially—as his crime of forgery was for such a small mount, could not have been very severe.

The statement that Fairchild was sent for by interested parties is denied, but his arrival here was very opportune, to say the least.

The Jerome News gives a different version of the affair, which is as follows:

After discovering that Miller was in Jerome, Constable Roberts* immediately started in to capture him. At about 8 o'clock, the hour at which he first found that Miller was in this neighborhood, Roberts went to Walnut Gulch, where Miller was at work some time for Ralph Dillon, the gentleman whose name he forged, and for which act he was in jail when he escaped. The constable went to the part of the trail leading to the Winningham mine, where it first strikes Walnut Gulch and about 300 yards from the mine. He took his stand about fifteen feet from the trail, and awaited patiently the coming of Miller, who, he thought, for reasons hereafter stated, would come there to get assistance from some of the men whom he had worked with. He had been there about one hour when he saw a man coming along the trail from Jerome, who occasionally gave a low whistle. The constable threw his gun—a double barreled shot gun—down on the man when he got opposite him, and commanded him to throw up his hands. After a little persuasion, he threw up his hands, when the constable went up to him, and found that it was Tom Woody, a miner who worked at the Winningham mine. Woody had a gun, a roll of blankets and a sack of grub. He was much excited and repeatedly asked the constable what was the matter, and requested that he be allowed to return to Jerome if anything was the matter, but the constable had been watching this man for the past two days and had noticed that he had daily visited the home of a relative of Miller's, who lives in Jerome, and it was for this reason he went to the trail to watch for Miller. Roberts compelled Woody to proceed on his way to the mine and to keep still. He remained there until 11 o'clock when he concluded that Miller, if he had been there to meet Woody, had become alarmed and moved away. He came to Jerome and again visited the gulch early on Friday morning and continued to keep a close watch out for his man during the day.

In the afternoon Detective Silvey and Deputy Sheriff Fairchild arrived from Tonto Basin, where they had gone from Winslow to intercept the escapes, upon information from the sheriff's office in Prescott that they had gone that way. About nine o'clock the deputy went to the mine and Woody was persuaded to go up the canyon after Miller. He was gone but a short time when he returned with the escape who gave himself up. Miller begged that he not be taken to Prescott, as he was afraid of being lynched, so the officers secured a team from J. L. Summers' livery stable and at 10 o'clock were going down to the Verde valley on their way to Flagstaff, having met Constable Roberts with their prisoner at the top of the hill leading to Deception Gulch.

Miller informed Roberts that he was to meet Woody the night the constable was watching for him on the trail and at the point where he was on the watch, but that he had seen Jim and hid.

Later information from Williams is to the effect that Parker did not stop at the

---

* Famed area lawman Jim Roberts.

sheep camp at all, but went around it, and that he neither secured ammunition nor a fresh horse there.

The confusion gets worse, but before we continue, it needs to be noted that Miller's claim that he was NOT at the Lynx Creek firefight shocked everyone, including the eyewitnesses to the battle, as shall be seen. His statement that the original plan of escape was to rob the treasury seems almost beyond belief—surely they would have known they would not have time for such a thing. Looking back in a historical context, it seems most likely that the ever-defiant Miller was once again sassing the people he believed to be his persecutors. Most people discount his denial of participation in the Lynx Creek firefight, and it is unlikely that the escapees truly thought they could get to the treasury. But as we have seen, Miller had a long history of shooting off his mouth in the face of adversity.

Was he telling the truth about three other convicts being in on the escape plans and not making it? We will never know. Likely candidates for such a plot would have obviously been Abe Thompson, John Rogers (who was still in jail at this time), and Richard Cross, but we will never know for sure.

Adding to the confusion over Miller's capture, the *Prescott Courier* ran the following accounts from two other newspapers on May 21, 1897:

> From Yavapai County Reporter Extra:
> At about ten o'clock tonight (Friday) forger and jail-breaker L. C. Miller, gave himself up to justice and law at the home of his sister, Mrs. Fred Haas, of this city.
>
> Under Sheriff Fletcher Fairchild, of Coconino county, a brother-in-law of Miller, had been sent for from Flagstaff, and to him Miller surrendered. It was through the efforts of his sister that Miller, who had been hiding in an old tunnel at the Winningham camp, just above town, in Deception gulch, for the past two days, was induced to give himself up. He is in a pitiable condition—weak from the wounds given him from the rifle of Deputy Munds in their encounter Sunday afternoon, which are not, however, of a serious nature, Miller having walked the greater portion of the distance from Lynx creek to this city.
>
> Miller confirms the reports of the encounter between the jail breakers on Lynx creek, Sunday afternoon, and says Parker carried him for some distance after his horse was shot from under him and he was wounded, but they agreed to separate, Parker leaving Miller and striking in a south-easterly direction, with Mexico, which was the point ultimately to be reached, in view.
>
> Miller and the Mexican left Parker and him almost as soon as they got of Prescott, and said Crown King country, where he had friends, was good enough for him. Miller was at once taken by Fairchilds, in a private conveyance, from town, as he was very much afraid of being lynched. He is now well on his way to Flagstaff, accompanied by Fairchilds and another officer.

The *Arizona Mining News* of May 18th has the following to say regarding the capture:

> Miller, the forger, who broke jail with Parker, the train robber, and the Mexican, was captured in Walnut gulch, one-half mile south of Jerome, last night about nine

o'clock by Constable Jim Roberts, of Jerome, Detective Silby of the A. & P. R'y, and Deputy Sheriff Fairchild, of Flagstaff, Coconino county.

Miller was in very bad condition and told Constable Roberts the following story of the escape and his experience since: The shots which Jailor Meador fired after the escaping prisoners took effect on Miller, one ball giving him a flesh wound in the side and the other taking a splinter from one of his shins. The one on the shin being the most serious and gave him much pain. He says that when they were about a mile from town he got down from the horse on which he and the Mexican were riding and hid in the brush; that he remained there until dark when he returned to Prescott and continued up the railroad until he came to Jerome Junction, where he laid all day in a ditch, continuing along the railroad that night, hiding in the hills during daylight and continuing toward Jerome during the night, arriving here Wednesday night about 10 o'clock.

He did not know that Lee Norris was dead until he got here, and he was very much affected when he learned that fact.

He says they did not receive any assistance from anyone outside of the jail in their escape.

That he was never near Lynx creek and that it must have been the Mexican who was there with Parker.

He says that Parker is a desperate man and is very bitter against Sheriff Ruffner, and says that he can willingly die if he can first kill him; that when they got to the stable he called for the sheriff and asked the stableman to go and hunt him.

Tom Woody, a miner working in the Winingham mine, is said to have provided for Miller's wants while the latter was secreted.

It gets worse. The *Flagstaff Sun-Democrat* carried the following account on May 20, 1897:

THE CAPTURE OF MILLER

Under Sheriff Fletcher Fairchild Apprehends Him Near Jerome

Under Sheriff Fletcher Fairchild and Detective Cade Selvey arrived in a buckboard from Jerome Saturday evening with Forger Miller, who escaped from the Prescott jail with Parker and the Mexican Carnellia. The prisoner was locked up in one of the steel cells of the county jail here, where he at present languishes.

The details of his capture are interesting. Under Sheriff Fairchild and Deputy Sheriff Martin Bugglin left here for Winslow last week and from there journeyed down into the Tonto Basin country, having received word from Sheriff Ruffner of Yavapai county that Miller and the Mexican were headed for that section. On reaching Tonto Basin no trace of the fugitives could be found and no word could be sent to Ruffner as to what the latest information relative to Miller's whereabouts was in his possession. A start was then made in the direction of Jerome, Mr. Fairchild believing that Miller would stop in that neighborhood on account of having a relative there.

On arriving at Jerome Mr. Fairchild went to the home of this relative and after a diplomatic talk succeeded in learning that Miller was secreted in the Jerome mountains about two miles away. After stating that unless Miller was turned over to him he would undoubtedly be captured by the Prescott officers and be brought there, where he would be sure to be lynched, the relative decided to direct Mr. Fairchild to the hiding place of Miller. Late Friday evening the relative in company with Mr. Fairchild set out for the fugitives retreat. On coming up with Miller he submitted peaceably to arrest and was seemingly glad to get away from the locality and out of reach of the Prescott authorities.

Friday night Mr. Fairchild and Cole Selvey started for Flagstaff with the prisoner, arriving here Saturday evening.

Or how about this version from the *Arizona Republican* of May 16, 1897:

Miller, one of the fugitives from the Prescott jail, was captured at Jerome early yesterday morning. On account of the feeling at Prescott, he was taken on his own request to the jail at Flagstaff. The capture was effected by Coconino county officials. Several versions of the capture were received here in the afternoon. According to one Miller gave himself up. It was said that he went to the railroad depot at Jerome, and sitting there a short time, unrecognized by anybody, went away. His manner aroused suspicion, and after he was gone he was remembered by descriptions of him. He was followed and taken without resistance. He had been shot in the leg. The wound, he said, had been inflicted by Jailor Meador as he was leaving the jail with Parker and the Mexican. The Mexican was shot through the body at the same time.

Norman Lackland of the railway mail service came in from the north last night. On his way down he met Under Sheriff Dillon of Yavapai county, who told him that Miller said as soon as he was out of town last Sunday he slipped from the horse he was riding and hid under a railroad bridge until night. As soon as it was dark he started for Jerome, near which place his married sister lives. The story of his escape preceded him. His brother-in-law, who was away from home when he reached his sister's house on his return, took down a rifle and was going to kill him. His sister pleaded for him and her husband at length consented to let him go unharmed if he would leave the community. He promised to do so and went away, but hid not far from the house. His brother-in-law caught his sister carrying food to him on Friday night and informed on him. He says that when he and his companions left the jail the only weapon they carried with them was the shotgun with which Parker had shot Norris, and there were only two or three shells loaded with bird shot for that.

If Miller's narrative is true in all its parts, the story told by the deputies on their return from the fight on Lynx creek divide on Sunday evening, is sadly compromised. That they killed a horse there is certain, but Miller could not have been there and could not have been shot and gallantly lifted by Parker on the horse behind him, as has been so graphically described.

Nothing was heard at Prescott of Parker. There was a rumor here last night that he had been surrounded in a cabin not far from Bill Williams' mountain and a fight with a large posse was in progress. The rumor could not be traced as far back as a telegraph office.

As we all know, that last paragraph was indeed just a rumor.

Chapter 7: Jailbreak and the Second Posse 219

The California newspapers generally relied on wire service reports to print on Miller's capture. This dispatch, from the May 16, 1897 *San Francisco Call*, is typical:

> Prescott, Ariz., May 16.—L. C. Miller, who accompanied Train-robber Parker in his recent escape from the jail here, was captured this morning near Jerome Junction, twenty-five miles north of Prescott. He was gaunt from suffering and lack of nourishment, and limped badly from a gunshot wound. Contrary to the generally accepted story, he was not shot while with Parker south of Prescott. His wounds were received at the hands of Jailor Meador while he was escaping. Meador fired three shots while the men were leaving the courthouse, and Miller then received two flesh wounds. He separated early from Parker and the Mexican. The latter was badly wounded by the jailer, and Miller believes he has crawled away in some thicket and died.
>
> Deputy Sheriff Fairchild of Coconino County arrested Miller without trouble. At Miller's request he was taken to the Flagstaff jail, as he feared a lynching if returned to Prescott.
>
> The posse after Parker is still reported near Williams, but the prospect of a capture is no better than heretofore. Through raids on sheep camps, Parker now has a fresh horse and is well armed.
>
> In the pursuing party are three of the best men Arizona could engage for such service.
>
> They are Commodore P. Owens*, Sheriff of Navajo County, renowned for bravery at Holbrook, where he single handed fought and killed four desperadoes in one battle; Sheriff Ralph Cameron of Coconino County, who knows every foot of the region, and Sheriff Ruffner of Yavapai County, who is so bitterly in earnest that he has offered $4000 reward on his own account. The posse is expected to run the fugitive into the impassable canyons that lead to the Grand Canyon of the Colorado.

Out of this confusing mess, historians have tended to favor the version that Miller surrendered at the home of his sister. The fact that Fletcher Fairchild would later collect the reward on Miller does much to bolster that story. But somehow or other, Thomas Woody was involved as well, as he was soon arrested for aiding and abetting a fugitive. From the *Prescott Courier* of May 21, 1897:

> Thos. Woody is under arrest in Jerome, and will have his preliminary examination today. He is charged with being an accessory after the fact to the crime of murder. Louis Miller is charged with murder, and Woody is the man who is said to have assisted in the concealment of Miller, while Miller was a fugitive from justice, near Jerome.

From the *Arizona Journal Miner*, May 26, 1897:

> Thomas Woody was arrested at Jerome yesterday, charged with assisting L. C. Miller to escape. District Attorney Ross went to Jerome last night to conduct the examination.

---

* This was famed lawman, Commodore Perry Owens.

From the same edition:

District Attorney H. D. Ross returned this morning from Jerome where he went to conduct the examination of Thomas Woody charged with having rendered assistance to L. C. Miller, an escape from jail. Woody was held under $500 bonds to appear before the grand jury. He furnished the bonds and was released. Woody and Miller were formerly employed together in working a mine.

Thomas Woody's court papers have survived and are interesting to read. The original criminal complaint accusing him of complicity reads as follows:

J. P. Dillon being first duly sworn, deposes and says; -
    That the defendant Thomas Woody is guilty of the crime of being an Accessory after the Fact, in the crime of Murder, committed as follows, to-wit: -
    That at the County of Yavapai, Territory of Arizona, on the 9th day of May, 1897, one L. C. Miller, willfully, feloniously, deliberately, and with his malice aforethought did make an assault on one E. L. Norris, and a certain gun which then and there was loaded with gunpowder and divers leaden bullets, and by him the said L. C. Miller had and held in his hands, he the said L. C. Miller did then and there willfully, deliberately, feloniously and with his malice aforethought shoot off and discharge at and upon the said E. L. Norris, thereby and thus striking the said E. L. Norris, with said leaden bullets, inflicting on and in his body a mortal wound; of which said mortal wound the said E. L. Norris then and there died.
    And that at the County of Yavapai, Territory of Arizona, on or about the 12th day of May, the said Thomas Woody being possessed of full knowledge that the said L. C. Miller had theretofore committed the crime of murder in form aforesaid did feloniously harbor and protect and maintain him, the said L. C. Miller.
    Contrary to the form and effect of the statute in such case made and provided and against the peace and dignity of the Territory of Arizona.
                                 J. P. Dillon
Subscribed and sworn to before me this 18th day of May, 1897.
                                 J. M. W. Moore
                                 Justice of Peace

The record of Woody's preliminary examination has also survived, although it is not known what his defense witnesses testified to. But to add to the confusion over how Miller was caught, pay attention to the names of the individuals who testified AGAINST Woody:

1897, May 20. Defendant Thos. Woody appearing in Court in charge of Depty. Sheriff Tom Elder and demanding that he be allowed to give bail the Court after due consideration and advice of Dist. Atty. Fix his bail at ($1,000.00) One thousand dollars for his appearance in Court at 2 o'clock on May 21st, 1897. Defendant left in charge of Depty. Sheriff returned in Court with W. O. Carrell and A. J. Winningham as bondsmen who justified the Bond and the Bond being approved by the Court, Defendant was released by Depty. Sheriff by order of the Court.

> Complaint filed by the Court with Warrant Subpoena issued for Fred Haas, Mrs. Haas and Joe Roberts on (illegible) of Territory subpoena issued for J. E. Winningham, J. Brown and E. P. Mayhew on (illegible) Dept.
> Fred Haas, Mrs. Haas and Joe Roberts sworn and testified on part of Plff. After the argument of District Atty. And E. M. Sanford for Defendant. The Court took the case under advisement until 6 o'clock p.m.
> At 6 o'clock p.m. in open court Dist. Atty. And E. M. Sanford and Defendant being present made the following order:
> It appearing to me that the crime of an accessory after the fact to the crime of murder has been committed and that there is sufficient cause to believe Thomas Woody guilty thereof. I order that he be held to answer the same and I have admitted him to bail to answer in the sum of five hundred dollars and that he be committed to the Sheriff of the County of Yavapai until he gives such bail.
> (name illegible)
Justice of the Peace

Ultimately, when the grand jury met in June, they decided not to indict Woody, and he was officially cleared. This was reported without comment in the court column of the *Arizona Journal Miner* on June 16, 1897.

While awaiting the action of the grand jury, Thomas Woody proved that he was as audacious as Miller himself—he applied for the reward. From the *Arizona Journal Miner* of May 26, 1897:

> Applications for the reward offered by the governor for the capture of the outlaw Miller are already beginning to arrive at the governor's office. Today a telegram was received by Governor Franklin from T. B. Woody of Jerome, claiming the reward and requesting that the claims of all others for that reward be discredited as Miller surrendered to him personally."—Phoenix Herald. Mr. Woody is just now under a cloud charged with aiding Mr. Miller to escape. If he succeeds in establishing his claim to the reward, it will be of great aid in clearing him of this charge.

The *Prescott Courier* of May 28, 1897 reprinted the following from Jerome's *Arizona Mining News* of May 22:

> The reward for the capture of Miller is claimed by six parties: Officers Roberts, Fairchilds, Selby, Tom Woody, Fred Haas and Miller himself says he is entitled to a share of it. There is only $833 to be paid for the capture of Miller, and if they all get a slice there will be but little for each.

The ever-defiant Miller was apparently arguing that since he surrendered and thus made possible his own capture, that he was entitled to the reward on himself! This was a show of audacity that is remarkable even today. Can you imagine, though, at how Minnie Haas felt over her husband trying to collect the reward on her brother?

The same edition of the *Courier* carried the following, which added even more confusion to the details over how Miller was captured:

> T. B. Woody has demanded, and seems to stand a chance of getting, the entire reward offered for the capture of Lou Miller. Woody is the man supposed to have harbored Miller during his stay near the Winningham camp, but now asserts that had he been left alone, Miller's surrender would have taken place before it did. He says that on the evening when Roberts came up the gulch, he was on his way to see Miller for the first time, and had every intention of taking him to town as his prisoner or as a corpse. He further states, and no one seems ready to deny it, that it was to him alone that Miller surrendered, and he intends to get the reward offered. It is known that Woody went up the gulch after the signal was given to Miller, and returned to where the other members of the party were awaiting him, with Miller, not as his prisoner, for no arrest had been made, but as the means by which Miller was compelled to lay down his arms. This makes the fifth claims for that reward.

Ultimately, Coconino County Under-Sheriff Fletcher Fairchild was awarded the entire amount of the reward. The July 23, 1897 *Courier* contained a reprint from Jerome's *Arizona Mining News* of July 17:

> Tom Woody informs the News that he did not receive any part of the reward paid to Fairchild for the capture of L. C. Miller. Tom says he wants it all or nothing.

Nothing further is known of Thomas Woody. Like so many others in that era, once he was out of the limelight, he probably took the opportunity to leave the area and start over somewhere else.

While the confusion over Miller's capture was raging, Jim Parker and Cornelia Sarata were continuing to elude the posses. Parker was riding into the Williams area, where he had many friends from his cowboying days. The May 21 *Prescott Courier* contained the following dispatches:

> Acting Deputy Sheriff Horace Yeoman returned to Prescott Saturday. The last he saw of Parker's trail was seven miles south of Williams. Yeoman has a force of men at work in Big Bug district to look after. He is confident that the men he and Deputy Munds had a fight with were Miller and Parker. He knows Cornellia well, as the latter cut wood for him a long time in the Senator section.

From the same edition:

> Sheriff Ruffner came in from the north Saturday night and went out again in the morning with six fresh horses. He says Parker is fortified in the Bill Williams' mountains, south of Williams; that he still has the white horse he rode out of Prescott. His shotgun was found with one empty cartridge in near the sheep camp where he got the Winchester and cartridges. Ruffner brought back the shotgun. In the same vicinity, Parker pulled the shoes from the white horse and ran the horse

for an hour or two with a band of bronchos to throw pursuers off the trail, but the trailers succeeded in following the trail of the white horse.

From the same edition:

Under Sheriff Dillon yesterday morning received the following telegram:
   Williams, May 14, 1897, 9:09 a.m.
         J. P. Dillon, Prescott, Arizona:
   Ruffner left here this morning. I am positive where Parker is; will have him in a few days, and possibly, at once; will try and keep you posted; have all help necessary; if we need anything will advise you. Hope to capture inside of two days.
                                   R. H. Cameron

From the same edition:

Special Deputies Lacey and Cannon brought in seven or eight horses on last night's train. They are animals which had been ridden leg weary by Sheriff Ruffner's posse.

From the same edition:

Under Sheriff Dillon received reliable news from Crown King yesterday that Cornellia, the Mexican, was still in that neighborhood.

From the same edition:

The stage-driver who came in from Crownd King last evening says the officers were sanguine of capturing the Mexican escape in that vicinity soon.

From the same edition:

Under-Sheriff Dillon has a task on hand of summoning about 150 witnesses to appear before the grand jury—with horse flesh a little scarce and in bad condition owing to vigorous pursuit of outlaws on available horses.

From the same edition:

A telegram was received in Prescott Saturday addressed to Deputy Sheriff Munds, stating that his mother was very sick in San Francisco. Munds is in northern Arizona on the trail of Parker.

Munds reportedly left the posse after that to go to his mother's bedside. From the same edition:

No set of men could have done more to recapture outlaws than have the sheriff of Yavapai county and his deputies. They have hardly known what sleep was since the occurrence; have been and are now doing all that human effort is capable of and the Courier believes that effort will eventually be crowned with success.

Artist J. E. Coker drew on his imagination and drew a very good picture of the recent fight on Lynx creek between deputy sheriffs and outlaws.

Unfortunately, the sketch is not known to have survived. From the same edition:

The Mexican was seen near Crowned King Thursday night. The Mexican's mother and family live in Nogales.

Report is that Chas. Genung, a good trailer and good shot, and who knows the country well, is on the trail of the Mexican and that he is personally acquainted with him.

Parker and his pursuers are now beyond a reasonable doubt in the rough wilds of the northern part of this territory, a region so isolated from the balance of the country that no definite news can be expected from it in less than two or three days. The posse will, in all probability, run the outlaw to cover, surround him and keep him there until he succumbs to thirst and hunter. This method could be pursued without loss of life, otherwise, we fear some one may be hurt, for Parker is a splendid shot and will hardly be taken alive.

Charles Genung was, of course, Yavapai County's legendary pioneer, miner, and scout who almost single-handedly settled the Peeples Valley, Yarnell, and Wickenburg areas. This clipping represents his only appearance in the Parker story.

Demonstrating once again how fast and furious rumors could fly in such a situation, the *Phoenix Herald* printed this tidbit on May 17, 1897:

From a gentleman who arrived from the north yesterday, it is learned that Sheriff Ruffner was in Prescott yesterday having come down from Williams. He spent but a short time in Prescott where he procured six horses, one of which was his favorite white horse which Parker rode off when he made his escape. Mr. Ruffner stated that Parker had given them the slip in the mountains between Williams and Flagstaff and that the posse was still hunting for the trail and would stay with it as long as there was a possibility of finding their man.

The Phoenix papers were still insisting that Sure-Shot had returned to Prescott. Even worse was this bit of gossip in the *Arizona Gazette* May 18, 1897:

News was received in the city last night that Cornelia, the Mexican who escaped with Parker and Miller from the Prescott jail, had been captured at the Crowned King mine.

Of course, Cornelia Sarata had not been captured at all, and in truth, the posse on his trail actually had no idea where he went.

Speculation that Parker would be almost impossible to catch if he reached the Bill Williams mountains proved true. He had done much cowboying in the area, and knew the region like the back of his hand. He had many friends in the area as well, and help him they did.

Many after-the-fact accounts of the Parker story have dwelled on the many "tricks" Parker used to elude the posse. Although some have been exaggerated, many were quite true. Parker seemed to be about the most resourceful outlaw to come down the pike in a long time. From the *Arizona Journal Miner* of May 19, 1897:

> Sheriff Ruffner came in on Saturday night's south bound train from his pursuit of Parker, the outlaw, and returned again to Ash Fork on the early north bound train on Sunday morning, taking with him eight fresh horses to continue the pursuit. Parker shows great shrewdness and cunning in his attempt to keep away from the officers. At one point in his trail they found where he had made a circle of several miles, crossing his own trail twice. In making the circuit, before coming to the point where he crossed his trail, he had muffled his horse's feet so that a different track would be found when he crossed from the original ones made. He also took the trouble to change the shoes on his horse once or twice, so as to confuse his pursuers. The shot gun which he took from the jail was found south of Williams, and it was learned that he had secured a new gun and plenty of ammunition. At one or two points on the trail, the officers seemed confident that they were close enough to the outlaw to be seen by him, but, of course, he managed not to be seen by them. It has been learned that he entered a miner's cabin near Lynx creek on Sunday and secured a supply of grub, and that he did not get any more till Thursday evening.
>
> Horace Yeomans, one of the posse who started out with Ruffner and Munds, was compelled to return on Saturday to look after his business. He discredits entirely the story told by Miller to the officers at Jerome and states positively that Miller was the man with Parker when he and Deputy Munds had the brush with them on Lynx creek. Mr. Yeomans is well acquainted with the Mexican, and would have recognized him had he been the man with Parker. Bedside, had he not known him, they could not have made any mistake in regard to him, as he had on a white shirt, and the man with Parker did not. Jailor Meador also says that he did not see Miller when he was shooting, but he thought he was shooting at the Mexican all the time.
>
> When Yeomans left the posse they were seven miles south of Williams, but it was rumored afterwards that Parker had crossed the Atlantic & Pacific railroad.
>
> At last accounts, Parker was still riding the white horse taken from Sheriff Ruffner's livery stable.
>
> The shot gun which Sheriff Ruffner brought back had still one loaded cartridge and an empty shell in it.
>
> One of the ruses adopted by Parker to throw his pursuers off his track, was to follow a band of range horses which he came across, having previously taken both of the shoes off the horse he was riding.
>
> ---
>
> Since the above was put in type, Al Galpin, of Phenix, who has been on the trail with the blood hounds, has returned on his way home, as it seems impracticable to follow the trail of Parker with the dogs. He left the posse on Sunday afternoon, and states that it is generally believed that Parker is still in hiding in the Bill Williams

mountains. He says that he has a host of friends in that section, who are protecting him in ever way possible. He says that whenever any of the officers leave Williams they are watched and their trail is followed. That threats are openly made against the officers by certain cow boys there. When Galpin went out with his hounds, he was followed, and at night, when they were in camp, his horse was stolen so that he could not follow the trail, and when he left the horse had not been recovered, although the man who stole it was known, as he had ridden the horse through Williams.

Parker succeeded in successfully throwing Sheriff Ruffner and posse from his trail on Wednesday, when they thought the chances of capturing him were very bright. After passing, east of Jerome Junction, Parker crossed the Verde river, avoiding Campbell's and Baker's ranch, where he was thought to be heading for, and made his way up into the Hell's Canyon country, where it is exceedingly rough and rocky. This was on Tuesday night, the officers leaving the trail near Jerome Junction on Tuesday evening to get the Indian trailers and fresh horses, and resuming the pursuit again on Wednesday morning.

Just as the moon was going down on Wednesday morning, Parker rode up to a ranch house between Hell's Canyon and Williams, awoke the occupants, a man and his wife, and compelled the latter to cook him some food, and secured a Winchester rifle and ammunition. In return for this, he told the man where he had cached $1,500 from the train robbery in February, and the man left the next day to secure it. He was seen in Ash Fork by the officers and he told of the circumstance while drinking, but proceeded to Peach Springs to secure the stolen treasure.

After considerable delay, Sheriff Ruffner and posse followed the trail to this ranch, and found the woman alone. She denied, at first, that any one had visited the place, or that she had cooked any provisions on Tuesday night, but after a long catechism from the officers, she admitted that some one had rode up there during the night, and had stolen a Winchester rifle and some ammunition. Parker also received some horse shoes there for his horse. The rancher, in his story, stated that Parker told them that he had had nothing to eat from the time he left the jail until he reached there.

The trail of the outlaw was getting so warm on Saturday night, that one of the Indian trailers quit the posse and the others left yesterday. A trail of two men, on foot, was found on Saturday evening, one of which was said by the Indians to be Parker's. The blood hounds were put on it, and followed it for some distance, when night overtaking them, they were recalled.

Sheriff Cameron was in Williams last evening, and just before the train pulled out on which Mr. Galpin left, he stated that a stock man came in and informed Cameron that Ruffner's white horse had been found with his throat cut. Whether this was reliable or not, he could not learn.

The rancher, at whose house Parker stopped on Tuesday night, stated that the outlaw told him that the officers had lost his trail, and that he intended to go into the Bill Williams mountains and remain in hiding there for some time—until the vigilance of the officers had eased—when he could safely make his escape.

The officers are not inclined to give full credence to the notice of intention of Parker to remain in the Bill Williams mountains for any length of time, as outlined to the rancher, and have accordingly scattered from the vicinity of Williams for the purpose of intercepting him. Other Indian trailers have also been secured to trail him.

> The horses which Sheriff Ruffner brought in on Saturday night were very much jaded and worn out.
> Word was received at the sheriff's office that Deputies Fairchilds and Selvey arrived safely at Flagstaff on Saturday evening with Miller and lodged him in jail there. They will join the other officers now in the pursuit of Parker.
> Ever since the three prisoners escaped, Under Sheriff Dillon has been kept hard at work, day and night, in organizing posses for the pursuit and in directing their movements, as reliable information is received. In all cases where officers are in pursuit of criminals they are flooded with alleged information, which, in nine cases out of ten, is misleading, while there is no end to the number of rumors which spring up on every street corner. To act with wisdom and prudence in cases of this kind, and not to overlook a genuine clue, requires experience, patience, and coolness, but Mr. Dillon has shown rare tact in his actions, and at the same time has been courteous to both press and the public, in giving to both any reliable information at his command. By being kept in as close touch as possible with the officers, he has been enabled to winnow the chaff from the various rumors afloat, and to act on those having the semblance of truth to them. Immediately on receipt of the news from Jerome that Miller was in that locality, he started for that camp, but was met en route by parties who informed him of Miller's capture.
> He states that the story told by Miller was told to Fred Haas, and was told voluntarily, and he is inclined to place more credence in it that is manifested by some others. Should the Mexican be apprehended, the truth of the story could be verified, or if not true, its falsity demonstrated.

Historically, the cowboys and country settlers are remembered as good people. Therefore, it has often been asked why they were so willing to help Parker the murderer. It must be remembered that Parker had not only been a friend of theirs in the past, but country settlers and cowboys had a natural distrust of city folk, and were always inclined to believe that their own were always innocent whenever the law came calling. In many respects, this point of view has never completely died out—comparisons to more modern day cases such as Leonard Peltier and Mumia Abu-Jamal are not out of order, as large numbers of people from their groups sincerely believe that these men were victims of massive frame-up jobs by the elite. Therefore, the cowboys and settlers were willing to do just about anything to protect their "brother," Parker.

Adding to this, Parker undoubtedly told many of them that he had gotten thousands from the train robbery, and offered or strongly hinted that he would give them some or all of it in exchange for aid. This one reported instance could not have been the only time. And by the time that the good Samaritans found out he had lied to them, he was long gone.

The following items appeared in the *Prescott Courier* of May 28, 1897:

> Deputy Sheriff Munds came in from the Flagstaff country Thursday night. He reports Sheriff Ruffner still in that section on the lookout for Parker, who is supposed to be in hiding in that part of the country. He says that Ed Gatling has been arrested and placed in the jail at Flagstaff on a charge of having fed Parker or given him assistance. Gatling was released from the Prescott jail on giving $1 200 bail. He is bound over

to appear before the grand jury on a charge of horse stealing. He is reported to have said that he had a horse for Parker when the latter needed it. This Gatling denied. Fairchilds had a talk with Miller and Fairchilds told Munds that Miller told him that he (Miller) never said the Mexican was shot in the court house by Jailor Meador.

So Miller was changing his stories yet again. As for Gatling (called Ad Gatlin in his court papers), he was never indicted or tried for aiding Parker—although he was brought up on the horse-stealing charge. From the same edition:

Mrs. George Ruffner was yesterday in receipt of a horseshoe from a foot of her now celebrated white horse, ridden away by outlaw Parker. The shoe formed the base or connection of a handsomely mounted pair of steer's horns. The shoe was picked up by the sheriff while following Parker's trail. The sheriff had it mounted with the horns as a memento of the valuable horse and the several horns of the dilemma which confronted the officers who followed the trail when the shoe was found. Mrs. Ruffner hopes that the shoe will be followed by the horse, and both horns of the dilemma met by the early capture of Parker. The Courier believes these happenings will soon follow.

From the same edition:

Thompson and Rogers, two prisoners in the county jail, were escorted to its photograph gallery yesterday and their pictures were taken. They are in jail on charges of train robbery and horse stealing, respectively.

Unfortunately, the photographs are not known to have survived.

Parker was such big news by this time that many unrelated stories were compared to the case. From the *Arizona Journal Miner* of May 19, 1897:

A man, apparently temporarily insane, created nearly as much excitement on the streets today as the jail escape did on Sunday. He unhitched Sam Hill's horse, attached to his delivery wagon, from the hitching post, jumped into the wagon and started off down the street at a break neck speed, followed by quite a crowd. He drove around for a block or two, when he stopped, laid down on his back in the street and commenced to yell. A man coming up near him, he jumped up, got into the wagon and drove off again. Don Coots and Ben DeLanty jumped into the wagon from behind, pinioned his arms, and held him while he was driven to the city jail. Prior to the man's taking Sam Hill's wagon, he entered J. L. Fisher's store, and in addition to his other clothing, had an overcoat on and a sheet thrown over it. His name is Ike Skillen. He is a very temperate, quiet man and his temporary aberration of mind is supposed to be due to illness, as he has been sick for several days.

From the same edition:

The shot gun, which Parker used with such deadly effect in escaping from jail, and which has since been recovered, was the one with which Deputy United States

Marshal John A. Donavan, a few years ago, shot and killed Counterfeiter Smith, an escape from the Prescott jail. It was with a charge from it also that Under Sheriff Dillon winged Murderer Hobart. Smith was killed at a distance of 115 yards, while Dillon emptied the contents of it into Hobart's arm at a distance of 95 yards.

From the *Arizona Republican* of May 19, 1897:

A passenger on yesterday afternoon's train from the north said he was told that word had reached Prescott that one of the posse pursuing Parker had come so closely upon him that in his flight the bandit had lost his hat. Al Galpin returned yesterday morning to Phoenix. He left the posse on Sunday afternoon. At that time it was believed that Parker had not yet gone out of the Bill Williams mountains. The jail breaker has a great many friends among the cowboys of not only that section, but in towns, who are ready to furnish him all assistance possible.

From the *Republican* of May 20, 1897:

Al Galpin, who has lately returned from the chase after Parker, illustrating the obstacles cowboys and sheep herders throw in the way of the pursuers, says that Parker would ride into a band of broncos and remove the shoes from his horse. The broncos would be driven along with him, thus obliterating his trail. In other instances the sheep herders had driven large flocks of sheep along his trail, utterly hiding it. The Indians could always pick it up again, but abandoned it, fearing to encounter the outlaw. They hunted him down after the Peach Springs train robbery and he swore then that he would shoot them if he ever got out of jail. When he escaped the Indians willingly joined in the chase, believing that he was a good man to be kept in a safe place. Then they took another view of it, knowing that Parker would not linger around for the sole purpose of killing them. When Steve, one of the Wallapai trailers, found the track getting warm, he stopped and in reply to exhortations to go on, said, "Me guess Jim shoot."

The *Arizona Gazette* May 19, 1897 ran an interview with George Thornton, a rancher from northern Arizona who had once employed Parker, and he reflected back on the Abe Thompson Gang:

George Thornton, one of the largest cattle owners in the territory, is in Phoenix, and in speaking of Parker yesterday said that the outlaw was in his employ for a year and a half and that he is one of the best vaqueros and horsemen he ever met. He is popularly called Jim, but his name is Flem Parker. Before coming to Arizona Parker hailed from Tulare where he had a reputation of being a tough citizen. He served two terms in San Quentin prison and upon his release the last time he came to Arizona. He is about 32 years of age. Previous to the train robbery Mr. Thornton said that Parker and other desperate characters committed many depredations, such as running off and killing cattle. He said that Parker had many friends in that section of the country among the cowboys and sheep men who will render him every assistance. He thinks the outlaw is now comparatively safe as he is in a region that is almost inaccessible, and it will be no very hard matter for him to elude the officers.

From the *Arizona Journal Miner* of May 26, 1897:

Heap Sabe Parker

A telegram from Kingman says "The Wallapai Indian trailers who have been on the track of Parker, the Rock Cut train robber and jail breaker, returned to Kingman this morning, saying the officers had been put on the wrong track by sheep men near Williams, and that they were not allowed to follow the trail they knew to be that of the outlaw. They are very much disgusted, and say that were they allowed their own way they would have captured Parker before he got near Williams. A sheep herder told the officers a cock and bull story and the scheme worked"

The officers tell a different story. They state that the trailers were not told who they were following. After being on the trail for several days, they came across certain signs which revealed to their minds that it was Parker on whose trail they were, and they quit it cold and left for home, as they are in mortal fear of Parker."

From the same edition:

The Pursuit of Parker
From Friday's Daily

Deputy Sheriff Johnny Munds, who has been in pursuit of Parker, ever since the jail break on May 9, returned on last night's train for a brief rest. The sheriff's posse are still in the vicinity of Williams, and still think that Parker is concealed in the mountain canyons of that section.

The rumor on the street today that Sheriff Ruffner's white horse had been killed by Parker, who had cut his throat, was without further foundation than that published in the Journal-Miner Monday. On Sunday night a man reported to Sheriff Cameron, of Coconino county, that such was the case, but the officers here had no confirmation of it since.

Marion Weston, of Chino valley, reported having discovered a white horse in the Hell canyon country, that was so poor and worn out that he could not bring it in, but was unable to give any definite description of it or of the brands on it.

Nothing really definite of Parker's whereabouts are known, or, if known to the officers, are not given out, since he left the rancher's house on the morning of Wednesday, May 12, where he secured his gun, ammunition, food and horse shoes.

J. N. Thacker, special detective for Wells, Fargo & Co., has issued a circular with a portrait of Parker printed on it, offering a reward of $1,000 for his capture. He gives his names as Fleming Parker, alias William Parker, age 31, and a native of Tulare county, California. He served a term of five years in San Quentin for burglary.

Wells Fargo had indeed issued their own wanted poster for Parker. This poster (see opposite illustration) has been reprinted many times to accompany various after-the-fact accounts of the Parker story. What is usually not added, however, is that Wells Fargo would ultimately refuse to pay the reward, as we shall see.

Look Out for
Train Robber and Murderer.

$1000 REWARD

For the Arrest and Conviction of

FLEMING PARKER

Who escaped from County Jail at Prescott, Arizona, on or about May 13, 1897. In making his escape he shot and mortally wounded the Deputy District Attorney.

DESCRIPTION.

Fleming Parker, alias William Parker, is now about 31 years of age; 5 feet 7½ inches high; weighs 165 lbs.; light grey eyes; brown hair; size of foot 6½ inches; teeth in fair condition; high, full forehead; round features; straight nose; small mouth; round chin; vacine mark on left forearm; mole back of neck; scar on left side of head. Usually wears his hat on back of his head; is a cowboy by occupation, and a native of Tulare County. His picture as given hereon is a perfect likeness of him. He has served a term of five years in San Quentin for burglary. When last heard of he was heading for Nevada or Utah; had a repeating rifle with him. He was arrested for attempting to rob the A. & P. R. R. train at Peach Springs, Arizona, and was being held for trial in the Prescott Jail when he escaped. His partner Jim, alias Harry Williams of Utah, was killed at the time of the attempted robbery. There is no doubt of his conviction if captured. If arrested telegraph Sheriff Ruffner, Prescott, Arizona, or the undersigned.

J. N. THACKER,
SPECIAL OFFICER, WELLS, FARGO & CO.,
SAN FRANCISCO, May 18, 1897.   SAN FRANCISCO

Wells Fargo put out this wanted poster for Parker after the jailbreak, and Detective John N. Thacker would later try to weasel out of paying the reward. (Courtesy of Sharlot Hall Museum)

From the same edition:

Two of the sheriff's posse came in from Williams last evening, bringing in several of the jaded horses which have been ridden in the search for Parker. The officers are still in the vicinity of Williams, but Parker's location is as much a mystery as if the earth had opened and swallowed him, although he is still thought to be in hiding in that vicinity.

From the same edition:

> Mrs. G. C. Ruffner left on this morning's train for the north. Her departure gave rise to a rumor that in a fight with Parker, her husband had been wounded, all of which was incorrect. Sheriff Ruffner would probably like nothing better than to get a chance to have a fight with Parker.

On May 20, 1897, the *Arizona Gazette* ran one of the most controversial news items about Parker to appear the entire time:

> #### OFFERED TO REWARD
>
> ##### Outlaw Parker Not Entirely Devoid of Humor
>
> A gentleman who came in yesterday from the north says that Sheriff Ruffner is persistently following the trail of Parker, although he had been sent on a false trail by a sheepman, a friend of the outlaw. Notwithstanding this fact the original trail was soon found and Parker was pressed so closely that he lost his hat and couldn't spare the time to stop and pick it up. The head gear was found by Ruffner who is wearing it as a souvenir of the outlaw. The Indian trailers not caring to serve as targets for Parker's bullets, returned home. They hadn't lost any outlaw and had troubles of their own. Knowing the Indians could not be relied upon in a possible scrimmage with Parker, Ruffner pushed on without them. While closely following the trail the sheriff noticed a piece of paper pinned to the ground. Prompted by curiosity he stopped and picked it up. It proved to be of deep interest to the officer, for it contained these words from Parker:
>
> "A reward of $1000 is offered by the undersigned for Sheriff Ruffner, dead or alive; dead preferred. An additional reward of $10 each, will be offered for the killing of the poodle dogs that have been on my trail."

This sensational item was picked up by the wire services and reprinted around the country, and down to this day it is often related as fact in after-the-fact accounts. A subsequent denial of the story simply did not become as widely circulated. From the *Phoenix Herald* of May 20, 1897:

> Deputy Sheriff Henry George returned this morning from the northern portion of the Territory where he went to secure witnesses for the District Court. He reports that the chase for Parker is still going on but that he is in the mountains and it has been some time since any trace has been had of him. The many reports that he pinned a note to the ground offering a reward for the killing of Sheriff Ruffner and that he had cut the throat of the white horse are entirely unfounded.

From the *Arizona Gazette* of May 21, 1897:

> Deputy Sheriff Henry George returned yesterday morning from a trip to Jerome after a witness. He says that Sheriff Ruffner and posse are pursuing Parker with untiring energy but have not as yet discovered the outlaw's hiding place on account of the many obstacles thrown in their way by Parker's friends. He said that

Chapter 7: Jailbreak and the Second Posse

the report that the outlaw had turned Sheriff Ruffner's horse loose was a mistake. He is still riding the horse he stole when he broke jail. The horse was shod and Parker with a cunning worthy of a better cause, cast the animal's shoes in order to better cover his trail. There are a very few horses that are shod in that section and for that reason it is a yard matter to follow the trail. Mr. George says that Parker was wounded, as when he stopped at the sheep camp where he secured his Winchester he had to be helped off and on his horse.

From the *Phoenix Herald* of May 22, 1897:

Deputy Sheriff Geo. Merritt and Joe Meyers of Yavapai county, arrived last evening from the north on the trail of the Mexican who escaped from the jail at Prescott with Parker and Miller. The Mexican is known to have left Crowned King five days ago in this direction and is believed to have been headed for the Globe country in which direction the Deputy Sheriff will go.

From the *Arizona Republican* of May 22, 1897:

Deputies Merritt and Nelson of Yavapai county arrived in town last night in search of the Mexican, Cornellia, who escaped from the Prescott jail with Parker. They were at the Crowned King where they learned that the Mexican had stolen a horse. They telephoned to Prescott and were directed to go on south, it seeming likely that the Mexican had given up the idea of hiding in the San Domingo country.

From the *Arizona Gazette* of May 26, 1897:

On Sunday there was a ripple of excitement as for a time it was thought Ben Belcher had accidentally discovered the whereabouts of Parker. It was through a Wells Fargo order for $10 sent from Maricopa to a woman here and bore the signature of Jas. Parker. Later it was ascertained that the Parker was an actual resident of Maricopa and not the desperado. Sheriff Ruffner is still on the chase but no news other than that Parker is supposed to be in the Bill William's mountains, has been received.
    R. W. Meador the brave jailor who was so severely wounded by the three escapes, has almost recovered. He made a desparate fight against great odds and managed to wound both Miller and the Mexican as they climbed the stairway. Three bullet holes in the wall testify to the accuracy and quickness of his aim.

The chase went on.

Cornelia Sarata was never recaptured and his fate was never ascertained. Of the two most likely scenarios of what happened to him, either one could be true. If Miller was telling the truth (and his word was highly dubious) that Sarata was badly wounded, he may have crawled away and died somewhere. Others have thought that he made it to Mexico with the willing aid of Arizona's beleaguered Mexican community, who were often known to help their brothers escape "white man's justice."

This author has seen it contended that the Arizona Territory requested the extradition of Sarata from Mexico, but there is no documentation for this. One later account states that Sarata's body was found two years later, but there is no corroboration for this either. The last news accounts of the pursuit of Sarata likewise expressed bewilderment. The *Prescott Courier* reported the following on May 28, 1897:

> Deputy Sheriff Merritt and Nelson have returned from Prescott, where they went in pursuit of the Mexican Cornelia. The impression appears that the fugitive has crossed into Mexico.

From the *Arizona Gazette*, May 26, 1897:

> The pursuit of Cornelia Asarta*, the Mexican who escaped from the Prescott jail, has been practically abandoned, as it is thought that he has crossed over into Mexico. It is more than likely that he is hiding in the San Domingo country, having joined the colony of criminals that live in that section.

The *Gazette* tried to sound a bit more optimistic on May 30, 1897:

> There is yet a strong probability that the Mexican who broke jail at Prescott with Parker and Miller will be captured as Sheriff Orme of this county and Sheriff Ruffner of Yavapai have each had two men out on his trail since the escape. He is thought to be in the Tonto country and if so will be caught sooner or later.

Finally, the *Gazette* ran the following cryptic news item on June 23, 1897:

> **WAS IT CORNELIA?**
>
> Half Starved Mexican Seen Near McDowell
>
> A gentleman who lives near McDowell reported at the sheriff's office that he met a Mexican about five miles from there a couple of days ago and from the man's condition and appearances was satisfied that he was either crazy or was a fugitive from justice. He gave a description of the individual which answered to that of the Mexican, Cornelia, who escaped from the Prescott jail with Parker and Miller. He said that he had gone into the hills to find a calf that had strayed from his place and while standing on a knoll saw a man peering over the top of a bush about a hundred yards distant.
>
> He watched him awhile and thinking that he may have met with some accident went over to him. The man was without hat, shirt or shoes and wore nothing except an old worn out pair of overalls. He was asked what he was doing there in that half naked condition, but he only answered by a shake of his head. Other questions were asked but he either could not understand or would not talk.

---

* This particular spelling error would later be used in several after-the-fact accounts.

> The gentleman thinking that the poor fellow was about half starved went to camp after some food and returned, accompanied by a couple of Mexicans, it being his intention to bring the individual into camp. The man was gone when he returned and although he scoured the neighboring country he could find nothing of him.

Another possibility appeared a few years later in an interview with famed lawman turned outlaw Billy Stiles (who still commands quite a following among "wild west" aficionados), conducted by the *Los Angeles Herald*, and appearing in the March 22, 1901 edition of that paper:

> TUCSON, Ariz., March 20---"Billy" Stiles, notorious in southern Arizona as a train robber, has returned from a trip to Mexico. Stiles has settled down to a peaceful life and has been looking up mining properties in Sonora. He secured a valuable gold property in the Altar district, which he thinks will become one of the greatest mines in Mexico. Stiles, while in Sonora, met the Mexican fugitive who escaped from the Prescott jail at the time Jim Parker and Miller escaped, when the district attorney of Yavapai county was killed by the jailbreakers. Stiles says that the Mexican bragged about the killing of the district attorney and stated that he put up the job for the jail delivery and looked after little details of the desperate work. The Mexican, as soon as he obtained his liberty, went direct to Mexico and was pursued through the greater portion of Arizona by a posse. Parker and Miller were captured in northern Arizona by George Ruffner, then sheriff of Yavapai county, and Parker was afterward hanged in the Prescott jail yard. Miller was sentenced to life imprisonment at Yuma. The Mexican was incarcerated in the jail at the time of the delivery for killing a miner at a mining camp in Yavapai county, and is considered a desperate character. Stiles says that he (Sarata) dislikes the "Gringo" as much as ever, and is reported to have killed a number of white men since he took up his abode in Sonora. Stiles has reported his meeting with the fugitive to the officers, and no doubt an effort will be made to capture the ubiquitous desperado who is making life hardly worth living for all Americans who cross the line."

The remainder of the article consists of Stiles denying rumors that he planned to take up again with his old outlaw buddies Burt Alvord and Bravo Juan, who were also in Sonora at that time.

So who knows? Cornelia Sarata may have made it to Mexico and lived out a full and free life there, killing Gringos. Or perhaps one of the many skeletons found in the Arizona desert in the ensuing years may have been his. Or perhaps neither of these theories is true. The fate of Sarata is one of the great enduring mysteries of the Parker story, unlikely to ever be solved.

Many years later, the *Journal Miner*, in its December 15, 1915 edition, reported that Dr. Harry T. Southworth had discovered in Granite Dells (near Prescott) an old coal oil can that contained a Colt revolver, a copy of the *San Francisco Examiner* from April 30, 1895, and almanac from 1900. The newspaper reported that authorities were speculating that this cache was related to the discovery several months earlier in the same vicinity of several human bone fragments, including a hip bone that looked like it has been grazed by a bullet. The *Journal Miner* added:

> It is also thought that the bones and the discovery yesterday may be connected with the escape of Jim Parker and two Mexicans during George Ruffner's reign as sheriff of Yavapai county. Parker, who killed Lee Norris in his escape from the county jail, was captured near Flagstaff and one of the Mexicans was taken into custody at Jerome. It is believed that the other Mexican made his escape to the border and into Sonora, but it is possible that he may have quarreled with his partners and was killed in the dells and his belongings left behind.

Of course this is highly unlikely, as the jailbreak occurred in 1897, not 1900! And of course, Louis C. Miller was not a Mexican! The passing of time was already giving people faulty memories.

On May 26, 1897, Samuel S. Preston, a white trading post operator on the Navajo reservation telegraphed authorities that he was in pursuit of Parker. As we know, Preston successfully captured Parker, and most newspapers had not gone to press in the interim between Preston's telegram and the capture. There were exceptions; and the *Arizona Gazette* printed an article on Preston's telegram that demonstrates just how quickly rumors can fly. As Preston himself never made any reference to the alleged incident in the *Gazette*'s May 27 article, it must be concluded that this version of the story is false:

> Flagstaff, May 26.—An Indian courier came in today with a message from a post trader living near the Navajo reservation north of this place, giving the information that Parker took dinner there yesterday. While the outlaw was eating three men made an appearance and surrounding the house called upon Parker to surrender. The outlaw jumped up and ran out the back way firing his Winchester at one of the men as he ran. The bullet struck the man in the arm. The other two discharged their revolvers at Parker and made for the brush followed by the taunting laughter of the outlaw who denounced them

Only known photo of trading post operator Samuel S. Preston, taken around 1892, presumably at his place of business. Although others would later try to dispute it, he was the one who finally captured Parker.

This is Samuel Preston's treading post c. 1897, around the time Parker was recognized here, which led to his capture.

as a pack of cowards. He coolly walked over to where the wounded man lay, and at the point of his gun forced the fellow to acknowledge who he and his companions were. The wounded man said they were cowboys and having come on Parker's trail accidentally concluded to effect his capture and claim the reward. Parker advised him, if he cared to live to leave his trail alone in the future and expressed regrets that it was not Sheriff Ruffner that he shot. He took the wounded man's revolver and ammunition and mounting his horse rode rapidly toward the Utah line.

As soon as the news was received Sheriffs Ruffner and Cameron and Deputy Fairchilds and the Indian trailers left for the reservation. It is generally believed a capture will be effected as the country is open and the trail can be followed without difficulty.

The reality of Parker's stop at Preston's trading post is quite different, and was recognized as such in short order, as few other papers printed this version of events.

The capture of Jim Parker was surprisingly restrained, considering the prior events. The *Arizona Journal Miner* summed it up simply on June 2, 1897:

NEVER FIRED A SINGLE SHOT

Parker the Train Robber and Murderer of Lee Norris, Surprised While Asleep and Captured

S. S. Preston and Ten Navajo Indians Effect the Capture Very Cleverly and Win the Twenty-Four Hundred Dollars Reward

From Friday's Daily

The old Prescott railroad depot, c. 1890s. It was here that Sheriff Ruffner brought Parker and Miller back, and where unproven folklore contends an angry lynch mob was waiting for them. (Courtesy of Sharlot Hall Museum)

Parker, the train robber, murderer and outlaw generally, who escaped from jail in Prescott on the afternoon of Sunday, May 9, was re-captured just after day break on Wednesday morning, May 26, about 70 or 80 miles north of Flagstaff. His captors were S. S. Preston, assisted by ten Navajo Indians.

News of the capture was received at the sheriff's office a little before eight o'clock last night.

Preston is engaged in merchandising in company with Hugh Campbell, formerly of Flagstaff, at Willow Springs. On Monday, Parker stopped at their place for dinner and was recognized by them. An Indian courier was immediately dispatched to Flagstaff with the information to the officers, and after Parker left, Preston secured the services of ten Navajo Indians, who were not only expert trailers, but brave men as well, and started on the trail, following it during Monday afternoon and all day Tuesday. Towards night on Tuesday, the Indians told Preston that they were close on the trail and that Parker had gone into camp. They proceeded cautiously until his camp was located, when they surrounded it and remained on guard all night. Just after day break, about 4:45 o'clock, they closed in on their game, when one of the Indians fired off his gun to awaken Parker, who was asleep. Parker jumped to his feet with his Winchester in hand, only to see eleven deadly guns pointed at him. He was taken completely by surprise, and Preston demanded him to lay down his gun, throw up his hands and advance six paces. Parker replied, "Is that you Fairchild?" when Preston answered no. Seeing that resistance was useless, Parker obeyed the mandate, contrary to all expectations, as it was thought that he would fight to the death. The Indians closed in on him, and bound his hands securely and the march to Flagstaff was commenced.

Immediately on receipt of the word at Flagstaff that Parker had been at Preston and Campbell's place on Monday, the posse started out on Wednesday afternoon, and were met at the Little Colorado river on Thursday by Preston and the Indians returning with their game. Parker was lodged in the Flagstaff jail about 7 o'clock last evening.

At the time of his capture, Parker had two fine black horses, one of which he secured on Miller's ranch* on the Tuesday night or Wednesday morning after his escape. Where he secured the other, has not yet been learned. It is now pretty definitely known that the white horse belonging to Sheriff Ruffner, and ridden by him from Prescott, was left somewhere in the vicinity of Miller's ranch, but whether he is dead or alive is not yet known.

It has also been learned that on Sunday evening when Deputy Munds had his brush with him on Lynx creek his horse ran up against a tree with him and his leg was pretty badly hurt. He had this wound also dressed at Miller's ranch the following Wednesday morning.

He had a Winchester and plenty of ammunition when taken. He was heading towards Lee's Ferry, on the Colorado river, with the evident intention of crossing into Utah, where he has a sister residing, and where he also formerly worked.

Of course, we know that Parker's sisters were not in Utah. The persistent rumors that Parker had come from Utah undoubtedly helped spawn the "Butch Cassidy" legend discussed in Chapter 11.

From the same edition:

PARKER AND MILLER

Lodged in the Prescott Jail Again at an Early Hour Sunday Morning

A Big Crowd Gathers Out of Curiosity, But No Demonstration.—Four Prisoners Shackled Yesterday

From Monday's Daily

It was just three weeks yesterday that three desperate men succeeded in making their escape from the county jail.

A little after midnight yesterday morning, two of them, Parker, the train robber and murderer of Lee Norris, and L. C. Miller, the alleged forger, were returned to their old quarters. They were brought in by Sheriff Ruffner, of this county, and Sheriff Cameron, of Coconino county, both of whom have been in pursuit of the former ever since their escape.

The story of Parker's capture by S. S. Preston and ten Navajo Indians has already been told in these columns.

It became noised around on Saturday evening that the prisoners would be in on the train due at 10:30 p.m. and it naturally attracted a large crowd to the depot. It went there solely out of curiosity, though, and not with any designs against the prisoners.

While Under Sheriff Dillon felt reasonably confident that no demonstration would be made against the outlaws, he took the precaution to advise the officers

---

* Probably the Hat Ranch, owned by Charley "Hog-Eye" Miller.

to have the train stop near the Half Way House, where carriages were in waiting for them.

The train was an hour and a half late, and it came through Whipple at a low rate of speed, and without whistling as usual. The prisoners were transferred to the carriages, and a hurried drive made for the jail. The train was detained then until the carriages had reached the corner of Mt. Vernon avenue and Gurley street, when it pulled into the depot.

The crowd, however, had been advised in the meantime of what was going on, and started for the court house. As the sound of footsteps were heard coming up the street, Miller remarked, "My God, they're coming to hang us." Parker fired off a volley of profanity, coupled with an obscene epithet at him, reproaching him for his cowardice, at the same time remarking, "You can't die but once any way." As the prisoners were taken through the entrance leading through the jail, Parker cast a rather sensitive look up the stairway, where he had so cruelly shot down Lee Norris, and where a big crowd of people had assembled. Aside from this, his actions were cool, and before being taken from the carriage, he even requested the officers to take them for a drive around town to give them some fresh air.

Parker, it is said, expressed to Sheriff Ruffner, very forcibly, his regrets at not getting an opportunity to shoot him. He also told him that had not the sheriff reached the camp of his (Parker's) captors at the time he did, he would have made another break for liberty, and confidently believed he could have succeeded in getting away from them, as he was not tied and had an opportunity to get a gun. He was only waiting, he said, to get his supper and to be sociable with his captors before making the attempt.

He told Sheriff Cameron that he will not be hanged, neither will he be at court when his case comes up, but just what he meant by this remark is not known.

In the Lynx creek fight on the Sunday evening that they escaped, Parker was shot in the leg below the knee. It was a spent ball that struck him and produced only a flesh wound which has about healed up. He says that the Mexican was more seriously wounded, having been shot through the fleshy part of the thigh. Miller was not shot at all, and none of the shots fired by Jailor Meador took effect.

Yesterday morning F. G. Breck and one of his employees went to the jail, at Sheriff Ruffner's request, and riveted heavy steel shackles on Parker and Miller and on Rogers and Thompson, charged with complicity in the train robbery, and they will hereafter be closely guarded. Parker complained that he was given an old and rusty pair of leg bracelets, while the others were shining ones, but beyond this he was silent and uncommunicative.

The *Prescott Courier* carried the news of Parker's capture on May 28, 1897:

PARKER CAPTURED

By S. S. Preston and Posse of Ten Indians

He Was Caught Napping

Special in the Courier

Flagstaff, May 27. — Parker, the train robber, jail breaker and murderer is now strongly quartered in jail in this town. He was captured yesterday morning by S. S. Preston and a posse of ten Indians at a point some sixty miles north of Tuba City. The day previous to his capture he had taken dinner with Preston, who carries on an Indian trading post about 90 miles north of here, in partnership with H. E. Campbell, of this town. After Parker had left and taken up his journey, Preston dispatched an Indian courier to Flagstaff to notify Sheriffs Cameron and Ruffner and he himself gathered together a band of trusty Navajo Indians and took the trail. They followed till they were about to locate the camp Parker had made for the night then, awaiting the break of day, stealthily surrounded him while he slept. The presence of Preston and his Indians was the farthest from Parker's mind, and he lay sleeping soundly as the posse gathered nearer and nearer and finally after each had taken his position, with Winchester in hand, one of the party fired and Parker sprang to his feet with gun in hand. He was completely surrounded and surprised that he realized the futility of further resistance and called out, Fairchilds is that you? Preston replied by a demand that he throw his gun down and advance which Parker reluctantly did. His hands were bound by the Indians with lashes and he was brought towards Flagstaff.

The party was met yesterday by Sheriffs Cameron and Ruffner and posse and, together with Preston, they brought the desperado into Flagstaff this evening.

When taken Parker had a Winchester, and plenty of ammunition and two horses which belong to parties living near Williams. He seemed to be considerably fatigued, and his long and rough trip has told on him, as well as upon the officers who have so closely followed him.

Preston, to whose energy and bravery Parker's capture is due, will undoubtedly receive the reward.

It is probable that Parker will remain in jail here till he is placed on trial.

From the same edition:

Now that Parker has been captured, it will not be amiss to state that private news was received in Prescott some days ago that Parker had stopped at a ranch, where a woman washed his wounded leg; that splinters of bone projected from the leg, and Parker stated that unless he had thrown the officers off the trail that he would be captured. It was also stated that Ed Gatlin was thrown in jail for buying medicine for Parker's wound. It was known that Parker could not travel long with such a wound. He is supposed to have sustained the wound in the fight on Lynx creek.

From the same edition:

There is the smile on the face of a hungry man who has eaten a good dinner; then there is the smile of the mental halluciationist whose best girl has accepted him and who thinks he is happy; then there is the smile of the fond parent, over the advent of another squaller into the household and the multiplication of misery on the face of the earth, but all of these smiles pale as the light of a candle before the mid-day summer sun when compared with the smile which is now on top in the court house and which can be seen on the face of George Ruffner, our gallant sheriff, who, on Saturday night last, at 12 o'clock landed Outlaws Parker and Miller, in the Yavapai county jail, hence that smile.

Sheriff Cameron, of Coconino, came down with Ruffner and the prisoners. The prisoners were manacled together. The crowd heard they were coming and gathered at the taxless* depot, but the prisoners and officers got off near Thos. Long's Half Way House, were driven in a hack through northeast Prescott and down the hill into the court house yard. As the officers assisted the prisoners to alight from the vehicle, which stood near the jail, about 100 men gathered around. There was no overt word (illegible) on the part of the crowd, but there had been enough foolish talk that, as the crowd pressed forward, Sheriff Ruffner firmly told them to stand back, that he could protect the prisoners. That if the crowd had wanted the prisoners they could have taken the trail and captured them; that he would now protect the manacled men in his charge. When Miller first saw the crowd approaching as he left the train, he exclaimed: "There they come to hang us." Parker said to him, "Try and have a little courage."

Parker was in good spirits coming down on the train; he is now sullen; Miller has been much dejected from the first. Parker says that he was shot in the court house by Meador; that the Mexican was with him in the Lynx creek fight, where the Mexican received a bullet through the right thigh, and Parker was struck below the knee on the inner right leg, the ball ranging down about five inches. Miller was not shot at all. Parker's wound has almost healed. Sheriff Ruffner killed three horses in the chase; that is, he bought them and left them for dead, or gave them away as worthless after the rides. The famous white horse ridden away by Parker is running on the range north of the A. & P. The railroad company has offered to bring home the horse free of charge. The saddle and bridle which Parker rode away with is now on a fine horse which Ruffner brought back. The saddle has a bullet mark in the rear which was caused by a shot from either Yeoman's or Munds' rifle in the Lynx creek fight. Had this shot been two inches higher it would have struck Parker in the small of the back and brought him down. The movement of his horse is probably what saved his life.

Parker says he left Miller outside of Prescott and left the Mexican soon after the Lynx creek fight. He says bullets flew thick and uncomfortably close in that fight.

And so the confusion over who was at the Lynx Creek firefight continued.

It should be noted that many after-the-fact accounts of the Parker story have alleged that Sheriff Ruffner bravely and successfully stared down a full-blown lynch mob when he brought Parker back to Prescott. As we can see, that was not the case. These stories undoubtedly started because some out-of-town newspapers did, in fact, overstate the ferocity of the crowd of spectators. Yavapai County authorities were clearly worried that a mob might materialize, but it did not happen.

In Western history, white trader Samuel S. Preston is remembered solely as the man who captured Parker. For those who have studied the history of Indian reservation

---

* For then-current political reasons, the *Courier* scornfully used the epithet "Taxless" to refer to the railroad every time a train apppeared in the news. This went on for several years.

trading posts, however, he is an important historical figure. Some after-the-fact accounts contend that Parker was recognized on the reservation by some Indians who went and told Preston. This is not true, either. In fact, the most interesting account of Parker's capture came from Preston himself, who gave an interview to the *Flagstaff Sun-Democrat*, which was published on June 3, 1897:

RECAPTURE OF JIM PARKER

S. S. Preston Apprehends the Wily Desperado

The End of a Hard and Desperate Chase—Mr. Preston's Daring Night Ride—An Interview with the Captor

Campbell and Preston's trading post is situated at Willow Springs, ninety miles northwest of Flagstaff. Parker when captured was heading for the Buckskin mountains, to reach which he had to cross the Colorado river at Lee's Ferry. When surrounded by Mr. Preston and the Indians he was within a few miles of the ferry and expected to cross it that morning.

A reporter for The Sun Democrat interviewed S. S. Preston, the captor of Jim Parker, and obtained the following authentic account of the affair. We believe it is the only correct account that has been published. Mr. Preston said:

"Almost sunup Tuesday morning, the 25th, I was awakened by Joe Lee, the man who works in our store, saying that there was a man outside who was very hungry and hadn't eaten for five days. I got up, dressed and invited the man in. On seeing the stranger, I felt certain I had seen him before somewhere, but couldn't place him. He came in and sat down near the stove, where he could watch everything. He seemed to me to be very nervous. He asked for some tobacco and he followed Lee into the store to get it.

"He came out and sat down again. Joe asked him if he'd heard whether they had captured the man who broke jail at Prescott or not. He said he had not, but didn't think they had. Lee related the circumstances of how they broke jail as he had heard it and told about Parker having killed Norris, and about the engagement on Lynx creek, where the posse had killed one of the prisoner's horses. When Lee said that one of them came back, picked up the Mexican and placed him on his own horse while twenty men were shooting at him, the man asked him who that was. Lee answered, 'Parker.' He laughed then. He asked a number of questions about the watering places, trails, etc. in that country, and said he was looking for some horses that had been stolen from him.

"After he eat breakfast he bought some chewing tobacco and a couple cans of fruit. He then stepped outside where his horses were. I told Lee as soon as the man had stepped out that I thought the stranger was Parker and that we had better take him in. But instead of Parker coming back to the store he got on his horse and rode off. This was about 7 o'clock.

"I then got on my horse and rode to Tuba to find the officers whom I thought were there. I did not find them, but met Nebeker, who is a Deputy Sheriff, and told him of Parker. I then returned to Willow Springs, and raising a posse of nine Indian trailers, whom I paid $15 apiece to accompany me, set out on Parker's trail. It was getting on toward evening when we left the trading post and we followed the trail until we came onto him the next morning, fifty miles from Willow Springs.

"The first thing we saw was his horse, picketed. We all dismounted and surrounded Parker, who lay in a little basinlike place asleep. A shot was fired by one of the Indians to awaken him.

"Parker jumped up, gun in hand, and hollowed, 'That's all right, boys; that's great!' I ordered him to lay his gun down and come up to where I was, and he said, 'Is that you, Fletch?' I replied, 'You lay that gun down and come up here.' He invited me to come down to where he was. I told him to hurry up or he'd be killed. Then he laid down his gun and started up. I went toward him and met him about twenty yards from his gun, and searched him. The Indians brought the horses around, we saddled up and came back to Willow Springs, arriving there about 1 p.m. We had dinner and rested our horses until 5 o'clock.

"I left the Indians here, procuring two others to help bring Parker to Flagstaff. We started out, and along about 9 o'clock in the evening, when five miles from the Little Colorado river, we met the Indian mail carrier on his way to Tuba. He told us that the Sheriff was on his way out and about seven miles on the opposite side of the river. I told Parker that we would meet the Sheriff on the other side.

Samuel Preston's assistant Joe Lee, c. 1894.

"We reached the river and crossed about 10 o'clock, camping for the night. I had the Indians unsaddle the horses while I watched Parker. He assisted in making a fire and once I stepped into the brush with him, about thirty feet from the fire, to get some wood.

"Along about half past ten some one on a horse rode up to within twenty or thirty feet on the fire. I first thought it was one of our Indians. I soon saw that it was a white man and that he was getting his Winchester out of the scabbard. I called out, 'This man is already under arrest.'

"'Oh he is' replied the horseman. 'Yes', I answered. He asked us if I was from Willow Springs, and when I told him I was he said 'all right'. Just then Parker spoke up and asked, 'Is that you, Ruffner?' He answered 'Yes.' This was the first intimation I had who the horseman was, other than that he must be an officer.

"About 1 o'clock in the morning Sheriff Cameron and Under Sheriff Fairchild came up in a buckboard, and at daylight we started for Flagstaff."

They arrived in town about 6:30 last Thursday evening and Parker was lodged in the county jail. Saturday together with Miller, who escaped with him, he was taken to Prescott, Sheriff Cameron accompanying Sheriff Ruffner with the prisoner."

Chapter 7: Jailbreak and the Second Posse

It is interesting to compare Preston's account with that of his Indian assistant, Joe Lee. Many years later in 1946, Lee gave a lengthy interview about his life to writer Gladwell Richardson. The interview did not get published until long after Lee's death at the Pioneer's Home in Prescott in 1952. Among many other things, Lee commented on the capture of Parker, although a few of his memories, especially about Parker's background, had clearly gotten a little fuzzy with the passing of time. The following is excerpted from the interview as it finally appeared in *Frontier Times* magazine in its February-March 1974 issue, under the name "My Wonderful Country":

> (George) McAdams had turned Willow Springs over to Samuel S. Preston to run on shares. The spring of 1897 Preston got me and Erne (Lee, Joe's brother) to build an addition to the old store building. It doubled the size, and we clay-plastered both the inside and outside stone walls. After the job was finished I remained a short while helping Preston and was there when the notorious Jim Parker came along.
>
> On February 8, 1897 Parker and one other outlaw robbed a Santa Fe train at Rock Cut in Yavapai County near Peach Springs. His henchman was killed by the express car messenger. Parker fled north to Diamond Creek where posses from three counties captured him. But he escaped a night camp, and his pursuit went on again until they took him near Grand Canyon's north rim.
>
> In May, awaiting trial, Parker escaped by knocking out the jailer and killing Assistant District Attorney Lee Norris. With him went two other prisoners. Lawmen hunted him for three weeks but he got clean away, alone. One of the other prisoners was recaptured but the second was never heard of again. Warning messages to look out for Parker were sent all over northern Arizona.
>
> Before dawn on May 25 a man woke me up kicking the bedside in the post living quarters. He said, "It's time for all working men to get up! I'm damned hungry and want to eat."
>
> Waking Preston in an adjoining room, I told him we had a tough hombre on our hands. Preston dressed and built a fire in the stove and cooked breakfast.
>
> While eating I mentioned having heard of Parker's escape from the Prescott jail, asking if they had caught him yet. Without batting an eye Parker replied, "No, I don't think so."
>
> Right there Preston gave me a warning look to shut up. He had seen Parker somewhere before and recognized him on sight. After breakfast Parker bought a sack of provisions, packed them on a black horse and rode off on another.
>
> Preston then told me who Parker was and got somewhat excited. A large reward had been offered for his capture. We didn't have any horses penned, so he sent me to round up some and to get several Navajos. We'd take out after Parker who was headed toward Lee Ferry. Yeipani, Deneh-nai, Atciddy-zhe, Chishey-yazzie, Denetcloth, Hosteen Tso, and Huskanahtza were the Indians I brought in. Preston made a deal to pay each $50 to help him capture Parker.
>
> Leaving me to run the store, they rode off north on a run. By the time they reached Cedar Ridge their horses were winded and they got fresh ones from Hosteen Tsissie Yazzie. Late that night while passing Bitter Seep the Navajos saw two black horses rope-staked on a wash called Deadman Canyon. Dismounting, they sneaked over into the wash and discovered Parker fast asleep. Preston went

up on one side of him behind a leveled six-shooter, and Deneh-nai was on the other side holding a cocked Winchester rifle. Then they woke him up.

With Parker disarmed, they cooked breakfast before starting south. Preston brought him to Willow Springs late that night and put him in a locked room with guards outside. The next morning Preston started for Flagstaff, Deneh-nai going along to help guard Parker. They crossed the Little Colorado River on Tanner Trail and camped in a flat that night.

They were sitting around a bright fire eating when Sheriff George Ruffner, leading a posse from his own Yavapai County and Flagstaff, spotted the smoke and rode in. Ruffner very nearly had a fit on discovering Parker lolling at ease in camp and not tied up. He wanted to secure the prisoner and take him over. This Preston refused because of the reward money offered for his capture. Preston was also a county deputy sheriff at that time and declared that Parker would be jailed in Flagstaff. Ruffner could take over from there legally.

They argued about this for an hour. Ruffner wanted Parker because he figured Preston would carelessly let him get away. Finally Preston agreed he could have Parker, provided Ruffner would personally pay him the Santa Fe's reward for Parker's capture, which was $800, and guarantee him the rest. Somewhat put out, Ruffner gave him his personal check for that amount and took custody of Parker, who was at once ironed.

Preston and Deneh-nai left camp towards Willow Springs, but instead of coming home they circled around and rode straight to Flagstaff. Late the next day Preston collected on Ruffner's check by a wire from Pollock's bank. That caused bad feelings between Preston and Ruffner, for the rewards once offered by the railroad, express company and Territory were never paid for Parker's capture. Parker was convicted and hanged June 3, 1898 in the Yavapai County jailhouse yard---not for robbery but for killing Norris.

Not having been paid yet for our stone work, I suggested to Preston that since he had all that reward money Erne and I should get our wages. For some reason that made him mad, but he paid me. He also canned me on the spot, not knowing I was quitting anyway to go back to work for George McAdams."

Joe Lee had to have been mistaken about one thing—since Preston would later claim all of the rewards, it had to have been Ruffner's own reward that he demanded from the Sheriff before turning Parker over to him. Details on the fight over the reward occur later in this chapter.

The *Mohave County Miner* reported on Parker's capture with just the basic details, but felt the need to editorialize about it on May 29, 1897:

Parker, the outlaw, has at last been captured and showed the white feather just the same as ordinary individuals. After making a desperate break for liberty and knowing that his life would not be worth a picayune if captured, it seems remarkable that this man should lay down his gun like an arrant coward. But it is nearly always the case that desperate criminals are extremely cowardly.

Again, those viewed as "bad men" by society were denounced no matter what action they took. If Parker had fought to the death, he would have been denounced as a monster. As he did not, he was denounced as a coward. Such was the way society's morals were kept up.

The *Phoenix Herald* editorialized May 28, 1897:

> Very few criminals ever get out of Arizona after once getting into it, without being apprehended. With all its hiding places and criminal population ready to help an escaping criminal, the character of the climate and country drives them from cover and then the Territory has numbers of the keenest and most fearless officers on earth who know the peculiarities of the country thoroughly and one can take every advantage in pursuit of a criminal. Very few ever get out of the Territory alive.

The *Arizona Gazette* likewise editorialized on May 29, 1897:

> There seems to have been considerable laxity on the part of the officers in hunting for Cornelia Arata, the Mexican who broke jail with Parker and Miller. The chase was centered on Parker and while the officers were scouring the country for the greater criminal the lesser malefactor leisurely made his escape and is now presumably in Mexico.

The *Gazette* further editorialized on May 30, 1897:

> Although Sheriff Ruffner was not the fortunate man to capture Parker, he gave the follow a hot chase and was still on the trail when the culprit was apprehended. Sheriff Ruffner is a brave man, a vigilant officer and he contributed more than his full share in bringing Parker back to jail.

In the same edition, the *Gazette* drew a comparison between Parker and an unrelated Salt Lake City case:

> Emulates Parker
> Salt Lake, May 29.—Richard Harvey, recently from California, was convicted of burglary last Monday and today was sentenced to prison for three years. While being handcuffed in the court room he made a break for liberty, knocked down several bailiffs and was finally shot and dangerously wounded by Deputy Sheriff Burt.

Most out of town newspapers drew on wire service reports, and were largely ordinary. To a routine account of Parker's capture, the *Los Angeles Times* added the following, almost certainly an unfounded rumor, on May 28, 1897:

> In his wanderings since his escape Parker visited his former haunts at Pine Springs, and while there he dug up the money which he got when he held up the train at Rock Cut and afterward buried. Parker told Miller*, the ranchman from whom he stole the rifle and ammunition, that he got $1500 out of the registered

---

* Charley "Hog-Eye" Miller.

letters. How he baffled the officers and completely hid his trail after leaving the Bill Williams Mountains he does not explain. Sheriff Ruffner's horse he turned loose in the mountains, and when captured he had two animals which he had appropriated near Williams. When captured he had a Winchester and forty rounds of ammunition, and only $7.50 in money in his possession.

Parker regrets the killing of Norris, but believed that it was Sheriff Ruffner that he shot at. Preston, who captured Parker, is an old-timer in Arizona and never before has made an arrest. He is modest, and takes his recent capture of the notorious outlaw as if it was but an every-day occurrence. No one has been permitted to interview Parker tonight, and there is no chance of his escape from this jail. The officers are elated over the capture without bloodshed, as it was thought that Parker would rather kill himself than be taken alive.

Again, Parker had not gotten anywhere near that much money in the train robbery. The *San Francisco Call* carried the following on May 30, 1897:

Prescott, Ariz., May 29.—It will be three weeks to-morrow since train-robber Parker left the Prescott jail over the dead body of young Lee Norris. To-night the desperado, along with Forger Miller, was brought back to his old cell, this time securely ironed hand and foot, and with no possibility of his escaping again.

Sheriffs Ruffner of Yavapai and Cameron of Coconino counties brought the prisoners from Flagstaff and landed them in jail here secretly and securely. The train was stopped two miles out of town, where the party was met by Ruffner's brothers with a closed carriage. Thus a great crowd at the station was disappointed and, possibly, mob violence prevented.

There was ample fear of the latter, for threats of lynching had been openly made. To-night Sheriff George Ruffner is a happier man than he has been for three weeks previous, as he has successfully concluded a most fatiguing series of travels after the worst desperado alive in Arizona.

A great crowd bid Parker good-by at Flagstaff and many expressions of admiration for his wonder nerve, and even sympathy for his present predicament, were expressed. Parker said to-day that he regretted killing Lee Norris.

"I had nothing against him," he said, "only I was rattled and was afraid he would wing me from the tower. However, what's done is done."

Parker was in fine humor and, on the train from Flagstaff, talked a good deal about his recent exploits. He said he had been three nights without sleep, or Preston and his Navajos would never have caught him napping. Unless Ruffner and Cameron had arrived just as they did he would have killed a few of the Indians easily and escaped again. He had his plans laid and was only waiting until his horse had been watered and fed.

United States Attorney Ellinwood claimed Parker as a Federal prisoner yesterday at Flagstaff, but Ruffner emphatically declined to turn him over, and after some sharp words Ellinwood left the city.

At Whipple, a short distance out of town, seventy-five determined armed men were assembled, expecting that Parker would be taken off the train there.

They were disappointed, but have vowed to have their way yet. During the ride through town the crowd at some places surrounded the vehicles in which were the prisoners. Miller in great terror cried out:

Chapter 7: Jailbreak and the Second Posse

"Oh, my God here they come; I knew they would do it."

"Shut up, you — fool!" roared Parker, and he gave Miller a kick with his manacled foot. Then he waved his hat at the crowd and called out:

"How do you do, boys? We're just riding about to get the air."

Extraordinary precautions had been taken against mob violence at every point, and Ruffner is happy to-night in successfully landing his man. Jim Parker's daring and sang froid are the talk of the city.

That account was almost certainly a mixture of fact and rumor. The ever-plucky *San Francisco Chronicle* somehow managed to get a reporter to Parker for an interview, which ran on May 29, 1897:

Flagstaff, Az. Te. May 28—Sheriffs R. H. Cameron of this county and George Ruffner of Yavapai will convey Jim Parker, the train robber and murderer to Prescott to-morrow. The feeling in Prescott over the escape of Parker and the killing of Lee Norris, an innocent bystander has subsided, and there is no danger of the desperado being lynched.

The recapture of this daring criminal closes the chapter in one of the hardest and most dangerous pursuits after outlaws ever chronicled. Parker was well known to the daring officers as a man lost to all regard for human life, who would willingly kill a dozen of his pursuers in an effort to increase his chances for escape. Nevertheless, through the rough hill country, across ravines and over boulder-covered foothills pressed on the officers, reckoning not of the danger to their own lives.

The particular part of Arizona through which Parker traveled afforded excellent places for concealment to an outlaw, and as the desperado has since related in his cold-blooded manner, more than once when he believed the officers close upon him, did he hide behind a convenient rock, and, rifle in hand, wait for their appearance to kill them. The officers deserve great credit for their efforts, and to Sheriff Cameron and to Sheriff Ruffner the law-abiding citizens of the Southwest owe a debt of gratitude.

As related in these dispatches yesterday, S. S. Preston, an old frontiersman, effected the capture of Parker. The cunning and desperate character of the man may be judged by the following, which he related this afternoon while being interviewed in the County Jail. After having surrendered to Preston, who disarmed him, he was placed on his own horse, unshackled, but guarded by the ten Indians. In this manner the party started for Flagstaff, 145 miles southward. When Campbell's trading post was reached, after a ride of forty miles, eight of the Indians were left at the post, and with the two remaining Preston proceeded with the prisoner on his way to Flagstaff. Unknown to the prisoner, an Indian courier was sent here to inform the officers of Parker's apprehension, as has been related. Sheriff Ruffner of Yavapai county, Sheriff Cameron and Deputy Fairchild responded, leaving Flagstaff at 2 P.M. on the day of the capture.

Parker states that after leaving the trading post with but the two Indians and Preston to guard him, the hope of escape from his captors increased. Preston carried his six-shooter on his left side in a holster on a loosely fastened cartridge belt. Parker planned to leisurely ride alongside of Preston, and, at an opportune moment snatch the pistol from the holster. The watchfulness of the Indians might prevent his carrying out the plan formulated to hold up his guards after securing the pistol. To test the redskins' alertness he rode close to them, and now and then would cause his horse to collide with the Indians' ponies. Their Winchesters were carried in scabbards, but at no time did they show anxiety and paid no attention to their prisoner's antics.

Noting all this, Parker felt that escape was within his grasp. His horse was jaded and tired as were those of Preston and the Indians. He concluded to go into camp with his guards, get a good supper and breakfast the next morning, and after breakfast make his escape. To make sure that his plans would not miscarry, after going into camp he kept up his usual good humor, joked and was thoroughly sociable with his captors. He even assisted in bringing brushwood for the campfire, and while thus occupied with Preston practiced his plan of snatching the six-shooter. He would frequently, while joking and laughing, bump up against Preston, who suspected nothing.

Satisfied that he could make his escape in the morning, Parker retired to rest with his captors. About 3 o'clock in the morning the party were awakened by the arrival of Sheriff Ruffner, having ridden on ahead of Cameron and Fairchild, who were in a buckboard. Parker's first words on seeing the rough-and-ready Yavapai Sheriff were "Well, is that you, Ruffner, you ___ ___ ___." If I had known you were coming I'd escaped long ago."

Sheriff Cameron and Under Sheriff Fairchild arrived on the scene at this juncture with the regulation hobbles and handcuffs. Ruffner informed Parker that he would see that there would be no further opportunity for his escape, and the desperado was securely bound hand and foot.

Parker now deeply regrets not having made his escape earlier in the evening, and with curses expresses his opinion of Ruffner. There was a reward of about $2400 offered for Parker, $333 of which Sheriff Ruffner offered. This last sum was paid to Preston this evening, and the balance will be turned over to him in a few days. Preston deserved great credit for the capture, and has richly earned the reward. Parker realizes that he has no chance of escape from the gallows, but keeps up his reckless good humor.

On May 28, 1897, the *San Francisco Examiner* also carried the news of Parker's capture. The account was routine, except that the paper described Preston as someone who *"had been acquainted with Parker when he was a vaquero for one of the big cattle companies here."* This seems unlikely, in view if the preceding details.

As noted earlier, the 1901 fire in Williams, Arizona destroyed the entire backfile of the *Williams News* up to that point, including its coverage of the Parker story. Gene Norris, a descendent of the Prescott Norris family who provided me much detail into the life of Lee Norris, also provided me with the text of the *Williams News* coverage of Parker's capture, the original of which had been found in the papers of one of his ancestors. It is an unusually flowery article, a mixture of fact and pulp, and gives an insight into what kind of newspaper the *News* must have been in 1897. It is also unique in that it gives the reporter's name, something generally not done in those days. It is clear that Luke North aspired to be a writer of greater fame than journalism—how else can one explain his use of the lynch mob rumor when he seems to have been an eyewitness to the arrival of Ruffner and Parker in Prescott, and surely saw that it did not happen?

Here, seen in its entirety for the first time since 1897, is the article on Parker's capture from the June 5, 1897 *Williams News*:

JIM PARKER IN JAIL

Sheriff Ruffner Lands His Man In Prison

SAD STORY OF LEE NORRIS

The Popular Young Attorney of Prescott, Arizona.—Heroism of Sheriff Ruffner
Prescott, June 3, 1897.
(Regular Correspondence of the News)
The event of the past week in Arizona was the capture of Jim Parker. Friday night I went to Flagstaff to see the bold, bad man of northern Arizona. Saturday I interviewed and photographed him in the jail at Flagstaff and then returned to Prescott with Sheriffs Ruffner and Cameron and their two desperate prisoners.

Parker is a beau ideal of bandits. If future paragraphs shall set him down as a monster in human shape, let these words stand as a testimony of the truth.

Jim Parker is no more than if quite the average in stature, but his compact build bespeaks tremendous energy and endurance. His features are regular, his face is intelligent and his blue eyes, though not large, are clear and keen. Except for a certain courseness in his face, partly the result of exposure to wind and sun, he is rather a handsome and altogether a dashing sort of young fellow. He has a good deal of personal magnetism and people like to talk with him. He has a clear baritone voice, looks straight at you when he talks and the romantically inclined ladies must, I am sure, find him a charming fellow. While his language is not polished, his conversation is engaging and his manner ingratiating, without the least display of bravado or affectation.

In the old days of "Gentlemen Dick" or of Robin Hood, Jim Parker would have been a hero among bad men. But these are prosaic times. Jim Parker was born two centuries too late, even for the border regions of the United States, "And, then, Arizona isn't quite the best place in the world for the real bad man from "Bitter Creek". All of them have been failures in this territory, and now even Jim Parker must end his brief career from the noose end of a rope. He will go to the gallows smilingly and will crack a joke with the hangman who arranges the knot.

He came nearer being lynched at Prescott Saturday night than he probably knows of. Seventy-five armed and determined men were lying in wait for the train at Whipple, where it usually slows up or comes to a stop. But Ruffner had arranged things differently, and both the crowd at Whipple and the one at Prescott station were fooled. However, as they rode through the streets to the jail quite a number spotted the vehicle and made a rush for it.

Miller quaked and trembled. "Here they come; here they come!" he cried, "I know they'd do it."

"Shut up, you _____ fool" shouted the undaunted Parker, giving his manacled twin a kick with his free limb. Then he turned to the threatening crowd, waved his hat to them and said:

"Hello, boys; we're having a little ride to get the fresh air.

* * * *

Parker laughs at the idea of his being captured by Preston. "It was George Ruffner who made a change in my plans," he says. "I never considered that Preston and the "navies" would give me much trouble when I got ready to go. I was waiting for my horse to get watered and fed. Then I'd have been on about my business and one or two 'navys' would have bit the dust and the rest taken wings to their heels. But, ____ it, Ruffner came too soon. He made a change all around."

Like all other bad men, Jim Parker made one fatal mistake—the killing of Lee Norris. He owns as much, "I had nothing against Norris," he says, "and I am sorry I killed him. I was a little rattled at the time and I was afraid he would wing me from an upstairs window. However, what's done is done."

* * * *

Artist's rendering of Erasmus Lee Norris, from the Detroit Free Press, June 11, 1897. (Author's collection)

The desperado's victim was one of the most popular young men of Prescott. Though but 28 years of age he was an attorney of acknowledged ability. A man of strong character, very pleasing personality, and, all in all, was abundantly equipped for an honorable and useful career. The hanging of a dozen Jim Parkers would never compensate for the untimely ending of one man like Lee Norris. He came to Arizona when but 17 years old with his brother, T. G. Norris, from his native town, Green Forest, in Carroll county, Arkansas. For several years he had been attending the University at Ann Arbor, Mich. He was in the literary department for some time, and then, in last June, graduated with honors from the law department. Soon after his arrival at Prescott he entered into a law partnership with District Attorney H. D. Ross. He was engaged to be married to a very charming young lady, who was also attending the Ann Arbor University, a Miss Burnice Smith, and the finding of a partly written loveletter to his sweetheart on his desk after he was shot, together with his directions to forward the letter as it was, so that she should know that his dying thoughts had been of her, was the most touching event of his tragic ending.

* * * *

Now, while there is a certain daredevil dash about Jim Parker that makes him an interesting character to dime novel reading youngsters and romantic school girls, men and women gifted with common horse-sense and some appreciation of such things as (unreadable) public safety and (unreadable) should be ashamed to indulge any mawkish sentimentality about such a villain and desperado as this man. He (unreadable) pressed, or Arizona will take a backward step in civilization.

> In reality, Sheriff Ruffner is the hero of the Jim Parker story—for how can a man be a hero who has no honor and no fine moral characteristics? Ruffner's exploits and dangers have been as great and even greater than those of Parker. He has captured for the second time Arizona's most desperate character and in just that measure he has served the whole territory. His magnificent defense of his prisoners on the courthouse steps Saturday at midnight, when he and Sheriff Cameron stood almost alone and boldly defied an angry mob bent on lynching Parker, was a finer piece of heroism than anything that will ever be found in the careers of all the Jim Parkers the fiends incarnate have ever produced.
> So I repeat, George Ruffner is the hero of the Jim Parker story—a story that is now almost ended.
>
> Luke North

The Detroit Free Press in Michigan, after a brief introduction, ran a lengthy excerpt from the *Williams News* article, but attributed the writing to Charles N. Stark, supposedly a former Detroit newspaperman. The article was accompanied by an artist's sketch of Lee Norris.

Parker and Miller were once again lodged in the Yavapai County jail under very heavy guard. The Grand Jury was to meet soon to formally indict. In the interim, the *Arizona Gazette* ran an interview with Henry F. Ashurst, a then-prominent attorney who would later become Arizona's famed statehood pioneer and U. S. Senator. In the interview, which ran on June 1, 1897, Ashurst recalled the Abe Thompson Gang:

> Henry Ashurst, the brilliant young orator of Bill William's mountain, and a member of the late legislative assembly, who spent the past two days in the city, returned home last night. Mr. Ashurst is well acquainted with Parker, the outlaw, who was captured a few days ago. He said Parker was formerly held to be a very quiet man. When he used to come in Flagstaff and Williams with a crowd of cowboys, he always behaved himself and never gambled or drank like the rest of his companions. This disarmed suspicion and he in nowise was connected with the numerous robberies that were taking place in that section. He made frequent visits to a spot where was known to be the rendezvous of the outlaws and this circumstance finally aroused suspicion and the discovery was made that Parker, the quiet and unassuming cowboy, was the leader of the gang.

From *Our Mineral Wealth* of June 4, 1897:

> Jim Parker states that had he known at the time of his capture that he had killed Lee Norris he would not have been taken alive. It would have been better for him and the coyotes had he made a loosing stand. T.L. Garner stated, just after the jail break, that he saw the tracks of Parker's horse leading towards Pine Springs but people were skeptical and the trail was not followed far. Parker states that he was at Pine Springs.

From the *Gazette* of June 5, 1897:

Sheriff Ruffner came down from Yavapai county yesterday to settle all obligations rendered by Sheriff Orme in sending two posses on the trail of Outlaw Parker. Sheriff Ruffner personally bore the entire expense incurred in capturing the escapes, as well as the reward offered for the outlaws.

From the *Arizona Republican* of June 6, 1897, this possibly apocryphal anecdote:

It will be remembered that on the Sunday noon the evasive Mr. Parker left Prescott mounted on Sheriff Ruffner's horse he called back in a spirit (unreadable) to the stableman who was in no humor for joking, and who had (unreadable) to dissuade him, "Just tell them that you saw me." Mr. Parker returned to Prescott the other day, as all the world knows, somewhat earlier than he expected. Sheriff Ruffner having finished riveting a pair of shackles on his feet in order to lessen the labor of communicating with him in the future, tapped him playfully on the shoulder and committed a gross plagiarism on the original remark of Mr. Parker, saying, "Just tell them that you saw me.

From the *Phoenix Herald* of June 1, 1897:

The boys about the Sheriff's office were this morning discussing the probability of soon having under their charge the desperadoes Parker and Miller, who have just been recaptured and are again in jail in Prescott. It was thought that it would be impossible to secure a jury to try the desperadoes in the northern portion of the Territory, and that it was very likely that they would be brought to Phoenix for trial on a change of venue. The jailors have already begun to look up their old Oregon boots and chains, and say that should those men be brought to this city they will be well cared for and no chances taken with them.

From the *Prescott Courier* of June 4, 1897:

Sheriff Ruffner desires the Courier to thank all friends who have assisted in tracking the outlaws. He desires those who have bills for services rendered to bring the bills in and he will pay them as soon as he can.

From the same edition:

Outlaw Parker received a letter from his sister yesterday. She lives in California and wrote after she saw the account of his capture in the papers.

From the same edition:

Outlaw Parker is a native of Tulare county, California. Has resided in Arizona about six years, but has been out of the territory several times during that time. He is said to have served two terms in San Quentin prison. He is about 33 years old. He is by trade a cowboy.

   Parker's parents were highly respectable people. His mother died when he was a boy. His father went insane after the death of his wife (Parker's mother) and

> died when Parker was about 15 years of age. Parker has no brothers, but has two sisters living. His father was Dan Parker, who was well known in Tulare county.
> Parker was raised by his grandfather, who is now living. In the letter he received from his sister, she said that the grand father was almost broken up from getting him out of scrapes and the whole family was disgraced.
> This information was obtained from a gentleman who knew the whole family. Parker has become a cowboy since he came to Arizona.

Again, the last part was obviously rumor, as Parker's grandfather was indeed deceased by this time.

From the same edition:

> Our Mineral Wealth, May 28:
> Ex-Register P. W. O'Sullivan has been appointed assistant district attorney in the place of Lee Norris, deceased. Mr. O'Sullivan is a staunch friend of silver and believes that America is big and wise enough to govern itself. Hope such men will always be favored in Arizona. If the east will recognize none but gold bugs the west should put a seeker for an office through his free silver catechism.

The June 11, 1897 *Courier* reprinted the following from the *Arizona Star* of Tucson, and added a comment:

> Sheriff Ruffner is the kind of officer that the law breakers fear, and he can rely upon the earnest co-operation of the people of the territory, for he is the prompt payer of rewards offered by him, as the recent capture of Parker demonstrates.—Arizona Star.
> Quite correct.

On June 15, 1897, the *Santa Fe Daily New Mexican* weighed in with this item:

> Albuquerque, N.M., June 13--- A.P. Frederick, postoffice inspector, will go to Las Cruces tomorrow night. During the gentleman's stay here, your correspondent called on him at his headquarters in the European, room 34, and found him busy with correspondence. Mr. Frederick said that he had just returned from Tonto Basin, north of Phoenix, where he had investigated trouble of a minor nature, but the culprit had made his escape. At Prescott he talked to Jim Parker, the train robber and murderer of Lee Norris at the time of his (Parker's) escape a month ago. Frederick urged that Parker should tell who was engaged in the train robbery besides himself, as it was no use to conceal information, but Parker was as "stubborn as a burro," to use the inspector's words. He insisted that he was not a party to the Peach Springs affair of six months ago. His trial will come up on next Friday, but whether on the first charge, or that of murder, Mr. Frederick could not say. Important affairs may call the inspector to other points south, but of the these the writer was enjoined not to make mention, though Mr. F. promised to divulge at the proper time.

The June 18, 1897 *Prescott Courier* reprinted the following from the *Williams News*:

> J. J. Stewart says that Jim Parker, the outlaw, was within three miles of Williams while the posse remained in town, undecided which direction to pursue. Mr. Stewart was prospecting on one of the two mountains northwest of town when Parker rode up and demanded something to eat. He was fed at the prospector's camp. The outlaw threatened Mr. Stewart with death should he attempt to betray him. Parker remained there several days. His night retreat was a big cave near the peak.
>
> Mr. Stewart told Guard Howe of his adventure with Parker, and Monday Mr. Howe and Constable Gray rode out to take a look at the cave, the existence of which had previously been known to only a few people. They found the cave. A small aperture leads slantingly down for twenty feet to a shelf of rock, the descent from which is perpendicular for thirty feet more. Messrs. Gray and Howe lowered themselves with ropes and flashed torches ahead of them to dissipate the Erebus-like gloom. At the bottom was a cavern as large as a house. The only sign of previous habitation were an old shovel and worn piece of rope.
>
> —Williams News.

The idea that Sheriff Ruffner had stared down a lynch mob to bring Parker to jail continued to spread. From the *Arizona Gazette* of June 15, 1897:

> The last number of the Police Gazette contains a graphic picture of Sheriff Ruffner defying a mob of would-be lynchers. The picture is highly suggestive of the early days of Arizona. The sheriff stands with a pistol in each hand and several others stuck in his belt. Surrounding the doughty official is a mob of cowboys, who quail before his drawn revolvers, and from the resolute gleam that shines from his optics. One of the number has a rope, which he seems anxious to drop under the mute appeal contained in the guns that stare him in the face. Dramatic color is lent by these startling headlines: "Sheriff Ruffner Defies a Mob; The Prescott, Arizona, Official Makes a Mob of Would-Be Lynchers Quail Before Him, and Finally Disperses the Marauders by His Coolness and Courage.

Unfortunately, that issue of the *Police Gazette* is not known to have survived.

The capture of Parker was solidly accomplished by Samuel S. Preston—It would be logical to assume that his collecting of the various rewards offered would be cut and dried, but it didn't work out that way. Instead, legal wrangling over much of the reward money would last long after Parker's death. There was also much resentment that a common citizen secured the capture instead of a lawman.

As we already know, Sheriff Ruffner grudgingly paid Preston the reward that he himself had offered. The next step was the reward offered by the Territory. The *Arizona Gazette* reported the following on June 1, 1897:

> The governor yesterday received notice from United States District Attorney Ellinwood, acting for S. S. Preston, the post trader who captured Parker, that the latter claimed the reward offered by the territory for the apprehension of the outlaw.

> The governor will order the reward paid as soon as the necessary affidavits are received. Preston has already received the $1,000 reward offered by Sheriff Ruffner.

From the *Arizona Republican* of June 2, 1897:

> S. S. Preston, the Willow Springs post trader who captured Parker, the train robber and murderer, arrived from the north early this morning. The object of his visit is to bring formal proof of his having earned the reward offered by the territory for the capture of the outlaw. There is no doubt that he did earn it, but his letter received at the governor's office last Monday asking for the $500 due him was lacking formality.

There were no further problems from the Territory, however, and Preston collected the reward. From the *Arizona Gazette* of June 8, 1897:

> The reward of $500 offered by Governor Franklin for the apprehension of Outlaw Parker was paid yesterday to S. S. Preston, who captured the escape.

The Territory's paying of the reward had some ripple effects, more humorous today than they were at the time. From *Our Mineral Wealth* of June 4, 1897:

> While at Phoenix, Sheriff Potts went before his royal highness Governor Franklin, and after a long siege induced him to offer a reward of $300 for the capture of Mouse, the murderer of Davis and Stearns. The Sheriff tried to have the sum of $500 offered, but the old man never before heard of Mohave county and he thought $300 for the apprehension of a double murderer was treating a small county like Mohave white as chalk. When Miller, the petty forger, broke jail $500 reward was offered by the governor. $300 is better than nothing. There is now a reward of $550 for Mouse, and a man with a good rifle can earn a good grubstake by putting him where the wind will whistle through his bones and do the county a lasting service.

From the *Gazette* of June 22, 1897:

> Governor Franklin yesterday received a letter from Albert Ruiz, assistant district attorney of Navajo county, requesting him to offer a reward for the arrest and conviction of John Gibson, the man who murdered Chas. B. Thompson on the 8th last. Gibson, he said, was in hiding somewhere in the vicinity of the Black river. The governor is somewhat doubtful about offering a reward for the murder's conviction, and thinks that as the officers know the hiding place of Gibson, they ought to make an effort to capture him and not wait for a reward to be offered. Since a reward was offered for the arrest of Parker and Miller, the Prescott escapes, he is being requested to offer rewards for the capture of every petty fugitive from justice.

Both Ruffner and the Territory of Arizona had made good on the rewards they had offered for the capture of Parker. It was a different story with Wells Fargo and the Santa Fe Railroad—Detective John N. Thacker refused to pay the reward he had offered on that now infamous Wanted poster that has been reprinted so often over the years. Thacker's legal excuse for weaseling out of paying was this—Wells Fargo was interested in Parker for the train robbery. As shall be seen in the next chapter, Parker was indicted for the train robbery, but never tried for it, the courts believing it would be silly to try him for the lesser crime after sentencing him to be hanged for murder. Consequently, without a conviction on record, the Rock Cut train robber had never legally been caught, the robbery was legally unsolved, and Wells Fargo and Santa Fe legally owed no one the reward.

It was the kind of legal loophole that only attorneys could cheer, and it spawned a spate of lawsuits, the details of which are regrettably sketchy, owing to lack of surviving court papers and newspaper disinterest in the cases.

Sheriff Ruffner, who was quite knowledgeable in law, saw the problem coming. The July 2, 1897 *Prescott Courier* reported that, at the close of Parker's trial, Ruffner got up and addressed the court with the following statement:

> Judge, before sentence is passed on this man, I request that this man be tried for train robbery; I had witnesses all here and was ready to proceed, and for some cause unknown to me, they were sent home, night before last. When this court opened the district attorney promised me and gave me his word, as a man, that if I would allow this man to be tried for murder first, he would have him tried for train robbery before this sentence was pronounced. This thing has already cost me $3000. There is $2300 on him if he is convicted of this train robbery and I ask that this sentence be suspended until he is so tried.

Ruffner's request was denied by the court. The Sheriff clearly had plans to try and claim the rewards, even though it was Samuel S. Preston who had actually captured Parker. There is no evidence one way or the other as to whether or not Ruffner attempted to claim the Territorial reward that had been paid to Preston. The same edition of the *Courier* editorialized:

> Sheriff Ruffner earned those rewards for the capture of Parker for train robbery. He certainly will get them if justice is done; but law is not always justice. Ruffner is out about $3000 on the escape and capture of Parker, actual expense.

On January 6, 1898, Samuel S. Preston filed suit against Wells Fargo for the reward it had offered. Reported the *Coconino Sun* (formerly the *Flagstaff Sun-Democrat*) on January 28, 1898:

> S. S. Preston, who on May 29, 1897, captured Jim Parker, the train robber, north of Willow Springs, in this county, has brought suit against Wells, Fargo & Co. for the reward offered for Parker's arrest. Parker had escaped from the Prescott jail and Wells, Fargo & Co. offered a reward of $1,000 for his capture. The express company now refuses to pay the reward, hence the suit. Preston is certainly entitled to the reward, as there is no disputing the fact that he arrested Parker and delivered him to the proper officer, but the express company wishes to avoid

the payment of the reward because Parker was convicted for murder instead of train robbery.

Court papers for the case of S. S. Preston Vs. Wells Fargo And Co. have survived and show that Preston and his attorney, Everett E. Ellinwood, made a very simple and logical argument—Wells Fargo and the Santa Fe Railroad had offered a reward for the capture of Jim Parker. Preston succeeded in capturing the outlaw and delivered him to the proper authorities. Therefore, Preston was entitled to the reward.

The case never made it to trial. On March 7, 1898, a stipulation was added to the court papers indicating that Preston and Wells Fargo had settled out of court, and the case was dismissed. As the newspapers did not report on the settlement, it is not known what the terms were, but it is probably reasonable to assume that Wells Fargo paid Preston a portion of the reward at least. It is sad that the details seem to be lost to history.

The papers from the Preston lawsuit show that Preston subpoenaed Coconino County Sheriff Ralph Cameron as a witness. That makes the following actions even more bizarre.

On June 15, 1898, roughly three weeks after Parker was hanged, Ralph H. Cameron filed suit for the reward. Instead of going after Wells Fargo, Cameron named the railroad as the defendant. The case was Ralph H. Cameron vs. Santa Fe Pacific Railroad. Granted, Cameron was on the posse trailing Parker, but it is outrageous even to this day, to claim that he earned any part of the reward. But then, audacity was a trait that Cameron was known for.

The court papers have not survived, so it is not known what argument Cameron used to justify his claim, but he almost had to, from a legal standpoint, contend that it was he, not Preston, who had apprehended Parker (and indeed, Cameron would make this claim in media interviews in later years). The newspapers did not cover the suit at all—Parker was now dead and therefore yesterday's news. Apparently inspired by Preston, Cameron retained Everett E. Ellinwood as his attorney.

On June 30, 1898, the railroad filed a countersuit against Cameron. The case was Santa Fe Railroad vs. Ralph Cameron and George C. Ruffner. Again, the court papers have not survived, so it is impossible to ascertain the grounds of the suit or what arguments were used, or why Ruffner was included when he was not a party to the original suit. Perhaps the railroad charged Cameron with harassment for filing a frivolous lawsuit. Perhaps Ruffner was planning his own suit, and Santa Fe hoped to discourage him with this action. The facts will probably never be fully known.

The two cases laid around in litigation for much longer than was customary in those days, and on March 22, 1899, both were transferred from Coconino County to Mohave County for trial. This is undoubtedly why the court papers have not survived. Throughout much of Arizona, detailed court records still exist from this period, but not Mohave County. Legal cases from Mohave County are quite difficult to piece together.

Make no mistake, Parker was captured by Samuel S. Preston. George C. Ruffner expended much effort, energy, and money trailing Parker, but he really had no claim to the reward. Ralph Cameron had even less claim, as he was nowhere in sight when Parker was caught. That makes the outcome of the case so bizarre and outrageous. The only news coverage pertaining to the case appeared in the *Coconino Sun* on April 15, 1899:

> R. H. Cameron returned from Kingman yesterday, where he has been attending court. He won his case, which entitles him to the reward offered by Wells, Fargo & Co., for the recapture of Jim Parker, the train robber, and which reward ex-Sheriff Ruffner also claimed.

Even without more surviving details, the words "travesty of justice" leap to mind. Somehow, some way, Ralph Cameron persuaded a judge that he was the one who had truly recaptured Parker. Imagine how both Preston and Ruffner felt!

As for the railroad's suit against Cameron and Ruffner, a surviving judgment docket at the Mohave County Courthouse shows that on April 6, 1899, the two defendants were ordered to pay Santa Fe a sum of $235.00. The railroad's legal fees, perhaps? If so, it makes these judicial decisions even more lopsided.

Many people attribute ridiculous lawsuits and outrageous judicial decisions to contemporary trends. This pair of cases shows that such foolishness goes back much, much further.

In January of 1903, a reporter for the *Washington Star* interviewed Ralph H. Cameron and asked him to relay the Parker story. This interview then appeared in newspapers nationwide through the wire services, and eventually appeared in part even in the *Williams News* on February 21, 1903. The unnamed reporter opened the article by describing Cameron as a *"modest, unassuming man"* (which Cameron most certainly was not), and then proclaimed that Cameron didn't want to talk about his adventures—but then did so just the same. The error in the article naming the town "Pete Springs" instead of Peach Springs was probably the fault of the reporter instead of Cameron, but Cameron certainly makes quite a number of his own errors—including, yes, that it was he and his posses who captured Parker both times. Cameron told the *Star*:

> That was perhaps the most thrilling experience in my life…Jim Parker was not a bad man at heart. Like many other young men he began wrong and developed rapidly. The police first became acquainted with Parker in Visalia county, California, where he was caught, while still a boy, stealing grain from the fields during harvest time. He was sent to San Quentin prison and served a term of five years. In the early 90s Jim Parker made his first appearance in Arizona as a cattle thief, and was the recognized chief of what was then known as the Thompson gang, whose headquarters was Robbers' Roost. This band consisted of Abe Thompson, Kid Marvin, and several half-breeds and Mexicans whose names were never known.

Thompson had been a railroad engineer and furnished the mechanical part of the plan to rob the Santa Fe trains. For several weeks Thompson, by drawings and illustrations, coached Parker in the management of a locomotive. It was the first chapter in a well-constructed plot to hold up an express train, a job that required great deliberation and daring. Jim Parker furnished all of that, for though a small man, with a kindly face, he was the most determined man when he set out to do a job that I ever saw. Parker told me afterward that he planned the robbery. Some time before the hold-up Parker went to Pete Springs, and purchased a ticket for California, taking with him his saddle and gun, giving it out generally that he was tired of the country and was going home. Three weeks after he left he returned on horseback, riding through the country, and joined the band in Robbers Roost. The scheme which they had planned was to hold up the train at Nelson, about eight miles from Pete Springs. Parker was to have one man with him to help him in the work, and as soon as they had secured the booty they were to go into southwestern Nevada and escape. Thompson and Marvin, as soon as they started on the expedition, were to go to Pete Springs, take a room in a prominent hotel, so that when the alarm was raised Thompson's gang would not be suspected, and Jim Parker, according to last accounts being in California, suspicion would be diverted from Robbers Roost.

But the best laid plans of mice and men are (illegible), as I will explain. The train showed up for Nelson in a box canyon, and Parker swung himself aboard the engine and held up the engineer and fireman and stopped the train. His partner was to uncouple the express car from the passenger coaches and signal by two shots when Parker would take the train up the canyon and they would dynamite the express car. When the train slowed up, the express messenger, fearing something wrong, grabbed his revolver and jumped from the train. He saw the cars uncoupled and was climbing back on the platform when he came face to face with the train robber. He shot him dead, and Jim Parker, hearing the two shots, concluded it was the signal, and pulled the throttle open and took the engine and mail car off. The mail car was ahead of the express car, which was unusual, but the mistake, fortunately, saved the Wells Fargo people a large sum of money, for the express car was left standing with the passenger coaches. Three miles from where the train stopped Parker brought the engine to a standstill and marched the engineer and fireman off, while he proceeded to rifle the registered mail pouch. He was expecting his partner every minute, but he did not materialize, and so, single-handed and alone, he calmly went through the mail, selecting the letters containing money and valuables. He then directed the engineer and fireman to go back and get the train, and he made for the bush. He came back, however, and hid along the railroad track as the train went by, and then hurried back to the place where he had left his partner, wondering in the meantime what had become of him. He found not a (illegible) of him, and, taking the horses, rode off to a deserted cabin, where he spent the night. The next morning he returned to the scene and, not finding his partner, made off for Nevada. A posse was immediately called and I was placed in charge of it. It included the sheriffs of Mohave and Yavapai counties and myself, the sheriff of Coconino county and seven deputies. We took up the trail from the place where the train had been held up and followed it for two days. Parker was a great cigarette smoker, and we found a place where he had consumed at least 100 cigarettes. We could tell from the trail that he had taken off his boots and wound his feet with clothing to protect them from the cold. He had evidently taken his boots off at night and his feet had swollen to such an extent as to prevent him from putting them on again. It was now only a question of time, we thought, before Parker would be taken. The trail led through a box canyon made famous in the days of Kit Carson, when he drove the Navajo Indians in there and compelled them to surrender. Our horses were tired and it became necessary to send back for fresh ones, and this, in my opinion, saved the lives of every one of the posse, for Parker and planned an ambush in this canyon, through which the trail led, that would undoubtedly have resulted in the death of every man. We could follow his trail in the snow into this canyon and over a sheer precipice of perhaps fifteen feet. The trail then ran straight to a waterfall, which had a drop of perhaps fifty feet. Parker had doubled on his trail and climbed the cliff and fortified himself in a position to command the entire range of the canyon. Had we ever gotten into this trap, as I have said, not one would have escaped, for Parker was a dead shot and well-armed. A delay of twelve hours, however, threw Parker off the track and he continued toward the Nevada line.

    In his escape toward the Nevada line Parker had planned to double on his track, or, at least, had an idea that it would be necessary for him to come back, for he had cached provisions here and there along the trail, which we discovered. The next day we pitched our camp in a bunch of cottonwoods by the side of Diamond canyon, and one of the deputies said he was going out to capture Parker. We all laughed at him and he took his gun and struck the bed of the stream and went toward Pete Springs. In a short time we were all thrown into a state of excitement by the return of the deputy, who stated that Parker was coming up the creek. I called the men together and secreted them in the bush and waited patiently for the train robber to make his appearance. He came in a few minutes, with his Winchester back of his head and whistling to himself. As soon as he got within twenty feet the nearest deputy jumped out and commanded him to throw up his hands, at the same time covering him with his Winchester. The rest of us made our appearance and Parker knew he was up against it and threw his rifle back. We secured him and started back for Flagstaff. Of course, there was great excitement at Pete Springs when we arrived.

    The prisoner was taken to Prescott and put in (illegible). He was tried in Yavapai county and sentenced to be hanged. While awaiting his sentence he made a bold escape from prison, killing the district attorney and severely beating the jailer. He was assisted in this escape by a Mexican and Marvin Miller. As soon as they broke jail they ran across the plaza to a livery stable kept by Sheriff Ruffner and stole two horses. Parker took the sheriff's horse, which was the best one in the county, and grabbed the Mexican up behind him and left town with the song 'Just tell them that you saw me, but didn't saw me sore'. They made for the big timber, and on the way Parker pushed the Mexican off in the brush, which looked like a shabby trick at the time, but the Mexican made good his escape and was never apprehended. Miller was caught at Jerome and jailed. Parker made for the Black Hills, and on the way we found where he had gone into a pasture, killed a yearling, and jerked the meat. He doubled on his track twice, and finally we located him in the lagoon country. It was here we received positive information at a trader's store that Parker had recently passed that way. The Indians were called in and offered $15 apiece to assist in his capture. Reinforced by these, we started out again and followed Parker, Indian-fashion, that is! We would rest during the day and trail him at night. Finally we came up to him in a small canyon, and found him sound asleep, with his forehead resting on his gun. He was completely surrounded and taken, and the march proceeded to Flagstaff, where he was jailed. Parker told me afterward that but for a coincidence he would have gotten away again. It was his purpose to ride alongside of an Indian when the horses were watered at the Colorado river, and snatching a gun from the holster, turn and shoot and get away, but when we reached the river another posse joined us and Parker gave up all hopes of escape. Yes, Parker was hanged, and I never saw a man die as game as he did. He made a speech on the scaffold and said it was all right, he deserved it, and after telling the boys good-by, tried the trapdoor and told them to let her go.

Ralph Cameron undoubtedly told much the same story to the judges in order to collect part of the reward. As we have seen in the previous chapters, Cameron's account here is riddled with errors, not only his proclamation that he and his deputies captured Parker both times, but also his absurd statement that Parker was sentenced to hang for the train robbery and *then* broke out of jail! Several of Cameron's more minor errors were later repeated by Williams historian Thomas E. Way, who undoubtedly knew Ralph Cameron personally.

CHAPTER 8

The Trial

The Grand Jury convened shortly after Parker's capture, and returned the expected indictments. It is not widely remembered today, but Parker was indicted for the train robbery as well as murder. From the *Arizona Journal Miner* of June 16, 1897:

> The grand jury returned indictments as follows: Against James Parker and Abe Thompson for train robbery; against Love Marvin for robbery; against E. E. Valdez for burglary.
>
> Brown Bros. vs. The Iron Springs Mining company. Case placed on calendar.
>
> At the opening of the court this afternoon the grand jury returned indictments against L. C. Miller for forgery, Charles Canaris grand larceny and Antonio Diaz for burglary.
>
> Parker and Thompson were brought into court and arraigned on a charge of train robbery and they were given till Saturday to plead.

Abe Thompson's case was ultimately separated from Parker's, but their indictment for the train robbery read as follows:

> In the District Court of the Fourth Judicial District of the Territory of Arizona, in and for the County of Yavapai, Territory of Arizona, —Plaintiff.
> vs.
> James Parker and Abe Thompson
> Defendants.
> In the District Court of the Fourth Judicial District of the Territory of Arizona, in and for the County of Yavapai, on this 9th day of June, A. D. 1897, James Parker and Abe Thompson are accused by the Grand Jury of the County of Yavapai, Territory of Arizona, by this Indictment of a felony, to wit: of willfully and maliciously making an assault upon a railroad train and upon a car of said railroad train for the purpose and with the intent to commit robbery upon and against a mail agent on said railroad train and in said railroad car of said railroad train committed as follows, to wit: That the said James Parker and Abe Thompson on or about the 8th. day of February, A. D. 1897, at the County of Yavapai Territory of Arizona, did upon a certain railroad train and upon a certain railroad car, the said railroad car being then and there one of the railroad cars of said railroad train, willfully, maliciously, and feloniously make an assault for the purpose and with the intent then and there to commit robbery upon and against one A. S. Grant who was then and there a mail agent on said railroad train and in said railroad car and which said mail agent was then and there in the employment of the United States of America in the

handling of its mail and was then and there engaged in the performance of his duty as such mail agent on said railroad train and in said railroad car and that the said railroad train was commonly known as the regular West bound passenger train and then and there being a railroad train of C. W. Smith, the duly appointed and acting Receiver of the Atlantic and Pacific Railroad Company, a corporation duly created, organized and existing under the laws of the United States, and the said railroad train and the said railroad car then and there being on the railroad track of the said C. W. Smith Receiver as aforesaid of the said Atlantic and Pacific Railroad Company; a further description of said railroad train and of said railroad car being to the Grand Jury unknown.

Contrary to the form and effect of the Statute in such case made and provided and against the peace and dignity of the Territory of Arizona.

H.D. Ross
District Attorney of Yavapai County, Arizona
Names of witnesses examined before the grand jury:
William Daze
J. A. Smith
Love Marvin

Love Marvin was also indicted for the robbery, but as already seen, he agreed to turn state's evidence and received a suspended sentence. His indictment, somewhat more detailed, read as follows:

In the District Court of the Fourth Judicial District of the Territory of Arizona, in and for the County of Yavapai.
Territory of Arizona, ----------------------Plaintiff.
    Vs.   INDICTMENT.
Love Marvin, ----------------------------Defendant.-------------------------------
In the District Court of the Fourth Judicial District of the Territory of Arizona, in and for the County of Yavapai, on this 9th day of June, A. D. 1897, Love Marvin is accused by the Grand Jury of the said County of Yavapai, Territory of Arizona, by this indictment of the crime of robbery, committed as follows to-wit: -
That the said Love Marvin, on or about the 8th day of February 1897, at the County of Yavapai, in the Territory of Arizona, in and upon one A.S. Grant did unlawfully, willfully and feloniously make an assault, and him the said A. S. Grant, unlawfully, willfully and feloniously, by means of force and violence, put in bodily harm and fear, and danger of his life, and many and divers letters and packages of the value of one hundred dollars, all the property of the said A. S. Grant, from the person and immediate presence and against the will of the said A. S. Grant, then and there unlawfully, violently, forcibly and feloniously, did steal, take and carry away; that a more particular description of the said letters and packages is to the Grand Jury unknown.

Contrary to the form and effect of the statute in such case made and provided and against the peace and dignity of the Territory of Arizona.

H.D. Ross
District Attorney of
Yavapai County, Arizona

Names of witnesses examined before the Grand Jury upon the finding of this indictment: Wm. Daze, - J. A. Smith, - Love Marvin.

Some confusion arose over Parker's legal representation early on. Earl M. Sanford had been the counsel for the train robbery defendants, but this was about to change, especially now that Parker was a murderer. From the *Prescott Courier* of June 11, 1897:

> When James Parker was brought into court yesterday to answer to the indictment of train robbery, Judge Hawkins asked Parker if he had an attorney. Judge Sanford arose and said he was Parker's attorney. Parker spoke up saying he did not want Sanford. Judge Hawkins asked Parker what he said and Parker repeated that he did not want Judge Sanford, whereupon Judge Hawkins appointed Joseph Morrison and Geo. A. Allen as Parker's attorneys.

Later portrait of Judge John J. Hawkins, who presided over the trials of Parker and Miller. (Courtesy of Sharlot Hall Museum)

While Parker and Sanford had definitely come to a parting of the ways, Sanford immediately disputed this account. He sent a note to the *Arizona Journal Miner*, which reprinted it verbatim June 16, 1897:

> Card from Mr. Sanford.
> Journal-Miner: The Courier this morning says that on yesterday morning I arose in court and said that I was Parker's attorney. I have been long enough in the profession to know whom I represent when I go into court. Parker and Thompson were jointly indicted; the court asked Thompson if he had an attorney. I replied that I was attorney for Thompson but not for Parker.
> E. M. Sanford

Red-faced, the *Courier* issued a retraction, which appeared June 18, 1897:

> Judge Sanford said to a Courier reporter yesterday that the item in yesterday morning's Courier was incorrect in reference to what took place in the court

room when Parker was brought into court to answer to the indictment of train robbery. When the question of attorneys for defendants came up Sanford stated that they (Parker and Thompson) being indicted jointly, he would appear for Parker for the purpose of the arraignment. Then it was that Parker said he did not want Sanford.

It will never be known why Parker wanted to change attorneys, although he would later tell reporters that Sanford had simply been taking his money and preparing an inadequate defense for him. This, of course, would have been unethical, and certainly very possible—attorneys in those days often deliberately tried to "throw cases" where their clients were extremely disreputable and "belonged" in prison. The legal profession had some different standards back then than they do now—standards that some people today, who are frustrated by rampant crime, would like to see return. On the other hand, it may have only been Parker's perception—it is doubtful his knowledge of judicial proceedings was very deep, despite his previous transgressions of the law.

This artist's rendering of Parker, which appeared in the *San Francisco Call* on June 26, 1897, is a full-length sketch, and therefore may have come from its unknown creator's imagination, inasmuch as there likely was not a photo of this kind for him to work from. (Author's collection)

Finally, in the interview where Parker made his remarks about Sanford (printed in Chapter 9), he used Sanford's alleged malfeasance as an excuse for the jailbreak. This is most revealing, and it doesn't ring true. Parker needed an excuse to justify his actions, and Sanford's alleged malice or incompetence was the best one he could think of.

From the June 15, 1897 edition of the *San Francisco Call*:

> It is reported that the Coconino County cowboys have raised $1000 for the defense of bandit Jim Parker and that a well-known Coconino County lawyer has been employed to assist in his defense.

This was likely just rumor, as Parker's attorneys were appointed by the court.

Parker's newly appointed attorneys were George Allen and Joseph E. Morrison, two of Prescott's most prominent members of the bar. They were highly regarded both in court and as town citizens. In later years, some folklorists—the ones who believe that Parker was Butch Cassidy's brother—have tried to depict them as mob lawyers, but this is untrue and calumnious. Allen and Morrison took their appointment seriously, and fought hard for Parker, harder than some citizens felt they should. The two attorneys took some strong criticism and ridicule for doing their jobs.

From the *Arizona Journal Miner* of June 16, 1897:

> Territory vs James F. Parker and Abe Thompson, train robbery; demurrers filed and overruled and Parker entered plea of not guilty. Thompson's attorney demands a separate trial, which was granted. Both cases set for trial Friday, June 18.

From the *Journal Miner* of June 23, 1897:

> Engineer Wm. Daze, Fireman Barto, Postal Clerk A. S. Grant and Detective Cade Selvey are in town to attend the trial of the alleged train robbers.

From the same edition:

> Abe Thompson was arraigned yesterday on a charge of train robbery, and today pleaded not guilty.

Surviving court papers show that, in addition to Daze, Bartoo, Grant, and Selvey, the Territory also subpoenaed as witnesses Frank Garner, Henry Loven, J. A. Smith, and John E. Ayers. Loven and Smith were law enforcement officials on the Mohave County posse, and Garner had been previously identified as the owner of the "race horse" stolen by Parker. It is unclear exactly who Ayers was. "Indian Jim Hardy," a trailer who was on the first posse, was also subpoenaed. After the cases were separated, an A. J. Harris was also subpoenaed to testify against Abe Thompson. This may or may not have been Mohave Deputy Asa Harris.

For his part, Parker subpoenaed two witnesses for his defense, identified in court papers as F. X. Cook and O. E. Manker. It is no longer known who these men were, or what they could have testified to that would have possibly benefited Parker in the train robbery case.

As already noted, Parker was never tried for the Rock Cut Train Robbery, making all of this legal wrangling a waste of time. After being sentenced to hang for murder, the court apparently deemed it to be superfluous to try Parker for any other crime.

It is well known that no witnesses were called for the defense at Parker's trial. Consequently, it has often been asked just what kind of a defense attorneys Allen and Morrison presented for Parker. It sounds like they didn't do anything at all, but this is not true. That Parker shot Lee Norris was beyond dispute, so the two distinguished jurists had no choice but to craft a defense based on the idea that, in its haste to put the notorious train robber and murderer on trial, the Territory of Arizona had violated Parker's rights under the law.

Contrary to popular belief, this was not a unique defense in its day. Generations of movies and pulp "Wild West" magazines have so entrenched the image of "frontier justice" into our minds that this sort of legal sophistication seems impossible, but in truth, the Arizona legal system of the 19th century was often more sophisticated than it has been made out to be. Because Parker had lawyers who were willing to go to bat for him, he received virtually the same legal rights he would have received in the present day. Even Parker himself seemed to realize that his attorneys were doing everything they could for him, for he retained George Allen and Joseph Morrison until the last day of his life.

Parker, Miller, and Cornelia Sarata were indicted jointly for murder, although the two trials were later separated (and, of course, Sarata had not been caught.) The text of the indictment reads as follows:

> In the District Court of the Fourth Judicial District of the Territory of Arizona, in and for the County of Yavapai.
> Territory of Arizona, -----Plaintiff,
> vs.
> James Parker, L. C. Miller and Cornellia Sarata,
> Defendants.
> In the District Court of the Fourth Judicial District of the Territory of Arizona, in and for the County of Yavapai, on this 7th day of June, A. D. 1897, James Parker, L. C. Miller and Cornellia Sarata are accused by the Grand Jury of said County of Yavapai by this Indictment of the crime of murder committed as follows, to wit:
> That on the 9th. day of May, A. D. 1897, at the County of Yavapai, Territory of Arizona, the said James Parker, L. C. Miller, and Cornellia Sarata did willfully, feloniously, deliberately, premeditatedly, and of their malice aforethought make an assault on one E. L. Norris, and a certain gun which then and there was loaded with gunpowder and leaden bullets and by them the said James Parker L. C. Miller and Cornellia Sarata had and held in their hands, they, the said James Parker, L. C. Miller and Cornellia Sarata did then and there willfully, feloniously, deliberately, premeditatedly and of their malice aforethought shoot off and discharge at, upon, and into the said E. L. Norris with said leaden bullets inflicting on and in the body of him one mortal wound; of which said mortal wound the said E. L. Norris then and there died, and so the said James Parker, L. C. Miller and Cornellia Sarata did in manner and form aforesaid willfully, feloniously, deliberately, premeditatedly and of their malice aforethought kill and murder the said E. L. Norris.
> Contrary to the form and effect of the statutes in such case made and provided and against the peace and dignity of the Territory of Arizona.
> H. D. Ross
> District Attorney of Yavapai County, Arizona
> Names of witnesses examined before the Grand Jury:
> R. M. Meador
> H. D. Ross

Parker's court papers have survived, and are voluminous, showing just how hard his attorneys fought for him with various appeals and motions. Perhaps Allen and Morrison recognized something that others didn't—how unfair it was that Parker was facing the gallows for a murder that, while unconscionable, was hardly premeditated, while calculating killers like Richard Cross were being saved by the Norton Act.

At any rate, Parker's court papers are far too lengthy to reproduce here, much as I would like to. So for the sake of expediency, we will have to hit the high points of the trial.

From the *Arizona Journal Miner* of June 16, 1897:

Parker and Miller in Court

At the hour of 4 o'clock on Tuesday, the time set for Parker and Miller to plead to the indictment of murder, the court house was packed full of people, all apparently anxious to get a glimpse at the now notorious couple.

The first move made by the attorneys for the accused, J. E. Morrison acting as spokesman, was to move that the shackles be removed from the prisoners. This was overruled, and an exception taken. Next was a motion to set aside the arraignment of the previous day, on the grounds that no copy of the indictment was served on the prisoners as required. One copy was furnished their attorneys, but in this the date was omitted, and counsel contended that inasmuch as there were two prisoners and two attorneys, there should have been two copies furnished. Judge Hawkins at first intimated that he would overrule this motion, but finally, to be on the safe side, he requested that copies of the indictment be furnished, and the prisoners were again placed on their arraignment, and took the statutory time to plead, being till 3 o'clock this afternoon.

At three o'clock this afternoon Parker and Miller were again brought into court to plead to the indictment, when a motion to set aside the indictment was filed. It alleged prejudice on the part of twenty members of the grand jury which returned the indictment, and, as the defendants had not been held to answer on this charge, they had no opportunity of challenging the venire. This motion was overruled, when a general demurrer was filed, which was also overruled. The prisoners were then ordered to stand up and plead, when each entered a plea of not guilty, and the case was set for trial at 10 o'clock Monday, June 14.

From the *Prescott Courier* of June 11, 1897:

During the time that Parker and Miller were in court yesterday the room was packed with people. Once the crowd rose and pressed forward against the railing until Judge Hawkins found it necessary to order all to be seated. When the time arrived to take the prisoners back to their cell, Judge Hawkins ordered those present to keep their seats until he gave them permission to leave the room, which he did as soon as the prisoners and guards were well down the stairs. This was done, of course, in order to prevent confusion, as the crowd came to see Miller and Parker and would have left the room at the same time with the officers and prisoners.

From the *Journal Miner* of June 16, 1897:

Parker and Miller's Case
From Monday's Daily

When the case of Parker and Miller was called in court this morning their attorneys filed a motion for a change of venue, alleging as their grounds for such action that defendants could not receive a fair and impartial trial in this county. In support of this allegation their own affidavits were filed, also the affidavit of R. C. Welsh of this county, and the affidavits of E. S. Clark, district attorney of Coconino county and M. J. O'Malia of Denver. Other sojourners in the town, it is alleged, were asked to make affidavits to the same effect, but refused as they stated that they could not discover anything in the feeling of the community to justify such a sworn statement.

The district attorney asked for time until 2 o'clock this afternoon to furnish affidavits in rebuttal of the above, which was granted.

At the above hour this afternoon a further postponement was had in the case till 10 o'clock tomorrow.

The application for a change of venue, submitted by Allen and Morrison follows:

In the District Court of the Fourth Judicial District of the Territory of Arizona, in and for the County of Yavapai.

Territory of Arizona,
   vs.
James F. Parker and L. C. Miller

APPLICATION FOR A CHANGE OF VENUE

COME NOW James F. Parker and L. C. Miller, the above named defendants, and file this their application for a change of venue, in writing, duly verified by them, asking the removal of this criminal action from this Court in which it is now pending, on the ground that a fair and impartial trial of said defendants cannot be had in said Yavapai County, where the said action is pending and show to the Court:

That in said action they are indicted and charged with the murder of one E. L. Norris, which said murder is alleged to have been committed in the City of Prescott, County of Yavapai and Territory of Arizona, on the 9th day of May, 1897, that to said charge they have pleaded not guilty and that they are advised and believe that, at the Bar of this Honorable Court they stand innocent men, until proven guilty beyond all reasonable doubt. That said E. L. Norris was on the said ninth day of May, 1897, the Assistant District Attorney of this said county.

Said defendants respectfully show to your Honor that the trial Judge of this Court, in delivering his customary charge to the Grand Jury which subsequently returned said indictment into this Court and in the presence of the panel of trial jurors drawn to try all actions which might be submitted to them at this June term of this Court and in their hearing, used the following language, relative to the crime charged in the indictment herein: "I desire to call the attention of the Grand Jury at this time to matters that have been taking place in this County. It is a matter of common knowledge, Gentlemen of the Grand Jury, that within a very recent time, the very steps of your court-house have been bestrewed with the blood of one of your best citizens. I charge you gentlemen, now, at this session of the Grand Jury, the very first thing you do, that you investigate the recent outbreak in the jail of this

County and that you investigate it thoroughly, taking up each and every part thereof and bring an indictment into this Court against each and every person connected therewith, so that the parties who committed the offence of killing one of your best citizens, here, right in the very hall of justice, may be brought to justice; so it may be brought out and the citizens of your county may know what is taking place here; what its citizens are going to do about conduct of this kind.

I charge you, gentlemen, to investigate first, upon your retirement, this matter, so you may know what has been going on; you may investigate it thoroughly and make a report thereon to the Court with all speed.

Now, gentlemen, you will be furnished with bailiffs, and you will be furnished with all the majesty of the law to support you in the conduct of your consideration. The Court will see that each and every offence which has been committed within this community will be given speedy trial.

I ask you, gentlemen, in the name of justice, in the name of law in the name of reason, that these matters be at once investigated, so that you may bring indictments into Court against persons who committed this offence and that they may be speedily tried and that the statutes and laws of this Country may be vindicated."

That, upon the conclusion of the said trial Judge's said charge to the said Grand Jury, that the body retired at about three o'clock P. M. on the afternoon of the seventh day of June, 1897, the same being the first day of the regular June Term, 1897, of said Court and that, about twenty minutes thereafter, the said Grand Jury returned into Court and presented the indictment in this case/ the filing mark of the Clerk of this Court, upon which shows that the same was filed at 3.30 o'clock P.M. on the said seventh day of June, 1897.

That within half an hour after the filing of the said indictment, the said defendants were brought into the presence of this Court, from the county Jail of said county, in the custody of the sheriff of said County, shackled and in chains and in said manacled condition, were placed upon their arraignment on said indictment. That upon the said arraignment, the said defendants, not having means wherewith to employ counsel, were represented by J. E. Morrison and G. Arthur Allen, attorneys at law, qualified to practice in said District Court, said counsel being appointed by this Honorable Court to appear for said defendants. That upon the conclusion of the reading of the indictment herein to the said defendants, they, through their counsel, took the statutory time to plead, to-wit: one day. That on the following day the said defendants were again brought into this Court, shackeled and manacled, for the purpose of pleading to the indictment herein and thereupon, the said counsel for the defendants directed the attention of this Court that the said defendants were in the presence of the Court and the judge thereof, in chains and said counsel moved the said Court to direct the sheriff of the said Count, who was then in Court with various deputies, wearing in the presence of the Court and the auditors there gathered, six shooters, hanging to belts which were bound around the bodies of said officers, to remove the shackles from the limbs of said defendants, while they were in Court, which motion of the defendants was then and there overruled.

That thereupon, the said defendants, upon being asked if they were ready to plead, by their counsel, filed a motion moving that the arraignment heretofore had on the said indictment be set aside, setting forth as grounds of said motion that neither they, the said defendants nor their said attorneys nor either of them had had delivered to them a copy of the indictment herein, as is required by law, which motion was, by the Court, then and there, overruled and, although said motion had been overruled and said ruling excepted to by the said defendants, the District Attorney of said County ignored the overruling of said motion and proceeded to re-arraign said defendants upon the said indictment and said defendants were again given the statutory time to plead to said indictment and thereafter, on the ninth day of June, 1897, the said defendants were again brought into this Court and thereupon, by their counsel, moved the Court that, not having been held to answer for the charge preferred against them in said indictment, said indictment be set aside on the statutory ground that a state of mind existed and did exist at the time of the finding of the said indictment and prior thereto, on the part of each and every of the Grand Jurors composing the said Grand Jury which returned said indictment, in reference to this case and to the said defendants and each of them which prevented them, the said Grand Jurors and each of them from acting impartially in this case and without prejudice of the substantial rights of these defendants and for the further reason that said indictment does not purport to show the names of the witnesses who were examined before the Grand Jury upon the finding of the said indictment; that thereupon, said defendants, by their counsel offered to submit evidence to substantiate and prove the allegations in said motion contained, which said motion to set aside the said indictment was by the Court overruled and the offer of the said defendants to submit evidence to prove the truthfulness of the allegations in said motion contained was then and there, by the said Court, denied and thereupon, the said defendants filed a general demurrer to the said indictment which said demurrer was then and there overruled and thereupon, the said defendants pleaded not guilty.

 Defendants further show to the Court that immediately after the death of the said E. L. Norris, rewards aggregating thousands of dollars were offered for the arrest of these defendants, dead or alive; that the sheriff of this County, personally, offered a large reward for the arrest of said defendants, dead or alive. That the said defendant Miller, upon being arrested not more than forty miles from the county seat of said Yavapai County was, by the officers making the arrest, taken out of said county of Yavapai and confined in the County jail of another county for several days, and that this was done because of the violent prejudice, bias and feeling which existed against said defendants for the crime with which they are charged, in the minds of the inhabitants of the said County of Yavapai and the many threats which had been made by the inhabitants of the said county to lynch and hang without judicial sanction the said defendants or either of them should they be returned alive to the said county seat of Yavapai County.

 That upon the night of the 29th day of May, 1897, when the sheriff of said county, together with other officers, was returning by rail to the city of Prescott, the county seat of said Yavapai County, with said defendants, the train which was carrying said officers and these defendants to said county seat was, by order of said officers, stopped outside of the city of Prescott and away from the regular railway depot in said city and said officers took said defendants, in a closed carriage, which was in readiness at said point where said train was stopped, to the county jail of said county, in said city of Prescott, fearing that the large mob which had gathered at the said railway depot to await the arrival of the train upon which these defendants were being brought in would do great bodily harm to these defendants and carry into execution the threats of lynching which had, before that time, been made, in the most public manner by the inhabitants of said county.

That upon arriving at said county jail, said defendants found there large numbers of the inhabitants of said county and the actions of the persons in said crowd were of such a demonstrative character, there being cries of "hang them" that the sheriff of said county, although accompanied by five or six officers well armed and he, said sheriff, being then and there, armed with a Winchester rifle, deemed it necessary and did make a personal appeal to the mob there gathered to restrain them from taking the said prisoners from him and his officer associates. That the other officers above mentioned, then and there, also deemed it necessary and did advise the crowd not to resort to violence towards said defendants and to make no effort to take said defendants from said officers' custody. Defendants state the fact to be that, had it not been for the determined stand taken by the said sheriff of said county and his associate officers, at the said last mentioned time and the fact that they, said defendants, were surrounded by the said officers, who were then and there armed to the teeth with Winchester rifles and six shooters, the said mob so assembled and surrounding said jail would have taken said defendants from the custody of said officers and would have, then and there, hanged them, because of the general public bias, prejudice, feeling and animosity which existed at that time in the minds of the persons composing said mob against said defendants, because of the belief that said defendants were guilty of the killing of the said E. L. Norris.

That to show to this Honorable Court the violent prejudice and feeling which exists against these defendants on the part of the sheriff of said county and his deputies, these defendants state the fact to be that upon being placed in this county jail on the 29th day of May 1897, the sheriff of said county caused each of said defendants to be shackled and, at all times since said last mentioned time down to the present date, to wit: the 13th day of June, 1897, the said defendants, when in said county jail, have had said shackels on them and from the said 29th day of May 1897, they have not been permitted by the officers to take a bath, be shaved or change their underclothing, notwithstanding the fact that counsel for defendants have requested said officers to furnish said defendants with proper clean clothing and to permit said defendants to bathe and be shaved.

That because of the killing of said E. L. Norris, said defendants being charged in this action with such killing, and the prominent standing and position occupied by the said E. L. Norris in Yavapai County and because of his being related to one of the leading families of said county and territory and because of the reward which was offered by the sheriff of said county for the apprehension of these defendants, dead or alive, and because the killing of the said E. L. Norris has occasioned such general comment and has attracted thereto great attention and condemnation of these defendants because of their alleged connection with said killing which is evidenced by the fact that the coming trial of these defendants is almost the only topic of conversation in the mouths of the inhabitants not only of the city of Prescott but of the entire county of Yavapai and beyond, there has existed and does now exist such a general prejudice, feeling, bias and animosity in the minds of the inhabitants of the said county of Yavapai against said defendants because of the said killing of the said E. L. Norris that a fair and impartial trial of this criminal action cannot be had in the said county of Yavapai where this action is now pending.

That upon the occasion of these defendants being taken from Court after having been arraigned upon the indictment herein, from the Court room of this Honorable Court, there was a large and tumultuous crowd present and threats and cries of "hang them" were then and there openly made.

WHEREFORE, said defendants pray that this honorable Court do make an order for the removal of this criminal action to a proper Court of a county, free from the objects above set forth.

James F. Parker
L. C. Miller

Territory of Arizona,)
)ss.
County of Yavapai)

James F. Parker and L. C. Miller, being first duly sworn, each for himself and not one for another, on oath deposes and says:

That they are the identical persons who are named as defendants in the foregoing application for change of venue; that they have read the foregoing application and that the facts therein stated are true of their own knowledge.

Subscribed and sworn to before me	James F. Parker
This 14th day of June, 1897.	L. C. Miller
Wm. Wilkerson	
Dep'y Clerk	

Repeating the idea that Sheriff Ruffner had stared down a lynch mob, which everyone in town knew to be false, certainly did not earn the defense any credibility with the court. What could Allen and Morrison have been thinking?

The supporting affidavits of citizens M. I. O'Malia, R. C. Welch, E. S. Clark, and attorneys Allen and Morrison themselves, have survived. As they are very similar in nature, we shall only reprint Clark's:

Territory of Arizona,)
)ss.
County of Yavapai.)

E. S. Clark, being first duly sworn deposes and says:

That he is a resident of Coconino County, Arizona but was formerly a resident of Yavapai County and is well acquainted with a great number of the inhabitants of said county.

That since the fourth day of June, 1897, he has been within the said county for the period of five days and during

Signatures of Parker and Miller, from their court documents.

that time has conversed with a large number of the inhabitants of said county with reference to the charge of murder against the defendants in the case of the Territory of Arizona against James F. Parker and L. C. Miller.

That almost without exception, every person with whom he has conversed has expressed the positive and decided opinion that said defendants were guilty of the murder of E. L. Norris and that they should be hanged and that, in the majority of cases, a violent and vindictive prejudice against these defendants has been betrayed; that since the indictment and arraignment of these defendants, affiant has been told by reputable and prominent citizens of Prescott and other parts of Yavapai County that unless the Courts move quickly in the trial of said defendants that lynch law might be resorted to. That the expressions to which affiant has listened, as aforesaid, have not been in the nature of mere passing comment or current rumor but have been declarations of fixed and unalterable opinions indicating deep seated prejudice and animosity against said defendants.

Yavapai County Attorney Henry D. Ross, who prosecuted Parker and Miller, in an undated photo. (Author's collection)

That by reason of the universal prejudice expressed to affiant as aforesaid, he does not believe that a jury could be secured within the said county of Yavapai by which defendants could have a fair and impartial trial but on the contrary believes that any jury impaneled to try this cause would be so influenced by the prevailing popular opinion and the free expression thereof that they could not give the defendant an impartial consideration of all the facts and circumstances in the case.

    Subscribed and sworn to before me   E. S. Clark
This 14th day of June, 1897.
    (unreadable)
    Notary Public.
My commissions expires Jany 17, 1898.

Representing the Territory in the trial were District Attorney Henry D. Ross and his new assistant, Patrick O'Sullivan, who had replaced Lee Norris as Deputy. O'Sullivan would have been forced to recuse himself today, but it was not to be so in 1897. Ross and O'Sullivan were not about to risk letting Parker get transferred to another county. They counter-filed several affidavits signed by many citizens of Yavapai County, all stating that they were not prejudiced and could give Parker a fair trial. The following is typical of them all:

In the District Court of the Fourth Judicial District of the Territory of Arizona, in and for the County of Yavapai.
Territory of Arizona,
    Vs.
James Parker and L. C. Miller

    We, the undersigned citizens of the said County of Yavapai, being first duly sworn, depose and say, each for himself and not one for the other:
    That we are well acquainted with the sentiment and feeling of the citizens, tax-payers and residents of the said County, with reference to the killing of Lee Norris; and that we have frequently heard the matter discussed: From what we know and have heard said about the case and the defendants therein, we are able to swear and do state upon oath that we believe the residents of the said County are anxious to have the defendants secure a fair and impartial trial; we further are of the opinion that there is no such feeling of prejudice and bias in this County as will prevent the defendants from having a fair and impartial trial; we further state that we have heard much talk in a general way of this matter, and that the opinion that the defendants can have a fair and impartial trial is founded upon such talk and statements made from responsible and tax-paying citizens of said County and men eligible for jury service. We believe that a great majority of the residents in the City of Prescott, eligible to jury duty, and most of the residents in the outside precincts of the county, can sit as jurors in the trial of the defendants and render a verdict according to the law and evidence. We further state that the city of Prescott and vicinity do not contain to exceed one-fourth of the citizens of said County eligible to jury duty; and that we are informed and allege the fact to be that the other three-fourths of the eligible jurors throughout the different portions of the County know very little of the case, and therefore could have no bias or prejudice."
    (signatures)

This particular affidavit bore the signatures of 59 people, including such leading citizens as Horace Yeoman, Ed Shummate, Harry Brisley, and *Courier* publisher Edward A. Rogers, who had obviously abandoned Miller, finally. The Territory submitted other affidavits as well, bearing multiple signatures.

Sheriff George Ruffner likewise filed an affidavit disputing the "lynch mob" account in the statement of Allen and Morrison. It reads:

In the District Court of the Fourth Judicial District of the Territory of Arizona, in and for the County of Yavapai.
Territory of Arizona,
    Vs.
James Parker and L. C. Miller
    Geo. C. Ruffner being first duly sworn, deposes and says: - I am the sheriff of the County of Yavapai, Arizona Territory: that I have read and heard read the affidavits of James Parker and L. C. Miller, J. E. Morrison and G. Arthur Allen; that I remember the night that I brought Parker and Miller into Prescott for Lodgment

in the County jail; affiant further says that there was probably between one and two hundred persons at the jail when I arrived there with the prisoners; that I was approached by two or three of the best and most influential citizens composing this crowd and was told that there was no danger; that the crowd was there from curiosity to see the defendants more than anything else: I further state that there was no overt act or effort on the part of the said crowd to interfere, or take said prisoners from my possession; that I verily believe that the said crowd was present through morbid curiosity, more than from any other motive;

I have heard a great deal of talk about the killing of Lee Norris, but the expression of all is that defendants be given a fair and impartial trial; there is no great prejudice, bias and animosity in the minds of the people of the County of Yavapai against the defendants; that very little is said or known of the case outside of the City of Prescott.

                    G. C. Ruffner

Subscribed and sworn to before me this 15th day of June, 1897.
                    Patrick J. Farley
My Commission expires Dec. 15 - 1900   Notary Public

The Grand Jurors filed an affidavit denying any prejudice on their part, and District Attorney Ross filed an affidavit attempting to discredit the sworn testimony of the earlier mentioned R. C. Welch. This one reads:

  Territory of Arizona
  Vs.
County of Yavapai
  H. D. Ross being first duly sworn deposes and says he knows one R. C. Welch: that said R. C. Welch was about the first of June A. D. 1897 arrested upon a warrant issued by Judge Donald Campbell upon an affidavit made by wife, Mattie Welch, for threatening to take the life of the said wife. That, he, Welch, was thereupon placed in jail with said defendants, Parker and Miller, and remained there with them three or four days and that if he made any affidavit concerning said case, it was after he was released from jail.
  H. D. Ross
Subscribed and sworn to before me this 15th day of June 1897.
                   William Wilkerson
                   Deputy Clerk Dist.
                   Court Fourth Judl.
                   Dist. Yavapai County Arizona

With this kind of legal muscle stacked against them, Parker and Miller didn't stand a chance for a change of venue. From the *Arizona Journal Miner* of June 16, 1897:

          No Change of Venue Granted.
When the case of Parker and Miller came up this morning, on the convening of court for hearing the application for a change of venue, the court room was crowded, every available seat in the main audience hall being occupied while a large number were compelled to stand for want of seats. Among the number

present were some ladies, attracted by a desire to get a view of the prisoners. The application for a change of venue, and the corroborative affidavits were ready by J. E. Morrison, and the voluminous quality of the documents showed that the attorneys propose to omit no point that will tend to benefit their clients. Not only was the subject matter of the application and affidavits voluminous, but the manner of their reading by the bright young attorney, was dramatic in the extreme. Mr. Morrison, it will be remembered, belonged to a very popular amateur dramatic club of Prescott, and in the various roles assumed by him he made decided hits. He exercised his histrionic ability to good effect in court this morning.

District Attorney H. D. Ross resisted the application for change of venue, taking the grounds that no such overshadowing prejudice and animosity existed against the defendants as the affidavits filed indicated. The court over-ruled the motion for a change of venue and the work of impaneling a jury was commenced this afternoon, in the case of Parker, as council asked that separate trials be allowed defendants, which was granted by the court.

It is ironic that this news article, so snide in its tone, demonstrated the very prejudice that Prescott's heavyweights were denying existed. Looking back in the context of history, it was an outrageous decision. The entire city of Prescott had been up in arms, understandably, over the murder of young Lee Norris—of course everyone had an opinion as to the defendants' guilt. In view of the overwhelming evidence against Parker and Miller, it is unlikely that going to another county would have resulted in acquittals, so what would have been the harm in giving them every opportunity? But the City fathers wouldn't hear of it.

A couple of interesting sidelights: Parker's court papers show that, when asked by Judge Hawkins if James Parker was his correct name, Parker snidely responded that no, his true name was "James F. Parker." After that, the remaining court papers listed the case as "Territory vs. James F. Parker Indicted As James Parker."

Also, the *Courier* of June 11, 1897, ran the following bit of foolishness:

The Kangaroo court convened in the county jail yesterday to hear the case of the Court vs. Jos. Morrison and G. A. Allen, charged with entering jail too often. The defendants are Parker's attorneys, but Parker was their attorney before the Kangaroo court. Not-withstanding, the latter's earnest pleadings defendants were found guilty. History will doubtless repeat itself when positions are reversed in the court above.

Apparently the prisoners in the Yavapai County jail, bored with nothing to do, had started engaging in parlor games. It also must have been a slow news day for the *Courier*.

On June 15, 1897, the trial of the Territory vs. James F. Parker commenced before Judge John J. Hawkins. Henry D. Ross and Patrick O'Sullivan represented the prosecution, and George A. Allen and Joseph C. Morrison appeared for the defense.

From the *Arizona Journal Miner* of June 23, 1897:

> Territory vs. James F. Parker, murder; the following jury impaneled to try the case: Wm. Seymore, Geo. B. Scammell, Jeff Davis, W. H. Strickland, J. A. Park, J. S. McDonald, Frank Ullery, Wm. Holliday, Wm. U. Cooper, W. A. Hughes, Patrick O'Donnell, P. A. Williams. Case on trial

Jeff Davis sometimes served as Undersheriff to George Ruffner. By today's standards, he would have been disqualified. Meanwhile, preparations were being made for Miller's separate trial. From the same edition:

> Territory vs. L. C. Miller: case called for trial. Venire of jurors exhausted and special venire issued for forty jurors to appear Monday, June 21st, and case continued to that day.

From the same edition:

> The venire for forty additional jurors was returned, and the work of impaneling a jury in the case of the Territory vs. L. C. Miller charged with murder, has been in progress. At 2 o'clock eighty-one jurors had been examined, out of which the panel of twenty nine was completed. The prosecution is allowed seven challenges out of this number and the defense ten, and a recess was taken till 3 o'clock to permit the attorneys to select their challenges.

Testimony commenced against Parker. From the same edition:

> Parker on Trial
> A jury has been impaneled to try the case against James F. Parker, charged with the murder of Lee Norris. The names of the men who swore to reach a verdict in accordance with the testimony and law will be found in the regular report of the court proceedings. The jury is composed of intelligent representative men, as will be noted from a perusal of the list. The impaneling of it was completed at 2 o'clock when the trial was commenced. The first witness sworn was Jailor R. W. Meador, who testified in detail in regard to the jail break, the escape of the prisoners, of Parker entering the jailor's room, securing a shot gun, and as he came out into the hall, leveling it on Lee Norris, who was on the stair way, and discharging it, when Norris fell, mortally wounded.
>
> At the opening of court this afternoon, the court room was crowded with spectators, among the number present being over a dozen ladies. As the trial progressed the crowd increased, until there was a perfect jam in the front part of the court room.
>
> It is not thought the case will last long, as there are few witnesses to be examined.

Messrs. Morrison and Allen are watching the interests of their clients very carefully, and although working without pay or hope of remuneration are as earnest and zealous as though there was a large fee at stake.

A noticeable feature of the trial is that nearly every attorney of Prescott is present to witness the trial, being customary of them to be in court only when cases in which they are personally interested are up for trial.

At four o'clock the prosecution had introduced all of its testimony and an adjournment was taken till 9:30 tomorrow, the jury being turned over to the custody of a bailiff.

In those days, transcripts of trial testimony were generally not kept after the trial was over unless it was clear that the convict defendant planned to appeal, which was not as common then as it is now. In Parker's case, his attorneys announced their intention to appeal afterwards, so the testimony was saved to show the higher courts that his trial was fair. Here, printed for the first time since 1897, is the surviving trial transcript of the testimony in Territory vs. James F. Parker:

The above cause came on to be heard Tuesday, June 15th. 1897, in the above court, all preliminary motions having been disposed of, and the Territory by the District Attorney H. D. Ross, and the defendant by his counsel J. E. Morrison and G. A. Allen both announcing ready, the jury was duly called, empanelled and sworn, to try the case, and the indictment having been read to them by the Clerk and the plea of "Not Guilty" stated, the following proceedings were had and evidence heard therein:
PROSECUTION. (June 16th. 2 P.M.)
By the Court - Mr. Ross, do you wish to make a statement? By Mr. Ross - I do not care to make any statement. By the Court - The Statute is you may, with or without a statement, introduce your evidence. By Mr. Ross - I do not care to make a statement. Call Mr. Meador.

Mr. ROBERT MEADOR, called on behalf of the Territory and duly sworn, testified as follows: -
DIRECT EXAMINATION BY MR. ROSS
Q What is your name? A R. W. Meador. Q Where do you live? A Prescott. Q How long have you been living in Prescott? A In and about here, a little over fourteen years. Q What official position do you occupy, if any, in this County? A Jailer at the County Jail. Q Have you been jailer of the County Jail here during the whole of this year? A Yes, sir. Q Do you know James Parker, the defendant? A Yes, sir. I do. Q Did you know one E. L. Norris, "Lee Norris? A Yes, sir. Q I will ask you who was attending the jail of this County on the 9th day of May, 1897? A I was. Q Please tell the jury what happened on that day with reference to E. L. Norris and this defendant Parker, in your own way.

A Well, on that day about one o'clock I was in the Sheriff's office; no one there but myself; I heard the jail door rattle; it was a usual thing when the boys wanted water down there or something; I went down, and opened my room and went in and got the key. And came out, and opened the first jail door; and the Mexican was standing there with a couple of buckets in his hand. He said he wanted water. I opened the door. Q Who was the Mexican? A Cornelia. Q Cornellia Sarata? A Yes, sir. That is the name. He came out and got a couple of buckets of water. Q Where did he go to get the water? A He went out to the well, just a little ways out. Q Did you open the jail door for him to come out? A Yes, sir, I opened the jail door. And I shut it again after he came out. I went and opened some screen doors that are out there, or iron doors, rather. And let him out there. He got the water. He came back. I locked those doors; he came right on towards the jail door, alongside of me. He had the buckets in his hand. I walked up to the jail door and looked in. I did not see anything unusual there. Just as I unlocked the jail door, to open it, he dropped his buckets and grabbed me, kind of pulled me back; just then Miller and Parker came running there, and scrounged through it. Q Who did? A Miller and Parker. I managed to get the door shut and locked again and got the key out; they passed on and went into my room, Parker and Miller. Q Where is that from the jail door? A Right there close to the jail door. They passed on to my room; I and the Mexican were scuffling in the door; he got the key away from me by that time, and was striking me with the key. Q Who was striking you with the key? A The Mexican. Just then I heard a noise; I looked around and saw Lee Norris coming down the steps, and Parker came out of my room with a shot-gun in his hand and threw up the gun and shot Norris right on the steps; Parker passed on up by me and Miller after him; they got about two-thirds of the way up the steps and the Mexican let me loose and broke and run after them up the steps. I stepped out of there, and took three shots at him as he went up the steps, at the Mexican. Q Where was the shot-gun? A It was in my room, right there next to the jail door. Q When Parker came out of the jail, where did he go to? A He went up the steps into the hall of the court-house. Q Immediately after he got out of the jail, where did he go to? While you and this Mexican were scuffling there? A He went right into my room there. Q That was where the shot gun was? A Yes, sir. Q Did you make any noise? A I hollowed when the Mexican grabbed me, to attract the attention of somebody. Q Whom did you see come to your rescue? A Lee Norris came running downstairs. Q What was said when he came down? A If he said anything, I did not hear him; if anybody else said anything, I did not hear them. Q Did you hear Parker say anything? A Not a word. Q Where was Mr. Norris when he was shot? A He was about half-way down the steps; he had just apparently turned around to go back. Q He was facing which direction? A He had turned to go back, still, I think, looking down that way. Q Who, did you say, shot him? A Jim Parker. Q The defendant in this case? A Yes, sir. Q In what County and Territory was that? A Yavapai County, Territory of Arizona. Q What month and what day of the month? A May the ninth, 1897.

Q What did Parker do after he shot Norris? A Went right on up the stairs. Q Did you follow him? A After a little bit I did, yes, sir. Q Did you see him any more? A I saw him just before he got to the fence, crossing right out here. Q Anybody with him? A There was the other two fellows on a little ahead of him.

By Mr. Morrison - I object to this line of examination; it is after the killing several moments; it is not material; it is not connected with the res gestae in any way; we ask that such testimony not be admitted; he has not connected it with the killing of the deceased in any way at all. By Mr. Ross - We want to show the flight of the defendant. By Mr. Morrison - I do not see that that cuts any figure at all. By the Court - The objection is overruled. By Mr. Morrison - Exception.

By Mr. Ross - Q What was he doing when you saw him? A He was running across, just as I saw him, a few steps before he got to the fence, he crossed the fence and went on towards Ruffner's stable. Q What direction is that from the court-house? A It is rather south-east. Q Have anything in his hand as he ran? A Yes, sir. Q What did he have? A A shot-gun. He had a gun in his hand.

Q How long had you known E. L. Norris? A Several months; I do not remember just how long. Q Take the witness.

CROSS EXAMINATION BY MR. MORRISON

Q When you heard the door rattle, on the ninth of May, about one o'clock as you have stated, who was in the sheriff's office, if anybody? A No one but myself. Q When you came through the hall, going downstairs, to the jail, who, if anybody, was in the hall? A I did not see anybody. Q Did you see anybody, from the time you left the sheriff's office, until the time that you went down to the jail door and opened the door and saw the prisoners? A I did not. That is, no one around the court house; I might have looked out on the street and saw some one passing; I don't remember that I did.

Q You went down there to this jail door alone, is that right? A Yes, sir. That is right. Q You unlocked the jail door? A Yes, sir. I did. Q The outer door? A Yes, sir. Q There are two doors? A Yes. There are. Q You unlocked the inner door after that? A Yes, sir. Q And this Mexican came out? A Yes, sir. Q He had the water buckets and went and got the water? A Yes, sir. Q He came back and just as you opened the inner door, was it— A Yes, sir, that is right— Q He grappled with you, is that right? A Yes, sir, that is right. Q How long was it, approximately, between the time this Mexican grappled with you and the time that you say this defendant came out of the jail? A It was a very short time. Q A very short time? A Yes, sir; I could not tell just how many seconds. Q Did this defendant come out running? A Why, no sir, he came out just as fast as he could get out. I and the Mexican were there in the door. Of course, he could not run out through the door. Q Was he shacked at the time? A He was not. Q There was nothing to obstruct—

By Mr. Ross - Object: incompetent, immaterial and irrelevant. By Mr. Morrison - We will connect it. By Mr. Ross - Makes no difference whether he was shackled or not.

By the Court - Go ahead; he may state.

By Mr. Morrison - Q There was nothing to impede his movements in the way of shackles or anything of that nature? A No, sir. There was not.

Q What did he do, as soon as he got out? A As soon as he got out of the jail? Q Yes, sir. A He went into my room there. Q What, if anything, did he do in your room, if you know? A I did not see him while he was in the room, of course. Q Mr. Meador, with reference to the time that Parker went into your room, when was it that the Mexican struck you over the head with the key? A It was just a very short time after Parker and Miller had went out until he got the key out of my hand and struck me with the key. Q What was the effect on you of this striking with the key? A He cut quite a place on my forehead. Q He cut quite a gash? A Yes, sir. Q How large is that key, about? A I can show you just as near — Q Just indicate? A about that long (indicating six or seven inches) I guess. That is the gash. (indicating right side of forehead) Q It is quite a good sized key? A Yes, sir, quite a good sized key. Q When the Mexican struck you over the head with the key, did the blood flow from the wound that was made? A Yes, sir. There was some blood came on my face. Q Was there very much of it? A Quite a little, yes, sir. Q You say the wound was right here? A Right there is the scar (indicating right side of forehead) yes, sir. Q Just underneath the hair there. Q The blood that flowed from that wound, flowed down your forehead? A Yes, sir. Q Did it flow into your eyes? A Yes, sir. Q What effect did it have on your vision at the time? A I could not see as well as I could if I hadn't any blood on there. Q Were your eyes pretty well filled with blood? A On, they wasn't closed, anything like that, with blood. Q Not closed exactly, but there was blood in your eyes? A Yes, sir. Q That blow was struck after this defendant had left the jail? A After he had just got out of the door, yes, sir. He was in my room about the time, I think.

Q With reference to the time that Parker entered your room after having left the jail, when did you first see E. L. Norris coming down the stairs? A While Parker was in my room, I heard a noise on the steps; I looked up and saw it was Lee Norris coming down; it was a very short time. Q How long after that, approximately, did Parker come to the door of your room with this shot-gun, as you say? A A very short time. Q As much as a minute? A No, sir, it was not that long. Q As much as thirty seconds? A I could not say; I do not think it was. Q Where was Lee Norris at the time Parker came back to the door of your room? A Right on the steps that goes down to the jail door. Q How far down the steps was he? A About half-way. Q About half-way? A Just about. Q What, if anything, was said at that time? A I did not hear anything. Q How long a space of time occurred between the time that Parker came to the door of your room and saw the deceased coming down the steps and the time that the shot was fired, as you say? A It was a very short time; he just came walking out of my room and shot. Q Couldn't you say, Mr. Meador, how long a time that was; couldn't you say approximately; was it a minute? A Oh, no, sir. Q Was it anywhere near like a minute? A No, sir. Q It was a very short space of time. A Yes, sir. Q Was it fifteen seconds? A I don't think it was, Joe. Q The fact of the matter is, just as soon as he saw Norris, he raised the gun and shot; is that your statement? A That is my idea of it, yes, sir.

Q I will ask you to show to this jury the exact position that this defendant Parker was in when he fired this shot, as you say, with reference to whether he was in the hall or at the foot of the steps, in your room, or in the door to your room? A He had just passed out of my room door into the hall, or through the hall kind of like that (indicating) Q He was standing in the hall when the shot was fired? A Yes, sir, he was in the hall. Sort of between the door and the foot of the stairs. Q I will ask you this: were you struggling with the Mexican at the time the shot was fired? A The Mexican had hold of me, yes, sir. Q Were you struggling? A In the door. Q Were either you or the Mexican on the ground? A Neither of us, no, sir. Q Standing up? A Yes, sir. Q Were you in the space between the outside door and the inside door of the jail? A Yes, sir. Q Were you right in that space there? A Yes, sir. Q Does the outside door of the jail open inwardly or outwardly? A Outwardly. Q How was that door standing at that time? A It was pushed open. Q It was pushed open? A Yes, sir. Q did that door swing clear around to the wall? A Yes, sir. Q When it is pushed open — A Around against my room; the room come together; it does not go plumb up against the jail; it strikes against the wall of my room.

Q Do you state it was this defendant that fired the shot that struck Lee Norris? A Yes, sir. Q In what position were you standing at the time that shot was fired? A Me? Q Yes, sir. A I was back, between the jail doors there, with my back next to the jail. Q Your back next to the jail? A Yes, sir. Q How long a time elapsed between the time that the Mexican started to grapple with you, and the time that the shot-gun shot was fired? A It was less than a minute, I think. Q Less than a minute, all together? A Yes, sir. Q In fact, it happened just as quickly as it could? A Yes, sir. Just as quick as they could go out of there and go into my room; they were some little time in the room, I don't know just how long. Q How far were you from Parker, approximately, when this shot was fired? A Not over eight feet at the outside. Q Not over eight feet? A Yes, sir. Q You say that you could not see at that time as well as you ordinarily do; is that right? A That is right. Q Just tell us the condition of your eyes at that time with reference to there being blood in them? A I say quite a good deal of blood on my face and in my eyes; of course I could not see as well as if it had not been there; but, then, I could see. Q You say that after this, when the Mexican was going upstairs, you fired three shots at him; is that correct? A Yes, sir. Q Did you hit him? A I do not think so. Q You don't think you did; can you tell this jury what the reason was you did not hit him? A I do not know that I can; I can just say I was trying to hit him. Q You were trying to hit him? A Yes, sir, I was. Q Isn't it a fact, if it had not been for the blood in your eyes, you would have hit that Mexican? A I might and I might not. I was somewhat excited, under the circumstances; it might have been I could not have hit him, if I had not had any blood on me. Q You are a fair shot with the six shooter? A Ordinary, shooting at a mark, I am. Q That was quite a mark? A Yes, sir. It was. Q How far were you from that Mexican when you fired those shots? A I must have been twelve feet. Q Were you standing still at the time? A I don't know that I was still; I was there, — Q Where were you, at the foot or side of the stairs? A I was at the side of the stairs, between my door, - you understand how it is down there, and the stair-case. Q You were firing at him through the balustrade that runs down? A Two shots over it, and one through. Q Ordinarily, if there had been a mark placed there, you might have been able to hit it? A Well, a reasonable sized mark, I guess I would, if I hadn't been excited or anything. Q Are targets that are used for pistol practice, are they as large a man? A No, sir. Q Not ordinarily? A No, sir.

Q When you opened the inside jail door, who, if any one, was there? A There was no one right close to the door. Q Who, if any one, was present; whom did you see? A You mean in the jail? Q Yes, sir; or anywhere around there. A The Mexican was right outside of the jail; you mean when I opened the door for the Mexican to come in? Q The first time you went down there? A There was nobody outside; Miller was standing inside, or sitting on a bench, I don't remember which; and the Mexican was standing there by a table with a couple of buckets in his hand. Q Was there anybody else there? A If there was anybody close there, I did not see them. Q Didn't see any of the prisoners around there? A Not close to the door; they were, of course, in the jail. Q You couldn't see them? A I don't remember whether I saw any of them or not; I did not pay any attention. Q Those are the only two you remember of seeing? A Yes, sir. Q Is that your statement? A That is my statement.

Q I will ask you, was it your ordinary custom, practice, to go to the jail door alone, when you desired to let out or put in, a prisoner? A Quite often, yes sir; when there was any of the boys, they generally went down with me. Q How many prisoners did you have in the jail at that time? A I think there was twenty-four or twenty-five, somewhere along there. Q What was the cause of this man Parker's detention in the prison? A He was accused of train robbery. Q You had a commitment for him? A Yes, sir.

By Mr. Ross— We object to that, not because we care, but think it immaterial and incompetent.

By the Court— Sustained.

RE— DIRECT EXAMINATION BY MR. ROSS

Q You say your room is just off from the jail door? What do you mean by "your room"? A The room where I stay at nights. Q Is that the room that Parker and Miller went into? A Yes, sir. Q Did you examine the condition of that room after this thing happened? A I went in there and saw how the condition was; they had thrown up the beds, at each corner, as though they were looking for a gun or something under the bed. Q What were you and this Mexican doing; were you making any noise? A I holloed for help. Q You were holloing for help? A Yes, sir. Trying to attract the attention of somebody. Q That was the time that Lee Norris came down? A Yes, sir. Q I wish you would tell the jury how you were held by the Mexican. A He just grabbed right around me, both arms, around my arms. Q Pinioned you? A Yes. Q That is all. By Mr. Morrison— That is all.

PATRICK J. FARLEY, called on behalf of the Territory and duly sworn, testified as follows: —

DIRECT EXAMINATION BY MR. ROSS

Q What is your name? A Patrick J. Farley. Q Where do you live? A Prescott. Q Where were you on the 9th. of May, 1897? A I was, about noon I was in the recorder's office, somewhere along about that time. Q What official position do you occupy? A Deputy County Recorder. Q I will ask you if you have ever seen the defendant James F. Parker before? A Yes, sir, I saw him, once before. Q I will ask you if you saw him on this day, the 9th. of May, 1897, about noon of that day? A I believe I did; I did not thoroughly recognize him, I just got a glance, the side of his face.

By Mr. Morrison— We object at this time, unless it is in some way connected with the killing of the deceased; it does not make any difference whether he saw him that day or not. By the Court— If you connect it— By Mr. Ross— We will connect it. By the Court— You may answer the question.

By Mr. Ross— Q Where were those gun shots from the recorder's office? A It sounded downstairs, from the sheriff's office, near the jail, or on the steps. Q About what time of the day was it? A It was about one o'clock. It may not have been exactly one; it was in the neighborhood of one o'clock. Q After you heard gun-shots, did you see anybody? A Yes, sir.

By Mr. Mr. Morrison— We object.

A I ran to get out of the recorder's office to go to the sheriff's office; I heard a gun-shot when I opened the door. I opened it about two inches; there was a shot fired, and a man holloed out loud that he was shot; I closed the door and pushed the man back that was behind me and told him to stay in; directly after that, there was three shots fired. Q Did you see anybody after that? A Yes, sir; I heard footsteps in the hall during the shooting; I kept my ear close to the door to hear what I could; I heard steps coming by on tip-toe and one acted as though he stopped in front of the door. Q Did you look at those people? A Yes, sir. I jumped up, and there was a gentleman at the window in the office, he said: They are gone. I jumped up right afterwards, they were by the water-closet, between the water-closet and the fence; I saw three men; the last man had a shot-gun in his hand; I thought at first he was an officer; and I looked back towards the sheriff's office and saw Meador coming with a gun in his hand, in his right hand, a pistol, a six-shooter, I think. He was rubbing the blood out of his eyes with his left hand; he was coming on a run. Q Did you see Lee Norris that day? A Yes, sir. Q Where did you see him after the shooting? A When Meador came to the door, I asked him if he was shot; there was blood all over his face; he said: No, I am not shot, I am not hurt. He looked after those people, they were just crossing the fence then; he said: That fellow has my shotgun. I looked and Parker had turned his face at that time just half-way around; I caught half of his jaw; I saw he was not an officer. I ran back towards the sheriff's office right away. In going close to the door of the sheriff's office, I recognized Norris' voice on the stairs, and I looked down, and he said: Pat, I am bleeding to death, get me a doctor, hurry up and save my life.

    By Mr. Morrison— Object to these statements of the deceased being introduced in evidence unless they tend to connect this defendant with this crime. There is a proper method of introducing a statement of that kind; we insist upon it. By Mr. Ross— We will prove this was a dying declaration of Mr. Norris. By Mr. Morrison— We would like to have it proven before it is entered. By the Court— Go ahead.

    By Mr. Ross— Q What did you do? A I asked him what doctor. Q You went after a doctor? A He said Doctor Davis or any doctor. I immediately ran for a doctor as fast as I could run. Q Where was he at that time? A He was in the space leading downwards on the steps, with his arms spread out; he was about half-way, possibly a step or two more than half-way down; it looked like he had fallen right there, helpless. Q That is all; take the witness.

CROSS EXAMINATION BY MR. MORRISON

    Q When did you first see these men you say were running with a shot-gun? After you heard those shots? A I saw them after I left the office. Q Where were they when you first saw them? A They were between the water-closet, in the court-house yard, and the fence. Q How long after that was it when you first saw Meador on this occasion? A Directly afterwards. Q How did you come to see Meador? A I went out on the back porch; I backed over on this side, so if there was any more shooting down in the hallway, I could get back in the shadow of the door, alternately watching towards the sheriff's office, and towards the side these people were running. Q It was not directly after that you saw Meador, because you had time to get in that position; how long was it; was it a minute, or — A Almost at the same time, as quick as I turned my head. Q I will ask you this question: how long, approximately, after you heard the cries, I believe you testified you heard cries? A Yes, sir. Q How long after that was it that you saw Meador rubbing the blood out of his eyes as he was coming along? A That was just, — I don't believe it was a minute, a very short time, a very short space of time. Q A very short space of time; will you tell this jury that it was not two minutes? A It was not over two minutes. Q It was not over two minutes? A No, sir. Q Was it about two minutes? A What noise have you reference to? Q The cries that you heard? A Cries after the shooting? Q No, sir. The cries you heard the first time. A It was not over two minutes. Q Your statement is, it was about two minutes; is that right? A Yes, sir. About two minutes. Let's see; it was not quite two minutes. It was over a minute; between a minute and two minutes. Q Between one minute and two minutes? A Yes, sir. It was not quite two minutes. Q How long after the first cry you heard was the first shot fired, about? A It must have been about half a minute. Q How long a space of time elapsed between the first shot and the firing of the first and the other three shots? A A very short space of time. Q Very short space of time? A Yes, sir. Q How were the three shots fired, the last three shots? A Fired in rapid succession. Q Indicate to the jury by patting your hands, about how they were fired. A Well, the first shot was fired, then (witness pats his hands to indicate) possibly ten or twelve seconds between the first shot and the three shots. Q You did not see any of these shots fired? A No, sir. Q You do not know anything about the actual immediate circumstances attending this killing, do you; the actual circumstances of the shooting? A I did not see a shot fired. Q You weren't there when the shooting was done? A No, sir. Q You weren't in sight? A No, sir. Q That is all.

++++++++++++

WILLIAM OSBORNE, called by the Territory and duly sworn, testified as follows: —
DIRECT EXAMINATION BY MR. ROSS

Q What is your name? A W. T. Osborne. Q Where do you live? A Prescott. Q Where were you on the 9th. of May, 1897? A I was working up here at Ruffner's stable. Q I will ask you if you have ever seen this defendant James Parker before? A Yes, sir. Q Did you see him on that day? A Yes, sir. Q About what time of the day? A Well, about one o'clock, I think. Q Who was with him? A Well, he was alone when he came in the stable up there.

By Mr. Morrison— if the Court please, we desire to object at this point; can it make any difference in this case what happened up at Ruffner's stable after this matter occurred; we are not charged with that sort of an offense but we are charged here with the killing of Lee Norris; we are not charged with having gone to Ruffner's stable and for committing other things — By Mr. Ross —We have not undertaken or tried to prove anything except the killing of Lee Norris; this evidence will be confined to that issue entirely. By Mr. Morrison— There is going to be an attempt right here to introduce other evidence on that subject; if it is going to be introduced, it is over our strenuous objections. By the Court— let us see.

By Mr. Ross— Q Did he have anything in his hand when he got at the stable? A Yes, sir, he had a shot-gun.

By Mr. Morrison— We object to that.

By the Court— Overruled; that is clearly a part of the res gestae. By Mr. Morrison— Exception.

By Mr. Ross— Q Did he remain there at the stable very long, how long? A Not very long; he came in the door; I had my attention drawn to the other side of the room at the time; he stepped in the door; I heard some one, and I turned around; he backed around in the corner, back of me, he had his gun down in this position (indicating)

By Mr. Morrison— Object. By the Court— Overruled. By Mr. Morrison— Exception.

A He motioned with the gun and told me to step out there between him and the door; I stood out; he says: You saddle a horse, you run and saddle a horse.

By Mr. Morrison— Object. By the Court— Overruled. By Mr. Morrison— Exception. By Mr. Ross—

Q What did you do? A I told him: Don't get excited about this matter; I will saddle a horse for you. He says: You run. I says: I aint going to run, but I will saddle a horse for you. I started to go out the door, and as I went out the door he poked me with the shot-gun.

By Mr. Morrison— They are proving an assault, if your Honor please.

A Sir? I started out in the stable where the horses were; I walked right along, of course, I went ahead of him; after I got out in the stable, I walked right through the stable; I didn't turn to the right nor left. I walked through. After I came out, — three or four stalls are here on the right, — Walter Ruffner was standing there with a gray horse, he just started to go in the stalls; this man did not pay any more attention to me; he paid his attention to young Ruffner; that released me; I walked out the back end of the stable and then came back. Q When did you last see the defendant, if you saw him after that? A Do you mean that defendant? (indicating Defendant) Q Yes, sir. A Yes, sir. I saw him after that. Q What was he doing? A He was getting on the horse; he got on the horse in the stable and rode him out, out the back door. Q That was the last you saw of him that day? A The last I seen of him when he went out the gate and turned down the alley. Q That is all.

By Mr. Morrison— We have been objecting to this evidence, and we want to say in reference to it, it is entirely incompetent and immaterial; it is not connected with the res gestae in any way, and nothing to do with the immediate circumstances attending this killing; it happens at least a block away, some time after the immediate killing; and we move this Court at this present moment to strike from the record, and from the testimony all of the evidence given by this witness.

By the Court— The motion is overruled.

EXCEPTION

By Mr. Ross— That is all. By Mr. Morrison— That is all.

+++++++++++

Dr. Barrett, called by the Territory, and duly sworn, testified as follows: —

DIRECT EXAMINATION BY MR. ROSS

Q Dr. Barrett, where do you live? A Prescott. Q What is your profession? A Physician and surgeon. Q How long have you been living in Prescott, Doctor? A Since the first of the year. Q Did you know Lee Norris in his life time? A Yes, sir. Q Did you see him on the 9th. of May of this year? A Yes, sir. Q Whereabouts? A In the room of the jailer in the court-house. Q How did it happen you saw him? A I was asked to go to the room to attend him; I heard he was shot. Q What was his condition, please tell the jury; have you got it there? A Here are some notes I took at the time of his death. Q You may use those to refresh your memory as to his condition. A Rooms of E. L. Norris, died 11:58 p.m. May 9th, 1897; he was six feet four inches in height; way about 180 pounds; fair hair; bluish gray eyes; cause of death was shock from gun-shot wound of the left chest. The complicated cause of decease was hemorrage of the left lung. The wounds were of small origin, located between the 7th. and 9th. left ribs, inclusive, three inches behind the axillary line. That is the line drawn from this point (indicating) down the side. Q Indicate on your person about where the wounds entered, if you know. A The wound occupied a circular space in vertical diameter of three inches, and five inches in horizontal diameter; the wound was just at this point here (indicating). Q Which way did that wound range? A I stated the wound was three inches in vertical diameter and five inches in horizontal diameter; it was a wound made up of a number of smaller wounds; there was excessive hemorrage at the sight of the wound and bloody expectoration, bloody spit from the lung, bleeding at the mouth beginning at four o'clock. I removed twelve small bird-shot from the wound and recovered four in the clothing; it was impossible to probe any of the wounds into the chest wall; but that some shot had entered the chest, entered the left lung, was beyond doubt. He never recovered from the first shock until he died. Q What was it that killed him? A The immediate cause of death was shock from the wound in the chest; accompanying cause, hemorrage of the left lung. Q Were you present when he died? A Yes, sir. Q At what hour? A 11:58, May ninth. Q When were you called in, what hour? A A little before two o'clock, between one and two o'clock; I did not record the time at which I was called; it was between those two hours. Q Doctor, which way did those shots range, you say it struck in the left side of the back; did it range down in the body, or up? A It ranged very slightly upwards; the shots I removed from the superficial wound were taken out, all of them, at points slightly further up than the laceration in the skin. Q That is all.

CROSS EXAMINATION BY MR. MORRISON

Q Was that wound a necessarily fatal wound, according to the best of your judgment? A Yes, sir. It is one of the most fatal wounds known to surgery, gun-shot wound of the lung. We have recoveries in some cases, but the proportion of recoveries is very small. Q Is it necessarily a fatal wound? A Yes, sir, that wound was. Q Did you assist in an autopsy, or post-mortem examination of this body? A No, sir. Q Do you know whether there was one held or not? A No, sir. I don't know anything about it. Q I think that is all.

By Mr. Ross— That is all.

+++++++++++

Dr. DAVIS, called on behalf of the Territory and duly sworn, testified as follows: —

DIRECT EXAMINATION BY MR. ROSS

Q Where do you live, Dr. Davis? A Prescott. Q What is your profession? A I am a regular graduate of medicine, physician and surgeon. Q Where are you practicing your profession? A Here in the city and county. Q Did you know Lee Norris in his life time? A Yes, sir. I did. Q I will ask you if you saw him on the 9th. day of May of this year? A I did. Q Where did you see him? A I saw him here in the basement of the court-house in the jailer's room. Q I wish you would tell the Jury his condition when you saw him? A I found him there suffering from a gunshot wound of the left chest, in a state of great collapse and approaching death. Q Did you examine the wound? A I did. Q Describe to the jury the condition of the wound at the different times you examined him? A I examined the wound a little after nine o'clock at night, not immediately

Chapter 8: The Trial

after it was inflicted. When he was being dressed, I inspected a group of perforations made by small shot covering a space of four or five inches in diameter, and among the others, there were two or three, or three or four larger perforations, evidently made by buckshot. The wound was situated in the lower chest, just below the shoulder blade, you understand it, just below the lower border of the shoulder blade. Q Did you examine that wound after Lee Norris was dead? A Yes, sir. Q Did you probe it? A I probed it with my finger; I made no incisions at all; I simply examined it while he was in the undertaker's care. Q What can you say about the condition of the wound? A In one of those wounds, by inserting my finger, and pushing it slightly upwards underneath the skin, I could find an opening into the chest cavity; the other two that I tried were most too small to admit of my finger without force, and I did not probe them any further.

CROSS EXAMINATION BY MR. MORRISON

Q Did you consider that a necessarily fatal wound when you first saw it? A I did. Q Was it a necessarily fatal wound according to the best of your opinion? A It was certainly. Q Did you remove any of the shot from that wound? A No, sir. The shot were removed before I was called in. Q Did you assist, Doctor, at any autopsy which may have been held on the body of the deceased? A No, sir; there was none held that I know of. Q You don't know? A I held this post-mortem examination myself, but not in the way of an autopsy, just a casual examination for my own information. Q Any other doctor there at the time you did this? A There was not. The undertaker was present only. Q That is all.

++++++++++

JOHN C. HERNDON, called on behalf of the Territory having been duly sworn, testified as follows:—

DIRECT EXAMINATION BY MR. ROSS.

Q What is your name? A John C. Herndon. Q Where do you live? A In Prescott, Arizona. Q Did you know Lee Norris in his life time? A Very well. Q I will ask you if you saw him on the 9th. day of May of this year? A Yes, sir. Q Did you see him after he was shot? A Yes, sir, between one and two o'clock. Q I will ask you if you were with him after that time until he died? A I was with him from the time I first went there and was with up until the time he died; probably during that time, five or six hours, I was in and out several times. Q Did you have any talk with him? A Yes, sir, a good deal.

By Mr. Morrison— Here is an attempt to introduce a dying declaration. We want to insist — By the Court— It will be under the proper rules. By Mr. Ross— We will lay the proper foundation.

Q I will ask you whether Lee Norris said anything to you about his condition, as to whether he would live or die? A He did. Q What did he say? A He made various expressions, I can repeat some of them. Q I wish you would do so. A He said: "I am dying. No man that suffers as I have suffered can live, possibly." He said: "There is no hope for me." And when some one remarked: "There is no entrance into the cavity," he called for a handkerchief and expectorated, and said: "Let me see it." There was blood on the handkerchief. He said: "There it is, boys; that settles it." Those were his expressions as I remember them. Q Did Mr. Norris tell you who shot him?

By Mr. Morrison— We object; the proper foundation has not been laid. By the Court— Overruled. By Mr. Morrison—Exception. We would like to know how long this was before his death. By the Court— I understood he stated the time.

By Mr. Morrison— No, sir. He said he was there for five or six hours, between the time he was shot and the time he died. He hasn't stated. By Mr. Ross— I will fix it.

    Q Mr. Herndon, how long after you went there and how long after Mr. Norris was shot, was it he first made these statements or some of them?
A I think the first statement, that "I am dying" was made within half an hour after I was at the room where he was, in the jailer's room down stairs. The last statement when he said: "There it is, boys; that settles it" was made about four o'clock in the afternoon; the other statements between the first and the last. Q I will ask you if you ever heard Norris say he was going to live? A I never heard him express any hope of living, or that he was going to live; no, sir. Q If you heard him say who shot him, I wish you would tell the jury.

By Mr. Morrison— Object. By the Court— Overruled. By Mr. Morrison— Exception. The proper foundation has not been laid.

A About five o'clock of the afternoon, I was in the room with him, I think, alone. I asked him the question "Lee, do you know who shot you?" He said: "I know it one of two men; I don't know who it was; it was either Parker or Miller"

By Mr. Morrison— We move that Mr. Herndon's testimony be stricken out on the ground that the proper foundation was not laid upon which to base a statement of as great importance as that. By the Court— Overruled. By Mr. Morrison— Exception.

By Mr. Ross— THE TERRITORY RESTS.

+++++++++

Recess until four o'clock p.m. jury being admonished as usual by the Court, and recess thence until Thursday, 10 a.m. June 17th., upon request of counsel for defendant; jury placed in charge of an officer sworn by the clerk, and jury duly admonished by the Court not to talk about the case, etc..

++++++++++

Thursday 10 a.m. June 17th. '97
Jury all present.
By Mr. Morrison— The defense has no testimony to introduce.
By Mr. Ross— That is all."

The evidence against Parker was damning, and the verdict of the jury brought no surprises, nor should it have. The lack of premeditation is the only argument that can be used in Parker's favor—in historical hindsight, he perhaps should have been charged with second-degree murder instead, but to an outraged city, this would have been unthinkable. The *Journal Miner* of June 23, 1897 recorded the inevitable:

PARKER FOUND GUILTY

The Jury Affixes the Death Penalty to Their Verdict

The Parker trial is over. As anticipated, it was short. The story of the killing of Lee Norris was short and it took only a few witnesses to tell it. Those placed on the stand by the prosecution were Jailor Meador, who told of the jail break and the shooting. Drs. Barrett and Davis, who testified to the character of the fatal wound, J. C. Herndon, and Osborn, the stableman in the employ of Sheriff Ruffner at his livery stable, who testified as to Parker getting the white horse, on which he made his famous ride.

Mr. Herndon testified in regard to Lee Norris' dying statement to the effect that it was either Parker or Miller who shot him.

The court room was crowded again this morning at the trial and on the opening of court the attorneys for the defense announced that they rested their case, without the introduction of any evidence.

The case was argued by District Attorney H. D. Ross and his assistant, P. W. O'Sullivan, for the prosecution and by J. E. Morrison and G. A. Allen for the defense, when the court delivered its charge to the jury. It lacked just a few minutes of 12 o'clock when the jury retired to deliberate on the case, and in whose keeping for the time being the life of a human being was introduced.

As Parker was being taken from the court room to the jail he made some jocular remarks to Sheriff Ruffner, but never indicated by word or emotion his feelings.

At 12:30 the jury announced that they had agreed upon a verdict, when Parker was again brought into court and the verdict was read as follows:

We, the jury, duly impaneled and sworn, find the defendant guilty of murder in the first degree and that he should suffer death. Signed Geo. B. Scammell, foreman. After the verdict was recorded it was read to the jury and being asked if that was their verdict as recorded, answered "Yes, so say we all."

Counsel for defendant immediately gave notice of a motion for a new trial. Wednesday, June 23. was fixed by the court as the date for pronouncing sentence.

Parker showed no emotion whatever when the verdict was read but sat in his seat unmoved, as he appeared all through the trial.

While he showed no outward sign of his feeling or emotions, he had already judged his own case and had rendered a verdict on it to himself and had also announced his verdict to his fellow prisoners. When he was taken back to the jail after the verdict of the jury had been rendered, one of the prisoners remarked, "Well, what did they do to you?" He replied, "Just what I told." Aside from that he made no comment on the result.

The *Courier* reported the result of the trail this way on June 18, 1897:

The Parker trial came to a close yesterday. The court room was crowded when the defendant was brought into court. Many ladies were present. District Attorney Ross and P. W. O'Sullivan spoke for the prosecution and J. E. Morrison and G. A. Allen for the defense. Judge Hawkins' charge to the jury was peculiarly fair and free from any sign of prejudice in the matter. The jury left the court room about 12 o'clock and returned in half an hour with a verdict of guilty of murder in the first degree, with recommendation of death penalty. Defendant's attorneys gave notice of motion for new trial. June 23rd was fixed as day for passing sentence. When the verdict of the jury was read to Parker, there was no change in his countenance or demeanor to show that his savage nature quailed under realization of the certain doom which was near at hand. It is stated, however, that as he was down stairs in the jail, he trembled and the muscles of his face twitched nervously, but he said not a word. The only testimony introduced, which the public is not already familiar with, was that of Hon. J. C. Herndon, who said that Lee Norris had stated that he did not know whether it was Parker or Miller who shot him.

The trial was the talk of Prescott. From the *Courier* of June 25, 1897:

> A life size picture of Outlaw Parker can be seen in the show window of Dillon's store and the subject of much comment. The popular verdict of "countenance" does not signify much, as nine men out of ten who look at the picture say it is not a bad countenance.

If that isn't prejudice, what is?

The *Arizona Gazette* reported a slightly different reaction that Parker gave after the reading of the verdict. While it does not contradict the reports from the Prescott newspapers, it is odd that they didn't print it if it actually happened. From the June 18 edition of the *Gazette*:

> The trainmen who arrived on the late train last night reported that when the verdict in the Parker case was brought in yesterday, Parker laughingly said to Sheriff Ruffner: "Well, Ruff, old boy, I see you are bound to make me the principal actor in a necktie party, but I'll bet you a hundred dollars to a doughnut that I'll never swing." Ruffner calmly replied that there was no danger that the people would be disappointed in the hanging.

The same edition editorialized:

> Justice, swift and certain, is being meted out to the outlaw and murderer, Parker. We commend the people of Yavapai county for their determined stand to stamp out such infamous crimes as the one committed by Parker.

Around this time, the Grand Jury wrapped up all of its business, and presented its report to District Court Judge John J. Hawkins. Most of it is routine legal issues, but one paragraph, rarely reported in later years, stands out. The entire report was published in the June 23, 1897 edition of the *Arizona Journal Miner*. The paragraph of significance:

> We could further report:
>   That we have investigated the recent jail break, and find that it was a premeditated and prearranged plan by one L. C. Miller, an inmate of the County jail at that time, and find that neither the Sheriff nor his deputies were in any way to blame, by carelessness or otherwise, and think they should be exonerated of any blame or criticism, whatsoever.

Historically, the idea that the jailbreak was planned not by Parker, but by Miller, is staggering. Historians and after-the-fact authors have always believed that the breakout was Parker's brainchild. The evidence and/or testimony that the Grand Jury based this on is unfortunately lost to history. They could have been in error, or failing that, it is not at all beyond the realm of possibility that the impulsive, hot-headed Miller, not known for his intelligence, was the mastermind, and that the opportunistic Parker simply took full advantage of the situation and his friend's stupidity. We will never know for certain.

The case of Territory vs. L. C. Miller began shortly after Parker's trial had ended. It was brief, and it interestingly had a slightly different roster of witnesses. As Miller did not later appeal his conviction, the trial transcript was not saved, which is unfortunate. All we have is newspaper coverage. From the *Arizona Journal Miner* of June 23, 1897:

> Miller on Trial for Murder
> The Miller trial has been in progress before the district court today. Richard Cross was on the witness stand this forenoon and testified in regard to the plot to break jail. He stated that he had been asked to participate in it but had declined. Miller was placed on the stand this afternoon on his own behalf and told the story of the escape but denied that any plans had been made previously. He stated that the matter had been talked of but he looked on it as more of a "josh" than anything else. Deputy Fairchild and Mrs. Haas were also on the witness stand for the defense. When the prosecution closed its case, Miller's attorneys made a motion that the jury be instructed to return a verdict of not guilty on the grounds that the testimony did not connect the defendant with the death of Lee Norris. This motion was overruled.
>
> The following is the list of jurors impaneled to try the case: John Crellin, George Kent, J. R. Alexander, John Warren, L. D. Bennitt, Charles Bennitt, A. L. Gibson, Joe Gibson, Charles Keator, J. R. Williams, E. W. Carroll, J. C. Tovrea*.
>
> At 2:30 both sides had rested their case and a recess of an hour was taken for counsel to prepare for argument.

It is odd that murderer Cross had not been called to testify in Parker's trial. Fairchild undoubtedly testified as to the manner in which he caught Miller, making it doubly tragic that a transcript has not survived, as it might have cleared up some of the confusion over that. Miller's court papers also show that Patrick J. Farley, William Osborne, and Drs. Davis and Barrett were subpoenaed to repeat the testimony they had given at Parker's trial. Very strangely, there is no record that jailor Robert Meador was called to testify.

The only indication of Fairchild's testimony appeared in the *Journal Miner* of June 30, 1897:

> Deputy Fairchilds, when on the witness stand in the Miller case, gave some testimony which would not be beneficial to Woody in the matter of getting the territorial reward offered for Miller. He stated that when he and Miller's sister were out hunting for Miller, they met Woody and asked him if he knew where Miller was.

---

* John Charles Tovrea was the brother of famed Phoenix meat-packing magnate Edward A. Tovrea. He managed aspects of his brother's business while living in Phoenix and Nogales, but he lived in Prescott for a time also.

He replied: "I do not, and if I did, I would not tell you for $5,000."

The jury for Miller was out for 16 hours, longer than Parker's jury had been. The verdict, however, was totally expected. From the *Journal Miner* of June 30, 1897:

> The Parker and Miller Cases
> The court room was crowded this morning on the opening of court, those present being attracted there by the prospective sentencing of Parker and the expected verdict in the Miller case.
> They were disappointed as to the former, and while the jury in the Miller case returned a verdict, it was also disappointing to very many. The jury found him guilty and fixed his punishment at imprisonment for life. The jury from the first stood eleven for this verdict to one for the death penalty.
> When Parker was brought into court, sentence was deferred until after his trial for train robbery. The latter case was called, when Parker's attorney made a motion to dismiss the case, on the grounds that the defendant had already been convicted of a crime, the penalty of which is death, and hence could not be tried again for a capital offense. The motion was overruled.
> Friday, June 25, was set as the date for sentencing each of the prisoners.

Yuma Territorial Prison mugshot of the mercurial Richard Cross, who was in jail with Parker in Prescott for a cold-blooded murder he committed in Jerome, but who drew a light sentence. (Courtesy of Pinal County Historical Society)

The courtroom in the old Yavapai County Courthouse in Prescott. Parker and Louis C. Miller were tried and convicted of murder here. (Sharlot Hall Museum)

The *Prescott Courier* of June 25, 1897, went into greater detail as to why the jury took so long:

> The jury in the case of Louis Miller, about being out 16 hours, agreed on a verdict at 9:30 o'clock yesterday morning, of guilty of murder with penalty of life imprisonment. The first ballot taken by the jury was on the charge of murder. The vote was: Guilty 11, not guilty 1. After balloting and jawing the night through this one juror still held out for his "not guilty" vote. He said that two men should not be hung for killing a man when only one of the men charged with murder had a gun. Most of the jurors were in favor of the death penalty. The one juror stood by his "not guilty" vote until a compromise on a life imprisonment verdict was made. When the verdict was made known in court Miller smiled, and well he might, for he had a narrow escape from the gallows. After he was led below, Parker was brought into the courtroom, clean shaven. He greeted his attorneys with effusion and smiles. His attorneys moved for a new trial; motion overruled. Motion was then made for arrest in judgment, which was also overruled. After some desultory talk on both sides Parker was taken below. In the afternoon Abe Thompson, charged with train robbery, in connection with Parker, was brought up and plead guilty to the charge. He is quoted as saying, after he left the stand, that he was not guilty, but plead guilty because he thought it best. Thompson and Miller will be sentenced Friday, June 25.

Abe Thompson, as a former lawman himself, obviously realized it was useless to fight the charge. It is too bad that this, his only surviving statement on the subject, is a defiant denial of involvement in the Rock Cut Train Robbery.

All that was left was the formal passing of sentence. From the June 30, 1897 *Journal Miner*:

> Parker and Miller Sentenced.
> From Wednesday's Daily
>
> Parker and Miller were in court again this morning, this time to receive the sentence of the court, for one of the most atrocious crimes committed in this county for years, the murder of Lee Norris.
>
> These criminals, and particularly the former, never fails to draw a crowd to the court room at every appearance, and as usual the room was crowded this morning.
>
> Parker was the first called on to stand up for sentence. He kept his eyes riveted on the judge during the reading of the sentence never showing the least sign of nervousness or emotion. He was sentenced to be hanged on Friday, August 13.
>
> Miller's sentence, in accordance with the verdict of the jury was imprisonment for life in the territorial penitentiary. The general sentiment in the community is that Miller as richly deserves the death penalty as Parker, although the latter fired the shot which snapped the cord of life in Lee Norris' body. The judge evidently entertained the same opinion as after the formal pronouncing of sentence he said, "And in your case, Miller, I desire to further say that it is to be hoped that Arizona may never be cursed with a chief executive who will show you any clemency."

After sentence was pronounced the prisoners were taken to jail and a death watch was immediately placed over Parker, and will remain until his execution unless an appeal is taken to the supreme court. The men selected for this are Jeff Davis and Miles Archibald. Immediately after the sentencing of the above the case of Richard Cross, who shot and killed Byron Jones, at Jerome, was called and a jury impaneled to try the case. A recess was then taken till 1:30 p.m. and at the convening of court Cross withdrew his plea of not guilty and entered a plea of guilty of manslaughter and sentence was set for tomorrow afternoon at 2 o'clock.

The crime committed by Cross was as atrocious even as that of Parker, as he lay in wait for his victim, pistol in hand and ready to shoot him down on his appearance. As the crime was committed prior to the passage of the celebrated Norton act, of the last legislature, a conviction could not be had for a greater crime than manslaughter to which he pleaded guilty.

The strikingly different fates of Parker and the cold, calculating Richard Cross cannot be overstated. The Norton Act and its poor wording had saved Cross and a number of other murderers throughout the Territory, which was an unintended consequence of its passage. Parker had killed Lee Norris after the passage of the Act. Literally a few weeks meant the difference between life and death for the two murderers who were in jail together. From the *Courier* of July 2, 1897:

Saturday last Judge Hawkins sentenced Cross, the Jerome murderer, to ten years in the penitentiary. The crime of which Cross was convicted for manslaughter was really one of the most premeditated and cold-blooded murders which ever took place in this county. The law passed by the last legislature saved the neck of Cross. Notwithstanding Cross's plea of guilty and the fact that the judge's attention was called to Cross's testimony in the Miller-Parker case, the judge gave the culprit the full penalty under the sentence, and the public will commend him for it.

The same edition covered the sentencing of Parker this way:

Parker and Miller were brought before Judge Hawkins yesterday morning for sentence. The court room was crowded, as it generally has been when either of those two celebrities have appeared. Parker appeared cool and collected. It is stated that he seemed struggling to smother a smile when the judge called upon him to stand up. When asked if he knew of any reason why sentence should not be passed upon him, he replied, "No, I don't think so." He was sentenced to be hanged Friday, August 13, an unlucky day and on an unlucky date, if tradition is right. When Parker was standing up for sentence, G. A. Allen, one of his attorneys, came into court and handed papers to J. E. Morrison, his assistant, which proved to be a notice of appeal, which was filed by clerk of court, and a copy handed district attorney. As the jury in the Miller case placed penalty at life imprisonment, the judge so fixed the sentence, not, however, without closing the sentence with: "And in your case, Miller, I desire to further say, that it is to be hoped that Arizona may never be cursed with an executive who will show you any clemency." A death watch has been placed upon Parker. Richard Cross, who murdered Byron Jones, at Jerome, in the most cold blooded manner imaginable, withdrew his plea of not guilty and plead guilty to manslaughter, the only charge under which he could be tried under the present law.

Before Parker was sentenced, Sheriff Ruffner arose and addressed the court as follows:

"Judge, before sentence is passed on this man, I request that this man be tried for train robbery; I had witnesses all here and was ready to proceed, and for some cause, unknown to me, they were sent home, night before last. When this court opened the district attorney promised me and gave me his word, as a man, that if I would allow this man to be tried for murder first, he would have him tried for train robbery before this sentence was pronounced. This thing has already cost me $3000. There is $2300 on him if he is convicted of this train robbery and I ask that this sentence be suspended until he is so tried."

Ruffner's words were in vain, and the witnesses went home. From the *Journal Miner* of June 30, 1897:

Mail Clerk A. S. Grant left on this morning's train for Los Angeles to resume his run on the A. & P. road. He was called here as a witness in the Parker train robbery case, as he was in charge of the mail car looted by the train robbers in February. Mr. Grant is an exceptionally good whistler, and during his stay in Prescott entertained a number of private audiences in this way.

An interesting tidbit from *Our Mineral Wealth* of July 2, 1897, demonstrating again Sheriff Ruffner's scorn for Mohave County's Hualapai Indian trailers:

Jim Hardy, the Indian trailer, had quite an experience at Prescott. It is thought he fell among thieves. Sheriff Potts sent him to Prescott, paying his way, to testify in the train robber cases that have occupied the time of the court lately. It seems he was not wanted in the cases, as Parker was not tried and Abe Thompson plead guilty. The Indian was then given a worthless paper with the sheriff's office of Yavapai county printed on the head and turned loose. The red man was allowed to ride on the cars to Ash Fork but no farther. He walked from the latter place to Kingman, 115 miles, without eating anything, and according to his own story he was heap hungry when he reached the first wigwam in Mohave county. The paper Jim carried was written as a joke, but Jim couldn't see it that way, and it has the appearance of being a darn mean trick. The sheriffs of the upper counties don't seem to have much confidence in the trailing abilities of these Wallapai Indians, we uns here, who know what they can do, are satisfied they have had no chance while being under the direction of these peaceable peace officers of the up counties. There has been several jail breaks here in Kingman, and each time these red trailers have been put on their track, and never have they failed to track their man, whether he had made one mile or fifty before the escape had been discovered. It is an easy matter to dig out of Kingman's jail but not to get away, owing to the skill of Jim Hardy and other Indian trailers to follow their tracks over rocks and even over the railroad ties. They are better than bloodhounds, and it is dollars to brass tacks that if Sheriff Ruffner had had Jim Hardy at hand when Jim Parker broke jail, there would have been little time elapsed between escape and capture, and that $3,000 he is out would have been in his official breeches instead of being scattered along Jim Parker's route.

From the *Mohave County Miner* of July 3, 1897:

Murderer Parker has obtained a stay for thirty days to enable his attorneys to perfect an appeal in his case to the supreme court. Yavapai county people may become impatient and give a hanging exhibition on July 4th. In cases of the Parker kind no appeal should be allowed.

Such sentiments were actually years ahead of their time, as modern day polls show large numbers of Americans support limiting appeals for criminals, or eliminating them altogether.

In many areas of America, mob lynchings were still very common, and would remain so for years to come. For whatever reasons, this was not the case in Arizona, which had only a few such incidents in its history. The Arizona Republican could not resist a little boasting about how civilized its citizens were, and in retrospect, I guess you can't blame them. From the June 26 edition:

NO LYNCH LAW HERE

Jim Parker, train robber and murderer, is to hang. Miller, who escaped from the Prescott jail with Parker, after the killing of Lee Norris, is to spend the remainder of his days in prison. This is quick justice, and a strong tribute to the law abiding character of the community.

In commenting upon the recent outbreak of savagery in Urbana, Ohio, a New York paper ignorant of the spirit which prevails in the southwest, said that if the Urbana lynching and its attendant horrors had occurred in Arizona public feeling would not have received such a severe shock. The only possible inference from this statement is that lawlessness triumphs in Arizona. The escape, recapture, trial and sentence of Parker and Miller are a sufficient refutation of the calumny. The people of Arizona are law abiding. Such horrible scenes as those enacted at Urbana, a supposedly "civilized" place, have never been witnessed in an Arizona town. Judge Lynch does not hold court in Arizona. He crossed the border years ago for more congenial fields in the east. Criminals here are, as a rule, given swift justice, at the hands of the territory's judicial officers. The pardoning power has been abused by governors of the territory, but public sentiment is opposed to such action. Arizona is a land of schools, of churches, of orderly, law respecting American citizens. This is more than may truthfully be said of many older American communities.

From the *Courier* of July 2, 1897:

Sheriff Ruffner, on Saturday last, accompanied by Deputy Sheriff Munds and two extra guards, left for Yuma prison in charge of the following convicts: L. C. Miller, sentenced to life imprisonment, for murder; R. Cross, to ten years' imprisonment, for manslaughter; Abe Thompson, robbery, 5 ½ years' imprisonment; Chas.

Yuma Territorial Prison mugshot of Louis C. Miller, taken upon check-in. (Courtesy of Pinal County Historical Society)

Canaris, grand larceny, three years; P. Kane, grand larceny, two and one half years; E. Johnson, grand larceny, two and one half years; E. Valdez, grand larceny, thirteen months, Emanuel Morales, an insane Mexican, was also taken to the asylum at Phoenix. Morales has a mania for doing washing. He would wash his own shirt several times a day. He was a great nuisance at Congress, from which place he was brought, and where, it is stated, he would enter houses at the most unseasonable hours and gather up washing without previous notice to owners and occupants. The result of such procedure was that he was shot at several times, by people who did not object to having their washing done through customary channels, but did object to the Mexican's methods.

Louis C. Miller was checked into Yuma Territorial Prison on June 28, 1897, as prisoner number 1300. His record has survived. His age was 27. His nativity was listed as Texas, his education was credited to both public and private schools, and oddly, his occupation was listed as an "engineer," indicating that he may have worked the railroad sometime.

Miller's expression was described as "open" and his complexion, "light." His height was 5 feet, 9 ½ inches. Color of hair, "light." Eyes, "gray." Weight: 144 pounds. His foot size was listed as 7, his head size 7 1/8, and his forehead "medium." He was listed as "intemperate" (meaning he used alcohol), and that he smoked. His religion was simply listed as Protestant.

Miller's body carriage was described as "erect" with a medium build. He had a scar on his left shin bone, caused by the bullet he received in the jailbreak. As for relatives, he listed his mother, Mrs. Clara S. Miller of Phoenix, instead of his brothers or sisters.

From the *Arizona Journal Miner* of July 7, 1897, a report from Yuma Territorial Prison:

M. J. Nugent tells the Phenix Republican that L. C. Miller, the Prescott murderer, is engaged in trundling a wheelbarrow laden with brick or mortar or something else equally heavy and sweat inspiring. Richard Cross, the slayer of Byron Jones, is practicing the tonsorial profession, and ex-Probate Judge Cluff, of Graham county, who was received last Wednesday night has been given charge of an insane convict. Cluff himself is believed to be not far from insanity.

One can still feel some sense of satisfaction over news like this, even more than a century after the fact.

Abe Thompson's Yuma Territorial Prison record has also survived, and gives us the only known description of the one-time lawman turned gang leader. He checked in to Yuma prison on the same day as Miller, as prisoner 1302 (Richard Cross had been 1301). He was 36 years old, and listed his nativity as Wisconsin. His education was listed as public schools in Wisconsin. Thompson listed his occupation as "engineer," again, indicating some railroad work (Ralph Cameron and some later historians have attributed Thompson's knowledge of the railroads to helping plan the Rock Cut Train Robbery). Thompson listed a secondary occupation as "Cowboy."

Yuma Territorial Prison mugshot of Abe Thompson, the only one to draw a prison sentence for the Rock Cut Train Robbery. (Courtesy of Pinal County Historical Society)

His expression was described as "open," and his complexion, "fair." He was 5 feet, 9 ½ inches tall. Color of hair, "brown." Eyes, "gray." He weighed 169 pounds. His foot size was 9, his head size 7 ½, and his forehead "high." He claimed to be temperate (he did not drink), said both of his parents were dead, and stated that he had two children (true). He also smoked.

Thompson's religion was listed as "Protestant." He apparently did not wish to embarrass his relatives, so he only listed his six year old son, Charles S. Thompson of Kingman as nearest relative. His body carriage was described as "erect," and "stout and well built." The record lists a scar on "point of right shoulder."

Abe Thompson and Louis C. Miller are the only known cohorts of Parker to have done time in the notorious Yuma Territorial Prison. An interesting tidbit—the October 9, 1897 edition of the *Arizona Sentinel*, the newspaper for Yuma—lists the town's postmaster's column for unclaimed mail at the post office. This was done in many cities to get people to come get their mail! The column from this date lists 2 letters for Abe Thompson! Apparently whoever was writing to him did not know how to address the letters to prison, and the postmaster apparently did not realize that Abe was incarcerated! One wonders if these letters ever found their way to Abe Thompson.

CHAPTER 9

The Long Road to the Gallows

While all of this was going on, Parker's sisters were frantically watching the California newspapers. The news that James Parker the train robber was actually Fleming Parker their brother had blindsided them, and it got worse after Parker became a murderer. Sister Margaret had apparently decided to write their brother off, but Martha and especially Sadie were griefstricken.

Sadie and Martha and their families were dirt poor. They could not afford to come to Prescott to be on the scene and visit their brother. After Parker was hanged, they couldn't even claim his body. The only details they could get of his case and his trial were the sketchy wire service reports in the California press. So they did the only thing they were able to do—they started writing letters to public officials in Arizona, pleading for aid in keeping their brother, who they loved dearly, from hanging. They could not bring themselves to believe that he was guilty of these terrible crimes. To Sadie and Martha, he was still "Flem," the brother they had grown up with.

It is nothing short of remarkable that a small handful of these letters have survived, and are in the Sharlot Hall Museum Archives. One cannot read these letters without getting a tear in one's eye, as the overwhelming grief continues to blast through the rough verbiage and terrible spelling down to this day. Like Parker himself, his sisters were poorly educated, and it makes the handwritten letters very difficult to read at times. I am surprised that these letters have not been used as source material by Parker researchers more than they have, as some of what we know about his early life comes from these documents.

It is not known how these letters survived, or how many hands they passed through before they were reposited at Sharlot Hall Museum. The first one is dated June 10, 1897, shortly before the start of Parker's trial. It is addressed to Sheriff George C. Ruffner; it is clear that Sadie had written to him previously, and that he had responded. The text:

> Los Angeles
> June the /10
> Mr. G. C. Ruffner
> Dear Sir
>
> Your letter of June the 3 Received last sadarday but I have felt so wearied I have bin unable to answer sooner   I thank you a thousand times for your Kindness

Chapter 9: The Long Road to the Gallows

and Symthey toward I and my Brother and would say I would be so glad to have my Darling Brother Photo   I think you are afuly Kind in Ofering to send it to me and I would like so verry much for you to let me Know about his trial   I can't see any thing about it in the Los Angeles times you cant relize how bad I fell about my Brother if I had tenn Million I would sacrfice the last dollar if I could only git him out of that trouble I think of others how they hafto have trouble as well as my self but seems as though I can not content my self any way I have had so much trouble any way but as you say I must try to Bear up and stand it for I have my little ones to raise and I hafto work very hard to suport them and I fell as though all I have is gone when I (illegible; either "loss" or "love") that Brother   I can't see how he could act so when he Knows his Sister loves him so well   if he had only stayed there and not Broke Jail I believe he would of come out allright for I never felt that he was in that train robbery of corse I don't Know I am only saying what I think

Poor fellow he has bin turned out in the world ever since he was twelve years old Mother and Father both died when we were verry young and we just had to do the Best we could and poor Flem he never had any raising like other Boys   it is So hard for me to give him up that way I try to Keep my self from studing about him but I can not he is on my mind the last thing at night and the first thing of a morning and I dream about him

It seems like the ones that try to live a Christian and do right by ever one is the ones that hafto suffer the most in this world now I would be so glad if you lit me Know about my Brother and his case

Hoping to here from you soon I am as Ever Resprectfully Yours
                            Mrs. Sadie Baker
                            Los Angeles Cal
                            780 (illegible; Elmere?) Ave

Sadie's next letter to Ruffner was written ten days later, and shows signs of mental deterioration due to panic and grief. Ruffner had apparently let her know that her brother's chances at his trial (which was about to start) were not good. This letter also gives us the only insight into their sister Margaret's attitude—she didn't really care what happened to Flem. The text:

                            Los Angeles Cal
                            June the 20/.97
                            Mr. G. C. Ruffner

Dear Sir   I will just hafto write you another letter as I fell that you will do as you said you would and it seems to do me so much good to write to you about my darling Brother now Mr Ruffner do Please Keep them from hanging him if you (illegible; possible?) can   I do believe it will be more for me than I can ever live over I am almost wild I can't relize that my Darling Brother would go and git into such great trouble as he has he Knows how it will torture me he often told me not to wearie about him but you Know Mr Ruffner I love that Brother So much that it is beyond my crontroll to Keep my self from wearing I just fell as though I canot live any longer if they should hang him

> 8, F.4, D.B.10
>
> Los Angeles
> June the 8/10
>
> Mr G. C. Ruffner
> Dear Sir
> Your letter of June the 3
> Recived last saturday but
> I have felt so worried I have
> been unable to answer sooner
> I thank you a thousand times
> for your kindness and Sympathy
> toward I and my Brother and
> would say I would be so glad
> to have my Darling Brother Photo
> I think you are a jolly kind in
> Ofering to send it to me and
> I would like to know very much for
> you to let me know about his
> trial I cant see any thing about

Leaves from letters written by Parker's sister, Sarah Jane "Sadie" Baker, to George C. Ruffner. (Courtesy of Sharlot Hall Museum)

Chapter 9: The Long Road to the Gallows

the most in this world now I would be so glad if let me know about my Boy and his case

hopeing to hre from you dear I am as Ever Respectfully Yours

Mrs Sadie Baker
Los Angeles Cal
780 Elmac ave

I want You if you ever come to Los Angles to come to our house it would do me so much good to talk with you about my Brother

my Youngest Sister is almost dead with sorrow they had to take her to the Doctor she has four little Children you might say all babies and she is verry low my other Sister she seems to Know how to Keep from wearing or the truth of it is she don't love Brother like I and my youngest Sister and she trys to hold us two up and tells us that Brother could of bin a good Boy just as well as to done thy way he has done

But I don't look at it this way I Know that it was bad compay that led him a Stray for any one that know his Father and Mother Know they were just as nice People as ever lived, but Mama died when I was thirteen then I took Care of my Brother and my two Sisters till my poor Father died then I was married at fiftenn and the rest was scaterd round one in a place and my Brother just wanderd round with bad compay and went away off out to Arizona when very young then I did not see him for a long time and then he came to me and stayed a while then he went Back again so you see I don't Know how he was or what he was doing But two years ago last may he came out here to see me and I and my husband Mr Boyd had bin Seprated a year and my Brother had not herd about it till a year afterwards so he came right out soon as he herd it and he took me home with him and my oldest Boy and if I liked it we was going to send for the other three so Brother fixed me a house all up nice and poor fellow is so good to me if he has a dollar and I want it he will give it to me and he would go with out so it was so lonesome and I got so sick I had to come home And I will always fell like if I had stayed with hijm I could of Kept him out of trouble I just cant think any other way. You don't know how good he has always bin to me and I always felt like as long as I had Brother I was allright   I have bin married one year last Oct to Mr Baker Brother has never saw him and Of corse you Know that makes me fell that much (illegible; probably "worse") I married and affull good man and he is highly theright (undoubtedly "thought") of by ever one that Knows him and you can just think how that makes me fell it seems to me likes he looks down on me because my Brother has done such affull crime   But he tells me ever day why Sadie he says what makes you fell that way I Know you cant help what you Brother has done he is affull good to me and my Children But I don't care how good a Step Father is it is not like their own Father

"well I must close for you will git tired of reading my letter and I beg of you to excuse me for telling you so much about my troubles as you are a Stranger to me but ever since I recived your letter it just seems like I am aquanted with you and I will never for git the Kiness and Rispect you showed toward me and my Brother
         Respectfully yours
         Mrs. Sadie Baker
         Los Angeles   780 (illegible; Elmere?) Ave

Apparently, Sadie was also writing pleading letters to Ruffner's Deputy Johnny Munds. Munds' wife, Frances, seems to have responded and asked her for information on her brother's life. Sadie responded, and this letter has survived as well. The text:

         Los Angeles Cal
         July the 19=97
         Mrs. John L. Munds

Chapter 9: The Long Road to the Gallows

Dear Madam
I just recived your letter Just a few minutes and will Answer your questions Just as Prompt and Just as near right as I can rember now my Brother was Borned in Tulari Co and my mother died in Confinement with her fifth child a Boy and she died in three weeks after it was Borned and my little Brother died one month after so there was us four little ones lift I was Just 13 years old and my Darling Brother Flem that has almost Killed me and (illegible; probably "ruined") my happiness for ever is Just 2 years and nine month younger than I and I was Just 34 last December and I have two more Sisters younger my youngest Sister name is Martha Rockwell her address is Reedly Cal and my other Sister name is Maggie Welch Visalia after Mother died Papa Sold our home place in Stokes Valley 18 miles from Visalia and he took us little ones and we all went to live with Grandpa my Mother Father and I was married there at 15 years old nothing but a small child and no mother to advise me or tell me what married life was and then I had to live with my husband folks for awhile and my Father was graguly loosing his mind over loosing my Mother and he could not Be contented any place so I moved to my self and I took my Brother Flem and my Younger Sister and my Aunt took my other Sister and my Father went to work for a man by the name of Smith and he worked there just about ayear as well as I can rember and my Brother never liked my husband nor neither did I allthoug I stood him for 15 years and had 4 Children by him well after Father worked there a year as I can Rember then he came to me and we Rented a farm him and my husband in Clark Valley in Freno Co and we saw papa acting so funny all the time but I never thought And there was a young lady got deeply in Love with Papa her name was (illegible; looks like Sofapha Duept) and so I told Papa I thought maby he would be better contented if he would get married he was Just almost Insane with sorrow about loosing Mama so he at last married and his wife and him lived there and we moved Just about a half mile from them and her and the three Children did not get along very well and Papa lived there with her about five months and he came by my house one day going to Visalia and I thought he looked so strange and he Kissed me good By and cryed I did fell so bad for I could see he was in trouble so the next Eve late about dark there was arunner came to our house and they said for us all to get ready that Papa was lost of corse if they had told us the truth I could never got ready well we got ready and rode all night and when I got there there was my poor Papa laid out he put up at his Unkle Green Parkers the only one of his folks I know of or ever saw and he has bin dead for 4 or five years and he took the Poison there and thought he could walk to Mama grave and the Poor fellar fell dead before he got there he left a letter to us Children telling us he could not live without Mama and what a Papa he said to do so But he could not help it so then there was my Brother and two Sisters left alone no Father or Mother so then what Property he had my husband Brother Jim Boyd Just (illegible; probably "swiped") from us and my Brother was turned out for his self and I Kept my Sister Pats and my Aunt took Mag well I could not tell you to save my life how come Brother to ever be a bad Boy but it was away out in the county and he got to runng with this one and that one seemed like he always picked on bad compay and he was always a cused of ever thing that happened don't matter what or where he was and he got to drinking and one scrape he got into was a Lie out and out he was working for a man by the name of Brown and

Brown hired him to go and get a load of Barly and it was not Browns so they arrested Brown for it and he turned States evedince on my Brother and got him into it so that is how he got into trouble that time and now Brown is in Penetiray or was and the time he was sent to Sanquntin you know your self if he had bin gilty we could not get him out of there* I forget I just cant bring it back to my mind Just how long it was but not only for a little while it don't seems to me like it was over two or three months but I don't say Postively for that has montreely sliped my mind I would tell you if I Knowed But that time if I rember just right you ask my Brother and tell him Sister said for him to tell you But that time they missed some Cattle up in the mountains there and of corse they all got to gether and (illegible; probably "Swore") Brother Flem drove them off and sold them and they sent him to Sanquntin well that is all the trouble I ever Knowed of

And after he came back from Sanquntin he went to live with Granpa in Antlope Valley where my Granpa lived when he died and Flem lived there for about a year I think maby longer and maby not quite a year I just don't exaly rember seemed like since Flem has got into that trouble I have forgot ever thing and I have weared till I am so (illegible; probably "frail") and so weak I cant hardly get around I am afraid I never can stand it I have begged and pleaded and prayed for that Boy if ever body Knowed the truth I do believe to my very utmost that they would sentence him Very lite I am not saying this because I have any hope for him for I have not for very few people stop to think now days we allway thought that he was the only Boy he was always a good Child and a Perfect Pet amongst us all it was not his Unkle got him out of that trouble it was his Porr old Granpa any how he got aquanted with a feller By the name of (illegible; looks like "Grome", maybe she meant Jerome?) Hamilton** and they got Flem to go with him and his Brother I think they stayed at the needle along time and then Flem went out to Arizona and worked for a man By the name of Sulcar till he acumatld some Propty of his own and then I did not here from him for years and years and then he came to see me in Tulari Co and stayed a short time and then he went back to Arizona and I did not here from him for a long long time again so in that mean times we moved to Los Angles and we had Just lived here one year when I and my husband seprated and I wrote ever where to get my Brother to help me but I could not here from him no place he was in Mexico at the time so I deeded my land over to my husband Mother and Father if they would take care of my Children till I could my self so I went to working out so some of Flems (illegible; probably "acquaintances") wrote to him about me and the Dear Boy came right at once to my asistince so he came to Santa Monica where I was working and Brought all 4 of the Children from Los Angles with him and he had got each of the Boys nice Suits and full suit out and out for them all and give them mony And then he thought it was to hard for me to work out so he Beged and Pleaded for me to go home with him so at last I was so glad to see him I concented But I could not get off till my month is up so he took my eldest Boy and went on and I went about two weeks latter he Bought me ever thing to make me (illegible; probably "comfortable") and give me money and I could Just go to the

---

*   Here, Sadie is apparently referring to the fact that Parker's conviction was later overturned by the California Supreme Court.

**   Here's the name of "Hamilton" again. See Chapter 1 and Chapter 12.

Store and get any thing in the world I wanted to and have it charged to him* And ever Body I saw spoke well of him out there and all thought anafull (illegible) of him I could not here a word about him and he had lots of stock of his own so I took sick and I had to come home and lift my Boy with him and then I got married and my Boy came home

He never had any change to go to School he was turned out in the world when Just a mere Boy and he always had the luck seems to mee to meet with the worst of compay he was always a Jolly fellar and always ready to help ever body if he had a cent and I love him Better than ever thing else in this world for I Know how his life has bin and I Know and would swear on my death Bed that he has bin acused of things that he never done and I just know as well as I know I am living that that old Abe Thompson Just talked him into Robing that train I don't want to Blame any body bit I know that much and some one put it into his head to Breake jail for I got a letter from him Just a few days before and I Know he did not have any Idea of doing so then he is not one half as bad as it is Reported I am a Christian and my only hopes of his life is in my Father hands and he Knows best

Now if there is any thing I haven't told you that you would like to know I will Kindly till you and I beg you as a friend as I did Sheriff Ruffner to not Bring me and my Sisters into it fer we are almost dead now and I am Just living for my Children sake I know I hafto stand it you ask me about his Parents Brothers and Sisters I don't know anything about papa folks as they are all in Kentuckey and they lost (illegible) he got (illegible) them they were all most dead and moved away he came to California with his Unkle when about 17 years of age his mother has one Sister and one Brother that is all the folks he has and his Father was a fine a man as ever lived and as well thought of as ever a man could be and never harmed no one and his Mother the same way and his Sisters is all well thought of I am the only one that has ever had any trouble and I can give any one all the witnesses that the want that I had a cause to seprate from my husband so Brother is the only one that has a thing hanging over him and I know that it is not borned in him it is Just bad compay that has led him astray you wanted to Know if Flem ever was in any love affair he was he loved a girl by the name of Melly Woody and I am so sory they did not mary for he would of settled down if he had but they fell out some way I never asked Flem about it you (illegible) has 16 years since Flem was with me and since he was in that trouble** and you Knoe any one forgets in that length of time I was not with him only a month when I went home with him

Now I think I have told you all I can think of and all you asked me if not Just write and I will tell you what ever I know and I have told you the plain truth if I had bin able I could put (illegible) through for (illegible) thing about Flem that is not true and for sending him up when he was innocent and now they make out like he is more to blame than anyone else that was into that trouble I hope you will find out that my Brother is not altogether to Blame for what he has done the Boy lost his Papa and his Mama and his Granpa and ever thing that happened it was onto him and seems like the Poor Boy has Bin Kicked down ever since his Parents died

---

* Sadie was apparently backward enough, and so trusting of her brother, that she seems to have had no realization that an "honest" ranch hand could not possibly have been so wealthy.

** Sadie clearly had no concept of time passage

7, F.4, D.B.10

Hedley July 16 1897.

My dear sister Sadie

I received your dear letter this morning was glad to git it. I hope you will git along all right. Take care of your self if I would loose you know I dont no what would become of me You are all the comfort I have got

this a[w]ful thing we have got how I stand it is Just killing me

Leaves from a letter written by Martha Rockwell to Sadie Baker. Both women were Parker's sisters. (Courtesy of Sharlot Hall Museum)

Chapter 9: The Long Road to the Gallows

Jack Kinlaid said he
would put up $100 if
some men would go and
old Harlor knows all
about the family he could
do a whole lot of
talking, do you think that
would help if I knew
it would I would start
out and try how get people
two help me raise the
money for him too go
on. well Sadie
write often and me all the
fresier you see about him.
I hope Mary is well and all
of you. Geaney is getting
along fine
  write soon. Your sister
                                  Martha

Well I am so tired I will close hoping you will excuse all mistakes and Poor writing I am as ever yours truley
                Mrs. Sadie Baker
P S I will send you a letter I got from my poor sister and you can see how she fells

Sadie had indeed enclosed a letter written to herself from her sister, Martha Rockwell. This letter has miraculously survived as well. Martha seems to have been even less educated than Sadie, for her writing and spelling are even worse. Here is the text:

           Reedley   july 16 1897
My dear sister Sadie
    I received your dear letter this morning was glad too git it I hope you will git along all right
    Take care of your self if I would loose you know I don't know what would be come of me you are all the comfort I have got
    This a ofel thing we have got to stand it is just killing me but god knows we cant help it I written a letter this morning too his Lawer and I written one a week ago but hant got no answer when I git a answer I will send it too you
    I told his Lawer to ask Flem if he wanted me too come and see if he did I would come
    I just wish I was able too go I would come by your place and we would go too gether I would leave ever one of my children with May but it is im posibull I couldn't raise money enough to go too save my life
    I hant able too do nothing I written and ask the Lawer how much would he save his life for oh my life is (illegible; probably "miserable")
    I think it looks ofel that we cant go too see the dear Boy
    Old Bill Hurtor you no him says what are you going too do just let him hang says if we would all make up a nough too pay his fair down there and back ne would   go down and talk and try too save him
    Jack Kinkaid said he would put up $40 if some men would go and old Hurtor knows all about the family he could do a whole lot of talking do you think that would help if I know it would I would start out and try too get people too help me raise the money for him too go oh well Sadie write often send me all the (illegible) you see about him   I hope Mary is well and all of you
Leancy is getting along fine
                Write soon your sister Martha

These sad, sad letters need no further comment from me, except to say that one thinks of the possibility, however remote, that Hurtor (if that was his name; Martha's writing is hard to decipher) might have been the one who informed the Prescott newspapers about Parker's background.

In the Archives of the Sharlot Hall Museum is another remarkable document, describing in sketchy detail the early life of Parker. It is written on lined paper for several pages, and then scrawled on stationary from the Yavapai County Board of Supervisors. The author alternates between ink and pencil, indicating it was written over a period of several intervals. Although it is unsigned (indicating it was never completely finished), it is clear from the outset that the author is Parker himself.

It is not known why he wrote this from his jail cell, or who he wrote it for. The opening sentence indicates that it indeed was written at someone's request—perhaps it was for his attorneys, or perhaps for a reporter who never published it. Like Parker's other few surviving statements, it is fascinating for what it says and frustrating for what it does not say. Parker does not discuss the train robbery at any length, undoubtedly because he was, at this time, professing innocence to the charges. In this document, Parker expresses a strong preoccupation with women, possibly one reason it was never used by the person who asked for it. It is not known exactly when it was written, although it ends very abruptly, indicating that it was possibly never finished.

Parker's handwriting is better than that of his sisters, but his spelling is abominable, demonstrating again the lack of any real schooling in the family. Here then, published for the first time in its entirety that I know of, is Parker's story as told by Parker himself:

> Well heare it is I was Bornd in California in Tularia County in the year of 1865* in the northern part of the County in the Sernavadres motontons on a small Stock ranch and stayed there till I was 5 years old thin my father sold out there and moved in the southern part of the County and bought a farm and there we lived 2 or 3 years and my mother died leaving my father with 4 children one sister older then me and to younger so he Sold the farm in a fue monts and moved back to the mountans and went into the Stock bisness and here come a (illegible; looks like dercith) and he lost the most of his Stock by hard (illegible) he saved a fue So he went wright a working to mak a living for us my oldest Sister took care of the other to children so things went a long untall the spring of 1870* then my father died and my oldest sister was married So she took my youngest sister to rase and my other sister went to my uncles to live and my grand father took me and it took all my father had to pay his dets except a fue head of horses which was divided betawean us children that left a head a pieace my grand father was all good to me but he had a old lady doing the house work and she had Children which could not git a long to gether and that made truble the old man would not whip me but he would give me sum hard talks and I was all to blame to heare the old (illegible; possibly "woman") tell the tale So one fine morning they sent me down to my uncles to take some ward to him so that was the last they saw of me I had a good horse and sadle so I drifted in to the northern part of Feresno Co and went to work for Miller and Lux so sevrl monts past befor they found out where I was so there I fell in with bad Company lernt to drink smoke gamble and run fast Ladies and go to (illegible) houses and was a little tuff for a cid so I worked there 2 years study and then went to my sisters to go to School to a lady teacher which was a bout 22 years old and there was a young man a (illegible) of about 20 so they were doing mor love making then School

---

* The year is clearly in error.

teaching so I only went one week until I had a nother Pard which was a bout my age we got ther one morning early which dident suat the marm and her lover it (illegible) as a cold winter morning so we would not leave the Stove and this lad threw me down on the flor and would bang my head to make me say I would leave the house so I told my Pard to hand me the fire poker and he dun so and I took him betwin the eyes with it and of he tumbeled so I got up and made a run for the door and as I hit the ground he lit on top of me so we had it out and I wone the battle by giting I stick of wood So that was the last of that school with me that was the winter of 1880 I went a head working for wages whe I could git enny thing to do and when I could not I made my Sisters my home until I was the of 19 and then I lit out a gin and went to work for Car and (illegible; possibly "Flegen") I only worked ther a fue monts until I had some trouble with to bruthers over ther Sister So we wet to settle it and settled it with a fight So they said they would have a (illegible; possibly "dance") that night and give me and a friend of mine a invitation so we go (illegible; possibly "dancing") not thinking but truble was all over So when we road up in the yard who Should we meet but one of the boys telling us that he forbid us coming in and turned back and went in the house so that was time to stop and Study but we finley made up our minds we would go in enny way So in we went to the front room they were dancing in a side room So as we got in the front room the thing titened we run into a shot gun in the hand of one of the Bruthers So he walked to the door and opened it but did not Step far enough to handle it So we started out and when we got up in a fue feet I jumped and grabed it and the little hing titened then for we had the hold forty to fight me and this one had it round and round after a long rasle I got the gun and throud it for the door and it lit in the door and at it we went running girls packing sticks of Stove wood to the men to beat us with finley my pard got his man down in the door with his head laying back over the gun and me and the rest was on our feet fighting but finley my man got me down on a (illegible) that set in the room So ther I was (illegible) to stay or Shoot my way out so a little shooting took place for them days the boys all packed Pistles So I got my hand under my back got my gun and shot the man which was on top of me and of he roled So just then a nother Party grabs the musle of the gun and of I pull her a gin giting the lad that my pard had down through the leg so that started the gang So we had the house to our sefves except the 2 men was Shot and they were doing ther Best to git out but we lost no time our Selves for we had all we wanted for we was beaten up bad we road a bout five miles and got our wonds packed up and then started out to keep out of the way of officers so we was on the dog for a fue days and was finly talked in to (illegible) of giving up to officers so we dun that and was taked off 40 miles to the county seet there we laid for 6 or 7 weeks before we could give bons and then I got out and settled things with the boys by paying ther dochter bill and giving them one $100 a piace So then I turned my self lose to take the world as she came I went to stealing a little and not working much so I finley fell in to it by stealing Cattle and Could not git out off it I was on the dog for 6 or 8 months and was finley Captured by too boys which was supposed to bee my friends but that is the way with friends they will all donn you for a fue dollars if they can so in I went a gin I give bale and got out right a way and was out a whill and Stood trile and was Convicted and sent to the pen for one year which I served and that was enuff for me When I got out I went into the northern part of the state and went to work worked there a fue monts and then went back to tularia Ca again and

Chapter 9: The Long Road to the Gallows

tried to settle down a gin I went to work for my grand father but evry body looked down on me but I stayed with it so me and my youngest Sister took Care off the ranch for the old man was a great hand for fast horses and was gone off racing most off the time so it was all left to us So I had not bin back long until I fell in love with a young lady and that was a gint her mothers will for her to go with me enny where but when She went to a dance She was my pardner in spite off the old womern and she would slip off and come over to see me I stayed with that for 2 years and my sister got married and left me and the old man a lone I had got sume Stock by that time and 160 acers off land but into it I gets a gin and that ase one thing that I knowed nothing a bout and I caied that for a long time trying to beet it but being Convincted there once I stood no chance for the Juge and Sheriff all had it in for me so I had to go to the Pen a gin then I appealed to the Supriam Cort and was orderd turned loose with out a trile there out broke a gin with out enny thing except one horse and sadle Sothen I drifted to losangeless Ca ther went to worke for wages and only worked a fue monts and got into a Saloon row and had not time to stop there for ther had bin a little Shooting there and I had no money to pay lawyers with so me and my friend took to the hills a gin and So we went to (illegible) Ca Cal but that part off the Cuntry we were broake had no money and 4 head of old poor horses there we stayed for a fue monts and Started for Arizona Te in the mont of Feb 1890* with 3 head of horses and $460 about 600 miles of desert a head of us got to the Cararada river with our pack horse giveout ther we sold too horses and my pard took the trane for prescott and I took the other hors and road to Prescott in for 4 days and ther I stayed until my money that we got for the 2 horses was gone and a bill on my horse for $5 and not a sent to git him out with So I Soaled my pistle for $8 and got the horse out and give the other 3 to my pard and I left the town without a sent in my pocket and did not know a sole in the Country I went about 100 miles and Stoped at a ranch for a fue days and helped ride a fue bronks and mad $15 and heard wher I could git a Job so I lit out for it as that was what I wanted at that time as I come to this Cuntry to make a anest living so I worked ther 8 or 9 months and saved my money then I heard of my grand fathers deth so I went to Califoria to see him for the last time and stayed a bout 2 weeks and back I come broak a userl and went to work a gin and worked study for 2 years and then wages was cut donn until a man could not make a living at that for he would not git by 5 or 6 monts work a year so I did not work for wages enny mor I went to trading for a living would bye and sell horses So I made money at that and had to friends that is what you might Call friends but they were not but I thought they were so we traided a round until we got a holt of a nuf of money to bye a band of horses and went to utough and bought them and paid our money for them and drove them back and went to braking them to ride but there was partys that would say we had stold them So we sold and traded them for Cattle and made money fast but our nabers all said we were robbing them that I don't denigh for if a man did not steal a little he would not Stay there long for they would steal what he had and he would hafto go on the bum and I will steal before I will bum so they finley raised a Stink was a gointoo put me in truble So me and one of the boys thought we had better leave the Cuntry for a fue days so we took 4 head horses and pulled

---

*   Parker's recollection of time is clearly off here.

for Nevada in the mont of Feb and feed was scarse and no (illegible) to bye feed for we were on the dog so our horses got verry poor and begin to give out on us So we got into white Pine Co Nevada there we went to work trading Cattle into Montania and worked at that until October and made for Arizona agin as we heard that things was all right so it took about on mont to come back so we made it back all right and had sum money and 9 head of good horses So we went to gethern our horses which we had left thare (illegible) trading for Cattle which we finley got a holt of severl dollars and me and the kid bought Abe out and finley I sold out to the kid and started for California to se a fue friends I had there so I went all over California about then pulled out for Nevada there I had a girl that I wanted to see so I stayed there 2 or 3 weeks and started for Arizona agin where I have last girl life and all by a boy that I have helped to git a long and lots of times give him the last Sent I had in my pocket but Still he will turn me in just to help him and git a fue dollars that is on this trane robbery which all of the trouble is about now if he had not told what he did I would of bin a free man to day but that was what he did not do So now I will give you the way this run happened after the trane Robery happened which I must arrested for I was on my road to a little town which is called peach springs on the (illegible) in Moharvia Co there I met a posey of about 6 men part of them was walipie Indins and they fired at me as soon as they saw me so I broke and run a wase and they kept firing at me as I went I run a bout one mile and then fired back at them 3 or 4 Shots and went on and they was on my trale for I had a good hors and could ride a way from them so they traled me for severl miles and over halled me and there I (illegible) a run for my self for a fue miles and they run me into the Snow so my horse could not go enny father so I pulled of my Saddle and turned my horse loose and took it a foot and a bout 20 men on my trale so I went for the Cararado River when it was verry rugh and hard to track a man and made it until the 7 day when I was over halled by 3 indins and a white man by the name of rogers and they had the drop on me before I knew that there was aman in fifty miles of me So I had to give up then so I dun that and we went back a mile or so and I told them I would not walk enny father if they wanted me that they would hafto git a horse for me to ride so they sent one Indin back for the posey after horses that was 20 miles so we camped there that night I knew the posey could not get there until 8 or 9 oclock the next morning so I took things easy for I had penty of time to get a way before they could make it so we got super as I had a little grub with me and the talked a while and thin pulled of my boots and laid down in front of the fire to take a nap and layed ther until a bout 4 oclock got up and had a cup of Cofey and put my boots on and then I Jumped over the top of the indins and grabed a gun and took the Camp and all of the guns they had so that made me 4 guns and 13 Catrages for the men all run when I got the first gun so I did not git to se what they had so I broke 2 guns up and took one and a pistle with me and away I went so I travled a bout 3 days without ennything to eat I then went back up the river and travld for 2 days and nights without enny thing to eat and then I run into a posey of five men which took me in so and brought me to Peach Springs there they put me on a train for Prescott and there I was put in Jale and I got a lawyer and give him all of the money I had to defind me and things went on smothe for a mont or so and finley I wanted to see him so I told the Jaler to tell him to come over and he did not come so I sent a gin and a gin and no lawyer Came and no friends Came to see me that went to shoe that my chance was small so I thought

> Well heare it is
> I was Borrnd in Caalifornia in Tularia County in the year of 1845 in the northern part of the county in the Sernavadeis mountians an a small stock ranch and stayed there till I was 5 years old then my father sold out there and moved in the suthern part of the county and bought a form and there we lived 2 or 3 years and my mother ded leaving my father with 4 children one sister older then one and to younger so he sold the form in a fue months and moved back to the mountains and went into the stock bisness and hear come a dreath and he lost the most of his stock up by hard weather he soved a fue So he went wright a mining to mak a living for us may aldest Sister tood care of the other to children so things went a long until the spring of 1876 then my father he died and my oldest Sister was maried so she took my yaungest sister to rase and my fathers sister went ...

Two leaves from the long, rambling statement Parker handwrote while awaiting trial for murder in Prescott. (Courtesy of Sharlot Hall Museum)

J. W. SMITH,................Chairman
THOMAS ROACH............Supervisor
JOHN WOOD.................Supervisor
CHAS. H. AKERS...............Clerk

OFFICE OF

THE BOARD OF SUPERVISORS,
OF YAVAPAI COUNTY.

Prescott, Arizona, _____ 189_

I then went back left the river and traveled for 2 days and nights without anything to eat and then I run into a party of horse men which took me in so and brought me to Peach Springs there they put me on a Train for Prescott and there I was put in Jail and I got a lawyer and gave him all of the money I had to defend me and things
and kindly I managed to see
so I told the ladies

Chapter 9: The Long Road to the Gallows 321

my onley chance was to get a way if I could so the only way was to go out at the Jale door and that I hated to do for the Jaler had always bin so kind to me but I thought we could attck him and not hirt him so we tackled him on the 9 day of may on Sunday a bout noon to git our liberty the only way to git a holt of him was for one to go after water so that put one man on the out side and he was to ketch the Jaler and the other 2 would run out and we would put him in side and lock him up and go (illegible) but we did not git him in for times got to (illegible) to waste there so we lit him go and left the Jale making for the stable to git horses that was 3 4 (illegible; possibly "hundred") yards a way but we made it all right and miller Jumped on a horse without a saddle and started out that left me and the other man there so I got a horse with a saddle on so I took the other man on behind me and lit out after miller so we went until we struck the out side of town ther the saddle turned with us and but I holt to the bridle and stoped the horse so we got the saddle on a gin and started on to Catch up with miller so we over halled him in a fue minits and he fell of his horse and said he was shot so bad that he could no travel so we left him in the brush in a bout 1 mile of town and we went on to make it we could so we went 12 or 15 miles and run into too officers they begin to shoot at us also finley they shot my pards horse and he started on a foot and they shot him in the leg so I turned to take him on behind me and I got a shot in the leg but I got him a behind and a way we went and we went 3 or 4 miles and saw that that would not do so I told him that one of us would hafto hide or they would catch us so he said that he would hide and I could go on so the way I went I road for 3 days and nights with out enny thing to eat and no hat so in that time I had reached the Bill Willims mountins so there I got a little grub and a hat and a gun and a way I went a gin so I travled north a cross a horse range for 30 or 40 miles with the shooes off of my horse or which I call my horse but it was the Sherffs horse so finley I turned for pine springs there I amed to change horses and git a beef so I made that Part of the country and killed a beef and took what I though I could use and then I struck Camp a way (illegible; back?) from the (illegible; matter?) and made no sine a round the (illegible; matter?) so ther I laid for 5 days then I Caught 2 horses and turned the one loose that I had road from Prescott and started northe east for for Colorado and made it for a bout 150 miles and noe one seen me that put me on the navihoe revashin and there I rode all night and at the brake of day I found my self in a indin Camp and in a bout 2 yards of a Store so I thought the best thing was to Put on a long (illegible; face?) and stop and git sum breakfast and a fue other things that I needed and tell them I was hunting horses so it went all right so I thought I got my stuff and lit out and travled about 75 miles that day and night and a bout 3 oclock I stoped and struck camp laid down and went to sleep and the first thing I knew I was waken by a shot so I Jumped up and grabed my gun but I could not see enny thing but I could hear them talking so my chance was small for I could tell that I was surondid by them so the only way was to give up so that I dun thinking maby I would git a Chance to git a way so they took me in there was 10 indins and one white man so back they went with me brought me back a bout 80 miles that day and there they met the Yavapie Shirff and too more Indin tralers so I seen it was off with me then for ther would be no chance to beat them so we stayed all night and started for Flagstaff the next morning so we made there by 5 or 6 oclock and I loged in Jale and was kept there a fue days and then took back to Prescott and loged in Jale a gin there

The document ends here, rather abruptly, unsigned, indicating that Parker may not have completed it, although if he wrote it shortly after his return to jail, there wouldn't have been much more to say.

Parker's version of his life story is difficult and frustrating to read. The document is, at different times, self-serving, seemingly honest, humble, proud, and boastful. Parker tries hard to depict himself as a poor victim of circumstances, yet is unable to restrain himself from bragging of his escapes, particularly from John Rogers.

Parker depicts himself as a simple ranchman who owned his horses and cattle, but yet felt the need to cryptically add that "there was partys that would say we had stold them." Parker denies participation in the Rock Cut Train Robbery, which is understandable since he was pleading Not Guilty at this time. But it is sad to note that he fails to even mention his shooting of Lee Norris in his account of the jailbreak. As he had pleaded Not Guilty to the murder charge, this may be understandable too, but Norris was still dead. Parker could have at least acknowledged an "unfortunate accident" during the jailbreak, but he fails to do so.

As seen in Chapter 1, a San Quentin prison record describes Parker's mental culture as "poor," and it is surely in evidence in this document. His spelling, grammar, and non-existent punctuation are bad even by the standards of illiteracy. He misspells words in one sentence, spells them correctly in another, and reverts to the incorrect spelling again later. He writes about things that seem to have no bearing on his story, as well as rinky-dink fights he was in.

The most interesting thing about Parker's account of his own life is his confession to participation in no less than two shooting incidents which are not reported anywhere else in Parker lore. One was at a dance in Fresno County wherein he said he was arrested but did no hard jail time. To date, I have not found any records of this incident. He also admits to having been involved in a saloon shooting in Los Angeles where he was apparently never wanted or suspected of participation. Without any further details on when this took place, it is impossible to determine which incident (undoubtedly one of many in those days) Parker was a party to, even if the action was reported in the newspapers.

It is interesting to note that Parker makes no mention of having known Sheriff Ruffner previously, even though strong circumstantial evidence suggests he did (see Chapter 2). Also, Parker corroborates Miller's contention that it was Sarata, not Miller, who was at the Lynx Creek firefight, even though the lawmen swore it was Miller they were shooting at. While I am still inclined to believe the lawmen, the truth will probably never be known for sure.

In summation, Parker's handwritten account of his own life is fascinating and disappointing at the same time. As a historical document, it is priceless, as very little exists of Parker's own words (and what little there is appears in this book). As far as insight into Parker goes, the document shows him to be a confused individual, with possible mental illness, affable in one sentence and sinister in another. Some of his writing is incoherent, but it obviously made sense to him at the time. The whole thing makes one wish for more, and there isn't any more.

In the late summer of 1897, a purported jailhouse interview with Parker went out over the wire services. It was unattributed, so I do not know its original source. So far, I have located it verbatim in the *Rock Island Argus* (from Rock Island, Illinois) of July 3, 1897; the *Roanoke Times* (from Roanoke, Virginia) of July 23, 1897; and the *Herald Democrat* (from Leadville, Colorado) of July 28, 1897. It did not appear in any Arizona newspapers.

This article makes some surprising allegations about Parker that appear nowhere else in Parker lore. Consequently, I am skeptical of the interview's content—did Parker really say such things? The text:

AN OUTLAW FOR LOVE

Jilted Jim Parker and His Lively
Career of Crime

A WILD CACTUS OF THE DESERT

His Daring Escape From an Arizona Jail
and His Reckless Ride, With the
Authorities of Three Counties on His Trail.
How They Ran Him Down.

"I've been brung up like a cactus, wild as they make 'em, and all my thorns set and I don't give a a ----- what they do with me, for it's an even toss whether it ain't as good to be under the earth as plunging around on top of it."

These are the sentiments of Jim Parker, train robber, murderer, and all round desperado. Jim is now safe in jail at Prescott, A.T., with indictments enough hanging over him to hang a dozen men.

He is a picturesque young ruffian, is Jim, both as to personal appearance and the choice of language. His career has been short, but tumultuous. It may be summed up briefly:

Jim Parker, born without regard to how the world might use him or he the world, at 12---alone and neglected---a weed by the wayside, trampled by the passerby; at 21, ignorant, audacious, savage, resentful of restraint, bittered; at 25 in love, with the wild sweeping passion of a strong nature unused to gentleness; at 26, with no star ahead and no memories to treasure, abandoned to the tide of recklessness, a convicted felon and an all round outlaw, with a heart for any fate.

Parker is a Californian. Thirty five years ago, on a little farm in Tulare county, he began life. Soon afterward his mother died, and when Jim was 12 years old his other parent expired, leaving the child nothing save debts and a worn out horse.

"For 23 years I've been alone, barring those two graves down in Tulare," says Jim, "and for 23 years I've been on the hustle."

But about his love affair. Little is known of that, for about it he will not talk. There are men whose love is fierce and changeless as the hate of an Apache. If it be hopeless, stand aside---something is certain to break. Jim Parker belongs to that class.

Somewhere in southern Utah lives a girl, Vole---he calls her---for whom his wild heart thrills. Vole does not care for Jim. It is not, however, that he is bad. She seems used to ill deeds and not disposed sharply to censure them, so they be bold and big.

After Vole said no and before he was 30, Jim drifted into Arizona. He had a way of acquiring horses and cattle bearing brands not his which brought him quickly into favor among frontier criminals, and before he had been in the territory six months he was the head of as ill-souled a gang of thieves as ever sat in saddles. Since then he has made Arizona his headquarters, and the criminal enterprises in which he is believed to have had a hand are so numerous that it isn't worth while to write them down. It will be sufficient to say that Jim was never known to neglect an opportunity, and that if any unfenced land has had more opportunities lying about than Arizona it ought to skip off the map.

The train robbery near Prescott on the 8th of last February may or may not have been the first job of the kind Parker undertook. He says nothing that throws any light on the subject, and the hold up was clever enough to an old hand at such business, and yet was not without features indicative of inexperience. For instance, it was a trifle bungling to let the messenger get the drop on Vole's brother, as Vole's brother doubtless thought as he quit thinking.

Parker was brought into Prescott from the Grand canyon on the 20th of February. On the 9th of May he escaped from jail.

"I wa'n't in a hurry," he said, when telling of the break, "because I didn't care a heap. I wa'n't much set on fussing about just to keep on breathing, but, of course, when a chance showed its head I somehow felt I might as well keep moving."

There were six prisoners in the plot to leave Prescott, though only three escaped. The break was planned for Saturday afternoon May 8, but Jailer Meadeor was attending strictly to business that afternoon, and the job had to be postponed.

Next day the opportunity came. Jailer Meadeor was on guard alone. A "trusty" prisoner--a Mexican named Cornelia--felled him, and as he did so Parker and a forger named Miller ran out. Cornelia followed.

After passing from the cage Jim Parker ran into the jailer's room and took possession of a double barrel shotgun. It was loaded with buckshot. Thus armed he dashed into the corridor of the courthouse, and while on the run caught sight of young Lee Norris on the stairs. Norris was assistant district attorney.

A moment later Norris was dead---shot by Parker.

He had come to the courthouse that afternoon to write a love letter to his sweetheart. It was found half finished on his desk, whence he had hurried, drawn by the cries of Meadeor.

The three criminals ran through the usual Sunday afternoon crowd near the courthouse, pursued by a fusillade of bullets from the jailer's revolver.

It takes a crowd a long time to collect its wits. Audacity stuns it, so no resistance was offered. The fugitives had an open path through the throng.

JIM PARKER ON THE RAMPAGE.

Unidentified artist's absurd sketch of "Jim Parker On The Rampage", which accompanied a highly dubious wire service story about Parker's purported girlfriend, "Vole". (author's collection)

Straight across the plaza they hastened and directly to the stables of the sheriff. The favorite horse of Mrs. Ruffner was standing there, saddled and bridled. Jim Parker jumped into the saddle, Miller clambered up behind him, and the Mexican got astride another horse. Then they raced away.

Not a hand was raised to stay them.

Jim Parker was in the lead, and he carried the shotgun at "ready", guiding the horse with his knees.

"We rode like h--l," said Jim, "and nobody cared to argy. I felt like a cyclone."

When it was all over and the three were out of Prescott and streaking for the hills, the crowd took a long breath, and about a half hour later the usual thing evolved---the posse.

Does anybody hear of "a posse" in these times without thinking of a body of cravens heavily armed and a safe distance behind?

The posse in this case was 100 strong, and not a soul hurt or was hurt.. But, Lord, how it threatened!

Parker met a traveler near Prescott.

"Stranger," said Jim, "back yan' you'll find a posse, I reckon. They think they're looking for us. I'm Jim Parker. Just tell them that you saw me."

About dusk two deputies of the sheriff---Mundo and Yeoman---overtook the runaways.

The officers opened fire at long range. Parker gave no answering shot. He had only one charge in his gun. The other had cut off a love letter. But he turned in his saddle and yelled defiance.

Two flashes and the roar of rifles.

The Mexican goes rolling in the dust. One bullet had pierced his thigh, the other had killed his horse.

Jim Parker, looking backward, called to the Mexican and leaped from the saddle. A ball plunked him in the leg, but he runs along to the heap in the dust and helps Cornelia to arise.

A few seconds later the wounded Mexican is behind Parker, Miller is riding the tail of Mrs. Ruffner's plucky horse, and the three refugees disappear.

Darkness had closed in, and the two deputies had failed.

Soon after the brush with the deputies, Parker rid himself of Miller and the Mexican and set to work to befog the pursuers.

"It was sort of recreation," said he. "I didn't care much if I was took, only I felt kind of duty bound to fool 'em if I could."

On Monday he traveled 45 miles from Prescott, and on Tuesday he journeyed back to within eight miles of his starting point, pursuing a bewilderingly circuitous route.

"Yes," said Jim, "I'm something of a mixer when it's wo'th while. I guess I must have shod that hoss as much as five times in two days."

At times the shoes of the horse were reversed, and at intervals Jim carried them in his coat pocket. It was not easy to follow him.

On the fourth day he reachhed the Bill William mountains, 80 miles north of Prescott. By that time the sheriffs of three counties, 50 other white men and a dozen expert Indian trailers were on the trail.

Of course he could not keep this up indefinitely. The end had to come sometime. It was when his horses were worn out and he himself was thoroughly fagged. He had thrown himself on the ground and gone to sleep. He woke to find himself in the center of a circle with ten rifles pointed at his heart.

Parker half arose and reached toward his shotgun. He glanced around the steel circle. Then he sat up, clasped his hands across his knees and exclaimed:

"Well, if this ain't h--ll!"

They bound Jim astride a horse and started for Flagstaff. On the way they met Ruffner.

"Old man," said Jim, "I'd like to plug you full of lead, but you see how I'm fixed."

When the party reached Prescott, a crowd of 500 persons was in waiting. It was in an ugly mood too. Crowds are ugly enough when a man like Parker is safely shackled.

There was talk of lynching, and Jim was not slow to hear the mutterings. He took off his hat and bowed in mockery of the multitude.

A few moments later he was within the cage whence he had escaped three weeks before.

"I reckon I'll swing all right enough," he said next day, "and I'm not saying I shouldn't. But I'm not the sort of fellow that steals from poor folks or does upon man on the quiet. I'd a heap rather I hadn't shot that boy, understand, and if I'd thought a second I wouldn't have plunked him."

This poorly written article is appalling, not only for its obvious factual inaccuracies on the events, but what about the interview? Did Parker really say these things? Based on what we have seen, the quotes do not even sound like him. And what of the other assertions—Parker entered a life of crime because a former girlfriend threw him over? And that the dead train robber was her brother??? Considering that Parker refused, even onto his own death, to reveal his partner's identity, it is difficult to believe he would say this to a reporter.

If Parker did make the statements attributed to him in this article, he probably decided to just have fun at the expense of a gullible reporter. But more likely, this dispatch is just a piece of "yellow journalism," crafted by a hack writer with an over-active imagination. I am suspicious of this article's veracity in all ways.

Parker was sentenced to hang on August 13, only a few weeks after his trial. But since he and his attorneys had announced their intention to appeal, most people knew that the execution would be postponed. In the meantime, the press was never very far away. Tidbits about Parker in jail, or various references to the case continued to appear in the *Journal Miner* and the *Courier*.

From the *Arizona Journal Miner* of June 30, 1897:

A letter was received at the sheriff's office yesterday from a Chicago woman, with an associated press telegram clipping from a Chicago paper giving an account of the conviction of Parker. The woman stated that her husband, James Parker, had left home four years ago, since which time she had heard nothing of him and was anxious to learn if the James Parker, convicted of the murder of Lee Norris, was her lost spouse. A photograph of her husband was also sent with the letter, but it bears no resemblance to James Fleming Parker.

From the *Prescott Courier*, July 2, 1897:

Young America is not so oblivious to passing events as the casual observer might suppose. A few days ago, in south Prescott, a horde of boys armed with paper cap exploding pistols, imitated the chase and capture of Outlaw Parker in quite a realistic manner. The chase took place through the bushy hills south of town, the boys rushing here and there through the brush, snapping their pistols whenever the supposed outlaw appeared in sight. The little boy who took the part of Parker led his comrades a long chase; in fact, he rather overexerted himself, as he had to stay in bed all the next day to recover from his fatigue.

From the *Journal Miner* of June 30, 1897:

The famous photo of Sheriff George C. Ruffner's prized white horse, Sure-Shot, taken after he was recovered from being stolen by Parker. (Courtesy of Sharlot Hall Museum)

Sheriff Ruffner expects to recover his famous white horse, which was ridden by Parker on his escape from jail, in a few days.

Sure-Shot had indeed been found, although exactly where is no longer known. As Parker no longer had the horse at the time of his capture, it is obvious he had let him go when the poor beast was too worn out to carry him any longer. Upon Sure-Shot's recovery, Sheriff Ruffner wasted no time in showing him off to an interested populace. From the *Courier* of June 15, 1897:

> Charlie Meadows is still bestirring himself to give a rousing wild west show in Prescott during the 4th of July celebration. Commodore Owens, Sheriff Ruffner, Virgil Earp and Frank Prothero, all men of note as criminal catchers and fighters, will ride as messengers in the Deadwood coach and Indian fight scene. The celebrated white horse, stolen by Parker, will also be in the melee. The coach to be used is an ancient Arizona relic; was driven in early days between Mohave and Prescott and shows scars of many a fight with bandits and Indians. The twenty Indians who will participate are of the Pima tribe, a tribe which has never received a dollar from the government and has never raised a hand against the whites.

From the *Journal Miner* of August 13, 1897:

> Sheriff Ruffner today took the famous white horse that Parker rode in his flight for freedom out on the hill and had a photo taken of him, from which an enlarged picture will be made. His arrival in Prescott has now been just a month since recovered, and appears to be again in good condition, and as full of spirit as ever, but the sheriff believes his staying powers are lacking. If there is anything sacred to Mr. And Mrs. Ruffner it is this animal, and he will never again be permitted to leave the city limits, or again be ridden on a long trip under any circumstances. He is certainly a noble beast, and no one knows it better than Parker, as the latter never took the bridle off him in four days and rode over 300 miles in that time without once feeding him. He should be pensioned like "Sandy," the famous horse of ex Sheriffs Mulvenon and O'Neill.

Parker's abuse of the horse demonstrated what he had sunk to. Once a highly respected ranch-hand who obviously took care of animals, to a killer who would let nothing stand in his way of escaping, not even taking the time to feed his escape animal. There is some strange irony here, in that some folklorists have tried to contend just the opposite in their after-the-fact accounts—that Parker cared for the horse so much that it slowed him down in his escape. Such is not the case.

From the *Journal Miner* of June 30, 1897:

> Parker's attorneys have filed notice of an appeal to the supreme court and have been granted thirty days to file bill of exceptions and statement of fact.

It is not widely remembered, but Parker, Abe Thompson, and Love Marvin were subsequently indicted on Federal charges in United States Court, of robbing the U.S. Mail, which was a Federal offense. As these were Federal charges, the plea bargain that Love Marvin had struck with the Territory was not applicable here. The Federal Grand Jury's report was printed in the July 21, 1897 *Journal Miner*. It is reprinted here in its entirety, simply because it evokes its era better than almost anything else:

> The United States grand jury submitted its final report yesterday and were discharged. The report is as follows:
> United States Grand Jury Room, Prescott, Arizona, July 13, 1897.
> To the Honorable J. J. Hawkins, Judge of the Fourth Judicial District in and for the Territory of Arizona:
> We, the United States Grand Jury impaneled in the above mentioned court for the adjourned term respectfully submit this our final report:
> We have examined a total of thirteen cases and have found true bills as follows:
> James Parker, for mail robbery.
> Abe Thompson, for mail robbery.
> Love Marvin, for mail robbery.
> John Lee, for selling liquor to Indians.
> Jose Sandoval, for selling liquor to Indians.
> J. F. W. Castillo, for selling liquor to Indians.
> We have dismissed five cases, as follows:
> H. L. Dyan, for selling liquor to Indians.
> Robert Meara, for selling liquor to Indians.
> Thomas Johnson, for selling liquor to Indians.
> Robert Brackett, for selling liquor to Indians.
> John Doe, for having unregistered still.
> We have referred the following cases to the next United States grand jury, the witnesses in those cases not being obtainable at the present time:
> Isidon Pens, selling liquor to Indians.
> John Daily, robbery on military reservation.
> Number of witnesses examined in above cases, thirty-one.

Ultimately, Parker, Thompson, and Marvin were never tried on the Federal charges, either. Thompson, who was in Yuma Territorial Prison on Territorial charges of train robbery, was the only one who ever served any hard prison time specifically for the Rock Cut Train Robbery.

The July 25, 1897 edition of the *San Francisco Call* printed an "amusing" tidbit regarding prisoner Jose Sandoval, mentioned above (and misspelled "Sandobal" in the article:

> Assistant United States Attorney Franklin, who returned yesterday from Prescott, whither he went to prosecute several cases against defendants accused of selling liquor to the Indians, brings with him the news of a very curious and painful mistake made by the jail officials there. Jose Sandobal, a Mexican, was convicted of selling liquor to the Hualapai and was sentenced to a short term in the penitentiary at Yuma. While still in jail awaiting transportation to Yuma, he asked that the sentence of the court be translated to him again, as he had imperfectly taken in its scope at the prior reading. The interpreter, a harness-maker named Calles, was sent for and given the document to read to Sandobal. Calles began reading, but before he had progressed very far Sandobal set up a tremendous howl and began dashing his head against the prison bars in a way that convinced his keepers that he had suddenly gone mad. It was some time before the prisoner could be quieted down, and then he asked piteously why he should be hanged for so small a crime as that of selling liquor to the Indian? This led to the discovery that the interpreter had been given the wrong document, and that he had been reading the death sentence of outlaw Jim Parker to the petty criminal. When the nature of the mistake was made known to Sandobal he laughed through his tears and declared that eighteen months at Yuma was like a perpetual siesta for him in comparison with Parker's sentence.

Or rather, it sounds more like the white jail officials were playing a practical joke on the beleaguered Mexican prisoner by switching the documents!

A few weeks after Parker's trial, Judge John J. Hawkins resigned his seat, although his reasons doubtlessly had nothing to do with the Parker case. From the *Courier* of July 23, 1897:

> Associate Justice Hawkins yesterday vacated his judicial seat in favor of Judge Sloan. Judge Hawkins is a democrat and Judge Sloan a republican; but, when a man occupies the position of a judge, he ceases to be a politician and bends his whole ability to the ends that justice may prevail in the court over which he is called to preside. This Judge Hawkins has done. No man can foretell his own future actions and is less able to foretell the future action of others; only by a review of a man's past actions can we judge him, while we hope the best for the future. Judge Sloan has not resided among us for a great while, but in that time he has won the utmost respect of all our citizens and the belief is general that he will fill his new position with credit to himself and to this section. He was sworn in yesterday morning by Judge Hawkins. Having taken his seat, Judge Sloan expressed his desire to consult the convenience of the attorneys in regard to court business. R. E. Morrison then arose and in a short talk paid a deserved complimentary tribute to the retiring judge and congratulated the bar upon the selection of Judge Sloan. Addresses in the same strain were delivered by ex Chief Justice Wright, Reese

Ling and Hon. T. G. Norris. Judge Sloan in reply thanked the attorneys for their courteous talks and expressed his high appreciation thereof, as did, also, Judge Hawkins, who followed Sloan, in a farewell talk from the bench.

From the *Journal Miner* of August 4, 1897:

The death watch over Parker has been discontinued, Judge Sloan deeming it unnecessary and expensive in view of the appeal going to the next supreme court, which meets in January.

On August 13, 1897, the *Courier* reprinted the minutes from a meeting of the Yavapai County Board of Supervisors, which included the following:

The bill of G. C. Ruffner for sheriff's fees, salaries, etc., for second quarter of 1897, amounting to $9,621.10, less $300, advanced by order of the court, was checked and on motion said claim was audited for $5,352.25 less the following $300, advanced by order of court, $200 advanced by board of supervisors, (transporting prisoners) and $59.80 for telegrams regarding prisoners escaped from county jail; paid by Board of Supervisors, leaving balance due G. C. Ruffner, $4,792.45.

From the *Journal Miner* of August 18, 1897 (obviously reprinted from the August 13 daily edition:

Today was the date originally fixed for the execution of Parker, the train robber and murderer of Lee Norris. Having taken an appeal to the supreme court, however, he is still in the enjoyment of his usual good health, his address being, County Jail, Prescott, Ariz.

From the *Journal Miner* of August 25, 1897:

A picture of Sheriff Ruffner's white horse, ridden by Parker in his efforts to escape from the officers, is on exhibition in Cook's jewelry store window.

On August 24, 1897, the *Arizona Republican* in Phoenix printed a fascinating article giving some first-hand insight into how the cowboys in Northern Arizona helped Parker to escape from the posse after the jailbreak:

HE WAS PARKER'S FRIEND

A Man Who Entertained Professor Creager on His Late Outing

Professors W. B. Creager and H. H. Brown returned on Sunday from an overland trip and outing in and about Flagstaff. Both are thoroughly tanned and one of them, Professor Creager, is repentant. He will never go abroad again in this fashion. He lost a horse and wandered about over the desert until he lost the directions and then himself. He left his fate to the superior judgment of a horse he was riding and was taken one afternoon to the ranch of a man named Jones who treated him hospitably and the next morning put him on the right road. He was surprised to learn that Jones was an old partner and warm friend of Parker, the convicted murderer, who, he says, is one of the noblest men God ever made. Jones said that Parker would have gotten away safely but for two things. The first was the killing of Norris. When Parker came among his friends on the range after his escape they held a meeting to consider the advisability of affording him active assistance. They decided that inasmuch as he had killed Norris the reward likely to be offered would be so high as to excite betrayal. Then again some of the cowboys were indignant because he had committed a needless murder and were apathetic regarding his fate. He remained with them some days and rode with them on the range. Jones believes that if he had stayed among them he might never have been taken and that his fatal mistake was made in trying to leave the country too soon.

Meanwhile, jailor Robert Meador continued to have trouble with his prisoners. From the *Courier* of October 15, 1897:

Saturday morning last, when Jailor Meador unlocked the jail and threw open the windows in the larger room in which Antone Rossi and several other prisoners were confined, he noticed Rossi standing by the sink and supposed he was washing himself, as Rossi stepped around to the end of the sink. When Meador went out the other prisoners called him back and directed his attention to Rossi's condition. He found that Rossi had broken an electric light globe during the night and attempted to kill himself with the broken glass. There was a four inch gash in his throat, which had severed his windpipe and he breathed through the gash; there were four gashes across the abdomen, through which the entrails protruded. Dr. McNally was called and sewed the man's wounds together; 12 stitches were taken in the throat and six in the abdomen. Rossi was taken to the county hospital. Report was, last evening, that he would recover if no complicating features appeared. It is also stated Rossi mixed a cup full of chloride of lime and drank it. The lime was in the jail for disinfecting purposes. Rossi was under arrest for assaulting his wife with a deadly weapon. His preliminary examination was to have taken place Saturday.

This coming on top of the Parker jailbreak must have been too much for Meador. He resigned shortly after. From the *Courier* of January 7, 1898:

R. W. Meador, who for five years past has filled the position of jailor and janitor of the county court house, has resigned that position. The position has never been filled by a more upright, faithful and highly respected man. It is safe to say that he has not been outside the walls of the court house over half an hour at a time during his incumbency of the position vacated.

The Parker story took a strange turn in January of 1898—Parker was caught planning another escape attempt. From the *Journal Miner* of January 12, 1898:

If current street rumors are true it seems that Jim Parker, the train robber and murderer, now in the jail under sentence of death for the latter crime, has not all the confidence in the world of the supreme court saving his neck. It is stated that a short time ago he succeeded in getting a file and with it cut one of the links of his shackles apart. Is was discovered though before he could take any advantage of it.

The rumors interested the *Courier*, which prompted them to go looking for more details. From their January 14, 1898 edition:

As various newspapers at hand contain a statement as to Outlaw Parker having filed his shackles off a few days ago, the reporter asked for particulars at the sheriff's office and learned that, on the 7th of last month it was discovered that Parker had filed a link in the chain connecting the shackles on his ankles. This link was filed from the end of the chain, the chain being refastened to the shackle by a stout string, so that the outlaw could walk around and seem securely hobbled. As he was in the habit of wearing rags about the ankle shackles, the rags covered the string which took the place of the filed away link, the absence of which could only be noticed on close inspection. The day the absence of the link was discovered, another prisoner was having shackles riveted upon him, when the officers inspected Parker's shackles and saw that he was tied only with a string. Parker laughed and said: "Well, boys, the hoss is on me this time." A larger and stronger pair of shackles was placed upon the desperate man.

From the same edition:

Outlaw Parker has had his shackles inspected daily since the new pair was placed upon him after he had filed the old ones in two.

The case dragged on.

The date for the Territorial Supreme Court to hear Parker's appeal was January 24, 1898. Interestingly, the attorneys on both sides of the case during Parker's trial were destined to repeat their roles before the High Court. Such appeals were handled then in pretty much the same fashion as they are today, which may surprise some people. Both sides filed briefs stating their positions (this also included the transcript of the original trial), and attorneys for both sides would present oral arguments before the High Justices. Then, the justices would consider the matter, and issue their ruling weeks or even months later.

From the *Arizona Gazette* of January 20, 1898:

THE PARKER CASE.

It May Be Prosecuted by District Attorney Ross.
The appeal case of Parker, the condemned murderer of Yavapai county, will come up in the supreme court on the 24th. The territory's interests have been conducted by District Attorney H. D. Ross of Yavapai county, under and by virtue of the supervision of Attorney General Frazier. The territory's brief was gotten up by Mr.

Ross and will be filed in a few days. Mr. Ross, if he so desires, will conduct the oral argument at the hearing on the 24th.

"I believe in letting these ambitious young district attorneys have a chance to win their spurs," explained Attorney General Frazier Tuesday.

Parker seeks to escape the death sentence on entirely technical grounds. One of the points his attorneys raise is that he was denied the full privilege of the law in the matter of jury challenges.

From the *Gazette* of January 23, 1898:

H. D. Ross, district attorney of Yavapai county, arrived in the city Friday night to remain some days attending to legal business. He is an able lawyer and looks carefully after the interests of the people of his county, who elected him by an unusually large majority. He will make the oral argument in the supreme court Monday in the Parker murder case. His brief, filed this week, in the same action, is said to be an able presentation of the case.

From the *Prescott Courier* of January 26, 1898:

J. E. Morrison and G. Arthur Allen, attorneys in the Parker case, leave tomorrow morning for Phoenix to represent their client before the supreme court. These gentlemen were appointed by the court to defend Parker, a defense wherein there is no compensation. They are making a good fight for their client.

From the *Arizona Journal Miner* of February 2, 1898:

George A. Allen was admitted to practice before the supreme court on Monday.

The same edition also reprinted an article from the *Arizona Republican* on the proceedings before the High Court:

PARKER'S CASE HEARD

The Slayer of Norris Had His Day in Supreme Court
The case of James F. Parker, appellant, vs the Territory of Arizona, respondent from Yavapai county, was partially argued in supreme court yesterday. This is the celebrated case of Parker, the train robber and murderer, under sentence of death at Prescott for the killing of Lee Norris last summer. Messrs. J. E. Morrison and George A. Allen appeared for the appellant. Both are young men. They were appointed to the defense of Parker and though they were not inspired by a big retainer, they conducted the case as skillfully and energetically as if a fee were in sight. They created a splendid impression in court yesterday and if Parker goes to the gallows he will go with the assurance that his last earthly business was not neglected.

The respondent was represented by District Attorney Ross of Yavapai county and Attorney General Frazier. The prayer of the appellant for a reversal of the judgment of the lower court is based on several allegations, some of which are startling and unusual. It is charged in the first place that the feeling and animus of the trial judge were manifested in his instructions to the jury; second, that the prisoner was brought into court shackled; third, that he had not been held to the grand jury for murder, but for train robbery; fourth that the court erred in overruling a motion for a change of venue made up on the ground of the inflamed popular feeling at Prescott at the time of the trial; and fifth, that the circumstances of the killing of Norris did not warrant a verdict of murder in the first degree.—Republican

From the *Arizona Gazette* of January 29, 1898:

George Arthur Allen sent an encouraging telegram last night to his client, Jim Parker, from Phoenix. He expected to have the case submitted today, and expressed hopes of a favorable result.

And Parker's day in the High Court was over, just like that. Nothing to do now but wait for the Court to hand down its decision, which would be at least several weeks in the future. From the *Prescott Courier* of January 26, 1898:

Attorneys Geo. Arthur Allen and Jos Morrison returned from Phoenix on yesterday morning's taxless.

Incidentally, substituting the word "taxless" for train was a political statement by the *Courier* over a topical issue that is not worth explaining here. They did it everytime they had to write about a train.

As with lower courts, the transcript of the hearing before the Arizona Supreme Court has not survived. However, the legal briefs have, and they make fascinating reading. As noted in the papers, Parker's attorneys, Allen and Morrison, appealed his conviction and death sentence on some unusual grounds, and never once did they try for sympathy from the Court (undoubtedly this was Parker's wish). This appeal argued simply that due to prevailing sentiment in Yavapai County, Parker had been denied simple rights that every other accused murderer was receiving.

Reprinted here, for the first time that I know of since 1898, is the appeal brief filed on Parker's behalf by attorneys George Allen and Joseph E. Morrison:

In The
SUPREME COURT
Of the
TERRITORY OF ARIZONA

JAMES F. PARKER
(Indicted as James Parker),
Appellant,

Vs.
TERRITORY OF ARIZONA,
Appellee,

The Defendant was indicted, without having been held to answer on the charge of murder, tried and convicted of the crime of murder in the first degree and sentenced to suffer the death penalty, at the June, 1897, term of the District Court, of Yavapai County, Arizona.

The following is a brief statement of the record so far as it is essential to the questions hereinafter presented:

At folio 1, of printed Abstract, Defendant was brought before the Grand Jury and J. E. Morrison and G. Arthur Allen were appointed to represent him as his attorneys.

At folio 10, Defendant was brought into open court for arraignment, in shackles; Court's attention directed to the fact, and Defendant's motion that they be removed denied; exception.

At folio 4, Defendant moved to set aside the indictment against him and offered to introduce evidence to substantiate the allegations contained in said motion; motion overruled and offer to introduce evidence denied; exception noted.

At folio 6, demurrer to indictment filed overruled and Defendant excepted.

At folio 6, motion for change of venue filed, argued, submitted and overruled; Defendant's exception noted.

At folio 6, testimony was taken on the trial and various exceptions to rulings were noted by Defendant, as appears from the statement of facts.

At folio 8, verdict of jury finding Defendant guilty of murder in the first degree and fixing the death penalty.

At folio 9, Defendant's motion for a new trial overruled and Defendant excepted.

At folio 9, Defendant's motion in Arrest of Judgment overruled and Defendant excepted.

At folio 9, Defendant filed written notice of appeal.

Assignment of Errors

The Appellant avers that there is error in said judgment and proceedings in this, to-wit:

ASSIGNMENT OF ERROR 1.

The Court erred in his charge to the Grand Jury.

ASSIGNMENT OF ERROR 2.

That the Court erred in denying Defendant's motion to have shackles removed from Defendant when he appeared in open court, upon his arraignment.

ASSIGNMENT OF ERROR 3.

That the Court erred in overruling Defendant's motion to set aside the indictment and offer to introduce testimony to substantiate the allegations in said motion contained.

ASSIGNMENT OF ERROR 4.

That the Court erred in overruling Defendant's motion for a change of venue.

ASSIGNMENT OF ERROR 5.

That the Court erred in refusing to instruct the jury as requested in Defendant's Instruction I.

ASSIGNMENT OF ERROR 6.

That the verdict found by the jury was contrary to the law and the evidence, in that the evidence does not support the verdict for the reason that no premeditation or malice of any character was shown.

ASSIGNMENT OF ERROR 7.

That the Court erred in overruling Defendant's motion for a new trial.

ASSIGNMENT OF ERROR 8.

That the Court erred in overruling Defendant's motion in Arrest of Judgment.

Defendant's Brief and Argument

The record shows that on the 9th day of May, 1897, in the City of Prescott, County of Yavapai and Territory of Arizona, a young man named E. L. Norris was shot, and subsequently, on said day, died from the effect of said shooting.

This Defendant, with one L. C. Miller and Cornelia Sarata, was accused of the crime of murdering said Norris.

On the 7th day of June, 1897, in the presence of the panel of trial jurors, summoned to try all causes at said term of court, the Trial Judge delivered the charge to the Grand Jury complained of in Assignment of Error 1.

At that time the blood of the unfortunate Norris was yet warm upon the Courthouse steps. The Grand Jurors, as well as the Trial Jurors, were immersed in a sea of popular prejudice and blinded by the spray of universal animosity against this Defendant. The strong and determined language of the Court certainly impressed upon the Grand Jurors the fixed conviction that it was their bounden duty to indict **this Defendant of this crime**, and as a result of the Court's charge ("I charge you, gentlemen, now, at this session of the Grand Jury, **the very first thing** you do, that you investigate the recent outbreak in the jail of this County, and that you investigate it thoroughly * * * and bring an indictment into this Court against each and every person committed therewith, so that the parties who committed the offense of killing one of your best citizens, here, right in the very hall of justice, may be brought to justice." * * *) within twenty minutes after their retirement, within the hour that said charge was delivered, the Grand Jury returned into court the indictment in this case.

We say that the said charge was a direct command; that the Grand Jury should investigate this matter **first** and that they should indict all persons connected therewith, and that the language as used tended to inflame the minds of the Grand Jurors against this Defendant, and the extraordinarily brief time spent by the Grand Jury in the investigation of such an important matter demonstrated the fact that said charge had the desired effect.

Within one-half hour after the indictment was returned into court the Defendant was brought into open court and placed upon his attempted arraignment. At that time he was shackled with steel chains. On the following day said Defendant was again produced in open court in a manacled and shackled condition, his lower limbs being bound together with steel fetters. The Defendant at that time, by counsel, directed the attention of the Trial Judge to his manacled condition and moved the Court that he direct the Sheriff to remove the shackles from his person, which motion was by the Court overruled and Defendant excepted. (Abstract of Record, folio 11.)

We contend that the action of the Court in overruling the last mentioned motion was palpable error, prejudicial to this Defendant. It is a well-settled rule of criminal law that every man charged with crime must be allowed the use of all his powers and faculties in his own defense when in open court upon the charge. The bringing of a man into court in fetters stamps upon him the brand of infamy, bearing as he does the symbol of the felon, impresses the common mind with a belief that he is a desperado or dangerous character, and arouses a prejudice and animosity against him. It violates one of his most sacred constitutional prerogatives.

'He has a right to appear in person, free from shackles and bonds.'
A & E Ency. Law, vol. , p. 812
People vs. Harrington, 42 Col. 168

As appears in Assignment of Error 3, upon the 9th day of June, 1897, this Defendant was again brought into open court for the purpose of pleading to the indictment and by counsel filed a motion to set aside the indictment herein, which said motion set forth that Defendant had never been held to answer upon the charge preferred against him in said indictment and that a state of mind existed and did exist at the time of the finding of the said indictment and prior thereto on the part of each and every of the Grand Jurors composing the Grand Jury which returned said indictment, in reference to this case and to the said Defendant, which prevented them and each of them from acting impartially in this case and without prejudice to the substantial rights of this Defendant, and for the further reason that said indictment does not purport to show the names of the witnesses who were examined before the Grand Jury upon the finding of this indictment, and thereupon Defendant offered to submit evidence to substantiate the allegation in said motion contained, and the Court then and there overruled said motion and denied said offer to produce testimony, to both of which latter rulings Defendant, then and there, in open court, excepted.

The Defendant was but invoking one of the fundamental safeguards of the criminal law, a right guaranteed him by our Penal Code, that of challenge to the Grand Jurors, on any ground which would have been good before the finding of the indictment, when the Defendant has not been held to answer.

As to the correctness of our position in asserting that there is prejudicial error in the last above mentioned action of said Court, we refer with absolute confidence to paragraph 1,513, subdivision 4, of the Penal Code of Arizona, which reads:

'The indictment MUST be set aside by the Court in which the Defendant is arraigned, upon his motion, in either of the following cases. If it be an indictment: * * *

"4—When the Defendant had not been held to answer before the finding of the indictment, on any ground which would have been good ground for challenge, either to the panel or to any individual Grand Juror."

The only method which the Defendant had of claiming his privilege of challenge to the Grand Jury, he never having been before that body upon the charge of murder, was by motion to set aside the indictment on statutory grounds, and the offer to introduce evidence to prove the allegations in said motion was in strict accordance with section 1.388, Penal Code, which says:

"The challenge mentioned in the three preceding sections may be oral or in writing and MUST BE TRIED BY THE COURT."

The ground of challenge to the individual members of the Grand Jury is statutory, according to section 1.387, subdivision 5, Penal Code, which is as follows:

"That a state of mind exists on his part in reference to the case or to either party which satisfies the Court, in the exercise of a sound discretion, that he cannot act impartially and without prejudice to the substantial rights of the party challenging."

As to the authorities sustaining this proposition, we refer primarily to the section of our Penal Code cited above; also to

People vs. Travers, 83 Col. 236.

People vs. Turner, 39 Col, 370.

The above cases clearly show that the facts which would entitle the Defendant to have the indictment set aside must be established by evidence or other proof. The action of the Court, while the Grand Jury was then in session, in denying the Defendant's offer to introduce evidence was manifestly in violation of this principle and of section 1.388, Penal Code, which says: "The challenge shall be TRIED by the Court." Defendant was thereby prevented from showing, by affirmative testimony, that he was never held to answer on the charge preferred against him in the indictment, and was never afforded an opportunity of challenge to that body upon said charge. If such were the fact, it will hardly be contended but that it was his statutory privilege to have the indictment set aside "upon any ground which would have been good ground for challenge."

We therefore say, and we urge, this proposition with all seriousness and sincerity upon this Honorable Court, that there was grave error in the ruling of the lower Court and thereby this Defendant had torn from under him one of the foundation stones of the structure of the criminal law, erected that every man shall have a fair and impartial trial when charged with crime, and shall be tried by a fair and impartial jury of his peers. This privilege is guaranteed him by the Constitution of the United States.

This flagrant violation of the law and utter disregard of this Defendant's rights is in exact keeping with the charge delivered by the Court to the Grand Jury (Assignment of Error 1), the almost indecent haste of the Grand Jury in charging and indicting this Defendant with this crime, and the subsequent appearance in open court of this Defendant manacled and shackled with bonds of steel.

This Defendant, as appears from his said motion to set aside the indictment herein, had never been charged with the murder of E. L. Norris by any court of competent jurisdiction. He was therefore without notice that this heinous charge had been preferred against him. Had he been advised that he was charged with this crime of murder he would unquestionably have exercised his right of challenge to the Grand Jurors, for he subsequently, by said motion alleges each and every of said Grand Jurors to have been prejudiced against him.

Subsequently this Defendant moved the Court that it grand a change of venue, on the ground that a fair and impartial trial of the charge against him could not be had in Yavapai County, and asked that the case be removed for trial to some county free from like objection.

The attention of Your Honors is respectfully, but urgently, directed to this motion. It is in statutory form, verified by this Defendant, and sets up numerous acts on the part of inhabitants of Yavapai County, Arizona, demonstrating that a feeling of bitter personal animosity existed towards this Defendant.

A few of the uncontradicted facts set forth in said motion are that the deceased, Norris, was a young man belonging to a prominent family of Yavapai County and was the Assistant District Attorney at the time of his death. That the charge of the Trial Judge, hereinbefore complained of, was delivered to the Grand Jurors, in the presence of the panel of Trial Jurors; that the Defendant was brought into open court shackled and in chains; the action of the Court in denying Defendant's offer to submit evidence in support of his motion to set aside the indictment; that immediately after the death of said Norris rewards aggregating thousands of dollars were offered for the apprehension of this Defendant, dead or alive; that when this Defendant was brought to Prescott, after having been taken into custody, a large mob of the inhabitants were assembled at the County Jail, and that were it not for the resistance made by the Sheriff and his numerous deputies, who were armed with Winchesters, shotguns and six-shooters, that said mob would have taken this Defendant and without warrant or authority of law, would have hanged him; that upon the occasion of this Defendant being taken from the courtroom, after having been arraigned, a large and tumultuous crowd was present, and threats and cries of "Hang him!" were then and there openly made.

The application was supported by the affidavits of M. L. O'Mailia, R. C. Welch, E. S. Clark, G.A. Allen and J. E. Morrison.

The paucity of corroborative affidavits is one of the strongest reasons why the allegations of the application are absolutely true.

As shown by the sworn statements of G. A. Allen and J. E. Morrison, attorneys for Defendant, a large number of the citizens and inhabitants of Yavapai County were approached and requested to make affidavits to the fact that this Defendant could not have a fair and impartial trial in Yavapai county, and that while they admitted that it was not possible that Defendant could have a fair and impartial trial, yet said that Defendant was guilty and should be hung anyhow.

As officers appointed by the Trial Court to represent this Defendant and see to it that his legal safeguards and prerogatives shall not be infringed upon, the attorneys in this matter felt bound to show to the Court the tremendous and universal prejudice which existed against this Defendant on account of his being charged with this murder.

Great confidence should be reposed in the affidavits of counsel appointed by the Court without compensation.

State vs. Mooney, 10 Iowa 506

The City of Prescott and the entire county of Yavapai was engulfed in a seething whirlpool of bitter prejudice, determined hostility and revengeful desire against this Defendant. Jurors brought from distant portions of the County could not possibly remain in the County Seat a day without being impregnated and saturated with the prevailing sentiment which was the only topic of conversation for weeks before the trial of this case. Threats were openly made to the attorneys in this case that if there was any considerable delay in the hanging of defendant that he would be taken from the county jail and lynched, all of which appears in the record of this case in the affidavits on motion for change of venue.

The affidavits presented by the Territory resisting said motion do not deny, specifically, the facts alleged in the sworn application. Certain parties testify to the conclusion that the defendant could have a fair and impartial trial. They allege no facts why it was so. On the contrary, the showing made by the defendant states innumerable facts, positively, from which no reasonable conclusion can be reached except as set forth in said application and affidavits.

The opportunities of the defendant's lawyers, engaged as they were in the performance of a sworn trust imposed upon them no officers of the Trial Court, and the diligence used by them in attempting to obtain corroborative proof of defendant's application show that they were much better qualified to testify to the almost unprecedented and universal prejudice and animosity which existed against this defendant than were the parties who made affidavits as against the application.

We direct your attention to the following authorities upon the action of the Court in overruling this motion.

State vs. Greer, 28 S. Va., 800
State vs. Hamilton, 10 Ind., 182.
State vs. Mooney, 10 Iowa, 506
Richmond vs. State, 10 Neb., 308
State vs. Nash, 7 Iowa, 347.
All of above authorities can be found in vol. 3, A. & E. Ency. Of Law, 97-99.
Steagal vs. State, 22Tex., App. 464.
Also cited in vol. 4, Ency. P. and P., p. 401

At this point we respectfully insist, in view of the positive showing made by defendant on his motion for a change of venue, that your Honors carefully scrutinize each and every act of the trial Judge from his forcible charge to the Grand Jury, in the presence of the panel of trial jurors down to the overruling of the last above mentioned motion. It is incumbent upon this Court to see that every material right of a defendant is protected; that his constitutional prerogatives are not ruthlessly torn from him, leaving him open to the tender mercies of an infuriated populace, groping in the bloody mist of deep-rooted and revengeful bias and animosity until, stricken down in the open field, reft of his constitutional safeguards and statutory protections, he falls a victim to the unreasoning wrath of a prejudiced community.

The Court erred in refusing defendant's instruction 1: "The Court instructs the jury that under the evidence in this case no deliberation or premeditation relating to the killing of the deceased, E. L. Norris, has been proven by the prosecution. The Court therefore instructs the jury that the Defendant in this case cannot lawfully be found guilty of murder in the first degree."

Act 17, page 52, Session Laws of Arizona, 1897, defines murder in the first degree as follows:

"All murder which is perpetrated by means of poison or lying in wait, or by any other kind of willful, deliberate and premeditated killing, or which is committed in the perpetration of an attempt to perpetrate arson, rape, robbery, burglary or mayhem is murder in the first degree, and all other kinds of murder are of the second degree."

The witness, Robert Meador, (pages 1, — — 13, Transcript of testimony) is the only eyewitness of the homicide produced by the prosecution. His testimony shows, if taken as wholly true, that no lapse of time whatever occurred between the time that Parker saw Norris and the firing of the fatal shot; that not a single word was spoken by any one present.

"Q.— How long a space of time occurred between the time that Parker came to the door of your room and saw the deceased coming downstairs and the time that the shot was fired, as you say?"

"A.— It was a very short time; he just came walking out of my room and shot. * *

"Q.— The fact of the matter is, just as soon as he saw Norris, he raised the gun and shot; is that your statement?

"A.— That is my idea of it, yes, sir.

(Pages 8 and 9. Transcript of Testimony: Meador's testimony.)

Probably no rule of criminal law is better settled than that premeditation or deliberation requires time, however short, before it can exist.

The testimony here discloses the fact that the defendant fired immediately upon seeing Norris and therefore the accessory elements of murder in the first degree, premeditation and deliberation, were wholly lacking in this killing. No malice, premeditation or motive is shown by the prosecution, and it will not be contended that the homicide was committed in the commission of any of the felonies set forth in said Act 17, Session Laws, 1897.

To sustain this position we rely upon the California rule as expressed in the following cases:

People vs. Dugull, 48 Cal, 85.

People vs. Williams, 73 Cal., 351.

People vs. Long, 39 Cal., 695.

The verdict returned by the Jury in this case (folio 8, abstract of record: assignment of error 6) is contrary to the law and the evidence.

The testimony of Meador (Transcript of Testimony, pages 7-8) shows that at the time the shot was fired, the blood was flowing from a gash in his forehead, down Meador's forehead and into his eyes. Meador says that he could not see as well then as he ordinarily could. He had been struck a violent blow upon the forehead with a key six or seven inches long. He was struggling with the Mexican (Transcript of Testimony, p. 9).

"There was a great deal of blood in his eyes; he was a good shot with a six shooter at a mark; he fired three shots at the Mexican at a distance of twelve and did not hit him; pistol targets are not as large as a man's body."

The conviction in this case is based upon the testimony of Meador. He was the only man who testified that Parker fired the fatal shot. Consider his condition at the time, according to his own statements. After having been struck over the head with a large jail key, with the blood streaming down into his eyes, and while struggling with a desperate Mexican he states that Parker fired the fatal shot, and yet directly afterwards at a range of twelve feet, although admittedly he is a good shot with a six-shooter, he is unable to hit the body of a man, while firing three shots at him.

And Parker was not the only man there besides the Mexican. Meador says (Transcript of testimony, p. 3);

"They passed on and went into my room, Parker and Miller."

As before referred to in the brief, according to Meador, Parker just came out of his (Meador's) room and fired. Therefore, Meador could have had but one brief glimpse of the man who fired the shot. Is it possible that a man in the condition in which Meador describes himself would have been able to state positively whether it was Parker or Miller who fired the fatal shot?

As to the condition of Meador's eyes at that time we refer to the testimony of witness P. J. Farley (Transcript of testimony, pages 17-18), who says that when he saw Meador upstairs in the hallway of the Court House, about two minutes after he heard the first cries from below, he was rubbing the blood out of his eyes.

Again in the dying declaration testified to by John C. Herndon (Transcript of testimony, p. 28) the deceased said: "I know it is one of two men, I don't know who it was; it was EITHER Parker or Miller."

We assert, and in this assertion we place implicit reliance in the unimpeachable integrity and wisdom of this Honorable Court, that such is not the class of testimony that will doom an American citizen to the felon's death upon the scaffold. The Territory must make out it's case, clearly and beyond a reasonable doubt.

As a matter of personal privilege we show to this Court that we were appointed by the lower Court, and it then became our sworn duty to defend this Defendant and to see to it that if he were convicted, such conviction should be obtained under the strict rule of the criminal law. We have brought this case here, not under a mistaken belief that every murder case must be appealed, but in the honest and firm conviction that the Court below has grievously erred and infringed upon the rights accorded a man charged with a criminal offence, in the several rulings complained of.

We are here as the last barrier which stands between this man and the shameful annihilation of a condemned murderer. We keenly feel and have diligently sought to perform the duty which the lower Court saw fit to repose in attorneys as young as ourselves, and we ask your Honors, respectfully but urgently, that you overlook our many errors, which undoubtedly appear in this brief; that you give careful consideration to the points suggested herein, and that you render such a decision as will comport with this Court's well-known character as the arbiter of the destiny of human affairs in our beloved Territory.

We ask that the judgment herein be reversed and that the cause be remanded for a new trial.

All of which is respectfully submitted.

J. E. Morrison
G. A. Allen
Attorneys for Appellant

Some of this, particularly the argument on premeditation, or lack thereof, is legally solid, but Parker's crime had so horrified the populace that it was pretty certain no court would have ever listened to this. The most embarrassing thing about this brief is Allen and Morrison once again trotting out the rumor that Sheriff Ruffner had stared down an angry lynch mob when he brought the prisoners back to Prescott. Everyone knew the story wasn't true, and it is a mystery why Allen and Morrison persisted in this.

Henry D. Ross, representing the Territory, filed his brief of rebuttal to all of the points, and it is reprinted here:

In The
SUPREME COURT
Of The
TERRITORY OF ARIZONA
January Term, 1898

JAMES F. PARKER
Appellant.
Vs.
TERRITORY OF ARIZONA
Respondent

Respondent's Brief and Argument

C. M. FRAZIER,
Attorney-General
H. D. ROSS,
District Attorney Yavapai
County, Ariz..
P. W. O'SULLIVAN,
Assistant District Attorney
Yavapai County, Ariz.
ATTORNEYS FOR RESPONDENT

Filed January 2nd, 1898,
L. Johnston
Clerk

In The
SUPREME COURT
Of The
TERRITORY OF ARIZONA
JANUARY TERM, 1898

JAMES F. PARKER, }
(Indicted as James Parker), }
Applicant, }
Vs. }
TERRITORY OF ARIZONA, }
Respondent, }

Respondent's Brief and Argument.

I.

The Territory of Arizona, Respondent herein, desires to make the point that the Supreme Court, upon the record as it appears before it now, can do no more than examine into the sufficiency of the indictment upon which the Defendant was tried. The Appellant undertaken to perfect his appeal under Act No. 71, entitled "An Act Relating to Appeals and Writs of Error from the District and Circuit Courts of the Territory to the Supreme Court 1897." And in pursuance of the requirements of that act have filed what purports to be an "Abstract of Record" and a "Statement of Facts," "Assignment of Errors and Brief." There is no bill of exceptions nor any proper statement of facts in the record as provided by paragraph 1870, Penal

Code of Revised Statutes of Arizona, 1887. Our contention is that the Act of 1897 applies solely to civil actions. This we say is evident because it provides for appeals or writ of error, and calls the parties "appellant or plaintiff in error." Right of appeal or write of error is a statutory right. Writs of error and assignments of error have never been known in the jurisprudence of criminal law, especially in this Territory. In civil procedure on appeal, Revised Statutes of Arizona, 1887, writs of error and assignments of error are especially provided for. Plaintiffs in error are there provided for. Paragraph 847, Revised Statutes, 1887, is "the party taking the appeal is called the appellant, the adverse party the appellee, Paragraph 848 is, "the party suing out a writ of error is called the plaintiff in error, the adverse party the defendant in error." In the Penal Code, paragraph 1,863 provides, "the party appealing is known as the appellant and the adverse party as the respondent." The Act of 1897 provides that the testimony "shall become a part of the record in said CAUSE;" cause of action means a controversy between individuals, because we demur to a complaint for the reason "that it fails to state facts sufficient to constitute a cause of action." We demur to an indictment for the reason "that it does not state facts sufficient to constitute any offence under the law." To hold that the Act of 1897 applies to appeals in criminal cases does violence to the language therein employed, besides requiring the clerk of the court wherein the case was tried to hazard the loss of the indictment—a most sacred paper—by sending it through the mails to the seat of the Supreme Court. Bonds of recognizance must suffer the same chances of loss.

For the reasons above stated we contend that the Court's investigation and examination of this case should be confined to the indictment and its sufficiency. If the indictment is found good then this appeal should be dismissed.

II.

The following is what we find to be, in succinct form, the facts as developed at the trial: The record shows that on May 9th, A. D., 1897, at about 1 o'clock p.m. Jailor Meador of the Yavapai County jail, opened the door of said jail for the purpose of permitting a certain Mexican prisoner (Cornelia Sarata) to enter the jail with a bucket of water. The Mexican grappled Meador as he was opening the door and a fierce struggle ensued, during which struggle Appellant Parker and one L. C. Miller escaped from the jail. During the scuffle between the jailor and said Mexican, the jailor cried for assistance; and one E. L. Norris, then in the District Attorney's office, in the same building, and who was then Assistant District Attorney of Yavapai County, in answer to the jailor's cry, rushed down the stairs leading to the jail door, and was shot in the back as he was retreating up the stairs, by Appellant Parker. Norris died from the effects of this shot. Jailor Meador was also seriously wounded in the struggle with the Mexican. Appellant Parker, carrying a double-barreled shotgun, and Miller and the Mexican, Sarata, then went to the livery stable of the Sheriff of Yavapai County, and the latter two, arming themselves with Winchesters, forcibly took horses from the employees of said stable and made their escape. After a long chase Parker was caught and tried for the murder of said E. L. Norris at the June term of court; was convicted of murder in the first degree and sentenced to be hanged. He appeals to this court and assigns eight specifications of error.

APPELLANT'S ASSIGNMENT OF ERROR

NO. 1

"The court erred in his charge to the Grand Jury."

"Section 1396, Penal Code of Arizona says: "The Grand Jury, being impaneled and sworn, must be charged by the court. In doing so, the court must give them such information as it may deem proper, or as is required by law as to their duties, and as to any charges for public offences returnable to the court or likely to come before the Grand Jury."

From the foregoing it will be seen that it was the duty of the court to charge the Grand Jury, and in so doing if he used strong and vigorous language, it was his duty and right to do so.

APPELLANT'S ASSIGNMENT OF ERROR
NO. 2

"That the court erred in denying defendant's motion to have shackles removed from defendant when he appeared in open court upon his arraignment."

Counsel for Appellant cite the case of People vs. Harrington, 42 Cal, 168, in support of this contention. An examination of that case shows that the prisoner was shackled during the entire trial and without sufficient cause. In the case at bar, the prisoner was shackled only twice during his arraignment. When his plea was taken and during the entire trial thereafter he was free of all restraint and incumbrance of every faculty and power that he possessed. Appellant Parker and L. C. Miller, who had broken jail, beaten and mutilated the jailor, killed and murdered Norris, were arraigned together. They were two desperate, hard characters. The officers of the law, appreciating that they had just escaped from them, leaving death in their tracks, might well feel that shackles were proper and necessary restraints. The Court, out of abundance of caution, and in part of the arraignment only, permitted the restraints upon the Appellant. In the face of the recent conduct of the Appellant Parker, the Bar and the Court itself had no guaranty of safety from harm or E. L. Norris' fate while in his unrestrained presence. Besides, his limbs were free and his every faculty was free during the entire trial.

APPELLANT'S ASSIGNMENT OF ERROR
NO. 3

"That the Court erred in overruling Defendant's motion to set aside the indictment and offer to introduce testimony to substantiate the allegations in said motion contained."

The contention of the appellant under this assignment of error is, that he was not examined by a committing magistrate and held to answer before the ending of the indictment, therefore had no opportunity to challenge the panel of the Grand Jury of any individual Grand Juror, and relies upon subdivision 4, paragraph 1513, Penal Code of Arizona. The record in this case fails to sustain Appellant's contention. It affirmatively shows (Appellant's abstract of record, pages 1 and 2), as follows: "Full panel of Grand Jurors present, sworn to answer as to their qualification, were examined and passed.

Prisoners James Parker and L. C. Miller being in custody, were ordered brought into court for the purpose of exercising their right of challenge to the panel or to any individual of the Grand Jury. The said James Parker and L. C. Miller, having no counsel, the Court thereupon for this arraignment assigned J. E. Morrison and G. A. Allen. There being no challenges, Court appointed foreman. The foreman being sworn and Grand Jurors being sworn, were duly charged by the Court, and the prisoners were remanded."

There is nothing in the record showing that Parker was not held to answer on this charge, and that being a matter of defense, it was incumbent upon him to show that he had not been held to answer. In the case of People vs. Travers, 88 Cal., 234, defendant introduced on his motion to set aside the indictment, on the ground that he had not been held to answer "an affidavit made by the County Clerk and one made by himself, which showed that he had not been held to answer when he was indicted and had no OPPORTUNITY to challenge the Grand Jury. No other evidence was introduced." Defendant Parker did have an opportunity to challenge the panel or any juror. He was in court before a jury was impaneled, represented by competent counsel. So far as the record shows, he was held to answer.

It is difficult to understand the exact meaning of Appellant's motion to set aside the indictment. This motion appears in abstract of record folios 4 and 5 in the nature of a challenge to the Grand Jury and jurors. Subdivision 4, paragraph 1313, Penal Code, is the same as Sec. 993, Penal Code of California, and provides that an indictment may be set aside "when the defendant has not been held to answer, before the finding of the indictment, on any ground which would have been good ground for challenge either by the panel or by any individual grand juror." In the case of People vs. Travers supra, the court uses this language: "This language clearly contemplates that the time for challenges has passed, and provides that a defendant may still prove any fact which, would have been good ground for challenge, if he had had an opportunity to interpose it at a time when a challenge was possible. But the fact which would have been good ground for challenge must be proven in the ordinary way in which the other facts are proven, by the introduction of evidence, either by the examination of the jurors or by other competent evidence. For this purpose of course defendant is entitled to the process of subpoena to compel the attendance of his witnesses but there is no process by which discharged grand jurors can be reassembled in the official character, and subjected to the original process of challenging. For the purpose of producing this evidence, a defendant would, no doubt, on proper showing, be entitled to a continuance; but in the case at bar there was no such showing. The Appellant did not make any affidavit of merits of diligence; nor did he by affidavit or otherwise show that he could produce a single item of evidence tending to show the disqualification of any grand juror. Indeed he did not make a regular motion for continuance, but seemed to rely upon the supposed right to have the Court reassemble the jury."

The record here fails to show that the Grand Jury that indicted Parker was in session at the time of the motion; fails to show a request that the Grand Jury be reassembled; fails to show that any subpoenas were asked for or issued for jurors or witnesses; fails to show any affidavits of merits of diligence; fails to show a single item of evidence tending to show the disqualification of any grand juror; fails to show that any motion for continuance was ever made. Besides, we contend, that the time for challenging the Grand Jury was before the indictment was returned, and for that reason the Appellant's motion, to set aside the indictment and challenge the Grand Jury, whatever may have been intended, in its present shape, is not in proper form. The motion at most only recites legal conclusions with reference to the state of the jurors' minds; it fails to set forth any fact "in the ordinary way in which other facts are proven."

Counsel for appellant in their brief, on page eight, referring to the action of the Court overruling their motion to set aside the indictment, say: "Defendant was thereby prevented from showing, by affirmative testimony, that he was never held to answer on the charge preferred against him in the indictment, and was never afforded an opportunity of challenge to that body upon said charge." In this statement counsel admit that "affirmative testimony" was necessary. They also admit and construe motion to be a challenge to the Grand Jury. They could have introduced affirmative testimony had they proceeded correctly to do so, but they could not challenge the Grand Jury, for the time of challenge had passed. Again, counsel show that the only pretense of any matter showing that defendant had not been held to answer appears in their motion to set aside the indictment. See Appellant's brief, page 9. This motion was not evidence nor proof of anything.

People vs. Travers, supra., cited by Appellant, is almost on all fours with this case. In the Supreme Court the lower court was sustained in refusing to set aside the indictment. The Travers case is not only against the defendant upon principle, but is very strong authority in favor of the respondent. The other cases cited by Appellant, People vs. Turner, 39 Cal., 370, is not an authority, for the reason that the record in that case showed that the Defendant had not been held to answer before the finding of the indictment. In that case, too, what was said upon motion to set aside the indictment, because the defendant had not been held to answer, was mere dictum, for the Court says, after deciding the case upon other points, that at the request of counsel the Court would "indicate an opinion upon the order of the Court below in overruling Defendant's motion to set aside the indictment." (Page 376.)

In the case of the People vs. Geiger, 49 Cal., 643, the Court says, at page 650: "The motion to set aside the indictment was properly denied. When the Grand Jury which found the indictment was empaneled, the defendant was in actual custody under a warrant of arrest issued by a magistrate, on a sworn complaint charging the defendant with the crime of murder, for which he was afterward indicted. But he had not then been examined by the committing magistrate. When the Grand Jury was about to be empaneled, the defendant was brought into court and was informed by the Judge that he might then interpose a challenge to the panel or to any individual Grand Juror, the Grand Jury then being present. But the defendant declined to interpose any challenge, on the ground that he had not been held to answer for any offence." At the proper time the Defendant moved to set aside the indictment, which motion was overruled by the Trial Judge. Defendant appealed, but judgment was affirmed by the Supreme Court.

We especially call the attention of the Court to this case as being right in point. The facts in said case, with respect to setting aside the indictment, are identical with the facts in the case at bar. The California statute on this point is identical with ours. To the same point we also cite cases of:

People vs. (unreadable)
Territory vs. (unreadable)
Territory vs. (unreadable)

Furthermore the attention of the court is called to the numerous affidavits on file in this case, sworn to by the grand jurors who found the indictment, setting forth emphatically that they had no bias or prejudice whatever against said Parker. These affidavits were made upon Appellant's motion for a change of venue, but they clearly show that it was not possible for the defendant to find any evidence whatever showing prejudice or bias upon the part of the jury that indicted him.

The authorities above cited clearly show that the defendant was protected in every step of the proceedings during his whole arraignment and trial. Certainly, nothing was done on the part of the Territory to prejudice any substantial right of his. Paragraph 2177, Penal Code of Arizona, is:

"Neither a departure from the form or mode prescribed in respect to any pleadings or proceedings, nor an error or mistake therein, shall render the same invalid, unless it have actually prejudiced the defendant or tended to his prejudice in respect to a substantial right."

APPELLANT'S ASSIGNMENT OF ERROR
NO. 4

"That the Court erred in overruling defendant's motion for a change of venue."

Parker's application for a change of venue was accompanied by the affidavits of E. S. Clark, G. A. Allen, J. E. Morrison, M. I. O'Mailia and R. C. Welch. Clark was a resident of Flagstaff, Coconino County; O'Mailia, of Denver, Col., R. C. Welch, of the County Jail, Yavapai County. Morrison and Allen were the attorneys of the Appellant.

Counter affidavits were filed by the Territory, and these affidavits were made and signed by nearly all of the leading business and professional men of Prescott; and, in fact, business men scattered all over the county. These counter affidavits were to the effect that Parker could have a fair and impartial trial in the County of Yavapai, and that there was no prejudice or bias manifested against him, or existing against him. As to the charge made by Counsel for Appellant, on page 10 of their brief, that a large mob congregated at the Court House for the purpose of lynching Parker, we refer you to the affidavit of George C. Ruffner, Sheriff of Yavapai County, on file in this case in which he flatly and in no uncertain tone contradicts this assertion.

A jury was procured in a very short time, and without any trouble, to try Parker, which goes to show that the application for change of venue was not based upon fact.

Change of venue is largely discretionary with the Trial Court, and such discretion will not be reviewed on appeal, except in cases of gross abuse. See the following cases;

People vs. Fisher, 6 Cal., 434.
People vs. Mahoney, 18 Cal., 180.
People vs. Cougleton, 44 Id., 92.
People vs. Pervue, 19 Id., 425.
People vs. Yoakum, 33 Id., 366.
People vs. Goldman, 76 Id., 337.

Affidavits upon a motion for a change of venue must state facts and cite instances from which the Court may deduce the conclusion that a fair and impartial trial cannot be had. Such conclusion is to be drawn by the Court and not by the Defendant, and his witnesses and the Court must be satisfied from the fact and circumstances positively sworn to in the affidavits and not to the general conclusion to which the Defendant or his witnesses may swear. To this point we cite the Last named cases, and, in addition, the following:

People vs. Barker, 1 Cal., 403.
People vs. Graham, 28 Id., 251.
People vs. Shuler, 28 Id., 490.
People vs. Lee, 5 Id., 353

APPELLANT'S ASSIGNMENT OF ERROR
NO. 5

"That the Court erred in refusing to instruct the jury as requested in defendant's instruction 1."

Counsel for Appellant maintain that the Court erred in refusing to instruct the jury that the defendant could not lawfully convicted for murder in the first degree for the reason that no deliberation or premeditation was manifested in the killing of said Norris. The deliberation and premeditation may be instantaneous. See:

People vs. Sanches, 24 Cal., 17.
People vs. Nichol, 34 Id., 211.
People vs. Long, 39 Id., 694
People vs. Williams, 23 Id., 544.
People vs. Cotter, 49 Id., 100.
State vs. Ah Mook, 12 Nev., 369
McAdams vs. State, 25 Ark., 403

The question of premeditation and deliberation is one which is peculiarly the province of the jury to determine. See:

People vs. (unreadable), 43 Cal., 552.

APPELLANT'S ASSIGNMENT OF ERROR
NO. 6

"That the verdict found by the jury was contrary to the law and the evidence in that the evidence does not support the verdict for the reason that no premeditation or malice of any character was shown."

The evidence in this case shows that Parker broke jail, armed himself with a shotgun, loaded with buckshot, and shot Norris in the back and while he was running from him. The evidence shows, and the jury found, that the shooting was deliberate and premeditated. Counsel for Appellant say that the evidence fails to show for a certainty who fired the fatal shot that killed the deceased. In view of this contention by counsel, we are greatly surprised that they have not sought to cast a doubt as to the death of the murdered Norris. Jailor Meador, as the evidence shows, saw Parker fire the shot that killed Norris. Other witnesses saw the gun in Parker's hand as he was fleeing from the jail.

With reference to Appellant's assignments of errors 7 and 8, we deem it unnecessary to occupy space in this discussion, for the reason that the ground has already been covered in the foregoing brief.

In conclusion we will say that the evidence in this case shows one of the most unprovoked and atrocious murders that was ever committed in our fair Territory. This evidence was heard by twelve good men and true, and Defendant was found guilty with the penalty of death attached. His trial was fair and impartial. He was represented by able and enthusiastic attorneys. He had the protection of every arm of the law. For the killing of young Norris, he should die the death that the jury and the Trial Court found he deserved. A speedy enforcement of the criminal laws of this Territory demands that the judgment of the Lower Court be sustained.

Respectfully submitted,
C. M. Frazier
Attorney-General
H. D. Ross
District Attorney, Yavapai County, Ariz.

> P. W. O'Sullivan
> Ass't Dis't Attorney, Yavapai County

The attorneys on both sides had presented their cases very well.

While everyone waited for the High Court's decision, life went on. There was a bizarre squabble at the Sheriff's office over Parker at one point. From the *Arizona Journal Miner* of February 16, 1898:

A WRIT OF MANDAMUS WANTED

> One of Parker's Attorneys Files a Complaint Against the Sheriff for Being Refused to See His Client
>
> There seems to be some friction between the sheriff's office and G. Arthur Allen, one of the attorneys for James Parker, according to an application filed in the district court today. Attorney Allen applies for a mandamus against the sheriff to compel that official to permit him to visit his client in the county jail for the purpose of interviewing and counseling with him whenever either may desire to do so.
>
> Mr. Allen's attorneys are Eugene B. O'Neill, and District Attorney H. D. Ross and Deputy District Attorney P. W. O'Sullivan. The papers in the case were served on Sheriff Ruffner this afternoon. Sheriff Ruffner could not be found by the JOURNAL-MINER representative, but Under Sheriff Dillon stated that J. E. Morrison, who is associated with Mr. Allen, as counsel for Parker, had free access to the jail and to his client whenever he wanted to go, but just why Mr. Allen was not allowed the same privilege was not clearly stated, although it may be at the hearing.
>
> The date for the hearing of the application was not set, but will be heard within the next ten days. The proceedings will be watched with interest, as the decision will determine just how far the authority of the sheriff may be exercised in his control of prisoners."

The *Prescott Courier* reported the incident in this fashion on February 18, 1898:

> G. A. Allen, one of the attorneys appointed by the court to defend outlaw Parker, complains that he is not permitted to visit Parker in the jail as often as he desires and his instituted mandamus proceedings to find out if there is any power to prevent such visits by him to his client. This is probably the correct thing from a legal standpoint, but from the standpoint of common reason, about the only desire which would actuate the ordinary mortal to see Parker, would be to see him pay the proper penalty of a life of lawlessness.

It is not clear what caused this dispute, or how it was resolved. The newspapers did not follow up, and I have found no court records pertaining to it.

From the *Courier* of February 25, 1898:

Jailor Morgan says that Outlaw Parker seemed quite jovial last evening and joked and laughed as if he felt in the happiest mood imaginable.

The story got stranger before it was over. The following item from the February 23, 1898 *Journal Miner* is usually never reported in the later after-the-fact accounts:

> PARKER PRETENDS BEING CRAZY.
> A radical change has come over the demeanor of Parker, the condemned murderer now in jail awaiting the decision of the supreme court in his appeal. For weeks he was quite morose and quiet, bordering on sulleness at times, and this has changed now to a feigning of insanity. Last night he is said to have made the county jail ring with echoes of his yells, apparently in line with other actions of feigned insanity. He goes about his cell and the corridor of the jail pretending to be picking up pins and other objects. It is expected that a decision will be rendered in his case next week by the supreme court.

Now, think about this for a minute. Today, if a prisoner started acting strangely, a thorough psychiatric exam would be ordered by the authorities, even if they thought he might have been faking. But in 1898, everyone, including the authorities and the newspapers simply assumed he was faking his insanity and refused to investigate any further. The *Journal Miner*'s approach to the story is jaw-dropping to this day. The *Courier* picked up the story in its February 25, 1898 edition:

> Regarding the report of Outlaw Parker's feigned insanity, Sheriff Ruffner says that Parker has been acting "nutty;" that he asked Parker last evening if he was trying to go crazy, and Parker replied, perfectly rationally, that he was not, that he always became flighty when sick with fever, and that he had been that way all his life. Parker is at present under medical treatment.

The *Journal Miner* closed the story this way in its February 23, 1898 edition:

> Parker says he is not feigning insanity but is always troubled with delirium, when suffering from an attack of fever. He says he has been this way all of his life. It will be in order now to prove that he had a severe attack of fever on the 9th of last May.

Very shortly after this, the Territorial Supreme Court announced its decision in the Parker case. The decision went as expected. From the *Arizona Republican* of February 24, 1898:

> PARKER MUST HANG.
> Decision of the Supreme Court in This and Other Cases.
>
> James F. Parker, the murderer of Lee Norris at Prescott, has not been hanged yet, but the rope was adjusted a little closer to his neck yesterday afternoon when the supreme court affirmed the judgment of the district court of Yavapai county

in which Parker had been convicted. The court was reconvened in the morning, but was adjourned until 2 o'clock, when it was announced that decisions would be handed down in several cases and would be reserved in others until a later meeting of the court.

The opinion in the Parker case was submitted by Chief Justice Street, who took occasion in announcing it to pass upon another matter, the manner in which the appeal had been brought.

The last legislature passed act No. 71, "an act relating to appeals and writs of error from the district courts and circuit courts of the territory to the supreme court," in which it is stated that it is not necessary to send up "a transcripted assignment of errors or other papers except as herein provided." The documents provided for include, among others, a copy of the testimony. The appeal in the Parker case had been taken under this act. The chief justice held that the act did not apply to criminal cases, but this case was one of so great importance, involving a human life, that the court had considered that a bill of particulars had been prepared and all proper forms of appeal had been complied with.

In the case of Samuel Donnelly, appellant, vs. the Territory, respondent, from Cochise county, the judgment of the lower court was reversed and the case was remanded for a new trial. The appellant is the principal owner of the Copper Glance mine and the head of a religious sect which is operating it. He was indicted, tried and convicted of aggravated assault in the punishment of a child.

In the case of George Cluff, appellant, vs. the Territory, respondent, from Graham county, the judgment of the lower court was reversed and the appellant was ordered discharged. The indictment against Cluff was held to be defective and the case of the prosecution irremedial. The appellant was probate judge and county school superintendent of Graham county. It was charged against him that he had presented to the county treasurer and had received money for a teacher's warrant whose face he had raised. The amount involved was small, but Cluff was convicted and sentenced to the penitentiary, a motion for a new trial having been denied. He was taken to Yuma, but was released last summer by Judge Baker of this district on a writ of probable cause, in the application for which the same facts of a defective indictment and insufficiency of cause were urged as in the hearing on appeal.

The judgment of the lower court was also reversed in the case of William Schultz, appellant vs. the Territory, from Yavapai county. Schultz is in the penitentiary, serving the longest possible term for manslaughter. If the tin-horn legislature had never convened he would likely have been sentenced to be hanged. Schultz and another man were charged with a brutal and cold-blooded murder several years ago. He was convicted, but the war office of the German government, of which he had been a soldier, interesting itself in his behalf, he was given a second trial. In the meantime the bill exonerating to some extent all persons then charged with murder was passed by the Nineteenth legislature, and when Schultz was tried again, he could be convicted of no offense greater than manslaughter.

In the case of Charles Hackett, appellant, vs. the Territory, respondent, from Yavapai county, the judgment of the lower court was affirmed. Hackett (colored) is also in Yuma for aggravated assault.

The article went on to list other decisions, but it is interesting to compare the Parker case with some of the others handed down that day. As seen in the article, a number of cases were overturned on technicalities that day, including the case of William Schultz, another Yavapai County murderer, who continued his winning streak, even though his life had earlier been spared by the Norton Act, just as it had been for Richard Cross.

The full text of the Supreme Court decision is as follows:

[Criminal No. 126. Filed February 23, 1898.]
[52 Pac. 361.]
JAMES F. PARKER, Defendant and Appellant, v. TERRITORY OF ARIZONA, Plaintiff and Respondent.

1. CRIMINAL LAW—APPEAL AND ERROR—LAWS 1897, ACT No. 71, DOES NOT APPLY TO APPEALS IN CRIMINAL CASES—Act. No. 71, supra, "relating to appeals and writs of error from the district and circuit courts of the territory of Arizona to the supreme court," has no relation to appeals in criminal cases.

2. SAME — SAME — SAME — PRACTICE — CHANGE IN — MURDER — REVIEW UPON IMPERFECT RECORD—REV. STATS. ARIZ. 1887, PENAL CODE, PAR. 1880, CITED—An appeal in a criminal case being erroneously taken under act No. 71, supra, this being the first session of the supreme court after the passage of the act, and paragraph 1880, supra, providing that the appellate court in criminal cases shall look into the record, and that the appeal shall not be dismissed if sufficient matter be contained in the record to enable the court to decide the cause on its merits, this court will not dismiss the appeal, or examine only into the indictment and judgment, where the charge is murder.

3. SAME — GRAND JURY — CHARGE — A charge to the grand jury, calling their attention to a recent jail-breaking in which a citizen had lost his life, and asking that they investigate all of the circumstances pertaining thereto, and to make an early report, but containing no reference to the defendant, subsequently indicted by such grand jury for the murder of the citizen, is not error.

4. SAME —TRIAL — SHACKLING PRISONER — HARMLESS ERROR — The shackling of a lawless, desperate character upon his first arraignment for murder is not reversible error where the record shows that the arraignment was set aside and fails to show that he was so shackled at the second arraignment of at any subsequent time during the trial.

5. SAME — INDICTMENT — SETTING ASIDE —APPEAL AND ERROR — RECORD— INSUFFICIENCY — REV. STATS. ARIZ. 1887, PENAL CODE, PARS. 1513, 1387, CONSTRUED. — Paragraph 1513, supra, provides; "The indictment must be set aside by the court in which the defendant is arraigned upon his motion in either of the following cases: . . . (4) When the defendant had not been held to answer before the finding of the indictment on any ground which had been good ground for challenge, either to the panel or to any individual juror [grand juror]." Paragraph 1387, supra, provides: "A challenge to an individual grand juror may be interposed if a state of mind exists upon his part in reference to the case or to either party which satisfies the court, in the exercise of a sound discretion, that he cannot act impartially and without prejudice to the substantial rights of the party challenging." This

right can only be exercised, after the indictment, by the defendant, when he had not been held to answer before the impaneling of the grand jury, and does not show that he was not then charged with the crime of murder, he cannot complain of the overruling of his motion to set aside the indictment.

6. SAME — SAME — SAME — MOTION — MUST BE SUPPORTED BY AFFIDAVITS OR RECORD. — Motions to set aside an indictment, unsupported by affidavit, and not showing the nature or character of the evidence upon which they are based, are insufficient. They must be based upon some facts appearing from the record or otherwise produced before the court.

7. SAME — CHANGE OF VENUE — PREJUDICE — SHOWING — TERRITORY V. BARTH, 2 ARIZ. 319, FOLLOWED. — It is not error for the trial court to refuse a motion for a change of venue supported by the affidavits of defendant, his co-defendants, and five others, including his two counsel, tending to show a prejudice in the county which would preclude a fair trial, where the same was met by affidavits of eighty-four citizens, including nineteen grand jurors, who found the indictment, denying the existence of such prejudice. Territory v. Barth, supra, followed.

8. SAME — MURDER — INSTRUCTIONS — PREMEDITATION AND DELIBERATION — EVIDENCE. — Where the evidence showed that defendant and others broke jail, and in the scuffle the jailer made an outcry, and one Lee Norris came to his assistance, but, on seeing defendant armed with a shot-gun, turned to flee, when defendant shot him in the back, it is not error for the court to refuse to instruct the jury that, under the evidence in the case, no deliberation or premeditation relating to the killing of Lee Norris has been proven by the prosecution, and therefore the defendant cannot lawfully be found guilty of murder in the first degree. It was the duty of the court, under proper instructions, to submit to the jury the question of premeditation and deliberation.

APPEAL from a judgment of the District Court of the Fourth Judicial District in and for the County of Yavapai. J. D. Bethune, Judge. Affirmed.

The facts are stated in the opinion.

J. E. Morrison, and George Arthur Allen, for Appellant.

C. M. Frazier, Attorney-General, H. D. Ross, District Attorney, and P. W. O'Sullivan, Assistant District Attorney, for Respondent.

STREET. C. J. —

1. The appellant, James F. Parker, was indicted at the June term of the district court in the year 1897, by the grand jury of Yavapai County, for the crime of murder, upon which he was tried and convicted June 17, 1897, the jury affixing to their verdict the death penalty, upon which judgment and sentence of death were entered. Appellant was confined in the county jail of Yavapai County, at Prescott, and while so confined, on the ninth day of May, 1897, with one L. C. Miller and Cornellia Surrota, a Mexican, also confined in said jail, made their escape by overpowering the jailer, Robert Meador. In the scuffle the jailer made an outcry, and one Lee Norris, assistant district attorney of Yavapai County, being at that time in the office of the district attorney at the courthouse, ran to his assistance. The appellant, Parker, had obtained a shot-gun from the room of the jailer, and had it in his hands, when Lee Norris made his appearance on the stairway leading to the jail, seeing which, he turned to

flee up the stairs when appellant shot him in the back, from which gunshot wound said Norris in a few hours died. Appellant, with his companions, went to a neighboring livery stable, seized some horses, and fled to the mountains. A sheriff's posse was organized, which gave pursuit, and, after a chase continuing many days, appellant was recaptured, and again placed in the jail of Yavapai County. Appellant has prosecuted his appeal under the provisions of act No. 71 of the nineteenth legislative assembly of Arizona, 1897, being an act "relating to appeals and writs of error from district and circuit courts of the territory of Arizona to the supreme court," and has certified up the evidence and papers and files in the case, without any bills of exception or statement of facts. In this proceeding counsel for appellant are in error, and have mistaken the method prescribed for appeals in criminal prosecutions. The act above mentioned has relation only to appeals in civil cases. By a careful reading of that act it will be observed that it was not the intention of the legislature to make the same applicable to appeals in criminal prosecution. It provides for appeals and writs of error, and speaks of plaintiffs in error and of appellees, neither of which terms is used in the statute designating the parties in criminal appeals, but are terms used in the statues with reference to civil appeals. In criminal appeals the parties are designated as appellant and respondent, and no provision is made for writs of error. That act dispenses with bills of exceptions. Criminal appeals are heard upon bills of exceptions and statements of facts. The provisions of that act can be made applicable to civil appeals, but cannot be made applicable to criminal appeals without further or additional legislation upon the subject. The appellate court, however, is required to look into the record, and the appeal shall not be dismissed if sufficient matter of substance be contained in the record to enable the court to decide the cause on its merits. Pen. Code, par. 1880. The court in this instance is disposed to go further, and to review all the errors complained of. This is the first session of the supreme court since the passage of act No. 71, and counsel have permitted themselves to be led into the mistake of conceiving the law applicable to criminal appeals, without having had the guidance of the court upon this question. Under such circumstances, the court does not feel like summarily dismissing the appeal, or examining only into the indictment and judgment, where the charge is so serious as that contained in this indictment. In making the investigation, however, the court finds itself embarrassed from the lack of bills of exceptions.

2. First. The first assignment of error is, that the court erred in its charge to the grand jury. We find no charge to the grand jury in the record, except in an affidavit of appellant and L. E. Miller, asking for a change of venue. But, referring to the language in that affidavit, and treating it as a matter properly before this court, the same as though it were contained in the bill of exceptions and statement of facts, we cannot find any language therein which refers to this defendant in any way. The attention of the grand jury is called to the recent jail-break, in which a citizen had lost his life, and asks them to investigate all of the circumstances pertaining thereto, and to make an early report upon the matter.

Second. The second assignment of error is, that the court erred in denying the defendant's motion to have his shackles removed when he appeared in open court upon his arraignment. As to the facts upon which that is based, the court is at somewhat of a loss, because of the lack of the bill of exceptions and statement of facts, for it appears from the minutes that the defendant was twice arraigned upon this indictment, — the first arraignment being set aside, and defendant was again arraigned; and it does not appear that he was in shackles at the time of the second arraignment. Paragraph 1106 of the Penal Code provides: "A person charged with a public offense shall not before conviction be subjected to any more restraint than is necessary for his detention to answer the charge," —which is but the common-law and constitutional right of a prisoner embodied in the statute. "It has, however, been the rule at common law that a prisoner brought into the presence of the court for trial, upon his plea of not guilty to an indictment for any offense, was entitled to appear free from all manner of shackles or bonds; and, prior to 1722, when a prisoner was arraigned or brought to the bar of a court to plead, he was presented without manacles or bonds, unless there was evident danger of his escape." People v. Harrington, 42 Cal. 176, 10 Am. Rep. 296, citing 2 Hale, P. C. 219; 4 Blackstone's commentaries, 322; Layer's Case, 6 St. Trials (4th ed., by Hargrave) 230; Waite's Case, 1 Leach, 36. The record does not disclose the fact that the prisoner was in shackles during any other period of his trial, nor is it asserted by his counsel that he was so shackled. The record reveals the fact that the defendant was a lawless, desperate character, who had to be guarded with the greatest care and vigor. Thousands of dollars reward were offered for his recapture, as well as for his original arrest for train robbery; and if it were a fact that he was in shackles at the time of arraignment, but not at the time of trial, the court could not consider that he had been unduly restrained of his liberty or deprived of his right to manage and control in person his own defense untrammeled, or that he was under such physical burdens, pains, and restraints as to confuse and embarrass his mental faculties.

Third. The third assignment of error is, that the court erred in overruling defendant's motion to set aside the indictment and his offer to introduce testimony to substantiate the allegations in said motion contained. Paragraph 1513 of the Penal Code: "The indictment must be set aside by the court in which the defendant is arraigned upon his motion in either of the following cases: . . .(4) When the defendant had not been held to answer before the finding of the indictment on any ground which had been good ground for challenge, either to the panel or to any individual juror [grand jury]." Subdivision 5 of paragraph 1387 provides: "A challenge to an individual grand juror may be interposed if a state of mind exists upon his part in reference to the case or to either party which satisfies the court, in the exercise of a sound discretion that he cannot act impartially and without prejudice to the substantial rights of the party challenging." This right can only be exercised after indictment by the defendant when he had not been held to answer before the impaneling of the grand jury, and was not present at the impaneling. Without the aid of bills of exceptions, we have to depend upon the minute entries of the paneling of the grand jury, which is as follows: "There being a full panel of grand jurors present, and having been sworn to answer as to their qualifications, and examined and passed, now, on motion of the district attorney, prisoners James Parker, Abe Thompson, et al., . . .having been held to answer and being in custody, were brought into court for the purpose of exercising their right of challenge to the panel of the grand jury, or to any individual grand juror, if any they had. And the said prisoners, James Parker et al.,. . .having no counsel, and stating to the court that they were unable to procure such, thereupon the court assigned counsel for said prisoners for this arraignment before the grand jury as follows: J. E. Morrison, G. A. Allen . . . There being no challenges, and there being twenty grand jurors present, the court appointed M. Bradley foreman of the grand jury, and, being sworn as foreman, and the grand jurors being sworn, were duly charged by the court and retired, and the said prisoners were remanded to await the action of the grand jury in their respective cases." It is argued by counsel that the defendant had been held only to answer to the charge of train robbery, and that his presence before the court at the time the grand jury was impaneled only gave him an opportunity to examine the grand jury in reference to the defendant on that charge. When we take into consideration the history of the killing, flight, and recapture of the defendant, as exposed by the record, one would naturally think that the defendant would have been apprised of the fact that he was about to be accused of murder; and, if he were possessed of any caution, he would be desirous of inquiring of the grand jury of the existence of any bias or prejudice in their minds against him in connection with that charge. The record, however, shows he was present at the impaneling of the grand jury, and does not show that he was not then charged with murder, which would effectually dispose of that assignment of error.

But, furthermore, paragraph 1388 of the Penal Code provides that such challenges may be oral or in writing, and must be tried by the court. At the time of arraignment the defendant made the following motion: "Come now the above-named defendants, and show to the court that neither of them was held to answer upon the charge preferred against them in the indictment in this case, and move to set aside the indictment herein upon the following challenge to the hereinafter-named individual grand jurors, the said grand jurors being members of the grand jury which found and returned said indictment, to wit: That a state of mind exists, and did exist at the time of the finding of said indictment, and prior thereto, on the part of E. H. Fredericks, W. A. Deering, J. H. Ehle, Mark Bradley, Frank Doggett, A. Falco, J. P. Bruce, R. H. Burmister, J. G. Allen, J. R. Dillon, J. W. Archibald, Joseph Johndrew, F. E. Jordan, J. M Croxdale, Robert Drynau, A. G. Oliver, E. E. Gregory, A. A. Moore, E. J. Austin, and John Smith, in reference to this case, and to the said defendants, and to each of them, which prevented the said above-mentioned grand jurors, and each of them from acting impartially in this case, and without prejudice to the substantial rights of these defendants herein; and for the further reason that said indictment does not purport to show the names of the witnesses examined before the grand jury upon the finding of said indictment. Wherefore, the said defendants pray that the said indictment be set aside and held for naught. And thereupon defendants' counsel did offer and ask leave to introduce testimony and evidence to substantiate the allegations in said motion to set aside the indictment contained. Said motion was then argued, and the court, being fully advised, overruled said motion, and overruled said offer of defendants to produce proof of said allegations in said motion contained, to which said action of the court, the defendants then and there, in open court, then and there excepted." The defendants did not introduce any affidavit in support of said motion. There is nothing to show whether the grand jury was then in session and could have been examined or not. There was nothing to show the nature and character of the evidence, nor anything, in fact, upon which to base the motion. Motions to set aside indictments must be based upon some facts appearing from the record or otherwise produced before the court. It is not sufficient for counsel, orally or in writing, to say to the court, "We move to set aside the indictment and ask for the privilege to make proof," without having laid a foundation for their motion. The cases cited by appellant—to wit, People v. Travers, 33 Cal. 236, 26 Pac. 88 and People v. Turner, 39 Cal. 370—bear out the views of the court in this particular, and we see no error in the court having overruled the motion to set aside the indictment.

3. It is further assigned as error that the court erred in overruling the motion for a change of venue. The motion was supported by the affidavit of defendant and his co-defendant, L. C. Miller, and the affidavits of five others, including the two counsel for the defendant, tending to show that such a prejudice existed against the defendant in Yavapai County as would prevent him from having a fair trial; and the same was met by the affidavit of eighty-four citizens of Yavapai County, including nineteen grand jurors who found the indictment, denying the existence of such prejudice. Upon the authority of this court, as established in the case of Territory v. Barth, 2 Ariz. 319, 15 Pac. 674, it cannot be said that the court erred in refusing to grant a change of venue.

The remaining errors complained of refer to the instructions of the court and the overruling of the motion for a new trial. Appellant principally complained that the court refused to give the following instruction at his request, to wit: "The court instructs the jury that, under the evidence in this case, no deliberation or premeditation relating to the killing of Lee Norris has been proven by the prosecution. The court therefore instructs the jury that the defendant in this case cannot lawfully be found guilty of murder in the first degree." We cannot see any error in refusing to give this instruction. An examination of the evidence clearly made it the duty of the court to submit to the jury, under proper instructions, which were given, the question whether the killing of Lee Norris was done with premeditation and deliberation; and the court committed no error in refusing to give that instruction.

We have carefully examined the full record, notwithstanding the failure of counsel to present the errors complained of by way of bill of exceptions and statement of facts, and have been led to do this, not only because of the earnest efforts of counsel, and their zealous and masterly way of arguing every objection, but from the importance of the case itself. We find no error which would warrant a reversal of the case itself. The judgment of the district court is affirmed.

Sloan, J., Davis, J., and Doan, J., concur.

The decision of the High Court was arguably very fair (this author still has trouble getting beyond the issue of premeditation), but it is also possible that the Court knew that public sentiment was still running high on the case. A decision to grant Parker a new trial could have conceivably resulted in rioting, or possibly a genuine lynch mob.

Following the decision, a new death watch was placed over Parker, which was rather ludicrous since Parker needed to have a new execution date set by the District Court. From the *Courier* of March 18, 1898:

> The death watch on Outlaw Parker state that Parker still appears to be in good spirits.

Attorneys Allen and Morrison petitioned the Supreme Court to rehear the case, which was largely a formality—they had to have known that the odds were heavily against them. From the *Journal Miner* of March 30, 1898:

> Those who expected that sentence would be passed on Parker today, for his wanton murder of Lee Norris in May, of last year, were doomed to disappointment. It appears that just prior to adjournment of the supreme court a motion for a rehearing of the case was filed before that body. This application simply means that the members of the supreme court are asked to reopen the case again and reverse their former decision. Supreme court does not meet again till April 15. So long as this motion is pending a remititur in the case can not be sent to the district court and in the absence of this remititur sentence will not be pronounced again, and Parker's attorneys hope to be able to prolong his life for several months yet, perhaps for a year.

The official motion for a rehearing displays the desperation of Allen and Morrison, who were fighting harder for their client than many attorneys of the day. The text:

IN THE SUPREME COURT OF THE TERRITORY
OF ARIZONA.

James F. Parker, appellant,
  Vs.
The Territory or Arizona,
  Respondent.

MOTION FOR RE-HEARING

COMES NOW the appellant herein and moves the Court for a re-hearing of this cause, and alleges:

That C. M. Frazier, Esq., whose residence if Phoenix, Arizona, H. D. Ross, Esq., District Attorney of Yavapai County, Arizona, whose residence is Prescott, Arizona, and P. W. O'Sullivan, Asst. District Attorney of Yavapai County, whose residence is Prescott, Arizona, are the attorneys for the respondent herein.

The appellant alleges that the grounds of his motion for such re-hearing and the reasons he assigns therefore, are as follows, to-wit:

First, that the Court, in deciding this case, held, upon assignment of error II that:

"The record does not disclose the fact that the prisoner was in shackles during any other period of his trial."

than upon his first arraignment, whereas, the record clearly shows that the defendant was in Court in shackles; that counsel directed the attention of the Court to that fact and moved that the Court order the removal of such shackles; that said motion was denied. The record discloses nothing further upon this subject. It is only by negative reasoning upon a subject on which the record is silent that the Court can arrive at the conclusion that the record shows that the prisoner was not before the Court in shackles on his trial. The record affirmatively shows, as above set forth that the prisoner was before the Court in shackles; that the Court declined to have them removed and therefore, as far as the record is concerned, it being thereafter silent upon the subject, the shackles remained upon the prisoner during all of the proceedings pictured by the record.

SECOND: The Court, in its written opinion, in ruling upon assignment of error III, quotes Par. 1513 P.C.:
"The indictment must be set aside by the Court in which the defendant is arraigned upon his motion, in either of the following cases: 4th: Where the defendant has not been held to answer before the finding of the indictment on any ground which would have been good ground for challenge either to the panel or to any individual juror."

In commenting upon this section under which the appellant moved to set aside the indictment and asked leave to introduce evidence as to the truth of the allegations contained in said motion, the Court says:
"This right can only be exercised after indictment by the defendant when he had not been held to answer before the impaneling of the Grand Jury and was not present at the impaneling".

With all due respect and deference, we respectfully insist that this Court has inserted into the Statute (P. C. 1513) a phrase which is not there and which it was not the intention of the Legislature to have there, to-wit: "and was not present at the impaneling". In our opinion this is manifestly incorrect and invading the domain of the Legislative branch of our Government. To illustrate our idea, in this connection, we respectfully submit the following example:

"A" is in the Court room in the presence of the Grand Jury when it is impaneled; he has never been held to answer and therefore, is charged with no felonious crime before that body but may be there simply as a spectator; the same Grand Jury subsequently indicts A. It will hardly be contended, as we believe, that A cannot have such indictment set aside under Par. 1513 P.C., Sub-Div. 4, upon proper showing, even though he was actually present at the empaneling. Yet by your Honors' construction and, if the words may be pardoned, alteration of said paragraph, he is absolutely precluded from taking advantage of said statute, for the simple reason that he was "Present at the impaneling".

Doubtless your Honors were greatly hampered in the consideration of this case by the absence of a bill of exceptions and statement of facts. This was, of course due to our unfortunate misconstruction of the Act of 1897, relating to appeals. However as the court was sufficiently interested in the case to give it careful consideration on the merits, we insist that the record should be taken as a whole and if there is any prejudicial error apparent upon the face of the record and of each and all of the proceedings, then the case should be reversed.

The written opinion says:

"The record shows that he (the prisoner) was present at the impaneling of the Grand Jury and does not show that he was not there charged with murder x x x"

The defendant below, in his motion to set aside, states affirmatively that he had never been held to answer on the charge of murder and he was denied the right to show that fact by evidence, over his objection and offer so to do. In the motion for a change of venue, the defendant below states, (unreadable) that he was never held to answer to the charge of murder. The record taken as a whole, therefore, shows in the strongest manner that the defendant below was never held to answer. The only other method by which he could have directed the attention of this Court to that fact was by way of a bill of exceptions, the absence of which your Honors have condoned.

Even if, as suggested in the decision, the defendant below was charged with notice by the "history of the killing, flight and recapture of the defendant" yet he (unreadable) not entitled to challenge any juror on the charge of murder. He had no more right to challenge than any spectator there in the Court room. But we must respectfully maintain that the first and only notice a man can have that a felony is charged against him is his arraignment upon an indictment, when he has not been held to answer.

This Court says further, in reference to said motion to set aside:

"The defendant did not introduce any affidavit in support of said motion" How could he have introduced an affidavit or any other evidence when the Court denied him that privilege? The Court below, as shown by the record, absolutely declined to hear evidence of any character and the action of the Court in so doing is one of the main grounds of error relied upon for a reversal. As we view it, this Court's decision says that it was absolutely necessary for us to do certain things. These we endeavored to do at the proper time in the Court below and the said Court denied us the right to instruct evidence, as your Honors say we should have done.

Again section 1519 P.C. "The motion to set aside the indictment of information shall be oral x x x "

How was the defendant below to verify or substantiate an oral motion but by offering to introduce evidence as to its truthfulness?

We are at a complete loss to understand how any other method of procedure could have been followed. It would be reversing the well established criminal procedure to say that evidence of a motion should be introduced before the motion itself is made. A criminal complaint is filed and then evidence is introduced; an indictment is returned and then evidence is introduced.

We respectfully direct your Honors' attention to Par. 1516 which is:

"The motion must be heard at the time it is made unless, for cause the Court, postpones the hearing to another time."

It is clearly the intention of the statute that this motion shall be tried by the Court the same as any other motion and the statute says that it MUST be tried.

We earnestly urge upon your Honors that this error is not of a trivial character; it strikes directly at the right of challenge; at the guarantee of the United States that every man charged with crime shall have a fair and impartial trial, as expressed in the Constitution, Article VI of Articles in addition to and amendment of the Constitution of the United States of America, which is follows:

> "In all criminal prosecutions, the accused shall enjoy the right to a speedy and public trial by an im-partial jury of the state and district wherein the crime shall have been committed. x x x x x"
> Most respectfully submitted,
> J. G. Morrison
> G.A. Allen
> Attorneys for appellant.

The April 20, 1898 *Journal Miner* reported simply that the motion for rehearing was denied. Surely no one expected differently.

While all of the business at the Supreme Court was going on, the *Arizona Republican* of March 15, 1898 partially reprinted an item from a non-surviving edition of the *Williams News*:

> C. Nick Stark of the Williams News recently visited Jim Parker in the Prescott jail. In a letter to the News, he wrote: The Yavapai bastile is particularly interesting at this time because it holds a distinguished prisoner---Jim Parker, the alleged train robber and murderer of Norris. Parker's escapades are still fresh in the public memory. He was "at home" to the News, whom Jailer Morgan kindly escorted to the bars. Parker greeted his visitor in his characteristic good natured, off-hand way and inquired for a number of his friends and acquaintances in this section. "Tell them I'm looking well and feeling just as good," said he smilingly. "I hope to get out of this scrape," he added, "but if I swing---why, I'll swing like a man." While the prisoner conversed with the News a stalwart guard patroled the narrow cell. The death watch is on Parker and his every movement is subjected to careful scrutiny. This espionage doesn't seem to worry the prisoner in the least, however. His attorneys, Allen and Morrison, are making a gallant fight for Parker's life. They have obtained a stay of execution, and Mr. Allen told the News that he feels hopeful of securing a commutation of the sentence of death.

The Spanish-American War had broken out by this time, and even the citizens of Prescott were paying attention to something other than the Parker case. The war seemed to even interest Parker himself. From the April 15, 1898 *Courier*:

> Outlaw Parker is said to be in improved spirits since the removal of the death watch and asks eagerly after the latest war news. He may have a chance to welcome fighting Bob Evans' first installment of Spanish in the lower regions.

All that was needed was formal resentencing and the fixing of an execution date. This came quickly. From the May 11, 1898 *Journal Miner*:

> The remittitur in the case of James Parker arrived from Phenix yesterday and Judge Sloan fixed Friday, June 3, between the hours of 9 a.m. and 3 p.m. as the date for his execution. Sheriff Ruffner has again placed a death watch over the condemned man.

Parker's time had just about run out. This time, the date would stick.

On May 25, 1898, the *Arizona Republican* reprinted a strange item from the *Jerome Mining News* (the original Jerome paper has not survived). The connection to Parker was clearly rumor, as it went unreported anywhere else, even in the Prescott papers:

> The Prescott opera house was partially burned down last Monday, the blaze being the work of incendiaries. While the fire was in progress, James Parker, the train robber and murderer in jail at Prescott under sentence of death, was discovered to be attempting to remove his shackles and it is thought the burning of the opera house was a portion of an attempt on the part of his friends to effect his escape.—Jerome News.

Preparations for Prescott's first hanging in a number of years commenced. From the *Prescott Courier* of May 20, 1898:

> The lumber has been ordered for the scaffold from which James Parker will be hanged. The hanging will take place in an enclosure at the east wall of the court house. The scaffold will be put up and tested on the first of June, the hanging to take place on the third. It will be a select affair which will be witnessed by only a few invited guests.

From the same edition:

> One of James Parker's attorneys tells the Courier reporter that Parker has a legal right to invite five persons to witness him hang.

It is no longer known if Parker exercised this right, and if so, who he invited. The newspapers seemed strangely uninterested in this.

Some of the detail of the preparations as reported in the papers to an interested public was relentless, and is difficult to read without wincing even today. From the *Journal Miner*, May 18, 1898:

HIS DOOM DRAWING NEAR.

Preparations Being Made for the Parker Execution —
A Carpenter At Work on the Scaffold

> Unless some unforeseen accident should happen, or unless the governor of the territory should interpose with a reprieve or commutation of sentence, the time of James Parker, murderer and alleged train robber, on earth is limited to two weeks and three days. The date for his execution has been set for Friday, June 3. Sheriff Ruffner has already commenced to make the preliminary arrangements for carrying out the sentence of the court, and a carpenter is now at work making the scaffold, the old one belonging to the county, and on which a number of murderers have expiated their crimes, having been destroyed by the court house fire.
>
> The laws of the territory require that the execution shall take place in an enclosure and accordingly Sheriff Ruffner has arranged to have an enclosure built

adjoining the court house on the east by building a fence eighteen feet high. Work will not be commenced on this until just a few days prior to the execution.

As the time for his execution draws near Parker shows decided signs of weakening and has become very reticent of late, although it is not thought that he will weaken to the extent of breaking down but will meet his fate bravely.

As a last resort, an application will be made to the governor by his attorneys for a commutation of sentence, but it will be done more as a matter of form than otherwise, as there are absolutely no grounds on which to base a request for executive clemency, and it is not believed that the governor will in any way interfere with the sentence of the court.

From the same edition:

On being sentenced to death James Parker, the train robber and murderer, remarked to some of the attaches of the sheriff's office: "Well boys I have not long to live now and I want to be furnished with the best food that can be had." His request is being complied with and instead of eating the regular prison grub his meals are sent to him regularly from a restaurant. He has roast turkey and all the delicacies of the season. He pays for the meals himself from his own funds.

The clock kept ticking. From the June 1, 1898 *Journal Miner*:

ONLY ANOTHER WEEK

James Parker's Lease on Life Rapidly Drawing to a Close

Only one more week on earth remains to James Parker, the outlaw, unless some unforeseen interference shall be made with the process of the law. The scaffold from which he will take his departure from the environments of earth has been framed, and is ready to be placed in position, and next week carpenters will be placed at work putting up the big eighteen-foot fence which will form the enclosure in which the execution will take place.

A female reporter of a San Francisco paper closed a three days' interview with him on Wednesday, during which she claims to have obtained a complete history of Parker's life, together with all the details of all the crimes he has ever committed. It is promised that this will be published in time for him to read it all.

While in the presence of other prisoners or that of the officials, Parker maintains an air of indifference, and even takes on an air of being jovial, but when he retires at night, he rolls and tosses around in his bed in a very restless manner. The strain and worry is commencing to tell on him, particularly during the past few days, and is plainly visible in the changed appearance of his countenance, as he is growing thin, despite the fact that he eats well. He admits now that he has no hope to escape the penalty of his crimes, and says he will meet his doom like a brave man.

The reporter was from the *San Francisco Examiner*, and the interview did not, in fact, appear until after Parker's death.

From the same edition:

Sheriff Ruffner has issued invitations to the execution of Parker next Friday. The hour fixed is 10 o'clock a.m.

A rare surviving copy of the *Jerome Daily News*, dated May 31, 1898 reported:

We acknowledge the receipt of an invitation from Sheriff Ruffner to attend the execution of James F. Parker, in the county court yard at Prescott, Friday, June 3, at 10 o'clock a.m.

These clippings regarding the invitations are important, as they seem to conclusively disprove a widely circulated myth that Ruffner forgot to send them out (see Chapter 11)! Regrettably, it is not known who all was invited to attend the enclosed hanging, but a few surviving clippings give some clues. From the *Journal Miner*, June 8, 1898 (remember, they were reprinting from earlier dailies):

W. H. Buck, of Phenix, came up on this morning's train to represent the Phenix Herald at the execution of Parker, returning to Phenix again this afternoon.
    City Marshal A. W. Galpin of Phenix came up to attend the Parker execution. Mr. Galpin was engaged in his pursuit for several days last summer.

From the same edition:

Sheriff Ralph Cameron came in on this afternoon's train to attend tomorrow's execution.

From the same edition, unsavory advertising:

Copies of the Weekly Journal Miner, containing a report of the execution of Parker, together with the other news of the week, can be obtained tomorrow at this office, or at the Corner drug store.

From the same edition:

IN THE SCAFFOLD'S SHADOW

    Parker Experiences a Change of Heart and Will Join the Church
Work was commenced today on the eighteen-foot high enclosure which is to surround the scaffold on which Parker will be executed on Friday. The temporary structure is being built on the east side of the court-house. While the officials have shut off the view of the work from the jail by closing the east side of it, the sound of the carpenters at their work can be plainly heard within the jail.
    Parker continues nervous and restless, and deep lines which are forming on his face tell plainly of the mental strain which he is undergoing, although he still maintains a calm demeanor when in the presence of others. The spirit of bravado

which has characterized him since his arrest has taken its departure, and in its place is that of (unreadable) and remorse. At his request, Father Quetu, of the Catholic church, visited him in the jail today, spending about half an hour with him, and as a result of his visit it is announced that Parker will be baptized tomorrow and will be received as a member of the church.

From the same edition:

THE APPROACHING EXECUTION

Arrangments for the Affair About Completed by the Sheriff.—Parker Maintains His Composure.
The arrangements for the execution of Parker tomorrow have been about completed by Sheriff Ruffner. The scaffold, which has been completed for some time is being placed in position within the enclosure adjoining the court house this afternoon.

Parker was baptized and received into the Catholic church this morning by Father Quetu, the only witness present being one of Parker's attorneys, J. E. Morrison. The latter, in speaking of the reports which have gained circulation in regard to Parker's being nervous, says that such is not the case but on the contrary he acts with the greatest composure and coolness. He says that he has given up all hopes of any intervention to save him and accepts the inevitable very philosophically.

A sister of the condemned man died only a few weeks ago, her death, it is said, being hastened by the knowledge of her brother's impending fate.

Six men arrived here last night, from Visalia, California, who are said to be old friends of Parker and who desired to see him once more. They are hunting for work, the dry weather in California having caused a scarcity of work there.

Nothing is known about Parker's six friends, but their appearance surely caused some worry and concern at the Sheriff's office.

I have not located any other newspaper reference for this, not even an obituary, but Parker's grief-stricken younger sister, Martha Rockwell, had indeed died. She actually seems to have passed away, probably of a broken heart, a few months earlier instead of a few weeks. The popular FindAGrave.com website lists her as having died in 1897 (obviously not long after she wrote that sad, surviving letter to her sister Sadie), and buried in a cold, unmarked grave in the Elbow Creek Cemetery near the small town of Ivanhoe in Tulare County, not far from Visalia. She was 25.

The June 3, 1898 edition of the *Courier* has reportedly not survived, but a couple of unidentified clippings pasted on paper by some anonymous individual in the Sharlot Hall Museum Archives are likely from that edition:

The scaffold upon which James Parker is to be executed at 10 o'clock today was completed yesterday. It is painted black. The steps leading up to the scaffold number 13, which, in this case, in certainly an unlucky number for Parker. The doomed man was baptized in the Catholic religion yesterday by Father Quetu. As serious a matter as the hanging of this man is, no good citizen regrets it, but all do regret that any man should become so wedded to evil that it becomes absolutely essential for public safely and the common weal to deal with him as a reasonless beast of prey. His fate should be a warning to others, who may thus be brought to realize that those who persistently sow the wind will surely reap the whirlwind.

Also unidentified:

It is stated that James Parker was playing poker yesterday while the ringing of hammers on the scaffold upon which he is to hang sounded in his ears.

From the *Arizona Republican* of June 3, 1898:

James Parker will be hanged at Prescott today. Quite a number of Phoenicians to whom a hanging is of more thrilling interest than a circus or minstrel performance, went north last night. Most of them were going on urgent business. They didn't think they'd go to the hanging. They wouldn't give a cent or walk across the road to see it. It is said that Parker is betraying a realization of the seriousness of his situation, but it is hardly expected that he will weaken to the extent of breaking down.

And then, it was over.

On June 3, 1898, the hanging of Fleming "James" Parker went off pretty much as planned. In those days, newspapers gave more "gory" details of executions than they do today, although the coverage of Parker's hanging was restrained when compared to that given other hangings previously. Comments are not needed from me; the reporters said it all. From the *Arizona Journal Miner* of June 8, 1898:

PARKER IS HANGED

Execution of a Confessed Train Robber and Murderer in the Court House Yard Today

He Meets His Fate With a Stoical Composure and Maintains an Outward Show of Courage

It was four o'clock this morning before James Parker, the condemned murderer, closed his eyes in sleep, on the last night for him on earth. Even then his sleep was fitful and broken and only lasted for a couple of hours.

Last night, for the first time since his incarceration, he asked for whiskey to stimulate him, and he drank freely though not to the point of intoxication of it. Sheriff Ruffner remained with him in his cell until long after midnight and Parker talked freely of his past life, telling the details of the train robbery, for which he was first arrested and which afterwards led to the murder for which he today paid the penalty with his life.

As stated, about four o'clock this morning he dropped off into sleep, but was up bright and early again for the day and partook of a hearty breakfast.

He was shaved this morning and was given a new black suit and white shirt, for his final appearance. Father Quetu, his spiritual adviser, visited him in the jail shortly after nine o'clock and spent about three-quarters of an hour with him administering spiritual consolation, which he received with apparent interest.

Shortly after 10 o'clock Sheriff Ruffner read the death warrant to him, and at 10:25 the march to the scaffold was commenced. Sheriff Ruffner had hold of his left arm while Deputy Jeff Davis held his right, Father Quetu and Deputies J. P. Dillon and Pete Boscha and ex-Deputy Johnny Munds, following them.

As Parker emerged from the gloom of the jail, in which he has been confined for more than a year, into the bright sunshine of an un-clouded Arizona sky, and his gaze rested on the instrument erected for his death, he was visibly affected and faltered for an instant. Quickly gathering his composure, though, as they were about to lead him up the stairs of the scaffold, he said: "Hold on boys. I want to look at this thing; I never looked at one before." Sheriff Ruffner permitted him to go under the scaffold and examine it and he spent a minute or two at it seeming to be especially interested in the mechanism of the trap which was to be the instrument within the next few minutes of transferring him from the environments of earth into the great unknown beyond.

During his examination of this he made several remarks to the sheriff but which were not audible to the spectators, who were ranged at some distance from the scaffold. After finishing his inspection of the scaffold from beneath, he walked with steady step up the stairs and getting on the trap stepped heavily upon it as if to try its strength. Seeing the heads of two nails, he remarked: "I will set my feet right on these two nails." He then took his slippers off, threw them carelessly on the floor of the scaffold. At this moment seeing J. D. Moore among the spectators, he saluted him with a smile, saying, "Hello, Jack! How are they breaking?"

As Sheriff Ruffner commenced to buckle the straps around his legs, he said, "Take your time, George, there is no use in putting them on; I am not going to straddle out; you needn't worry."

When his arms and legs had been pinioned, Under Sheriff Dillon told him that if he had anything to say he could do so now, when he said: "I have not much to say. I claim that I am getting something that ain't due me, but I guess every man who is about to be hanged says the same thing, so that don't cut no figure; whenever the people says I must go, I am one who can go, and make no kick."

The black cap was then drawn down over his face when he said, "Hold on, I want to shake hands with the boys."

The cap was removed, when he shook hands with all on the scaffold, saying that he had no ill feelings toward any one. After shaking hands with all he motioned to Jailor Morgan and shook hands with him a second time, holding his hand for a few seconds, remarking: "It's all off; tell the boys (meaning those in the jail) that I died game and like a man."

The black cap was then again drawn over his face, and Under Sheriff Dillon was adjusting the rope while Sheriff Ruffner had his hand on the level of the trap prepared to spring it, when he said: "Don't get excited; George you put her on."

Although Under Sheriff Dillon had the rope already adjusted properly, Sheriff Ruffner gave it a pull and at the same moment sprung the trap, when Parker shot downward six feet, the whole thing being done so quickly that the spectators could scarcely watch the movements.

The trap was sprung at exactly 10:31, after which there were several convulsive twitches of the legs after the body fell, which were the only motions perceptible.

Drs. E. W. Dutcher and J. R. Walls were the official physicians in attendance and timed his pulse. At the expiration of ten minutes and fifty-four seconds life was declared extinct and the body was taken down. An examination of it showed that the neck was broken in the fall.

When the black cap was removed his features appeared perfectly natural, with the exception of the open eye lids and a slightly drawn appearance to his mouth. The body was at once removed to Undertaker Logan's establishment, where it was viewed by a number of people this afternoon, and was buried at the expense of the county in the potter's field at 4 o'clock.

The arrangements for the execution were complete in every detail and the affair passed off without a single break of hitch, reflecting credit on the sheriff's office.

In addition to the sheriff and his force of deputies, who assisted him, the execution was witnessed by Sheriff Cameron of Coconino county; Marshal Galpin, of Phenix; Chief of Police Prince and ex-Sheriffs Lowry and Mulvenon.

The crime for which Parker died today was the murder of Lee Norris May 9, 1897, while making his escape from jail. He had been arrested in February 1897 for train robbery, committed on the line of the Santa Fe Pacific railroad near the Mohave county line, the penalty of which, if convicted, was death.

On the date above mentioned, he with L. C. Miller and a Mexican, overpowered Jailor Meador and escaped jail. Norris, who was assistant district attorney, was engaged in writing a letter in his office at the time and in response to Meador's cries started to his help and was shot down on the stairs, receiving wounds from which he died at midnight.

Parker has since admitted his guilt, as well as that of train robbery.

Certainly Parker was one of the calmest, most collected individuals to face the hangman, and that rattled some people, and may actually be a factor in why his story continues to fascinate people today. The *Prescott Courier* reported it this way on June 10, 1898:

From Saturday's Daily
At 10:31 a.m., June 3, 1898, James Parker, the life-long law-breaker and self-confessed train robber and murderer, was hanged in the court-house yard at Prescott. The manner in which he met his death was typical of the desperado that he was—cool and unflinching. The history of the crime for which he was executed is fresh in the minds of our readers, being the murder of Lee Norris on the court-house steps by Parker while Parker, Louis Miller and Cornelius Serata were escaping from jail. Norris heard the noise, went down the stairs to see what the trouble was, and was shot down in cold blood, the escaped prisoners running over the body of the dying man. Parker was then in jail for robbing a train near Peach Springs, in which robbery Parker's comrade robber was killed outright. Parker was captured after an exciting chase by Sheriff Ruffner. When he escaped from jail, he rushed for the Plaza stables, mounted Ruffner's white horse, and rode it several hundred miles before he was recaptured in northern Arizona by Mr. Preston and a lot of Navajo Indians, Ruffner being close on his trail at that time. H. D. Ross and Assistant Prosecuting Attorney Patrick O'Sullivan prosecuted him, while Attorneys George

Arthur Allen and J. G. Morrison were appointed to defend him, and did so in a conscientiously professional and creditable manner. He was sentenced to death by Judge Hawkins in June, 1897. An appeal was taken to the Supreme court; the decision of lower court was sustained, and May 31, 1898, Judge Sloan fixed the date for Parker's execution. He had hope to the last that something would occur to save him, as when eating his last breakfast on earth he remarked that he expected to eat another breakfast the next morning. As usual in such cases, he was well dressed, clean shaven and washed, and barring a sinister expression in his eyes, was a good-looking man with a well-shaped head. He drank some whiskey a few hours previous to his execution, but not sufficient to intoxicate. Father Quetu was his spiritual comforter and ascended and stood with him on the scaffold. A few minutes past 10 o'clock, Sheriff Ruffner read the doomed man the death warrant. He shook hands with all the prisoners and his attorneys before he left the jail. Then, accompanied by Father Quetu, Under Sheriff Dillon, Deputies Jeff Davis, Pete Bascha, and Assessor John Munds, Parker entered the scaffold enclosure about 10:25. He seemed to be a little dazed as he stepped out from the shade into the glaring sunlight, but he instantly assumed a fearless front which he maintained to the last. He said as he approached the scaffold: "Hold on, boys: I want to look at this thing; I never looked at one before.: He was allowed to walk under the scaffold, which he inspected leisurely and slowly, saying that it seemed to be all right. He ascended the scaffold with steady step, and even smiled as he reached the platform. While adjusting himself on the center of the trap door he said, "I will set my feet on the heads of these two nails." He then leisurely drew off his slippers, looked out among the spectators, and seeing J. D. Moore, smiling, called out: "Hello, Jack! How are they breaking?" As Ruffner was strapping his legs, he said: "Take your time, George. There is no use in putting them on; I am not going to straddle you; you needn't worry." He also stated that he bore no ill will to anyone present. Under Sheriff Dillon then told him that he could talk, if he had anything to say. He said: "I have not much to say. I claim that I am getting something that ain't due me, but I guess every man who is about to be hanged says the same thing, so that don't cut no figure; whenever the people say I must go, I am one who can go, and make no kick." The black cap was quickly drawn over his face, when he exclaimed: "Hold on; I want to shake hands with the boys." The cap was removed; he shook hands with all present; wished them well; winked at Jailer Morgan, who came up and again shook hands with Parker, who said to Morgan: "It's all off; tell the boys that I died game and like a man.: He looked around and admonished those present not to get excited. He asked who was adjusting the replaced cap and the rope; when told that Under Sheriff Dillon was, he requested that Ruffner do it. Ruffner stepped up, adjusted the rope, when Parker exclaimed from beneath the black cap, "you're choking me, George." Ruffner then instantly sprung the trap and at 10:31 the trap door fell, and the body shot through the opening. The man's lower limbs were noticed to slightly draw up twice. Drs. Dutcher and Walls then stepped up and in just 10 minutes and 54 seconds pronounced life extinct. The man's neck had been broken by the fall. Ruffner sent for a cot, and the body was cut down and placed thereon. Then came a rush up the scaffold by relic hunters, who cut the rope into small bits and divided the same with their friends. The body was then taken to Logan's undertaking parlor. Burial was had in the potter's field and Sheriff Ruffner drove the hearse.

People who have attended numerous executions say the hanging of Parker passed off as creditably as any affair of the kind they ever saw. There was not a single happening to mar the clock work-like culmination of the laws' demands. The irrepressible small boy was in evidence around the enclosure where Parker was hung; he cut numerous holes through the thin planks of the enclosure and looked on with one eye. The scaffold and enclosure were immediately taken down after the execution.

These articles seem to identify all of the people on the scaffold with Parker, but subsequently, certain historians have asserted that the photos of the execution show a Deputy named Shorty Lacy and ex-Mayor Morris Goldwater on the scaffold as well. I find these claims to be suspect at best; if Goldwater had participated especially, the papers would have surely reported it.

Since both of Prescott newspapers pretty much agreed on what Parker's last words were, it is reasonable to assume they were reported accurately. Naturally, as reports drifted farther from Prescott, they lost something in the translation. This report from the *Coconino Sun* (formerly the *Flagstaff Sun-Democrat*) of June 4, 1898 shows all the earmarks of being culled from second-hand sources:

JAMES PARKER HANGED

The Condemned Man Died Game and Danced a Jig on the Scaffold
Prescott, June 3. — James T. Parker was hanged this morning at 10:31. His neck was broken and he was pronounced dead in 10 minutes and 45 seconds and cut down four minutes later. The hanging took place in an inclosure 18 feet high built for the purpose adjoining the court house on the east. The scaffold was black. He entered the enclosure at 10:25. Father Quetu led the procession, sheriff Ruffner on the left, deputy sheriff Jeff Davis on the right of the condemned. Before mounting the scaffold Parker inspected it thoroughly and expressed his satisfaction. He then mounted the scaffold, danced and pulled of his slippers. Ruffner asked if he wished to speak when he said: "Well boys I haven't got much to say, you are here to see something and I am not the kind of a man to disappoint you. I want to say that I am not justly punished but when the people say 'take it' I am ready to be taken. I will die game. Now boys don't get excited, take your time, let her go."

Undersheriff Dillon then pulled down the hood, strapped his hand and legs, he then asked the cap to be raised to shake hands with his friends which was granted and with smiles he shook hands with all on the scaffold. He seemed to be in the best of spirits, ate a harty breakfast at 8:30. When undersheriff Dillon was adjusting the rope Parker enquired who it was, then called, "you put her on yourself George," meaning Ruffner.

Parker died game and evidently to sheer force of will power had overcome the signs of weakening which were apparent for the past few days as evidenced by the following from the "Journal-Miner."

The rest of the article consisted of reprints from earlier *Journal Miners*. Unfortunately, this poor translation of Parker's last words hit the wire services and were reported in other papers as well.

The *Mohave County Miner* likewise reported the hanging on June 4, 1898, but their coverage was adequate but ordinary, containing no variations worthy of reprinting here.

The June 4, 1898 *Arizona Republican* carried an account of the hanging with very colorful language, as well as a critique of Parker's idiosyncratic behavior on the gallows:

THE END OF PARKER

Train Robber and Murderer Died Dissatisfied

In an Address from the Scaffold He Believed the Punishment Too Loose a Fit for His Crime

Prescott, Ariz., June 3.— (Special.) — The morning of the day set for the execution of James Parker, train robber and murderer, dawned warm and bright. No unusual stir about the court house conveyed to the casual observer that any extraordinary event was pending, although the new enclosure of rough pine boards adjoining might have hinted of something. Early in the day, however, crowds possessed with the morbid curiosity always attendant upon such occasions began to throng the premises, increasing as the time set for the execution approached.

Sheriff Ruffner's instructions provided for the execution between the hours of 10 and 2, and with commendable appreciation of the proprieties of the occasion, he had his arrangements completed. Parker spent a restless night, but in the waking hours of his last day on earth, was more collected. He received the last rites of the church just before going to the scaffold. This last structure was a substantially constructed affair, the well braced cross beam from which the rope depended being painted black.

About 10:15 Sheriff Ruffner and his deputies made a final inspection of the platform, testing the rope and satisfying themselves that the noose would slip and hold properly. At 10:25 Parker, attended by his spiritual adviser, Father Quetu, and under the personal conduct of Sheriff Ruffner and a deputy, left his cell and entered the yard wherein the gallows was erected. He appeared remarkably collected under the circumstances, and remarked as his eyes fell upon the scaffold, "Well, I see you have got it painted black." As his attendants turned his steps toward the stairs leading to the platform, he said, "Hold on; let me see what this thing looks like," and proceeded with much indifference to inspect the under side of the trap, weight, etc. He walked up the steps quietly between the sheriff and a deputy and took his place at once upon the trap, testing the stability with a stamp or two of his feet.

He was neatly dressed in black, with white shirt, collar and black tie. He put aside the offer of assistance of a deputy to remove a light pair of slippers he wore, doing it himself—a suggestive action of one whose frequent boast had been that he would die "with his boots on." He looked carefully at the pinioning of his arms and legs, buttoning his coat and vest himself in order to admit of a free adjustment of the belts, maintaining a desultory conversation during the process, and repeatedly urging the attendants "not to get excited"—a warning for which there was no occasion.

Before adjusting the cap Sheriff Ruffner asked if he had anything to say, and he replied briefly that "he supposed the people would be satisfied now that they had what they were looking for; that he felt, however, that he had not deserved the extreme penalty of the law. He thanked the sheriff, the jailor and his attendants generally for their courteous treatment during his incarceration, shaking hands with all upon the platform and making an especial wish to Ruffner, his relentless Nemesis, of "all the good luck in the world." The subdued tone of his remarks was evidently a relief to the officials, as it was feared that he might display at the last something of the bitter animosity he has felt and evidenced, and vent it in a vicious harangue. Whatever reason for his mild behavior, it removed what would have been a most objectionable feature of the execution.

As Deputy Sheriff Dillon adjusted the cap and placed the noose about his neck he asked who was doing it. Upon being told "Dillon," he said, "Let George do it," which request was complied with, and Ruffner attended to another detail in the final disposition of the criminal who has given him more trouble than all the rest of his charges together. The sheriff adjusted the noose with no uncertain hand, provoking the half stifled exclamation, "It is too tight," the last words James Parker spoke, for with a quick motion Ruffner stepped back, laid his hand to the lever, and quicker than the eye could follow the detail Parker shot down through the trap.

For a full half minute the body hung, slowly turning this way and that, then convulsive twitchings of the limbs and labored heavings of the chest showed the effort of the life spirit to resume its sway. Perceptibly the efforts decreased, until the body hung perfectly limp and motionless, and at the expiration of eight minutes Drs. Dutcher and Wall pronounced life extinct.

With little delay the body was cut down, placed in the box near at hand, and the dramatic career of James Parker was closed. Parker's appearance and demeanor in the execution yard were on the whole disappointing to those who had expected to see him carry himself with the same defiance that has characterized him since his introduction to the public through his bold attack on the A. & P. mail train.

There was a conspicuous absence of any manly appreciation of his position, and his apparent indifference to his surroundings impressed the observer as the result of dulled faculties and imperfect comprehension. His last few words were entirely without character, and his comments as the details were carried out, were made in a trivial way that failed to impress the hearers with any great amount of sympathy.

There could be no regret in the minds of any who looked on, at the demands of justice being satisfied. The disposition to sympathize over the untoward fate of a man who had proven himself a brave, if reckless character, was considerably dissipated by his characteristic behavior at the last.

Sheriff Ruffner and his deputies are to be congratulated upon the efficient way in which they carried out the details of their disagreeable duty. Once started, there were no delays and it was carried through without a halt and with all the speed commensurate with complete and satisfactory results.

The crime for which Parker died was the murder of Lee Norris at Prescott on Sunday, May 9, 1897. The killing of Norris was an incident in the escape of Parker, L. C., Miller and a Mexican from the Yavapai county jail, where Parker was awaiting trial for an attempted train robbery in Mohave county early the previous March. Until that time Parker was known throughout the territory as a cowboy somewhat reckless and daring, but with no especial criminal tendency. One of his companions was killed by an express messenger. Parker and the others were followed by Sheriff Ruffner of Yavapai county and Sheriff Cameron of Coconino. He was captured, but before he was landed in jail, he escaped. He was soon recaptured by Sheriff Ruffner and taken to Prescott to await trial in federal court.

About noon on Sunday, May 9, 1897, in the absence of Sheriff Ruffner and all his deputies, Jailor Meador opened the door of a cell in which Parker, Miller and a Mexican were confined to allow the Mexican to go after a bucket of water. He had been often warned against opening the door unless accompanied by another officer. The Mexican left the cell and Meador locked the door. When the Mexican returned Meador unlocked the door. At that instant the Mexican seized him from behind and obtaining possession of the heavy key began beating him over the head. Parker and Miller ran out. They went into the sheriff's room and secured guns. All this occurred in the basement. In order to get out of the building they had to go upstairs to the hallway of the first story of the court house. When Parker reached the foot of the stairway Norris, the assistant district attorney, who had been in his office, attracted by the racket below, had started down. Parker ordered him to turn and go back. Norris did so, but in turning Parker discharged one barrel of a double-barreled shotgun inflicting a wound from which Norris died within a few hours.

After the shooting Parker, Miller and the Mexican ran up the stairs and toward Sheriff Ruffner's livery stable. The sheriff's horse was saddled and bridled, but the other horses were loose in a corral. Parker and Miller ran into a stable room and secured another gun. Then they compelled the stable boys to catch, saddle and bridle another horse. The crowd was gathering so fast that the outlaws could not wait for another, but Parker on the sheriff's horse and Miller and the Mexican rode off, singing, "Just Tell Them That You Saw Me."

This occurrence subverts an eastern theory that the average Arizonian is always armed. Before the shot that killed Norris was fired the city marshal and another officer within less than a block of the jail were aware that trouble was going on, but neither had his gun. When the outlaws rode away in the face of a hundred men there was not a gun in the crowd. As they were leaving somebody, a sympathizer of the fugitives, opened the outer gate of the corral, allowing the horses to escape, so delaying pursuit. The outlaws rode south and were soon out of sight. Fifteen minutes later a posse was after them, but it took a wrong one of four roads. Other posses dispatched later followed wrong trails. Later in the afternoon Deputy Sheriff Munds, who had in the meantime returned, started in pursuit with two men. They came upon the fugitives on the summit at nightfall. There was an exchange of shots, and the outlaws disappeared in the darkness. Being unable to pursue them, the officer returned to town and the next morning a systematic search, lasting more than a month, was begun.

Miller, who had separated from Parker in Lonesome valley the day after the escape, was captured a week later near Jerome, where he was hiding in the vicinity of relatives. He was tried at the June term of court in Yavapai county and was sentenced to the penitentiary for life. Not long ago he attempted to escape, but was taken back wounded.

The Mexican has never been seen. It is supposed by some that he made his way into a Mexican settlement in the western part of the territory and was assisted out of the country. Others believe that Parker and Miller killed him to get rid of him and threw his body into an abandoned mining shaft.

Parker worked his way back to the cattle and sheep ranges in Coconino county, where he received assistance from friends who further aided him by throwing obstructions in the way of the pursuers. He lingered among his friends for some time and then made his way toward Utah.

An Indian post trader, attracted by the reward, enlisted a dozen Navajos and taking up the murderer's trail from a point where he was known to have been twenty-four hours before, followed it toward Lee's Ferry. They came upon the outlaw one morning just as he was getting up and he surrendered without resistance. He was so nearly out of danger that he had relaxed his vigilance.

He was brought back to Prescott, put on trial at the June term, was promptly convicted and sentenced to be hanged. An appeal was taken, but at the January term of the supreme court the judgment of the lower court was affirmed and Parker was re-sentenced to be hanged yesterday.

Parker was about thirty years old and had lived in the northern part of the territory several years. He has four sisters, one single and three married, living in California. Within the last two weeks Governor McCord has received appealing letters from them asking for a commutation of the sentence. They were joined in the petition by persons in Prescott and Parker's friends elsewhere in the north.

Some erroneous data, to be sure, but the *Republican's* flowery approach makes for fascinating reading.

The June 4 *Arizona Gazette* covered the hanging in routine fashion, but they added an interview with one of the witnesses, who speculated on Parker's motive for his behavior on the gallows:

W. H. Smith, a well-known resident of Prescott, arrived in Phoenix Friday night. He was one of those who attended the Parker hanging and said:

"Parker was undoubtedly a brave man. He died without showing a sign of nervousness and when Deputy Sheriff Dillon started to put the noose around his neck he asked that Sheriff Ruffner do it."

Concerning the report that a half dozen California friends were in Prescott with the purpose of liberating Parker, Mr. Smith said:

"I noticed that Parker seemed to take everything very leisurely. He looked at the gallows and examined its parts, walking under it, and seemed to take a long time in which to do it. If he was expecting any outside assistance and was endeavoring to gain time it was evidently of no use, as no demonstration was made."

It was stated in this connection that one of Parker's friends visited him in prison the day before the execution occurred. Of this, however, Mr. Smith had no positive knowledge.

From the same edition:

Al Galpin and Will Buck returned from Prescott Friday night, having witnessed the hanging of James T. Parker. Mr. Buck brought with him a section of the rope with which Parker was hung.

Other newspapers around Arizona, California, and other parts of the country dutifully reported on Parker's hanging, but used wire service reports that were culled from the Arizona reports that have been reprinted. *The San Francisco Examiner*, known for its sensationalism under William Randolph Hearst, did take the time to describe Parker in this manner on June 4:

> The murderer of Lee Norris and train-robber who spread terror throughout the Southwest for several years paid the penalty of his crimes on the gallows at the jail in Prescott, Ariz. Yesterday. Parker was one of the most daring and picturesque bandits in the Southern country. He looted trains, battled with Sheriffs, killed officials, broke jail and distinguished himself in every variety of border crime.

Perhaps the strangest thing was the behavior of the *Visalia Daily Delta* and the *Tulare County Times*, both of which also used only some brief wire service reports. No details about Parker's family or friends or anything like that. For some reason, they had lost interest in their home town boy.

From the June 8, 1898 *Journal Miner*, a very poignant clipping:

> James Parker was buried yesterday afternoon in the potter's field at the county's expense. About a dozen people attended the funeral. The hearse was driven by Sheriff Ruffner in whose custody he has been for nearly a year and a half.

Even though Parker probably wouldn't have cared, Sheriff George Ruffner stayed with his old friend to the last. This clipping, though, has confounded historians for years, many wondering exactly where Parker is buried. The article sounds like Prescott had a separate graveyard for paupers and other undesirables, but historical records show no such burial place in existence.

In reality, the "Potter's Field" is a section of Prescott's Citizens Cemetery, which was the City's only graveyard at that time. As the poor and disreputable were looked down on, this section on the east end of the graveyard was viewed by society as a separate graveyard, even though it was within the same walls as the "respectable" graves. Old records for the Citizens Cemetery actually show where Parker is buried.

Fleming "James" Parker was buried in an unmarked grave in a row of the Potter's field in Citizens Cemetery that was reserved for hanged criminals buried at county expense. He was buried next to the notorious D. W. Dilda, who had been hanged in 1885. Next to Parker are the graves of Hilario Hidalgo and Francisco Renteria, who were jointly hanged in 1903. All of these graves were unmarked, but in recent years, concerned individuals have placed small rock walls around the grave sites, and for many years, this author kept these four graves clear of weeds. On September 9, 2016, I and members of the Ruffner family placed a small marker at the approximate location (possibly the exact location) of Fleming Parker's grave. It undoubtedly never had one before. Elisabeth Ruffner, widow of Lester Ward "Budge" Ruffner, and her daughter Melissa (both prominent Prescott historians) joined me in helping pay for the

On September 9, 2016, a headstone was placed at the grave of outlaw Fleming "James" Parker in Citizens Cemetery in Prescott. From left to right are Parker Anderson, Elisabeth Ruffner, and Melissa Ruffner. (Author's collection)

tombstone, and the small ceremony was also attended by Julie Holst and Bob Bakken of the Yavapai Cemetery Association. There was no press coverage due to concern that it might attract vandals to the cemetery.

A few interesting tidbits in the wake of Parker's hanging—from the *Journal Miner* of June 8, 1898:

> The extra edition of Friday's daily issue containing an account of the Parker execution being exhausted, parties desiring it can be accommodated with copies of the weekly on Wednesday of this week.

From the June 15 *Journal Miner*, an item that does not seem as funny today as it did in 1898:

> Pete Boscha's boy, Richard, who witnessed the execution of Parker, showed the boys at Congress the other day how the thing was done. He erected a scaffold, trap and all complete and then used a rat to represent Parker, pulling the trap and ending his life at the end of a rope.

The *Mohave County Miner* of June 11, 1898 contained a truly bizarre item that appeared nowhere else, not even in the Prescott newspapers:

> Prior to his execution James Parker confessed everything in connection with the robbery of the Santa Fe Pacific train at Rock Cut and the subsequent murder of Lee Norris to Sheriff Ruffner. His confession exonerated Abe Thompson from all participation in the robbery. He says that Thompson knew of the intended attempt to hold up the train, but refused to have anything to do with it. The man killed by the messenger was picked up in Nevada. His name we have forgotten as it was a peculiar one. The man had been around the globe and was probably a rounder. The belief has been general that Abe Thompson put up the job to rob the train but Parker's confession is worthy of credence. Thompson is serving a five year sentence in Yuma for complicity in the holdup.

Artist's illustration published in the *San Francisco Examiner* on June 4, 1898 to accompany its interview with Parker.

These fanciful artist illustrations accompanied the *San Francisco Examiner's* interview with Parker, which was published on June 5, 1898. (Author's collection)

June 3, 1898. Sheriff George C. Ruffner strings up the noose on the scaffold while other officials look on. Parker has not yet ascended the scaffold. (Courtesy of Sharlot Hall Museum)

If Parker did indeed say this to Sheriff Ruffner, it would appear that the doomed man was trying to help his old friend Abe Thompson in his last hours, showing an uncharacteristic sense of honor. It was for naught, though, as since Thompson had pleaded guilty, no appeals were filed in his behalf. Abe Thompson remained in prison for the time being.

As previously seen, the *Journal Miner* reported that a female reporter from a San Francisco paper had interviewed Parker for three days. On June 5, 1898, two days after Parker was hanged, the *San Francisco Examiner* ran the interview. William Randolph Hearst apparently deemed it to be not too newsworthy, as the brevity does not indicate anything near three days worth of talks. Brace yourselves for a shock:

GRIM CONFESSIONS OF THE LATE JIM PARKER,
NOTED COWBOY BANDIT
Disclosed His Romantic Career on the Road to an "Examiner" Writer
a Few Days Before He Was Hanged

Prescott (Ariz.), June 5. — Jim Parker, the noted cowboy train robber and murderer,

Yavapai County law enforcements confer among themselves. Parker has still not been brought onto the scaffold. The bearded man is Father Alfred Quetu, the Roman Catholic priest who baptized Parker the night before. (Courtesy of Sharlot Hall Museum)

was hanged here on June 3d for killing Lee Norris, Assistant District Attorney for Yavapai county, on May 9, 1897, in an attempt to break jail with a Mexican and a white man named Miller. Parker became embroiled in a shooting melee, in which Norris was shot. His dying statement was to the effect that the shooting lay between Miller and Parker. Parker had the only gun.

Parker had been in San Quentin twice—for stealing grain, two years, and for hog-stealing, three years. He was pardoned after eighteen months.

I was received by Parker quite cordially. He related his experiences as though he were telling a pleasant story, except the killing of Norris, which he regretted exceedingly. He said: "I robbed the train for revenge. The trains killed two fine horses of mine in the fall of '95. They were worth $150. They offered in settlement $10 for both. I refused and swore revenge. I had a partner, who was killed. Of course I would never tell his name. He came from a good family.

"We went to the train by horseback and tied our horses three miles above the point of the hold-up, walked back to the rock cut, flagged and slowed down the train, got on behind the tender and ordered the fireman to cut off; but we made a blunder and spoiled it all.

Parker kicks off his shoes as deputies prepare to pinion him on the scaffold. Note the corner of the old Knights of Pythias building in the upper left-hand corner of the photo—this building is still standing. (Courtesy of Sharlot Hall Museum)

Parker calmly chats with the officials on the scaffold after he is pinioned (the equivalent of a full-length strait-jacket) to keep him from struggling. His death is only seconds away. (Courtesy of Sharlot Hall Museum)

Joseph P. Dillon pulls the black hood over Parker's head. Note in background, Sheriff Ruffner's hand is on the lever. (Courtesy of Sharlot Hall Museum)

Fleming "James" Parker is hanged. (Courtesy of Sharlot Hall Museum)

"We succeeded in the second attempt. The express agent lay down back of the train and shot my partner, but I ran the train ahead three miles and came back with the fireman, flagman and express car. I saw I was a man short, but got in and took some registered letters. I had no dynamite. It was with my dead partner, so I lost a big pile. It was a poor job.

"Then I ordered the engineer to go ahead. I rode three miles with both horses, then did away with my gun, mask, clothing and one horse, and rode twenty miles. At the end of this long stretch I changed my horse for a new one and started back.

"There was no evidence against me; but when ten miles from town I saw six men in the road ahead. They never called for me to halt, but commenced shooting at me. I never intended to run, there being no evidence against me, but I had to fly. I struck out for a mile to a lone cedar and tried to locate the parties but it got too hot. I pulled loose my six-shooter three times, loaded it and stuck it in the scabbard and yelled for them to come on. After another eight miles, when the snow got too deep, I saddled and went northwest towards the Colorado river on foot.

"After four days they caught up. There were one white man and three Indians. I had to back down and threw the six-shooter belonging to my friend into the river. My friend was not known to be in this trouble. His name was Kid Marvin, and he turned State's evidence at Flagstaff. The fool told because he got scared. Rogers was the man that arrested me.

"I lay down until 3 o'clock, smoking cigarettes, and then suddenly turned, jumped over the guards, grabbed a gun and tried to kill Rogers. He rolled over too quick. I tried the lever, but it would not work. I grabbed another gun, which was empty, and ordered Rogers to pull off his six-shooter and lay it down where I could get it. He laid it on the ground and begged me not to kill him. The Indians rolled into the creek. I wanted to kill Rogers because he was a traitor. I befriended him in trouble and spent money on him, which he never paid back.

"I walked two days and when nearly starved I ran into Ruffner and six men, who got the drop on me. After eating supper I went to Peach Springs. Broke jail because I had no chance. My lawyer, Sanford, took $150, every cent I had, and would not come to see me and get witnesses. Friends who owed me went back on me. The Kid squealed, and all was up.

"I made the arrangements for escape when Jailer Meador brought in some water for a Mexican. The signal was given to the effect that all was right in the guards' room. We made for the door. The Mexican caught the jailer in his strong arms. I caught the left side and Miller the right. Norris was shot as we passed up stairs. I did not know he was killed until I was brought back. Miller had one horse and myself and the Mexican had to ride double like the wind. The Mexican pushed the saddle on the horse's neck and we both fell off. The pursuers caught up. Miller fell twice and swore he was shot to pieces. I put Miller behind me and rode to the brush to hide him. Munn shot the Mexican's horse twelve times before it was killed. Finally we saw that we would get caught, and the Mexican hid. I rode through Lonesome valley to Cherry creek and back to Bull Williams mountain for grub and money. At Cataract I laid five days, waiting for friends and money to leave the country, but gave it up. I had two fresh horses east of Little Colorado to Navajo post, where I got breakfast and some tobacco. I went ninety miles and lay asleep in a gulch until 3 in the morning, when I heard a shot. I was surrounded by a post trader and a lot of Indians. We met Ruffner at the Colorado river. I intended getting loose until I saw Ruffner.

"They took me to Flagstaff to save me from hanging by a mob. On the way to Prescott I got off at Whipple Barracks and took a carriage to the jail. Four hundred men were lined up in front. I was shackled and brought before the Grand Jury. I had not been shaved nor changed my clothing for six weeks. The Judge instructed the jury to find an indictment at once. I was indicted in ten minutes.

"I don't feel hard toward the officials. A change of venue saved my neck for a time. I am sorry for my sisters, I being the only black sheep of the flock. I am not afraid to die. When I get to the scaffold and have to go, will say, 'Well, boys, you may consider this a picnic, but I don't, as I am not able to help myself, so here goes.'

"I am no Christian, nor a heathen. My parents were not religious. Have only goodwill to all officials and have been treated like a man. Have nothing to regret but Norris' death. I would give my life to have him back, if that would do any good."

L. L. W."

Parker's interview seems honest in spots and very self-serving in others. The most shocking thing about it is Parker's alleged motive for the Rock Cut Train Robbery—he said he had a grudge against the railroad for killing two of his horses. That simply does not jibe with the rest of the surviving evidence about Parker's life and his known gang affiliations (he fails to even mention his friend, Abe Thompson). Furthermore, if this were true, Parker surely would have said something earlier, or there would likely be some record of the dispute. But there is none. It must therefore be concluded that Parker said this to the reporter in an effort to tell the nation that he really did not deserve to be hanged.

Parker could not possibly have known what a legacy he was crafting for himself with this interview. In the ensuing decades, fully half of the after-the-fact accounts of the Parker story have used the "revenge against the railroad" story, despite its lapses in logic. Parker said the horses were killed in 1895? He sure waited a long time to take his revenge!

It is interesting to note that Parker claimed to have indeed had a prior relationship with John Rogers. If that were widely known, and it seems to have been, that worked against Rogers when Parker escaped from him!

The interview, fascinating and maddening (like Parker himself), makes one ache for the entire three day interview, which has not survived. But no matter what one thought of him, Fleming "James" Parker was gone.

CHAPTER 10

Life After Parker

Of course, the world does not stop for anyone's death. It does not even pause for a moment. The same was true of James Parker, even though his story had mesmerized so many. Parker was now dead, but the other participants in his story lived on, and in this chapter, we will examine, where known, the fates of some of Parker's friends and adversaries. A surprising number of "the good guys" in this story went on to lofty, successful positions in Arizona history, and while this was probably not due to their behavior in the Parker story, I'm sure this didn't hurt.

After his hanging was over, and the deceased was buried unceremoniously in a pauper's grave, Parker was not easily forgotten. For a while afterwards, newspapers in Prescott drew comparisons on new crimes to Parker. From the *Courier* of June 10, 1898, a reprint from an earlier edition of the *St. John's Herald*:

> "Broncho Bill" and his companion, Bill Johnson, who held up a train on the Southern Pacific near Belen, New Mexico, recently, are now in hiding in the southern part of this county, in the Black river country. Well-known parties have had long interviews with them. Both men have flesh wounds. They showed one person over $7,000, the proceeds of their recent raid. As these outlaws have added murder to their former crime of train robbery, by killing Deputies Vigil and Bustamante, of Valencia county, the express company will probably be forced to send Detective Thacker et al, after them. As these officers are not well acquainted with the country, the firm of Broncho & Co., will probably continue to do business. The case of Parker, the Prescott murderer, is exactly similar. His captor has a suit pending against the express company, in the district court of Coconino county, for the reward offered for Parker's arrest and which was fairly earned. Should the party now enjoying the cool breezes and fine scenery of the White mountains be caught, they will then be first tried for murder, and thereupon the express company will refuse to pay any reward for their apprehension, for the reason that they "were not convicted of the crime of train robbery."—St. Johns Herald.

From the *Arizona Journal Miner* of June 15, 1898:

Another white horse figures in a killing scrape. The slayer of Jim Keenan rode to Prescott on a white horse.

From the same edition:

Chapter 10: Life After Parker

White seems to be a favorite color with criminals. When Parker escaped from jail he made his famous ride on a white horse. Frank Stewart, who shot Dr. McNally is also mounted on a white steed in his flight to escape arrest.

But comparisons such as these did not last long, as life went on and new horrors replaced the old, as they do in every city.

Over a year after Parker's hanging, the Federal United States Court realized that they still had his train robbery charge on the Docket. They decided to logically clean house. From the *Journal Miner* of August 9, 1899:

> The United States docket was cleared of three old cases yesterday. Two of them were timber trespass cases placed on the docket during United States Attorney Rouse's administration. The other was the train robbery case of James Parker. The latter having paid the death penalty for murder was removed beyond the jurisdiction of the United States court, hence could not be tried for train robbery.

The Federal charges remained in place for Abe Thompson and Love Marvin at this time, but neither was ever brought to trial.

Many years later, when interest in the "Frontier era" and the "old West" began to manifest itself in motion pictures and dime novels, people started to think about Jim Parker again.

A retrospective of the story appeared in the *Journal Miner* on May 29, 1923, which read:

PARKER DANGLED AT ROPE END
QUARTER OF A CENTURY AGO

George Ruffner is meditating these days on old times. He recalled yesterday that it will be just a quarter of a century next Saturday since, under orders of the district court, he took James Parker to a "quiet and convenient spot" and hanged that train robber and murderer until he was dead, dead, dead.

Parker's capture after a famous getaway, took place just 26 years ago last Saturday near the southern rim of the Grand Canyon, after a long chase.

The train robber was incarcerated in the Yavapai county jail in 1897. He escaped one day, walked to the north door of the court house, and there met Lee Norris, brother of T.G. Norris and at that time deputy prosecutor. Parker shot Norris dead, went to a stable where Ruffner had left his saddle horse, the famous Sureshot, took the horse and rode north. After a thrilling chase, Ruffner captured the bandit, who now was doubly at outs with the law over the killing of Norris.

Parker was brought back and landed in jail on May 26, 1897. A year and one week later, Ruffner hanged Parker on a scaffold erected on the plaza exactly opposite where the Journal-Miner now stands. Ruffner himself sprung the trap.

"And that one hanging," said the sheriff, "was enough for me."

On February 11, 1930, the *Journal Miner* ran another retrospective of the story, with a headline that strongly suggested that they interviewed George C. Ruffner for the piece, even though it offers no direct quotes from him. Ruffner, although getting on in years, had actually returned to the position of Sheriff in this era. This article is invaluable, as it seems to be the only really solid piece of evidence that Ruffner and Parker had once been friends on the range. It reads:

ANNIVERSARY OF FAMOUS MAN HUNT IN WHICH SHERIFF TRAILS FORMER PARTNER RECALLED BY G. C. RUFFNER

Last night marked the thirty-third anniversary of the start of a manhunt from this city that contained all the romantic and thrilling elements of Owen Wister's Virginian and similar sagas of this colorful country.

It was the anniversary of Sheriff George C. Ruffner's start on the night of Feb. 10, 1897 to capture Jim Parker, train robber, and only five years previous to that date a saddlemate and partner in many a cattle roundup in the country north of here.

In 1893 Sheriff Ruffner was pushing cows for old man King, founder of the present King outfit in Chino Valley. Parker was a cowpoke for the old Thornton outfit in the same district at the same time. During roundups both frequently found themselves working the same country together, eating from the same chuck wagon and sleeping side by side.

WERE CLOSE FRIENDS

A close friendship grew between them and there was considerable mutual respect and liking.

Then the cowboy Ruffner was elected sheriff. And on February 9, 1897 the cowboy Parker and a partner robbed a Santa Fe train at Deep cut this side of Pete Springs near Kingman. Parker's partner was killed during the affair but the former succeeded in making his escape with some money.

Sheriff Ruffner was immediately notified of the robbery. On the following day he and Deputy Johnny Munds, now deputy at Clemenceau*, left by Santa Fe for the scene of the hold-up. They unloaded their horses at Deep Cut the night of the tenth with the surrounding country covered with more than a foot of snow and bitterly cold.

After breakfast early the morning of the 11th, Parker's horse tracks in the snow were located and the hunt started with Special Deputy "One Eye" Riley accompanying Ruffner and Munds. That breakfast proved the only real meal until the night of the (unreadable).

START THE TRIP

The hunt was started with the three men traveling light, carrying nothing but a little barley for their horses and (unreadable) flour and a little water for themselves. Speed, they figured, so essential that not even an extra blanket was carried along, this despite the bitter cold.

The trail was followed for three days, with the hunters sleeping in the open each night and close to only a small fire. The second night they had some supper with practically no food in between. Horses were not hobbled but kept close to camp.

---

* Today, Cottonwood, Arizona.

In the meantime a white man and several Indians, hearing that the Santa Fe railroad had offered $1,000 reward for the capture and conviction of Parker had started out to effect his capture. Parker had left his horse which had given out and was captured by this white man and Indians afoot and almost starved. He escaped, though, that night, Feb. 14, 1897, when refusing to go further he forced his captors to camp.

Awaiting his chance, he took a gun from the white man, while the latter was asleep and scaring the Indians off, made his escape.

About 2 o'clock the afternoon of Feb. 15, 1897, he was captured in Diamond Canyon by Sheriff Ruffner and Riley. Munds had gone ahead thinking he would stop Parker at a river ford.

When captured Parker was walking up a stream in an attempt to hide his tracks. He was carrying a Winchester over his shoulders and a six-shooter was buckled to his waist. Ruffner, concealed by a rock ordered him to halt as soon as Parker came within effective pistol range.

Parker did so, and when ordered to drop his rifle and unbuckle his six-shooter and strap also drop it, complied. No sooner had he done this than Riley took & shot at him but missed. Ruffner then ordered Riley to stop shooting.

KILLS ATTORNEY

With all concerned, prisoners and captors, practically in a starved and worn out condition, the trip back to Pete Springs was made. Parker was placed in the county jail here but in May of the year he was captured he escaped from the jail killing Lee Norris, at the time assistant county attorney, on the way out.

He was re-captured and the following year hanged for the murder of Norris.

As Parker was never tried and convicted for the Santa Fe train robbery but hung for the murder of Norris before the other charges were tried in court, it was at first feared that Sheriff Ruffner would not receive the $1,000 reward, which citizens of the district felt he richly deserved. But the Santa Fe dispelled these doubts by paying him the full amount offered for Parker's capture and conviction.

That last paragraph may have been an error on the part of the *Journal Miner*, as it was published by different people this many years later. Or perhaps Ruffner in this interview simply decided to claim that he received the reward, figuring no one would remember any differently. As honorable a man as Ruffner was, it is not beyond the realm of possibility that he could have stretched the truth just a bit when telling a story, and that is not necessarily wrong. The fight over the reward money had been embarrassing to Ruffner, Ralph Cameron, and Samuel S. Preston, and Ruffner may have decided it was better not to dredge that up again, especially when there is no evidence that Ruffner received *any* reward money from *any* of the parties who had offered it.

Three days later, the *Journal Miner* ran a followup that contains some interesting tidbits. From the February 13, 1930 edition:

ANCIENT HOTEL BLOTTER TELLS OF ESCAPE OF JIM PARKER FROM LOCAL JAIL AND LONG CHASE BY POSSEMEN

The recent story of the capture of Jim Parker, train robber, by Sheriff George C. Ruffner in 1897 had a repercussion yesterday when Judge McLane, in going over an old hotel register, discovered a notation regarding Parker's later escape on Sunday, May 9, 1897.

The notation was made on a blotter of the old Sherman Hotel register and was opposite the register list for the same day almost 33 years ago. The Sherman House is now known as the Laurel Hotel.

The note, written in ink, says as follows: "Sunday, May 9, 1897. This day three prisoners escaped from the county jail, killing Judge Norris's brother, who died nine hours later."

"A posse is now after them. Parker, train robber, Otto Miller, another white man and a Mexican are the culprits. Miller shot at Lynx Creek six hours later by officers.

"10th—Parker crossed Agua Fria six hours ahead of posse. 11th—Parker aiming for Mogollon mountains. Miller at large, also Mexican."

Judge McLane states there is only one discrepancy in this entry. The Miller mentioned was a brother of the escaped prisoner, whose name was Louis Miller and not Otto. Otto at the time was employed by the Santa Fe railroad as an engineer.

The register is interesting in other ways as a comparison with modern hotel registers. In the left hand corner it states, "All money, jewels, coats, valises and other valuable must be left at the office and checks received for them, otherwise the proprietor will not be responsible for any loss.

BAR BILLS LARGE

In the center was the name of the hotel and under it the words "Rates $1.50 per day." On the upper left hand corner was the name of the proprietor, G. H. Schuerman.

A second register of the Pioneer Hotel, also owned by Schuerman starts its dates off with November, 1884. It is in ruled form with the lines made by rule and pencil and meals and lodging are marked in each square with a figure "1". Both registers are regular brief books without the more modern loose leaf arrangements.

Included in the bills are money due for room, meals and bar refreshments. One guest shows a lodging bill for $6.25 and a bar bill for $17.25. Another has a lodging bill for $1.50 checked against him, with a bar bill for $6.50.

Meals at the hotel were 50 cents apiece and Judge McLane, an oldtimer in this city, states that the hotel had three long tables 25 persons and that these were full up at all three daily meals.

Many of the names are of oldtimers in this district and a good portion of them were known to Judge McLane who stated that some of those that lived at both the Pioneer Hotel and Sherman House are still alive and living in Prescott. The home town of most of these registrants are listed next to their names and include cities in practically every state in the union. A pretty good illustration of the variety of characters that made up the early population of this city.

In relation to the Parker entry, Judge McLane stated that he still has the leg irons worn by the train robber when captured as well as the key he used in making his escape with the other two.

Where did Judge McLane obtain these valuable souvenirs? This is not known; possibly Sheriff Ruffner had given them to him in a gesture of friendship. Do the leg irons and the key that jailor Meador was beaten with still exist? Do Judge McLane's descendents have them? This is not known either; if they do, they have chosen to keep quiet about them. For all we know, they could well be treasured family heirlooms somewhere.

From the *Courier* of September 15, 1931:

ARTICLES SHOWN

So that delegates to the United Indian War Veterans convention might see what Prescott looked like years ago, Mark Cardiff of the Bashford-Burmister company has rigged up a pioneer display in one of the company's show windows.

The articles on display are drawing a lot of attention. Some of the visiting old timers who fought the Apaches in this part of Arizona, using Fort Whipple as a base for operations, recognize the scenes portrayed in the photographs shown.

Of great interest also is an old Sherman House hotel register. The book is opened at the registration for Sunday, May 9, 1897. On the opposite side of the register sheet is the following entry in a bold hand:

This day 3 prisoners escaped from the County Jail, killing Judge Norris, who died 9 hrs. after.

A posse is now after them. Otto Miller, Parker, train robber, and a Mexican are the Culprits.

Evidently later, the following entry was made:

"Miller shot at Lynx Creek 6 hrs. later by officers. Parker crossed Agua Fria 6 hrs. ahead of posse. Parker aiming for Mogollon mountains. Miller at large, also, Mexican." This Mexican's name was Candelaria.

"Judge Norris" referred to was Lee Norris, then assistant district attorney. He was a brother of T. G. Norris, of the Prescott law firm of Norris, Flynn, and Patterson and Byron M. Partridge. The "culprits" later were hanged on the plaza.

Numerous bills, part of the records of George H. Schuerman, are shown also in the window. Also a license issued him by the Western Interstate Protective Association of Liquor Dealers on March 21, 1900. There is a Pioneer hotel register (unreadable) and H. Schuerman, opened at January, 1885.

Here is something of real interest. "Territory of Arizona, Turkey Creek Quartz Mining company, December 30, 1864. I hereby certify that T. P. James has acquired an irrevocable title to 300 feet in the lode known as the Little Grant lode in this district by claim No. 14 south of Discovery, the same being recorded in book No. (unreadable) page 81, of the records of this district, Charles Taylor, recorder, by Henry Clifton, deputy."

Surprisingly clear is a large photograph of the council between General Crook and Geronimo out in the open woods.

Three old guns on display, one of them with a barrel about 2 inches in diameter, and the bore nearly as large, the barrel, strapped to its wooden stock with heavy wire, seem old enough to have chin whiskers. They were crude firearms common (unreadable) they were plenty effective in a pinch.

Miss Kate T. Cory, Arizona artist, has three studies on display in the same window. One of them is of an Indian chief, holding a peace pipe.

If a person might be inclined to find fault with Gurley street now, "just let him take a look at the same street in the early '70's with its small frame shacks, dirt thoroughfare and other evidence of a real frontier town."

Another display of equal interest to the visitors here for the Indian War Veterans reunion and convention and Prescott residents young and old is that to between in the window of the McLane & McLane realty agency in the Bank of Arizona building.

Here Judge Charles McLane, city magistrate, has arranged some of the articles which form his private collection, the majority of them dating back to the days of the old west in this part of the country.

Prominent among the articles is the old pistol used by the famous scout, Jim Bridger, while another is the rifle used by another equally famous character of pioneer days, Black Jack, Jr. This has 32 notches on the stock, so closely cut as almost to be overlapping. Whether these represent 32 Indians who "bit the dust," or are the result of Black Jack's arguments with pioneer whites could not be learned.

Another gun which holds the attention is an old flint lock, while several additional pieces of early American (unreadable) are displayed.

On the more peaceful side, Judge McLane has displayed the old pipe made for Governor Tzitla, one of the territorial governors who made his home here. It is of German manufacture with a bowl which would hold an ordinary tin of tobacco, at on firing. It has a hinged cover and is deeply carved, the date 1700, being out into the bowl.

An old wick scissors used in early days to trim the wicks of oil burning lamps, is shown and there is a boot jack in the form of a huge black bug used in early days by D. Levy, the first of that family to locate in Prescott.

Of almost equal interest but of more recent origin is a fair-sized bottle of coarse gold washed from the sands of Lynx creek by Judge McLane when he first removed here from San Francisco.

A few years later, the *Prescott Courier* ran its own retrospective on Parker. From the May 8, 1937 edition:

FAMOUS PARKER CASE RECALLED

Although the old courthouse and many other once famous landmarks of Prescott and most of the men who built them are gone, the tradition and history associated with these famous buildings and famous Yavapai men is still available to the present, and intensely interesting to those who take time to delve into it.

Sunday, May 10, is the fortieth anniversary of the escape of Jim Parker from the Yavapai county jail in the old courthouse, which stood where the present one now stands. At that time Yavapai included what is now Coconino county, and was full of daring bandits and tough hombres in general, as was the rest of Arizona. Jim Parker was one of the most famous bandits of his time.

Old timers say that Parker's career, as far as Arizona was concerned, started in the late '80's, when he was hired by Tom Wagner, owner of the old Bar Cross ranch near Williams, as a cowhand. Wagner was always a staunch friend of Parker's and maintained that a certain "Kid" Garner turned his thoughts to banditry.

One time Parker failed to return to the ranch and soon afterward report came that the Santa Fe train had been robbed of a shipment of gold near Peach Springs, which some claimed was $90,000. The correct amount was probably nearer $30,000. In this robbery, Garner was killed, and Parker was reported to have been seen among the bandits. Wells Fargo posted a $1500 reward for the arrest and conviction of Parker for the robbery. Henry Hartin, who was in Prescott then, stated that Parker only got $5 from a registered letter.

Sheriff George Ruffner, who was known for getting his man, went out after Parker, finally overtaking him on Diamond creek, northeast of Seligman, and got the drop on him. Parker came back to Prescott peacefully, but did not tell where the gold was hidden.

Parker was never tried for robbery, as he escaped from jail before his trial came up. One day he asked the jailer, Bob Meador, for a drink of water. A Mexican, Cornelia Sarata, hit Meador over the head with a large key, and smeared blood in the jailer's eyes. Meador yelled loudly for help, but by this time, Parker had taken his keys, freed the Mexican and another prisoner, Lew Miller, picked up the jailer's double-barrel single-shot shotgun, and headed for the nearest door.

Deputy county attorney Lee Norris coming to the aid of Meador, was coming down the stairs as Parker and his companions were leaving. Parker ordered him to keep quiet and turn around. When Norris made a dash up the stairs, Parker let him have it with both barrels, shooting him in cold blood. The buckshot was left imbedded in the wall until the building was torn down. With the unloaded shotgun, Parker held up a livery stable, and rode out of town on Ruffner's best horse, Sure Shot, a fine white animal.

After a long chase, in which Parker used all of the tricks known to the range in eluding the officers, putting his horse's shoes on backwards and others, he was finally captured at Tuba City by Preston, owner of the trading post and deputy sheriff, and several Indians. Parker had almost escaped from Preston, when Ruffner rode on to the scene and stopped him.

Parker was finally hanged in an enclosed space on the plaza, without ever telling where the gold was hidden. The Wells Fargo reward was never paid as Parker was never tried and convicted of robbery, but was tried for the more serious charge or murder instead.

Some people claim to have found a few golden eagles in Parker's cave near Williams, but old timers of Yavapai say that the yellow loot lies buried someplace in the hills of Northern Arizona.

All right, who the hell is Kid Garner? The unknown author was clearly a friend of Tom Wagner, who had died several years earlier, so the whole story was second hand or even third hand. I suspect that "Kid Garner" is a misnomer for Love "Kid" Marvin, who was definitely NOT the dead train robber. As for "Parker's cave," who knows? There is no way of knowing for sure where the fleeing murderer hid out from the posse, and at least one old news article did allude to a cave.

It has been difficult finding information on Parker's family after he was hanged, but thanks to the miracle of genealogy websites like rootsweb, we have some meager information. Parker's sister, Sarah Jane "Sadie" Baker, had written plaintively to Sheriff

Ruffner and to Frances Munds about how she didn't think she could go on if her brother was hanged. Instead, she had to live with her pain and grief for another 52 years, passing away on November 20, 1950 at the age of 88, in Los Angeles. She is buried in Evergreen Cemetery there.

Margaret "Maggie" Welch, Parker's younger sister, died on August 30, 1940 in Santa Cruz at the age of 72. She is buried in the Pioneer Cemetery in Watsonville. Her husband, William A. Welch, had passed away on June 12, 1934.

As noted before, Parker's youngest sister, Martha Rockwell, actually died in late 1897 before her brother hanged. A broken heart undoubtedly contributed to her passing at the age of 25. She is interred in an unmarked grave in the Elbow Creek Cemetery in Ivanhoe in Tulare County. Her husband, Wallace Rockwell, died on January 24, 1945 in Fresno County, not far from Visalia, at the age of 78. Their son, also named Wallace Rockwell, died on July 8, 1965 at the age of 71.

Nothing is known of what they did in the years after their brother's death. All had children, which means that Parker likely has living relatives yet today. If so, they have never stepped forward to try and get in on their ancestor's notoriety and you can't really blame them.

There is a grave in the town cemetery in nearby Reedley for Curtis J. Boyd Sr.. This is almost certainly Sadie Baker's first husband and father of her children, Curtis Jackson Boyd. He died in 1951, Next to him is the grave of Minnie Boyd who died the same year, certainly his second wife (who was 18 years younger than he). Parker's maternal aunt, his mother's sister Litha Boyd (she had married a Boyd as well) is also buried in the Reedley Cemetery, having died in 1919.

Homer Dailey Woodard, the Visalia rancher whose steer and possibly other cattle had been stolen by Parker and Philo Johns in 1885, died in Visalia in 1908.

Woodard claimed to be a descendent of William Williams, a signer of the Declaration of Independence.

Alfred Balaam, who was Sheriff of Tulare County when Parker was arrested with Philo Johns for stealing Homer D. Woodard's steer, died in Farmersville, California on January 17, 1919. He was 79 years old. He lived to hear of Parker's eventual hanging, but any thoughts he may have had are not recorded.

Judge William W. Cross, who had presided over both of Parker's early trials in Tulare County, died unexpectedly of heart failure on July 27, 1901.

Parker had always claimed that he had been framed by Walter Brown on the 1890 wheat-stealing charge, and alleged that all of the law enforcement personnel, including Cross, were biased against him because of his earlier cattle-rustling conviction. Without rock-solid evidence on the case (which, as seen in Chapter 1, was largely Brown's word against Parker's), it is difficult to comment, but Judge Cross remained a solid, respected citizen of Visalia until his death.

Tombstone of Judge William W. Cross.

Judge James S. Clack, who defended Parker against the wheat-stealing charge in 1890 and who successfully appealed Parker's conviction to the California Supreme Court, but later sued Parker for non-payment of his bill, died on July 30, 1934 in Visalia.

Clack had gone on to become Justice of the Peace for Tulare County, and served 19 years in that capacity. He had also run unsuccessfully for District Attorney in 1910. At the time of his death, he was still remembered as one of the great legal minds in Tulare County.

Judge James S. Clak's burial vault.

William B. Wallace, the District Attorney who prosecuted Parker and Philo Johns for stealing Woodard's steer, went on to a prominent career in Tulare County. He later became a Superior Court Judge there, and died in 1926 at a ripe old age.

Tulare County Sheriff Eugene W. Kay, who was ordered by the courts to seize Parker's land during Clack's suit against Parker, died on December 11, 1940 in San Francisco.

Attorney Oregon Sanders, who defended Philo Johns at his cattle-rustling trial, died in San Francisco on July 19, 1903 of unknown causes at the age of 53. He is buried in the Modesto Citizens Cemetery in Modesto, California.

Jerry Sullivan, the pioneer rancher whom legend contends employed Jim Parker and George Ruffner as ranch hands at the same time, died in 1929 at the age of 86.

The legend is probably true, but there are no known surviving statements by Sullivan about Parker. His death set off a highly publicized (locally) legal battle over his estate when his 84-year-old brother Dan, who lived in Congress, Arizona, filed suit to contest the will.

Tom King, who with his brother Charles owned the large King Brothers ranch in Chino Valley where both Parker and Ruffner reportedly worked as ranch hands, died around February 11, 1932 on his ranch. He was 62 years old.

Both Tom and Charles had been born in London, and came to America where they learned the cattle business from their uncle.

John R. Robinson, a Coconino County rancher and cattleman from the 1880s and 1890s, died in the Arizona Pioneer's Home in Prescott on June 1, 1937 at the age of 83.

While his name does not appear in any written accounts of the Parker story, he almost certainly knew Parker and George Ruffner in their cowboying days, considering his business and the time period he plied his trade in.

Tom Wagner, the rancher and cattleman who had employed Parker in the early 1890s, died February 24, 1926 of pneumonia at Mercy Hospital in Prescott at the age of 63. He was one of the best known cattle stockmen in Arizona, and wasn't that much older than Parker. He later went to work for the Coburn Brothers, as foreman for their huge cattle interests throughout the state of Arizona and into Mexico. He is buried in Citizens Cemetery in Prescott, not far from Parker himself.

George C. Ruffner made Prescott his home for the rest of his life. Even though a definitive biography has yet to be written, he lives on in the memories of old Yavapai, where he is still spoken of reverently. He was a pillar of the community in every sense of the word.

After hanging his old friend Jim Parker, Ruffner did not have time to rest. Only three days later, a psychotic prospector named A. A. Stewart shot and wounded Dr. John Bryan McNally, and Sheriff Ruffner was off on another arduous manhunt. Such was the life of a Sheriff in old Arizona. Ruffner was succeeded in the office in late 1898 by his Deputy Johnny Munds. In the election of 1900, Ruffner tried unsuccessfully to regain the office after candidate Virgil Earp bowed out of the race.

Following this, he settled down to the life of a respectable businessman, running his livery stables, and engaging in many local philanthropic activities. In 1906, he acquired one of two local undertaking parlors, sent his brother Lester to mortician school, and let him operate it. The Ruffner Funeral Home remained in the family until the 1980s, and even today, it still bears the family name out of reverence.

In 1922, George C. Ruffner was getting on in years, but he had a hankering to get his old job back. He ran for Sheriff of Yavapai County once again, 24 years after leaving the position. He won, and remained in the office with the exception of 1924-26 until his death in 1933. Now you need to think about this; a man who served as Sheriff in the era of stagecoaches, train robberies, and horseback posses returned to the job in the era of automobiles, Prohibition, and bootleggers. He handled both eras very well, and there are very few public figures about whom such a thing can be said.

Probably the greatest tribute we can put to him here is to reprint his lengthy obituary coverage from the *Prescott Courier*, beginning July 23, 1933:

GEORGE RUFFNER CALLED TO REST

County's Most Picturesque Character, Sheriff Over 40 Year Period;
Dies Sunday Morning

George C. Ruffner, 71, Arizona's most picturesque pioneer character and her oldest peace officer, both in point of years and in service in office, succumbed at Mercy hospital at 6:15 o'clock yesterday morning, within 35 or 40 minutes after he had been brought back here from the Agua Caliente Hot Springs, death being caused by an attack of pneumonia which followed a severe case of inflammatory rheumatism, from which Sheriff Ruffner had suffered for less than a week.

Taken ill shortly after he returned from his last active duty, when he returned the three alleged kidnappers of C. G. Riesbeling and A. L. Owen from Brainerd, Minn., a week ago Sunday night, the sheriff was removed by ambulance to the springs on Tuesday. Saturday morning he was said to be resting more easily and to be recovering, but later in the day the pneumonia attack developed and his brother, Lester Ruffner, left at once with the ambulance to bring him back to Mercy hospital for treatment.

Sheriff Ruffner, who suffered several previous rheumatic attacks, had complained first of pain while he was returning with his adopted son, George S. Ruffner, deputy sheriff, with the trio, and it is believed the cramped quarters of the car in which the peace officers and their prisoners rode may have aggravated the attack.

His death, following so closely upon that of E. A. Kastner, which occurred the previous night, and of Dr. Harry T. Southworth, a week ago Sunday, left residents of this city grieved and shocked beyond words, since few of his friends had realized his illness was so serious.

Pioneer residents of this county and state possibly will miss Sheriff Ruffner more than any others of his multitude of friends, since his loyalty to these aged men and women had been one of the loveliest of his characteristics and in his death, they, as well as the members of his family, the city, county and state, have suffered a grievous loss.

Mr. Ruffner, who had been a resident of Arizona for more than half a century, was a native of Mason, Ill., where he spent the early years of his life. The west called him, however, when he was only a lad of 18 and he removed to Arizona, going first to Maricopa county and then removing on May 1 of the following year to Yavapai county, where he had made his home since that date.

He first was employed as a cowboy in the Mayer and lower Agua Fria districts, forming some of the friendships which endured during the remaining years of his life. Later, he went to the Chino Valley district and from there entered into the teaming business, driving his teams with freight from Witherville station, on the old railway line, to Jerome. His loads largely were coke for the smelter at Jerome and copper matt, back to the railway line.

Varying this occupation, the late sheriff then turned to mining, working at Hackberry at one time, and then was employed at the old Boggs smelter near Mayer. During this period of his youth, he met the late Tom Taylor, and J. S. Douglas, who had been among his closest friends down through the years.

Ruffner's first duties as a peace officer came in 1893, when he was appointed a deputy sheriff by the late Sheriff Jim Lowery, serving under him in that capacity, and incidentally, as a deputy county assessor, for two years. His work as deputy assessor covered the listing and valuation on the county's property in the northern part of the state, which then included the greater part of what now is Coconino county.

In 1894, nearly 40 years ago, he was elected sheriff of this county for the first time and served over a period of 18 years in all, being re-elected in 1896, in 1922, 1926, 1928, 1930 and again, for the last time, in 1932.

He was married in April, 1891, to Miss Mary R. (Molly) Birchett of Tempe, who survives him. The Ruffners, having no children of their own, adopted the son and daughter of Van. A. Reichard upon their mother's death, and raised them as their own.

In addition to his widow, these two, George S. Ruffner, deputy sheriff, and Mrs. Gladys McDonald, survive him. Other survivors include Mrs. McDonald's two children, Milliecent and Robert Marshall McDonald, one brother, Lester Ruffner, of this city, a sister, Mrs. Alma Rigg of Denver, Colo., two brothers, Andrew Ruffner of Ohio and Ed Ruffner, living in the old home at Mason, Ill., his nephew, Lester Ward Ruffner, and a niece, Mrs. Mary Lou Vaughn, and a number of nieces and nephews residing in the east.

Funeral services for Sheriff Ruffner will be held Wednesday morning at 10:00 o'clock at the Lester Ruffner funeral home, 303 South Cortez street, with services there and at Mt. View, where he will be laid close to two of his former friends, the late Bill Mulvenon and the late Jim Lowery, both of whom served this county in the office of sheriff. The local lodge of Elks, of which Mr. Ruffner was a charter member, will hold services at the grave, it is expected.

His body will lie in state at the funeral home tomorrow from 3 o'clock in the after noon until 9 o'clock tomorrow night in order that all his former friends may see him and bid him a final farewell.

Among those from outside the city who will be here for the services will be Governor and Mrs. B. B. Moeur, who will drive north early Wednesday morning. Mrs. Isabella Greenway also is expected to be here for the services and has instructed that her headquarters here be closed during the time of the funeral. Others include Mrs. Ruffner's brother-in-law and sister, Mr. And Mrs. A. J. Houston, her brother and sister-in-law, Mr. And Mrs. Joe Birchett, another brother, John Birhcett, and a nephew, Kenneth Houston, all of Tempe.

SAYS PIONEERS FEEL RUFFNER LOSS KEENLY
By Celia Colwell

Our friend, our brother, our old pioneer, George Ruffner, is gone. We old pioneers cannot walk into his office and receive his greeting, his cheer and help, as we did almost daily.

His gifts at Christmas time, his assistance of cars at all times, we remember, as the golden rainbow, on a dark cloud.

We feel our loss and we are just a little more lonely as we walk down the hill, but we know that George has only gone ahead, to make a new trail, and will greet us when we cross the divide.

HALT BUSINESS FOR FUNERALS

Out of respect for two of Prescott's leading citizens, E. A. Kastner and Sheriff George Ruffner, who were taken in death during the week-end, Mayor Charles F. Robb has requested all business houses and offices of the city to remain closed for an hour during each of the funerals, that for Mr. Kastner being set for 10:00 o'clock tomorrow morning and that for Sheriff Ruffner, for 10:00 o'clock on Wednesday morning.

The Piggly Wiggly-Kastner store will remain closed during all of tomorrow but will reopen for business as usual on Wednesday morning.

Tomorrow afternoon after 3 o'clock and until 9 tomorrow night, the body of Sheriff Ruffner will lie in state at the Lester Ruffner funeral home in order that all his friends may see him once more and bid him a final "goodbye."

RECALL ARREST OF JIM PARKER

With the death early yesterday of Sheriff George C. Ruffner, some of the stirring events of his life were being recalled today by old time residents and by the peace officers who served with him during the long years he was in office here.

Among these possibly the most thrilling was the chase for, arrest and execution of Jim Parker, train robber and old time close friend of the sheriff.

Parker, who had punched cows in Yavapai county with Sheriff Ruffner in the eighties, had been arrested for the train robbery and the theft of registered mail and was being held in the county jail, which then was in the old court house on the Plaza.

On May 9, 1897, Parker made a spectacular break for liberty, taking with him Louis Miller, serving a term for forgery, and a Mexican, Cornelia Sarata. The trio met resistance from the late Bob Meador, then a jailor, overpowering and injuring him severely. Meador's calls for help attracted E. L. Norris, assistant district attorney and brother of the late T. G. Norris, who rushed to his aid, only to be shot down and killed by Parker.

The three then made their way across the Plaza to the old Plaza stable, where the fire hall now stands, where they stole three horses, Parker making off with Sure Shot, Ruffner's own and favorite mount.

The sheriff at the time was at Congress Junction and on being notified, left immediately for Prescott, the Santa Fe turning over to his use a light engine which brought him to the foot of the hill, where another light engine from Prescott was waiting to bring him the rest of the way.

The break occurred just at noon, and about 4:30 Sheriff Ruffner was on his way, on horse back, after them. Two of his deputies, Johnny Munds and Horace Yeomans, already had taken the trail of the three desperadoes and had had a brush with them at Lynx Creek, where one of the horses was shot.

Parker left his companions when he reached the McCabe district, and although he had used every ruse possible, including the re-shoeing of Sure Shot, putting his shoes on backwards in an attempt to mislead his pursuers, Ruffner kept up a relentless pursuit, following the trail to the Colorado river country, where he came upon and captured Norris' slayer.

He returned Parker to Prescott, where he was hanged in July of the following year, 1898. The two men remained friends, despite the fact that Ruffner was among those who sought Parker's execution, and on the night before the hanging, the sheriff remained in the cell during the long hours with his former range companion.

In his office, among the trophies of his political life, Sheriff Ruffner had an enlarged and tinted photograph of Sure Shot, the horse he had loved and the horse he eventually pensioned and sent to pasture in the Salt River valley. He also had one of the horse's shoes, cast during the long race for escape and picked up by Ruffner as he trailed Norris' slayer. Sure Shot, by the way, lived to be nearly thirty years old.

Other trophies included two framed commissions, hanging on either side of a copper plaque showing his membership in the local Elks lodge. The one commission was presented him on November 28, 1894, when he first was elected to the office of sheriff, and the other was his last commission, signed November 26, 1932. The copper plaque was made for him and presented by the late Tom Taylor, superintendent of the United Verde smelter, who had been his close friend over a long period of years.

A framed photograph of Sheriff Ruffner and Mr. Taylor, taken not long before the latter's death, also held a place of honor in the office, along with a photograph of the sheriff's last six-horse team and his last 22-mule team, reminiscent of his teamster days in and near Prescott, and a number of other pictures, water colors, crayons, photographs and oils, of running and bucking horses, while on his desk stood a lovely bronze of a horse, the work of E. Framiet, a French artist, which was presented him by James S. Douglas, president of the United Verde Extension Mining company, also a friend of half a century. Ruffner's photograph, taken at his desk during his first term in office also is among this interesting collection.

Another thrilling incident in the late sheriff's life is brought to mind by the old hat, with its bullet pierced brim, and a battered watch, which for years have hung on the wall over his head.

The watch is one which saved the life of the late Dr. John McNally when he was shot at by a man named A. A. Stewart. This shooting occurred in the doctor's office about where the Music store now is. Stewart, believing he had killed the physician, then fled across Granite creek and, that night, while attempting to steal a horse, met and shot Billy Doering in the hand.

Sheriff Ruffner was on his trail by that time and had tracked him to the Turkey creek district, even outdistancing Stewart and arriving at a camp he felt sure the man would visit before the miner got there. Ruffner was sitting on the porch of the bunk house when he saw Stewart pull up and ask one of the women there where he might get something to eat. She directed the man to the cook house and the sheriff waited for him to get settled in the place and then started toward the other house to place him under arrest. Stewart, however, had seen the officer approaching and opened fire, one of the bullets piercing the hat Ruffner was wearing.

Stewart made another break in the dark, hitting for the Big Bug country, with the relentless officer close on his trail. He came upon him the following day and then sent friends of Stewart's to the man, who believed he had killed Dr. McNally, to explain that the physician had not been injured and to ask him to come out, unarmed, to meet the sheriff, who also would put aside his guns. Stewart complied with the sheriff's request and submitted to arrest without further trouble. He was sentenced to serve 15 years in the state penitentiary, then located at Yuma.

The Parker incident only recently was used as the basis of one of the department of justice stories being broadcast over a national radio hookup.

The Parker story was remembered even then, as it seemed to be regarded as the pinnacle of Ruffner's law enforcement exploits. To my knowledge, the radio dramatization referred to has not survived. What a shame.

As with many historical figures, much folklore has come to exist about Ruffner, which is too bad since the facts of his life are so compelling on their own. For example, a folklore version of the story of A. A. Stewart exists, with some variations in detail, and with the shooter's name inexplicably changed to "Bugger Bennett." Based upon my own research, I have ascertained the Stewart name to be correct.

From the *Courier* of July 26, 1933:

FINAL TRIBUTE IS PAID RUFFNER

State Mourns as Body of Pioneer Yavapai County Sheriff
Is Laid at Rest in Mt. View

Grief stricken friends and fellow peace officers from every corner of the state gathered here this morning to pay final tribute to the memory of Sheriff George C. Ruffner, 71, who died at Mercy hospital early Sunday morning and was laid at rest in Mt. View cemetery, following services held at 10:30 in the funeral home of his brother, Lester Ruffner.

Business in Prescott was halted for the period of the services and the county offices were closed from 10 o'clock until noon out of respect for his memory, while the flag on the county court house hung at half staff.

At the funeral home, the services for Mr. Ruffner were held by members of the local lodge of Elks, of which he had been a charter member, and the ritual of the lodge also was read at the grave, no other services being held.

The pall bearers, all men who had served with the late sheriff as deputies over a long period of years, included Deputies John Munds of Cottonwood, C. C. Edwards, of Clarkdale, Bob James of Seligman, Carl Lambertine of Ash Fork, Harley Miller of Congress Junction, and Van A. Reichard, formerly undersheriff and life long companion of Sheriff Ruffner.

Other peace officers, representing every county of the state were here for the sad service, while Governor Moeur, accompanied by Mrs. Moeur, represented the state of Arizona at the funeral.

Flowers sent from friends and admirers from every part of the southwest were banked about the casket in which the veteran peace officer lay at his last rest and messages of condolence have been received by thousands by the grieving family. Among those were the cabled sympathies from James S. Douglas, from Paris, France.

Sheriff Ruffner, who had been a resident of this county for more than half a century, succumbed early Sunday to an attack of pneumonia, which had developed only the previous afternoon while he was at Agua Caliente Hot Springs, where he had been taken earlier in the week to treatment for inflammatory rheumatism. Notified of the sheriff's condition, his brother, Lester Ruffner, and son, Deputy Sheriff George S. Ruffner, left at once to return him here. He died within about half an hour after arriving.

Born in Mason, Ill. In 1862, Mr. Ruffner removed to Arizona when he was only 18 years of age and came to Yavapai county in 1881 to make this county his home. He was a cowpuncher during those early years, later branching into the teaming business and working, as well, as a miner and mill man. In 1893 he first served as a peace officer, being appointed a deputy sheriff during that year by the late Sheriff Jim Lowery. The following year, 1894, he first was elected to the office of sheriff and served in that capacity for nearly 13 years, being re-elected in 1896, 1922, 1926, 1928, 1930, and, for the final time, in 1932.

Sheriff Ruffner is survived by his widow, Mrs. Mollie Ruffner, his son, George S. Ruffner, a daughter, Mrs. Gladys McDonald, two grandchildren, one sister, Mrs. Alma Riff of Denver, his brother, Lester Ruffner of this city, and two other brothers, Andrew Ruffner of Ohio and Ed Ruffner of Mason, Ill.

The funeral arrangements for Sheriff Ruffner were handled by A. Lee Moore of Phoenix, who was assisted by W. H. McLellan of this city, G. E. McMillan of Jerome and C. R. Van Marter of Kingman.

Six Arizona sheriffs were among those in attendance. They were Arthur Vandervier, Flagstaff; Tom W. Voelker, Bisbee; J. R. McFadden, Phoenix; Ernest Graham, Kingman; J. F. Belton, Tucson; and Charles E. Byrne, Globe. Others in attendance included Undersheriff W. S. Ingalls of Yuma; Maricopa Deputies Lone Jordan and Cal Bouse; W. W. Cook, former sheriff of Maricopa county; J. E. Wilkie, secretary of the Arizona Peace Officers' association, Phoenix; George O. Brisbolse, chief of detectives, Phoenix; W. P. Mahoney, Santa Fe special officer, Winslow; and Oscar Roberts and J. C. McGrath, Phoenix peace officers.

Very few men have had a final send-off like that. This probably speaks more for George C. Ruffner than anything I could say.

Ruffner's wife, Mary "Molly" Ruffner, passed away on February 17, 1949.

Johnny Munds succeeded George Ruffner as Sheriff in late 1898, and ultimately carved out his own name in law enforcement until 1902. A number of significant events happened on his watch.

Munds was the Yavapai County Sheriff who unsuccessfully pursued Tom Ketchum after the latter gunned down two men in a store in Camp Verde in 1899. Ketchum was later apprehended and hanged in New Mexico for unrelated crimes. Many western historians believe that Ketchum was the well-known outlaw who was known as Black Jack in that era—others are not so sure it was he. The full truth will probably never be known.

Johnny Munds was also Sheriff when the legendary, catastrophic fire of 1900 hit Prescott, destroying almost the entire downtown.

After leaving law enforcement, Munds ventured into ranching and mining, and in later years, worked for the United Verde Mining Company. He reportedly went to Japan for a while as part of the United States' effort to help that nation rebuild after World War II, helping to teach the citizens how to build mines the way America did.

He died in 1952 at the age of 83, having outlived his only son, who passed away the year before. He was survived by two daughters. His *Courier* obituary, incidentally, recounted his role in the Parker story, and noted that "A Picture of the hanging is still in Goldwater's store in Phoenix and Munds and other officers are in the picture on the scaffold."

Munds' wife, Frances, also made a name for herself in Arizona history. She entered politics, which was still almost unheard of for a woman in those days. Frances served as State Senator in the Legislature for several years, and had the distinction of being only the second female State Senator in America up to that time. The days when Parker's sister Sadie pleadingly wrote to her for help were long in the past. Frances Munds died in 1948.

Joseph P. Dillon, who, as Undersheriff, acted as the hoodsman at Parker's hanging, went on to become a major influence in the Democratic Party in Yavapai County as Arizona approached statehood. As hard as it is to believe today, Arizona was a stronghold of the Democrats back then.

Dillon was also an important member of Prescott Elks Lodge No. 330 B.P.O.E., and from 1906-10 served as manager of Prescott's legendary Elks Opera House (a.k.a. Elks Theatre).

In September of 1922, Dillon briefly became Sheriff of Yavapai County himself, appointed by the Board of Supervisors to the post upon the unexpected death of Sheriff Warren G. Davis. Dillon only served a couple of months, as his old boss George C. Ruffner would be elected Sheriff again that November.

Dillon passed away in 1933 at the age of 69. The cause was a cerebral stroke.

One of Sheriff Ruffner's deputies was Matthew P. "Shorty" Lacy, who participated in the first posse, and likely the second posse as well.

Shorty Lacy later went on to become a Special Officer for the Santa Fe railroad, and he passed away in the railroad's Coast Lines Hospital in Los Angeles in April 1938 of a heart attack. He was 65.

The *Courier*'s obituary for Lacy noted his involvement in the Parker case with a brief recap. He was buried in Mountain View Cemetery in Prescott.

Another deputy under Sheriff Ruffner was Jeff Davis, who also served on the jury that convicted Parker of murder, and participated on the scaffold at Parker's hanging. He continued on as deputy under succeeding Sheriffs, and spent many years in law enforcement.

Jeff Davis was paralyzed by a stroke in early 1922, and lingered in this condition until June 10, 1922, when he passed away.

Former Coconino County Sheriff Ralph Cameron is not widely remembered today, which is unusual as he went on to achieve the greatest success in life of anyone connected to the Parker story. His ambition, his penchant for self-promotion, and driving need to keep himself in the public eye put him over.

After leaving the Sheriff's office in late 1898, and after winning his lawsuit for the Parker reward in 1899, Cameron dabbled in mining and ranching, and served a term on the Coconino County Board of Supervisors from 1905-1907. But he was far more ambitious than this.

In 1908, Ralph Henry Cameron was elected as Arizona's Territorial Delegate to the United States House of Representatives as a Republican, defeating incumbent Marcus A. Smith. Arizona's battle for admission to statehood had already begun at this time, and Cameron, at least publicly, put himself at the forefront of this fight. Cameron's name was on the front page of Arizona newspapers on a regular basis in connection with the approaching statehood at this time, but most Arizona historians tend to believe today that Statehood was achieved more through behind-the-scenes manipulations, politicking, and deal-making, which Cameron was not a party to. Consequently, Cameron is remembered more as a figurehead for the Statehood movement, rather than an active participant, although with his ego, Cameron himself may not have realized this. In fact, most Statehood historians don't even bother to mention his name anymore.

Cameron served until Statehood in 1912 voided his office of Territorial delegate. He then returned to mining and acquired extensive interests.

Not content with being out of the public eye, Ralph Cameron ran for the U. S. Senate in 1920, and was elected. His stint in Washington was unimpressive, as he spent much of his time waging a personal war on the ever-expanding National Park system, which he viewed as an encroachment on private property rights and mining interests (particularly his own mining interests). He had spent over 20 years in court trying to prevent the Grand Canyon from being preserved as a National Park, and is considered a major villain in the history of the Grand Canyon—one whom Canyon historians go out of their way to avoid mentioning.

This author finds it a bit odd that Ralph Cameron has not been rediscovered in recent years, as numerous Republican politicians have become extremely critical of America's National Parks for the exact same reasons. In this way, Cameron was ahead of his time.

As he had largely made himself a one-issue U. S. Senator, he was defeated for re-election in 1926 by Carl Hayden. He attempted to run for Arizona's other Senate seat in 1928, but was also defeated. He tried once more for a Senate comeback in 1932, but failed.

After that, Cameron returned to mining, and ultimately moved to North Carolina and Philadelphia. He died on February 12, 1953 at the age of 89. He was buried in the American Legion Cemetery at the Grand Canyon, near where much of his mining activity had been.

Fletcher Fairchild, the Coconino County lawman who collected the reward for capturing his brother-in-law Louis C. Miller, succeeded Ralph Cameron as Sheriff, but he didn't last long.

Fairchild spent the last three months of his life in the Territorial Asylum in Phoenix after being declared insane before he died October 23, 1899. Details are almost nonexistent beyond this, and family descendent Carol Powell says that family lore contends that Fairchild's kin broke into the various courthouses soon after and destroyed all of the paperwork connected to Fletcher's case. Who knows?

Coconino County Deputy Martin Buggeln, who rarely got his name spelled correctly in the newspapers, went on to purchase the Bright Angel Hotel at the Grand Canyon after leaving law enforcement in 1900. He sold it again in 1905, but stayed at the Grand Canyon where he went into ranching.

Buggeln died on November 29, 1939, in Williams. He was 72 years old. An obituary for him, from an unidentified newspaper clipping in my files (I suspect it is from the Williams News), mentions his service under Coconino Sheriff Ralph Cameron. In doing so, this obituary asserts that Cameron "almost singlehanded captured the notorious Parker gang in 1896." Cameron's boasting did carry weight, didn't it?

A Deputy United States Marshal named Frank Morrell, who hailed from the Williams area, served on the first posse and probably also the second posse. He was a widely respected lawman in northern Arizona, and had many friends. Therefore, the circumstances of his death at the age of 36 are truly bizarre.

A few days before Christmas 1898 not all that long after the Parker story had ended, Morrell was in the Palace saloon in Williams around 1:00am, and got into an angry argument with an unidentified patron. Williams Constable Ed Hardesty happened to be nearby, and tried to calm the men down. Morrell then pulled his gun and shot at Hardesty, missing him. Hardesty returned fire, killing Morrell instantly.

Constable Hardesty turned himself in to Coconino County Deputy Martin Buggeln, and shortly after that, a coroner's inquest jury ruled the shooting was in self-defense, and freed Hardesty. The Constable was deeply grieved, as he and Morrell had been friends and brothers in the Odd Fellows lodge.

Morrell was buried in a family cemetery, the Ferguson/Morrell Cemetery, which is a small enclosure adjacent to Mountain View Cemetery on Willow Creek Road. .

Former Mohave County Sheriff John C. Potts died on April 10, 1914 in Kingman. He was 76. According to his obituary, he had been stricken with an attack of paralysis of some kind a few days prior to his death.

After leaving the office of Sheriff, Potts had remained a prominent citizen in Mohave County, and at the time of his death, he was Chairman of the Mohave County Board of Supervisors.

Maricopa County Sheriff Lin H. Orme left the position later in 1898, but did not live long after that. He died on September 24, 1900 at the age of 52, of "an affection of the brain."

One of the best known trading post operators on the Navajo reservation was Samuel S. Preston, the man who captured Parker for the last time, and who had to go to court to get the reward the railroad had offered.

He stayed in the business for years after that, but eventually changed locations for it, and finally retired and left Arizona in 1918 for Carrollton, Kentucky, where he passed away of a liver ailment in early April 1932.

Preston's assistant Joe Lee, died at the Arizona Pioneer Home in Prescott on February 25, 1952, and is buried in their cemetery.

After resigning from the bench in 1897, Judge John J. Hawkins went on to a number of highly placed positions, among them, he was a member of the seventeenth legislative assembly in Arizona, President of the Arizona Bar Association, and most notably, Vice President of the American Bar Association.

There are no known surviving comments about the Parker case from Judge Hawkins, and as he rose, he certainly had no personal need to make any. He eventually retired to Los Angeles, where he died May 1, 1935. He was 80 years old.

Yavapai County District Attorney Henry D. Ross, who prosecuted Parker, Miller, Richard Cross, and others, went on to a long distinguished legal and judicial career in Arizona. He continued on as District Attorney until statehood for Arizona was achieved in 1912, when he was unexpectedly appointed an Associate Justice of the first State Supreme Court of Arizona. In 1915, he became the Chief Justice of the High Court, and held that position until his death on February 9, 1945, at the age of 83.

Ross was truly one of the pioneers of the State of Arizona, and a detailed retrospective of his life is long overdue. In honor of the long term Chief Justice, his body lay in state in the State Capitol rotunda prior to his burial in Phoenix.

Patrick W. O'Sullivan, who succeeded Lee Norris as Deputy District Attorney, and who helped Henry D. Ross prosecute Parker, went on to hold various other positions in Prescott. He served as City Attorney from 1899 to 1900, and became County Attorney himself in 1912, and served roughly five years in that office.

In 1935, he declined an appointment to the United States Circuit Court of Appeals in San Francisco. He died August 11, 1941 of a cerebral hemorrhage while walking down the street. He was 74.

Attorney John C. Herndon, law partner of the Norris brothers, and who testified at Parker's trial, died in his sleep on April 10, 1906 of unreported causes at the age of 56.

Well-liked and respected in Prescott, his pallbearers were a who's who of Yavapai County legal personnel, including Morris Goldwater, R. M. Burmister, James R. Lowry, Richard E. Sloan, John J. Hawkins, and Robert E. Morrison. He is buried in Prescott's Masonic Cemetery.

George Scammell was a native of Ireland when he arrived in Prescott in 1897, shortly before he was called to jury duty in the Parker case. Assuming the position as Foreman of the jury, it was he that read the guilty verdict to the court.

Scammell opened a hotel call the Three Mile House in Prescott, which he ran until 1909. In March of that year, he rode into town one day and walked into the Bashford-Burmister store, and asked to pick up a suit of clothes that he said an angel named Hobolow ordered for him. When informed there was no suit for him, Scammell became angry and walked outside, calling into the air for Hobolow to appear. Someone called the police and Deputy Joe Cook arrived and arrested him for insanity. These were the days when acting the least bit eccentric got you picked up by the authorities.

According to the *Prescott Journal Miner* of March 10, 1909, Scammell was brought before a Probate Judge (they handled insanity cases because if you were declared insane, your property went into probate to be disposed of just as if you had died), and was promptly ruled insane and shipped off to the Territorial Asylum in Phoenix. Scammell had told the Judge that he belonged to the Hobolow Christian Association, which was run by angels, and that his guardian angel Hobolow was a nephew of the Archangel Gabriel. He claimed that when the angels were not in his presence, a woman with a large razor was constantly trying to kill him, even in the jail. Scammell also apparently refused to eat after being brought in. He was also tubercular, which may have contributed to his delusions.

After being sent to the asylum, his estate went into probate and was sold off, as he had no known relatives. As with Fletcher Fairchild, George Scammell did not last long in the asylum. He died there in December of 1909. He was 63. In Arizona and many other places, life expectancy was interestingly (and perhaps conveniently?) not very long if you were institutionalized. There was no treatment for mental illness in those days either.

J.M.W. Moore, the Prescott Justice of the Peace who presided over the arraignments of Parker, Abe Thompson, and the other criminals in this story and held them for action by the Grand Jury, died in May of 1944 at the ripe old age of 97. His death was due to "the infirmities of age," according to his obituary.

Moore had held a variety of legal and judicial posts in his lifetime, and had also engaged in mining. He had been the Register of the U.S. Land Office, appointed by President Theodore Roosevelt, until the office was moved from Prescott to Phoenix.

He was buried in the Odd Fellows Cemetery in Prescott.

Everett E. Ellinwood, the attorney who represented both Samuel S. Preston and Ralph Cameron in their lawsuits for the Parker reward money, died August 8, 1943 in Phoenix at the age of 81.

At the time he accepted these cases, he had returned to private practice after serving for several years as U.S. District Attorney for the Territory of Arizona, appointed to that post by President Grover Cleveland. In 1907, he had moved to Bisbee, Arizona after accepting a position as primary attorney for the Phelps Dodge mining corporation. He was also a delegate to Arizona's Constitutional Convention in 1910 during the preparation for Statehood.

Ellinwood had also run for Governor of Arizona in 1926, but was defeated in the Democratic primary by George W.P. Hunt. He had many other accomplishments.

After quitting his position as Yavapai County jailor, Robert W. Meador dabbled in a variety of professions, including mining and hotel managing. But he did not settle into anything permanent.

In his advancing years, Meador became sort of a local "old codger," who would spend his days on the Courthouse Square, spinning stories of old Yavapai to children, passersby, and the many friends he had in town. These stories almost certainly included how he was bushwhacked by Parker, Miller, and Sarata.

Meador never married and had no children, although his obituary listed a surviving niece, a Mrs. E. C. Pierce of Azusa, who he had not known until she tracked him down several months prior to his death.

Robert Meador died in his room at the Dial Hotel on May 22, 1933 at the age of 79.

Horace R. Yeomans, a member of the second posse and owner of the horse stolen by Miller and Cornelia Sarata, died of pneumonia on February 11, 1927.

Patrick J. Farley, the Court Clerk who overheard the shooting of Lee Norris, and who called the doctors, died August 8, 1919 in the Consolidated Hospital in Humboldt, Arizona.

Farley had served in numerous minor judicial offices over the years, and for a while had also been the City Editor of the *Arizona Journal Miner*.

Publicly, Parker tried to blame his jailbreak on his attorney, Earl M. Sanford, who (according to Parker) was taking his money but planning to send him up the river for the Rock Cut Train Robbery. Such a claim is impossible to prove, of course, although in those days, it was not uncommon for court-appointed lawyers to deliberately give inadequate defenses to unsavory clients. In any event, it was still very weak justification for the jailbreak, but then, Parker was always trying to excuse his actions, always trying to place the blame on others. He only faced his past square on when he was on the scaffold.

As for attorney Earl. M. Sanford, his fate is shrouded in mystery. He eventually moved to East Orange, New Jersey. In 1915, he went into financial decline, and the

Prescott (formerly *Arizona*) *Journal Miner* of September 24, 1915 reported that he had probably committed suicide. The edition quoted his wife as saying: "Last Friday my husband ran out of the home with a razor in his hand, wildly saying that he would end it all. Because of my crippled condition, I was unable to stop him." The police were also quoted as saying that Mrs. Sanford had been "without food or sleep for four days and nights, and was in a pitiable condition of exhaustion waiting for her husband to return." The area around his home was extensively searched without finding Sanford dead or alive.

Nothing further was said for nearly three weeks after that, until the *Journal Miner* reported on October 10, 1915 that it had received a letter from Sanford's son, Earl A. Sanford, reporting that his father was, in fact, alive. No further details were given.

Four years later, the *Journal Miner* reported the death of Mrs. Sanford in Phoenix, Arizona, in its November 12, 1919 edition. She was run down by an automobile while crossing a street. In her obituary, it was stated that her husband, E. M. Sanford, had died "about three years ago in Phoenix shortly after his return to Arizona from New Jersey after an absence of many years."

I have been unable to ascertain the particulars of Sanford's death at this time. If any of his descendents read these words and wish to fill in the blanks for a future edition of this book, I invite their input.

Undated photo of Arizona Territorial Governor Benjamin Joseph Franklin, whose brief time in office was marred by the Parker case. He offered a reward for Parker's capture on behalf of the Territory. (Library of Congress)

Benjamin Joseph Franklin was Governor of the Arizona Territory at the time of the Parker story. He had previously served as a U.S. Congressman from Missouri from 1875-1879 (two terms) before being appointed to the Arizona Territorial Governorship by President Grover Cleveland in 1896.

Governor Franklin was not well liked by Arizona residents, and he did not last long in the position. Franklin left office on July 22, 1897, less than a month after paying the reward for Parker's capture to Samuel S. Preston that he offered on behalf of the territory. It is worth noting that of the three rewards offered for the jail escapees, Governor Franklin was the only one who did not try to get out of paying.

Benjamin J. Franklin died in Phoenix on May 19, 1898, only a couple of weeks before Parker's hanging. He was 59.

Tragedy continued to strike at the Norris family. Only a little more than a year after Parker's murder of Lee Norris, his brother B. F. Norris, living in Green Forest, Arkansas, died unexpectedly August 18, 1898.

Meanwhile, their brother Thomas G. Norris continued to remain a prominent attorney in Prescott, a pillar of the community. When he died in May of 1932, his death made the front page of the *Journal Miner*. Unlike his brother Lee, who was shipped back home to Arkansas, T. G. Norris was interred in the mausoleum at Mountain View Cemetery in Prescott. He was 76 years old.

The surviving Yuma prison record for Abe Thompson shows nothing extraordinary; no time in solitary, no escape attempts, or anything else. From the *Phoenix Herald* of March 2, 1899:

> Walter Bauch of Coconino this morning received a cane, the gift of Mr. John Clarke, of Flagstaff but at present a guard in the territorial prison. The cane is a fine piece of workmanship being made of common brown paper with an ironwood head and silver trimmings. It is the work of Abe Thompson, a train robber, now serving a term in the prison at Yuma.

Abe Thompson obviously chose to behave himself in prison. It paid off; on August 11, 1900, he was paroled by Territorial Governor Nathan Oakes Murphy. It cannot be pointed out enough that, contrary to popular belief, pardons and paroles were almost as easy to obtain then as they are today. Abe Thompson's parole came approximately a year before his sentence would have been up.

The whereabouts of Abe Thompson after his release are unknown at this time. In his book, The Parker Story, author Thomas E. Way contends that Thompson perpetrated another train robbery single-handedly between Prescott and Ash Fork. Way also admits to having heard two differing versions of this story. In one, Thompson becomes the first and only person to be hanged specifically for a train robbery in Arizona on the strength of the statute that was rarely used. In the other, author Way claims to have seen an article that alleged that Thompson was killed by the U. S. Marshal who apprehended him. The article Way cites quotes the unidentified Marshal as saying: "His horse wouldn't let me load the body on him so I had to tie him to my horse. Then I rode his horse and led mine. I had to deliver the meat to get paid."

Did Abe Thompson really rob another train? I have looked high and low for documentation for this story, and have come up empty. If it is true, it definitely did not happen in Yavapai County, and I am 99% certain it did not happen in Arizona. Unless someone reading my words can fill in the blanks with data from another state, I am ready to proclaim this story to be a myth. I suspect the article that Way saw (which

I have yet to locate as well) came from one of those old pulp western magazines like *Sheriff Magazine*, which used to pass off all manner of folklore as fact. That quote about "delivering the meat" even sounds like something from an old Wild West magazine. It is unlikely that a U. S. Marshal, even in Frontier days, would have used language like that to a reporter.

If this story is a legend, then whatever did become of Abe Thompson? Perhaps he went back to Wisconsin, or perhaps he headed for Kentucky to try and hook up with his children again. Without any clue, it is impossible to trace. Somebody probably knows Thompson's fate; he had two children. Theoretically, he could still have grandchildren living yet, and especially great-grandchildren. If so, they have chosen (understandably) to keep quiet about their notorious ancestor.

There is a cryptic article in the October 23, 1907 edition of the *Hartford Herald*, the newspaper of Hartford, Kentucky, reporting the accidental river drowning deaths of a man named Abe Thompson and his young daughter Hattie. It is unlikely this is "our" Abe Thompson, but I mention it here because it is not impossible, considering Abe apparently had family in Kentucky. If this were him, it would mean that he would have remarried and had another child.

In 1909, the U. S. Government dropped the Federal charges against Thompson, which he had never been tried on. A letter in the old U. S. Postal Service records in the national archives, from a postal examiner named William H. Ramsey to the U.S. Attorney General, reads as follows:

Pensacola, Fla., Feb. 20, 1909.

The Attorney General,
    Washington, D.C.

Sir:
In compliance with Department instructions regarding pending cases to which the United States is a party, or in which it has an interest, I have the honor to submit the following information:

Criminal Case No. 395, Docket No. 1, Page 183.
The United States
    vs
Abe Thompson.
    The Post Office Department is interested.
    Pending in the District Court for the Fourth Judicial District of the Territory of Arizona.
    The indictment was filed July 13, 1897.
    The defendant is charged with being an accessory before the fact to the robbery of a person instructed with the U. S. mail, to wit, one A. S. Grant. The robbery is alleged to have been committed by one James Parker in Mohave county on Feb. 8, 1897, and to have been accompanied by an assault with firearms.

The last action was taken on July 24, 1900, and consisted in entering motion of U. S. attorney and order continuing the case for the term.

On June 19, 1897, this defendant was indicted by a territorial grand jury for robbery, concerning the same matter as that referred to in the U. S. indictment. On June 23, 1897, he pleaded "guilty", and was sentenced, on June 24, to a term of five years and six months in the territorial prison.

I recommend that this case be dismissed. The U.S. attorney concurs. I did not see the post-office inspectors, as both were absent from their headquarters on an official trip.

Very respectfully,
Wm. H. Ramsey
Examiner.

POST-OFFICE DEPARTMENT   Report No. 49

This letter makes no reference to any known criminal case that Thompson might have been involved with following his release from prison, as it surely would have if Thompson had been involved in another train robbery.

On the genealogy website of *Ancestry.com*, there is posted a draft registration card from 1942 for Abe Thompson's son, Charles Samuel Thompson. It states he was born on May 29, 1893 in Peach Springs, Arizona—the year seems to be a little off from other accounts, but the Peach Springs reference shows it is undoubtedly him. It is the only data I have found on him. The card lists him as working at Hawthorn Farm in Libertyville, Illinois. The Lake County Historical Society has informed they can find no data on him as ever having been a resident there, indicating he was a drifting farm worker, who traveled around wherever work could be had. I have no further information on Charles, nor do I know when or where he died either.

Also on *Ancestry.com* is a Thompson family tree, posted by someone identified only as Shadowin, who claims to be a distant Thompson relative. However, this individual does not know the fate of Abe and his son Charles either, although it makes an interesting note that Abe's other unidentified child was a female!

Lack of more data on Abe Thompson has been very frustrating for me. He comes off as a fascinating individual, good or bad. One aches for more detail, but the data just isn't there.

As noted earlier, the eventual fate of Love Marvin is unknown. As he seemed to be a drifter, there is no known documentation as to his origin prior to his escapades with the Abe Thompson Gang. This also makes it virtually impossible to trace him in any way.

After his prison sentence was suspended indefinitely, he seems to have understandably left the area for parts unknown. The Federal indictment against him remained in effect, but he was never brought to trial. Years later, these charges would be dropped. The *Arizona Journal Miner* of July 8, 1907 reported activity in United States Federal court, and contained the following:

Action was taken as follows during this session: Upon the request of J. L. B. Alexander, United States attorney, twelve cases on the old calendar were dismissed, some of them dating back to 1891. The following were affected by this order:

Henry M. Marvin, indicted for selling whisky to Indians in 1891; William K. Jones, indicted on a similar charge in 1893; Thomas Burns, D. R. Reley and James Walsh, indicted for conspiracy for the restraint of trade, in 1894, in connection with the A. R. U. strike on the Santa Fe; Love Marvin, indicted in 1897, on the charge of accessory to robbery of the mail; Joe Soto, indicted in 1907 for selling whisky to Indians; Jack Finney, indicted in 1897 on the charge of robbery; R. E. Stevens, indicted in 1895 on the charge of receiving stolen goods; J. F. W. Costello, indicted in 1897 on the charge of selling whisky to Indians, and Val Polly, indicted in 1902 on the charge of receiving stolen property.

In asking that these cases be dropped, the United States attorney said that those indicted had left the territory and it was impossible to locate them at the present time.

Here, some confusion begins. In the United States Postal Service records in the National Archives, there is a letter from William H. Ramsey, a postal examiner, asking the U.S. Attorney General to dismiss the charge again Marvin. The letter is dated nearly two years later—apparently some red tape delayed the dismissal after the judge granted it. The letter reads as follows:

Pensacola, Fla., Feb. 20, 1909.

The Attorney General,
    Washington, D.C.
Sir:
    In compliance with Department instructions regarding pending cases to which the United States is a party, or in which it has an interest, I have the honor to submit the following information:

Criminal Case No. 396, Docket No. 1, Page 163.
The United States
    vs
Love Marvin.
    The Post Office Department is interested.
    Pending in the District Court for the Fourth Judicial District of the Territory of Arizona.
    The indictment was filed July 13, 1897.
    The defendant is charged with being an accessory before the fact to the robbery of a person instructed with the U. S. mail, to wit, one A. S. Grant. The robbery is alleged to have been committed by one James Parker in Mohave county on Feb. 8, 1897, and to have been accompanied by an assault with firearms. This mail was in the custody of A. S. Grant.
    The last action was taken on July 13, 1897, when the indictment was filed.

On June 9, 1897, this defendant was indicted by a territorial grand jury for robbery, concerning the same matter as that referred to in the U. S. indictment. On June 23, 1897, he pleaded guilty, and the sentence was suspended indefinitely. James Parker mentioned above as the principal in the robbery, was hanged in 1898 for a murder committed in breaking jail at Prescott.

I recommend that this case be dismissed. The U.S. attorney concurs..

Very respectfully,
Wm. H. Ramsey
Examiner.

POST-OFFICE DEPARTMENT   Report No. 50

Nothing further is known of Love Marvin.

Louis C. Miller always seemed to be the man who just couldn't stay out of trouble. It didn't stop with his imprisonment, either. His surviving record, along with news clippings, show that Miller was an incorrigible prisoner with a long string of infractions inside the Yuma Territorial Prison.

His record shows that on January 20, 1898 (which was even prior to Parker's hanging), Miller was put in solitary confinement for 17 days for "refusing to work and attempting to escape." Yes, attempting to escape! The fact that Miller was in his present predicament BECAUSE he had tried to escape from jail was lost on him. Determined not to serve out his life sentence, he made another break for liberty.

The *Prescott Courier*, of January 26, 1898, gave more details, reprinted from an earlier edition of the *Arizona Gazette*:

> Louie Miller, sentenced from Yavapai county for complicity in the jail delivery at Prescott, attempted to escape from the penitentiary at Yuma Thursday morning. He secured a suit of clothes belonging to Assistant Superintendent Hatch, which was hanging in the office within the inclosure and scaling the wall pulled out for the Sonora line. In a short time men were scouring the valley and he was captured by Frank Green and Julio Martinez. It appears that Miller hurt his leg while scaling the prison wall, and was unable to travel fast. When found he was seated near the road under the shade of a tree or brush. Some praise is due the young men captured him as the reputation Miller holds made it a dangerous job to go in search of him.—Arizona Gazette.

It is not known if Parker heard about Miller's escape attempt, and it is unlikely he would have cared if he did.

Miller's speedy recapture was not the end of his story. His prison record tells us that he was returned to solitary confinement for one day on April 8, 1898 for fighting. The details are not known.

On January 15, 1899, Miller was once again placed in solitary confinement for 13 days for "possessing citizen's clothing." Where he got the clothing was unknown, apparently even to the prison authority. The punishment for possessing such contraband may seem unduly harsh, but think about it. Why would he want civilian clothing in prison? It seems pretty obvious that he was planning another escape attempt.

On April 11, 1899, Louis C. Miller escaped from Yuma Prison for the second time. This time around it was a little more complicated. From the *Yuma Sun* of April 14, 1899:

> About 3 o'clock last Tuesday afternoon, while a number of convicts were employed in loading wagons with building stone at the prison quarry, two desperate characters, Smith and Miller, made a break for liberty and succeeded in getting away. They were working on the east side of Prison hill, near the Gila river, and both men started at the same time. Jumping over a steep embankment, they had but a short distance to go to get under cover of the thick underbrush of the Gila river bottom. S. W. Bayly, who was guarding the working force, fired several shots at the fleeing fugitives, but the brush was so thick and the distance so great that none of the shots took effect. During the excitement which followed the escape of Smith and Miller, "Frenchie," a lifetimer, who was working in the prison garden between the Gila and Colorado rivers, took advantage of the situation and faded out of sight. "Frenchie" left his prison clothes in the garden, but his future plans and present address, like those of Smith and Miller, is at present unknown, except to himself and will probably remain a mystery for some time to come.
>
> A posse of guards immediately took the trail of the fugitives and have followed them closely ever since. Armed men have closely guarded the river and railroad, leaving the only avenue of escape across the desert, which is almost impossible for men without provisions who are not acquainted with the country.
>
> All three of the escapes are considered bad men and if they succeed in getting provisions, arms and ammunition their capture will be a difficult matter.
>
> Of the three men, Miller is probably the hardest character. He was serving a life sentence for implication in the murder of Lee Norris in Prescott three years ago, when the noted outlaw Parker headed a jail break. He made an attempt to escape about a year ago by scaling the prison wall, but injured his ankle in the fall on the outside and was captured in the valley a few miles below town.
>
> Smith was serving the last end of a ten year sentence for burglary and is considered as an exceedingly desperate character. He also attempted to escape from the prison last year when Frank Armour headed an unsuccessful outbreak.
>
> "Frenchie" was doing time for killing a couple of Mexicans in a quarrel over some burros. While he has a splendid record as an exemplary prisoner, he is not considered "easy" by any means.
>
> Mr. Bayly took the blame for the outbreak upon himself and resigned his position as guard, yet it does not seem right to censure him for this unfortunate occurrence, as he was not responsible for such a great number of desperate characters being outside the prison walls, where the temptations to take a chance at dodging Winchester bullets from a rifle in the hands of even a crack shot is more than most men with any ambition can withstand.—*Yuma Sun*, April 14."

The Sharlot Hall Museum Archives possesses some newspaper clippings about this jailbreak that are undated and the newspaper unidentified. I have not yet deduced which paper they came from, but suspect that some were from the *Arizona Gazette*. Another clipping:

Hallen, the trusty who escaped from Yuma a few days ago, is thought to have gone direct to Mexico. The report comes from Yuma that he was not in collusion with Smyth and Miller. He was in the garden when he made off. He was not under guard even. Miller and Smyth are believed to be heading east along the line of railroad. They are all three still outside the walls.

Another unidentified clipping:

It is reported that Sam Bailey, the Yuma penitentiary guard in charge of Miller and Smyth at the time of their escape, has resigned. The resignations should have commenced higher up the line. Who authorized, ordered or permitted those two men to be taken outside the walls of that institution? Citizens of Arizona are asking this question. When answered then start the resignations.

Another unidentified clipping:

THE YUMA ESCAPE

It Looks as if the Governor Must Become Keeper of the Prison

Yesterday Governor Murphy received a letter from the penitentiary at Yuma, informing him of the escape of Miller, Smith, and Hallen, and the circumstances of their going. The latter is simply told. The convicts were outside the yard at work on what is known as the rock pile. They broke and ran, soon getting into the brush and disappearing, the shots of the guard whistling close about them.

The Governor yesterday afternoon telegraphed to learn if there had been any recapture, but up to the time of closing the executive chambers had received no reply from Yuma.

There were three escaped, Louis Miller, sentenced for life for murder; Smyth, an eight-year burglary man, committed Nov. 1896, and Frank Hallen, sentenced March 1898 to five years. The latter was a trusty.

It is more than a puzzle to many persons here to know why such a desperate criminal as Miller was permitted to go outside the walls for any purpose. This puzzle is not confined to citizens. It has strongly pervaded the precincts of the executive chambers and Governor Murphy proposes to hold the prison officials to a strict accountability, for his escape, above all others.

It seems but a short time ago since Miller was one of another escaping party from that institution, and his recapture was no easy task. With that escape in view, in connection with his sentence and well-known criminal tendencies and desperate character, it looks almost like a crime on the part of some one in authority down there to again place in his way the avenue of escape. Harsh words now will not help matters any, but the people of the territory, having paid high for protection against this man, will certainly now look to the governor for some deliberate action toward better provisions against repetitions of this and other criminals escaping.

From the *Arizona Journal Miner* of April 19, 1899:

> Rewards of $25 each have been offered for the capture of L. C. Miller and the other two escapes from the Yuma penitentiary.

That really was not very much, considering who Miller was, and considering the stir that the escape caused.

Another unidentified clipping details the eventual capture of Miller and Smith, who did not get very far in the seven days they were out:

> Tucson, Ariz., April 18.—Miller and Smith, two of the desperate convicts who eluded their guards at the territorial penitentiary at Yuma, several days ago, and in quest of whom determined and experienced officers and trailers have been scouring the country in all directions, were captured here yesterday morning by the station agent and turned over to superintendent Brown, of the penitentiary, who, with a posse, came here and took them to Yuma.
>
> At daybreak yesterday morning the wife of the station agent, who had arisen, discovered the convicts passing by, and being convinced who they were, wakened her husband, who in turn aroused his friend, the section boss. They proceeded to outfit a hand car with paraphernalia of war and manning it with a crew of section laborers, with themselves in command, they swooped down upon the plodding, unsuspecting refugees from justice.
>
> (Line missing)
>
> Smith, having no arms, and being almost worn out with tramping and lying in hiding in the Gila river bottom. From the time they escaped from the penitentiary until they were captured, they had been almost entirely without food, subsisting only on such herbs as they could make use of. The men had secured some cast off citizen's clothing, but still wore their convict hats, which had been cut and made to resemble hats."

The *Yuma Sentinel* reported the capture this way:

> Smith and Miller after enjoying liberty for a week—and not the best liberty in the world either now languish in the "snake den." They were captured last Monday by the station agent and section boss at Aztec, about seventy miles from Yuma. Guard Will Buck, who was one of the searching party, flagged a freight train at Aztec for Yuma about 5 o'clock in the morning mentioned and about 15 minutes later a telegram was received by Superintendent Brown that Smith and Miller had been captured. The convicts evidently knew that Mr. Buck was in Aztec and when they saw him take the train, tried to pass on, but the station agent and section boss, from descriptions sent out, knew them to be the escapes. They were taken without any resistance. Superintendent Brown and James Graham landed them at home on Tuesday, where they will perhaps remain without any more chances to escape.

Surprisingly, Miller's record shows that he was put in solitary confinement only seven days for this escape.

At Miller's original sentencing, Judge John J. Hawkins had said that he hoped Arizona would never be "cursed" with a Governor who would show any clemency to

Miller. Judge Hawkins lived to see those words become a reality. Now think about this: Miller was convicted of murder and sentenced to life. He had two escape attempts under his belt. And despite this, Governor Nathan Oakes Murphy took pity on Louis C. Miller and commuted his sentence to twenty years in 1902. The *Arizona Journal Miner* expressed outrage on May 8, 1902:

> Louis Miller's Sentence Commuted
> Governor Murphy has commuted the sentence of Louis C. Miller from life to twenty years. Miller was one of the parties connected with the jail break May 9, 1897, in which Train Robber Parker killed Lee Norris. In his application for a commutation, says the Republican, he is supported by the superintendent of the prison, who believes that a sentence of twenty years will meet the ends of justice. The governor has gone into the case very fully and he believes that at the end of the time to which the sentence has been commuted, Miller will have been sufficiently punished, since there are grave reasons to doubt whether he ever intended to aid in the killing of Norris. Miller was 29 years old when convicted.
>
> The Republican's reference in the above as to the grave doubts whether he ever intended to aid in the killing of Norris, is about as senseless and flimsy a pretense as ever was advanced in connection with an exercise of clemency. Of course Parker himself, who was hanged for the murder, had no idea of killing Norris. They simply went to the jailor's room, armed themselves with the best weapons they could find for the purpose of shooting any one who might interfere with their flight. Norris, hearing the cries of Jailor Meador, started to investigate its cause, and in this way it so happened that he became their victim.

Miller continued to be far luckier than he was smart. When all was said and done, he now had hope that he might actually live to see his release in a few years—a twenty year sentence allowed him to apply for a parole far sooner.

While Miller was in prison, his mother passed away in Phoenix. Her obituary ran in the *Arizona Republican* of May 30, 1906:

> DEATH OF MRS. MILLER.—Mrs. Clara S. Miller died yesterday at the family residence, No. 14 North Sixth avenue. She was sixty-eight years old and was well known in both Phoenix and Prescott, these two cities having been her home for the last twenty-one years. She was respected by all who knew her as a good woman and a devoted mother. The funeral will be held this afternoon at 4 o'clock from the family residence and interment will be made in the Masonic cemetery. She is survived by the following named children, all of whom will be here to attend the funeral: Will Miller and Charles Miller, both of whom are engineers in the employ of the S. F. P. & P. railroad; B. O. Miller of Douglas, an engineer on the E. P. & S.W. railroad; Mrs. Fred Haas of Douglas and Otto V. Miller of this city.

The data in this obituary show conclusively that this was Miller's mother. The omission of her wayward son Louis had to have been deliberate, out of respect for the deceased.

Since it looked more and more like Miller would be eventually released from prison, he decided to get ready for it. He took a course in civil engineering in an effort to qualify himself for a job once he was out. From the *Prescott Courier* of May 27, 1907, a truly bizarre reprint from the *Yuma Examiner*:

Miller's Education

All the wealth of Mrs. Russell Sage of New York, will never buy greater happiness for any life which it may reach than that which came like a (unreadable) yesterday to L. C. Miller, one of the boys "on the hill," when he opened a treasure chest received from that philanthropic woman and found it to contain a superb set of civil engineering instruments valued at $650.

In surveying the site of the new Arizona penitentiary at Florence, Miller will have an important part and this will give him his first opportunity of employing the apparatus which has brought the first joy to ten irksome years of life within prison walls.

Every person who makes a mistake pays the natural penalty. This is the great law. Only the superior man will make of his adversities stepping stones to better things. Out of the wreck and ruin of his life Miller has accomplished a work which gives promise of yet leading him to a high destiny.

When Miller was sentenced from Prescott June 27, 1897, to life in the Yuma penitentiary for murder, the clear-headed, big-hearted fellow realized that in a moment of passion he had taken a stencil of ink and blotted out for him and his all the sunshine of the world. On May 8, 1902, when his sentence was commuted from life to twenty years he began to see a ray of hope and to busy himself with the question of what he might do with what should be left him of life. He decided that he would not leave prison as he had entered it, handicapped by a lack of education, but that he would leave with a constructive knowledge of some practical work. Receiving the encouragement of prison authorities he decided to take a course of civil and mechanical engineering through correspondence with the Armor Institute, Chicago. He set about the business at once and so earnestly did he study and so aptly acquire the knowledge he sought that two weeks ago he was graduated with the phenomenal record of never having returned an examination paper on which he did not receive a grade of 100 per cent.

These were honors that, as a student of West Point, would have permitted him to have been graduated as a first lieutenant in the corps of engineers. This, too, is an honor, convict though he be, which entitles him to membership in the American society of engineers, and membership in numerous polytechnic and scientific societies of the nation, to which only men of scholarly attainments are eligible. Miller is now thirty-seven years of age and has only a trifle more than two years to serve. He will then have served twelve years and a half and the remaining years are forgiven him for good behavior.—Yuma Examiner.

The *Journal Miner* had covered the story as well, albeit with so many typographical errors that one wonders if the typesetter had a few drinks prior. From April 6, 1907:

Down in Yuma, shut in with many other prisoners, by the bare brick walls of the Territorial penitentiary, is Lee Miller, a convict, who, when his term expires, will emerge with his life ambition gratified, thanks to the generosity of Mrs. Russell Sage.

Miller, in 1879, was incarcerated in the Bisbee jail, awaiting trial on the charge of forgery. Confined with him were James Parker and the latter's companions, who had held up a Santa Fe train. One night, led by Parker, all escaped. An attempt by Lee Norris, a clerk in the court house, to stop the jail breakers, resulted in his being shot to death by Parker. The jail breakers made good their escape for the time being but were eventually re-captured. Parker was hanged and Miller was given a life sentence. This sentence was afterwards commuted to twelve years' imprisonment, by ex-Governor N. Oakes Murphy.

Miller's great ambition was to become a civil engineer, and during the time he has been confined in the penitentiary he has thoroughly studied to fit himself for this profession. A letter to the wife of the now deceased billionaire, Russell Sage, interested her, and she sent the prisoner, who will be released in another two years, a full set of engineer's instruments, so that Miller, when he emerges from his confinement, will be in a position to take up immediately his chosen profession.

How did a Prescott newspaper turn Prescott into Bisbee? Or "Louis" into "Lee" or 1897 into 1879?

It wasn't long after that when Louis C. Miller, in spite of his abominable track record was paroled. The *Journal Miner* gave it considerable play in its July 20, 1907 edition:

2 CONVICTS FROM YAVAPAI TO BE PAROLED

Plea of Miller Recalls Memorable Jail Break Here

At a recent meeting of the Board of Control, held in Phoenix, paroles were recommended for Louis C. Miller and William Connors, both serving terms in the Territorial penitentiary in Yuma for murders committed in this county. Miller has two more years to serve and Connors has served about five years of an eighteen year sentence.

Miller, it will be remembered, was one of the principals in a jail break here, Sunday, May 9, 1897, in which Attorney Lee Norris, brother of Attorney T. G. Norris, lost his life. While Miller did not fire the fatal shot, it was generally conceded that he was the leader of the jail break and equally guilty of murder with James Parker, the train robber, who fired the shot that killed Norris.

On May 9, shortly after noon, Miller, who was in jail on a forgery charge, called to Jailor R. W. Meador, and asked him to allow Cornelius Sarata, a fellow prisoner, out of the jail to secure a bucket of fresh water. The jailor allowed Sarata to get the water from a well underneath the steps of the south entrance of the court house. Sarata returned with the bucket of water, and while Meador was engaged in opening the jail door, Sarata attacked him from behind, and while they were struggling Miller and Parker pushed through the door, Sarata hit Meador on the head with the jail door key, inflicting an ugly wound.

During the struggle between Meador and Sarata, Parker ran into the jailor's room and secured a double barreled shot gun, loaded with buckshot. Attorney Norris, who was in the district attorney's office at the time, was attracted to the jail door by the jailor's call for help, and as he reached a point near the foot of the stairway leading to the jail, Parker fired one charge of the shotgun into his body, inflicting wounds from which he died before midnight.

Miller, Parker and Sarata made good their escape after Jailor Meador had fired three shots at them as they ran up the stairs, without effort. The escapes secured mounts in Ruffner's livery stable, then near the southeast corner of Cortez and Goodwin streets. They rode across the mountains, in the direction of Lynx Creek, pursued by ex-Sheriff John L. Munds, who was then deputy sheriff under Sheriff George Ruffner. Munds sighted the fugitives before sundown, crossing the Lynx Creek and Big Bug divide, and although he was about 400 yards distant from them, succeeded in shooting the horse on which Miller and Sarata were riding, dismounting them. He fired several shots at Parker before he disappeared over the divide, mounted on a very fast horse, one of the bullets making a hole in the saddle in which Parker was seated.

Parker escaped in the darkness to the Black Hills and succeeded in making his way to Coconino county, where he was given shelter by friends, and later furnished with fresh mounts. He was later arrested by an Indian agent with a posse of Indians, tried, convicted and hanged for the murder of Norris.

Miller escaped on foot in the direction of Jerome, where he later surrendered to his sister and brother-in-law, who turned him over to the officers. He was tried and convicted of murder in the first degree, all of the members of the jury, with the exception of one, being in favor of the death penalty. He was sentenced to imprisonment for life, and a few years later the sentence was commuted to twenty years. Since his incarceration in the penitentiary he has studied engineering, and has secured a diploma from one of the correspondence schools. He has been a model prisoner of late years and only a few months ago he was presented with a set of engineering instruments by Mrs. Russell Sage, who had heard of his studious habits.

Sarata escaped on foot to Mexico, and was never apprehended. He is said to be still at large in that country.

William Connors, who also asks for a parole, was tried and convicted of the murder of George W. Bryan, an aged resident of the White Piccacho mining district. The crime was committed on or about January 4, 1903. A few days later he was arrested at Morristown by A. A. Johns, then under sheriff, while trying to make his escape from the country on horseback. Connors reached Morristown well mounted and armed. Under Sheriff Johns reached the place a short time before and apprehended Connors as he was walking into the wash room of the hotel, after setting his Winchester against the wall. Johns had the drop on him before he was aware of his presence. Connor's surrender was a very reluctant one, as he had already vowed that he would not be taken alive.

Connors is not about 45 years old. He has been a model prisoner since his incarceration in the Territorial prison, and this had much to do with the recommendation of the Board of Control for his pardon.

The *Courier* was less interested. They simply reprinted a short dispatch from the *Tempe News* on July 26, 1907:

Miller and Connors Paroled
Acting upon the recommendation of the board of control, Governor Kibbey yesterday pardoned Carmeon Mendibles from the territorial penitentiary, and paroled L. C. Miller and William Connors.—Tempe News, July 18.

The news that Miller had reformed was widespread. He seems to have been offered a civil engineering job down in Bisbee, in Cochise County, not far from the Mexican border. On August 1, 1907, the *Courier* reprinted the following item from the Tucson Post:

> Louis C. Miller was in the city Wednesday en route to Bisbee to accept a position as civil engineer. Mr. Miller is well qualified for the position and will undoubtedly give satisfaction to his employers.—Tucson Post.

Newspapers in Tucson did not say much with regard to the Parker story, so it is astonishing to see that they found Miller's passing through town to be newsworthy. It had to have been due to the news of his "reform," and that Mrs. Sage, the wealthy New York philanthropist, had believed in him.

It is to be presumed that Miller started his new job in Bisbee. The details are not known to have survived. All was quiet for a while, but it was inevitable that the man who couldn't stay out of trouble was back in trouble again. From the *Prescott Courier* of June 1, 1908:

> Louis C. Miller is under arrest in Bisbee on charge of false registration. He is a paroled prisoner of the Yuma penitentiary.

What that means is, Miller had foolishly attempted to register himself in the Great Register (the equivalent of registering to vote today). Then as now, ex-convicts were not allowed to vote until their citizenship was restored. Why Miller had tried this, or whether he was so ignorant he did not know the law (despite his past as an ex-Constable), is not known.

From the *Courier* of June 13, 1908, a reprint from the *Tucson Star*:

> **MILLER HELD TO GRAND JURY**
>
> Louis C. Miller was held to await the action of the grand jury on the charge of illegal registration in Bisbee. His bond was fixed at $500, but as yet he has been unable to furnish bondsmen to guarantee his appearance and he remains in jail.
>
> Miller is a paroled convict, with about nine years to serve, and it is expected that his being held to the grand jury will be sufficient grounds upon which to return him to the territorial prison at Yuma.
>
> To prevent Miller being sent back to Yuma, however, his friends, so it is understood, will appeal to Governor Kibbey in his behalf to allow him another chance to show that he is deserving of the clemency exercised by the governor when he paroled Miller last summer.—Tucson Star."

The original criminal complaint filed against Miller reads as follows. I am not sure who John Foster was—possibly the County Recorder:

> In the Justice's Court, Precinct No. 2.
> Cochise County, Arizona Territory

Before me, John W. Hogan, Justice of the Peace in and for said Precinct.
TERRITORY OF ARIZONA,
    Plaintiff }
    Vs.   }
            }   CRIMINAL COMPLAINT

Louis C. Miller,
    Defentant }

TERRITORY OF ARIZONA,   } as
County of Cochise,   }

On this 25th, day of May, A.D. 1908, personally appeared before me, a Justice of the Peace, John Foster, who being by me first duly sworn, complains and says: That on or about the 15th day of April A. D. 1908, in the County of Cochise, Territory of Arizona, one Louis C. Miller, did then and there willfully, unlawfully, and feloniously cause, procure, and allow himself to be registered in the great Register of the City of Bisbsee, Cochise County, Arizona, knowing himself to be not entitled to such registration, he the said Louis C. Miller having been convicted of a Felony;
    all of which is contrary to the form of the Statutes in such cases made and provided and against the peace and dignity of the Territory of Arizona.
    Said complainant therefore prays that a warrant may be issued for the arrest of said
        Louis C. Miller, and that he be dealt with according to law.
           John Foster
Subscribed and sworn to before me this 25th day of May, 1908.
        John W. Hogan
        Justice of the Peace in and for said Precinct in said County.

For reasons that are not clear, the charge was later dismissed by the court. Perhaps he had successfully pleaded ignorance of the law and Justice Hogan had mercy on him. Once again, Miller had landed on his feet.

Miller must have suffered a downward spiral of some kind after that. It is not known what circumstances caused it—perhaps he lost his job, perhaps other factors occurred. But for whatever reason, Miller was obviously in need of money late in 1908, and he returned to some of his roots. Believe it or not, he forged a check. The fact that check forging was what had started the chain reaction of bad luck he had undergone before was lost on him; he did it again, and was arrested before he could skip town. The victim was a man named Frank Schmidt.

Miller's Grand Jury indictment reads:

IN THE DISTRICT COURT OF THE SECOND JUDICIAL DISTRICT OF THE TERRITORY OF ARIZONA, IN AND FOR THE COUNTY OF COCHISE.

The territory of Arizona,   )
    -- vs--   )   INDICTMENT

Louis C. Miller   )   NO. 1605
)

     Louis C. Miller is accused by the Grand Jury of Cochise County, Territory of Arizona, by this indictment, found on the 11th day of May, A. D. 1909, of the crime of obtaining money by a false pretense, committed as follows, to-wit; The said Louis C. Miller, on or about the 13th day of December A. D. 1908, and before the finding of this indictment, at the County of Cochise and Territory of Arizona, did willfully, unlawfully, knowingly and feloniously, and with intent to cheat and defraud one Frank Schmidt of the sum of fifty dollars, lawful money of the United States of America, make, sign, and deliver to the said Frank Schmidt a certain false and bogus check upon the Miners and Merchants Bank, of Bisbee, Arizona, in the words and figures following, to-wit: "Bisbee, Ariz., 12th 1908 No. _____ Miners and Merchants Bank, Pay to the Order of Schmidt & Toland $50.00 Fifty dollars $50.00 Dollars J. R. Miller," it being then and there the fact, as the self defendant then and there well knew, that the said Miners and Merchants Bank had no funds nor credits with which to pay said check nor applicable thereto, by reason whereof the said defendant did then and there obtain from the said Frank Schmidt the sum of fifty dollars in lawful money of the United States of America.

Miller was brought to trial in Cochise County; there were no dismissals this time. The June 6, 1909 edition of the *Tombstone Epitaph* recorded that Miller's attorney tried to get him freed on a writ of habeas corpus, but that failed. And, from the same edition:

> In the case of the territory vs L. C. Miller, charged with forgery, the jury returned a verdict of guilty. A peculiar circumstance arose in the case, when the court read the verdict handed him by the foreman of the jury which read "not guilty," but as it happened the foreman had signed the wrong blank, and the jury was ordered to return to the jury room and correct its error, which was done, the same being made to read, "guilty." The defendant, no doubt, imagined himself again a free man for the time being, but the same was only a brief duration.

Miller's surviving court papers are not especially detailed, so little is known about the jury makeup except that the foreman was named Alfred Hoagland.

Louis C. Miller was headed back to Yuma Territorial Prison, and everyone knew it. His official court sentence reads:

> The District Attorney Jno. S. Williams, Esq., and the defendant in person and by counsel W. B. Cleary, Esq. And J. T. Kingsbury, Esq. Came into court and this being the hour for sentence herein, the Court says: "Louis C.Miller, stand up. On the 11th day of May A. D. 1909, you were indicted by the Grand Jury of this county for the crime of obtaining money under false pretense. To this indictment you pleaded "not guilty." On the 3rd day of June A. D. 1909, you were given a fair and impartial trial, in this court, before a jury of your peers, and said jury returned into open court their verdict, finding you guilty in manner and form as charged in the indictment. Have you anything to say or legal cause to show why the judgment of this Court should not be pronounced against you?" The defendant replied: "I have

Yuma Territorial Prison mugshot of Louis C. Miller, taken upon his arrival in 1909. (Courtesy of Pinal County Historical Society)

Yuma Territorial Prison mugshot of Louis C. Miller in 1909, after the guards shaved his head. (Courtesy of Pinal County Historical Society)

nothing to say." No legal cause being shown or appearing to the court, the Court doth render its judgment: That, whereas, you Louis C. Miller having been on the 3rd day of June, A. D. 1909, after a fair and impartial trial in this Court, found guilty by a jury of your peers, of the crime of obtaining money under false pretense,

IT IS ORDERED, ADJUDGED AND DECREED that you Louis C. Miller are guilty of the crime of obtaining money under false pretense and that you be punished therefore by imprisonment in the territorial prison of the Territory of Arizona, for the term of six (6) years commencing from the date of sentence herein, viz: the 8th day of June, 1909.

AND IT IS FURTHER ORDERED that you be, and you are herby, remanded to the custody of the sheriff to be by him safely delivered into the custody of the proper officers of said territorial prison, and that a certified copy of this order and judgment shall be sufficient authority for the said sheriff to take, keep and deliver you, Louis C. Miller into the custody of the warden of said territorial prison of the Territory of Arizona and shall be sufficient command unto the warden of the said territorial prison of the Territory of Arizona, to receive and safely keep you, Louis C. Miller in said territorial prison of the Territory of Arizona, for the term of six (6) years commencing from the date of sentence herein, viz: the 8th day of June, A. D. 1909.

TERRITORY OF ARIZONA,   )
) as
County of Cochise,   )

I, GEO. B. WILCOX, Clerk of the District Court of the Second Judicial District of the Territory of Arizona, in and for the County of Cochise, do

hereby certify the above and foregoing to be a full, true and correct copy of the judgment and order in the case of the TERRITORY OF ARIZONA vs. Louis C. Miller made and entered in record in said Court on the 8th day of June, A. D. 1909.
   Witness my hand and the seal of said Court this 8th day of June, A. D. 1909.
         GEO. B. WILCOX, Clerk
            By P. (handwriting unreadable), Deputy Clerk

The *Bisbee Daily Review* carried the sentencing on June 9, 1909, in a story which carries some notable factual errors (strange, considering this had become a local story):

L. C. Miller, who was convicted of passing a worthless check at Lowell, was also arraigned for sentence. He is the man who has had two penitentiary sentences to serve before this. On the first occasion he broke jail, but was recaptured. After his second sentence he frustrated a jail break and was paroled with six years of his sentence unserved. Today Judge Doan sentenced him to Yuma for 9 years and the remaining period of his unexpired term is added to this sentence so that he will have to serve fifteen years in the Arizona penitentiary.

The judge in Miller's trial was Fletcher Doan, who in 1899 had presided over the legendary Pearl Hart stagecoach robbery trial. From the same edition:

The motion for a new trial in the case of L. C. Miller was taken up and argued at considerable length by the attorney for the defendant and the matter was taken under advisement by the court.

From the same edition:

Deputy Sheriff Wheeler accompanied by two guards left this morning for Yuma, taking three prisoners, L. C. Miller, who was sentenced to serve six years, and who had been making his threats that none of the officers would be able to land him in Yuma, S. F. Williams, one year for grand larceny and David Foster, eighteen months for forgery.

Miller had obviously returned to his regular habit of sassing his perceived tormentors. Did he really think he would have an opportunity to escape after boasting of his intention to do so?

He was booked into Yuma Territorial Prison June 9, 1909 as prisoner number 3020. His record shows that 45 cents was found on him upon his arrival. He was described this way: His age was 39 years upon his return to prison, his religion was listed as Protestant. His height was 5 feet 8-7/8 inches, his weight 145 pounds. His complexion was "light," his expression "open." Size of head, 7-1/8. Forehead: Medium. Color of hair: light. Color of eyes: Gray. Size of foot: 7. His scars were listed this way—scar over left eye, scar over right eye, scar over left ear, bullet wound right calf, several moles on back, vaccination mark on left arm.

The prisoner's occupation was listed as both "miner" and "engineer," and was listed as a smoker. He listed his nearest relative as Lola Howard of Douglas. Carol Powell has told me that she was the daughter of one of his sisters—perhaps this niece was the only relative speaking to him at this time?. The fact that he did not list any of his siblings would seem to indicate that he had rejected them, or they had rejected him (probably the latter).

At the time Miller was incarcerated, Yuma Territorial Prison was getting ready to close its doors for good. A new territorial prison was being built at Florence, which is still in operation today. On August 29, 1909, Louis C. Miller was transferred to Florence. He was one of the first inmates at what is today the Arizona State Prison in Florence.

On January 15, 1910 or 1911, Miller was put in solitary confinement for "insubordination." But again, Miller ended up luckier than he was smart. Despite his lengthy negative past, his sentence was commuted on August 28, 1912, and he was freed. Furthermore, Governor George W.P. Hunt officially restored Miller's citizenship on September 28, 1912! Maybe someone had told him about Miller's previous arrest for false registration.

On October 31, 1913, the *Prescott* (formerly *Arizona*) *Journal Miner* reported the death of Miller's brother, Baldwin O. "Tobe" Miller, without referring to Louis at all:

TOBE MILLER IS KILLED IN A COLLISION

ENGINEER FORMERLY OF THIS CITY MEETS HIS DEATH NEAR SPOKANE, WASHINGTON

Meager advices by telegraph were received Wednesday by Otto Miller of this city of the death of his brother, "Tobe" Miller, which occurred at Spokane, Wash. In a railroad wreck. It is the supposition that the unfortunate man was in a collision, while performing his duties as an engineman on his locomotive.

The deceased for many years was a resident of this city, where he was employed by the S.F., P. & P. railway. He was a careful engineer, and a splendid citizen, having the faculty of making friends through his genial personality, and his strict attention to the performance of any duty to which he was entrusted. He left this section some years ago. His death has caused expressions of sincere regret in this community where he had near relatives and scores of friends.

As for Louis C. Miller himself, his bad luck continued to haunt him. Apparently trying to start over somewhere where no one knew him, he drifted up to Park City, Utah and adopted the name of Charles J. Parker. It is very interesting that he would take the surname of "Parker"—it is almost as if, psychologically, Jim Parker were still haunting him. That would, of course, be understandable, since meeting Parker in jail had been the worst thing to happen to Miller in his life up to that point. One would like to know what the initial J stood for!

Under the name of Charles Parker, Miller went to work at the Daly Judge mine in Park City, Utah. It is not known how long he worked there. Then came the most shocking news of all. Some people might have called it retribution for the bad life he had led; others would say it was more of the ill fortune that had plagued Miller all of his life. From the *Park City Record* of November 29, 1913:

Another of those awful and apparently unavoidable accidents happened at the Daly Judge mine at 12:15 Thursday morning, resulting in badly maiming one man for life and perhaps two. Nick Soret, stope boss, and Charles Parker, miner, were at work in the 907 stope. The latter was drilling and evidently bored into a missed hole. The explosion which followed shattered the right hand of Mr. Parker, later necessitating its amputation, and his face was so badly peppered with rock that he will lose one of his eyes, and the attending physician fears the sight of the other is destroyed. Mr. Soret was not so badly injured. His head and face were badly cut and he may lose the sight of one of his eyes, though the doctor hopes to save it. Both men are at the hospital, where every attention and care is being bestowed upon them. Mr. Parker is a single man, and has been in the Park but a short time. Mr. Soret is a man of family, and has been employed at the Judge for the past five years.

The same day, the *Salt Lake City Tribune* reported the accident this way:

PARK CITY, Nov. 28----Last night, while at work in the Daly-Judge mine, Charles Parker and Nick Soret were severely injured by picking into a missed hole and causing an explosion of dynamite.

Parker was peppered with rock and fine dirt about the head, face and hands and it is questionable, according to local physicians, as to whether his sight can be saved. His hands and arms are also badly mangled and it is feared that one of his arms will have to be amputated.

Soret was much more fortunate than his fellow-worker and escaped with minor injuries. His condition is not considered serious, although he was badly shaken up from the force of the blast.

The two men were at once taken to the local hospital, where they were given every possible attention. Word from there this afternoon was to the effect that they were both getting along as well as could be expected.

On December 6, 1913, the *Park City Record* ran the following update:

Charles Parker, the unfortunate victim of the "missed hole" explosion at the Daly Judge last week, is in a precarious condition. Both eyes are completely destroyed, and he is suffering from many severe injuries, besides the amputation of his right hand. He surely is to be pitied in his awful plight. Nick Soret, the other victim, is getting along splendidly and will suffer no permanent injury.

So, after living a life of self-induced troubles that eventually led him to leave Arizona, Louis C. Miller was now blind and crippled. News eventually reached his old haunts of Prescott, where he had once broken jail with Jim Parker. This is logical, since his brother Otto still lived there, and others still remembered him.

While the newspaper misidentified the state initially, the following appeared in Prescott in the *Journal Miner* on December 13, 1913:

LOUIS MILLER IS INJURED IN MINE EXPLOSION

J. H. Robinson received a telegram yesterday evening from Park City, Colo., giving information of a mine explosion that had taken place in which Louis Miller was a victim. The latter was reported in a serious condition. His right arm was blown off, necessitating an operation as necessary to amputate the remaining portion. Miller's wounds on the body were regarded as indicating he would not recover.

    The unfortunate miner was a resident of this city many years ago, and is a brother of Otto Miller, a resident. Only a short time ago another brother, "Tobe" Miller, also a former resident, lost his life in a railroad accident while engaged as a locomotive engineer in the State of Washington.

The *Journal Miner* followed up the story on December 31, 1913:

HORRIBLY INJURED IN UTAH MINE EXPLOSION

Mrs. Minnie Haas, at Park City, Utah, writes to her brother, Otto Miller in this city, giving additional particulars of the sad accident that overtook Louis Miller, a brother, a short time ago when the latter was the victim of a missed hole explosion in a mine where he was the timber man.

    Miller lost both eyes, his right hand has been amputated and it is believed the left one cannot be saved. He was otherwise injured, and his escape from instant death is considered as a miracle. He was going into the mine to perform work in his line when directly in front of the missed hole the explosion occurred. The blame is supposed to be due to the shift that was at work at the time.

It has been asked of me if I am positive the unfortunate miner in these news articles is the same Louis Miller who broke jail with Parker. After all, as infamous as Miller was, wouldn't the *Journal Miner* have recounted his notorious deeds? Logically, one would think so, but yet the identification of Miller's relatives—brother Otto, and sister, Minnie Haas, prove conclusively that the disfigured miner was indeed Louis C. Miller. So how does one explain the *Journal Miner's* decision not to remind readers of his past?

There can only be one explanation. Even in those days, it would have been difficult to kick a man when he was down. Miller had lost his eyes and his hands, virtually a death sentence in those more primitive times. Opportunities for the handicapped simply were, for the most part, non-existent. The *Journal Miner's* expression of sympathy for Miller and their refusal to dredge up his past constituted an act of forgiveness, truly spectacular by the standards of the era. The *Courier* from this particular era has not survived, so it is not known what coverage, if any, they gave to Miller's plight.

Some time later, on February 14, 1914, the *Park City Record* ran a new update:

Mrs. Minnie Haas, who came from her home in Bisby, Arizona, several weeks ago to help cheer and comfort her brother, Mr. C.J. Parker, who was so badly injured recently by an explosion at the Daly Judge, leaves this afternoon for her home, being called hither by the illness of her baby. The lady has had more than her share of trouble. It was but recently that she lost her husband, who for seven years was blind, through an accident similar to the one which befell her brother. When news of the latter's misfortune reached the lady , she immediately came to Park City and has been with him constantly since her arrival, proving a great source of comfort to the sufferer. Mr. Parker, not withstanding the fact that he is hopelessly blind, and crippled by the loss of one of his hands, is cheerful in his affliction. He is still at the local hospital, where everything possible is being done for him, but he will surely miss the company and attention of his devoted sister.

The fate of Minnie's husband, Fred Haas, is discussed later in this chapter.

However, after Miller had recovered as much as he possibly could without his eyes and hands, he got married for the first time in his life. Obviously determined to continue living, Louis C. Miller married Emma A. Schultz on March 25, 1914, according to his surviving marriage license. According to the license, Miller was 43 years old by this time, and his bride was 25 years old, a noticeable difference in ages. Emma had been Louis' nurse in the hospital, and this clearly blossomed into romance. Things were a lot different in those days—today, it would be a violation of professional ethics for a nurse to enter into a romantic affair with a patient. Such a nurse would be expelled from the profession today, but in 1914, no one thought anything of it.

The marriage ceremony was performed by Pastor T. P. Cook of the Methodist Episcopal Church in Park City. The marriage license was signed by two witnesses, Tom Baker and Mamie M. Balding, indicating it was a very private ceremony instead of a full wedding. Moses C. Taylor, County Clerk of Summit County, Utah, also signed the marriage license. By the time the marriage occurred, Miller had clearly owned up to his real name, apparently realizing that his marriage might not be valid if he wed under a phony name.

In spite of this, there is no evidence that anyone in Park City, Utah, ever realized that Louis Miller, the blind and injured miner, was the same Louis Miller who had been sent to prison as an accessory to one of the most notorious murders in Arizona history up to that time. In fact, circumstances would seem to suggest that he never even told his wife of his past, which means that Emma Schultz, young, trusting, and in love, married a man she never really knew, even though she thought she did.

The Utah newspapers thought this was all a very beautiful love story. From the *Salt Lake City Tribune* of undetermined date:

> Blind Park City Miner Weds Nurse Who Soothed Him Back to Life
> **HERE ON HONEYMOON**
> Bride and Groom Talk Enthusiastically of Happiness That is Theirs
> Declaring that his reward had been directed by the hand of God, L.C. Miller, totally blind, who nearly lost his life in a Park City mine explosion last Thanksgiving Day, told yesterday of his romance with Miss Emma Schultz, a nurse at the hospital where he was soothed back to life, which led to their marriage on Wednesday. The marriage was the culmination of a romance which lasted more than three months and during a part of that time, Miller was not expected to live.
> Miss Schultz, formerly of Denver, reached the Miners' hospital at Park City about two weeks after Miller had been taken there, following his accident in the

mine. She was immediately assigned to his case and at once a strong attachment was formed between the couple and they became inseparable, although at no time in the early stages of Miller's confinement in the hospital was hope held out for his ultimate recovery. Besides rendering him totally blind, the explosion blew his right hand completely off.

Released From Hospital

In the last month and a half, Miller began to show steady improvement, and about a week ago he was released from the hospital. His arm is still in bandages and his eyes are not only completely closed, but his face is burned with powder marks. The marriage took place in Park City Wednesday at the parsonage of the Rev. T.P. Cook of the Methodist church, who officiated.

Mr. And Mrs. Miller are in Salt Lake for a few days at the Peery hotel. Suit for damages in the sum of $30,000 has been filed by attorneys for Miller against the Daly-Judge Mining company, the corporation by which he was employed at the time of the accident. Miller said yesterday that he would probably remain in Utah until his damage suit is settled in the courts.

Miller, who has been a miner all his life, began employment in the Daly-Judge mine last summer. The explosion which resulted in the loss of his eye-sight and one hand was caused when Miller, working with a pick, struck a cap in a missed hole loaded with six sticks of dynamite.

Charmed With Utah

Relating his experiences yesterday, Miller said Utah had come to have a personal charm for him in the few months he had lived and worked here last summer and fall and that, before the explosion, he had been seriously thinking of making a permanent home in the state. His home originally was in Bisbee, Ariz., where he has relatives and where he intends to go with his wife to spend the remainder of his days. Mr. Miller said the accident at Park City was the first he had ever suffered as a miner and that prior to that he had never had to lay off from work a day because of accident or sickness.

Mrs. Miller is apparently as happy as her husband. She said yesterday, just as Miller had said, that she felt that their marriage had been the will of the Lord and that she knew when she first saw Miller at the hospital that she must go through life with him and help to make the world happy for him.

What a beautiful love story! What would the people of Park City and Salt Lake have said if they had known who Miller really was?

The *Park City Record*, also deeply touched by this story, weighed in on March 28, 1914:

Those who had occasion to visit the Miners Hospital since the accident at the Daly Judge mine, which cost L.C. Miller, known up to this time as L.C. Parker, his eyesight, could not but notice the sincere devotion and gentle attention, that Miss Emma Schultz, one of the best nurses ever at the local hospital, gave to the unfortunate man. Every spare moment was given by Miss Schultz in an endeavor to make the burden of Mr. Miller lighter, and day and night the sufferer was shown every attention and waited upon with that tenderness and care that is always prompted by a big heart and a noble desire to alleviate suffering and assist the sadly afflicted. Because of this devoutness, a mutual love sprang up between patient and nurse, and Wednesday last in the dinning room of the hospital, Rev. T.P. Cook of the M.E. church, pronounced the words that made Mr. Miller and Miss Schultz man and wife. The happy couple left on the afternoon train for Salt Lake, and later will go on to Phoenix, Arizona, where they will make their home. The well wishes of the Park City people go with the happy couple, and fortunate indeed is Mr. Miller in winning so good a woman, and The Record wishes for both every happiness that is sure to come from true love, even though the eyes see not.

The remainder of this article was a verbatim reprint from the *Salt Lake Tribune*.
Miller had indeed filed suit against the Daly Judge Mining Company for his injuries. The suit was filed before he had married Emma, on January 19, 1914, but did not end until afterwards. The court papers have survived in the Summit County (Utah) Courthouse. The original complaint reads:

IN THE THIRD JUDICIAL DISTRICT COURT OF THE STATE OF UTAH
IN AND FOR THE COUNTY OF SUMMIT

Louis C. Miller,   Plaintiff
         Vs.
The Daly Judge Mining Company,
a Corporation, and James
McDonnoll,   Defendants

Plaintiff complains of Defendants for cause of action alleges:
1. That the defendants Daly Judge Mining Company is and at all times herein stated was a corporation, owning and engaged in operating a certain mine in Park City, Summit County, Utah, known as the Daly Judge Mine, and that at the time of the Commission of the grievances herein complained of the Defendant McDonnell was employed by said defendant Company as "Shift Boss" so called, and as such had immediate supervision and control over the employes of said Defendant Company working at the same place on the opposite shift from the one on which Plaintiff was employed, as hereinafter set forth and had immediate direction and supervision over the manner of doing said work at said place.
2. That immediately before the occurance hereinafter set forth, plaintiff was an able bodied man, 42 years of age, a miner by trade, earning and capable of earning $3.25 per day.
3. That said Daly Judge Mining Company contains a large number of drifts, stopes, and other openings, which the Defendant Company was engaged in working and operating, on and for some time prior to the 28th day of November, 1913, and that for the purpose of breaking down rock and other materials in said drifts, stopes, and other openings, the defendant Company caused a large number of holes to be drilled in the face and other portions of said drifts and openings, which said holes were filled with dynamite, or giant powder, and exploded by means of fuse and caps, commonly called blasting; that a large

number of said drill holes was made in the same opening, and after the same had been filled with giant powder or dynamite, they were fired or exploded simultaneously; that by the rules of the defendant company at the time herein complained of, it was made the duty of the employes of said defendant engaged in such blasting, to count the number of reports resulting therefrom and compare the number of reports with the number of holes so charged, for the purpose of ascertaining whether all the holes charged with dynamite or giant powder had in fact exploded, and if there were fewer explosions than the number of holes so charged, it was the duty of such employes to report to the shift boss as "missed holes" the difference between the number of explosions and the number of holes so charged; and it was also made the duty of all said shift bosses, including defendant McDonnell, before going off shift, or ceasing work, for that day, to report the number of "missed holes" in each of said openings respectively to the men going to work on the opposite shift.

4. That on the 28th day of November, 1913, plaintiff was, and for some time prior thereto, had been in the employ of defendant Daly Judge Mining Company, working as a machine man, engaged in operating a certain machine drill in what is known as stope No. 907 on the 900 level of its said mine; that on the night of the 27th and early morning of the 28th of November, 1913, plaintiff was working on the night shift at said point, but had been ordered by said defendant temporarily to cease operations with said machine, and to assist the timber man in timbering said stope; that in order to properly place the timbers therein, it was necessary first to level the bottom of floor of said stope by picking and removing certain earth and rock therefrom.

5. That defendants at said time carelessly and negligently failed to keep the place where plaintiff was so employed in a reasonably safe condition in the following particulars, to-wit: That said defendants carelessly and negligently suffered and permitted a certain drill hole near the face, at the bottom of said stope No. 907, which had been filled with dynamite several days before said 28th day of November, 1913, and which had failed to explode, and notice of which as a "missed hole" had been duly reported to said defendants herein, to be and remain in such condition, without taking any action to cause the same to be discharged or exploded, or the condition in said stope otherwise rendered reasonably safe, and carelessly and negligently permitted plaintiff and others of its employes to continue their work in said stope without warning, or otherwise apprising them of the existence of said missed hole, and the dangerous condition of said stope as a result thereof.

6. That on the early morning of said 28th day of November, 1913, to-wit, at about the hour of one o'clock, while plaintiff was engaged in assisting the timber man to timber said stope No. 907 as aforesaid, and while he was engaged in picking rock from the bottom near the face of said stope for the purpose of properly placing the timbers, as aforesaid, and while he was exercising due care and caution for his own safety and without any fault or negligence on his part, and having no knowledge or notice of the existence of said unexploded blast or "missed hole" in the bottom of said stope, which had theretofore been drilled and filled with giant powder or dynamite, but which at the time of blasting had failed to explode, and which defendants with knowledge and notice of its existence, had carelessly and negligently permitted to remain

unexoloded, his pick came in contact with the powder in said hole, and the same exploded with great force, causing the rock, earth, and other materials in said stope to be shot and forced violently into the face of plaintiff, and against various parts of his body, as a result of which both of his eyes were blown out, the hearing in both ears badly impaired, numerous cuts and bruises were made on various parts of his face, his right arm was so badly lacerated and injured that it had to be amputated at a point between the wrist and elbow, his left hand was badly cut and bruised, and a large number of cuts and bruises made upon his legs; and he was thereby rendered sick, sore, and lame, and has suffered and will continue to suffer great pain and injury, and has been rendered helpless to earn his living, all to his damage in the sum of Fifty Thousand Dollars.

Wherefore plaintiff prays judgment against the defendants for the sum of Fifty Thousand Dollars, together with his costs in this behalf incurred.

Snyder & Snyder
Attorneys for Plaintiff

STATE OF UTAH

ss.

County of Salt Lake

BISMARCK SNYDER, being first duly sworn, deposes and says: I am one of the attorneys for plaintiff in the above entitled action. I verify this complaint on behalf of said plaintiff because he is absent from and not a resident of the county of Salt Lake, State of Utah, where I reside, and because of conversations had with said plaintiff I am familiar with the facts in this case. I prepared the foregoing complaint, know the contents thereof, and the same is true according to my best knowledge and belief.

BISMARCK SNYDER
Ray S. Bowman
Notary Public

On January 24, 1914, Miller had to file an Impecunious Affidavit attesting that he was poverty stricken, and could not bear his legal costs, a necessary move in order to persuade the Court to add them to any judgment he might receive. The affidavit was signed by Miller with an 'x' because he could no longer write, and his sister, Minnie Haas, signed as a witness before the Notary Public, Robert Dalgleish. The court papers also show that Summit County Sheriff John C. Coffey delivered the summons to George Lambourne, Secretary of the Daly Judge Mining Company, and to James McDonnell on January 30, 1914.

The Daly Judge wasted no time in firing back. Their attorneys, "Booth, Lee, Badger, Rich & Parke," filed a Petition of Removal, in which they denied responsibility for Louis Miller's injuries; denied that James McDonnell was even on duty as shift boss that fateful night; charged that by enjoining McDonnell (a resident of Utah) to the suit by name, Miller's attorneys were attempting to keep the suit in the State courts instead of United Stated Federal courts, where most claims against mines were fought because mine headquarters were usually out of state (in fact, the headquarters of the Daly Judge were in

New Jersey). The Daly Judge petitioned the Court to have McDonnell's name removed from the suit, and the case remanded to the United States District Court. The Petition was filed February 17, 1914.

It is probably true that attorney Bismarck Snyder was trying to keep the case in local courts, where Plaintiff Miller might stand a better chance. Then as now, Federal Courts tended to favor big corporations in cases such as this.

James McDonnell, undoubtedly at the behest of his employer, also filed an affidavit February 16, 1914, denying he was present when Miller's accident occurred. It reads:

> James McDonnell, being first duly sworn, deposes and says: that he is twenty-five years of age, and is and at all times hereinafter stated was, an employee of the Daly Judge Mining Company, working in the mine of said company at Park City, Utah; that he is, and at all times hereinafter stated was, a machine man and worked as such except at such times as he did relief work for timberman, and at times acted as shift boss in the place or absence of one Pat Holland, a regular shift boss; that he was acting as temporary shift boss in the place of said Pat Holland on the day shifts on the 25th and 26th day of November, 1913; that he was not shift boss or acting as such or working in the mine of said Daly Judge Mining Company on the night of November 27th and early morning of November 28th, 1913; that Louis C. Miller, the plaintiff in said action and known to the employees of said company under the name of Charles Parker, met with an accident and was injured in said mine working on the night shift on the night on November 27th and early morning of November 28th, 1913; that during said shift on the night of November 27th and early morning of November 28th, on which the said plaintiff was injured, affiant was not the shift boss, was not working in said mine and the said Louis C. Miller was not on affiant's shift and was not under any control, charge or supervision of affiant, and that at the time said Louis C. Miller met with his injuries aforesaid affiant had no control, jurisdiction, charge or supervision whatever or in any manner over the said Louis C. Miller or over the work or duties or labor in any manner of the said Louis C. Miller, and at the time the said Louis C. Miller met with his injuries, to-wit: the shift of the night of November 27th and early morning of November 28th affiant had no authority, control or supervision over any of the employees whatever of the said Daly Judge Mining Company, nor was affiant working in said mine at the time the said Louis C. Miller met with his injuries, aforesaid.
>
> And affiant further states that after the said Louis C. Miller filed his complaint in said cause and named affiant as one of the defendants therein affiant interviewed the said Louis C. Miller and asked him why the said Louis C. Miller had named him, this affiant, as one of the defendants, and the said Louis C. Miller advised affiant that he was instructed not to discuss his case and referred affiant for any information he desired to his attorney.
>
> James McDonnell
> Subscribed and sworn to before me this 16th day of February, 1914.
> Bertha H. Cannon
Notary Public

In addition to this, the Daly Judge had their Park City mine superintendent,

George S. Krueger, file an affidavit on the same day denying that McDonnell was on duty that night.

The mine's legal maneuvering worked. The suit was dismissed by Judge Frederick C. Loofbourow on March 7, 1914 with the court costs charged to Miller ($500, which the Daly Judge paid), and transferred to the Federal court, where the whole thing started all over again.

The papers for the Federal case of "Louis C. Miller vs. The Daly Judge Mining Company, a corporation, and James McDonnell" are reposited in the National Archives, Rocky Mountain Region located in Denver, in Record Group 21, Records of the United States District Courts. It is case file no. 3594. They are interesting reading.

The first thing to occur in the case once it reached the District Court for the United States was for Miller's attorney, Bismarck Snyder, to file a new Motion to Remand, asking that the case be moved back to State court because McDonnell's name on the case prevented Federal jurisdiction (the reason Snyder had enjoined him by name in the first place). The legal wrangling went on.

But as Miller and Snyder had feared, the atmosphere in the United States District Court was more hostile than it had been in the state court, and they were clearly feeling heat for enjoining McDonnell to the case as co-defendant, even though he was nowhere near the scene of the accident. Obviously on the advice of his attorney, Miller himself filed an affidavit, which reads:

> LOUIS C. MILLER, being first duly sworn, deposes and says: I am the plaintiff in a certain action now pending in the United States District Court for the District of Utah, in which the Daly Judge Mining Company and James McDonnell are defendants, which said action has been removed to said court by said defendant Daly Judge Mining Company from the district court of the Third Judicial District for the County of Summit, State of Utah. I have heard read the petition for removal filed on behalf of said Daly Judge Mining Company, and the affidavits of James McDonnell and George S. Kruger attached thereto. The statement in said petition for removal to the effect that at the time of filing said complaint I well knew that said James McDonnell had not committed any acts of negligence and had not in any manner or degree contributed to my injury is not true, for the fact is that while said James McDonnell was acting as shift boss for said defendant Daly Judge Mining Company on either the 25th or 26th day of November, 1913, the existence of the missed hole which caused my injury was directly reported to him, and he failed and neglected after receiving such notice either to cause said missed hole to be discharged or exploded, or to cause the existence thereof to be reported to the next shift or any subsequent shift upon which I was working; that as a result of such negligence, and the negligence of said Daly Judge Mining Company in not causing said hole to be so exploded or the existence thereof reported after it had knowledge thereof, when I was performing the duties which I was ordered to do for said defendant, and having no knowledge or notice of the existence of said missed hole, I picked into the same and it exploded, causing my injuries, as fully set forth in my complaint. It is not contended by me that said James McDonnell

was a shift boss on the same shift that I was working on, but I do contend that for the reasons herein and in my complaint set forth, the said James McDonnell was negligent in failing to cause the existence of said missed hole to be reported, or to cause the same to be discharged, and that his said negligence contributed directly to my injuries aforesaid. The said James McDonnell is made a party herein because I am advised by my attorneys and verily believe that a joint cause of action exists in my favor against both said defendants Daly Judge Mining Company and James McDonnell.

Louis C. (X) Miller

> Subscribed and sworn to before me
> This 4th day of March, 1914.
> Robert Dalgleish
> Notary Public

Miller, unable to write, had signed the affidavit with an 'x', while the notary filled in his name. Attorney Snyder also filed an affidavit:

BISMARCK SNYDER, being first duly sworn, deposes and says: I am one of the attorneys for plaintiff in the above titled action. Before this action was brought I consulted fully with said plaintiff and with other persons familiar with the facts and circumstances in connection with the accident which resulted in the injuries complained of in his said complaint. After such consultation I determined the manner of bringing this suit and the allegations to be contained in the complaint, and prepared said complaint accordingly. This action is brought against both defendants, because after a full consideration of the facts as they were explained to me, I have advised the plaintiff that, in my opinion, his cause of action is joint against both defendants; that both of said defendants are liable to him in damages for the injuries he has sustained, and that both of said defendants can be properly joined as parties defendant in this action.

The allegations in the petition for removal herein, to the effect that this action is brought against Defendant McDonnell fraudulently, and for the sole purpose of defeating the jurisdiction of this court, are not true.

BISMARCK SNYDER

> Subscribed and sworn to before
> me this 11th day of March, 1914.
> (name of notary illegible)

It probably would have been an open and shut case in Miller's favor in the State court, but now in Federal Court, the plaintiff was clearly on the defensive. On March 30, 1914, the Daly Judge Mining Company filed a eight-page response to the suit, denying all claims of liability, and contending that missed holes are fairly easy to see for experienced miners, and therefore, Miller's accident had been caused by his own carelessness in not looking where he was picking.

While it is normal that the mine offered up such a defense in court, there may be some truth to the allegation. Under his new identity in Utah, Miller claimed to have been a lifelong experienced miner, but today we know that was not the case. Therefore, if missed holes are visible at all, Miller may not have known what they looked like. I am in no way defending the Daly Judge, because it is true that the missed hole should have been known of and dealt with by the shift bosses. However, in fleeing his sordid past, Miller passed himself off as a seasoned miner instead of a novice. If he had told his employers he was new at mining, they may have stationed him elsewhere while he learned the details of the trade.

Things did not look good in court for Miller, not only from a legal viewpoint, but if the Daly Judge was going to defend itself by claiming Miller was not an experienced miner after all, it was reasonable to assume they might start digging into his past as well. So, when the attorneys for the Daly Judge offered him an out-of-court settlement for a fraction of what he was asking, Miller and attorney Snyder accepted. A Stipulation was filed in the case on April 9, 1914, in which Miller agreed to drop James McDonnell as co-defendant in the suit, and to withdraw his Petition of Remand. In exchange, the Daly Judge would settle the suit for $3,750.00. Naturally, that was a lot more money in 1914 than it is today, but it was still not enough to care for a man who could never work again for the rest of his life. Nevertheless, the case was over.

Later that year, Louis C. Miller returned to Prescott for a visit, for the first time since his murder conviction. His reasons are not known; perhaps he missed the town he had spent so many years in, and obviously his brother Otto had informed him that public sentiment against him had waned considerably since 1897. In his present condition, it had become safe for Miller to return. From the *Journal Miner* of June 17, 1914:

UNFORTUNATE MAN
Mr. and Mrs. Louis Miller, the former the victim of a sad mine accident in Utah several months ago arrived in the city yesterday from Wickenburg, returning recently from the above State. Mr. Miller has recovered sufficiently to be able to walk, but the sight of both eyes is gone, as well was his right hand blown off. He was formerly a resident of the city, and is well known.

At this point, details on the remainder of Miller's life are a bit sketchy. Carol Powell has told me that her family's tradition contends that Louis later invested in a string of movie theaters in Washington state, but she has not been able to confirm this. Louis and Emma had a child together, a son named Granite, born July 17, 1919, and who died February 11, 1976. The United States Census of 1920 shows Louis, Emma, and five month old Granite living in Portland, Oregon, and this is apparently where they stayed.

The blind Louis C. Miller had truly been able to escape his past. In 2011, thanks to leads provided to me by Carol Powell, I had the pleasure of meeting Dora Silberman, Miller's great-grand-daughter (grand-daughter of Granite), still living in the Portland area. She provided me with some insight into Miller's years in the Pacific Northwest. At one point he owned a grocery store in Seattle, Washington, at 817 8th Avenue. In Portland, he owned an apartment house at 192 ½ Grand Avenue, where he and his family lived for a time.

Most important, Miller drew on his German ancestry and became a local orator and activist for German pride during the years during and following World War I, giving speeches and writing letters to the editor of the *Portland Oregonian*. He wrote and published a German pride song in 1915 called "The Teutonic Barrier," for which he received a congratulatory letter from the German embassy. Most interesting, he always stated that he had come from Arizona, almost as if he were (consciously or subconsciously) daring someone to discover his past.

Dora Silberman provided me with copies of some of her great-grandfather's letters to the *Portland Oregonian* and other papers. They are undated, but are interesting reading, all dealing with World War I issues:

> PORTLAND, Sept. 28.---(To the Editor.)---I hope you can find space in your esteemed paper for an Arizonian's views on certain phases of the Administration or rather mal-administration of the Democrats.
>
> A review of the Wilson-Bryan Administration constrains one to exclaim how long, O Lord, how long must we submit to the weak, maudlin, foreign diplomacy and hyper-profligacy and medieval policies of the Democrats in Washington? Could anything be more nauseating to an American than the part this Government has played in the Mexican muddle?
>
> President Wilson's methods concerning Mexico remind me of Buchanan's Administration just prior to the Civil War, when all the arms and other munitions of war were taken from the Federal arsenals in the North and distributed throughout the Southern States. In fact, about all President Wilson has accomplished in the Mexican trouble is that he has indirectly, by his vacillating policy armed and ammunitioned most every greaser in Mexico.
>
> In a few short months the Democrats have practically undone the years and years of good work and upbuilding by the Republican Administrations in the Phillipines. Under Democratic methods a great majority of Filipinos are fast reverting to the conditions that obtained under the old Spanish regime. Are we to be embroiled with far-away Turkey simply because the Ambassador from that country stated a few unvarnished facts, a statement we all know to be absolutely true?
>
> I repeat, sir, that a review of the Democratic administration of public affairs constrains one to exclaim how long, O Lord, how long must we submit to the classroom methods and antiquated policies of the Democrats in Washington
>
>   LOUIS C. MILLER
>   166 ½ Fargo Street"

Another one:

> Portland, April 24---(To the Editor of the Telegram.)---The deplorable fiasco staged in Paris a couple of years ago, wherein the five great I Ams started out to boss the world, reminds me of the "Ten Little Indians", that is, we have—
> Five little statesmen
> Crammed full of lore;
> One got peeved,
> And then there were four.

Four little statesmen
   Failed to Agree;
One quit the game,
   And then there were three.
Three little statesmen
   Feeling Mighty Blue;
One went home
   And then there were two.
Two little statesmen
   On the dead run;
One tumbled down
   And then there was one.
One little statesman
   Standing by his gun;
The thing went off
   And then there were none.
   It is certainly great, after eight years of Wilsonitis, to again have a Republican administration in Washington. Gosh! I should say it is.
         LOUIS C. MILLER
            42 N. Twenty-first Street, City.

Still another one:

PORTLAND, Dec. 8---(To the Editor)---Shall Congress at its next session appropriate a large sum of money for the construction of more battleships of the super-dreadnought type for the American Navy?

Undated later photo of the now-blind Louis C. Miller, probably taken in Portland, Oregon, after he turned his life around and became a respectable citizen. (Courtesy of Dora Silberman)

In view of the world war now raging, and the possibility of our being drawn in to the conflict, the problem of sea power becomes of unusual importance.

The proposition of naval increase rests upon three main issues. First, is the heavily armed and armored battleship the most efficient and effective naval unit?; second, is the building of more warships justifiable for economic reasons?; third, is an increase of our Navy necessary for defensive and offensive purposes?

During the Spanish-American war monitors were tried and found wanting. It was American battleships and American cruisers that hunted down and destroyed the Spanish fleets. Again, when the Japanese, before a declaration of war against Russia, and under cover of darkness, sent a flotilla of torpedo-boats into the harbor at Port Arthur, thus torpedoing several Russian warships, the cry went up that the battleship was doomed; that the big ship was no match for that scorpion of the sea, the torpedo-boat; but it was clearly demonstrated, in that war, that except under the most favorable conditions, torpedo-boats and destroyers were absolutely helpless against battleships or cruisers. It was Japanese battleships that destroyed Russian sea power in the Far East.

We now hear it loudly proclaimed from various quarters of the globe that the submarine has relegated the battleship to the scrap pile. Unquestionably the submarine is of great value for harbor and coast defense, but out on the open sea, where the great battles for naval supremacy will be fought, the frail submarine cannot cope with the battle fleets.

The Germans are a brave and resourceful people, and no doubt have employed their submarines to the full capacity of those boats, yet today English battleships dominate the North Sea and English Channel, isolating Germany from the rest of the world, thus depriving that country of supplies most needed for carrying on the war.

In consideration of all these facts, we can safely assume that the battleship is still the most efficient and effective naval unit.

The economic aspect of the proposition requires an analysis of expenditure of the amount appropriated. It is generally agreed that the profit of the warship builder is about 4 per cent of the cost of the vessel. Further investigation will discover that a major portion of the balance is disbursed among the very ones who need it most, i.e. the miners who extract from mother earth the copper and iron ores which go into the construction of the ships, the smelter men who melt the ore and the numerous army of mechanics and artisans who design and build the ships.

I submit that it is not the gold hoarded in bank and treasury vault, but it is the money in circulation, that brings happiness and comfort to the American people. Our high financiers and psychological statesmen may point to this hoarded gold as the true measure of prosperity, but to the man who works it is the money he earns that clothes and feeds himself and family; therefore, the greater the amount of work the more money in circulation, consequently the greater the welfare of that army of toilers who bear the burdens of our Government.

Is an increase of our naval strength necessary for defensive and offensive purposes?

Is our Navy strong enough successfully to engage any possible enemy? If not, then assuredly we should make our fleet strong enough to carry the Stars and Stripes to victory against the sea power of any hostile country.

I am aware there are advocates of peace at any price who declare the only purpose of our Navy should be for police duty and to show the flag in distant climes. A glance back through the pages of history of the rise and fall of empires will disclose that peace at any price means peace at an exorbitant price; that peace at any price means peace at cost of National honor; that peace at any price means peace at loss of national integrity, and in its ultimate analysis peace at any price means peace at sacrifice of National liberty.

Our naval establishment is opposed by another class—those visionaries who exultantly announce there will be no more wars, that watchful waiting and peace treaties will solve all international difficulties. It may be in the remote future the race will attain a full realization of the brotherhood of man and universal peace; but we are to deal with the problems of today, therefore it would be well for every American to understand that to maintain our position among the nations of the world we must be prepared to meet any eventuality; hence, if the time comes when we must send our ships against an enemy let us have fleets strong enough to meet any foe; if that time should come, all who are acquainted with the history of the American navy will know that when our squadrons go into action the signal firing from the masthead of the flagship will be, as it always has been, full speed ahead, close in.

LOUIS C. MILLER
192 ½ South Grand avenue

Chapter 10: Life After Parker

Another one:

Editor The American-Reveille:
In view of the rational and patriotic stand taken by the American-Reveille in the matter of national defense, I am sending you a copy of a reply to Sen. W.L. Jones' request for the views of the people of this state on preparedness. Hoping this may be of interest, I am

Yours respectfully,
LOUIS C. MILLER
Wahl. Wash.

Hon. W.L. Jones, Washington, D.C.
Sir: I take pleasure in responding to your request for the opinions of individuals of this state in the matter of military and naval preparedness. I also heartily commend your frankness and plan to discover the attitude of the people of your state in a matter so vital to the nation.

I can state my position in a very few words, and that is: If we are to maintain our status as an independent and sovereign people, determined to work out our destiny in our own way, we most assuredly should have an adequate military and naval preparedness. To say otherwise would be equivalent to declaring that our large cities do not need a police force or a fire department. Hence the principal question at issue is, what is adequate preparedness? Now it would be about as rational for you, I or any other layman to attempt to decide this point as it would be for a Papago Indian to attempt to instruct Edison in electrical engineering, or Newcomb in astronomy.

There are really two distinct questions involved. The first: Do we require an adequate national defense? This question is for the people, through their national legislators to decide. The other question is, what is adequate preparedness? This problem is for the military and naval experts to work out.

As it is most apparent that the people have decided to have an adequate national defense there only remains the question of adequacy.

For my part, I have supreme confidence in the honor, competency, and patriotism of our military and naval experts.

Yours very respectfully,
LOUIS C. MILLER

Another one:

PORTLAND, Oct. 1---(To the Editor) Permit me to say a few words on what I consider to be the most important question for the consideration of the voters at the coming election. I believe a little study and thought will disclose the fact that the numerous measures and amendments to be voted on are of secondary importance to one dominant question at issue.

A question every voter should ask himself before casting his vote, i.e. does he approve of the methods and policies of the Democratic party, or does he believe the American people will be best served by a return of the Republican party to power?

The answer to that question will depend to a great extent on the vote of the Progressives.

I postulate that a majority of the Progressives are at heart and in principle Republicans, and that the Progressive party cannot win; further, that a vote for a Progressive party candidate is in effect a vote for the Democratic party.

Remember that a vote for the Democratic party indicates the voter's approval of Mr. Bryan's Columbian treaty, whereby Brother Bryan would purchase the friendship of all Latin America by paying as tribute a trifling sum of $25,000,000 to Colombia.

A vote for the Democratic ticket approves the canal toll exemption repeal measure, wherein the Democrats not only brazenly repudiated their own National platform, but on the demands of a foreign government servilely surrendered American rights in the canal.

A vote for the Democratic party is a vote for a continuance of our Mexican policy—watchful waiting—which means further destruction of American property (About 43 per cent of the wealth of Mexico is owned by Americans), the wanton murder of American citizens, and all the hideous brutalities of a guerilla warfare carried on by a mongrel semi-savage people.

A vote for the Democrats mean acquiescence in that party's policies in the Philippines, measures which if carried out will make chattel slaves of a large majority of the natives of those islands, slaves to be exploited by and for the benefit of the educated class.

A vote for the Democratic party is a vote of approval for the Democratic tariff tinkering, the free importation of Chinese eggs, New Zealand butter, etc., and a war tax to cover the inefficiency and profligacy of the Democratic leaders, and a vote for the Democratic party is an expression of approval of that spawn of a darker age, the spoils system.

Therefore it behooves every voter to consider well whether he can afford to vote directly or indirectly for the Democratic party.

LOUIS C. MILLER
166 ½ Fargo Street

Another one:

PORTLAND, July 6.---(To the Editor) ---Now, since the so-called peace treaty with it's interwoven league covenant has been signed and the chief advocate of internationalism, Woodrow Wilson, is on his way home let us pause and consider what has been accomplished by the men so inaptly termed the Big Three.

If we fairly and fearlessly apply the accumulated knowledge of all the centuries that have gone in analyzing the work accomplished we cannot but feel that June 28, 1919, will go down in history as the blackest day in the annals of humanity.

For centuries the genii of India churned the Indian ocean and only succeeded in bringing forth a white elephant. So the Big Three labored and travailed for months and brought forth a monstrosity, a hideous thing that makes the United States of America a vassal state to Great Britain, even as it makes China a vassal state to Japan.

Since that greatest of all disasters that ever befell this country, the election of Woodrow Wilson in 1912, our ship of state has drifted into strange waters. Guided by incompetent helmsmen our ship no longer bravely breasts the turbulent waves but has sought shelter in a stagnant pool, where all is miasmic and enervating. And this brings up the query, whither are we drifting? Is this great republic to be dragged down into the same mire that destroyed the mighty Roman empire? When Augustus usurped the functions of the Roman senate he started that empire on the decline that led to ruin. Even so will it be with our country if Wilson and his followers succeed in coercing the senate into accepting that nauseating league covenant.

Some time ago General Villa, the Mexican bandit, asserted that Americans were white Chinamen. If Villa was speaking in the present tense I challenge the assertion. But if we was merely prognosticating I am (qualifiedly) inclined to believe that he called the turn. Because if we continue to allow our national and international policies to be shaped in the fashion now urged, it will not be long before we shall be as low in the scale of national life as is China, Egypt, or India.

Never before has our country faced such grave dangers as it does today. Therefore it behooves every true patriot to assert himself in behalf of those senators who are so valiantly fighting to maintain our American institutions and this great republic.

As for me, I am for unalloyed Americanism and prefer to be guided by Washington rather than Wilson, by Lincoln rather than Lloyd-George and by Roosevelt rather than Clemenceau.

LOUIS C. MILLER
587 Washington Street

Another one:

Portland, March 15---(To the Editor of the Telegram)---A Portland paper recontly exultantly declared that 90 per cent of the people are in favor of the proposed League of Nations. Well, suppose they are, that does not prove anything. It merely affirms the fact that the masses never have been right. Turn back the pages of history and nowhere and at no time can it be found that the masses were right. It is this mental inertia of the people that makes it possible for a man like Wilson to succeed, because he does not appeal to reason or intelligence, but rather to the mollycoddle, emotions of the gullible masses.

Furthermore, if the league is put through as planned it will surely fail, just as other similar combinations have failed before, and for the self-same reason. The intentions of these self anointed wise ones may be all right, but they are ignoring prime factors in the equation, the irreconcilable, racial, social and economic differences between the various nations.

It is not necessary to call upon the remote past for evidence, for at the outbreak of this war there was a triple alliance between Germany, Austria-Hungary and Italy. But on a show down Italy backed water and took the first favorable opportunity to attack her former allies. Why? Because there is nothing in common between the Italians and the Teutons. So with the Bulgars and Turks. They laid down their arms without compunction as to the result such action would have upon their allies. And why? Because there is nothing in common between the Bulgars, Turks, and Germans. There was also an understanding between England, France, and Russia, yet Russia quit and violated her promises and pledges to the allies for the same reason. And so will any league or polyglot combination fail,not only fail but surely lead to trouble, and more trouble. Therefore our only hope is that there will be enough steadfast patriotic senators to resist this nonsensical clamor of the masses and get us out of this miasmic jungle in which we find ourselves as a result of blindly following an ignis fatuus chasing leader.

L.C. MILLER

Among the papers Dora Silberman shared with me was a poem that Louis C. Miller had written on the occasion of the birth of his son Granite in 1919. The proud father penned the following:

GRANITE EVEREST MILLER

I have stood upon the highest peaks,
Where the air was wondrously pure.
And I have gazed upon the ocean
As it surged against the shore.
I have heard the wild roar of the wind
On the desolate plains of the West;
But nowhere such a treasure do I find
As in Granite, my Son Granite Everest.

I have traveled in many strange lands,
Through desert and forests and jungle.
I have list to the call of the wild,
And with millions in cities have mingled.
I have stood on a ship's burning deck
With a smile and a hope for the best,
For out of the storm and the wreck
Came Granite, my Son Granite Everest.

I have felt the hot blast of the cannon
On the field of carnage and blood.
And I've answered to the call of the stricken
Where Pestilence and the Grim Reaper stood.
I have knelt by the side of the dying,
And have gently laid them to rest;
But now, homeward to loved ones I'm flying,
To Granite, my Son Granite Everest.

Written by L.C.M. July the 18th. 1919. Granite was born July 17th.

Hon. Granite Everest Miller. Mr. Granite E. Miller. G.E. Miller. G.E.M.

Ladies and Gentlemen, and you too Democrats, I have the pleasure of introducing the distinguished speaker from the great state of Oregon, the Hon. Granite Everest Miller. Great and prolonged applause.

Born July 17th. 1919. Granite Everest Miller, and I Louis C. Miller am his dad, and Emma, bless her, is his mother. So Be it.

A strange document indeed, showing Louis daydreaming about how important his son might be someday, and apparently allusions to himself being a war veteran, which he never was. Which war? In his new life, did he tell his wife Emma and his new friends that he had served in the Spanish-American War? He actually was in Yuma Territorial Prison at the time.

Louis C. Miller died in Portland on March 29, 1932 of cardiac failure. His wife Emma was the informant on his death certificate, and listed him as having been a civil engineer (mining) for 25 years. This indicates that she was either protecting her husband's reputation even in death, or more likely, she never knew of his disreputable past.

Miller's obituary in the *Portland Oregonian* of April 1, 1932 reads simply:

MILLER—Funeral services for the late Louis C. Miller of 709 Hoyt st., Friday, April 1, at 11 A.M., at the Chapel of Miller & Tracey. Interment Lincoln Memorial Park. BR 2691.

Hill in Lincoln Memorial Park, Portland, Oregon. The grave of Louis C. Miller is near the bottom, while the grave of his wife Emma is several rows up. (Author's photo)

Emma Miller later married again, her second husband being a man named Herrington (the family does not know his first name). Emma Schultz Miller Herrington is also buried in Lincoln Memorial Park in Portland, only a few rows up from her first husband. Mr. Herrington is not buried beside her, and I have no knowledge of his fate. Louis and Emma's son Granite Everest Miller is buried elsewhere in the same cemetery. He would serve in World War II and later became a cab driver. He was killed in an auto accident in 1976, probably never knowing his father's real background.

One interesting final note—Carol Powell provided me with a photocopy of Miller's burial record from Lincoln Memorial Park. On it, somebody has handwritten "famous Arizona outlaw," showing

Grave of Louis C. Miller in Lincoln Memorial Park in Portland. So this is where he ended up. (Author's photo)

Grave of Louis Miller's wife Emma, who may have never known of her husband's notorious background. Her second husband, Mr. Herrington, is surprisingly not buried next to her and it is unknown where he is. (Author's photo)

Grave of Granite Everest Miller, the son of Louis C. Miller. (Author's photo)

that someone else at some time (before Carol and I came along) made the connection in the years since his death.

In a first draft of this book, before I learned the details of Louis Miller's fate, I concluded this section by stating that Miller, in retrospect, comes off almost as repellent as Parker himself. I used strong words, but upon reflection, it can be stated that if it is true that you reap what you sow, then Miller paid a heavy price for his misdeeds and his attitude. Plus, he used his misfortune to finally turn his life around and become a respectable citizen who gave back to his community. So, if the city of Prescott was able to forgive Miller in his lifetime, then surely we all can do so from a historical perspective. May he rest in peace.

Louis Miller's brother Otto has been a difficult person to do research on, owing mainly to the fact that there was more than one Otto Miller in Arizona. In my files, I have a news clipping that even addresses the confusion over having more than one man with the same name appearing in news articles. An Otto Miller also served time in Yuma Territorial Prison, but judging by the data on him, he was definitely not Louis' brother. Louis' brother Otto also reportedly worked as a newspaper printing assistant both in Prescott and Phoenix.

An Otto Miller was also arrested for a string of minor sex crimes in Maricopa County in the early 20th century—I strongly suspect this is, in fact, Louis' brother, but I cannot prove it to my satisfaction, so I won't go into the details here. Aside from his brief arrest after the Prescott jailbreak, there is only one other verifiable skirmish with the law that Louis Miller's brother Otto was involved in. From the *Journal Miner* of February 3, 1909:

OTTO V. MILLER IS PRISONER OF SHERIFF

Accused of Fraudulence
Taken in Custody At Douglas

Sheriff Smith is expected home today from Douglas with Otto V. Miller, a former resident of this city, charged with felony. Miller was arrested in Douglas Sunday, on an indictment returned by the last grand jury of this country. The indictment was one of several other secret ones returned against persons absent from the county when the grand jury was in session.

According to rumors the indictment grew out of a questionable transaction in which Miller is alleged to have sold a mining claim in which he had no interest to a man named Thomas L. Rice for the sum of $150. Another report is that Miller appropriated moneys to his own use advanced to him by Rice to do assessment work on a mining claim in the Santa Maria district while he was working on an adjacent claim belonging to himself.

Miller was raised from a mere boy to manhood in this city. He is a printer by occupation. He was at one time foreman of the Tucson Star and is well known to the printers and newspaper men of the territory, having been engaged at various times in all the principal printing and newspaper offices.

Miller is a brother of Lew Miller, who was a principal in the Parker jail break here several years ago in which Deputy District Attorney Lee Norris was shot and killed. Parker and Miller were convicted of murder in the first degree, the former paying the penalty of his crime on the gallows, Miller being sentenced to the territorial prison in Yuma for life. Miller's sentence was later commuted to twenty years. He was released on parole last year. Since then he has been arrested twice. He is now alleged to be in jail in Tombstone awaiting shipment to the territorial prison.

From the *Journal Miner* of February 17, 1909:

Otto V. Miller, charged with obtaining $120.10 under false pretenses from Thomas R. Rice a year ago, was bound over to answer before the next grand jury under

> $500 bonds by Justice of the Peace McLane yesterday. In default of the required bonds Miller was remanded to the county jail.
>
> Miller is accused of securing the money from Rice on the representation that he had perfected the location of a group of mining claims in the Santa Maria district last year. He is alleged to have left the district before finishing the work after he procured the money from Rice.
>
> He was arrested in Douglas two weeks ago and brought here by Sheriff J. W. Smith.
>
> Miller formerly resided in this city. He is a printer by occupation. He is well known all over this territory and New Mexico, having held positions of trust on many of the principal newspapers of the southwest.

When the Grand Jury met in June, they indicted Otto Miller for "obtaining money under false pretenses," but the manner in which he had done it made it a misdemeanor, unlike his brother Louis' check forgeries, which were felonies.

Otto Miller decided not to fight it. From the *Journal Miner* of June 16, 1909:

> Yesterday's session of the district court was of brief duration, and but a few cases were considered.
>
> Otto Miller withdrew his former plea of not guilty of obtaining money under false pretenses, and pleaded guilty. He will be sentenced today.

Miller's court papers show that he was sentenced to six months in the Yavapai County jail and fined $158.00. According to Carol Powell, Otto Victor Miller died in Los Angeles on September 30, 1945.

Louis and Otto were not the only family members who ran afoul of the law. Carol Powell has also provided me with information that their sister Florence was once arrested in Navajo County, Arizona for operating a "house of ill repute." Much later, she died in Prescott in 1944 and is buried in Mountain View Cemetery under the name of Florence Laney.

In further tragedy, their railroading brother William died of a heart attack while at the throttle of a train outside of Wickenburg on July 14, 1945. He is buried in Greenwood Cemetery in Phoenix, not far from their mother, Clara Miller.

It is not known whether Margaret Sage (Mrs. Russell Sage), the multi-millionairess who was benefactor to Louis C. Miller in prison, ever learned of his failure to succeed in life following his release and her generous gift to him of surveying equipment. She died in New York on November 4, 1918 at the age of 90. As one of the wealthiest women in the world at that time, her death made national news.

Following her husband's death, she became a major philanthropist in America, giving millions to charity and establishing foundations to improve social conditions in the United States. It still is not known how Louis Miller's case came to her attention.

Mrs. Sage was a descendent of Colonel Henry Pierson, founder of the public school system in America in 1787.

After the notoriety of their involvement in the Parker case, Louis Miller's sister Minnie and her husband Fred Haas moved far away to Douglas, Arizona, near the Mexican border. There, Fred opened a German beer hall and also became a hotel proprietor. He apparently worked in the mines also, as Carol Powell has told me he was blinded in a mining accident a few years before his death (ironic, as this is what happened to his wife Minnie's brother Louis). This was also noted in the *Park City* (Utah) *Record* in writings about Minnie's visit to her brother Louis.

Fred Haas, who was born Johann Friedrick Haas, died in Douglas in the Windsor Hotel, which he owned, of chronic inflammatory nephritis on March 15, 1912 at the age of 44. He and Minnie had a daughter, Audrey, who was born in 1905. She passed away on May 8, 1972 in California.

In an ironic footnote, Fred Haas and Minnie Miller had married in Prescott on January 21, 1896, and their witnesses were Sheriff George C. Ruffner and Joseph P. Dillon.

After Fred's death, Minnie continued to work on her own, generally at menial tasks reserved for women in those days. As we saw, she rushed to her brother Louis' bedside when he was crippled and blinded in the Park City mining accident.

She died February 9, 1935, but the cause and location of her death are not known at this time.

Because he committed his murder of Byron Jones only a few weeks prior to Parker's gunning down of Lee Norris, the cold-blooded Richard Cross was indeed spared by the Norton Act, as we have already seen. Convicted of manslaughter instead or murder, Cross became eligible to apply for a pardon in 6 ½ years only, and he received it. Richard Cross walked out of Yuma Territorial Prison a free man on Christmas Eve 1903. Knowing that he was in jail with Parker, it is impossible not to be struck by the vast difference of fate the two killers met.

Richard Cross moved to Los Angeles after that, and apparently married, but like most habitual criminals, his temper got the best of him. From the *Prescott Courier* of May 9, 1907:

> —Los Angeles papers which came in yesterday state that Dick Cross, who fired four shots at his wife, one of the shots wounding her, has been found guilty of assault with intent to murder. Cross, it will be remembered, is the man who killed a man at Jerome, in this county, and who was sentenced to serve ten years in the territorial prison at Yuma. He was a barber."

Cross served two years in Folsom Prison and was released. His whereabouts after that are unknown.

Colonel Edward A. Rogers, pioneer newspaperman and publisher of the *Prescott Courier*, died in October of 1922 at the age of 68. Considered something of a rogue in his lifetime, he is generally well-remembered by Prescott historians. His misguided friendship with Louis C. Miller while Miller was Constable is the only real blemish on his reputation.

Prescott attorney T.W. Johnston, who had represented Louis C. Miller during his trial for shooting John Wallace in 1894, died May 4, 1899 at the Girard Hospital in Philadelphia, reportedly following an unspecified operation. Johnston was also defense attorney for the murderer Richard Cross, and successfully got his charges reduced to manslaughter following the passage of the controversial Norton Act.

T.W. Johnston was buried in Columbus, Mississippi, his former home.

J. Ralph Dillon, Louis Miller's friend whom Miller had defrauded by forging a check in his name (the offense that fatefully landed Miller in the same cell as Parker), died in New York City of pneumonia on March 31, 1902. Dillon had left Prescott for the Big Apple to open a brokerage business. He certainly did not last long after he started.

George A. Allen, Parker's lead Defense Attorney, continued his private law practice afterwards. On December 31, 1901, he died of pneumonia at the age of 44.

He reportedly was a British expatriate, and almost all of his relatives were in England.

Dr. E. W. Dutcher, one of the doctors who pronounced Parker dead following his hanging, died only 3 ½ months later on September 24, 1898, from spinal meningitis caused by severe burns he had received in a September 7 fire in Prescott.

His body was shipped to Allegheny, New York for burial in his family's plot.

The Right Reverend Monsignor Alfred Quetu, the Catholic priest who baptized Parker just before he was hanged, died on September 30, 1930, in old Carthage on the Mediterranean shores of north Africa. Word of his death did not reach Prescott until almost a month later.

Father Quetu had been one of the pioneering clergyman of old Prescott, having taken over the Prescott parish in 1886, and he oversaw the building of the first Sacred Heart church in Prescott at the corner of Marina and Willis streets (the building, no longer a church, is now the home of Prescott Center for the Arts, a prominent community theater). Father Quetu also oversaw the building of the Catholic Church in Jerome, still a landmark in that town.

Father Quetu was about 70 at the time of his death. He had left Prescott in the early 20th century, going first to San Juan Capistrano and then to Carthage. An interesting document survives from his years at San Juan Capistrano. It is a portion of a diary by another priest there, Msgr. John O'Sullivan, who knew Father Quetu. A portion of this diary was given to Elisabeth Ruffner, a historic preservation activist in Prescott whose husband, Lester "Budge" Ruffner, was George C. Ruffner's nephew. This excerpt is used here with her permission.

Msgr. O'Sullivan's diary entry here seems to be dated February 25th, 1911, a Sunday. It reads:

> Today I heard Father Quetu tell of Jim Parker who was hanged in Prescott, Arizona some ten years ago. The subject was introduced by Sam Wilson's remarking that he had received a postcard from France the other day containing a picture of the hanging. Father Quetu's account was in substance as follows: "Parker had held up a train near Kingman, and about a week later was caught on the Navajo Desert by two deputy sheriff's from Kingman. They, wanting to prepare supper, ordered Parker to sit on a stone nearby while they went about getting the meal. Watching his chance he suddenly made a dash for the guns which had been laid near, and catching up one aimed it at them and warned them not to move until he had backed off far enough to make his escape in the dark. The deputies then came to Prescott and told what had happened.
>
> George Ruffner, who was sheriff of the county in his search for him some days afterwards, was riding along the edge of the Grand Canyon which is considerably north of Prescott, when looking over the edge of the canyon he saw Parker only a short way down the cliff. He was walking along with the rifle straight across both shoulders and holding the butt of it in one hand and grasping the barrel in the other. Ruffner had known him for many years for they had been cowboys together and always on good terms. He called down to him, "Jim, drop that gun and come up here."
>
> Parker immediately recognized the voice and immediately answered, "Is that you, George?" without turning his head.
>
> "Yes," Ruffner answered.
>
> Then Parker dropped the gun by releasing it from both hands at once and letting it fall down behind him, and started to climb up the side of the canyon. When he reached the top he was rolling a cigarette and when he got near enough said, "George, give me a match. I haven't had a smoke for days for want of a match."
>
> Of course he got it and went back to Prescott with Ruffner. While he was in jail, which was under the courthouse, a Mexican prisoner asked to go out to the well under the front steps for two buckets of water. The jailer let him out and when he returned, and as soon as the jailer had opened the front door with a big brass key, the Mexican suddenly dropped the two buckets, grabbed the key and wrenching it from his hand struck the jailer over the head with it, felling him to the floor and slightly stunning him.

Then Parker and another prisoner named Miller rushed to the door and dashing into a room connected with the sheriff's office, grabbed up a couple of rifles and started off. A brother of the district attorney named Joe Norris, hearing the noise because the jailer had gotten to his feet and begun shooting. He could not see well because of the blood in his eyes kept running down. Parker commanded him to stand still but Norris turned to run and Parker shot him dead and ran to escape.

George Ruffner was not only sheriff but was also the livery stable keeper and undertaker as well and had a fine white horse named Sure Shot. When ever Ruffner came to the jail, Parker would ask him, "Well George, how is Sure Shot?"

Sure Shot was always well, and Parker would add, "That's right, keep him in good shape, for I'm going to take a ride on him one of these days."

So when he reached the street he went straight to the stable and forced the one man there to saddle Sure Shot for him. Then the Mexican and Miller both together mounting another horse they all rode through the streets, where there were about fifty men near, but not one with a gun. As they passed Parker called out to them, "Just tell them you saw us."

Immediately a posse was formed to follow them and they were traced to the neighborhood of the Little Jesse Mine, where Miller was shot in the leg and fell from his horse. Parker then seeing Miller holding his hands in the air came back to him cursing, boosted him up on Sure Shot and galloped off in a shower of bullets without being touched.

For many days they tracked him. He tied gunnysacks on the horse's feet to prevent him making tracks. He then took off all the shoes and nailed them on backwards to make it appear the horse was going the other way. But at last the horse gave out and he continued on foot finding himself in the Flagstaff Reservation. Meanwhile, his photographs had been sent all over the country, and a storekeeper where he had gone to buy some tobacco and canned goods recognized him. When he left the store the clerk armed half a dozen Indians with rifles and sent them out after him. A few hours later they found him fast asleep with his gun clasped in his arms. Sneaking up to him they all surrounded him and pointing their guns straight at him, had one of the party shoot his gun up in the air. Upon awakening he saw there was no use to fight sohe simply said, "Boys, you've got me," and went with them. Miller was also taken, but the Mexican was never seen again. He was then tried and condemned to death.

Then the Salvation Army and some Methodists used to visit the jail and pray for him in front of his cell, until he got tired of it and he complained to Ruffner, who had them leave the man alone. Ruffner told me and I, waiting a few days, told Ruffner I would like to call to see Parker, and said I would not mention religion to him unless he wanted me to. So I called to see him, and told him if he had any things to do such as writing letters I would do it for him. He was much pleased and looked for my visits regularly, so that when I was away at Jerome or Congress, he would ask for me.

Finally one day he said to me, "It's a week tomorrow, isn't it—Next Friday?"

"Yes," I said.

"Well don't you think I'd better get ready—I don't want to die like a dog—I want to be baptized."

"That's up to you," I answered him. "I said I would not mention the subject of religion unless you wanted me to. Do you want to be baptized by the Methodists or any of the other churches, or do you want to be a Catholic?"

"Oh," he answered, "I want to be a Catholic."

"Why is it—what is the reason you want to be a Catholic?"

"Why, for the reason, out in Nevada I got all bust up once and was brought to a Sister's Hospital and to lay there a long time. While I was there I began to think how those sisters worked all the time for others that were sick—not for a few years, but all their lives, and that without any salary or other reward except for the expectation of getting their pay for it in the next world, I thought that if there was any right religion these people had it. And again if there is a next world and I die like a dog I'll surely go to hell, and if there isn't a next world it won't do me any harm to be baptized."

I then began his instruction and baptized him the day before he was to die.

I was there the next morning and was talking to him when Ruffner came up in his silk shirt sleeves, with a big paper sticking out of one hip pocket and a big bottle of whiskey sticking out of the other.

"I guess it's getting pretty near time, Jim, and the judge gave me this here paper which he says I've got to read it to you."

Then taking the death warrant out of his pocket, Parker came over and looking over his shoulder they spelled it out between them, going over the whole thing together. Then Ruffner pulled out the bottle of whiskey and offered it to Parker, but he said he wouldn't take any. When Ruffner held up the bottle and said "Here's to you, Jim," and took the biggest drink I ever saw a man take.

Then the three of us went out a crawler through a window into the enclosure where the gallows was. On coming into the sunlight, which he had not seen for a long time, Parker staggered a little, which gave rise to the rumor that he was drunk, but I know that he was not. When he looked up at the gallows he asked Ruffner to "show him how this thing worked," which Ruffner did. When it came to the black cap, he insisted that Ruffner do it, for there had been a rumor that Ruffner had not treated him well, and he wanted to show the people there that he had nothing against him. He said an act of contrition just as the black cap was going on him.

That afternoon Ruffner got out his best hearse and finest pair of horses to bring his body to the graveyard. I was the only one that followed the hearse. When we reached the cemetery there was only Mrs. Mills, who went to every funeral, and ten strange hard looking cowboys. I learned afterwards they had come from California, and had been there a long time watching for opportunity to get Parker out of jail, but had not succeeded.

When I was through with my prayers, I started for my buggy, but Ruffner stopped me and commanded me to go back and say something. I reminded him that it wasn't easy to do that under the circumstances, but he insisted so strenuously, that I decided to risk a few words rather than the chance of being hot. I spoke as I could to suit the occasion to my unknown assembly. When I was finished, Ruffner said, "Thank you". Taking out his big red handkerchief he cried as if his heart would break.

This is a fascinating account, though we must remember that Father O'Sullivan was recording Father Quetu's comments from memory some time after it happened. It is interesting to note that Quetu claims that Parker did indeed know whose horse he was stealing, which, as we have noted before, seems a bit hard to believe but certainly not impossible.

At the end, Father Quetu hesitated to speak at Parker's funeral because, even though he had baptized Parker, it is against Church doctrine to speak well of a reputedly evil man even at a funeral. In the last paragraph, Quetu says he risked saying a few words rather than risk being hot. Is this a typo? Did he mean "shot"? Did Father Quetu think the distraught Sheriff Ruffner was going to shoot him? We will never know what went through the minds of the men that fateful day.

Mike Hermann, the old codger of Groom Creek who claimed that the jail escapes had robbed him of three bottles of whiskey, was considered to be quite a local character in his day. He always seemed to have a story about being persecuted. Maybe true, maybe not. From the *Arizona Journal Miner* of December 13, 1899:

> An unsuccessful attempt was made last night to rob Mike Hermann at his road station on Groom creek, six miles south of town. About 9:30 o'clock two Mexicans entered the place, one with a six shooter and the other with a murderous looking dagger. Hermann was alone in the front room, at the time, sitting in a chair, and the Mexicans no doubt concluded that he was the only person in the building at the time and would be easy prey for them. The man with the dagger advanced toward him and suddenly sprang forward and seized Hermann with his left hand, while he raised the knife in his right hand to strike him a blow with it. Mr. Hermann, who is a veteran of the civil war, and who had not only faced bullets but had been struck with them, was not to be stampeded as easily as they imagined. He always carries a six shooter where he can lay his hand on it conveniently, and as the two men entered the door he sized them up and immediately placed his hand on his six shooter, and when the man attacked him he drew the weapon. Simultaneously with doing so Ike Chandler, who was in a back room, appeared at the door between the two rooms, and the sight of him and of Mike's gun unnerved the would-be murderers and they fled precipitately. As they left Mr. Hermann fired four or five shots at them, one before they got outside of the building, and as the bullet could not be found anywhere in the building he thinks he hit one of the men.

A veteran of the Civil War, Hermann had been struck by a shell fragment which left him with a bad scar on his face. He also had an amputated leg; according to his obituary, a huge boulder fell on him while he was placer mining, crushing the leg. He reportedly laid pinned under the boulder for 24 hours before someone found him.

Hermann died November 22, 1904. He had no relatives, and he was buried in Prescott's Citizens Cemetery, not far from the grave of Parker, the man who supposedly robbed him of whiskey.

From the *Arizona Journal Miner* of July 20, 1898:

> N. E. Bartoo, one of Captain O'Neill's company of Rough Riders, who enlisted at Williams, is now running the engine on the little road from Baquiri to the front of the American army. Bartoo is a first class engineer, leaving the Santa Fe Pacific to become a soldier. When Baquiri was taken, the Spanish tried to disable the engine, but Bartoo helped to put it together in short order.—Albuquerque Democrat.

Nelson Bartoo was, of course, the fireman on old No. 1, the train robbed by Parker. He later became one of the legendary Rough Riders during the Spanish-American War, and attached to Buckey O'Neill's squad at that!

On October 31, 1946, the *Prescott Courier* ran the following:

> County Attorney Palmer C. Byrne is in receipt of a letter from Don Steffa, general manager of Vallecito Mining company, Inc., of California which digs into an exciting period of Prescott's past and is self-explanatory:
>
> October 21, 1946
>
> District Attorney
> Prescott, Arizona
> Dear Sir:
> Some time early in 1898, a deputy district attorney was shot and killed in the jail at Prescott by Jim Parker, a train bandit who had engineered the holdup of a Santa Fe passenger near Nelson in February 1897.
>
> If it is not putting you to too much trouble, will you be kind enough to furnish me with the name of the murdered deputy; also, the name of the sheriff who later hanged Parker? I believe his name was Ruffner. Parker attended his own necktie party in 1898.
>
> The foregoing inquiry is made at the request of Mr. Nelson Bartoo, who lives near here, and who was a foreman on the train which was held up. He is 76 years old and, I imagine, the only surviving member of the train crew that went through a rather thrilling experience.
>
> Bartoo was a member of the Rough Riders under Captain "Bucky" O'Neill, served in the Cuban campaign, and was standing by the side of Capt. O'Neill when the latter was killed by a sniper's bullet. I think you will find Bartoo's name on the metal plaque on the side of the O'Neill monument in your city park.
>
> Bartoo is trying to piece together his memoirs and I have offered to give him such little assistance as I can.
>
> Thanking you for any courtesies you may extend in the matter, I beg to remain,
>
> Very truly yours,
> Don Steffa
> Murphys, Calif.

A few days later, on November 2, 1946, the *Courier* ran a letter to the editor in response to this, from Ralph Bolyne on Copper Basin Road. In it, he quoted the story verbatim from the book *Arizona, the Youngest State*, from McClintock's histories (see Chapter 12). If Nelson Bartoo did complete his memoirs, I have found no evidence they were ever published.

On June 18, 1948, the *Courier* reported that he would attend the 50th anniversary reunion of the surviving Rough Riders in Prescott on June 24-25, 1948. He was living in Altadale, California at the time. He died August 18, 1949 in Whittier, California.

I have been unable to ascertain the fates the rest of the train's crew, Alexander Summers, Albert S. Grant, and William Daze, let alone Ed Allen, the Rock Cut track watchman.

As previously seen, a man named Ward Pritchett was briefly detained for complicity in the Parker jailbreak, apparently because he made some jocular remarks that were interpreted as sympathetic to the escapees. Pritchett was released soon after, as there was no evidence at all to connect him to the breakout.

Pritchett was only a minimal figure at best in the Parker story. Ordinarily, I wouldn't even print his fate were it not for the manner in which he died. On September 11, 1906, the *Prescott Courier* printed the following, originally from the *Oaxaca Herald* in Mexico:

Ward Pritchett Killed at Los Ocotes Mine

Without the slightest warning, the lumber laiden rafters of the carpenter shop at the Los Ocotes mine collapsed last Tuesday afternoon, instantly killing Ward Pritchett, fatally injuring an assistant and seriously injuring another workman. Mr. Pritchett was the son of Dr. D. W. Pritchett, of this city, and one of the best known mining men in the state.

The accident happened at 3:45 in the afternoon. Mr. Pritchett was on his way from one of the buildings to the office of the mine and was called into the carpenter shop by one of the workmen, who asked to be shown in regard to a certain piece of work he was doing at the time. Mr. Pritchett was marking off a plank and explaining the work when the rafters gave way and two carloads of lumber crashed on the heads of the men. A large plank struck Mr. Pritchett on the back of the head breaking his neck. One of the two other occupants of the room had his head badly crushed, and while he still lives his death is expected at any time. The other workman was badly cut and bruised but will live.

The body was at once taken to Ejutla and prepared for burial and was interred the following evening.

David Ward Pritchett was born in St. Louis, Mo., thirty-three years ago. He came to Mexico seven years ago and has worked in various parts of the republic. Last December he went to the Los Ocotes as master carpenter and has been engaged in that capacity since that time. He was a jovial, good natured man who was popular with all of his associates, and who was favorably known in many mining camps in the republic. He was unmarried, leaving to mourn his loss his father and mother, who are in the United States; two brothers, George and Gordon Pritchett of this city, two sisters, Mrs. W. H. Dudley of Oaxaca, and Mrs. Sadie Wilbanks of Chihuahua.—The Oaxaca Herald, Oaxaca, Mexico, Sept. 2, 1906.

All the parties mentioned in the above article are former residents of Prescott. Ward Pritchett did the press work on the Courier for some months and was a member of the Prescott fire department.

Chapter 10: Life After Parker

Wells Fargo Special Agent and detective John Nelson Thacker, who issued the infamous Wanted poster on Parker and then refused to pay the reward, also appears as a character in numerous Southwest "law and order" stories from the late 19th century. Therefore, it is odd that, to date, very little of any substance has ever been written about him and his career. As of this writing, Detective Thacker does not even have a Wikipedia entry.

John N. Thacker died on January 3, 1913 at the age of 76, and is buried in the Holy Cross Cemetery in Colma, California. Prior to joining Wells Fargo, he had served as Sheriff of Humboldt County, California from 1868 to 1870.

By 1957, former Mohave County Deputy Asa Harris was probably the only man still living who had participated in the posses that pursued Parker, and he undoubtedly knew this. Therefore, he began to seek out newspaper reporters to tell his own version of the story, and he found an eager listener in Carle Hodge, a reporter for the *Arizona Republic*.

John Nelson Thacker.

The Hodge interview with Harris appeared in the December 30, 1957 edition of the *Republic*, and it is jaw-dropping to this day! It reads (reprinted with permission):*

> Couple of Trifling Errors Ended Jim Parker's Career
> In Banditry
> By Carle Hodge
>
> KINGMAN---Jim Parker underestimated a railroad guard's aim.
>
> Worse, later, the bronc tamer and train bandit fatefully overestimated his own stamina. He fell asleep.
>
> It was, as Asa (Ace) Harris recollected the other day, the last error Parker could enjoy. His first came in 1896 when the cowboy returned from Utah ranges with a stranger named Williams.
>
> One snow-dusted November dusk, the pair ignited a pyre of old ties on the Santa Fe tracks a half-dozen miles east of Peach Springs. When the 8 p.m. express snorted to a stop, they forced the fireman to uncouple the engine, then stripped the mail car.
>
> . . .

---

* From the *Arizona Republic*, December 30, 1957. © 1957 The *Arizona Republic*. All rights reserved. Used by permission and protected by the Copyright Laws of the United States. The printing, copying, redistribution, or retransmission of this Content without express written permission is prohibited.

UP TO THEN all went well---except that a Santa Fe shotgun messenger fired at Williams with immediately fatal consequences.

Unaware, Parker waited in hiding for hours for his partner, a delay on which Harris still blames the getaway's failure.

That same night the Santa Fe wired Harris, then and for years after a Mohave County deputy, for help. A railroad detective in a one-car special---a locomotive and boxcar---picked him up with his Indian tracker, a microscopic-eyed Hualpai known as Captain Hardy, and their horses.

Former Mohave County Deputy Asa Harris spins tall tales for the *Arizona Republic* in 1957.

At daybreak they saddled up at Peach Springs and sniffed up the scent. Fifteen miles later, at sundown, they overtook the lagging Parker in a clearing.

• • •

RIFLE FIRE crackled.

"I can't shoot from a horse that's jumpin' around," Harris sighs, to this day a little miffed. He missed the fugitive, but blasted off his saddle cantle.

Parker, afoot, somehow vanished. So did the detective.

"I guess," Harris says, "he remembered some railroad business he had to look after."

A few hours later, Ace and his tracker met Yavapai County Sheriff George Ruffner and a posse, but it was noon the next day before they again spied Parker, wading down Diamond Creek, a gun over his shoulders.

"Jim! Meeting's up! Come on out. I don't want to kill you," Harris shouted.

Apparently Jim didn't want him to, either, because he went meekly to a federal cell in Prescott.

However, Parker had some allergy to trials. Before his came up, he disturbed the old cow-town's Sunday somnolence by clobbering a jailer with a coal bucket and helping himself to keys and arms.

He shot down and killed an assistant county attorney who, hearing the commotion, wandered into the jail. Then he raced across the plaza to Ruffner's livery stable and rode off on one of the sheriff's own horses, a big gray.

Quickly, Harris and Captain Hardy highballed on their special, this time to Prescott and thence down the tortuous "Peavine" line to Congress.

FOR SIX days, with Ruffner and his men, they pursued the fleeing killer. At the Verde River he momentarily mystified them by unshoeing the big gray in midstream. But Harris pointed out evidence on the opposite shore was clearly that of a grain-fed animal, not the local range variety.

Possemen sacked out at a sheep camp, and discovered the next dawn Parker had sat on a butte watching them, not 300 yards away.

Word was out, meantime, that there was a $1,000 bounty on the escapee, breathing or otherwise. When finally he dropped exhausted and slumbered in the Navajo Country northeast of Flagstaff, the posse hot behind, Indians surrounded him.

• • •

AT HIS hanging for the assistant DA's murder, the strayed ranch hand joked with spectators.

Harris had many adventures after that as a deputy, but never another customer like Jim Parker. Not that the old lawman lives on memories. At 88, still 6 feet tall and straight as a gunstock, he goes to work each morning at 6 as timekeeper at the county garage.

Some time ago---it was 1915---he happened to be on the West Coast. Doctors prematurely gave him a brief time to live.

"This kicking off is all right," Ace Harris told them. "But, dammit, don't bury me in California."

I am sure that Asa Harris was a good man, and it is not my wish to denigrate his memory. But this does not change the fact that his statements are appalling. Perhaps he still felt burned because he sold ammunition to Love Marvin (who doesn't even appear as a character in Harris' "story") prior to the train robbery. Perhaps he was simply envious over all of the attention the other lawmen got in the Parker case. Whatever the reason, it is clear that in the twilight of his life, Asa Harris felt the need to reinvent the Parker story with himself as the hero.

Most embarrassing of all, Harris couldn't even get the incidental facts right. The train robbery occurred in November? Sure-Shot was a big gray?? And by saying he took the train to Congress, Harris inadvertently places himself far Southeast of Kingman, exactly the opposite direction from where Parker was going. Harris' knowledge of Arizona geography was apparently failing him.

A couple of weeks later, on January 10, 1958, the *Arizona Republic* printed a letter to the editor in response to the Harris interview. This letter, from Samuel S. Preston's widow, is far more interesting than anything Harris had to say:

Editor, the Arizona Republic:
Articles of or pertaining to Arizona history, printed in the Arizona Republic are always of a great deal of interest to me. In the issue of Dec. 30, I read Carle Hodge's interview with Mr. Harris of Kingman with a personal interest. I would like to add a bit in the way of further information on that article.

The Navajos did not capture Jim Parker. Samuel S. Preston, an early day trader among the Navajos and operating a trading post at Willow Springs at that time, was the man who took him into custody and with a Navajo Indian accompanying him, brought Jim Parker to a distance south of the Little Colorado River where they were met by Ruffner and his deputies from Prescott.

It came about this way. Jim Parker was in a camp as he said, in a secluded spot in Echo Cliffs near Bitter Seep (now called Bitter Springs) on what is now Highway 89. That is some 50 miles north of Willow Springs. He was low on provisions and rode into Willow Springs for supplies. Mr. Preston recognized him from descriptions posted and took him into custody, hiring a Navajo Indian to accompany them to Flagstaff. In the meantime, or during the travel, Mr. Preston in some way got word to the authorities in Flagstaff who in turn contacted Mr. Ruffner of Prescott and was met by the latter at the aforesaid place.

WHEN PARKER CAME to Willow Springs, he had his horse's feet or hoofs wrapped in sheepskin to disguise tracks and mislead any trailers. During the trip, he told Mr. Preston that the loot of the holdup was cached in the cliffs near about where he had been camped. The loot consisted of personal jewelry---watches, rings, etc., along with the money taken from the baggage car. To date I have never heard of anyone finding any trace of this loot, but often wonder now, with so many people passing in that area, the new road to Glen Canyon having been built, and with Geiger counters and other magnetic gadgets of modern times, if someday someone may come upon this layout if Parker told the truth. I have a copy of the San Francisco Examiner dated Jan. 13, 1898 which gives an account of Jim Parker's keen attempts for freedom after he had been tried and sentenced. He was not tried on the robbery charge, but tried and convicted on the murder charge.

I was married to Mr. Preston in October 1904 and went to Willow Springs as a bride living there until February 1905 when Babbitt & Preston bought from C.H. Algert his store at Tuba City and we moved there, opening for business February 13, 1905. Willow Springs store was abandoned at that time and has never been in operation since. The walls of the old store and living quarters are still standing.

After Mr. Preston's death, Ivanhoe commandery at Prescott, of which he was a member, sent me a letter of commendation for his valiant service in capturing Jim Parker.

LAURA A. RUNKE
Flagstaff

I do not know at this time which newspaper Mrs. Runke had, but it was surely not the *San Francisco Examiner*. I have checked the cited issue without finding the article she refers to, as well as the other San Francisco papers in case she had gotten confused.

Asa Harris died in October of 1958 at the age of 89. At the time of his death, his son Bill was Undersheriff of Mohave County.

Historian Roman Malach's book *Peach Springs* (1975; Mohave Pioneers Historical Society) is a history of that municipality. It strangely does not mention the Parker story, even though the train robbery was a major event in the town's history.

But in a section on old-time Hualapai Indian Army Scouts, author Malach expounds on an ex-scout who went by the name of Kate Crozier, who died on August 11, 1961 allegedly at the age of 118! His age was unproven and seems hard to believe, but who knows?

Malach claims that Kate Crozier was an Army Scout under General George Crook, and that he was also with General Miles when Geronimo surrendered in 1886. But more interesting to us, the February 1949 issue of *Arizona Police* magazine (to be discussed in more detail in Chapter 12) contains an interview with Johnny Munds in which he identifies one of the Indian trailers who tracked Parker as Kate Crozier.

If this was the same man (and it probably was), and if he really did live until 1961, he almost certainly was the last surviving person to have had anything to do with the Parker story, regardless of whether or not he was 118. Roman Malach states that Kate Crozier was blind the last 40 years of his life.

A first-hand newspaper clipping reprinted on page 202 identifies one of the Indian trailers as "Indian Kate"—this may indeed have been Kate Crozier.

Prescott Justice Henry W. Fleury was not a figure in the Parker story, as he died in Prescott on September 2, 1895 of Bright's disease, long before Parker became news. However, he was a pivotal figure in the early career of Louis C. Miller. Fleury served off and on as Justice of the Peace, and as such, Constable Miller brought all of the petty miscreants he arrested before Fleury for sentencing, including "Red," whose arrest led to the shooting of Miles Archibald.

Judge Fleury had been one of the original pioneers of Prescott, having come to Arizona in 1864 with the original Governor's party as a secretary when they arrived to settle the newly proclaimed Territory. After Prescott lost the Capitol of the Territory in later years and all the Government officials went back East, Fleury was the only one to stay in Arizona. He held a variety of positions, and reportedly was the one who inspired Sharlot M. Hall toward her work in historic preservation.

When Fleury died, no less a man than Territorial Governor Frederick A. Tritle served as one of his pallbearers.

Utah attorney Bismarck Snyder was not a figure in the Parker story, but he represented the blind and crippled Louis C. Miller in his lawsuit against the Daily Judge Mine in 1913-1914.

It is interesting to note that Snyder died on February 15, 1919, a victim of the Spanish Flu pandemic that decimated the United States and the world, killing millions, following World War I. His father must have been an old-time Utah Mormon polygamist, as the popular *www.FindAGrave.com* website lists Snyder as having 34 brothers and sisters!

Although ex-Chief of Police Miles Archibald was not a pivotal figure in the Parker story, enough has been said about him in this book that he warrants an epilogue in this chapter. What ever became of Archibald? There are no records in Yavapai County, and previous researchers have come up empty-handed on the question. But at last, the truth is known.

1897 found the ex-lawman still living with his mother in Prescott. From the *Arizona Journal Miner* of March 31, 1897:

> The residence of Mrs. Archibald was consumed by fire this morning at 4:30 o'clock. At the time the fire was discovered, the only occupant of the house was her son, Miles, who was only awakened by the smoke entering the room he occupied, and in getting out lost nearly every thing he had that was not hurriedly picked up. The origin of the fire is supposed to have been from a defective flue or the bursting of a lamp that was burning in the room at the time. Nothing of value was saved, and the loss will reach at least $1,500, covered by $1,000 insurance. The Toughs received the record, and a conspicuous fact in connection with the blaze was that there were not over seven firemen, out of 100 on the rolls of the four companies, in attendance.

He had obviously returned from San Francisco, and as seen in previous chapters, he was on the street when Parker, Miller, and Sarata made their escape. Archibald was also identified as one of the men appointed to oversee a death watch on Parker.

Archibald's arm must have healed up fairly well since 1894, because late in 1897, he left Prescott for good to take a job as a prison guard at Yuma Territorial Prison. There is some bittersweet irony in nothing that Miles Archibald served as a guard at the prison at the same time that Louis C. Miller, who had once shot him, was a prisoner there. At any rate, Archibald never looked back when he left Yavapai—he started a brand new life for himself in Yuma. From the *Arizona Sentinel*, a Yuma newspaper, of November 13, 1897:

> Mr. Miles O. Archibald and Miss E. Cunningham of Yuma were married in Los Angeles last Tuesday, returning home Wednesday evening. Mr. Archibald is employed as a guard at the prison and is an industrious and trustworthy young man. The bride is one of Yuma's most beautiful and accomplished young ladies, a niece of Mrs. Nellie Cashman, the popular landlady of the Hotel Cashman. The SENTINEL joins the many friends of the happy young couple in extending congratulations.

As noted before in Chapter 6, it seems that Archibald had a previous marriage under his belt before moving in with his mother. This latest marriage, in which the bride was a member of a famed family, would last until her death.

From the *Sentinel* of April 8, 1899:

> Mrs. Miles Archibald, the wife of the captain of the yard on the hill, left Wednesday for a visit to San Francisco.

From the *Sentinel* of June 6, 1900:

> Mrs. M. O. Archibald left last Friday for the Coast where she will spend the summer. Mrs. Archibald contemplates a trip to Dawson to visit Miss Nellie Cashman, her aunt.

From the *Sentinel* of September 19, 1900:

> Mrs. Miles Archibald returned Saturday where she spent the summer, very much improved in health.

While in Yuma, Archibald served a term as Chairman of the Yuma County Republican Party. From the *Sentinel* of November 14, 1900:

> The SENTINEL desires to say that Miles Archibald, as chairman of the republican county central committee, conducted a clean and able campaign, and considering the difficulties under which he was obliged to work, the result is not at all to his dis-credit as a political organizer and manager. The dissention within the party made the position of chairman a disagreeable one to fill, and rendered it impossible to accomplish the results desired, or what would have been accomplished had the party been united and all working in harmony. It is certainly to be regretted that such a state of affairs existed. Under the circumstances we want to say it is to Miles Archibald's credit that he managed to preserve his temper and equilibrium throughout the campaign.

From the *Sentinel* of August 28, 1901:

> Miles O. Archibald, captain of the guard of the Territorial prison, left on Monday for Dawson City, where he will join his wife, who had been in Dawson for some time visiting her mother. Mr. Archibald has been an attaché of the prison for about five years, and this is the first vacation of any duration he has taken. He will be gone about three months, and during his absence his position will be filled by W. H. Buck.

For some reason, Archibald decided to stay in Dawson City, and quit his job at the prison. From the *Sentinel* of October 9, 1901:

> A private letter from Miles O. Archibald, former captain of the guard at the territorial prison, states that he has decided to remain in Dawson permanently.

Time marched on, and Archibald ventured into other areas of interest. From *The Copper Era*, a newspaper of Cochise County, of October 9, 1902:

> Miles Archibald, a well-known miner of Arizona has recently returned to Bisbee from Klondike. He is of the opinion that the cream of the Klondike has been skimmed for the reason that the country is of glacial formation.

The year of 1904 found him back in Yuma. From the *Arizona Sentinel* of March 16, 1904:

> Miles Archibald and Joe Alvarado have opened a cigar stand in the place formerly occupied by Manual Molina. Mr. Archibald has purchased a half-interest on Alvarado's fruit stand on the corner of Main and Second streets. They will run the two places.

And then, he got his old job back. From the *Sentinel* of December 16, 1904:

> Miles Archibald, formerly captain of the guards at the territorial prison, has again taken employment on "the hill" as a guard.

And then, the inevitable tragedy struck. From the *Sentinel* of December 22, 1904:

> Miles Archibald, of the firm of Archibald, Webster and Co. returned from Los Angeles last week. Mr. Archibald was called to Los Angeles by the sickness of his wife who died last week.

They had only been married seven years. Once again, Miles was alone. He stayed on in Yuma, though. It is not known what firm the article refers to, but it seems that Archibald had many oars in the water at this time.

From the *Sentinel* of October 17, 1906:

> Miles Archibald has received the appointment as a mounted inspector in the customs department for this district, with headquarters in Yuma. The position is a good one and goes to a good man.

From the *Sentinel* of June 5, 1907:

> Miles Archibald, employed in the U. S. Customs service, has been transferred to Nogales and left for the line city Sunday.

Back in Prescott, the *Courier* ran this bit of news June 22, 1907:

> Miles Archibald, formerly of Prescott, is trying to get the position as postmaster at Yuma, Arizona. Opposing him as an applicant for the same position is Dick Stanton, a Rough Rider. Archibald is now a mounted deputy customs collector.

It appears that he did not get the job, as he retained his position with the Customs Service.

From the *Sentinel* of December 9, 1908:

> The custom house at Yuma has been placed in charge of Miles O. Archibald pending the arrival of the new deputy collector to succeed P. J. Sullivan.

Archibald seems to have settled on work with the U. S. Customs as his permanent line of work. In 1909, he also married for the third time. From the *Sentinel* of April 22, 1909:

> Miles O. Archibald, U. S. Customs inspector for this district, was married Tuesday by Probate Judge DeVane, to Grace E. Larkin. The SENTINEL extends congratulations.

After that, nothing further is known of Archibald, except that he stayed in Yuma for the rest of his life and eventually began operating a hotel there. He died in 1925 at the age of 55. His obituary from the *Yuma Sun* of December 11, 1925:

Chapter 10: Life After Parker

The funeral of Miles Archibald who died suddenly Wednesday afternoon at the Bon Air Hotel, 156 ½ Main Street, of which he was proprietor, will be held at 3 o'clock today from the undertaking parlor of O. C. Johnson on Second Avenue. It is expected that his sister and aged mother from Los Angeles will be in attendance and also his former wife, Mrs. Virginia Archibald.

Mr. Archibald, who was born in Nova Scotia 55 years ago, had come here from Prescott some 30 years ago and was for years in the U. S. Customs service along the border. He was widely known among the older element of this city and valley and has been engaged for several years in the hotel business here.

Virginia was undoubtedly his first wife from Prescott.

The latter part of Archibald's life was much quieter than his earlier life had been, but he led it with dignity and honor. Perhaps being shot had led him to reassess where he was going. If so, it was not all for nothing. Miles Archibald had a good life. We should all be so lucky.

CHAPTER 11

Myths, Legends, and Unverifiable Stories

The vast majority of well-known figures from the Old West have had the misfortune of having their stories fall into folklore in the ensuing years. When they do, the stories usually take on new details, embellishments, and outright fabrications. This has been helped along by Hollywood, writers of western fiction and "fact," and others who seek to romanticize the Old West; to make it seem more glamorous than it really was; to make us believe in a way of life that never really existed. After the Internet era began, it got even worse with dubious history websites and blogs.

One book, for example, could not possibly hold all of the wild myths and legends that have sprung up about the Earps, Jesse James, Bat Masterson, Billy the Kid, Wild Bill Hickok, et al. Some of these legends are so ludicrous that it is amazing that anyone believes them, but they do. In rare instances, the central figure of a story will himself be responsible for the spreading of falsehoods—a lot of the lavish Wyatt Earp stories were started by Wyatt Earp, for instance.

Fleming "James" Parker, though not as famous as the above men, has still had his story revised and embellished by time and legend. A number of fanciful stories exist about him, some of them blatantly and provably false, while others could possibly be true but are unverifiable. As some of these Parker legends are widespread, we need to examine them here. Some, in fact, are so widespread that the reader may be surprised to learn there is no documentation for them at all.

One of the most widespread legends about Parker is that he was the last man to be hanged in either Prescott or Yavapai County. This is absolutely untrue for either location. In Prescott in 1903, two Mexicans, Hilario Hidalgo and Francisco Renteria, were hanged on the Courthouse Square in Prescott, in virtually the same location Parker was put to death. Hidalgo and Renteria had been convicted of killing Charles Goddard and Frank Cox, the proprietors of a popular stage stop known as Goddard Station near New River. Unlike Parker, they were not allowed to appeal their sentences, and swung into eternity scarcely six months after the horrible crime.

As for the rest of Yavapai County, a Hualapai Indian named Dixon Sujynamie was hanged at Fort Whipple (near Prescott) in 1925 for killing a taxi driver named Albert Cavell for his money and his car. He was truly the last man to be hanged in Yavapai County.

The long-held notion that Parker was the area's last hanging is undoubtedly based in public attitudes of the day. In actuality, Parker was the last *white* man to be hanged in old Yavapai. In those days, the average white citizen did not consider Mexicans and Indians to be even remotely human; no, to their way of thinking (and for decades afterwards), Hidalgo, Renteria, and Sujynamie were not "men." In the present day, it is hard to comprehend an era when such racial attitudes were so solidly entrenched, but that is the way it was, and there is no "nice" way to describe it. It is as simple as that.

The legend of Parker being Prescott's last hanging has started to fade in very recent years, no doubt due to the fact that some Western historians have rediscovered the Goddard Station murders, which had otherwise been long forgotten.

Another very widespread legend concerns Parker's alleged motives for the Rock Cut train robbery. According to this story, Parker was a respectable, hard-working cowboy who owned a small string of horses. Then one day, wouldn't you know it, a train ran over two of them. When the railroad offered Parker a ridiculously low settlement for his loss, he refused the sum and proceeded to rob *the very same train* for revenge!

Sound familiar? As we saw in Chapter 9, Parker told virtually this same story to a reporter from the *San Francisco Examiner*, which published the interview on June 5, 1898, two days after Parker's hanging. Many years of retelling has given the legend additional "details." Most after-the-fact accounts of Parker's story that utilize the "revenge against the railroad" legend have embellished the tale to further contend that Parker only robbed the train of the amount he felt his horses were worth; and that, due to the image of "simple justice," public opinion in Prescott was strong in Parker's favor until the murder of Lee Norris.

Since the story originated with Parker himself, that would seem to give it strong credibility, and is undoubtedly the reason the legend has lasted so long. Many after-the-fact accounts have utilized the "revenge against the railroad" story, but despite its origin, the tale falls apart under close scrutiny.

To begin with, there is no other documentation for it beyond Parker's own words, which cannot be considered overly credible. From the days of his earliest crimes in California, Parker always tried to depict himself as a victim of circumstance, which, after four major crimes he was arrested for, started to strain the boundaries of believability. Furthermore, if Parker's alleged grudge against the railroad was so well-known that it swayed public opinion, the newspapers would have surely picked up on it. They did not.

If Parker robbed the train for "simple justice," he would surely have told this story earlier than two days before his hanging. There is no evidence that he did, even though it would have made for a powerful legal defense. As Parker was in mail contact with his sister, Sadie Baker, he would have surely told her that he was a victim of circumstances. Instead, as we have seen, Sadie made it clear in her letters to Sheriff Ruffner that she did not believe her brother was involved in the robbery at all.

We have seen the long string of testimonials as to Parker's gang activity. Even if one were to dismiss the confession of fellow gang member Love Marvin as lacking in credibility, it is not so easy to ignore the published statement of rancher George Thornton and then-Williams attorney Henry F. Ashurst, who were quite vivid in their descriptions of the cattle rustling that Parker was involved in. Both men were highly respected members of their communities, and would have had no reason to lie.

On top of that, the first news dispatch to identify Parker by name (appeared in the *Arizona Journal Miner* of Feb. 17, 1897) referred to him as "a well-known desperado." The *Flagstaff Sun-Democrat* (Feb. 18, 1897) related how Parker, Abe Thompson, and others "had for several years terrorized the law-abiding ranchmen in the vicinity of Peach Springs and kept up a continual round of pilfering and petty stealing …" Let us recall also that Mail Clerk Albert Grant, in his newspaper interviews, stated that Parker made off with nine packages of registered mail—he did not stand around counting out a specific amount of money to take.

I have always found the story hard to swallow also because, would horses really stand still on a railroad track while a train bore down on them? Trains didn't move all that fast in those days, but I guess it did happen sometimes. There is a small notation in the *Mohave County Miner* of April 14, 1894 that reads:

> Three horses were killed by the cars in the cut above town a few days ago. We have not learned who the owners were.

This raises the question, were these Parker's horses? Is the mentioned "cut" the Rock Cut, and is that why Parker chose that location for the robbery? Does this clipping prove the story? It is easy to let one's imagination run wild with this clipping, and many people will think it says more than it actually does. I certainly cannot prove these were not Parker's horses, but I still don't believe it. There was no follow-up in the Miner either, to help us along. As a Mohave ranch-hand, however, Parker certainly would have heard about the accident.

The "revenge against the railroad" story also asks us to believe that an honest cowboy seeking justice would suddenly metamorphose into the mad-dog killer of Lee Norris. This just doesn't make sense. It is clear that Parker, in initially telling this story, was simply trying to convey the message to anyone who would read his interview that he really didn't deserve to be hanged. He could not have possibly known, however, how successful he was in crafting his own legacy. A number of reputable historians have accepted this legend as fact, and I expect my rejection of it to cause considerable controversy.

A truly bizarre legend, accepted as gospel in some quarters, contends that Parker was a member of the Butch Cassidy gang (The Wild Bunch), and probably was also Butch Cassidy's brother. This particular opus is unique in that it not only contradicts the facts, it contradicts virtually all of the other legends about Parker as well.

When told, this flimsy story goes on to describe Parker as a "long rider" for the Wild Bunch. Now, "long rider" is a term used by Western folklorists to describe a member of a rustling gang whose tentacles stretch across several states rather than just locally. The term was almost certainly never used in real life during the period. The legend further contends that Parker was born in 1874 in Circleville, Utah—the change of date and location of Parker's birth are necessary to this story to make him Butch Cassidy's brother.

The story spirals out of control as it goes on, informing us that Parker participated in the Wild Bunch's bank robbery at Montpelier, Idaho before being dispatched to Arizona as the gang's representative and spy. One night in a Williams saloon, we are told, a conveniently unidentified cowboy sidled up to Parker and said: "You know, you're a dead ringer for Butch Cassidy. If I didn't know different, I'd say you was him. You fellers brothers or just shirt tail kin?" Parker allegedly sneered: "Friend, you are a damned flannel mouth!" and walked away. And wouldn't you know it, the next morning the cowboy was found mysteriously murdered! Yeah, right.

Finally, the story concludes by informing us that, after both the Rock Cut train robbery and the jailbreak and murder of Lee Norris, "mysterious money" flowed into Prescott to pay for expensive attorneys for Parker's defense, a sure trademark of the Wild Bunch! Aside from how silly the whole story is, it needs to be remembered that George Allen and Joseph E. Morrison were appointed by the court to defend Parker. Both men were highly respected in the Prescott community. It is insulting down to this day to depict them as little more than mob lawyers, but since when have tall-tale spinners taken such things into account?

There is no evidence to support any part of the Butch Cassidy legend, needless to say, but it has shown remarkable endurance over the years. Some of its staying power may possibly be attributed to the fact that it was endorsed by Gladwell Richardson and Lowell Parker. Both men were considered among the foremost Western historians of their eras, although time has not been kind to either man's work, and if they didn't research any better on other subjects than they did with Jim Parker, it is easy to see why.

The Butch Cassidy legend may have originated in Coconino County, as Sheriff Ralph Cameron figures prominently as the hero in the story, instead of George Ruffner. In the legend, it is Cameron who figures out the connection between Parker and the Wild Bunch; it is Cameron who strikes the trail after Parker; and it is either Cameron or one of his men who finally apprehends Parker following the train robbery. For all we know, it may have even been Cameron who started this story, since he was known to exaggerate in his favor throughout his life.

Exactly how the legend originated is unknown, but it probably had much to do with the fact that Butch Cassidy's real name was Robert Leroy Parker. Tall-tale spinners probably put two and two together and came up with 65, and the story gathered additional "details" as it went from mouth to mouth. The Wild Bunch's hideout was reportedly dubbed Robber's Roost, a name which has also erroneously been attributed to the hideout of the Abe Thompson Gang (which was actually known as Thompson's Cabin).

Solid research into Parker's past by Thomas E. Way, Philip J. Rasch, and Harold Edwards has done much to diffuse the Butch Cassidy legend in recent years, but it still pops up every now and then. The most recent appearance of it that I have seen was an allusion to it in Richard Patterson's otherwise excellent book, *The Train Robbery Era* (Pruett Publishing, 1991). In it, Patterson describes Parker as a "hard-case from Utah" who "may have been kin" to Butch Cassidy.

One of the most widely repeated stories about Parker concerns his alleged last request. On the night before his hanging, Parker was asked by Sheriff Ruffner what he wanted for his last meal, so the story goes. In reply, the doomed man purportedly said: "The meal doesn't interest me, but there's a little dolly down there on Whiskey Row . . ." A saloon girl named Flossie, a favorite of Parker's, who worked and "sold her wares" in the Palace Bar. Ruffner proceeded to procure her for one hour for his one-time friend.

This story has a terrible case of the cutes, which is always a bad sign. As often as it has been repeated, many will be surprised to learn that there is no documentation for it. In fairness, it should be noted that there is no evidence to disprove it either. The story may be true, but I reject it for several logistical reasons.

In the first place, the *Arizona Journal Miner* (June 8, 1898) reported that on the morning of his hanging, Parker "partook of a hearty breakfast," but that doesn't necessarily disprove the Flossie legend—perhaps Sheriff Ruffner let his old friend have both Flossie and a last meal. But there are other factors to consider in examining this story.

Prior to his hanging, Parker had not been a free man in Prescott or anywhere else for 1½ years—he had either been in jail or on the run from posses. Most historians say that saloon girls were a dime a dozen who moved in and out of towns on a fairly regular clip in those days, so it seems hard to believe that Flossie would have still been around after 1½ years. In fact, some historians say that it is a Hollywood myth that prostitutes worked in saloons at all in the old west—that they were relegated exclusively to the red light districts in almost every town in real life.

Furthermore, we also know that Parker had lived in and near Peach Springs in Mohave County for several years prior to the train robbery. While he could have easily visited Prescott and Whiskey Row, it seems more likely that he would have ventured into Kingman or Williams (both of which were much closer and had wild reputations) whenever he wanted women or liquor. Despite another persistent legend to the contrary, there is no solid evidence that Parker ever lived in Prescott. If he did, and I'm not saying he didn't, it couldn't have been for very long.

Finally, it strains the bounds of believability that the saloon girl in question, *always* called Flossie, would have a name that sounds so similar to the word "floozie." Think about it.

The "doomed man asking for a whore" legend has attached itself to other prominent hangings of the era as well, including that of Tom "Black Jack" Ketchum in New Mexico in 1901. In that version, interestingly enough, the Sheriff declines the request.

Another popular legend, almost always told in conjunction with the Flossie story, alleges that Sheriff Ruffner was very absent-minded! According to the version usually told, on the morning of Parker's hanging, the Sheriff realized with horror that he had forgotten to mail out the invitations! To rectify this, he sent a playing card from his personal deck to every invited witness. Only those with cards from the deck of his pattern were admitted to the gallows yard.

This is another story with a bad case of the cutes. As already seen, the *Arizona Journal Miner* on June 1, 1898—two days before the hanging—reported that: *"Sheriff Ruffner has issued invitations to the execution of Parker next Friday."* And they were reprinting from a daily edition earlier in the week! And don't forget, a rare surviving copy of the Jerome Daily News, dated May 31, 1898, acknowledges receipt of an invitation to the hanging! Finally, we have seen that a number of invited guests, including Ralph Cameron and Al Galpin, were from out of town. A "playing card" invitation sent out the morning of the hanging could not possibly have reached them in time, let alone allowing them enough time to get ready and go!

This evidence pretty much buries the "playing card invitation" legend, but it has shown remarkable duration over the years. Even staunch admirers of George Ruffner have repeated this story, and this puzzles me. I guess the opus sounds very romantic somehow, but I have just the opposite reaction. I find the story demeaning—if Ruffner were that incredibly forgetful, he could not possibly have been as effective a lawman as we know he was.

Like the Flossie story, the "playing card invitation" legend has attached itself to other hangings in the Southwest as well. In fact, the Sharlot Hall Museum archives actually has a playing card that was purportedly used as an invitation to the 1925 hanging of Dixon Sujynamie at Fort Whipple. As I have not yet studied that case in depth, I won't comment, but forgive me if I remain skeptical.

I also have a fuzzy memory of seeing this "playing card" bit dramatized in some old western movie or TV show when I was a child. Unfortunately, I no longer remember the name or the actors.

Several after-the-fact accounts contend, without listing any sources, that the night before he was hanged, Parker told George Ruffner that he wanted him, the Sheriff, to be the one to pull the trap. Parker is usually quoted as saying that he wanted to be put to death "by a real man."

Traditionally, the Sheriff always did pull the trap at hangings. Still, there is nothing to disprove this story, although admittedly, the quote seems a bit out of character for Parker.

One story I have never seen in print, but have heard several times from oral tellers, alleges that Sheriff Ruffner pursued Parker with such determination after the jailbreak mainly because Parker had stolen his horse, Sure-Shot! Otherwise, he might have been inclined to let his old friend go.

This story is told in the same semi-jocular vein as the "playing card invitations" legend, and is from the "nothing comes between a man and his horse" school of western lore, popularized in old B movies and horse operas. But frankly, I find the story offensive, for it seems to contend that Ruffner really didn't care that a man had been murdered, but was outraged over the theft of his horse. We know for a fact that the Sheriff had more character than that, and if he really had this kind of attitude, he would not have lasted very long in the position!

I am amazed when I hear people who claim to admire Ruffner tell this story, as if it were somehow flattering and "colorful" to him. Is it just me?

Some museum archives are plagued with old, typewritten, unsigned, sourceless accounts of certain events, apparently written by people who felt they had some pertinent data to offer and wanted to preserve it. Needless to say, these anonymous typists really didn't do anyone any favors, since they kept themselves and their sources a secret.

The Sharlot Hall Museum Archives has a number of such documents. Some pertain to the Parker case; I have identified two of them as having been culled from news accounts of the day. Two others are more difficult. Unusually brief, the pages relate short anecdotes about Parker that could be true, but since the typist chose anonymity, and chose to leave out his source, they are historically worthless.

The first such sheet seems to take place after one of Parker's arrests, probably after Sheriff George Ruffner took custody of him from Samuel S. Preston. It reads simply:

> The Indians surrounded Parker—when Ruffner came up they were about to eat—R. put handcuffs on P. He was asked: "Why can't he eat first?" "I know this man"—said Ruffner, he can eat with the hand cuffs on.

The second sheet purports to offer up a quote by well-known Prescott miner Homer Wood, who purportedly witnessed Parker's hanging. The sheet says in its entirety:

> Homer Wood: Parker said—"Who's pulling the trap (Joe Dillon Was), I want Ruffner to pull the trap." He wanted Ruffner at his burial—Father Queter (sic) officiated—spoke so low Ruffner didn't hear him—George said—"Damn you, why can't you say something?" Ruffner was very nervous. Father Q. repeated—louder.

Chapter 11: Myths, Legends, and Unverifiable Stories

The various writings of Williams historian Thomas E. Way, particularly his book *The Parker Story* (Prescott Graphics, 1981), contain a number of interesting stories about Parker that may well be true but are no longer independently verifiable. The most notable tale relays an incident in which Parker, working as a cowhand for rancher Tom Wagner, saved Wagner's life. The story goes that one day the rancher was charged by an angry cow. Wagner ran for his life but was cornered on a precipice. Parker, riding nearby, saw what was happening and managed successfully to rope the cow and pull it down, saving his boss from certain doom. Author Way gives no source for this story, and it appears nowhere else but in his writings, but he does acknowledge having personally known Wagner in his youth. Perhaps Wagner himself relayed the story to Way at one time. There is certainly nothing to say it isn't true.

Way was one researcher who believed that Parker made his first forays into Arizona years before his first documented appearance in the early 1890s. In fact, Way contends that Parker and George Ruffner, already friends, both entered Prescott's legendary first July 4th rodeo in 1888 (Prescott is famed for hosting the "world's oldest rodeo," held annually since 1888). As Way based much of his writings on the recollections of people who had known both Ruffner and Parker, who is to say this isn't true? I love this particular legend—it is a tragedy that full entry records for this rodeo have not survived to either confirm or deny the story.

In the same book, author Way also describes two specific incidents of rustling that were attributed to Parker while he was with the Abe Thompson Gang. As the gang committed many acts of rustling and thievery, these stories may well be true, but again, there is no surviving corroborative evidence.

According to the first story, Constable Jim Kennedy of Williams hired Parker to break a string of wild horses that he had purchased and hoped to sell. During that time, several were stolen, but Parker was not suspected in the thefts until some time later, after it was discovered he belonged to the Abe Thompson Gang. This story appears only in Thomas Way's writings, and as he claimed to have known Jim Kennedy personally, he may well have gotten this story first hand, but if so, he fails to specify this.

The second story alleges that one dark night in Seligman, forty horses were stolen from a loading pen and driven West. Seligman is not far from Parker's known haunts in Mohave County, but Seligman is in Yavapai, so Sheriff Ruffner formed a small posse and took off after the thieves. When the two rustlers saw the posse closing in, they abandoned the horses and escaped. The horses were recovered, and the members of the posse were certain that one of the two rustlers was Parker.

More about Thomas E. Way and his writings appears in Chapter 12.

Above, Prescott mayor Morris Goldwater, whom folklore has long contended was the hoodsman at Parker's hanging, even though he does not resemble the man doing the job in the hanging photos. Below, Joseph P. Dillon, who was the actual hoodsman, and a comparison of this photo to the hanging photos show it is indeed he. (Both courtesy of Sharlot Hall Museum)

A bone of contention among researchers of the Parker story has been the question: Did Morris Goldwater (ex-Prescott Mayor, prominent citizen, and uncle of legendary U. S. Senator Barry M. Goldwater) participate in the hanging of Parker? Whenever the photos of Parker's hanging appear, the short, mustachioed man pulling the hood over Parker's head in Photo #5 is almost always identified as Goldwater, even though the man in question does not look like the former Mayor. All of the first-hand newspaper accounts of the execution state that Undersheriff Joseph P. Dillon was the hoodsman, and indeed, an examination of other surviving photos of Dillon easily confirm that it was he.

The question of Goldwater's alleged participation still remains, however, because other historians have contended that an unidentified man standing to the far right of Photo #5 is actually Goldwater. This man doesn't look much like Morris either, but who is to say for sure?

On the other hand, if a citizen as prominent as Morris Goldwater had a role in the hanging, surely Prescott's newspapers would have made note of it. Yet, while both the *Journal Miner* and the *Courier* go into great detail describing who was on the platform with Parker, Goldwater is not mentioned at all. Furthermore, since the ex-Mayor did not hold any official office at that particular time, it seems unlikely that he would have been invited to participate as anything other than a spectator, unless Sheriff Ruffner included him out of friendship.

It is certain that Morris Goldwater was not the hoodsman. Although I cannot say with 100% certainty that he did not participate in some "official capacity," it would seem from the surviving evidence that his presence is just a legend.

CHAPTER 12

Other Writings

For someone who has been repeatedly described as an "obscure outlaw," Fleming "James" Parker has certainly had enough articles written about him over the years in Western magazines, anthology books, and amateur history essays. All of these, needless to say, have displayed varying degrees of accuracy (and some have displayed no accuracy at all). Some of these writings have also done much to keep the varying myths and legends about Parker alive. At the same time, it should be noted that perhaps Parker would indeed be forgotten if it had not been for these various historians, writers, and folklorists.

This chapter lists and analyzes some (by no means all) of the after-the-fact writings about Parker that have appeared in the ensuing years since it all happened. Some of them are adequate, some of them are straightforward, and a few are truly bizarre.

Thomas E. "Spike" Way, a historian from Williams, who also served as that city's Justice of the Peace from 1941 to 1976, wrote a number of books and magazine articles about Northern Arizona history, including several pieces on Parker, eventually culminating in his book, *The Parker Story*, (Prescott Graphics; 1981). For many years, Way was considered an expert on Parker, and his book is the only other book I am aware of that deals exclusively with the Visalia-born outlaw.

Although I never met Thomas Way personally, I owe him a debt of gratitude for introducing me to Parker. It was *The Parker Story* that first piqued my interest in Jim, or Flem, and led to the research that you now hold in your hands.

Author Way was unique in his way in that he tried to base his writings about Parker not on unverified legends, but on solid evidence. By his own admission, *The Parker Story* is based on the recollections of men he had known in his youth who had known both Parker and George Ruffner, as well as on a file folder on Parker possessed by the Sharlot Hall Museum Archives. Unfortunately, judging by the content of the book, Way apparently assumed, wrongly, that this file folder contained all of the Museum's holdings on Parker. By making this assumption, as it appears he did, he missed out on a lot of interesting material that was right in front of him.

The Parker Story tells quite a number of personal anecdotes about Parker and Ruffner and their friendship, including conversations they purportedly had. It is reasonable to conclude that Way obtained these stories from the men who had known them. Unfortunately, in an apparent effort to prevent excessive book length, Way fails to state who told him what. The result is a number of fascinating anecdotes without sources, a few (by no means all) of which I have alluded to in the course of this book. It would be great to know, for instance, who assured Way that Parker was in Arizona long before his first documented appearance in the early 1890s, but such information appears to be lost. Way did not seem to realize that, without specific sources named, these stories are not worth very much to historians.

Way contends that one of the spreads worked by Parker and Ruffner was The Hat Ranch near Williams, owned by a man named Charley "Hog-Eye" Miller. Again, no documentation, but I have no reason to disbelieve it. Newspaper accounts from 1897 on the story did refer to "Miller's ranch" near Williams, and this was probably it.

In recounting the pursuit of Parker through Williams, Way states that after Parker abandoned Sure-Shot, he stole fresh horses from his old friend Tom Wagner and a Williams livery stable owner named Sanford Rowe. All quite likely true, but no solid documentation.

The book does contain some factual errors as well, but nothing really serious (the book uses Ralph Cameron's depiction of Parker swinging onto the passing train instead of forcing the watchman to flag it; he identifies the Mohave County Sheriff as Bill Lake instead of John C. Potts; and a few other mistakes). Perhaps the most serious error in the book is Way's claim that Parker was caught the first time by Deputies "One-Eye" Riley and Martin Buggeln. *The Parker Story* was the best written work on Parker up to its time, and despite its flaws, I recommend reading it in conjunction with this book if you really like this story (it is out of print, but some Southwest libraries still carry it).

Author Way had previously written magazine articles on Parker, including one in the long-defunct magazine *Scenic Southwest* in 1941, as well as a lengthy 1952 article in my possession of unidentified origin, which appears to have originated in a long-defunct publication from Ash Fork. These articles varied in quality, as Way had not completed all of his research at these writings. The Sharlot Hall Museum Archives also has a cassette tape of a lecture Way gave in 1974 on various subjects, Parker included.

Thomas E. "Spike" Way died in April of 1992, at the age of 82.

I have, in my files, a photocopy of an unidentified magazine article, from 1929, detailing anecdotes about the Yuma Territorial Prison (only about 20 years after the closing of the prison). The article is titled "Prison Days on the Arizona Frontier," by John S. Gorby.

The write-up refers to Louis C. Miller as a prisoner (called "Lou Miller" in the article), but very strangely does not connect him to Parker, and states he was in Yuma simply for forgery! Gorby states that Miller tried to escape twice from jail in Prescott before arriving at the prison.

Gorby goes on to refer to Miller's interest in becoming a surveying engineer, and states that "Captain Ingalls" advised him to study mathematics, which he did. He then took a correspondence course in surveying, and was given the highest grade ever issued by that particular school, according to Gorby.

The author does refer to Mrs. Russell Sage's gift of surveying instruments, but closes his story by saying that he started drinking and gambling after his release, sold his instruments to pay his debts, and disappeared.

John S. Gorby's account of Miller is so muddled and strange that it casts the rest of his article into question. Admittedly, I have not taken the time to confirm or deny his other prison anecdotes, but at this point, I am treating them with a grain of salt.

In 1930, the State of Arizona issued an official, four-volume edition titled simply *History of Arizona* (Record Publishing; 1930), edited by former Territorial Governor Richard E. Sloan and an advisory council. The set consists of Arizona's background in numerous areas.

A brief section recounts the Parker story, in routine fashion, although it erroneously attributes Parker's capture (after the first posse) to Ralph Cameron, and states that it is known that Cornelia Sarata died of the wounds he received in the jailbreak (if such information was ever known by anyone specific, the evidence has long since disappeared).

Richard E. Sloan wrote his memoirs in 1932, simply titled *Memories of An Arizona Judge* (Stanford University Press; 1932). Recounting his days as a judge in Prescott, he briefly mentions the Parker story. The only notable thing about his account is that he states that Parker's hanging took place beneath the window of his chambers.

In the mid-1940s, Prescott Postmaster and pioneer citizen Gail Gardner gave a series of lectures on the Parker story to various clubs and organizations in Prescott. He addressed the subject in a discourse given at the Prescott Kiwanis Club on May 31, 1945, in a program chaired by Les Childers.

Gardner also did his presentation about Parker for the Rotary Club on March 22, 1946. County Attorney Palmer Byrne was chairman for the program, and Greenboro, Pennsylvania newlyweds Mr. And Mrs. Milton Goldstein were introduced. They were visiting Prescott after honeymooning in Mexico, and were presented with a bouquet of flowers by A.M. Crawford.

Gail Gardner likely did his presentation elsewhere, also.

On July 1, 1949, in time for Prescott's annual Frontier Days and rodeo, the *Courier* ran an article entitled "Old-Timers Here Recalled 1898 Hanging of Jim Parker." This piece, whose author is unidentified, would be repeated verbatim in the *Courier* for the next several years at rodeo time.

The article alleges itself to be based on interviews with Johnny Munds, as well as Henry Hartin, a gentleman who had once served as a deputy to Sheriff Ruffner, and who was probably a member of the Parker posse, even though the original news articles did not mention him. In later years, Hartin became kind of a local "old sage," who regaled younger generations with stories about the wild and woolly days of Prescott.

Unfortunately, this reflective newspaper article does not offer any direct quotes from Munds or Hartin. However, the article claims that Hartin "is credited with obtaining for Sheriff Ruffner a horse that would 'stand the gaff' after the sheriff had worn down a much lauded blooded race horse in a matter of a couple of hours in the grueling pursuit."

The remainder of the article is just a basic recounting of the Parker story, although it does say that the second posse consisted of over 100 men, and states, wrongly, that Parker was still riding Sure-Shot when captured.

Henry Hartin died in June of 1952 at the age of 73.

Again, the Sharlot Hall Museum archives contains many photocopies and portions of photocopies of various historical articles from the 20th century, which were filed there by previous archivists who were not as thorough as archivists are today. Among them is a portion of an article simply titled, "Jim Parker, Outlaw" by an author named W. R. King. M.D., that allegedly appeared in the February 1949 issue of *Arizona Police*, a periodical with which I am unfamiliar. I presume it was a law enforcement journal along the lines of *Sheriff Magazine*.

As the surviving article is incomplete, it is impossible to pass judgment on it. However, this surviving section contains a statement attributed to Johnny Munds, describing the first posse to trail Parker after the train robbery. The quote reads as follows:

> After much circling we cut the fugitive's tracks and followed them down the jagged defiles of the Diamond Creek Canyon. But this fellow Parker was a slippery gent and after we had tracked him down Diamond Creek to where it sends an off-shoot into Farley Canyon, night closed down upon us again.
> All of us took up the chase next morning at daybreak, and it took us into the Meriwitica country there where the creek runs into Spruce Canyon. We found the skunk's saddle and rifle in the forks of a pinion tree; he had discarded them to lighten his load.
> We trailed him to the Farley House where he had bedded down that night and on down Diamond creek to the Colorado river.
> I had become separated from the rest of the boys when I sighted Parker in the shallows of the Colorado river some distance below its mouth. An hombre whose name I did not then know caught up with me. I fell down the bank breaking my thumb so I handed my gun to this new acquaintance. 'Go down and help them

> capture Parker,' I said to my companion but he did exactly the opposite and turned out to be a confederate of Parker's.
> Stack your guns,' I heard him bawl out the order to the Indian scouts who were closing in. They did just this and now Parker, who had somehow become unarmed, grabbed a gun and started shooting at the now unarmed Indians.

I cannot prove that the above quote was truly said by Johnny Munds. However, I have no reason to doubt its authenticity, either. If genuine, it showed that Munds still believed, in 1949, that John Rogers deliberately aided Parker.

Author King asserts that the posse also contained a Mohave County deputy named "Smith," as well as a Federal Marshal from Williams named Frank Morrell. He also says that the Indian trailers in the posse were named Two Lilly, Captain Crook, One Eyed Jack, Bally Curtin, and Kate Crozier. King gives no source for this information, but if he truly interviewed Johnny Munds for this piece, the data may be accurate. If so, remember again that Indian trackers were generally given their ridiculous names by their white "masters."

Roscoe G. Willson was a writer of western lore who had a newspaper column in the *Arizona Republic* for many years, from the 1940s on. Like many historical columnists of his day, Willson had a certain amount of repute in his field.

On August 21 and 28, 1949, Willson devoted two of his columns (which was known as "Arizona Days and Ways") to the Parker story. These articles represent a surprisingly adequate account of the basic facts of the story (I say "surprisingly adequate" because these were the days when legends and folklore about the Old West were especially running wild). The account was undoubtedly even more compelling when it appeared in 1949, because the story had not yet been retold quite as often as it has today, although no one had really forgotten Jim Parker.

One item of interest: Referring to newspaper accounts that stated, after the jailbreak, that Parker rode Sure-Shot out the back of the stable into the alley, Willson notes that one old-timer who was there (and who Willson apparently spoke with) claimed that Parker rode out the front door into the street.

In my files is an unidentified clipping allegedly lifted from McClintock's *History of Arizona*. It purports to give brief descriptions of all of Arizona's train robberies, Parker's included.

It is an interesting read, but not extraordinary. It has been reprinted a number of times elsewhere as well.

In August 1950, *Sheriff Magazine* published a biography of Ruffner entitled "George C. Ruffner: Frontier Sheriff," by Toni and Robert McInnes. *Sheriff Magazine* was a periodical aimed largely at law enforcement personnel, and consisted of the latest law enforcement news, as well as write-ups on famous original cases of yore, and biographies of famous lawmen. The magazine has long since ceased to publish.

The McInnes piece is an example of an article that is better known than the periodical in which it appeared. As Ruffner biographies have been surprisingly few, many western writers have utilized the Sheriff piece as source material, and copies of the article are quite prominent in various archives (I have even seen one painstakingly handwritten copy of the entire article).

The McInnes article deals largely with Ruffner's first term as Sheriff of Yavapai County, and fails to even mention his late in life return to the position. It is unfortunate that this piece has been regarded as the definitive biography of George for so long, because it contains a number of inaccuracies, anecdotes about Ruffner without sources, and also represents the first written appearance that I have seen of a number of legends, including the "Bugger Bennett" story, as well as the image of Ruffner and Parker riding into Prescott together in 1881.

In dealing with Parker, the Sheriff article recounts the story in fairly routine fashion, but erroneously states that Parker was hanged on his original date of August 13, 1897. It repeats the old story that Parker asked Ruffner to perform the hanging, and alleges that Ruffner once said that Parker was "the first and last real man he ever knew to come from Bakersfield, California." It is a very dubious-sounding quote that doesn't even get Parker's hometown right.

According to the McInnes', the usual Sheriff's posse under Ruffner consisted of deputies Johnny Munds, Van Reichard, Harley Miller, Henry Hartin, Butch Lambertine, John Merrit, and Tot "Soupbone" Young. No source is given.

The life story of George C. Ruffner is still waiting to be told in decent form, and it is to be hoped that someone will do it justice someday. The famed lawman deserves better than the McInnes piece gave him, and it is to be desired that the article be retired from use as source material.

The book *The Arizona Story* (Hastings House; 1952) by Joseph Miller did something bold and original for its era—it related its historical anecdotes by basing them on original newspaper coverage of the events! Needless to say, the book didn't become overly popular, as the idea of utilizing original sources was even more scoffed at then than it is today.

There is a chapter on the Parker story. As it bases itself on the coverage the *Prescott Courier* gave the story in 1897-98, the account is reasonably adequate and not bad at all. The only problem with it is brevity; there simply aren't as many details as one might like.

Three years after covering the Parker story in its Ruffner biography, *Sheriff Magazine* took another stab at it in its June 1953 edition. The results were very different than the McInnes version had been. The article, "Long Rider," was written by Gladwell Richardson.

From the 1940s through the mid-1970s, the Flagstaff-based Gladwell "Toney" Richardson was considered one of the foremost Western writers of his era. He wrote hundreds of articles for a variety of Southwest periodicals, sometimes under his own name (as in the "Long Rider" article), but more often under a variety of pseudonyms that he used, including Maurice Kildare, John R. Winslowe, Ormand Clarkson, Calico Jones (!), George Blacksnake (!!), Cary James, Laramie Colson, Pete Kent, Buck Coleman, Charles McAdams, Higgs Meador, John Robert Ringo, Frank Warner, Warren O'Riley, Grant Maxwell, John S. Haines, and Don Teton. If you have ever read any articles in old magazines by any of the above authors, you have read the work of Gladwell Richardson. He also wrote scores of dime novels in addition to his voluminous "non-fiction" work.

Southwest historian Gladwell Richardson, a very influential man in his day, but the years have been quite unkind to his work following his death. (Author's collection)

In an interview that appeared March 5, 1973, Richardson bitterly told *The Arizona Republic* that he had no time for "so-called Western writers who wouldn't know the south end of a cow going north." It is therefore ironic to note that in the years since his death in 1980, the work of Gladwell Richardson has fallen into considerable disrepute in western academia. The reason for this is simple—Richardson belonged to the old school of historians that believed a story's longevity was a testament to its accuracy. Today, most scholars believe, and I concur, that just the opposite is true.

There is no better example of Richardson's errors than his *Sheriff Magazine* article on Jim Parker. The title in itself, "Long Rider," is a dead giveaway to its content—it is a lengthy endorsement of the Butch Cassidy legend.

In the article, Richardson takes us through all of the staples of that particular fairy tale—Parker came from Utah, was probably Butch's brother or close relative, was recognized as such by an ill-fated Williams cowboy, etc., etc., etc. No part of the legend is left out. Incidentally, Richardson attributes the capture of Parker (after the train robbery) to Coconino County Deputy Bill Hicklin (whoever *he* was!).

The article goes on to describe George Ruffner's horse, Sure-Shot, as a "black mare" (oh, come now!). According to Richardson, just before the jail break, Parker told Ruffner: "Mighty fancy mare—How's to let me take a canter on her?" Ruffner is said to have replied: "I don't doubt you'd like to, but some other time, though, Jim." Parker responded,

"Okay, next week will do." The point of this foolish story is that Parker knew enough to grab Sure-Shot when he broke out of jail.

As usual with retellings of this particular myth, the article tells us that Coconino County Sheriff Ralph Cameron figured it all out; mysterious money flowed into Prescott to pay for Parker's attorneys; etc. But if you're going to tell a whopper, as Gladwell Richardon does, you need to make it interesting. "Long Rider" commits the cardinal sin of being <u>dull</u> on top of its fabrications. Since the story is flimsy, Richardson wastes a great deal of ink describing how cattle were rustled, what trails thieves regularly used, etc. None of this is even remotely interesting.

Gladwell Richardon undoubtedly contributed to the public's lasting interest in western lore, and it brings me no pleasure to report that "Long Rider" is my personal nomination for worst after-the-fact account of Parker's life ever written. Since most academians have also stopped taking his work seriously, I must conclude that his other writings aren't much better. Richardson's dogmatic insistence that the West is littered with lost and buried treasures that are just waiting to be discovered has also cost him brownie points in the years since his death.

Richardson, who was the son of a trading post operator on the Navajo reservation, kept an enormous collection of files on numerous subjects, from which he drew on when writing his articles. This collection is now reposited at Northern Arizona University. It is very impressive, but when you examine it, it becomes crystal clear what its creator's researching habits were. Almost all of the files consist of clippings of after-the-fact accounts of their subjects—the kind that Richardson himself wrote.

His file on Parker, for instance, consists solely of a few later newspaper and magazine clippings, and a typewritten proposal for another Parker article to be written under his pseudonym of Maurice Kildare (if he wrote and sold that article, and he may well have, I have not yet located it). There are no old, first-hand clippings or photocopies at all, and certainly nothing he could have used to justify the "Butch Cassidy" legend.

I am not as down on Gladwell Richardon as I probably sound, simply because he was a product of his time. For many years, historians did believe that oral legends were more historically accurate than primary sources. It is a belief that has started to fade in recent years, thankfully, although it still has some adherents. Richardson did score a few coups in his career—his interview with Joe Lee (see Chapter 7) was one of them.

Gladwell Richardon's influence in his field was considerable in his lifetime, and it is reasonable to assume that his endorsement of the "Butch Cassidy" legend did much to keep the story alive. This is unfortunate, as this story has bedeviled Parker researchers for many years.

Richardson died on June 14, 1980, at the Fort Whipple Veterans Administration Center in Prescott.

On May 15, 1964, the *Prescott Courier* published a "Centennial" issue, marking the 100th anniversary of Prescott's incorporation as a town. The issue contained a number of historical stories, including a full page recounting of Parker's hanging.

The page contained four of the six known photos of the hanging (and, as usual, misidentifies the hoodsman as Morris Goldwater), as well as photos of Parker's wanted poster, as well as the portrait of Sure-Shot. Accompanying this was a short article entitled, "Fleming Parker Was Last Victim of Rope Within Prescott City Limits," once again repeating that old myth. The author of the piece was Jim Garner, who, years later, would become editor of the *Prescott Courier*.

Garner describes Parker as a "resourceful, but stupid, type." The article is noteworthy, though, as the earliest written account of the "Flossie" legend that I have seen.

Parker made the first of several appearances in *True West* magazine in the September-October 1964 edition. This article, titled "Jim Parker's Revenge," was written by Tom L. Coleman, who claimed to have been an eight-year old boy in Prescott when all the excitement happened in 1897.

Coleman's account is one of the strangest I have encountered in Parker folklore. With the exception of Parker's own 1898 jailhouse interview with the *San Francisco Examiner*, this is the earliest printed version of the "revenge against the railroad" legend that I have seen. However, it is a bizarre variation of that legend that I have not seen repeated since.

In his version of the legend, Coleman contends that Parker robbed the train not to avenge the death of his horses, but to avenge the deaths of horses belonging to a friend of his! This friend is identified as Jim Hamilton, and it was he who had two horses killed in a train accident, according to Coleman. The railroad only offered $30. apiece for the horses, far below their worth.

The article tells us that Parker was chief assistant to Hamilton on the latter's ranch, and he was outraged by the railroad's treatment of his boss. You guessed it, he robbed the train to avenge Hamilton.

Well, if you are going to tell a whopper, make it interesting. But there is virtually no evidence to support the "revenge" legend in its usual form, and there certainly isn't to support this version, which stands alone in Parker folklore. The name of Jim Hamilton appears in no other accounts, although as seen in Chapter 1, Parker did apparently know someone by this name in early Visalia.

Continuing on, Coleman claims that the robbers jumped the train when it stopped for water at a water tank. He also identifies George Ruffner's horse as "Surefoot"; and claims that Parker was captured for the last time not by Samuel S. Preston, but by an Indian agent named "Bly."

Tom L. Coleman closes his article by telling us that he and his father were among the spectators at Parker's trial, and that he was disappointed to see that Parker "was a quiet, peaceable looking man of rather heavy build." Coleman also says that he and the other kids in town were looking forward to seeing the hanging until it was learned that the gallows would be surrounded by a big board fence.

Several people have brought to my attention the fact that the book *Echoes Of The Past Vol. 2* (Yavapai Cowbelles; 1964) contains a reference to a Jim Parker.

This book consists of a number of essays written by people (mostly women) who were settlers and residents in the old west; these essays were written many years after the fact, when the authors were getting on in years.

One essay describes the author's trip to the Verde Valley by wagon, with a sick husband, seven children, and other members of the wagon train. Their guide, who rode on ahead looking for signs of Apaches, was a man named Jim Parker, described as "rough and ready," and "fearless."

It is possible, of course, that Parker hired out as a wagon guide in his cowboying days. There is nothing to say that he didn't. But as this has never been alleged anywhere else, I have a strong hunch that the guide in this story was a different Jim Parker. It's not like this was an uncommon name.

A journal of western lore called *The Southwesterner* ran a brief account of the Parker story in April 1965. This periodical, long defunct, is so forgotten that when I asked to look at it at the Northern Arizona University Special Collections department, I was told that I was the first person in many years to request it.

The article was written by Mike Tenney, and is headlined, "Parker Did All Right Robbing Trains, but Hanged for Killing." It is a brief recount of the basic facts, although Tenney claims that one of Parker's aliases was "Jim Davis," and that he got away with $1500 from the train robbery.

On July 1, 1965, the *Phoenix Gazette* ran an interview with an elderly woman named Mrs. Ethelle Morris, then 78, who claimed to have been a witness for a number of historically significant events in Prescott history, including the catastrophic 1900 fire, which she erroneously places in the 1890s. She also claimed to have worked as a clerk in Morris Goldwater's store.

She discusses Parker's jailbreak, and intimates that she was on the street when Parker and the other two jailbreakers rode by. (If so, she was only 11 years old at the time). However, her memory of the story served her ill, as she told the reporter that Parker broke out by reaching through the bars, grabbing a deputy's gun, and shooting him.

Unknown artist's illustration of the jailbreak, which appeared in the long-denfunct periodical, the *Southerner*.

Some Southwest libraries still have copies of *Portraits of the Past*, a 1968 self-published book by students at Sunnyside High School in Tucson. These students, members of the school's History Club, each wrote essays for the book on a number of Arizona historical figures.

A Junior named Dave Burchell wrote his essay on George C. Ruffner, and gives space to the Parker story. However, Burchell lists as his only source the Toni and Robert McInnes biography from *Sheriff Magazine*, and indeed, the essay comes off as a marginally reworded version of that too widely circulated article. Enough said.

In October of 1971, the Arizona Friends of Folklore, a group operating out of Northern Arizona University, decided to run their own article on the Parker story in their official publication, *AFFword*. This periodical consisted largely of old western legends and analysis pieces, and despite the group's name, they maintained that most of their stories were largely true.

That was a mistake. The *AFFword* article on Parker was nothing short of a total disaster. Entitled "Jim Parker: Train Robber and Murderer," this piece is second only to Gladwell Richardson's old "Long Rider" article on my personal list of worst after-the-fact accounts of Parker's life. The author was Wilfred Babcock, a Kingman-based old-timer who contributed many folksy compositions to *AFFword*.

Babcock's article is a verbatim repeat and embellishment of the outrageous story that Asa Harris fed to the *Arizona Republic* in 1957. The story repeats every one of Harris' tall tales, right down to the geographical error of placing Congress north-east of Kingman (it is actually far Southeast). Babcock must have known Harris, and must have hung on every word the aging ex-deputy ever spoke.

Wilfred Babcock adds some heavy embellishments to Harris' story as well. Whether these inventions were purely Babcock's, or if Harris had spoken these details at one time as well, is not known. Babcock glowingly describes "Ace" Harris as "one of the greatest peace officers our Southwest ever saw." He contends that Harris always took up the trail after outlaws because Mohave County Sheriff John C. Potts was too old and sick to adequately discharge his duties any more (absurd, as the original newspaper accounts specifically place Potts as the leader of the Mohave posse).

Author Babcock must have been aware that most versions of the Parker story have George Ruffner as the hero, as he goes out of his way to make Ruffner look like a fool. At one point, Babcock contends that after riding hard after Parker all day, Harris came across the Ruffner posse—sound asleep! Later, after the jailbreak (which is accomplished when Parker hits the jailor over the head with a bucket of coal), we are told that George Ruffner refused to accept that a certain horse's footprints belonged to Sure-Shot, and needlessly delayed the posse three hours—until Harris points out that the horse's droppings were grain-fed, and could only be Sure-Shot! And yes, Babcock repeats Harris' description of Sure-Shot as a "big gray." And of course, Harris captured Parker all by himself!

Babcock also showers praise on Harris' sidekick, the Indian trailer "Captain Hardy," calling him "one of the world's greatest trackers." He writes: "They entered the great forest and ever and ever this great Captain Hardy never lost this man Jim Parker." Lavish praise indeed.

I could go on and on, but what's the point? The *AFFword* article is an embarrassment, unworthy of the organization that published the piece. Babcock must have idolized Asa Harris, and there is nothing wrong with that, except that he let his admiration blind him to his hero's shortcomings, such as tall-tale spinning.

Interestingly, six months later in April 1972, *AFFword* reprinted Thomas E. Way's old 1941 *Scenic Southwest* article on Parker, with the excuse that it was to demonstrate how much influence an individual storyteller has on common material. It was a strange move, and I have to wonder if perhaps Way had seen the Babcock article, was outraged by it, and demanded equal time.

On June 24, 1973, Yavapai County Deputy Sheriff George McMurran was shot and killed by deer poachers he was attempting to arrest. After the outrage over the shootings died down, Prescott old-timers started discussing the fact that they could not remember a County law enforcement official being killed in the line of duty in their lifetimes. An alternate Prescott newspaper, called simply *The Paper*, ran an article about this on July 4, 1973, written by Ken Wayman.

The Paper interviewed several old-timers, including Gail Gardner, Orville Bozarth, and Lester Ward "Budge" Ruffner (George C. Ruffner's nephew). They concluded that the last time such a thing had occurred was the shooting death of Deputy John Murphy in 1886 (it was actually 1885) by the murderer D.W. Dilda (misidentified as William Dilda in the article).

This write-up concludes by recalling the Parker story as well, since Parker had slain Deputy District Attorney Lee Norris. The article names the dead train robber as "Jim Williams" (from the wanted poster). After the jailbreak and murder, Wayman says that Cornelia Sarata (unnamed in this article) died many years later in Mexico. He also attributes Parker's capture on the Navajo Reservation to George Ruffner instead of Samuel S. Preston, and adds that Parker "was taken off the train at Ft. Whipple to avoid a mob which was intent on lynching Parker."

Famed historian and poetess Sharlot M. Hall made only one reference to the Parker story in her writings that I know of. It appears in the diary she kept while on her well-known tour and camping trip in the vast wilds of Northern Arizona in 1911. This diary was published many years later under the title *Sharlot Hall on the Arizona Strip* (Northland Press; 1975).

In her diary, when camping by Willow Springs, Sharlot Hall notes that about 100 yards from her campsite were the ruins of Samuel S. Preston's old trading post, and further notes that this was where Parker was recognized and ultimately captured by Preston.

1911 really wasn't all that many years after Parker's hanging. After Preston (who was still alive at that time) vacated the trading post, apparently no one else took it over, or ever tried to convert the building to other uses. Note Laura Runke's account of this in Chapter 10 as well.

The now defunct Prescott-based publication *Westward* ran an article on the Parker story on July 18, 1975 entitled, "Despite Sister's Pleas, Fleming Parker Was Last Prescott Hanging," by Paul Perry.

The only thing noteworthy about the piece is that it is one of the very few after-the-fact accounts to utilize quotes from the surviving letters of Sadie Baker, Parker's sister. I have always been amazed that more researchers have not used this material.

Aside from this, the rest of the article is routine. And, of course, it is not true that Parker was Prescott's last hanging.

In my files is a photocopy of an unidentified after-the-fact article on Parker, headlined "The Sheriff and the Outlaw, They were Friends," by longtime Prescott journalist Claudette Simpson. I estimate the article appeared circa 1976 from some now-defunct Prescott publication.

Most of the article is an adequate retelling of the basic facts, although at the end, it does once again give us the "Flossie" legend, as well as the story that Parker asked Sheriff Ruffner to pull the switch so he could die at the hands of "a real man."

Lowell Parker (no relation to Fleming-Jim) wrote a column for the *Arizona Republic* for many years, in which he expounded whimsical and entertaining stories of old Arizona. As a Western writer, Lowell Parker had a high reputation and was enjoyed by millions of readers who automatically assumed he knew what he was talking about.

But Lowell was a historian of the old school, who believed that oral legends were more accurate than documented research, and many of his columns consisted of the same old folklore that had been circulated for decades.

Needless to say, the ensuing years since his passing have not been kind to him, and a comparison of Lowell Parker to Gladwell Richardson would not be inappropriate. This is further driven home by Lowell's columns of Sept. 7-9, 1976—three columns devoted to Jim Parker, in which the columnist dredges up once again the "Butch Cassidy" legend.

Western sage and storyteller Lowell Parker, highly regarded in his day, but history has not been kind to his work. (Author's collection)

Lowell offers nothing new to the feeble fable, but simply repeats verbatim all of the staples of the legend—that Parker was Butch's brother, the dead Williams cowboy, mysterious money flowing into Prescott, etc. etc. ad nauseum. Lowell Parker's description of Sure-Shot as a "black mare" is a dead giveaway that the columnist used Gladwell Richardson's old "Long Rider" article in *Sheriff Magazine* as source material.

Interestingly, at two points Lowell acknowledges that some people believe that Jim Parker was just a cowboy gone bad, but hastens to reassure us that "all evidence" points to Parker having been the Wild Bunch's agent in Arizona. This is typical of purveyors of the Butch Cassidy legend, most of whom have taken on a smug "we know something you don't know" kind of attitude.

In closing, Lowell Parker observes that if the Wild Bunch had any mourners at Parker's hanging, they went unnoticed.

Lowell Parker is now deceased, but I am unclear as to when he passed on.

The October 1976 issue of *Sheriff Magazine* (still as dubious as it ever was) ran an article it claimed was reprinted from the July 14, 1923 issue of the *Coconino Sun* (I did not locate the original article in that issue, by the way), entitled "Old Time Arizona Sheriffs," by an author using the ridiculous *nom de guerre* of Jem M'Kem (One Who Knew Them).

Jem recounts various anecdotes about the title characters, including George C. Ruffner. In briefly recounting the Parker story, Jem erroneously places the action in 1900, and contends that after the jailbreak, Ruffner pushed on alone after Parker and "trailed the bandit for 200 miles across the Mogollon Mounts and Painted Desert to the Navajo Reservation," where he finally captured Parker.

One note: If Jem really wrote this in 1923, and if he had really known them, he would have also known that Ruffner had returned to the Yavapai County Sheriff's office even as he wrote his words, but he fails to mention it. In light of this, and my failure to locate the original article on its purported date, I am suspicious of the article's veracity in all ways.

The January 13, 1978 edition of the defunct Prescott magazine *Westward* contained a recounting of the Miller-Archibald shooting, under the title of "Wild, Wild, Wild West in Prescott." As the author, Claudette Simpson, draws heavily on old *Journal Miner* coverage, the account is reasonably accurate.

One oddity: Simpson apparently failed to realize that Louis C. Miller was the same man who would later break jail with the legendary Jim Parker, as she fails to allude to it.

In 1979, Sally Munds Williams self-published a book she had written about her parents, Johnny and Frances Munds. The book was rather audaciously titled *History of Valuable Pioneers of the State of Arizona*.

In a section describing her father's years as Deputy to Sheriff Ruffner, Ms. Williams recounts the Parker story in some detail. It is not a bad rendition, probably due to her obvious reliance on the *Journal Miner's* coverage for details.

A couple of interesting notes, Ms. Williams contends that during the second posse, her father and Sheriff Ruffner kept plying potential witnesses with $50 bills for information on which direction Parker went. She also twice describes Louis C. Miller as "an awful coward."

On September 13, 1979, a Flagstaff-based publication called *The Northlander* published an unflattering biography of Ralph Cameron, covering his life from his days as Sheriff of Coconino County to his one-term in the United States Senate. The author, Ralph Sorgenfrei, depicts Cameron as a power-hungry megalomaniac, thirsting after money and influence most of his life.

Sorgenfrei at one point quotes Cameron from a 1910 interview that the one-time Coconino Sheriff allegedly gave to a reporter named James B. Morrow. I have not been able to locate the original interview, and Sorgenfrei does not name the publication, so I cannot verify the authenticity of the quote, although I have no reason to doubt it. In his remarks to Morrow, Cameron takes full credit for capturing Parker after the Rock Cut train robbery:

> I tracked Parker into the Grand Canyon. At daylight of the fourth morning, a one-eyed man and I saw Parker leisurely walking down a creek. We hid in some willow brush and when he came along we threw our guns into his face.

Ralph Henry Cameron was certainly not above making such an outrageous statement to enhance his own reputation.

For the first time since 1964, *True West* magazine returned to the Parker story in its January-February 1980 issue. This article, written by William B. Secrest, was titled, "Tell The Boys I Died Game."

Secrest is one of the better authors of western lore, who is still very active. He was one of the first to return to researching primary sources for his articles, and his essay on Parker, while admittedly not spectacular, is a decent account of the basic facts, and will certainly suffice for anyone who has not heard the story.

I am very much an admirer of William Secrest.

The pulp western magazine *Real West* took its turn at the Parker story in its July 1980 issue, with an article entitled "Jim Parker: Good Cowboy Gone Bad?" by Matt Dodge. The result was truly bizarre.

Dodge clearly relied on old *Journal Miner* coverage for most of his writing, so that makes three-fourths of this article very good, but simultaneously, Dodge also endorses the Butch Cassidy legend! How Dodge could research original sources and still come to that conclusion is beyond me, and I have to wonder if he actually knew better and just thought that bringing in Butch Cassidy would increase his chances at selling a magazine article.

Matt Dodge describes Parker as "curly haired" and says: "Jim and Butch were skilled cowboys, had similar physical characteristics, and a pleasing manner that impressed strangers. They could have been brothers or cousins. Maybe they were. After all, Jim Parker was born and raised in southern Utah, right in Butch's old Circleville neighborhood."

After dispensing with this tripe, Dodge goes into a long but generally accurate account of the Rock Cut Train Robbery, the pursuit by posse, and the jailbreak and murder of Lee Norris. In fact, if only Dodge had left Butch Cassidy alone, this would be on my list of excellent after-the-fact articles on Parker.

But regrettably, Dodge returns to Butch Cassidy in the latter part of the article by postulating that at the time Parker was captured on the Navajo reservation, he was likely making his way to a Wild Bunch hideout, "Robbers Roost Number Seven, (which) was on the east side of the Colorado River, about 15 miles below Dandy Crossing near the junction of the San Juan river."

Dodge then goes back to describing Parker's trial and hanging quite accurately. Then, Dodge finishes up by talking about the "mysterious money" that supposedly paid for Parker's attorneys, and contends that Butch Cassidy and the Wild Bunch robbed the Paymaster of the Pleasant Valley Coal Company at Castle Gate, Utah on April 27, 1897, not all that long after Parker's train robbery! Dodge also says that the Wild Bunch robbed a bank at Belle Fourche, South Dakota on June 28, 1897, very shortly after Parker was sentenced to hang! The reader is supposed to believe these could not possibly be coincidences, which they, of course, were. I suppose I have to grudgingly give the author some credit (if that word is even applicable here) for trying to add something new to this fairy tale.

Dodge also has the audacity to quote from the book *Butch Cassidy: My Brother* by the outlaw's sister, Lula Parker Betenson, even though she makes no mention anywhere of having a brother named Jim. The ambiguous quote Dodge uses regards her brother Butch's motives for his crimes. This brazen choice also makes me think that deep down the author knew the Butch Cassidy legend was not true, but used it anyway. Too bad; this article shows real promise gone awry by poor choices on the part of the author. Some of the verbiage Matt Dodge uses in the Butch Cassidy segments is very similar to Lowell Parker's *Arizona Republic* articles four years earlier, indicating he used this for source material as well.

The Sharlot Hall Museum archives possess a written transcript of a speech given by one Danny Freeman in 1982 to the 20th anniversary gathering of a group known as the Prescott Corral of the Westerners. Freeman's topic was the life of George C. Ruffner, and it appears that he probably drew on the infamous McInnes article for source material, as so many others have done.

Naturally, Freeman devoted much of his speech to the Parker story, which he tells in fairly routine fashion, right down to the "Flossie" story again, and the legend that Parker asked Ruffner to perform the hanging. Aside from this, there are some interesting variations in Freeman's text:

Freeman contends that Ruffner and Parker, while they were friends, worked for a rancher named Jerry Sullivan, whose Double O spread ran from Prescott to Seligman.

He further states, erroneously, that Parker was captured for the last time on the Navajo Reservation by Ralph Cameron instead of Samuel S. Preston.

In a very interesting and probably true sidelight, Freeman contends that legendary Prescott pioneer and "cowboy poet" Gail Gardner, as a boy, tried to witness the hanging by peering through a knothole in the board fence, but would keep getting pulled away by guards.

Freeman finishes by saying that Sure-Shot, crippled for life by Parker's abuse, was sent to a green pasture in the Salt River Valley by Ruffner, where he lived out his days and was eventually buried. The site, according to Freeman, is now the Arizona Biltmore Hotel. This anecdote, which I have no reason to doubt, reportedly originated with Ruffner's nephew, Lester Ward "Budge" Ruffner.

The Spring 1982 issue of the quarterly journal of the *National Association and Center for Outlaw and Lawman History* (reportedly affiliated with the University of Wyoming), contained a lengthy, more detailed than usual article on Parker by Dr. Philip J. Rasch, a writer of Western lore who was ahead of his time by researching original sources.

Dr. Rasch's article, simply entitled "Fleming 'Jim' Parker, Arizona Desperado," is a mixture of the usual legends (Flossie, the playing card invitations, etc.) and some surprisingly solid research. The result is one of the better after-the-fact accounts of Parker's life and career.

The article gives a decent account (albeit very abbreviated) of Parker's early life, something most later articles never do. The incident with John Rogers is included, which is unusual for these later accounts, and the whole thing is remarkably good.

There are a few glitches (Miller's name is misspelled "Lew C. Miller"), but this article is quite worthwhile despite a few lapses into legend.

I understand that Dr. Philip J. Rasch is now deceased, but I do not know when he passed on.

On June 1, 1983, the *Prescott Courier* published a special insert recounting various significant events in the city's history. The Miller-Archibald shooting is briefly recounted, without naming either man. It simply stated that in 1894, the Chief of Police and Constable dueled over the custody of a prisoner, and that both of them missed. This is not quite true, of course, but the account adds sarcastically that "Tombstone had the good shots."

This special insert also reprinted one photo of Parker's hanging.

The August 1985 issue of *Arizona Highways* contained a small write-up by Bob Boze Bell (today, the publisher of *True West* magazine) in which he relates a story, attributed to Gail Gardner (who was still alive), in which Sheriff George Ruffner allegedly snuck up on an unidentified miscreant by wrapping his bedroll and hat up into a pack, wrapping a bandana around his head, and hobbling into the unsuspecting vermin's camp looking like an old Indian or miner with a packhorse.

Although the outlaw is unidentified in the text, an artist's rendition of the scene accompanies the blurb, with a caption identifying him as Jim "Thumbing" Parker. The idea that Parker's nickname was "Thumbing" is something I've seen nowhere else, and I find it difficult to believe that Gail Gardner would have told the Parker story in this fashion, as he certainly would have known better. Since the outlaw's name was unidentified in the article text, perhaps Bell just assumed it was Parker being talked about?

On Oct. 1, 1985, the *Prescott Courier* published a historical account of Parker's life and hanging, the first of many they would run over the years. The article, "Last Hanging-Those Who Sow the Wind Must Reap The Whirlwind," was written by *Courier* Staff Writer Bonnie Walker.

The article quotes extensively from the old *Journal Miner* coverage, and overall is an adequate, if unexceptional, account of the story. At one point, though, Walker notes with puzzlement that there was no community discussion in 1898 over the ethics of capital punishment. That's the trouble with too many historical writers—they judge the past by the enlightened standards of the present. In the 19th century, the death penalty was universally regarded as just. The idea that it might not be did not start to come into its own until the 1950s.

An article on Parker, entitled "Bad Company Led Him Astray" by then-museum archivist Sue Abbey, appeared in the *Sharlot Hall Gazette* in September 1987, a publication put out by the Sharlot Hall Museum in Prescott.

The article is better than usual, owing to Sue Abbey's decision to quote from Sadie Baker's letters, and she is also the only author I know of (prior to this book) to quote from the manuscript on his life written by Parker himself from his jail cell.

Owing to its exclusive reliance on original documents, the Abbey piece is quite good. It is too bad it was not more widely circulated.

The *Prescott Courier*, in its June 1, 1988 edition, published another special insert, briefly recounting various stories from the city's history.

This time around, they reprinted Jim Garner's account of the Parker story verbatim from the May 15, 1964 edition.

The *Prescott Courier* revisited Parker again in its "Days Past" column of April 24, 1989. "Days Past" is a weekly column that runs to this day, expounding old stories of Yavapai County.

This column, written by Steve Brennan, recalls anecdotes about all of Yavapai's frontier-era sheriffs, although his paragraphs on George C. Ruffner are largely devoted to the Parker story. Unfortunately, Brennan's account is simply a retread of the "revenge against the railroad" legend. He also repeats the fallacy that Morris Goldwater was the hoodsman at Parker's hanging.

The *Tucson Citizen* newspaper went into book publishing in 1990 with *Arizona Territory: Baptism in Blood* by Paul L. Allen and Peter M. Pegnam. This photo-laden book contains many colorful stories of old Arizona. It has a lot of great stories that should be told, but…..

This is one of those books that is frustrating to read because it mixes solid research with folklore. For example, a chapter on female stagecoach robber Pearl Hart goes to considerable effort to separate fact from folklore and says so, which is terrific, but at the same time, the chapter on Parker is dreadful.

Titled "Badge Came Between Friends," the authors give us the "revenge against the railroad" story, Flossie the floozy yet again, the playing card invitations, and the story that Parker wanted Ruffner to pull the switch so he could die at the hands of a "real man." The authors also contend that Louis C. Miller was captured in Chino Valley instead of Jerome. Then, in an abrupt switch, the essay concludes by describing Parker's hanging in detail, and accurately! The chapter is accompanied by a photo of Ruffner and a fake wanted poster for Parker which contains the exact same words as the genuine poster—why didn't they just reprint the real thing?

The three-volume reference book set, *Encyclopedia of Frontier Biography* by Dan L. Thrapp (Arthur H. Clark Company; 1990) contains a brief entry on Parker. It claims that he served his full five years at San Quentin, was arrested in Tuba City after the Yavapai jailbreak, and (of course) was the last man to be hanged on the Courthouse Plaza in Prescott. Well, I suppose it could have been a lot worse.

In 1990, the *Jerome Traveler* tackled the Parker story twice in one year. The *Traveler* was a tourist-oriented periodical that regaled its readers with stories from old Yavapai. For my money, the articles run hot and cold. Some are excellent, while others tend to lapse into legend and folklore.

The May 1990 issue contained a biography of George C. Ruffner, with much space devoted to Jim Parker. Under the headline of "Sheriff Ruffner, Yavapai County's Pioneer Lawman," author Bill Roberts (then the publisher of the *Traveler*) recounts the usual Ruffner stories, with much of the material clearly cribbed from the old McInnes article in *Sheriff Magazine*.

In the September 1990 edition of the *Traveler*, Parker got his own article under the headline, "Outlaw Fleming Parker and Williams." In both pieces, the references to Parker are almost word-for-word identical. Although Roberts never lists his sources, he seems to have had several for Parker. Much of the account seems to have been based on Thomas E. Way's book, *The Parker Story*, which is good, but other paragraphs come straight from legend. Once again, we get the usual yarns about Flossie the floozy, and Parker's "revenge against the railroad."

Bill Roberts attributes Parker's capture after the train robbery to Deputy One-Eye Riley. And in a truly bizarre turn, both articles claim that the gallows upon which Parker was hanged now rest, preserved, at the Sharlot Hall Museum. I have been told categorically by museum personnel that this is not true.

On May 20, 1990, *The Arizona Republic* ran a lengthy historical article headlined, "Gallery of Rogues and Characters," by Michael Clancy. In it, Clancy rattles off brief descriptions of various Arizona eccentrics, criminals, and unusual events, throughout Arizona history. For reasons known only to Clancy, he takes a potshot at Yavapai County's beloved poet-historian Sharlot M. Hall and her famous copper dress.

Also in his list of "rogues and characters," Clancy refers to the Parker story, but only offers up the legends of the "playing card invitations" and "Flossie," and lets it go at that.

In its December 1990 issue, *True West* magazine tackled the Parker story again. The article, by Mary G. Stano, was entitled, "The Lawless Trail of Fleming Parker," and contains a few oddities.

To begin with, author Stano tries (unconvincingly) to tell her readers that Parker's lawless ways, including his association with the Abe Thompson Gang, do not conflict with the "revenge against the railroad" story, and that both stories are therefore true. I suppose that is theoretically possible, but I find it highly unlikely, especially in the wake of no solid documentation for the "revenge" story.

Stano goes on to recount the Rock Cut Train robbery, identifies the dead robber as "Henry Williams," and claims he was shot by two disgruntled passengers who apparently decided to play hero.

After George Ruffner brought Parker back to Prescott from the Navajo Reservation, Stano contends that an angry lynch mob of about 200 people, brandishing rope, descended on the Courthouse and demanded that Parker be turned over to them. Ruffner bravely stood his ground, and the crowd dispersed. This story is obviously a variation of one that circulated at the time of Parker's arrest, as already noted, but in reality, there really was no attempt to storm the Courthouse.

Finally, Stano recounts the "Flossie" legend, and describes the saloon girl as "red-haired." In between all of this is some fairly decent writing; as a whole, the *True West* piece comes off as a nice try that doesn't quite work because of its lapses into folklore.

Mary G. Stano had previously written a shorter piece on Parker, covering much of the same territory, that appeared in the *Nevadan* on July 9, 1989. That article was simply called "Peach Springs Train Robber."

The Train Robbery Era (Pruett Publishing; 1991) is an excellent book by Richard Patterson, recounting most of the west's known train robberies in encyclopedic form. There are also detailed entries on most of the known train robbers themselves.

Patterson's entry on the Rock Cut train robbery is about the least impressive in the whole book. Apparently this robbery didn't interest him as much as the others. This is further evidenced by his description of Parker as a "hard case from Utah" who "possibly was kin" to Butch Cassidy.

Come on, Richard, you know better than that. And if you don't, you should.

I have in my possession a thin paperback entitled *Wild West Characters* by Dale Pierce (Golden West Publishers; 1991). It gives one-page thumbnail sketches of 113 western personalities, regarded by the author as colorful or eccentric. The brief profiles range from the old standbys like Billy the Kid, Wyatt Earp, Butch Cassidy, Joaquin Murieta, Pancho Villa, and Geronimo, to such names as Dennis Dilda, Pearl Hart, Old Man Clanton, Brigham Young (say what??), Buckey O'Neill, Tom Mix (!), Morris Goldwater (!!), Richard McCormick (!!!), and (gak!) Sharlot Hall.

Books like this are generally sold exclusively at tourist souvenir shops and are not recommended for serious researchers. Pierce is actually described in his bio as an expert on bullfighting! One of his brief profiles in this book is George C. Ruffner, but the page consists mostly of the Parker story. It is told in very brief, routine fashion, but Pierce just HAD to add the Flossie legend to it! Why is this unproven bit of trivia so fascinating to so many people?

The book *Desert Lawmen,* by Professor Larry D. Ball (University of New Mexico Press; 1992) is devoted to an exhaustive study of the various Sheriffs of New Mexico and Arizona, prior to statehood.

The text is unusually excellent, dredging up names and criminal cases that had not been discussed for many years (any book that makes reference to "Army" murderer Philip Lashley gets high marks from me). My only quibble with the book is that Professor Ball relies on just a few too many after-the-fact accounts for his stories, and it occasionally shows.

In writing about Yavapai County Sheriff George C. Ruffner, Ball refers to Parker twice by his father's name, Dan Parker. He also refers to the "Flossie" legend (without using her name this time), and repeats the story of Parker asking George to pull the switch because he wanted to be hung by a "real man."

Despite these glitches, the book is well worth reading.

Parker appeared again in the *Prescott Courier's* "Days Past" column on September 14, 1992 in an article headlined, "Death Not As Social As It Used To Be," written by John Plestina.

The article dealt with purported hanging "etiquette," with regard to invitations and the like. Plestina also includes some "humorous" anecdotes about what happened at various Arizona hangings. Some of it is marginally true, other parts are total folklore.

Two pictures of Parker's hanging are used to illustrate the article, and Plestina's text makes use of—naturally—the "playing card invitations" legend when referring to Parker's hanging. This article in a waste of time.

Only two weeks later, on September 28, 1992, the *Prescott Courier* carried the Parker story again in its "Days Past" column. This time, it was disguised as a biography of George Ruffner, entitled "Sheriff's Story: How The West Was One," but as with other Ruffner write-ups, the author, Roland Schmidt, spends most of his space dealing with Jim Parker.

Parts of the write-up are okay, but there are a few peculiarities. After the Rock Cut Train Robbery, Schmidt says that "wearing an Indian disguise, Ruffner rode bareback into Parker's camp and arrested him without gunplay." This truly bizarre assertion appears nowhere else in Parker folklore, and it is unknown where Schmidt picked it up.

Schmidt also states that jailor Robert Meador had only one-eye (certainly possible, but I've seen this nowhere else), and he unfortunately recounts the story of "Flossie" again, as well as the story that Parker asked Ruffner to hang him so he could "die at the hands of a real man." He also states that Ruffner finally found Sure-Shot "beside the road." Uh . . . okay.

The Schmidt article is a mixture of fact and folklore, and should have had references to more Ruffner stories than just Parker. Won't somebody please, PLEASE write a decent biography about the famed lawman?

The book *Mountain Town* by Platt Cline (Northland Publishing; 1994) is a large, lengthy history of the town of Flagstaff, written by one of that city's most prominent historians.

Although Flagstaff is not the first city one thinks of when contemplating the Parker story, the book contains quite a lengthy account, told from the point of view of Coconino County officials such as Deputy Fletcher Fairchild. It is quite good and generally accurate, clearly taken from the accounts of the *Flagstaff Sun-Democrat* and the *Coconino Sun*. Unfortunately, this leads to the book's one error on Parker—the Flagstaff papers had erroneously recorded his last words on the gallows, and the same inaccurate quote is therefore in this book.

Parker again appeared in the *Prescott Courier's* "Days Past" column on March 17, 1996, under the headline, "Tell the Boys That I Died Game . . .Like A Man." The author was Jeff Kellum.

The column once again repeats the "revenge against the railroad" legend, and Kellum also makes use of a few other "minor" inaccuracies that have appeared over the years in other after-the-fact accounts. On the whole, this write-up is not very impressive.

The book *Manhunts and Massacres* (Arizona Highways; 1997) contains a variety of essays about sensational Arizona criminal cases of old, including the 1903 Goddard Station murders, the Guadalupe Canyon massacre (which ultimately led to the death of Newman Haynes "Old Man" Clanton), and of course, Parker.

The essays were written by various authors. The chapter on Parker, written by Leo W. Banks, is surprisingly decent, probably due to his clearly relying on original sources instead of after-the-fact accounts. Banks packs a lot into his brief chapter; his only errors are that he states that it is unknown how Love Marvin's court case turned out (he received a suspended sentence), and that the identity of the Mexican who broke jail with Parker and Miller is unknown (come on, it's Cornelia Sarata!).

Banks also briefly alludes to Parker's hanging in his book *Rattelesnake Blues* (Arizona Highways; 2000) in a section describing the behavior of doomed murderers on the gallows.

The "Days Past" column in the *Courier* attempted to dispel the myth that Parker was Yavapai County's last hanging in an article that appeared February 8, 1998, written by Pat Atchison, who at that time was head of the Yavapai Cemetery Association, and overseer of Citizens Cemetery where Parker is buried.

Atchison devotes most of the column to the Hidalgo-Renteria hangings of 1903, but does write briefly on the Parker story in order to dispel the obvious myth.

The *Prescott Courier's* "Days Past" column returned to the Parker Story yet again on June 7, 1998, with an article entitled "Fleming Parker: 'I Will Steal Before I Will Bum'," after a statement Parker made in the long letter he wrote from jail. The author was former Sharlot Hall Museum Archivist Sue Abbey.

As she did with her Parker write-up in the *Sharlot Hall Gazette* in 1987, Abbey quotes extensively from the surviving letters by Parker and his sisters. The article is good, but this time, Sue Abbey was constrained by limited newspaper space, and this piece is not quite as informative as her earlier piece had been.

In the year 2000, there was a spurt of new interest in the Parker case, helped along to a certain measure by, immodestly, myself. Once a year, Sharlot Hall Museum's Blue Rose Theatre, headed by the renowned historian and businesswoman Jody Drake, recreated the trial of a well-known criminal case in Yavapai County history. This mock trial, presented in cooperation with members of the local legal profession, usually was presented in a courtroom in the Yavapai County Courthouse. The cast usually consisted of local attorneys and prominent citizens.

In 2000, the trail of James Parker was chosen. I had not yet completed my research when I wrote the script for the trial, and I did not yet have the transcript of the testimony, so I based the dialogue on the newspaper accounts of the case. The *Prescott Courier* ran an advance article by Mark Duncan on the *Law Day* recreation of April 24, 2000, briefly recounting the Parker story, and advising the public that the trial recreation was forthcoming.

On April 28, 2000, the recreation took place. Directed by Blue Rose member Katherine Gosney, Judge Hawkins was portrayed by myself, Prosecutor Henry D. Ross was played by attorney Mark Willimann, Patrick O'Sullivan by attorney Dan DeRienzo, while Parker was portrayed by Sharlot Hall Museum assistant curator Rob Bates. George A. Allen was played by attorney Bruce Rosenberg, and J. E. Morrison by attorney Mark Drutz. Attorney Marc Hammond, who dabbles in theatre occasionally, played jailor Robert Meador, while Sharlot Hall Museum Education Department head Warren Miller portrayed George Ruffner.

The recreation was successful, and the *Courier* covered it on May 1, 2000, although reporter Mark Duncan seemed surprisingly interested in the two attorneys who strayed from the script in order to improvise jokes. The jurors and other witnesses were portrayed by other members of Prescott's legal community.

The renewed interest in Parker in Prescott in the year 2000 continued that summer when Sharlot Hall Museum's Blue Rose Theatre presented *Until The Last Dog Is Hung*, a play dramatizing Jim Parker's life. The script was written by myself, but as I had not yet completed my research on Parker, I must confess to a few minor historical inaccuracies, including a depiction of Parker spending time in Prescott in his cowboy days, something which many historians accept, and which MAY have been true, but is not documented with any certainty.

The format of the play is thuswise: The script dramatizes Sheriff George C. Ruffner conversing with Parker in his cell one hour before his hanging. We then proceed to flashbacks of various incidents in Parker's life, including his friendship with Ruffner, his membership in the Abe Thompson Gang, etc. As it is my own work, I am in no position to pass judgment on it, but the play was well-received by audiences.

I also directed the show, and played Abe Thompson. Parker was portrayed by Sharlot Hall Museum archivist Michael Wurtz, while Ruffner was played by local actor Thomas Kayn. Theatre student Heather Elliott played Molly Ruffner, while Blue Rose regular Paco Cantu played a country settler boy who aids Parker in fleeing the posse.

The *Prescott Courier* reviewed the play on July 13, 2000, and critic Sandy Moss gave it a positive review and briefly recounted the Parker story.

With all of this new interest in Parker, I was asked to write a new article on him for the *Courier's* "Days Past" column. It ran July 9, 2000, under the headline, "James Parker, a Legendary Badman of Old Yavapai."

Again, as it is my own work, I cannot pass judgment on it, but I like to think that I recounted the basic facts as accurately as I could with what space I had.

One after-the-fact account of the Parker story that I consider genuinely impressive appeared in the October 2000 edition of *Wild West* magazine. The article, "A Rope For Cowboy Fleming Parker," written by Harold L. Edwards, is surprisingly well-researched, and shows clear signs of the author having a genuine interest in the subject matter, an ingredient which is sorely lacking in so many articles of western lore.

Edwards traces Parker's early scrapes with the law in California, through his ranchwork, and into Arizona. Despite the obvious limitations of space, the author crams quite a bit of detail into the piece, and it is well worth reading. The only noticeable thing absent from the piece is Parker's friendship with the man who would later become his nemesis, Sheriff George C. Ruffner.

There are a few very minor glitches, including some name misspelling (Love Marvin becomes Love Martin in this article for instance, an error that would be repeated in later accounts because of this article), and Edwards is in error when he states that it is not known where Parker is buried. These things aside, the *Wild West* article is one of the best pieces written on Parker in recent years. Harold L. Edwards is to be commended for a job well done.

I responded to the Edwards article with a letter commending him, and asking Edwards if he had found any further detailed documentation on Parker's friendship with George Ruffner, since he had not alluded to this in the article. The letter appeared in the August 2001 edition of *Wild West*, and Edwards responded that he had found, up to that time, no evidence at all that the two were friends

---

The only detailed account of the life of Louis C. Miller that I had seen prior to the writing of this book was written, immodestly, by myself and appeared in the *Prescott Courier's* "Days Past" column on November 12, 2000. It was titled, "L. C. Miller: The Man Who Broke From Jail With James Parker."

I am in no position to judge my own work, and while constrained by limited newspaper space, I did try to recount Miller's story from the Archibald-Wallace shootings through the jailbreak with Parker through his final stay in Yuma Territorial Prison in 1909.

In the article, I asked if any readers and historians had any data on Miller after 1912. There were no responses. I had not met Carol Powell or Dora Silberman at that point.

While researching the Parker story, I became interested in the story of Richard Cross, the cold-blooded murderer who was in jail with Parker, and who received a light sentence because of the Norton Act. I was struck by the vastly different fates the two killers met.

In 2001, I wrote a play about Richard Cross which was performed by Sharlot Hall Museum's Blue Rose Theater, and was entitled *Murder Dismissed*. The play was directed by Jody Drake, and I wrote a scene which took place in jail between Cross and Parker. Jim Parker was again portrayed by Michael Wurtz, as he had been in *Until The Last Dog Is Hung*. I portrayed Richard. Other performers included Natasha Ragsdale, Kristina Velasco, and Davey Neighbors.

Prior to the play's premiere, I wrote an article about Cross in the *Prescott Courier's* "Days Past" column, which ran July 29, 2001 under the title, "Loophole In The Law Saved Man From Hangin' Tree," which was not my doing. In the article, I again drew the necessary comparison between Richard Cross and James Parker.

Jim Parker appeared in the *Courier's* "Days Past" column once again on January 6, 2002, in an article written by myself in which I described how difficult it often is to sort facts from folklore in well known stories. In using Parker as an example, I made note of the true story and then contrasted it with the "revenge against the railroad" legend, the "Butch

Cassidy" legend and also with Asa Harris' widely circulated version of the story, in which he had proclaimed himself to be the hero.

In the article, I advised researchers who are faced with conflicting accounts of stories to gather up ALL information they can first, and then go about sorting through it second. That way, the pieces of the puzzle usually fall into place easier.

In its March 2002 issue, the *Carroll County Historical Quarterly* responded to a query I had made of them by reprinting newspaper coverage of Parker's murder of Erasmus Lee Norris from the *Green Forest Tribune*. They also reprinted my original message to them.

Twenty years after running Dr. Philip J. Rasch's article on Parker, the quarterly journal of the National Association for Outlaw and Lawman History, Inc., of the University of Wyoming, ran another excellent article on Parker, in its July-September 2002 edition.

The author this time was Professor John D. Tanner, Jr., who had become interested in the Parker story after finding the early newspaper clippings on the Rock Cut Train Robbery wherein officials speculated that the caper was pulled off by George Musgrave, whom he was researching for a book of his own (*Last of the Old-Time Outlaws*; University of Oklahoma Press; 2002).

Professor Tanner's article on Parker, drawing almost exclusively from original sources, is quite excellent, one of the best after-the-fact accounts to date. Tanner, in his detailed research, came up with far more data than he was able to use in the article, particularly concerning Parker's early life in Visalia. I am deeply grateful to him for sharing his research with me, which has added a great deal to this book and what we know about Parker.

The Hotel Vendome, a historic lodging place in Prescott, stages "fun" tourist-oriented events for its guests from time to time. In November of 2002, the Vendome's owners staged something called "Sleeping With the Ghosts at the Vendome," a guest-participation mystery performed by Murder Ink, a Phoenix group.

Ink's actors played various western characters in entirely fictional sketches throughout the Hotel—although the fictitious aspect was largely downplayed. According to the November 7, 2002 edition of the *Courier*, one of the sketches depicted George Ruffner in a shootout with "Black Bart." Other historic characters involved in the tomfoolery were Theodore Roosevelt, Bucky O'Neill, Morris Goldwater, Father Alfred Quetu, and Fleming Parker. I do not know what they had Parker do.

Only a couple of weeks later on November 17, 2002, Prescott historian Jim Lockwood premiered his new slide show presentation on the Parker story at Sharlot Hall Museum. The program was called "Law and Outlaw: Sheriff George Ruffner's Personal Horse Thief." I was there; it was pretty good. The *Prescott Courier* ran a brief article promoting it as an upcoming event on November 10, 2002. Written by an unidentified author, this article does make the error that Parker was the last legal hanging in Prescott.

Mr. Lockwood continues to present this program at clubs and organizations to this day. He also gave this presentation at the Sharlot Hall Museum Western History Symposium on September 30, 2006.

On February 23, 2003, the *Courier's* "Days Past" column ran an article on Abe Thompson written by myself, under the headline "From Lawman to Lawlessness: the Variable Abe Thompson." In the article, I summarized in abbreviated form most of the information on Abe that appears in Chapter 3 of this book.

As far as I know, this article was the first time anything had been written in detail on Abe Thompson, and I have noticed with a combination of being both flattered and dismayed that it has been reprinted a number of times without authorization on "wild west" sites on the Internet. Well, I guess devotees of outlaw lore DO get excited whenever something new is said, since new information is usually rare.

"Days Past" once again returned to the Parker story on December 14, 2003 in a piece entitled "Another Twist on the Story of James Fleming Parker," written by Carol Powell, who is a distant relative of Louis C. Miller.

In the article, Powell describes how Coconino County Deputy Fletcher Fairchild went out of his way to get Miller to surrender safely at Jerome, probably because Miller was Fairchild's brother-in-law (Fairchild had once been married to Miller's half-sister Pearl, who was deceased by 1897).

One unfortunate side note to this article was the *Prescott Courier's* worded headline, identifying Parker as "James Fleming Parker." His real name was Fleming Parker, but he adopted the alias James Parker, or Jim Parker, after arriving in Arizona! Regrettably, this error has found its way into a number of other after-the-fact accounts of the Parker story down to the present day because of this headline.

One of the most prolific western authors of the early 21st century is R. Michael Wilson, who has written many books in a short period of time on criminal cases from the old West. On the whole, his output is very impressive and well-researched, although a few glitches do sneak in.

Wilson's book, *Crime and Punishment in Early Arizona* (Stagecoach Press-RaMA Press; 2004), impressively recounts EVERY legal execution in the Arizona Territory prior to Statehood, as well as Arizona's surprisingly few lynchings! The book also prints complete lists of all prisoners at Yuma Territorial Prison, as well as Florence Prison prior to Statehood in 1912. There is also a list of all Territorial Sheriffs in Arizona.

There are some minor errors in his coverage of Parker. First off, Wilson states erroneously that Parker was hanged on June 10, 1898 (it was actually June 3). He says that Parker and Jim "Harry" Williams (name taken from the wanted poster) robbed the train, but makes no mention of Abe Thompson and Love Marvin or the gang. When Parker breaks out of jail, the Mexican is identified as Cornelia Asarta instead of Sarata. Wilson says that at the time of his death, Parker was described as five feet seven and one-half inches in height, weight 165 pounds, with light grey eyes and brown hair. Since the only descriptions I have found of Parker were from early in his life, I'm not sure where Wilson got this. He also repeats the legend that Parker was the last man hanged on the Courthouse Plaza in Prescott, even though he writes later in the book about Hilario Hidalgo and Francisco Renteria, who were hanged there in 1903.

Most of Wilson's research clearly came from the *Journal Miner*, and despite these minor flaws, it is a good account overall.

R. Michael Wilson followed up this impressive book with an even more ambitious one, *Murder and Execution in the Wild West* (Stagecoach Books-RaMA Press; 2006). This time, Wilson not only reprints the above book almost verbatim, but includes all known hangings in Colorado, Idaho, Montana, Nevada, New Mexico, North Dakota, South Dakota, Utah, and Wyoming!!! California is not included for some reason, but all of this makes for a very thick book that is great fun to read for the Wild West aficionado.

The segment on Parker is reprinted almost word-for-word from the first book.

Wilson revisited the Parker story yet again in his book, *Frontier Justice in the Wild West* (Globe Pequot Press; 2007). This book is less ambitious, but still has some great stories and photos. Regarding Parker, Wilson wrote a new account which took a step backward from his previous writings because it contains a few more errors. He repeats the erroneous execution date of June 10, 1898, and this time he identifies Parker's partner as Jim "Harry" Williams alias Charles or John Creighton "sometimes spelled Crayton." He says both men worked for the Arizona Cattle Company and lived together in a cabin owned by the company (say what??). According to Wilson, Parker and "Williams" enlisted the help of cowboys Abe Thompson and Love "Martin" when they decided to rob the train. There is no gang in this account.

During the first posse, Wilson identifies John Rogers as Tom Rogers, Martin Buggeln as Martin Buglin, and Deputy One-Eye Riley as Ed Riley (which could be true for Riley). During the jailbreak, Wilson again identifies Cornelia Sarata as "Asarta."

R. Michael Wilson seemed to have done some extra research on Parker for his third attempt at the story, and in the process, just got a little confused.

Wilson took on the story for the fourth time in his book, *Great Train Robberies of the Old West* (Globe Pequot Press; 2007), a lesser but still entertaining book delivering just what the title promises. The section on Parker is reprinted almost word for word from *Frontier Justice in the Wild West*, but Wilson does try to correct a couple of his previous errors. This time, he does have Parker and "Williams" living at Abe Thompson's cabin (which they were), and he gets Love Marvin's name right (although he does add that it is "sometimes spelled Martin").

Covering much of the same territory, Wilson wrote about Parker yet again in his book, *Legal Executions in the Western Territories, 1847-1911* (McFarland; 2010), covering all known executions in Arizona, Colorado, Idaho, Kansas, Montana, Nebraska, Nevada, New Mexico, North Dakota, Oklahoma, South Dakota, Utah, Washington, and Wyoming!

Writing on Parker this time, Wilson still erroneously lists June 10, 1898 as Parker's hanging date. In this version, Parker and Jim "Harry" Williams still worked for the Arizona Cattle Company and "enjoyed the thrilling life of the cowboy, but there was never enough money." When they decide to rob the train, they enlisted the help of Abe Thompson and Lovell "Love" Martin (we are back to Martin again).

Wilson repeats his misspellings of names, including Sarata as Asarta, and says that Abe Thompson was convicted of being an accessory to the train robbery (he actually plead guilty). The rest of this account repeats most of what appeared in his previous books.

In 2011, Wilson independently reprinted his 2004 book *Crime and Punishment in Early Arizona* with a few revisions and corrections, via Amazon's *www.CreateSpace.com* service. He still has Parker's execution date wrong, and refers to Cornelia Sarata as "Asarta." He also says that, at the time of capture, Parker's "leg had been hurt in one of the earlier encounters with the posse when his horse ran against a tree, but the wound had been well dressed."

R. Michael Wilson is an impressive author and researcher, and his few errors are no doubt due to his writing about too many things simultaneously. Under those kinds of circumstances, occasional mistakes are inevitable.

In 2013, Wilson self-published (through Amazon's CreateSpace) another book entitled *Wells Fargo & Company vs. The Train Robbers 1870-1912*, in which he chronicles the dozens of train robbery cases that Wells Fargo fell victim to, as well as backgrounds on the company and the railroads! His section on the Rock Cut Train Robbery covers mostly the same territory as his previous accounts, including his previous errors (Parker's erroneous execution date, Asarta, Love Martin, etc.). But this time he pads it with a lot of detail on how the robbers planned the caper, most of it clearly taken from Love Marvin's confession—though he still persists in calling him Love Martin!!! Wilson also adds that Parker had finished well in Prescott's 1895 rodeo (which could be true but I have seen no documentation), and refers to train fireman Nelson Bartoo as "Bartee".

But 2015 brought author Wilson's most ambitious work yet; a self-published (through Amazon's CreateSpace service) volume called *Train Robbery in North America*. It consists of summaries of ALL known and recorded train robberies in the United States, Canada, and Mexico!!!! From the first recorded robbery in 1855 through—I kid you not—2012 (it still happens occasionally), they are all here. This is arguably Wilson's crowning achievement, regardless of any minor errors. His section on Parker is reprinted almost verbatim from his 2013 book above.

Sharlot Hall Museum's Blue Rose Theater revived my play on Richard Cross, *Murder Dismissed*, on August 5-6 and 12-14, 2005. This time, the show was directed by Gail Mangham, and Steve Clark replaced me in the role of Cross. Because of some casting difficulties, I played Parker in his cameo with Cross! Other cast members were Jody Drake, Errol Reed, and Kaileena Martin.

On July 31, 2005, in advance of the show, the *Courier* reran my 2001 "Days Past" article contrasting the fate of Richard Cross with that of Parker.

2006 saw yet another anthology book of old Arizona stories, this one titled *Outlaw Tales of Arizona* by Jan Cleere (Globe Pequot Press; 2006). It bears the mark of many recent books of its kind, in that the author successfully digs up good stories that should be remembered, but solid research on them falls short. Among the "outlaws" Cleere writes about are the Apache Kid, Pearl Hart, Charles P. Stanton, Augustin Chacon, James Addison Reavis, and a few others. There is also a chapter on Parker.

Jan Cleere's primary source for her chapter on Parker seems to have been Thomas Way's book, *The Parker Story*, as she repeats a number of details that had previously appeared only in Way's writings. Nevertheless, she also throws in the "revenge against the railroad" legend, and the "Flossie" story.

She also claims that, during the second posse, Parker left Sure-Shot with his old friend Tom Wagner, and that he was also sheltered for a time by old employer Charley "Hog-Eye" Miller. She also states that the terrain outside Williams was so rough that the trackers had to put booties on their bloodhounds to keep their feet from getting ripped up. She spells Miller's name as "Lewis C. Miller" and says Cornelia Sarata's name is sometimes spelled "Asarta."

I had always thought that the long, bizarre story of Louis C. Miller would make a good play. I pitched it to Jody Drake, and Sharlot Hall Museum's Blue Rose Theater staged *Another Kind of Miller* on October 13-14, 20-21, 2006. It was directed by Melanie Reed, who also played Marie Castro.

This play depicted Miller, bedridden and blind, speaking of his sordid past to Emma Schultz (which he may never have done in real life), whom he would later marry. The show was plagued with production problems, and I ended up playing Miller although I had not intended the role for myself. We ended up having him speak of his past as a monologue to an unseen Emma. Tedd deLong played Miles Archibald in a flashback, Bob Wright played John Wallace, and Mark Payne made an excellent Parker.

Prior to the show's premiere, the *Courier's* "Days Past" column ran an article by Carol Powell describing how she and I met and pooled our information on Miller, enough to piece together much of his life. It was titled, "Two Sides to the Story of Louis C. Miller's Double Life."

Tucson-based historian Jane Eppinga took a different approach to lawlessness in her book *Arizona Sheriffs: Badges and Bad Men* (Rio Nuevo Publishers; 2006) by concentrating on the lives of the lawmen instead of the lawbreakers. She also delves into a number of 20th century cases that haven't been written about as much yet. She also gives a list of all known incidents in Arizona history where Sheriffs or Deputies were killed in the line of duty, as well as a list of all known Arizona Sheriffs in history!

This is all wonderful, until you read her short segment on George C. Ruffner and Fleming Parker. Here, we are given the old standbys once again—the Flossie legend, the playing card invitations, and the notion that Parker wanted Ruffner to pull the switch. Eppinga also says Parker came from Bakersfield, California, and in a caption to Photo #5 of the hanging, again identifies the man on the far right as Morris Goldwater.

Reading all of this made me very frustrated. The last 30 years have seen a great deal of solid research on Fleming "James" Parker, all of it easily had. There is absolutely no excuse for these fairy tales to still be in active circulation at this late date (2006), but they are. It is made worse here because Jane Eppinga is a reputable historian, and there is a lot of worth in much of this book. This unfortunately gives the Parker folk tales new credibility that they don't deserve. It is my hope that she will make some needed corrections here in future editions of this book.

The Internet search engine Yahoo has a page called Yahoo Answers where people can ask questions about anything at all, and people can "blog" answers, all anonymously. Sometime in 2007, someone posted the question:

"Why was louis miller arrested?"

The question was that simple; no details from the poster about Louis Miller's background, and since this is a common name, was the person referring to the man who broke jail with Parker?

A "blogger" named Marilyn N responded with a summary of this Louis Miller's story, neatly summed up, written in such a way that I suspect she used my "Days Past" column on Miller as source material.

This page is still on-line as I write this, but whether it is when you read this is anyone's guess. The web page is at:

http://answers.yahoo.com/question/index?qid=20071202184100Aaj4Owo

---

On April 8, 2007, Carol Powell wrote another "Days Past" column entitled "They Were Just A Railroadin' Family," describing the lives of some of Louis C. Miller's brothers, and briefly alluding to Louis himself. Since then, she has also written individual articles on Louis' brothers William and Baldwin "Tobe" Miller.

Again, there have been a lot of Western anthology books in recent years where the authors dig up fascinating stories and then fail to take the time to fact check . Another one is *Gold, Greed, & Glory* by Sedona-based writer Kate Ruland-Thorne (Publish America; 2007). I had a blast reading the book, the stories are wonderful, and it is great they are being remembered, but regrettably, folklore does creep in to the text.

Ruland-Thorne devotes a section to a George Ruffner biography, but in recounting his life, she gives us the inaccurate "Bugger Bennett" legend again. When she gets to the Parker story, she says that Ruffner and Parker first met and became friends on a ranch out in Big Bug, near Mayer, owned by Jake Miller (who had been one of the first men to explore Arizona as a member of the Walker party). A number of historians have given locations where the two friends met, but this is the first time I've heard this one. She also says that "It was Parker who introduced Ruffner to the wild life of Prescott's Whiskey Row and the lure of the gambling tables." Certainly possible, perhaps even likely, but not heavily documented.

The author recounts details of Parker's early life accurately, but by the time she gets to the jailbreak, she writes that Ruffner "found the townspeople enraged and ready to form a lynching party." She also repeats an error first told by Thomas E. Way that two Navajo Indians recognized Parker from his wanted poster and notified Samuel S. Preston (unnamed in this book) who in turn notified Sheriff Cameron.

Ruland-Thorne claims that Parker was hanged on June 8, 1898 instead of June 3, an error that has been made before due to misunderstandings by later historians on how "weekly" editions of newspapers operated. She recounts the "Flossie" legend yet again, proving once more that this unlikely tale is by far the most often repeated story about Parker. This time she actually offers a new quote from Parker. "Well, I don't want any damn last meal," Parker is said to have snarled. "I'd like one of my girl friends on Whiskey Row to visit me." In repeating another legend, she quotes Parker as saying "I want to die like a man, and I want a man I respect to pull the lever," meaning Ruffner.

I always find it depressing to see authors and books, which have so much going for them in many ways, lapse into carelessness in others. Kate Ruland-Thorne does list some of her sources at the end of the book, including the old McInnes piece from *Sheriff Magazine*. This piece of malarkey is still misleading researchers 60 years after it was written. She also used Sue Abbey's 1998 "Days Past" article as a source, which is fine, but I smiled wistfully upon realizing she did not use my "Days Past" articles, which she certainly would have been aware of.

In the *Courier's* "Days Past" column of June 8, 2008, Carol Powell wrote a new piece about how Fletcher Fairchild went out of his way to obtain the peaceful surrender of his brother-in-law, Louis C. Miller. It was titled, "The Lawman and the Outlaw."

An "old west" newspaper-periodical entitled *Chronicle of the West* has been published out of Show Low, Arizona for a number of years now. It prints fairly simple renditions of western stories and reprints from old newspapers. It is entertaining stuff for the armchair western enthusiast, although it may come up short for devotees of detailed books like the one you are reading right now.

Chronicle of the West also syndicates very short (about two minutes) radio shows, in which the group's leader, Dakota Livesay, expounds "old west" stories backed by "exciting" music. These sketches are also for sale on CD from the organization.

In June 2008, one of these brief radio sketches relayed the Parker story. It sums it up fairly nicely for something running only two minutes, except Livesay errs when he says Parker broke out of jail TWICE (he must have been confused by Parker's escape from John Rogers), and he also he says that George Ruffner was the one who captured Parker on the second posse.

The *Chronicle of the West* output is decent fun for the lighter western aficionado. You can find them at *www.chronicleofthewest.com*.

On June 20, 2009, an Internet blogger calling himself The Nite Tripper posted a slightly cropped photo of Parker's hanging on the photo-sharing website *www.flickr.com*. In the caption, this individual wrote that the train robbery was a failure because "the accomplice died from his wounds and Parker lost the stolen money." In relating the jailbreak, the Tripper describes Louis Miller as a "forgerer" (you don't have to know how to spell to post on the Internet), and says that Parker "shot and killed the district attorney in the courthouse square."

There were two anonymous blog responses to the photo, one by someone named "sclopit" who says, "Parker looks remarkably collected for somebody who is about to die."

Sounds like "sclopit" was skeptical of the photo's authenticity, but as we know, Parker was indeed unusually calm and collected!

The Nite Tripper's blog was reprinted (misspelled words and all) anonymously in an undated entry on Parker at the popular *www.FindAGrave.com* website.

In the early 21st century, a group of Old West re-enactors formed in Prescott, calling themselves "The Regulators and Their Shady Ladies." They perform mock gunfights, comic old west sketches, and the like. They perform in re-enactment tournaments around the country, and once a year they get to block off Whiskey Row in downtown Prescott to host an annual tournament themselves called "Shootout on Whiskey Row."

The *Courier* covered their 2009 "Shootout on Whiskey Row" on July 26, 2009, and the author, Doug Cook, also wrote about Parker. I did not attend the tournament that year, so I don't know if the Regulators performed the Parker story, or if Regulators President George Ranz (quoted by name) told Cook the story. Whatever the case, the facts are all wrong. Cook says that Parker was the leader of a gang of outlaws in Yavapai County, and that Sheriff Ruffner shot Parker in a gunfight and arrested him. Then, the Sheriff and a Constable got into a fight over custody of Parker, and the Sheriff was shot! Whoever was responsible for this tale seems to have gotten the Parker story confused with Louis Miller's shooting of Miles Archibald. Accompanying the article was a picture of Parker's wanted poster, and a photo of his hanging.

The *Courier* must have caught hell from somebody over this brand new telling of the Parker story, because a few days later, a different *Courier* reporter phoned me to ask for the straight story, because they knew I would have it. Shortly after that, the paper printed a small correction blurb, and they rewrote the offending paragraphs in the on-line version of the original article.

Ah yes, 111 years after his death, Parker had not lost his ability to stir up controversy!

Shortly after that, and totally unrelated, Sharlot Hall Museum's Blue Rose Theater revived my old 2000 play, *Until the Last Dog is Hung*, which performed on August 14-15, 20-22, 2009. We cleaned up some of the errors I had made in the original script nine years earlier, and the production was well received once again.

Jody Drake directed the show this time, with Martin Miller as Parker, Thatcher Bohrman as George Ruffner, Sara Day as Molly Ruffner, myself as Abe Thompson as I had been in the original production, and Thatcher's son True Bohrman as the country settler boy.

The *Courier* gave the play a positive review in an article on it by Karen Despain, which appeared August 14.

In line with the production of the play, the *Courier* ran a column in its "Days Past" section on August 16, 2009 written by me entitled "In Search of Fleming Parker, Robber and Murderer." In it, I described a trip I had made in August 2008 to Visalia, California, with the purpose of visiting the graves of Parker's parents, the tragic Daniel Parker and Mary Elizabeth Parker. While there, Terry Ommen, who helped me with some of the research for this book, showed me around.

At the Visalia Cemetery, I also found the grave of Fleming Work, Parker's grandfather. I did not mention it in the article, but I also found the grave of Judge William W. Cross, and the mausoleum crypt of Judge James S. Clack.

A website devoted to Visalia history had previously noted my visit in a posting dated September 9, 2008. It described me as a "stranger" who had "slipped into town" to research Parker. As of this writing, the site is located at: *http://visaliahistory.blogspot.com/2008/09/historic-happenings-newsletter-under.html*

On October 4, 2009, Parker was briefly mentioned in a letter to the editor of the *Arizona Republic* that was written by me. I was responding to an earlier editorial column by E.J. Montini in which he wrote about a woman, Kathee Austin, who wished to convert to Catholicism in time for her terminally ill Catholic husband, Bill Austin, to see it before he died, but the Church (which requires months of hard study and teaching before conversion) would not expedite the process.

In the letter, I compared the situation to how Fleming "James" Parker converted and was baptized by Father Quetu before he was hanged. There is no evidence that Parker was studying the faith in jail in the months leading up to his execution. How times change, I said.

In 2013, the Sedona Historical Museum (in Sedona, Arizona) published the book, *From Oxen to Oxides* by John Fletcher Fairchild, the son of Fletcher Fairchild the Coconino County lawman. This book is the first printing of the younger Fairchild's autobiography, which he had completed shortly before his death in 1982.

An appendix to the book reprints a few articles about Fletcher Fairchild aiding in the capture of his brother-in-law Louis C. Miller that were written by Carol Powell for *rootsweb.com* and other sites. Her writings have always been accurate.

There is a website at *www.tomrizzo.com*, where Tom Rizzo blogs on various "wild west" stories. He posted a blog on the Parker story on February 5, 2014. It is simplistic, but it pretty much sticks to known facts and is surprisingly decent.

Parker made an appearance in a history column in the *Arizona Republic* (the Phoenix newspaper) on April 1, 2014, an apt date for an article like this. The author, John Stanley, apparently did a little on-line research regarding Parker's early days, which was okay, but then gives us yet again the "revenge against the railroad" story. Stanley writes: *"So many stories have grown up around Parker over the years that it's not easy to separate fact from fiction. True or not, though, some of these stories bear repeating."* But why, John? If we know certain stories are not true, why repeat them as if they are?

Stanley then concludes with the Flossie story, and adds, *"Maybe it happened, maybe it didn't."* Come on, people who want to learn Southwest history deserve better than that!

As this book goes to press, I have become aware of a new oral legend (spread from mouth to mouth) making the rounds of Prescott, that contends that the ghost of Parker haunts the old Knights of Pythias building across the street from the Courthouse plaza where he was hanged. Today, this historic building houses the Tis Art Gallery and some law offices upstairs. What the ghost story tellers are unable to explain is *why* Parker's spirit would haunt this edifice, as he is not known to have ever had any connection to it, aside from the fact that it was in view of the place where he died.

The State of Arizona employs an Official State Historian, and for many years, history professor Marshall Trimble has held this job. He does good work, and he also goes around making personal appearances, singing cowboy songs and telling folksy stories, and yes, he is very entertaining. His knowledge of the "old west" is vast, but his schedule does not always allow him to dig as deep into already established stories as one might like.

Marshall Trimble has a regular question and answer column in *True West* magazine, and has written numerous books on Arizona history, several of which have short chapters on the Parker story. Unfortunately, when telling this tale, he relies heavily on past written accounts and folklore. It is mystifying why so many otherwise fine historians go awry when relating the story of Jim Parker.

Trimble's book, *Roadside History of Arizona* (Mountain Press Publishing Company; 1986, and reprinted in 2004) is very ambitious and entertaining, with many great stories of locations around Arizona and how they got their names. When writing about Prescott, the author deals briefly with Jim Parker, utilizing the "revenge and the railroad" story, the playing card invitations, and Flossie. It is the only weakness in this very well-done book.

In his 1989 book, *Arizona—A Cavalcade of History* (1989; Rio Nuevo Publishers), Trimble deals with the story briefly again, utilizing the "revenge against the railroad" story; the playing-card invitations; that Parker specifically requested George Ruffner to be the one to hang him; and of course, Flossie the floozy. Trimble also states that Louis C. Miller (actually unnamed in this account) was caught in Chino Valley, and that George Ruffner sneaked Parker into Prescott by a back route to avoid an angry lynch mob waiting at the station—this has been an oft-told tale, but this version adds that, when the mob realized they had been bamboozled, they marched to the jail and ordered Ruffner to turn Parker over to them. When the Sheriff refused, the mob dispersed. All variations of old folk tales.

By 1997, Marshall Trimble had clearly become acquainted with Thomas Way's book, *The Parker Story*. In Trimble's book, *The Law of the Gun* (Arizona Highways; 1997), he writes a chapter on George C. Ruffner, but devotes most of it to the Parker story. However, this time he thankfully abandons the above legends and tells a fairly decent account, clearly using Way's writings as source material (and including a few of Way's own errors). However, Trimble attributes Parker's capture after the train robbery (the first posse) to One-Eye Riley and Martin Buggeln, and identifies the dead train robber as Windy Wilson. With the jailbreak, Trimble spells the names of the other two participants as Lewis Miller and Cornella Sarata. He also describes Sure-Shot the horse as being Arab, a claim I have seen nowhere else. In this account, we are also told that Parker offered a reward of ten dollars to his cowboy friends who were helping him for every bloodhound they killed, forcing the owner of the bloodhounds to quit the posse and go home.

Trimble continues this account by stating that after turning Sure Shot loose, Parker was given a good horse by his old friend Hog-Eye Miller, owner of the Hat Ranch. Samuel Preston is not a character in this version, as we are told that two Nanajo Indians recognized Parker and alerted Coconino County Sheriff Ralph Cameron. After sneaking up on Parker with his posse, Cameron says, "Mornin' Parker," to which the fugitive replies, "Reckon it ain't so good for me." After Sheriff George C. Ruffner arrives to take possession of Parker, the fugitive allegedly told him, "Where in hell would I have to go to find a place where you wouldn't be?" To which George responds, "That's exactly where you'll be when I finish ridin' herd on you!"

Trimble concludes this version with the old standbys, the playing card invitations and the visit from Flossie. Then, Trimble adds that Parker was Prescott's last hanging, and that this was because Sheriff Ruffner pressed Territorial officials to move all executions to the Territorial Prison in Yuma. I have never seen that alleged before. While executions were indeed later moved to the Territorial (and late State) prison, this did not happen for a number of years yet, and as we know, Parker was not Prescott's last hanging.

The Arizona State Historian gave the Parker story another try in his book *Arizona Outlaws and Lawmen* (The History Press; 2015). In this one, Trimble uses a marginally reworded version of his writing from *The Law of the Gun*, using mostly Thomas Way's version as source material. This time, though, Trimble gives a name to the train Express Messenger, Jim Summers (instead of Alexander Summers as it actually was). In both of these most recent efforts, Parker's execution date is erroneously listed as June 8, 1898 yet again. This most recent chapter yet again closes with the playing card invitations opus, and the visit to Parker by Flossie (the legend that just won't die).

Marshall Trimble also briefly recounted the Parker story in a blog post dated July 2, 2015 on *www.truewestmagazine.com*, the website for *True West*. He again repeats the tale of Flossie, and the story that Parker announced from the scaffold that there was only one man he respected enough to pull the lever—George Ruffner.

I briefly mentioned the Parker story in my book, *Cemeteries of Yavapai County* (Arcadia Publishing; 2013) in a paragraph noting the grave of Joe Lee in the Pioneers Home Cemetery in Prescott. Lee, as we have seen, was the assistant to trading post operator Samuel S. Preston, who captured Parker the second time. The paragraph includes a photo of Lee's tombstone.

Parker made his DVD debut in 2015, in a production called *Legends of Whiskey Row*, put together by Norman Fisk. It was designed to be sold mostly to Prescott tourists, and recounts numerous "colorful" stories of old Prescott, but unfortunately many of the stories are taken from folklore. While corny narrations (by Fisk himself) are spoken, we see silent dramatizations of the various gunfights and altercations, performed by the Prescott Regulators and others. Sections of this DVD have been posted on YouTube by Fisk as well.

The section on Parker states that he did his first term in San Quentin when he was 15 (he was actually 20). The DVD then recounts the basics of the story, but then tells us one thing that separates the Parker story from other hangings—Flossie, of course! In recounting the tale, we actually see on screen a lawman hanging a blanket over the jail cell in order to give Parker and Flossie some privacy!

A sensational title clearly designed to sell books, *Wild Women of Prescott, Arizona* by Jan MacKell Collins (The History Press; 2015), unfortunately masks a truly excellent and well-researched book on prostitution in old Prescott. The author makes use of voluminous sources to paint a compelling picture of the "red light district," but in doing so, the author addresses the legend of how Parker asked Sheriff Ruffner to procure his favorite lady of the evening, Flossie, for one hour as his last wish.

Collins refreshingly admits there is no documentation for the legend, but yet admits a strong fondness for it, and states, "In other words, if it isn't true, it ought to be." I know the author personally and have much respect for her, but I must disagree. The absurd Flossie legend has bedeviled serious researchers of the Parker story for decades, causing them to waste many hours trying to nail down a definitive source for it, and coming up empty. I remain at a loss as to why this tale holds such a strong fascination for people—would these same people be as charitable if a soon to be executed murderer made the same request *today* and it was granted? I doubt it very much—more likely, we would be hearing screams of anger and moralistic disgust.

It is time for Flossie the floozy to rest in peace.

In my own book, *Wicked Prescott* (The History Press; 2016), I recount a large number of colorful stories of old Prescott, mostly law and order and crime stories from bygone eras. I endeavored to include details of all 11 of Prescott's legal hangings, including that of Jim Parker. As it is my own work, I cannot review it without bias, but I will say that I feel I wrote a very good and accurate summary of the case.

In October of 2016, Yavapai County celebrated the 100th anniversary of its Courthouse in Prescott, which had been built in 1916 on the site of the previous Courthouse where Parker, Miller, and Sarata had made their jailbreak. Historical exhibits were unveiled in the Courthouse on October 16 for permanent display, including several enlarged photos of Parker's hanging, along with a narrative written by Elisabeth Ruffner.

Every October in time for Halloween, the Prescott Center for the Arts community theatre hosts an elaborate stage production entitled "Ghost Talk", which consists (mostly for comedy) of ghosts regaling the audience with colorful stories of old Yavapai (mostly culled from area folklore). It is largely a burlesque, and is quite fun and entertaining as long as you don't take the stories too seriously. For the 2015 and 2016 Ghost Talks, Parker's hanging was briefly dramatized, narrated by an actor playing the ghost of Father Quetu.

Epilogue

Fleming "James" Parker was never married, and is not known to have had any children. Consequently, his line of the Parker name has ceased to exist. However, Parker's three sisters did have children, and it is likely they in turn had children as well, as so on. Therefore, it is very likely that Parker does have blood relatives living today.

If so, they either are unaware of their ancestry, or more likely, have chosen to keep quiet about it. If any of them are reading my words here, I wish to say that it is my hope this book has brought them a better understanding of their infamous ancestor. Parker cannot be referred to as a "good" man, but at the same time, he was also not the inhuman monster that he has been depicted as for so long.

Readers of this book are invited to send me their comments and input. If you have any further data, I would be very interested in adding it to a future edition of this book. I can be reached at P. O. Box 1285, Prescott, AZ 86302, or e-mail me at *parkerr86302@yahoo.com*.

www.ingramcontent.com/pod-product-compliance
Lightning Source LLC
Chambersburg PA
CBHW081213170426
43198CB00017B/2599